The Tutorverse
MAKING THE UNIVERSE BRIGHTER, ONE STUDENT AT A TIME

New York City SHSAT: 1,000+ Practice Questions

4th Edition

New York City SHSAT: 1,000+ Practice Questions
4th Edition
Revised February 2019

Published in the United States of America by:

The Tutorverse, LLC

222 Broadway, 19th Floor

New York, NY 10038

Web: www.thetutorverse.com

Email: info@thetutorverse.com

For information about buying this title in bulk or to place a special order, please contact us at info@thetutorverse.com.

ISBN-13: 978-1-7321677-4-2
ISBN-10: 1732167745

Neither the author or publisher claim any responsibility for the accuracy and appropriateness of the content in this book, nor do they claim any responsibility over the outcome of students who use these materials.

The views and opinions expressed in this book do not necessarily reflect the official policy, position, or point of view of the author or publisher. Such views and opinions do not constitute an endorsement to perform, attempt to perform, or otherwise emulate any procedures, experiments, etc. described in any of the passages, excerpts, adaptations, cited materials, or similar information. Such information is included only to facilitate the development of questions, answer choices, and answer explanations for purposes of preparing for the SHSAT.

Table of Contents

New York City SHSAT: 1,000+ Practice Questions

4th Edition

Welcome

Dear Students, Parents, and Educators,

The 2019 SHSAT brings refreshed material to last year's redesigned test. The test will again include literary passages (excerpts from novels, short stories, and poems) in the reading comprehension section of the test. In addition, compared with the 2017 test, there will be more reading comprehension questions and fewer revising and editing questions.

The key to success on this test remains access to better practice and expert advice. This is why we've filled this workbook with over 1,000 practice questions – more questions than on 10 actual tests! – and numerous test-taking tips. We've identified core concepts and crafted questions for each topic designed to help reinforce understanding. Within each topic, questions build on fundamentals and grow progressively more challenging. Our questions help to build confidence, test mastery, and introduce new concepts, skills, and knowledge.

This workbook will help students to identify skills and concepts requiring further development. This workbook will also provide students with ample practice for many of the core concepts seen on the SHSAT. Whether you use this workbook for independent study or with a professional tutor or teacher, we believe that the practice you will receive will benefit you both on the SHSAT and beyond.

This revision includes significant updates to the reading comprehension subject and is based on guidance released by the New York City Department of Education.

Best wishes, good luck, and welcome to The Tutorverse!

Regards,

The Team at The Tutorverse

How to Use This Book

Overview

The purpose of this workbook is to provide students, parents, and educators with practice materials relevant to the SHSAT. The primary goal of this workbook is to provide students with copious practice and to serve as an introduction to new words, concepts, and skills, wherever necessary. In addition, this workbook includes information with respect to the test's structure and content – and includes tips, suggestions, and strategies.

About the New York City SHSAT

The SHSAT consists of 114 questions that must be answered within 180 minutes. The test is split into two sections: English Language Arts and Mathematics. A total of 20 questions (10 from each section) will <u>not</u> be scored. Students will <u>not</u> know which items are not being scored. There is no time limit for either section – students need only complete the entire test within the 180-minute time limit.

The test is required for admission to the following schools:

- 🐟 The Bronx High School of Science
- 🐟 The Brooklyn Latin School
- 🐟 Brooklyn Technical High School
- 🐟 High School for Mathematics, Science, and Engineering at the City College
- 🐟 High School of American Studies at Lehman College
- 🐟 Queens High School for the Sciences at York College
- 🐟 Staten Island Technical High School
- 🐟 Stuyvesant High School

<u>Note</u>: The Fiorello H. LaGuardia High School of Music & Art and Performing Arts *does not* require the SHSAT. Instead, the school requires a separate, audition-based application process, which is not in the scope of this workbook.

The SHSAT is usually administered near the end of October, with registration opening at the beginning of the school year. The exact date of the test varies by year and is determined earlier that calendar year, usually in the spring or summer. Therefore, it is important to check with the student's guidance counselor or with the New York City Department of Education to find out the exact date of the test.

There are, generally, several different places to take the test – at least one per borough. Again, it is important to check with the student's guidance counselor and/or the New York City Department of Education to determine the precise locations of the testing centers.

Organization

This workbook is organized into four main sections. Each section is designed to accomplish different objectives. These sections and objectives are as follows:

- 🐟 Practice Test 1 (Diagnostic)
  This section is designed to help students identify the topics requiring the most practice. The practice test should be used as a gauge to estimate the amount of additional practice needed in each topic.

- 🐟 English Language Arts
  English Language Arts is the first practice section in this workbook. This section contains practice for writing (revising/editing) skills and reading comprehension questions found in the first section of the test.

The Tutorverse

☞ Mathematics
Math is the second practice section in this workbook. There are many topics in this section, which are organized as indicated in the table of contents. These include, algebra, geometry, statistics, and more.

☞ Practice Test 2
The final practice test helps to familiarize students with the format, organization, and time allotments they should expect on the SHSAT. This test should be taken once students have completed Practice Test 1 and have spent sufficient time answering the appropriate questions in the practice sections.

At the beginning of each of the above listed sections are detailed instructions. Students should carefully review these instructions, as they contain important information about the actual test and how best to utilize this workbook.

Strategy

Every student has different strengths and abilities. We don't think there is any one strategy that will help every student ace the test. Instead, we believe there are core principles to keep in mind when preparing for the SHSAT. These principles are interrelated and cyclical in nature.

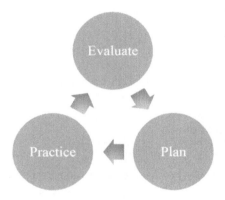

☞ Evaluate
A critical step in developing a solid study plan is to have a clear idea of how to spend your time. What subjects are more difficult for you? Which types of questions do you frequently answer incorrectly? Why? These and many other questions should be answered before developing any study plan. Practice Test 1 is just one way to help you evaluate your abilities.

☞ Plan
Once you've taken stock of your strengths and abilities, focus on actions. How much time do you have before the test? How many areas do you need to work on during that time? Which areas do you need to work on? How many questions (and of which type) do you need to do each day, or each week? The answers to these and other questions will help you determine your study and practice plan.

☞ Practice
Once you settle on a plan, try to stick with it as much as you can. To study successfully requires discipline, commitment, and focus. Try turning off your phone, TV, tablet, or other distractions. Not only will you learn more effectively when you're focused, but you may find that you finish your work more quickly, as well.

☞ Reevaluate
Because learning and studying is an ongoing process, it is important to take stock of your improvements along the way. This will help you see how you are progressing and allow you to make adjustments to your plan. The practice test at the end of this workbook is designed to help you gauge your progress.

The Tutorverse

Help

Preparing for a standardized test such as the SHSAT can be a difficult and trying time. In addition to challenging material, preparing for a standardized test can often feel like an extra responsibility. For these reasons, it's important to recognize when students need extra help.

Some students may find material in this workbook to be challenging, or even entirely new. Encountering something new in this workbook is completely normal. In fact, it's better to encounter something for the first time while practicing in this workbook than to be surprised by it on the actual test!

We encourage you to reach out to trusted educators to help you prepare for the SHSAT. Strong tutors – like those that teach with The Tutorverse – teachers, and mentors can help you with many aspects of your preparation. These educators can help you evaluate and reevaluate your needs, create an effective plan, and help you make the most of your practice.

Looking for a tutor?

Look no further – we're The Tutorverse for a reason! Have a parent or guardian send us an email at **info@thetutorverse.com** and we'll see how we can help!

The Tutorverse

Practice Test 1 (Diagnostic)

Overview

The first step in an effective study plan is to know your strengths and areas for improvement.

Use this practice test to assesses your mastery of certain skills and concepts that you may see on the actual test. There are several differences between this practice test and the actual test.

The practice test is scored differently from how the actual test is scored. To replicate an actual test-taking scenario, the practice test includes all 114 questions students will see on the actual test. Note that 20 of these (10 from each section) will not be scored on the actual test.

Because of these differences, this practice test should be used to gauge your mastery over skills and concepts, not as a gauge of how you will score on the actual test. Instead, use the results of this test to determine which topics to focus on.

Format

The practice test includes the following sections:

Practice Test Section	Questions	Time Limit
English Language Arts	57	90 minutes *suggested
Mathematics	57	90 minutes *suggested
Total	**114**	**180 minutes**

* The time limits indicated above are recommendations only. The actual test consists of 57 English Language Arts questions and 57 mathematics questions to be completed in 180 minutes. Students are not required to finish the test in any particular order, nor are they limited to a certain amount of time for each section. How students choose to split that time up between sections is entirely discretionary.

Answering

Use the answer sheet provided on the next page to record your answers. You may wish to tear this page out of the workbook.

The Tutorverse

Practice Test Answer Sheet

Section 1: English Language Arts

1. Ⓐ Ⓑ Ⓒ Ⓓ   13. Ⓐ Ⓑ Ⓒ Ⓓ   25. Ⓐ Ⓑ Ⓒ Ⓓ   37. Ⓐ Ⓑ Ⓒ Ⓓ   49. Ⓐ Ⓑ Ⓒ Ⓓ
2. Ⓔ Ⓕ Ⓖ Ⓗ   14. Ⓔ Ⓕ Ⓖ Ⓗ   26. Ⓔ Ⓕ Ⓖ Ⓗ   38. Ⓔ Ⓕ Ⓖ Ⓗ   50. Ⓔ Ⓕ Ⓖ Ⓗ
3. Ⓐ Ⓑ Ⓒ Ⓓ   15. Ⓐ Ⓑ Ⓒ Ⓓ   27. Ⓐ Ⓑ Ⓒ Ⓓ   39. Ⓐ Ⓑ Ⓒ Ⓓ   51. Ⓐ Ⓑ Ⓒ Ⓓ
4. Ⓔ Ⓕ Ⓖ Ⓗ   16. Ⓔ Ⓕ Ⓖ Ⓗ   28. Ⓔ Ⓕ Ⓖ Ⓗ   40. Ⓔ Ⓕ Ⓖ Ⓗ   52. Ⓔ Ⓕ Ⓖ Ⓗ
5. Ⓐ Ⓑ Ⓒ Ⓓ   17. Ⓐ Ⓑ Ⓒ Ⓓ   29. Ⓐ Ⓑ Ⓒ Ⓓ   41. Ⓐ Ⓑ Ⓒ Ⓓ   53. Ⓐ Ⓑ Ⓒ Ⓓ
6. Ⓔ Ⓕ Ⓖ Ⓗ   18. Ⓔ Ⓕ Ⓖ Ⓗ   30. Ⓔ Ⓕ Ⓖ Ⓗ   42. Ⓔ Ⓕ Ⓖ Ⓗ   54. Ⓔ Ⓕ Ⓖ Ⓗ
7. Ⓐ Ⓑ Ⓒ Ⓓ   19. Ⓐ Ⓑ Ⓒ Ⓓ   31. Ⓐ Ⓑ Ⓒ Ⓓ   43. Ⓐ Ⓑ Ⓒ Ⓓ   55. Ⓐ Ⓑ Ⓒ Ⓓ
8. Ⓔ Ⓕ Ⓖ Ⓗ   20. Ⓔ Ⓕ Ⓖ Ⓗ   32. Ⓔ Ⓕ Ⓖ Ⓗ   44. Ⓔ Ⓕ Ⓖ Ⓗ   56. Ⓔ Ⓕ Ⓖ Ⓗ
9. Ⓐ Ⓑ Ⓒ Ⓓ   21. Ⓐ Ⓑ Ⓒ Ⓓ   33. Ⓐ Ⓑ Ⓒ Ⓓ   45. Ⓐ Ⓑ Ⓒ Ⓓ   57. Ⓐ Ⓑ Ⓒ Ⓓ
10. Ⓔ Ⓕ Ⓖ Ⓗ   22. Ⓔ Ⓕ Ⓖ Ⓗ   34. Ⓔ Ⓕ Ⓖ Ⓗ   46. Ⓔ Ⓕ Ⓖ Ⓗ
11. Ⓐ Ⓑ Ⓒ Ⓓ   23. Ⓐ Ⓑ Ⓒ Ⓓ   35. Ⓐ Ⓑ Ⓒ Ⓓ   47. Ⓐ Ⓑ Ⓒ Ⓓ
12. Ⓔ Ⓕ Ⓖ Ⓗ   24. Ⓔ Ⓕ Ⓖ Ⓗ   36. Ⓔ Ⓕ Ⓖ Ⓗ   48. Ⓔ Ⓕ Ⓖ Ⓗ

Section 2: Mathematics

58. 59. 60. 61. 62. (grid-in answer boxes, digits 0–9)

63. Ⓐ Ⓑ Ⓒ Ⓓ   74. Ⓔ Ⓕ Ⓖ Ⓗ   85. Ⓐ Ⓑ Ⓒ Ⓓ   96. Ⓔ Ⓕ Ⓖ Ⓗ   107. Ⓐ Ⓑ Ⓒ Ⓓ
64. Ⓔ Ⓕ Ⓖ Ⓗ   75. Ⓐ Ⓑ Ⓒ Ⓓ   86. Ⓔ Ⓕ Ⓖ Ⓗ   97. Ⓐ Ⓑ Ⓒ Ⓓ   108. Ⓔ Ⓕ Ⓖ Ⓗ
65. Ⓐ Ⓑ Ⓒ Ⓓ   76. Ⓔ Ⓕ Ⓖ Ⓗ   87. Ⓐ Ⓑ Ⓒ Ⓓ   98. Ⓔ Ⓕ Ⓖ Ⓗ   109. Ⓐ Ⓑ Ⓒ Ⓓ
66. Ⓔ Ⓕ Ⓖ Ⓗ   77. Ⓐ Ⓑ Ⓒ Ⓓ   88. Ⓔ Ⓕ Ⓖ Ⓗ   99. Ⓐ Ⓑ Ⓒ Ⓓ   110. Ⓔ Ⓕ Ⓖ Ⓗ
67. Ⓐ Ⓑ Ⓒ Ⓓ   78. Ⓔ Ⓕ Ⓖ Ⓗ   89. Ⓐ Ⓑ Ⓒ Ⓓ   100. Ⓔ Ⓕ Ⓖ Ⓗ   111. Ⓐ Ⓑ Ⓒ Ⓓ
68. Ⓔ Ⓕ Ⓖ Ⓗ   79. Ⓐ Ⓑ Ⓒ Ⓓ   90. Ⓔ Ⓕ Ⓖ Ⓗ   101. Ⓐ Ⓑ Ⓒ Ⓓ   112. Ⓔ Ⓕ Ⓖ Ⓗ
69. Ⓐ Ⓑ Ⓒ Ⓓ   80. Ⓔ Ⓕ Ⓖ Ⓗ   91. Ⓐ Ⓑ Ⓒ Ⓓ   102. Ⓔ Ⓕ Ⓖ Ⓗ   113. Ⓐ Ⓑ Ⓒ Ⓓ
70. Ⓔ Ⓕ Ⓖ Ⓗ   81. Ⓐ Ⓑ Ⓒ Ⓓ   92. Ⓔ Ⓕ Ⓖ Ⓗ   103. Ⓐ Ⓑ Ⓒ Ⓓ   114. Ⓔ Ⓕ Ⓖ Ⓗ
71. Ⓐ Ⓑ Ⓒ Ⓓ   82. Ⓔ Ⓕ Ⓖ Ⓗ   93. Ⓐ Ⓑ Ⓒ Ⓓ   104. Ⓔ Ⓕ Ⓖ Ⓗ
72. Ⓔ Ⓕ Ⓖ Ⓗ   83. Ⓐ Ⓑ Ⓒ Ⓓ   94. Ⓔ Ⓕ Ⓖ Ⓗ   105. Ⓐ Ⓑ Ⓒ Ⓓ
73. Ⓐ Ⓑ Ⓒ Ⓓ   84. Ⓔ Ⓕ Ⓖ Ⓗ   95. Ⓐ Ⓑ Ⓒ Ⓓ   106. Ⓔ Ⓕ Ⓖ Ⓗ

The Tutorverse

Practice Test 1
(Diagnostic)

Section One: English Language Arts

Recommended Time Limit: 90 minutes

Revising/Editing

Questions 1-10

The Revising/Editing section is in two parts: Part A and Part B

Revising/Editing Part A

Directions: Read and answer each of the following questions. You must recognize and correct errors in conventions of standard written English in sentences or short paragraphs. Mark the best answer for each question on the answer sheet.

1. Read this sentence:

> The dog chased after the soccer ball with a bushy, wagging tail.

Which edit should be made to correct this sentence?

    A. move *bushy* after *the* and before *dog*
    B. move *with a bushy, wagging tail* before *the soccer*
    C. move *with a bushy, wagging tail* after *dog*
    D. move *with a bushy, wagging tail* after *chased*

2. Read this sentence:

> Temperatures in Hawaii can be much, much warmer than Antarctica.

How should this sentence be revised?

    E. Temperatures in Hawaii can be much, much warmer than all of Antarctica.
    F. Temperatures in Hawaii can be much, much warmer than those in Antarctica.
    G. Hawaii's temperatures can be much, much warmer than Antarctica.
    H. Hawaiian temperatures can be much, much warmer than Antarctica.

3. Read this paragraph:

> (1) Since chili was my sister and my favorite food, we decided to enter the chili contest at the county fair. (2) We spent hours of our time looking over recipes before finally deciding upon and cooking the most promising sounding one. (3) During the contest, we were nervous when the judges tasted our chili, since their faces were inscrutable. (4) In the end, our's was the most popular chili at the contest, beating out even those of famous local chefs.

Which pair of revisions need to be made in the paragraph?

    A. Sentence 1: change **sister** to **sister's**
          Sentence 4: change **our's** to **ours**
    B. Sentence 1: delete the comma after **food**
          Sentence 2: delete **our**
    C. Sentence 1: change **sister** to **sister's**
          Sentence 3: delete the comma after **contest**
    D. Sentence 3: delete the comma after **contest**
          Sentence 4: change **our's** to **ours**

CONTINUE TO THE NEXT PAGE

The Tutorverse

Revising/Editing Part B

Directions: Read the passage below and answer the questions following it. Each question asks how best to improve the writing quality of the passage and to correct errors so that the passage follows the conventions of standard written English. You may reread the passage if you need to. Mark the **best** answer for each question.

Dream On

(1) Martin Luther King, Jr.'s "I Have a Dream" speech is one of the most famous speeches of the 20th century. (2) Part of the reason for this fame is due to the different techniques King used throughout the speech.

(3) Throughout his speech, King made references to a number of carefully prepared sources. (4) King delivered this speech on August 28, 1963, in Washington, D.C., in front of a crowd of over 250,000. (5) His speech called for an end to racism and equal rights for all Americans. (6) These included Shakespeare, the Bible, Abraham Lincoln's Emancipation Proclamation, the Constitution, and the Declaration of Independence. (7) He alluded to these other sources because he thought that they would help make his speech more effective and interesting.

(8) As he spoke to the crowd, King felt that the audience was not reacting as he had hoped. (9) It was then that King departed from his carefully written speech, improvising instead and not following his prepared speech, making it up as he went along. (10) King drew on his years as a preacher and spoke the following unforgettable words: "I have a dream." (11) King delivered his first sermon at Ebenezer Baptist Church in Atlanta, Georgia, in 1947.

(12) The rest of his speech, in which King expanded on this idea of a dream, was improvised. (13) He described a world in which people of all races and backgrounds lived together peacefully. (14) He told his listeners, "I say to you today, my friends, that in spite of the difficulties and frustrations of the moment, I still have a dream!" (15) The crowd roared in approval.

(16) Part of what made King's speech so effective was his use of a speaking tactic called anaphora. (17) This is the repetition of a phrase at the beginning of sentences. (18) Though it was unplanned, King repeated the statement "I have a dream" eight times throughout his entire speech. (19) By using this technique, he was able to help his audience imagine the society he dreamed of.

(20) King also used the volume of his voice to help capture the attention of his audience. (21) Sometimes, he would raise the volume of his voice, speaking loudly, confidently, and passionately. (22) Other times, King would lower the volume of his voice, speaking more quietly, peacefully, and sometimes even sadly.

(23) King's speech on the steps of the Lincoln Memorial represented an important turning point in America's history. (24) Thanks to the powerful techniques King used throughout his speech, he was able to moved the hearts and minds of an entire generation.

4. Where should sentence 3 be moved to improve the organization of the second paragraph (sentences 3-7)?

   E. between sentences 4 and 5
   F. between sentences 5 and 6
   G. between sentences 6 and 7
   H. to the end of the paragraph (after sentence 7)

CONTINUE TO THE NEXT PAGE

The Tutorverse

5. Which transition should be added to the beginning of sentence 8? *C*

    A. Clearly,
    B. Besides,
    C. Nonetheless,
    D. Consequently,

6. Which revision of sentence 9 uses the most precise language? *E*

    E. It was then that King began to improvise, coming up with a new speech on the spot.
    F. It was then that King began to make things up as he went along, not following his prepared speech.
    G. It was then that King improvised and did not following his prepared speech, making things up as he went along.
    H. It was then that King departed from his carefully written speech, improvising instead of following his prepared speech.

7. What is the best way to combine sentences 16 and 17 to clarify the relationship between ideas? *C*

    A. Part of what made King's speech so effective was his use of a speaking tactic called anaphora, not the repetition of a phrase at the beginning of sentences.
    B. Part of what made King's speech so effective was his use of a speaking tactic called anaphora, and the repetition of a phrase at the beginning of sentences.
    C. Part of what made King's speech so effective was his use of a speaking tactic called anaphora, which is the repetition of a phrase at the beginning of sentences.
    D. Part of what made King's speech so effective was his use of a speaking tactic called anaphora, because of the repetition of a phrase at the beginning of sentences.

8. Read this sentence. *H*

> Together, these tactics had the effect of drawing the audience even more deeply into his words.

Where should this sentence be added to best develop the ideas in the sixth paragraph (sentences 20-22)?

    E. before sentence 20
    F. between sentences 20 and 21
    G. between sentences 21 and 22
    H. at the end of the paragraph (after sentence 22)

9. Which edit is needed to correct sentence 24? *A*

    A. change **moved** to **move**
    B. change **was** to **has been**
    C. delete the comma after **speech**
    D. change **generation** to **generations**

10. Which sentence presents information that shifts away from the main topic and should be removed? *F*

    E. sentence 8
    F. sentence 11
    G. sentence 15
    H. sentence 19

CONTINUE TO THE NEXT PAGE

The Tutorverse

Reading Comprehension

Questions 11-57

Directions: Read each passage below and answer the questions following it. Base your answers only on information contained in the passage. You may reread a passage if you need to. Mark the best answer for each question.

The Cold

In the city, the cold is
thin and vain.
He hurtles down the streets—
no time to waste! work to be done!—
5   (rushing,
preening),
his gleaming suit of ice,
and his granite topcoat,
and his cufflinks
10   Like one perfect snowdrop each.

Someone walks by
(Is that you?)
He narrows his eyes
and points a finger,
15   (it looks like you)
a single silver saber[1],
in a single sweeping gesture—
whhtt! whhtt! whhtt!—
shearing through feather and wool and bone
20   Like a blade across the face.

The buildings stand taller, sharper as he passes,
polished and menacing.
The avenues type themselves with snow,
white on black
25   (or is it black on white?)
because they have important news—
The cold is here!
The cold is here!—
and the frozen bridge arches splendidly across the river
30   Like a diamond necklace laid against the sky.

In the country, the cold is
Soft. Soft.
She skates across the fields—
abundant,
35   lush—
her fleecy white coat
trimmed with last year's leaves and a brooch of sleepy swallows,
and her magnificent hoary[2] cloak,

---

[1] **saber**: a sword with a curved blade
[2] **hoary:** a greyish white color

CONTINUE TO THE NEXT PAGE

The Tutorverse

and her shimmering earrings
40 Like three new snowflakes each.

She tilts her wrists slightly as she walks by,
Taking care to ruffle the chimney tops.
One red bird on a branch
announces her sweep through the fields—
45 chill-y! chilly-chilly-chilly chill-EE! —
as she smooths every furrow,
rounds every rooftop
furs every point,
turning bone to feather and wool.

50 A city car winds up a driveway,
  (Is that you?)
and stops. The doors open.
  (it looks like you).
She peers more closely and before the wind can take a breath,
55 swoops through the open car, clasping the visitors in her blowsy embrace,
pressing their city-cold, close, against her bosom.
The birds nestled comfortably there take umbrage[3], take flight,
and in their splendid flap and dissent: snow,
like laughter, brilliant and shattered, swirling up into the sky.

60 They meet twice a year:
Once in fall to make their plans,
once in spring to say goodbye.

---

[3] **umbrage**: offense

11. How does the similar construction of the sentence in lines 1-2 and the sentence in line 31-32 contribute to the meaning of the poem?

   A. It introduces the two people whose dialogue make up the poem.
   B. It shows that winter has a similar form regardless of location.
   C. It suggests that people in the city are vainer and more arrogant than people in the country.
   D. It contrasts the sensation of cold in the city and in the country.

12. The comparison to a blade in lines 20 helps show that the cold in the city

   E. can be deadly to the people it touches.
   F. penetrates multiple layers of clothing easily.
   G. disfigures people, by leaving scars on their faces.
   H. causes animals to lose their fur, and birds to lose their feathers.

CONTINUE TO THE NEXT PAGE

The Tutorverse

13. Read lines 3-6 and lines 33-35 from the poem. *A*

> **He hurtles down the streets—**
> **no time to waste! work to be done!—**
> **(rushing,**
> **preening),**

> **She skates across the fields—**
> **abundant,**
> **lush—**

How do these lines contribute to the development of a central idea of the poem?

A. They suggest that the cold takes on characteristics of the local setting.
B. They highlight that the cold is occurring in similar settings.
C. They suggest that the cold in the city and the cold in the country move in similar ways.
D. They reveal that the cold in the city and the cold in the country are attempting to meet each other.

14. How do the poet's descriptions of outer appearances in lines 7-10 and lines 36-40 contribute to the central idea of the poem?

E. They highlight the excellent taste that the cold in the city and the cold in the country show in their choice of outfits.
F. They emphasize the degree of chill that occurs in both the country and the city, based on the many layers that people are wearing.
G. They contrast the sleek, sharp nature of cold in the city with the cozy, comfortable cold of the country.
H. They show how wealthy people in the city and people in the country are based on their outer attire.

15. Read lines 29-30. *D*

> **and the frozen bridge arches splendidly across the river**
> **Like a diamond necklace laid against the sky.**

How does the simile contribute to the development of ideas in the stanza?

A. It emphasizes how wealthy people in the city are by describing their jewelry.
B. It describes a present that the cold of the city intends to give to the cold of the country.
C. It supports the city avenues' excitement at the arrival of winter.
D. It shows that winter in the city can be beautiful as well as menacing.

CONTINUE TO THE NEXT PAGE

The Tutorverse

16. What impact does the repetition of the phrases "(Is that you?)" (lines 12, 51) and "(It looks like you)" (lines 15, 53) have on the meaning of the poem? F

   E. They suggest that winter is directly addressing the reader.
   F. They present a romantic connection between the cold in the city and in the country.
   G. They imply that winter is targeting a specific person with cold winds.
   H. They reveal the confusion that the cold feels at the crowds of people in the city.

17. Read lines 43-45 from the poem. A

> One red bird on a branch
> announces her sweep through the fields—
> chill-y! chilly-chilly-chilly chill-EE! —

   The figurative language in these lines convey

   A. the playful personality of the cold of the country, through the sound of a bird call.
   B. how winter is a harsh and difficult season to animals and people alike.
   C. how weak the cold is in the country side, compared to the cold of the city.
   D. the extreme cold that characterizes winter in the country, as evidenced by the suffering of wildlife.

18. Read lines 54-56 from the poem. G

> She peers more closely and before the wind can take a breath,
> swoops through the open car, clasping the visitors in her blowsy embrace,
> pressing their city-cold, close, against her bosom.

   The personification in these lines suggest that the cold in the country is

   E. a reckless force that moves without thinking.
   F. unaware of the existence of cold in other places.
   G. eager for opportunities to meet the cold in the city.
   H. fond of visitors from other locations in the world.

19. In the last stanza (lines 60-62), how does the repetition of the word "once" affect the tone of the ending? C

   A. It reinforces a joyful tone as the cold of the country remembers meeting the cold of the city.
   B. It establishes a light-hearted tone by ending on a joke between the two entities.
   C. It creates a somber tone by emphasizing how rarely the cold of the country and the city are able to meet despite their desire.
   D. It suggests a frustrated tone as the cold of the country and the city are separated by distance.

CONTINUE TO THE NEXT PAGE

The Tutorverse

A Garden Masterpiece

1   Claude Monet's *Water Lilies* are some of the world's most renowned Impressionist pieces. *Water Lilies* is not a single painting, but rather a series of over 250 oil paintings, inspired by Monet's flower garden.

2   Monet and his contemporaries, including Camille Pissarro, Auguste Renoir, and Edgar Degas, were known as Impressionists, and were the first to challenge the conventions of Parisian art. At the time, artists depended on patronage and institutional acceptance to determine success. Exclusive academies, like the École des Beaux Arts, focused on classical and realistic art. Artists depicted idealized landscapes inside of a studio, and focused on developing their technical skills to create hyper realistic depictions of dramatic though fantastical scenes. Impressionists turned this tradition on its head: they focused on emotions, freedom of expression, and ordinary subjects.

3   Monet captured what he saw as it was happening. He began to refine his landscape paintings in the 1890s with series paintings including *Haystacks*, *Poplars*, and *Rouen Cathedral*. In these series, Monet painted the same site over and over, trying to capture how the appearance of the space changed at different times of the day. Light and shadow were important to Monet, and he used light primers instead of dark ones to create an array of tones.

4   Starting in the late 1890s, Monet primarily focused on the water lily pond in his garden at his Giverny estate in Normandy, France. He had designed the pond himself, composing the placement of weeping willows and bamboo trees as if creating a work of art. "My finest masterpiece," he once said, "is my garden."

5   From 1899 onward, Monet repeatedly used the garden as artistic inspiration. He wanted to capture every impression he observed. The resulting paintings epitomize the Impressionist style, because they capture the sensation of the landscape rather than exactly what was there. Monet focused on perception and feeling rather than on capturing the smallest details.

6   One of Monet's goals was to create the illusion of water without a horizon. These paintings focus on the surface of the water rather than the land and sky. In fact, Monet only shows the land and sky in the reflection of the water. Instead of illustrating objects in the landscape in great detail, Monet allows individual petals, leaves, and ripples to blend in with their surroundings in a beautiful hazy blur.

7   As he labored over the series, he began to experiment with the scale of the work. Some of the paintings were done on extremely large canvases. Monet wanted to evoke the feeling of peaceful meditation in the midst of a flowering aquarium. The vast expanse of the canvas was meant to give the illusion of a wave with no horizon and no shore.

8   Monet had two distinct compositions of the water lilies. The first one shows the edge of the pond and its vegetation, which is seen in the Japanese Bridge painting. The second form only includes the surface of the water with the flowers and reflections. In the second type of composition, the elements are closeup in a tight frame.

9   When he was eighty-two, Monet discovered he had a cataract and could not see with his right eye. He painted the last of the series including "Water Lilies and Japanese Bridge" right before his death. Although Monet was losing his vision, the quality of his artwork did not suffer. Since he sought to capture the sensation and perception of a moment rather than the exact forms, these works reflected his experience of impaired vision in moving, emotional ways.

CONTINUE TO THE NEXT PAGE

The Tutorverse

10 At the time of his death, Monet was wealthy and well-respected. ~~He had created almost 300 water lilies~~ paintings over the course of his life. Over 40 of them were in large format. Monet offered what would be his last water lilies series to the French government on November 11, 1918, as a symbol of peace. The French government installed his last water lily series at the Musée de l'Orangerie in Paris in 1927, a few months after Monet's death, where they remain today. It was the culmination of thirty years of painting the water lilies.

11 There is no equivalent to Monet's masterpiece. Today, Monet's *Water Lilies* are considered to be some of the early twentieth century's greatest pieces. The paintings are exhibited all over the world in galleries including the Metropolitan Museum of Art and Museum of Modern Art in New York, the Musée d'Orsay in Paris, and the Art Institute of Chicago and attract millions of visitors a year. The dollar value of these works reflect their popularity; one of the paintings, "Nympheas," sold for $54 million in a recent auction.

20. Which statement best describes the central idea of the passage? F

    E. Monet escaped his early poverty by creating extremely valuable works of art.
    F. Monet was a pioneer of the Impressionist movement, and is known for the series *Water Lilies*, which portrays his focus on perception rather than realism.
    G. Monet was a provocative artist who hated the official art institutions of Paris, and painted landscape paintings outdoors to challenge traditional artists.
    H. Monet was a determined artist, and miraculously completed the last of the *Water Lilies* series despite developing a cataract and becoming nearly blind.

21. Read this sentence from paragraph 2. C

> **Artists depicted idealized landscapes inside of a studio, and focused on developing their technical skills to create hyper realistic depictions of dramatic though fantastical scenes.**

What role does this sentence play in the overall structure of the passage?

    A. It explains the artistic background of the Impressionists, who once studied at these academies, in order to show the evolution of their artistic style.
    B. It contrasts the way art schools were structured before and after the Impressionist era.
    C. It gives context to the Impressionist movement by describing the traditional aesthetics that Impressionist art rebelled against.
    D. It emphasizes the similarities between Impressionist art and the works of the previous era.

22. What is the most likely reason the author uses the word "idealized" in paragraph 2? H

    E. to highlight the realism and technical skills of traditional artists in landscape painting
    F. to emphasize how important the work of traditional artists was to the development of Impressionism
    G. to suggest that people only respected art that was done of nature and landscapes rather than ordinary subjects
    H. to show how traditional artists were painting their ideas of what nature should look like rather than on how nature makes people feel

CONTINUE TO THE NEXT PAGE

The Tutorverse

23. According to the passage, Monet painted the same scene over and over again because   D

    A. he was a perfectionist, and it took many tries to capture every detail in the painting.
    B. each of the paintings was valuable and able to sell for large sums of money.
    C. his eye cataract prevented him from seeing and painting clearly.
    D. he wanted to study how the appearance, light, and shadows in a space changed over time.

24. How does paragraph 5 support the development of the central idea?

    E. It describes how his paintings embodied his artistic concepts.
    F. It highlights his reputation for painting repetitive artworks.
    G. It reinforces the wealth of his experience in painting gardens all over Europe.
    H. It emphasizes his passion for his garden by showing how he thought it was his finest masterpiece.

25. Which evidence best supports the idea that Monet's art was about perception and not accuracy?

    A. "Monet had two distinct compositions of the water lilies." (paragraph 8)
    B. "Although Monet was losing his vision, the quality of his artwork did not suffer." (paragraph 9)
    C. "He had created almost 300 water lilies paintings over the course of his life. Over 40 of them were in large format." (paragraph 10)
    D. "Monet offered what would be his last water lilies series to the French government on November 11, 1918, as a symbol of peace." (paragraph 10)

26. Which of the following most likely describes the work of an Impressionist painting?   G

    E. a carefully planned, detailed painting of a grand building, like a cathedral
    F. a realistic painting of a mountain with painstakingly drawn waterfalls and glaciers
    G. a painting of a home that creates feelings of warmth, happiness, and comfort
    H. a painting that shows a fictional location of extreme beauty and natural perfection

27. Which sentence best explains why Monet experimented with different size canvases for his paintings?

    A. "The vast expanse of the canvas was meant to give the illusion of a wave with no horizon and no shore." (paragraph 7)
    B. "The first one shows the edge of the pond and its vegetation, which is seen in the Japanese Bridge painting." (paragraph 8)
    C. "The second form only includes the surface of the water with the flowers and reflections." (paragraph 8)
    D. "There is no equivalent to Monet's masterpiece." (paragraph 11)

CONTINUE TO THE NEXT PAGE

The Tutorverse

The Rule of Law

Equality for All

1 Today, many societies are governed by laws and legal principles rather than the whims of a ruling regime. These legal principles help settle conflicts and ensure the orderly conduct of various interpersonal interactions. Government based on legal principles is often referred to as the rule of law.

2 The rule of law stands in contrast to systems of government that grant ruling power to those with the most power. Unlike in the latter, in the former, everyone is bound by the same rules and laws that govern the society. In the former, everyone, from the poorest pauper to the wealthiest baron, must adhere to codified laws. Even the administrators of the government – the prime ministers, presidents, and statesmen – are bound by the rule of law.

A Rare Practice

3 The rule of law is a fairly new concept. For centuries, many societies were organized as stratocracies, plutocracies, or monarchies. These societies conferred ruling authority on the powerful. In a stratocracy, such as the ancient Greek city-state of Sparta, society is governed by warriors, and power is held by those with the greatest physical strength. In a plutocracy, such as the Italian republics of Venice and Florence during the Middle Ages, ruling power is derived from economic wealth. For nearly two thousand years, the emperors of China ruled with absolute authority in the form of a monarchy, with power derived from the divine. In many such societies, the ruling class often lived by an entirely different set of laws than those governing the ruled.

4 Yet even in the distant past, the seeds of modern rule of law were being sown. The ancient Greek philosopher Aristotle was a fervent advocate for it. He stated that "it is more proper that law should govern than any one of the citizens" and that "if it is advantageous to place the supreme power in some particular persons, they should be appointed to be only guardians, and the servants of the laws." Similar rumblings also surfaced in ancient China in the form of the legalist school of thought. Han Fei, a political philosopher of the second century BC, wrote in his seminal work that "the intelligent ruler...makes the law measure merits and makes no arbitrary judgment himself." Despite the logic of Aristotle and Han Fei's arguments, few societies at the time actually practiced the theories advanced by these legalists.

A Shining Light

5 Some thousand years later, King John of medieval England signed the Magna Carta. This document would help the rule of law flower. It would go on to limit the power of the English monarchy and establish the rules and laws governing the people of England. It would go on to serve as a framework for other societies aspiring to the rule of law.

6 One notable example of the Magna Carta's influence can be found in the Constitution of the United States. The framers of the Constitution wanted to ensure that no individual, no matter how talented or persuasive, could ever rise above the law. This sentiment rose largely from their study of history. It was also influenced from their personal experiences with the then-King of England. The founding fathers of the early American republic limited the power of the president by incorporating the concepts of "checks and balances" within the Constitution. The Constitution separated the federal government into three branches: the executive branch (led by the President), the legislative branch (run by Congress), and the judicial branch (headed by the Supreme Court). As the highest law in the land, the Constitution ensured

CONTINUE TO THE NEXT PAGE

The Tutorverse

that each branch and its leaders were bound to the rule of law. The power of each branch was "checked and balanced" by the roles and powers given to the other branches of government.

7 During the 19th and 20th centuries, the United States rose to become a world superpower. As a result, other countries attempted to replicate the Constitution and the rule of law it reflected. Governments in Latin America, Eastern Europe, Africa, and Southeast Asia attempted to use the rule of law to form the same "checks and balances" within their own governments.

8 American rule of law, which had its roots in medieval English governance and ancient political philosophies, consequently became the new norm in global politics. As a result, a concept that once existed in practical obscurity went on to dominate global governance.

28. Which statement best describes the central idea of the passage?

   E. All countries should adopt the rule of law.
   F. Rule of law is a good idea that has not been successfully put into practice.
   G. Rule of law was invented by the American government in the form of the Constitution, and has been adopted by other countries following the American example.
   H. Rule of law is a concept that was created in ancient times but only put to practice in recent human history.

29. Read these sentences from paragraph 2.

   The rule of law stands in contrast to systems of government that grant ruling power to those with the most power. Unlike in the latter, in the former, everyone is bound by the same rules and laws that govern the society. In the former, everyone, from the poorest pauper to the wealthiest baron, must adhere to codified laws.

   What do these sentences reveal about how political leaders can act in a society governed by rule of law?

   A. They are just as accountable to laws as the average citizen.
   B. They still have the power to make all decisions regardless of the law.
   C. They are held accountable to stricter laws than the average citizen in their nation.
   D. They must follow codified law in most instances, but may override it under certain circumstances.

30. How does paragraph 3 fit into the overall structure of the passage?

   E. It helps provide context for how the rule of law is different from other kinds of government.
   F. It argues for how other types of government have been more successful than the rule of law.
   G. It demonstrates how other political systems have failed before the arrival of the rule of law.
   H. It indicates that the idea of rule of law had been born thousands of years ago.

CONTINUE TO THE NEXT PAGE

The Tutorverse

31. The author would most likely agree with which of the following statements?

~~A. Aristotle was a more influential philosopher than Han Fei.~~
~~B. The strongest people in society should be the ones to lead it.~~
~~C. A society ruled by the wealthy is preferable to one that is ruled by a single person.~~
(D.) The American Constitution was heavily influenced by a similar document in medieval England.

32. Which sentence from the passage best conveys Han Fei and Aristotle's perspectives regarding rule of law? H

E. "These legal principles help settle conflicts and ensure the orderly conduct of various interpersonal interactions." (paragraph 1)
F. "…society is governed by warriors, and power is held by those with the greatest physical strength." (paragraph 3)
G. "the emperors of China ruled with absolute authority in the form of a monarchy, with power derived from the divine." (paragraph 3)
(H.) "…wanted to ensure that no individual, no matter how talented or persuasive, could ever rise above the law." (paragraph 6)

33. Paragraph 5 contributes to the development of the central idea of the passage by

~~A. illustrating how a monarchy's power increased and the rights of the king became supreme.~~
B. conveying how much societies governed by monarchies and plutocracies resisted the use of rule of law.
C. highlighting the difference between theory and practice in societies that first adopted rule of law.
(D.) emphasizing the historical moment where rule of law was put into effect rather than remaining a theoretical concept.

34. Read this sentence from paragraph 7. E

During the 19th and 20th centuries, the United States rose to become a world superpower. As a result, other countries attempted to replicate the Constitution and the rule of law it reflected.

What does this statement reveal about how other nations viewed the U.S. Constitution?

(E.) They were convinced by it that rule of law could be implemented in reality, to great effect.
F. They saw it as fundamentally flawed, and made modifications based on its mistakes while still preserving the spirit of rule of law.
G. They feared it as a symbol of the United States' superpower status in the 19th and 20th centuries.
H. They tried to undermine its power by claiming that it did not truly follow the of rule of law.

CONTINUE TO THE NEXT PAGE

The Tutorverse

Prove It!

1   For thousands of years, people have tried to explain nature. They often did so in creative ways. Norse mythology explained thunder as the sound of the god Thor ragefully hitting things with his hammer, Mjölnir. In Japan, earthquakes were blamed on a giant catfish named Namazu, who was said to be trapped beneath the islands. Hawaiians ascribed volcanic activity to the goddess Pele, a beautiful but vengeful deity. All over the world, people used myths and fantastical tales to explain the world around them. Today, however, our understanding of nature has advanced significantly beyond these stories. This is thanks, in part, to the development of the scientific method.

2   The scientific method is a rigorous process that is used to prove specific claims. Scientists begin by carefully observing the phenomenon, as well as doing prior research, before coming up with a hypothesis, or claim. To test this hypothesis, scientists then create and conduct an experiment, collect data, and analyze it. Using the resulting information, they conclude whether the hypothesis was true or false. Their results are not assumed to be true, regardless of their reputation. Instead, other scientists may analyze their work for inconsistencies, and recreate the experiment to check if the conclusions are valid. An example of this is the famous case of the Piltdown Man. In 1912, an amateur archaeologist claimed to have found the evolutionary 'link' between ape and man. Later testing showed that the skull was artificially created by combining skull fragments from a human and an ape. On the other hand, when Gregor Mendel's famous discoveries about genetics were criticized for being false, analysis of his records and methods confirmed the validity of his results. Indeed, repeatable and observable uses of the scientific method have helped advance our understanding of the world around us.

3   The scientific method has been especially helpful in formulating our understanding of gravity. Gravity is a natural force that pulls objects toward one another. Gravity is the force that keeps the planets orbiting around the sun, and the moon orbiting around the Earth. It is also the force that allows objects, like meteorites, to "fall" to the Earth. Since gravity is a force that cannot be perceived directly by our five senses, at one point in history, people did not realize that gravity was responsible for these events. They believed that some supernatural being controlled all-natural events. Then, in the 1600s, Galileo Galilei conducted a famous experiment that changed people's understanding of how the world works.

4   Galileo was an early supporter of the scientific method. He used carefully designed experiments to study the ways gravity affected lighter versus heavier objects. Prior to his famous experiment, people still believed that heavier objects fell faster to the Earth than lighter objects. After all, a hammer will hit the ground faster than a feather, when both are dropped from the same height at the same time. Galileo, however, suspected that there was more to these scenarios than met the eye. He set out to test his hypothesis by employing the scientific method.

5   According to historical accounts, Galileo climbed to the top of the Leaning Tower of Pisa[1] with two heavy balls. These balls, though of similar shape and size, had different weights. When Galileo dropped these two balls from the Tower, he found that they hit the ground at the same time. This experiment led Galileo to conclude – rightly – that all objects will fall the same rate of acceleration, regardless of their weight.

6   Galileo's famous experiment not only encouraged people to conduct more experiments using the scientific method, but led to findings that became a cornerstone of modern physics. Today, we know that the reason the feather will fall more slowly than the hammer is because of air resistance, not because of its weight. Since the feather has a relatively large surface area, molecules in the air play a large part in slowing down the feather's descent. Similarly, because the hammer has a smaller surface

---

[1] **Leaning Tower of Pisa**: a tall tower in Italy

CONTINUE TO THE NEXT PAGE

area than the feather, the effect of molecules in the air on the hammer's descent is less than the effect of molecules in the air on the feather's descent.

7 Incredibly, in 2017, scientists reproduced this experiment in a satellite in outer space. Scientists wanted to see if the results of Galileo's experiment could be more precisely reproduced in the absence of air resistance. Their results confirmed Galileo's findings – and demonstrate how the scientific method can illuminate truth.

35. Which statement best describes the central idea of the passage? *D*

   A. Myths and legends help people understand natural phenomena more accurately.
   B. Galileo's experiment at the Leaning Tower of Pisa helped to define gravity.
   C. The scientific perception of why things fall has evolved through time.
   D. Using the scientific method has helped people better understand natural phenomena.

36. Why does the author describe several myths in paragraph 1? *G*

   E. to illustrate the central idea that nature has inspired myths from many different cultures
   F. to prove that natural phenomena is inherently mysterious and can only be understood through stories
   G. to highlight the simplistic and fanciful nature of early understandings of natural phenomenon
   H. to emphasize how far humanity's understanding of gravity has evolved

37. In paragraph 2, the words "repeatable" and "observable" are used to highlight *A*

   A. how the scientific method leads to dependable and objective findings.
   B. how experiments must be carried out by specific, talented scientists to be valid.
   C. that conclusions from scientific method experiments are usually the result of luck.
   D. that scientists enjoy repeating the same experiment over and over again.

38. Read this sentence from paragraph 4. *F*

   Galileo, however, suspected that there was more to these scenarios than met the eye.

   What is the most likely reason the author uses the word "suspected"?

   E. to show that Galileo had a suspicious and paranoid personality
   F. to highlight how Galileo used the scientific method to generate a hypothesis
   G. to emphasize how Galileo's theories have been overturned in later years due to lack of sufficient evidence
   H. to reinforce how similar to Galileo's reaction was to other scientists' perception of free fall

CONTINUE TO THE NEXT PAGE

The Tutorverse

39. How does paragraph 5 help develop the central idea of the passage? *B*

    A. It presents a solution to the scientific questions posed in a prior paragraph.
    B. It illustrates an early historical example of the scientific method yielding important information.
    C. It contrasts the way scientists used the scientific method in the past and present.
    D. It details a historical experiment that was not supported by later re-enactments.

40. Which conclusion is best supported by the information in paragraph 6? *E*

    E. On the moon, where there is no air, a feather and hammer will fall to the ground at the same speed.
    F. If a feather and hammer are the same weight, they will fall to the ground at the same speed.
    G. If a feather and hammer are made from the same materials, they will fall to the ground at the same speed.
    H. A hammer will fall faster than a feather under any circumstance.

41. How does paragraph 7 support the development of the central idea? *C*

    A. It emphasizes the progress that has been made in the field of physics research.
    B. It reveals how Galileo's results were determined by the location of his experiments.
    C. It highlights how Galileo's experiment led to a valid conclusion because it was reproducible by others.
    D. It shows how experiments have changed since Galileo's time, despite being inspired by the idea of the scientific method.

CONTINUE TO THE NEXT PAGE

The Tutorverse

Adapted from *The Scarlet Plague*

by Jack London

1 When he could eat no more, the old man sighed, wiped his hands, and gazed out over the sea. With the content of a full stomach, he waxed reminiscent.

2 "To think of it! I've seen this beach alive with men, women, and children on a pleasant Sunday. And there weren't any bears to eat them up, either. And right up there on the cliff was a big restaurant where you could get anything you wanted to eat. Four million people lived in San Francisco then. And now, in the whole city and county there aren't forty all told. And out there on the sea were ships and ships always to be seen, going in for the Golden Gate or coming out. And airships in the air – dirigibles and flying machines. They could travel two hundred miles an hour. When I was a boy, there were men alive who remembered the coming of the first airships, and now I have lived to see the last of them, and that was sixty years ago."

3 The old man babbled on, unheeded by the boys, who were long accustomed to his garrulousness, and whose vocabularies, besides, lacked the greater portion of the words he used. It was noticeable that in these ramblings, his English seemed to break out into better construction. But when he talked directly with the boys it lapsed, largely, into their own uncouth and simpler forms.

4 "But there weren't many crabs in those days," the old man wandered on. "They were fished out, and they were great delicacies. The open season was only a month long, too. And now crabs are accessible the whole year around. Think of it – catching all the crabs you want, any time you want, in the surf of the Cliff House beach!"

5 A sudden commotion among the goats brought the boys to their feet. The dogs about the fire rushed to join their snarling fellow who guarded the goats, while the goats themselves stampeded in the direction of their human protectors. A half-dozen forms, lean and gray, glided about on the sand hillocks and faced the bristling dogs. Edwin arched an arrow that fell short. But Hare-Lip, with a sling such as David carried into battle against Goliath[1], hurled a stone through the air that whistled from the speed of its flight. It fell squarely among the wolves and caused them to slink away toward the dark depths of the eucalyptus forest.

6 The boys laughed and lay down again in the sand, while Granser sighed ponderously. He had eaten too much, and, with hands clasped on his paunch, the fingers interlaced, he resumed his maunderings.

7 "'The fleeting systems lapse like foam.' That's it – foam, and fleeting. All man's toil upon the planet was just so much foam. He domesticated the serviceable animals, destroyed the hostile ones, and cleared the land of its wild vegetation. And then he passed, and the flood of primordial life rolled back again, sweeping his handiwork away – the weeds and the forest inundated his fields, and now there are wolves on the Cliff House beach." He was appalled by the thought. "Where four million people disported themselves, the wild wolves roam to-day. Think of it! And all because of the Scarlet Death--"

8 "Tell us about the Red Death, Granser," Hare-Lip demanded.

9 "The Scarlet Death," Edwin corrected.

---

[1] **David & Goliath**: a biblical story about how David defeats Goliath, a much larger and more powerful enemy

CONTINUE TO THE NEXT PAGE

10 "An' don't work all that funny lingo on us," Hare-Lip went on. "Talk sensible, Granser, like a Santa Rosan ought to talk. Other Santa Rosans don't talk like you."

11 The tale began.

12 "There were very many people in the world in those days. San Francisco alone held four millions—"

13 "What is millions?" Edwin interrupted.

14 Granser looked at him kindly.

15 "I know you cannot count beyond ten, so I will tell you. Hold up your two hands. On both of them you have altogether ten fingers and thumbs. Very well. I now take this grain of sand—you hold it, Hoo-Hoo." He dropped the grain of sand into the lad's palm and went on. "Now that grain of sand stands for the ten fingers of Edwin. I add another grain. That's ten more fingers. And I add another, and another, until I have added as many grains as Edwin has fingers and thumbs. That makes what I call one hundred. Remember that word—one hundred. Now I put this pebble in Hare-Lip's hand. It stands for ten grains of sand, or one hundred fingers..." And so on, laboriously, and with much reiteration, he strove to build up in their minds a crude conception of numbers. As the quantities increased, he had the boys holding different magnitudes in each of their hands. For still higher sums, he laid the symbols on the log of driftwood; and for symbols he was hard put, being compelled to use the teeth from the skulls for millions, and the crab-shells for billions. It was here that he stopped, for the boys were showing signs of becoming tired.

16 "There were four million people in San Francisco—four teeth."

17 The boys' eyes ranged along from the teeth and from hand to hand, down through the pebbles and sand-grains to Edwin's fingers. And back again they ranged along the ascending series in the effort to grasp such inconceivable numbers.

18 "That was a lot of folks, Granser," Edwin at last hazarded.

19 "The world was full of people. The census of 2010 gave eight billions for the whole world—eight crab-shells. Eight crab-shells there, yes, eight billion people were alive on the earth when the Scarlet Death began."

42. In paragraph 2, how does the phrase "To think of it!" affect the tone of the paragraph?

E. It creates a marveling tone by suggesting that the things Granser once saw now seem unimaginable.
F. It creates a sullen tone by suggesting that Granser feels his loss of the world of his youth was an injustice.
G. It introduces a nostalgic tone by showing how much Granser misses being young and healthy.
H. It establishes a tone of contentment by showing how satisfied Granser feels with his meal.

43. How does paragraph 2 support the development of the plot?

A. It highlights the fantastical nature of the setting, as the story takes place on a different planet.
B. It establishes the setting as a realistic depiction of present times.
C. It reveals the setting is a time in the distant past, and compares it with the present.
D. It introduces the setting as a time in the possible future, and contrasts it with the present.

CONTINUE TO THE NEXT PAGE

The Tutorverse

44. Which excerpt from the passage best supports the idea that the boys do not fully understand Granser's way of speech?

    E. "It was noticeable that in these ramblings, his English seemed to break out into better construction." (paragraph 3)

    F. "'Tell us about the Red Death, Granser,' Hare-Lip demanded. 'The Scarlet Death,' Edwin corrected." (paragraphs 8-9)

    G. "'There were very many people in the world in those days. San Francisco alone held four millions—' 'What is millions?' Edwin interrupted." (paragraphs 12-13)

    H. "'That was a lot of folks, Granser,' Edwin at last hazarded." (paragraph 18)

45. Read this sentence from paragraph 3.

The old man babbled on, unheeded by the boys, who were long accustomed to his garrulousness, and whose vocabularies, besides, lacked the greater portion of the words he used.

The word "garrulousness" in the sentence conveys

    A. how annoying and frustrating the boys find Granser's stories to be.

    B. how trivial and unimportant Granser's rambling seemed to the boys.

    C. that Granser is being uncharacteristically talkative in this moment in the story.

    D. that Granser has become grumpy and irritable in disposition due to old age.

46. How do the details in paragraph 4 about the setting help support the development of the plot?

    E. It emphasizes the superiority of the current world as compared to the society of Granser's youth.

    F. It suggests that there are fundamental similarities between the world of Granser's youth and his current circumstances.

    G. It demonstrates that the boys are fascinated by Granser's stories about the past.

    H. It shows that not all the ways in which the world changed after the Scarlet Plague were for the worse.

47. Read this sentence from paragraph 5.

But Hare-Lip, with a sling such as David carried into battle against Goliath, hurled a stone through the air that whistled from the speed of its flight.

What is the most likely reason the author included the reference to David and Goliath?

    A. to portray the boys as significantly weaker beings than the wolves they face, and show how difficult it was for them to win the battle

    B. to emphasize the primitive nature of the boys by comparing them to characters from Biblical times

    C. to demonstrate the terror that the boys feel at the arrival of the wolves

    D. to show the boys' experience and confidence in dealing with dangerous predators in the wild

CONTINUE TO THE NEXT PAGE

The Tutorverse

48. Read this excerpt from paragraph 7.   E

> **"'The fleeting systems lapse like foam.' That's it – foam, and fleeting. All man's toil upon the planet was just so much foam."**

How does the metaphor in this sentence help support the theme of the passage?

- **E.** It implies that regardless of effort and progress, the outcomes of all human labor is temporary.
- **F.** It demonstrates how human systems had become so numerous that people lost their individuality.
- **G.** It illustrates how the human world was destroyed by pride when the sea levels rose.
- **H.** It shows the advancement of human technology in controlling weather and tidal patterns.

49. What do paragraphs 10 and 15 convey about the relationship between Granser and the boys? C

- **A.** They highlight the friction between the boys and Granser, who disagree constantly.
- **B.** They show how patient the boys are with Granser, despite his old age and feeblemindedness.
- **C.** They reinforce how patient Granser is with the boys, despite their ignorance and disrespect towards him.
- **D.** They reveal the irritation that the boys feel towards Granser, who is dependent on them for food.

CONTINUE TO THE NEXT PAGE

The Tutorverse

Helping Others Pays Off

1 For many, choosing a career path can be a scary task. There are many things to think about when considering different job opportunities. Oftentimes, it is hard to find a job that has all one's desired qualities. For example, a job that pays well can often be stressful or require long hours or advanced degrees of study. A job that is too easy might not be satisfying or stimulating enough, even if it pays well.

2 One potential option, which many have pursued in recent years, is the career of a registered nurse (RN). RNs perform a diverse set of duties. In general, RNs coordinate and provide care and education to patients and their families. In addition to caring for the body, some RNs also provide emotional support to their patients. RNs may choose to work directly with patients in bedside roles, or to provide care more indirectly. The opportunities are not limited to home or hospital, either: nurses can be found in clinics, schools, and even in prisons. Depending on personal preference, RNs can work exclusively with people of a specific age range or medical condition. Because there are so many options for specialization, RNs can choose to work in different environments. They can often choose roles that best suit their interests and strengths.

3 According to the United States Department of Labor's Bureau of Labor Statistics (BLS), the occupation is also one of the fastest growing in the healthcare economy. The BLS expects the opportunities for RN positions to grow 16 percent from 2014 to 2024 – an astonishingly high rate of growth exceeding most other occupations! As the world's population continues to grow and people continue to live longer, demand for healthcare professionals such as RNs is also expected to grow. As the population ages, more and more people will require both preventative care and management for chronic conditions, like diabetes and obesity. As a result, average compensation for RNs – already among the highest in the nation – is expected to rise.

4 RNs experience their fair share of challenges, however. Many RNs work long shifts, sometimes as long as 13 hours in a row. This is a practice that jeopardizes the safety of nurse and patient alike. In addition, due to the nature of their work, RNs are more exposed to pathogens and diseases than other people. Employers and RN advocacy groups recognize these challenges, and are now working together to address them.

5 Despite such drawbacks, RNs appear happy with their careers. In one study conducted by a healthcare staffing company, 90% of nurses surveyed indicated that they were very satisfied with their career choice, and over 80% plan to remain in this career for their lifetime. In a career-satisfaction interview, one nurse explained that she loves her career because of the "joy [in] caring for my patients, and the trust that develops with that relationship. [My patients] fulfill me, and I help provide them with the care they deserve." Another explained that "some of the most interesting people I have ever met came into my life because I'm a nurse."

6 Though requirements vary from country to country, prospective RNs in the United States have two options. Candidates can either obtain a minimum of an associate's degree in nursing, or they can receive a diploma from an approved nursing program. After these educational requirements are met, registered nurses must also pass the National Council Licensure Examination-Registered Nurses exam. If they choose to go on to obtain a Master's of Science in Nursing, they could potentially oversee other nursing staff and perform more high-level duties.

7 Many find that these requirements are a small price to pay to be a part of such a well-respected and well-compensated profession.

CONTINUE TO THE NEXT PAGE

The Tutorverse

Healthcare Sector Job Growth, 2006-2016

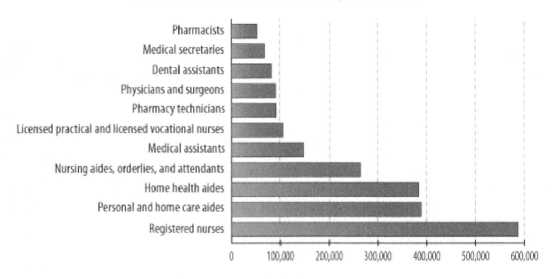

Source: Bureau of Labor Statistics, 2016

50. Read this excerpt from paragraph 1.

    ...a job that pays well can often be stressful or require long hours or advanced degrees of study. A job that is too easy might not be satisfying or stimulating enough, even if it pays well.

    The parallel structure of the two lines

    E. reveals that nursing is a job that has many perks as well as detractors.
    F. emphasizes how most jobs have benefits and drawbacks, even if the specifics are different.
    G. reinforces that jobs that are well-paid will never be satisfying in other respects.
    H. stresses a contrast between the nursing profession and other types of careers.

51. Which of the following best tells what this passage is about?

    A. a summary of the necessary steps a new graduate must take to begin a nursing career
    B. an overview of the different specializations within the field of nursing
    C. the benefits and attractions of a career as a registered nurse
    D. the challenges and drawbacks of a nursing job

52. How does the information in paragraph 2 support the development of the central idea?

    E. It highlights the overwhelming number of duties that RNs are responsible for.
    F. It shows the diverse settings that RNs may be found working in.
    G. It emphasizes the physical nature of an RN's daily duties.
    H. It reveals the range of possibilities that are available to RNs.

CONTINUE TO THE NEXT PAGE

53. Which conclusion is best supported by the information in paragraph 3?

  A. The nursing occupation is growing quickly because of funding from the United States Department of Labor.
  B. The number of nursing opportunities rises and falls with people's lifespans.
  C. The rising demand for nurses is caused by a high rate at which people are leaving the profession.
  D. Though nursing positions are increasing, the average salaries nurses make is remaining the same.

54. What is the primary role of paragraph 4 in the structure of the passage?

  E. It offers supporting examples to the ideas introduced in paragraph 3.
  F. It introduces a new topic that is further elaborated in paragraph 6.
  G. It explains a counterargument to the main claim before challenging it in paragraph 5.
  H. It summarizes information found in the rest of the passage.

55. What is the most likely reason the author includes the quotes in paragraph 5?

  A. to provide a new supporting argument to the overall claim
  B. to convince readers that the long road to becoming an RN is worth it
  C. to confirm the accuracy of the numbers in the study results
  D. to offer personal anecdotes that support the statistical evidence

56. How does the graph provide additional support for the ideas in paragraph 3?

  E. Average compensation for RNs is expected to rise in ten years.
  F. The cost of healthcare is expected to continue rising.
  G. People are living longer than ever and staying sicker for longer.
  H. The demand for RNs far exceeds the demand for other healthcare jobs.

57. With which statement would the author of this passage most likely agree?

  A. The effort needed to become a registered nurse is well worth it.
  B. Being a registered nurse is a rare occupation with no drawbacks.
  C. The educational requirements for people to become a registered nurse are unnecessary.
  D. It will take a registered nurse little time to pay off the debt from their student loans.

CONTINUE TO THE NEXT PAGE

The Tutorverse

Section Two: Mathematics

Recommended Time Limit: 90 minutes

IMPORTANT NOTES: (1) Formulas and definitions of mathematical terms and symbols are not provided. (2) Diagrams other than graphs are not necessarily drawn to scale. Do not assume any relationship in a diagram unless it is specifically stated or can be figured out from the information given. (3) Assume that a diagram is in one plane unless the problem specifically states that it is not. (4) Graphs are drawn to scale. Unless stated otherwise, you can assume relationships according to appearance. For example, (on a graph) lines that appear to be parallel can be assumed to be parallel; likewise for concurrent lines, straight lines, collinear points, right angles, etc. (5) Reduce all fractions to lowest terms.

Mathematics – Grid-In Questions

Questions 58-62

Directions Solve each problem. On the answer sheet, write your answer in the boxes at the top of the grid, starting *on the left side of each grid.* Print only one number or symbol in each box. *Do not leave a box blank in the middle of an answer.* Under each box, fill in the circle that matches the number or symbol you wrote above. *Do not fill in a circle under an unused box.*

58. $|15 - 51| - |150 - 510| - q = 100$

In the equation above, what is the value of q?

-424

59. What is the value of x in the equation

$9 - 2(x + 5) = 3x - (5 - 5x)$?

$\dfrac{2}{5} = x$

60. Janelle has taken 4 tests so far and has an 87 average. She is taking two more tests, each of which will be scored out of 100, with no extra credit. If she wants her final test average to be 90, what is the lowest she can score on one of the tests?

92

61. What is the perimeter, in inches, of a rectangle with an area of 108 square inches if its width is 3 times its length?

62.

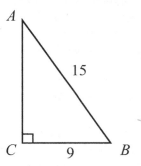

In units squared, what is the area of the right triangle shown above?

67.5 units

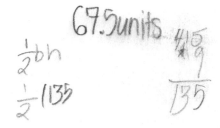

CONTINUE TO THE NEXT PAGE

The Tutorverse

(handwritten top) $4\bar{t} = 87.4$
$2\bar{t} = 2x$

(handwritten) $A = \dfrac{4.87 + 2x}{6} > 90$

Mathematics – Multiple Choice
Questions 63-114

Directions Solve each problem. Select the best answer from the choices given. Mark the letter of your answer on the answer sheet. You can do your figuring in the test booklet or on paper provided by the proctor. DO NOT MAKE ANY MARKS ON YOUR ANSWER SHEET OTHER THAN FILLING IN YOUR ANSWER CHOICES.

63. What is the solution set for $-1 \le -2f + 1 \le 9$?

A. *(number line -9 to 9, segment from -4 to 1, closed dots)*

B. *(number line -9 to 9, segment from 0 to 4, closed dots)*

C. *(number line -9 to 9, segment from 1 to 4, closed dots)*

D. *(number line -9 to 9, segment from -2 to 4, closed dots)*

(handwritten work)
$-1 \le -2f + 1 \le 9$
$-1 \qquad -1 \qquad -1$
$\dfrac{-2}{-2} \le \dfrac{-2f}{-2} \le \dfrac{8}{-2}$
$1 \ge f \ge -4$

64. Phone Company A charges $50 + 3x$ dollars for a phone plan, where x is the number of minutes spent talking. Phone Company B charges $60 + 2x$ dollars for a phone plan, where x is the number of minutes spent talking. What is the price at which both companies charge the same amount?

E. $10
F. $20
G. $30
H. $80

(handwritten: Counting)

65. William, Xing Mei, Yuki, and Zack run a race. In how many different ways can they finish?

A. 4
B. 16
C. 24
D. 32

(handwritten: Averages)

66. Olu has taken four tests so far in her math class. Her scores on these tests are 94, 100, 88, and 80. The score on her final exam will be counted twice in her mean. What is the lowest score she can get on her final exam and have a mean score of no less than 92?

E. 90
F. 95
G. 97
H. 100

(handwritten)
$\dfrac{362 + x}{4} = 92$
$362 + x = 368$

(handwritten: Ratio)

67. On a blueprint of a school, $\frac{1}{4}$ inch represents 24 feet. If the cafeteria is 60 feet long, what is its length, in inches, on the blueprint?

A. $\dfrac{3}{8}$
B. $\dfrac{5}{8}$
C. $\dfrac{3}{4}$
D. $1\dfrac{1}{4}$

(handwritten: $\frac{1}{2}$ in = 12)

(handwritten: $t_1 + t_2 = 192$)

68.

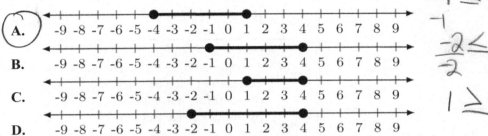

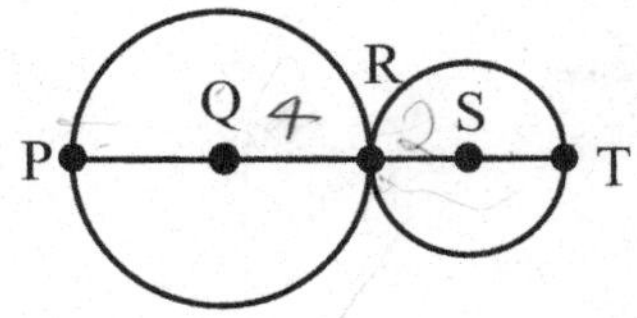

In the above figure, the two circles are tangent at point R. The length of PR = 8. The area of the circle with center Q is 4 times larger than the area of the circle with center S. What is the length of QS?

E. 6
F. 8
G. 10
H. 12

(handwritten: Geom.)

CONTINUE TO THE NEXT PAGE

The Tutorverse

(why?)

69. Darius ran $\frac{1}{6}$ as many times around the track as

    Ezekiel. Darius ran around the track $2\frac{2}{3}$ times.
    How many times did Ezekiel run around the track?

    $\frac{8}{3} \cdot \frac{6^2}{1} = 16$

    A. $\frac{4}{9}$

    B. $\frac{2}{3}$

    C. 14

    D. 16

70. A decagon has 10 sides and 10 angles. What is the average number of degrees in each interior angle of a decagon?

    $(10-2)180$
    $8(180) = 180$
    1440

    E. 140
    F. 144
    G. 1,400
    H. 1,440

71. The table below shows a relationship between x and y values.

x	0	2	4	6	8
y	1	5	9	13	17

    Which of the following equations describes this relationship?

    A. $y = 0.5x + 2$
    B. $y = x + 1$
    C. $y = 2x + 1$
    D. $y = 3x - 2$

72.
$$|x - 3 \times 5| = 6 + y$$
$$|9 - y + 6| = 21$$
    In the equations above, $y < 0$. Which of the following could be the value of x?

    E. -15
    F. -3
    G. 3
    H. 15

    $9 - y + 6 = 21$
    $-y + 15 = 21$
    $\quad -15 \quad -15$
    $y = -6$

73. The probability of picking a piece of dark chocolate out of a bowl of candy is $\frac{5}{6}$. Which of the following could NOT be the number of pieces of candy in the bowl?

    A. 6
    B. 11
    C. 24
    D. 30

74. Two pyramids are glued together base to base. The area of each base is 25 in.^{2}, and the height of one of the pyramids is 3 in. The other pyramid is twice as high. What is the total volume of the combined figure?

    E. 50 cu. in.
    F. 75 cu. in.
    G. 100 cu. in.
    H. 125 cu. in.

75. If $a = \frac{2b^3}{c}$, what happens to the value of a when both b and c are doubled?

    A. a is not changed.
    B. a is doubled.
    C. a is tripled.
    D. a is multiplied by 4.

76. In a class poll, 24 students chose pizza as their favorite food, 15 students chose hamburgers, and 1 student chose neither. What fraction of the students polled chose pizza?

    E. $\frac{3}{5}$

    F. $\frac{4}{5}$

    G. $\frac{3}{8}$

    H. $\frac{5}{8}$

    $\frac{24}{40} = \frac{6}{10} = \frac{3}{5}$

CONTINUE TO THE NEXT PAGE

The Tutorverse

77. What is the value of $\sqrt{16+9}-\left(\sqrt{16}+\sqrt{9}\right)$?

A. −2
B. 0
C. 2
D. 4

78.

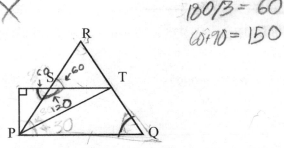

In the above figure, triangle PQR is equilateral, S is located at the midpoint of PR, and T is located at the midpoint of QR. What is the degree measurement of angle PST?

E. 120°
F. 125°
G. 135°
H. 150°

79. At noon, Bradley began steadily increasing the speed of his car by 2 miles per hour every minute. At 12:15 p.m., he realized he was going 15 miles per hour over the speed limit. If his speed at noon was 40 miles per hour, what was the speed limit at 12:15 p.m.?

A. 55
B. 60
C. 65
D. 70

80. $(2+3)\times(4-2)^2$

If the parenthesis were removed from the above expression, what would be the change in the value of the expression?

E. There will be no change in value.
F. a decrease of 4
G. a decrease of 10
H. a decrease of 18

81.

Pete's Living Expenses

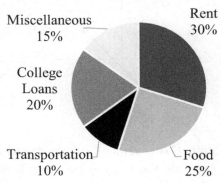

The graph above shows the distribution of Pete's $1,200 living expenses. Pete has two roommates and splits the cost of rent with them equally, so the amount he pays for rent is only part of the total rent for the apartment in which he lives. What is the total rent for Pete's apartment?

A. $360
B. $720
C. $1,080
D. $1,333

82. A piece of paper is used to make a cylinder (without a top and bottom) that is 8 inches long and has a radius of 1.5 inches. Assuming no part of the paper overlaps, what is the area of the piece of paper?

E. 12 sq. in.
F. 24 sq. in.
G. 12 π sq. in.
H. 24 π sq. in.

83. A number is increased by 30%, and then the new number is increased by another 30%. What is the percent increase from the original number?

A. 60%
B. 69%
C. 160%
D. 169%

CONTINUE TO THE NEXT PAGE

The Tutorverse

84.

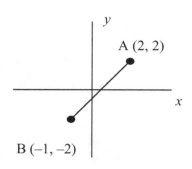

Point C (not shown) is the midpoint of segment AB. What is the y-coordinate of point C?

  E. −1.0
  F. −0.5
  G. 0
  H. 0.5

85. The area of square *ABCD* is 4 times larger than the area of square *WXYZ*. If the area of square *WXYZ* is 9, what is the difference between the length of a side of square *ABCD* and the length of a side of square *WXYZ*?

  A. 3
  B. 4
  C. 6
  D. 12

86. Assume that the notation $\perp (q, r, s, t)$ means "Multiply q and r, then add the product to s and divide by t." What is the value of $\perp (2, 6, 4, 8) + \perp (4, 7, 2, 6)$?

  E. 7.0
  F. 7.5
  G. 8.0
  H. 8.5

87. If $0 < y < 1$, which of the following statements must be true?

  A. $y^2 > y^3$
  B. $y > 0.5y$
  C. $y > y^3$
  D. All of the above

88. When the sum of a list of integers is divided by the mean of the integers, the result is x. What does x represent?

  E. the sum of the integers
  F. half the sum of the integers
  G. the mean of the integers
  H. the number of integers in the list

89. Express 6.925×10^{-5} in standard form.

  A. 0.00006925
  B. 0.0006925
  C. 6.92
  D. 692,500

90.

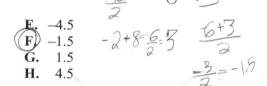

On the number line above, X is located at −10, Y is at −2, and Z is at 8. M (not shown) is the midpoint of $\overline{XY}$, and N (not shown) is the midpoint of $\overline{YZ}$. What is the midpoint of $\overline{MN}$?

  E. −4.5
  F. −1.5
  G. 1.5
  H. 4.5

91. Wesley and two of his friends are driving cross country nonstop and have agreed to take turns driving in 7-hour shifts. Each person will drive for one shift, and take two shifts off to rest. If Wesley's first shift starts at 6:00 a.m., at what time will Wesley complete his third shift?

  A. 5:00 a.m.
  B. 6:00 a.m.
  C. 7:00 a.m.
  D. 8:00 a.m.

CONTINUE TO THE NEXT PAGE

The Tutorverse

92. Triangle *GHI* is similar to Triangle *JKL*.

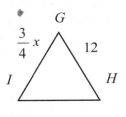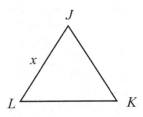

What is the length of side *JK*?

E. 8
F. 9
G. 15
H. 16

93. If A is the set of all integers that can be written as $x^2 + 1$, where *x* is a nonzero integer, which of the following integers is in set A?

A. 16
B. 35
C. 82
D. 99

94. On a number line, what is the midpoint of a line segment beginning at –17 and ending at –3.5?

E. –6.75
F. –10.25
G. –13.5
H. –20.5

95. The length of a painting of a tree is $\frac{2}{9}$ of the length of the actual tree. If the length of the painting of the tree is 16 inches, what is the length, in inches, of the actual tree?

A. $3\frac{5}{9}$

B. $19\frac{5}{9}$

C. $20\frac{4}{7}$

D. 72

96.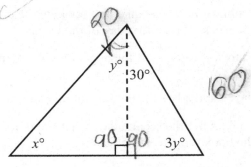

What is the value of *x* in the above figure?

E. 20
F. 40
G. 60
H. 70

97. $\dfrac{(-3)^3 - (-2)^5}{(-4)^2 - (-1)^2} =$

A. $\dfrac{5}{12}$

B. $\dfrac{1}{3}$

C. $\dfrac{2}{3}$

D. $\dfrac{7}{12}$

98. Will bought a textbook. Sales tax was 8%. If he was charged $6 for sales tax, what was the cost of the textbook before tax?

E. $6.48
F. $48.00
G. $69.00
H. $75.00

99. If $4(x - 5) = 28$, what is the value of *x*?

A. 2
B. 5
C. $8\frac{1}{4}$
D. 12

CONTINUE TO THE NEXT PAGE

100. Latonya must read an entire book by the end of the week. On the first day of the week, Latonya reads $\frac{1}{4}$ of the book. On the second day, she reads $\frac{1}{3}$ of the remaining pages in the book. After the second day, what fraction of the book remains to be read?

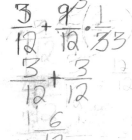

E. $\frac{1}{12}$

F. $\frac{5}{12}$

G. $\frac{1}{2}$

H. $\frac{7}{12}$

101.

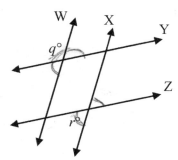

In the above figure, lines W and X are parallel, and lines Y and Z are parallel. What is the sum of q and r?

A. 90°

B. 180°

C. 270°

D. 360°

102. Charlize knows that she has $4.31 in her piggy bank in quarters, nickels, dimes, and pennies. She takes out 12 quarters, 9 dimes, 6 nickels, and 5 pennies. Which of the following could be the coins left in her piggy bank?

E. 1 nickel and 1 penny

F. 1 dime and 1 penny

G. 1 dime and 1 nickel

H. 1 quarter and 1 penny

The Tutorverse

103. A motorcycle tire has a radius of 1 foot. If the motorcycle travels at a speed of 6,300 feet per minute, how many revolutions will each tire make in 2 minutes?

A. 500

B. 1,000

C. 2,000

D. 2,500

104. What is the value of the numerical expression $\frac{9\times10^6}{3\times10^4}$ in scientific notation?

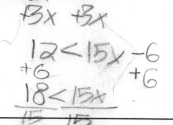

E. 3.0×10^2

F. 3.0×10^1

G. 3.0×10^0

H. 0.3×10^2

105. $$7 - (3x - 5) < 9x - (6 - 3x)$$

What is the solution to the inequality shown above?

A. $x > \frac{8}{9}$

B. $x < \frac{8}{9}$

C. $x < \frac{6}{5}$

D. $x > \frac{6}{5}$

106. On an xy-plane, the center of a circle is located at the origin. A line segment is drawn from one side of the circle to the other, through its center, and represents the circle's diameter. If the line segment begins at point $(2, -3)$, what are the coordinates of the other end of the line?

E. $(3, -2)$

F. $(-2, 3)$

G. $(-3, 2)$

H. $(-2, -3)$

CONTINUE TO THE NEXT PAGE

107. If w, x, y, and z are all positive integers, then which of the following proportions is the only one that is <u>not</u> equivalent to the other three?

A. $\dfrac{x}{y} = \dfrac{w}{z}$

B. $\dfrac{w}{y} = \dfrac{x}{z}$

C. $\dfrac{x}{w} = \dfrac{z}{y}$ ✓

D. $\dfrac{zw}{yx} = \dfrac{2}{2}$ ✓

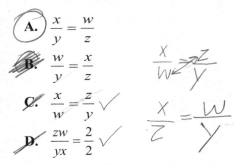

108. If the degree measures of the angles in a triangle are in the ratio 2:3:4, what is the degree measure of the largest angle?

E. 90

F. 80

G. 45

H. 40

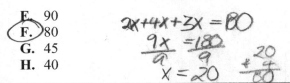

109. A jar contains 21 marbles: 6 red, 7 green, and 8 brown. 5 marbles are removed from the jar. The probability of picking out a brown marble is now 50%. How many brown marbles were removed from the jar?

A. 0

B. 1

C. 2

D. 4

110. It takes Maritza 25 minutes to read a 25-page magazine. If Maritza always reads at a constant rate, what fraction of the magazine remains to be read 15 minutes after she begins?

1 pg per minute

E. $\dfrac{1}{4}$

F. $\dfrac{2}{5}$

$\dfrac{15}{25} = \dfrac{3}{5}$

G. $\dfrac{3}{5}$

$\dfrac{2}{5}$

H. $\dfrac{3}{4}$

111. 9, 5, 9, 11, 9, 9, x, 5, 1, 5

In the list of 10 numbers above, the mode is 9 and the median is 7. Each of the following could be the value of x EXCEPT

A. 2

B. 3

C. 4

D. 5

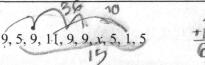

$7 = \dfrac{61 + x}{10}$ 70

112.

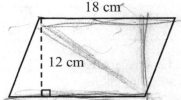

What is the area of the parallelogram above?

E. 108 sq. cm.

F. 216 sq. cm.

G. 324 sq. cm.

H. 432 sq. cm.

113. In a certain regular polygon, the interior angles have a total degree measure of 1,800°. How many sides does the polygon have?

A. 12

B. 11

C. 10

D. 9

114. The sum of five consecutive even integers is 110. What is the sum of the smallest three of these five integers?

E. 18

F. 26

G. 60

H. 84

THIS IS THE END OF THE TEST. IF THERE IS TIME REMAINING, YOU MAY CHECK YOUR ANSWERS TO BOTH PARTS 1 AND PART 2.

ENSURE THAT THERE ARE NO STRAY MARKS, PARTLY FILLED ANSWER CIRCLES, OR INCOMPLETE ERASURES ON THE ANSWER SHEET.

The Tutorverse

Scoring the Practice Test

Using your answer sheet and referring to the answer key at the end of the workbook, calculate the percentage of questions you answered correctly in each section by taking the number of questions you answered correctly in that section and dividing it by the number of questions in that section. Multiply this number by 100 to determine your percentage score. The higher the percentage, the stronger your performance in that section. The lower the percentage, the more time you should spend practicing that section.

Note that the actual test will not directly evaluate your score based on percentage correct or incorrect. Instead, it will convert the raw number of questions answered correctly into a scaled score. This scaled score will be used to compare your score with the scores of other students.

Record your results here:

Section	Questions Correct	Total Questions	Percent Questions Correct
English Language Arts – Revising/Editing Skills	_____	10	_____%
English Language Arts – Reading Comprehension	_____	47	_____%
Mathematics	_____	57	_____%

Carefully consider the results from your practice test when coming up with your study plan. Each question is labeled with a topic that can be referenced in the practice sections of this workbook. If, for example, a Fraction question was particularly challenging, think about spending more time on the Fraction topic of the Mathematics section.

Remember, it is not uncommon to encounter new words, concepts, or types of questions on this test. You've already taken a most critical step: finding out what you don't know. The next step is to spend time practicing your skills in these areas. And remember – you don't need to do it alone. You can reach out to a trusted educator – a parent, teacher at school, or tutor – to help you along the way.

The Tutorverse

English Language Arts

On the Actual Test

On the English Language Arts section of the SHSAT, you will encounter three types of questions:

- 🎓 Revising/Editing Skills – 9 to 11 questions total
    - o Stand-Alone (Part A)
      There will be several stand-alone questions that will ask students to revise and/or edit a given sentence or paragraph. Students must do so based on their knowledge of standard English convention. These questions are all multiple choice, and each question has 4 possible answer choices.
    - o Passage-Based (Part B)
      There will be one passage followed by several questions that will ask students to revise and/or edit different parts of the passage. Students must do so based on their knowledge of standard English convention. These questions are all multiple choice, and each question has 4 possible answer choices.
- 🎓 Reading Comprehension – 46 to 48 questions total
  This section will contain 6 passages, each followed by 6 to 10 questions. There will be one poem and 1-2 works of literature on the test. The remaining 3-4 passages will be non-fiction (explanatory or argumentative passages). These questions are all multiple choice, and each question has 4 possible answer choices.

Thus, there are a total of 57 questions on the actual English Language Arts section of the test.

There is no specific time limit during which students must finish the English Language Arts section. Instead, students have 180 minutes to complete both the English Language Arts and Mathematics sections of the test. Generally, students should spend approximately 90 minutes on each section. However, this guideline should be adjusted based on a student's strengths.

In This Practice Book

The practice questions in this workbook mirror closely those found on the actual test in terms of content, presentation, and style.

The questions within the Revising/Editing following section of this workbook grow progressively more difficult. For example, question 1 will generally be less challenging than question 5. The Reading Comprehension questions are not presented in order of difficulty.

English Language Arts practice consists of the following sections:

- 🎓 Stand-Alone Revising/Editing Skills
- 🎓 Passage-Based Revising/Editing Skills
- 🎓 Reading Comprehension

There are additional instructions and recommendations at the beginning of each of these pages, which students should review before starting each practice section.

The Tutorverse

Stand-Alone Revising/Editing Skills

Overview

The Stand-Alone Revising/Editing Skills section of the test asks students to read a given sentence or short paragraph. Students must then identify an error in the sentence or short paragraph and choose the best revision/edit to correct that error. These questions assess a student's understanding of standard conventions used in the English language.

On the Actual Test

Students will likely see only a few Stand-Alone Revising/Editing Skills questions, which consist of sentences or short paragraphs followed by a prompt to correct for a specific error. The student must find the error, then answer the question to fix the error. These errors have to do with violations of standard writing conventions used in the English language. For example, the errors could deal with the proper use of punctuation, with number-agreement, or with the appropriate placement of modifiers. The test will avoid ambiguous or debated grammar topics.

In This Practice Book

Many students today do not receive formal training in grammar. Instead, many students rely on intuition to determine the proper way to write. In lieu of providing grammar lessons per-se, the Stand-Alone Revising/Editing Skills section breaks out practice questions by topic. As students work through each topic, they should learn the basic rules of each topic and how to apply them in various ways to a sentence. Explanations for why an answer choice is correct or incorrect can be found in the answer explanation section of the workbook and serve as a practical lesson in standard writing conventions.

Note that on the actual test, students won't necessarily be explicitly told the topic being assessed.

How to Use This Section

We recommend that students practice several sections per week in preparing for the test. This includes reading the answer explanations carefully to understand the reason why answer choices are correct or incorrect. It is extremely important to understand *why* a sentence or short paragraph is written incorrectly, and what can be done to correct it. Perhaps most importantly, it is necessary for students to be able to recognize why certain revisions correct an error, while others do not.

As you work your way through this section, you may come across new words and phrases, especially those that describe the grammar or writing convention topics being tested. There are many online and in-print resources that can help students further develop proficiency in revising and editing skills. In addition, be sure to reach out to a trusted educator (like those at www.thetutorverse.com) for help learning new or confusing words or concepts.

Remember that on the SHSAT, there is no penalty for guessing. If you don't know the answer to a question, take your best guess.

The Tutorverse

Pronoun Clarity

Pronouns must clearly refer to an antecedent: a specific person, place, or thing.

1. Read this sentence:

> The manager gave the punctual and high-performing employee her bonus.

Which edit should be made to correct this sentence?

A. change **her** to **a**
B. change **her** to **his**
C. change **her** to **its**
D. change **her** to **it's**

2. Read this sentence:

> Many people like to shop the sales immediately after their Thanksgiving Day dinners, though they are short and often not very good.

Which edit should be made to correct this sentence?

E. change **they** to **those**
F. change **they** to **these**
G. change **they** to **some**
H. change **they** to **the sales**

3. Read this sentence:

> As the stranger approached the agoraphobic man (who was trying his best to avoid people), he said, "Excuse me, please."

Which edit should be made to correct this sentence?

A. change **he** to **it**
B. change **he** to **him**
C. change **he** to **anyone**
D. change **he** to **the former**

4. Read this sentence:

> Though they agreed to clean up the apartment together, Sarah told Melissa that she had made the bigger mess.

Which edit should be made to correct this sentence?

E. change **she had** to **they had**
F. change **she had** to **they have**
G. change **she had** to **Melissa had**
H. change **she had** to **Melissa's**

5. Read this sentence:

> The engineer knew that if she wasn't pumped out soon, the extra water would sink the ship.

Which edit should be made to correct this sentence?

A. change **she wasn't** to **it wasn't**
B. change **she wasn't** to **he wasn't**
C. change **she wasn't** to **they weren't**
D. change **she wasn't** to **those weren't**

6. Read this paragraph:

> (1) Jordan had been sick more than six weeks ago, with a fever, a cough, and a runny nose. (2) Though he had all but gotten better, he still couldn't get rid of his cough. (3) Not knowing what else to do, he asked Jake what to do. (4) He suggested that, perhaps, he should visit the doctor.

Which sentence should be revised to clarify an unclear pronoun?

E. sentence 1
F. sentence 2
G. sentence 3
H. sentence 4

7. Read this paragraph:

> (1) Clyde and Billy had hoped to carry out their heist in the middle of the night. (2) He suggested that they jackhammer through the bank's vault. (3) They did so, but somehow failed to anticipate that doing so would attract unwanted attention. (4) Thus, the burglars were caught before they were able to penetrate the vault.

Which sentence should be revised to clarify an unclear pronoun?

A. sentence 1
B. sentence 2
C. sentence 3
D. sentence 4

Modifiers

Modifiers are words or phrases that describe something else, and can sometimes be confusing or ambiguous when arranged in certain ways, as with misplaced, dangling, or squinting modifiers.

1. Read this sentence:

> It has been shown that reading more quickly improves one's vocabulary.

Which edit should be made to correct this sentence?

A. delete **more**
B. delete **it has been shown that**
C. change **improves** to **enhances**
D. move **quickly** after **vocabulary**

2. Read this sentence:

> While playing the lead in *Hamlet*, the audience groaned as the actor delivered yet another boring and uninspiring performance.

Which edit should be made to correct this sentence?

E. move **the audience groaned** before **while**
F. move **while playing the lead in Hamlet,** after **actor** and add a comma before **while**
G. move **while playing the lead in Hamlet,** after **audience** and add a comma before **while**
H. move **the actor delivered yet another boring and uninspiring performance** before **while**

3. Read this sentence:

> Shining from a new coat of car polish, Jeremy wondered to himself how many compliments his car would earn him.

Which edit should be made to correct this sentence?

A. delete **to himself**

B. move **shining from a new coat of car polish,** after **him** and delete the comma after **polish**

C. move **shining from a new coat of car polish,** after **his car** and add a comma before **shining**

D. move **shining from a new coat of car polish,** after **Jeremy** and add a comma before **shining**

4. Read this sentence:

> Corey eagerly watched the kitten nervously take its first wobbly steps, dripping with anticipation.

Which edit should be made to correct this sentence?

E. delete **eagerly**

F. delete **nervously**

G. switch **eagerly** and **nervously**

H. delete **, dripping with anticipation**

5. Read this paragraph:

> (1) On the last day of February, Forrest wanted to see whether or not it was finally warming up outside. (2) To find out, he donned his favorite coat, which he had received for his birthday, and headed outdoors. (3) He shut the door behind him, locked it, and started walking to the nearby library. (4) Collecting into tiny pools, Forrest watched the icicles hanging from the trees slowly melt onto the sidewalk.

Which sentence should be revised to correct a misplaced modifier?

A. sentence 1

B. sentence 2

C. sentence 3

D. sentence 4

6. Read this paragraph:

> (1) The family attorney told Amber McCoy that there would likely not be a better offer from the Hatfields. (2) As a result, Amber signed the unfavorable agreement with a grudge. (3) Even as she signed the agreement, she swore that the Hatfields had not heard the last of the McCoys, and vowed to get even. (4) It was in this way that a generations-long feud began between the two families, which were once neighborly with each other.

Which sentence should be revised to correct a misplaced modifier?

E. sentence 1

F. sentence 2

G. sentence 3

H. sentence 4

The Tutorverse

7. Read this paragraph:

> (1) Ms. Cortez said after the science lesson that the students would be able to enjoy a break. (2) For almost the entire morning, the students had been studying for the upcoming state test. (3) Ms. Cortez knew that many of her students were losing focus, since the material was very dense and dry. (4) With as much energy as she could muster, Ms. Cortez pressed on, trying her best to engage the class and make it as interesting as possible.

Which sentence should be revised to correct a misplaced modifier?

- **A.** sentence 1
- **B.** sentence 2
- **C.** sentence 3
- **D.** sentence 4

Tenses, Mood, & Number

In every sentence, the verbs must agree in tense (past, present, future, etc.), mood (indicative, imperative, or subjunctive), and number (singular or plural).

1. Read this sentence:

> When he realized he was going to be late for class, Terence is jumping out of bed and frantically searched for his backpack.

Which edit should be made to correct this sentence?

- **A.** change **is jumping** to **jumped**
- **B.** change **is jumping** to **will jump**
- **C.** change **is jumping** to **will be jumping**
- **D.** change **is jumping** to **has been jumping**

2. Read this sentence:

> It took the camp counselors over an hour to find Tanya, who will hide beneath the canoes after listening to the scary ghost story.

Which edit should be made to correct this sentence?

- **E.** change **will hide** to **is hidden**
- **F.** change **will hide** to **has been hiding**
- **G.** change **will hide** to **will have hidden**
- **H.** change **will hide** to **had been hiding**

3. Read this sentence:

> Be sure to call your grandmother tomorrow morning and you tell her what happened today.

Which edit should be made to correct this sentence?

   A. change **you tell** to **tell**
   B. change **you tell** to **told**
   C. change **you tell** to **telling**
   D. change **you tell** to **you told**

4. Read this sentence:

> If you are a billionaire, then I would be Mickey Mouse!

Which edit should be made to correct this sentence?

   E. change **are** to **is**
   F. change **are** to **was**
   G. change **are** to **were**
   H. change **would be** to **was**

5. Read this paragraph:

> (1) Around the nation, incidents of cyberbullying have risen dramatically. (2) Our school is not invulnerable to the pernicious effects of cyberbullying. (3) Therefore, at the next school assembly, a traveling theater troupe will be presenting on what cyberbullying is, and what we can do to recognize and stop it. (4) It is imperative to the safety of students that all teachers and students are present.

Which sentence should be revised to correct the mood of a verb?

   A. sentence 1
   B. sentence 2
   C. sentence 3
   D. sentence 4

6. Read this sentence:

> To others, Brent makes a ceremony of his morning coffee routine, as the beans, water, and various implements are treated like holy treasures by him.

Which edit should be made to correct this sentence?

   E. change **as the beans, water…by him** to **as he treats the beans, water, and various implements like holy treasures**
   F. change **as the beans, water…by him** to **having treated the beans, water, and various implements like holy treasures**
   G. change **as the beans, water…by him** to **with the beans, water, and various implements being treated like holy treasures by him**
   H. change **as the beans, water…by him** to **since the beans, water, and various implements are being treated like holy treasures by him**

7. Read this paragraph:

> (1) Though many people are interested in investing, few know enough about investing to do it well. (2) Many people wrongly assume that because something happened in the past that it will continue to happen in the future. (3) Dominic, for instance, will have been continuing to invest in the stock market in the future because he had been receiving unusually high returns in the past. (4) This is a psychological phenomenon that fuels speculation and inflates the price of stocks.

Which sentences should be revised to correct an inappropriate shift in verb tense?

   A. sentence 1
   B. sentence 2
   C. sentence 3
   D. sentence 4

Possessive Nouns & Determiners

In order to show proper possession, students must use nouns, pronouns, and determiners appropriately.

1. Read this sentence:

> Because they can earn the most tips during weekend nights, the waitresses favorite shifts tended to be during Friday and Saturday nights.

Which edit should be made to correct this sentence?

A. change **waitresses** to **waitress**
B. change **waitresses** to **waitress'**
C. change **waitresses** to **waitresses'**
D. change **waitresses** to **waitresses's**

2. Read this sentence:

> Dexter's uncanny ability to understand advanced math and science earned him the moniker "boy genius," which would stay with him for much of his' life.

Which edit should be made to correct this sentence?

E. change **his'** to **their**
F. change **his'** to **its**
G. change **his'** to **his**
H. change **his'** to **his's**

3. Read this sentence:

> Marisa was eventually able to prove to her roommate, Jordan, that her's was the right way to do dishes.

Which edit should be made to correct this sentence?

A. change **her's** to **hers**
B. change **her's** to **she's**
C. change **her's** to **hers'**
D. change **her's** to **there's**

4. Read this sentence:

> The publisher believed that the book, with it fresh take on a popular fairytale, was going to be a bestseller.

Which edit should be made to correct this sentence?

E. change **it** to **its**
F. change **it** to **it's**
G. change **it** to **their**
H. change **it** to **the**

5. Read this sentence:

> Yuki, always responsible and self-reliant, felt that it was her responsibility to have stopped the leaking hose, not there's.

Which edit should be made to correct this sentence?

A. change **there's** to **theres'**
B. change **there's** to **their's**
C. change **there's** to **theirs'**
D. change **there's** to **theirs**

6. Read this paragraph:

> (1) Camillas preference for pink was apparent, as everything she owned was one shade of pink or another. (2) Hers was a closet filled to overflowing with salmon scarves, coral coats, and strawberry shoes. (3) Her favorite item, though, was a blush-colored beret, which she wore whenever she had the chance. (4) In fact, she liked the beret so much that she rarely left home without it.

Which sentence should be revised to correct for an inappropriately used indicator of possession?

E. sentence 1
F. sentence 2
G. sentence 3
H. sentence 4

7. Read this paragraph:

> (1) After the housing crisis in 2008, the value of many people's homes plummeted. (2) It took nearly 10 years for the values of those homes to recover. (3) Cassidy's and Kaleb home, which they purchased together in 2007, lost nearly 50% of its value in just one year. (4) Fortunately, the value of their home has nearly bounced back to the price they paid in 2007.

Which sentence should be revised to correct for an inappropriately used indicator of possession?

A. sentence 1
B. sentence 2
C. sentence 3
D. sentence 4

Subject-Verb Agreement

In a sentence, the verb number must correspond with the subject number (i.e. singular vs. plural).

1. Read this sentence:

> The camp for boys are situated by a lake some five hours away from the closest town.

Which edit should be made to correct this sentence?

A. change **are** to **is**
B. change **are** to **were**
C. change **boys** to **boy**
D. change **town** to **towns**

2. Read this sentence:

> Doris' forgetfulness became a real liability when she forgot where she kept her passport and were late for an important flight.

Which edit should be made to correct this sentence?

E. change **were** to **is**
F. change **were** to **was**
G. change **were** to **will be**
H. change **were** to **have been**

The Tutorverse

3. Read this sentence:

> Every member of the local labor union were instructed to participate in the strike.

Which edit should be made to correct this sentence?

A. change **were** to **are**
B. change **were** to **was**
C. change **were** to **have been**
D. change **participate** to **participates**

4. Read this sentence:

> Everybody in Kaisha's class were afraid of snakes, so the science teacher changed the class project to be about the lifecycle of frogs, instead.

Which edit should be made to correct this sentence?

E. change **were** to **was**
F. change **were** to **have been**
G. change **were** to **will have been**
H. change **changed** to **changes**

5. Read this sentence:

> The CEO decided that the financial and operational functions of the company is so interrelated that a combined department should be created.

Which edit should be made to correct this sentence?

A. change **is** to **has been**
B. change **is** to **might be**
C. change **is** to **was**
D. change **is** to **are**

6. Read this paragraph:

> (1) Though people make appointments and schedule events, life often gets in the way. (2) Despite one's best intentions, one often finds that one must reschedule or cancel even the most important engagements. (3) This frequently happens to me when my coworker and close personal friend schedule a mid-afternoon coffee break with me. (4) Although the two of us want to break for coffee, we're often too busy to stop working.

Which sentence should be revised to ensure that a subject and verb agree in number?

E. sentence 1
F. sentence 2
G. sentence 3
H. sentence 4

7. Read this paragraph:

> (1) Even though it was bedtime, neither Grace's three daughters nor her son are ready for bed. (2) This was partially due to the fact that each of the four children had raided the freezer and ate an entire pint of ice cream each. (3) Instead of brushing their teeth and taking baths, the children ran around banging on pots and pans, energized by frozen cream and sugar. (4) Neither Grace nor her husband knew what to do but wait.

Which sentence should be revised to ensure that a subject and verb agree in number?

A. sentence 1
B. sentence 2
C. sentence 3
D. sentence 4

Frequently Confused Words

In English, there are many words that are pronounced the same way but have very different meanings. Many of these words, called homophones, are often used incorrectly in written English.

1. Read this sentence:

In order to test the recruits' meddle, the coach always ran a particularly exhausting practice during the first week of tryouts.

Which edit should be made to correct this sentence?

A. change **meddle** to **metal**
B. change **meddle** to **medal**
C. change **meddle** to **mettle**
D. change **meddle** to **muddle**

2. Read this sentence:

Weather or not a contestant wins the grand prize is dependent solely on luck.

Which edit should be made to correct this sentence?

E. change **solely** to **soulfully**
F. change **Weather** to **Wither**
G. change **Weather** to **Wether**
H. change **Weather** to **Whether**

3. Read this sentence:

Not able to except the fact that she was actually going to jump out of a plane, Jamie could not bear to look as she took the plunge on her first skydiving adventure.

Which edit should be made to correct this sentence?

A. change **bear** to **bare**
B. change **bear** to **beer**
C. change **except** to **expect**
D. change **except** to **accept**

4. Read this sentence:

One must be careful not to veer off course when traveling threw a dense fog.

Which edit should be made to correct this sentence?

E. change **off** to **of**
F. change **course** to **coarse**
G. change **threw** to **through**
H. change **threw** to **thorough**

5. Read this paragraph:

(1) Austin never knew that he had a particularly green thumb until his knew roommate, Frankie, moved in. (2) Frankie made a real effort to grow a few plants in the window box beneath the kitchen window. (3) But no matter what she did, her plants never flowered. (4) Meanwhile, Austin's jungle by the living room window was doing so well that the plants blocked most of the light from entering.

Which sentence should be revised to correct an incorrectly used word?

A. sentence 1
B. sentence 2
C. sentence 3
D. sentence 4

The Tutorverse

6. Read this paragraph:

> (1) The persistent cough, which he had been unable to shake for more than a week, had taken a toll on Marius. (2) His once sweet voice was now horse, ravaged by the ceaseless hacking. (3) There would be no way he could sing at tomorrow's concert. (4) Every attempt to sooth his throat – cough drops, teas, medicines – was pursued earnestly, though ultimately, in vain.

Which sentence should be revised to correct an incorrectly used word?

    E.   sentence 1
    F.   sentence 2
    G.   sentence 3
    H.   sentence 4

7. Read this paragraph:

> (1) My aunt was a smooth-talker who could usually get her way. (2) There was once a time when I saw her somehow convince the bank manager to wave a fee that had been applied to her account. (3) There was another time when she managed to convince the waitress at a restaurant to give our table a free taste of their famous dessert. (4) Then, of course, their was the time when she simply asked a baker for a free cookie, and got it!

Which sentences should be revised to correct an incorrectly used word?

    A.   sentences 1 & 2
    B.   sentences 1 & 4
    C.   sentences 2 & 3
    D.   sentences 2 & 4

Logical Comparison

In a sentence where a comparison is being made, the corresponding nouns being compared must be logically equivalent.

1. Read this sentence:

> The weight of a dire wolf is greater than domesticated lapdogs.

Which edit should be made to correct this sentence?

    A.   change **weight of a dire wolf** to **dire wolf's weight**
    B.   change **weight of a dire wolf** to **weight of some dire wolves**
    C.   change **than domesticated lapdogs** to **than a domesticated lapdog**
    D.   change **than domesticated lapdogs** to **than that of a domesticated lapdog**

2. Read this sentence:

> Many believe that pizzas made in New York City are superior to Chicago due to differences in the water used in the dough-making process.

Which edit should be made to correct this sentence?

    E.   change **to Chicago** to **to Chicago's**
    F.   change **to Chicago** to **from Chicago**
    G.   change **to Chicago** to **from Chicago's**
    H.   change **to Chicago** to **to those made in Chicago**

3. Read this sentence:

> After a year of practice, the chef finally concluded that Dara's ability to make delicious sauces was better than anyone else.

Which edit should be made to correct this sentence?

- **A.** change **anyone else** to **anyone**
- **B.** change **anyone else** to **anyone else's skill**
- **C.** change **anyone else** to **anyone else's sauce**
- **D.** change **anyone else** to **anyone he had ever seen**

4. Read this sentence:

> Like yesterday, the front page of today's newspaper was plastered with news of the politician's corruption and lies.

Which edit should be made to correct this sentence?

- **E.** change **yesterday** to **the day before**
- **F.** change **yesterday** to **the previous day**
- **G.** change **yesterday** to **yesterday's cover**
- **H.** change **today's newspaper** to **today's paper**

5. Read this paragraph:

> (1) Though lead has been shown to be detrimental to everyone's health, it is particularly damaging to the neurological development of children. (2) This is why people must take steps to become aware of sources of lead poisoning and remove them from the household. (3) In older homes, lead can be found in plumbing, paint, and even in the cupboard. (4) For example, the amount of lead in crystal glassware is much higher than normal, everyday glassware.

Which sentence should be revised to correct an illogical comparison?

- **A.** sentence 1
- **B.** sentence 2
- **C.** sentence 3
- **D.** sentence 4

6. Read this paragraph:

> (1) In many respects, New Yorkers can be an argumentative bunch. (2) One example is about whether the bagels at one shop are better or worse than bagels at another. (3) Another example is about whether the West Side is better than living on the East Side. (4) New Yorkers have even been known to argue about which hotdog truck is the best!

Which sentence should be revised to correct an illogical comparison?

- **E.** sentence 1
- **F.** sentence 2
- **G.** sentence 3
- **H.** sentence 4

The Tutorverse

7. Read this paragraph:

> (1) Potassium is one of the most important nutrients to maintaining one's health, and can be found in a variety of foods. (2) The amount of potassium found in a kiwifruit is comparable to a banana. (3) However, the amount of potassium found in a kiwifruit pales in comparison to that which can be found in a cup of spinach. (4) Still, the amount of potassium in spinach is second to that of the king of potassium: the avocado!

Which sentence should be revised to correct an illogical comparison?

    A.   sentence 1
    B.   sentence 2
    C.   sentence 3
    D.   sentence 4

Subordination & Coordination

The logical use of conjunctions is referred to as subordination and/or coordination (depending on the types of conjunctions used, i.e. subordinating or coordinating conjunctions). These questions test the student's ability to identify and correct illogically used conjunctions.

1. Read this sentence:

> Products with more reviews sell more than products with fewer reviews, but stores want shoppers to leave reviews.

Which edit should be made to correct this sentence?

    A.   change **but** to **and**
    B.   change **but** to **for**
    C.   change **but** to **so**
    D.   change **but** to **yet**

2. Read this sentence:

> The car had been taken to the mechanic's to be repaired only yesterday, for it nevertheless broke down today while I was driving to the supermarket.

Which edit should be made to correct this sentence?

    E.   change **for** to **and**
    F.   change **for** to **or**
    G.   change **for** to **so**
    H.   change **for** to **yet**

3. Read this sentence:

> During juggling six bowling pins and a sword, the street performer wowed the tourists.

Which edit should be made to correct this sentence?

A. change **During** to **Because**
B. change **During** to **Whenever**
C. change **During** to **Whether**
D. change **During** to **While**

4. Read this sentence:

> The real-estate developer needed to choose between either the bigger building in a quiet neighborhood and a smaller building in a more bustling part of town.

Which edit should be made to correct this sentence?

E. change **and** to **or**
F. change **and** to **nor**
G. change **and** to **for**
H. change **and** to **from**

5. Read this paragraph:

> (1) Amie's parents never missed a parent-teacher conference, and were very involved in her studies at home. (2) She knew that her parents cared a lot about her grades, though they always asked her about how she was doing in school. (3) Amie expected her parents to be very angry when she did poorly on the big math test, for her parents were in fact more concerned than upset. (4) Together, they sat down and talked about what happened, and how she might be able to do better next time.

Which sentences should be revised to correct an inappropriately used conjunction?

A. sentences 1 & 2
B. sentences 2 & 3
C. sentences 3 & 4
D. sentences 1 & 4

6. Read this paragraph:

(1) Whenever a movie generates more than $100 million in box office sales, the movie studio automatically considers creating a sequel. (2) As soon as a movie generates $200 million in box office sales, however, different departments begin working on turning the idea of a sequel into a reality. (3) So that other teams can begin their work, it's very important that the writing team come up with a solid outline of the movie's story. (4) Though the casting department might pick the wrong actors, so too might the costume department come up with the wrong style of clothing without a clear storyline.

Which sentence should be revised to correct an inappropriately used conjunction?

E. sentence 1
F. sentence 2
G. sentence 3
H. sentence 4

7. Read this paragraph:

(1) The diner, who was both picky and rude, was not popular among the restaurant's staff. (2) He had been known to not only send food back to the kitchen and to also tip poorly. (3) In addition, he neither smiled hello nor waved goodbye, instead giving a curt nod in the general direction of whomever had the misfortune of serving him. (4) In the absence of any other information, the staff assumed that he was either a miserable person or was having one bad day after another.

Which sentence should be revised to correct an inappropriately used conjunction?

A. sentence 1
B. sentence 2
C. sentence 3
D. sentence 4

Within-Sentence Punctuation

Commas, colons, semicolons, and dashes are used in sentences to separate different parts of speech. Knowing when to use which form of punctuation depends on the context.

1. Read this sentence:

David always said he only needed two things to be happy, friends and family.

Which edit should be made to correct this sentence?

A. delete the comma
B. change the comma to a colon
C. change the comma to a period
D. change the comma to a semicolon

2. Read this sentence:

Because she had recently moved to a new town Melissa was sometimes lonely.

Which edit should be made to correct this sentence?

E. add a colon after **town**
F. add a comma after **town**
G. add a semicolon after **town**
H. add a comma before and after **recently**

3. Read this sentence:

> Some parts of the American Southwest are suffering from a drought; umbrellas are a common sight during the monsoon months in India.

Which edit should be made to correct this sentence?

A. change the semicolon to a comma
B. change the semicolon to a dash
C. change the semicolon to a colon
D. change the semicolon to a period and capitalize **umbrella**

4. Read this sentence:

> The sleek stealthy cat pounced on the unsuspecting mouse.

Which edit should be made to correct this sentence?

E. add a comma after **sleek**
F. add a comma after **stealthy**
G. add a comma after **pounced**
H. add a comma after **unsuspecting**

5. Read this paragraph:

> (1) It is almost impossible to say which single scientific discovery has had the greatest impact on humanity. (2) Throughout the millennia, there have been countless scientists who have worked to discover the truth about the world around us. (3) Take, for example, Galileo Galilei, a famous sixteenth century scientist. (4) His discoveries have helped shape our modern conception of the universe and our place in it.

Which sentence should be revised to correct improperly used punctuation?

A. sentence 1
B. sentence 2
C. sentence 3
D. sentence 4

6. Read this paragraph:

> (1) Seth was very excited for the long, three day weekend. (2) He was initially planning to simply stay home and play videogames. (3) However, his friend, Travis, suggested that they go get burgers and watch a movie that Saturday, instead. (4) To Seth, this was a great plan; if they could get a ride!

Which changes should be made to correct improperly used punctuation?

E. Sentence 1: delete the comma after **long**
Sentence 3: delete the comma after **Travis**
F. Sentence 3: delete the comma after **friend**
Sentence 4: delete the comma
G. Sentence 2: add a comma after **home**
Sentence 3: delete the comma after **however**
H. Sentence 1: change **three day** to **three-day**
Sentence 4: change the semicolon to a dash

The Tutorverse

7. Read this paragraph:

> (1) After the blaze had been extinguished, the firefighters met with law enforcement officials to understand what had happened. (2) The investigators were perplexed that the brick building on the corner, spontaneously caught fire. (3) Since there was no lightning in the area, and the building was not connected to a gas line, they concluded that the fire was a product of arson. (4) Now, police knew that they were hunting for a criminal.

Which sentence should be revised to correct improperly used punctuation?

A. sentence 1
B. sentence 2
C. sentence 3
D. sentence 4

End-of-Sentence Punctuation

The questions in this category focus on the appropriate use of punctuation to conclude a sentence.

1. Read this sentence:

> Do you know what will be covered on tomorrow's quiz!

Which edit should be made to correct this sentence?

A. change the exclamation point to a period
B. add a period before the exclamation point
C. add a question mark after the exclamation point
D. change the exclamation point to a question mark

2. Read this sentence:

> Someday, I would very much like to travel to New Zealand?

Which edit should be made to correct this sentence?

E. add a period after the question mark
F. change the question mark to a period
G. add a period before the question mark
H. change the question mark to an exclamation point

3. Read this sentence:

> The hockey game was the most exciting game I had ever seen?

Which edit should be made to correct this sentence?

A. add a period after the question mark
B. add an exclamation point after the question mark
C. change the question mark to an exclamation point
D. add an exclamation point before the question mark

4. Read this sentence:

> Miranda asked, "Why is no one ever ready"?

Which edit should be made to correct this sentence?

E. add a period between **ready** and the closing quotation mark
F. move the question mark between **ready** and the closing quotation mark
G. add a period between **ready** and the closing quotation mark and delete the question mark
H. move the question mark between **ready** and the closing quotation mark and add a period after the closing quotation mark

5. Read this sentence:

> Did Allison really say, "I believe in mermaids?"

Which edit should be made to correct this sentence?

A. change the question mark to a period
B. add a period after the closing quotation mark
C. move the question mark after the closing quotation mark
D. move the question mark after the closing quotation mark and add a period between **mermaids** and the closing quotation mark

6. Read this paragraph:

> (1) Reid had dreamed of climbing Mount Everest for much of his childhood. (2) Who knew that, one day, he would make his dream come true! (3) Not only did Reid climb the mountain, but he did so in record time! (4) He would go on to inspire countless other climbers around the world to pursue their dreams.

Which sentence should be revised to correct for an inappropriately used punctuation mark?

E. sentence 1
F. sentence 2
G. sentence 3
H. sentence 4

The Tutorverse

7. Read this paragraph:

> (1) The students were all very excited for, if not also a little bit nervous about, the upcoming field trip. (2) Few of them had ever set foot in another state, and fewer still had been away from home for more than a day or two. (3) Because of this, there were many questions? (4) What should the students pack in terms of clothing? or snacks? or money?

Which sentence should be revised to correct for an inappropriately used punctuation mark?

A. sentence 1
B. sentence 2
C. sentence 3
D. sentence 4

Punctuating a Series

Depending on the context, writers must use commas, colons, semicolons, or dashes to separate items in a list or series.

1. Read this sentence:

> The term "succulents" can refer to a number of different plants; such as the baby jade, giant agave, and pincushion cactus.

Which edit should be made to correct this sentence?

A. change the semicolon to a dash
B. change the semicolon to a colon
C. change the semicolon to a period
D. change the semicolon to a comma

2. Read this sentence:

> During my career, I have worked in three different places: Seattle, Washington, Chicago, and New York City.

Which edit should be made to correct this sentence?

E. change the colon to a semicolon
F. change all three commas to semicolons
G. change the commas after **Washington** and **Chicago** to semicolons
H. change the colon to a semicolon and delete the comma after **Seattle**

3. Read this sentence:

> The three coworkers: Cheryl, Blake and Daniel; often argued about the right way to perform their shared responsibilities.

Which edit should be made to correct this sentence?

A. change the colon to a comma
B. change the semicolon to a comma
C. change the colon and semicolon to commas
D. change the colon and semicolon to dashes

4. Read this sentence:

> Before you leave for vacation, remember: close the windows – set the alarm – and lock the door.

Which edit should be made to correct this sentence?

E. change the colon to a comma
F. change the dashes to commas
G. change the colon to a semicolon
H. changes the colon and the dashes to semicolons

5. Read this sentence:

> When determining the path of a projectile, it is important to consider several factors; velocity, or the speed that the projectile travels; acceleration, or the rate at which the velocity changes; and the effect of gravity on both the velocity and acceleration.

Which edit should be made to correct this sentence?

A. change the semicolon after **factors** to a colon
B. change the semicolon after **travels** to a colon
C. change the semicolon after **travels** to a comma
D. change the semicolon after **changes** to a comma

6. Read this paragraph:

> (1) There are many sources of stress in people's lives, including school, work, and bills. (2) With so much going on, it's no wonder that many people cite holidays as another stressor. (3) Instead of worrying, loathing, or dreading holidays, people should instead remember the opportunities that holidays bring. (4) Days off from work or school are the perfect opportunity to spend time with friends and family, donate time, money, or goods to charitable organizations and otherwise relax by the fireplace with a good book.

Which sentence should be revised to correct for an improperly punctuated list?

E. sentence 1
F. sentence 2
G. sentence 3
H. sentence 4

7. Read this paragraph:

> (1) Thanks to delivery services, budget-friendly dining options, and a plethora of alternatives, cooking at home is fast becoming a dying art. (2) What once was a staple of human existence – preparing, cooking, and serving food – seems at times to be a relic of the past. (3) Still, for some, cooking is more a joy than a chore. (4) Cooking is one of my favorite pastimes, it relaxes, rejuvenates, and refreshes my mind; it affords me an opportunity to work with my hands; and it provides me with something delicious to eat.

Which sentence should be revised to correct for an improperly punctuated list?

A. sentence 1
B. sentence 2
C. sentence 3
D. sentence 4

Parenthetical Expression & Nonrestrictive Clauses

Nonrestrictive clauses and parenthetical expressions refer to those elements of a sentence that are unessential to the sentence's core meaning.

1. Read this sentence:

> The nearby residents questioned why the boat (that was docked at the end of the pier) remained there through the winter when other boats usually left for warmer waters.

Which edit should be made to correct this sentence?

A. delete both parentheses
B. replace both parentheses with dashes
C. replace both parentheses with commas
D. replace the first parenthesis with a dash, and replace the second parenthesis with a comma

2. Read this sentence:

> Miniature golf which is also known as "mini golf" is a game that is popular with children and adults alike.

Which edit should be made to correct this sentence?

E. add a comma after **game**
F. add a comma between **golf** and **the closing quotation mark**
G. add an open parenthesis before **and** and add a closed parenthesis after **alike**
H. add a comma after **Miniature golf** and add a comma between **golf** and **the closing quotation mark**

The Tutorverse

3. Read this sentence:

> Judge Lemon who was famous for throwing the book at repeat offenders, surprised the courtroom with her leniency.

Which edit should be made to correct this sentence?

A. delete **who**
B. add a comma after **Lemon**
C. remove the comma after **offenders**
D. add an open parenthesis before **with** and add a closed parenthesis after **leniency**

4. Read this sentence:

> Unable to decide which color to paint the walls (turquoise was so calming, but ocher so warming) the client instructed the interior decorator to flip a coin.

Which edit should be made to correct this sentence?

E. add a comma after **walls**
F. add a comma before **the client**
G. change the parentheses to commas
H. add a comma after **decide** and add a comma after **walls**

5. Read this paragraph:

> (1) Grandfather decided to sell his house and drive around the United States in the recreational vehicle, that he loved. (2) He did so abruptly, giving almost no notice to the rest of the family, shocking everyone when they discovered his plans. (3) It was up to the rest of the family to sort through his belongings, put things in storage, and sell the rest. (4) The family was amazed to find in grandfather's attic an antique steamer trunk which had crossed the Atlantic on the *Mayflower*, still intact and in good condition.

Which pair of revisions should be made to properly offset nonrestrictive clauses?

A. Sentence 1: delete the comma after **vehicle**
   Sentence 4: add a comma after **trunk**
B. Sentence 2: delete the comma after **abruptly**
   Sentence 3: delete all commas
C. Sentence 2: delete all commas
   Sentence 3: add a comma after **up** and **family**
D. Sentence 1: add a comma after **house**
   Sentence 3: delete the comma after **storage**

6. Read this paragraph:

> (1) Frank was under the mistaken impression – probably caused by his unfamiliarity with the local culture that the food on display was free. (2) So, Frank reached out, grabbed a morsel, and ate it with relish, smiling as he did so. (3) It was then that the store owner – or, at least, an employee at the store – began shouting angrily at Frank. (4) Frank did not know what he had done wrong, and looked around in confusion.

Which sentence should be revised to properly offset a nonrestrictive clause?

E. sentence 1
F. sentence 2
G. sentence 3
H. sentence 4

7. Read this paragraph:

> (1) Doctors and nurses must not only be skilled and highly trained, but must also be able to communicate with their patients. (2) Part of their responsibilities is to understand their patients – to know what might be causing pain or discomfort. (3) The questions – that confuse patients the most are those that are phrased in medical jargon that only trained professionals understand. (4) The best medical professionals are those that can relate to patients as fellow humans – as fellow laymen who do not think and speak in medical terms.

Which sentence should be revised to properly offset a nonrestrictive clause?

A. sentence 1
B. sentence 2
C. sentence 3
D. sentence 4

Unnecessary Punctuation

Punctuation must only be used where required.

1. Read this sentence:

> Cheetahs, are one of nature's most effective hunters, possessing both stealth and speed.

Which edit should be made to correct this sentence?

A. delete all commas
B. add a comma after **stealth**
C. add a comma after **effective**
D. delete the comma after **Cheetahs**

2. Read this sentence:

> Over the roar, of the crowd, Curtis yelled, "Doesn't this music rock, Nelson?"

Which edit should be made to correct this sentence?

E. delete all commas
F. delete the comma after **roar**
G. delete the comma after **rock**
H. delete the comma after **yelled**

3. Read this sentence:

> Investment in scientific and medical advancement, is something that experts, on all sides, of the political spectrum, tend to deem important.

Which edit should be made to correct this sentence?

A. delete all commas
B. delete the comma after **sides**
C. delete the comma after **spectrum**
D. delete the comma after **advancement**

4. Read this sentence:

> Some research, suggests that the rise of 24-hour-a-day news stations contributes to feelings of nervousness, and anxiety, among the elderly.

Which edit should be made to correct this sentence?

E. delete all commas
F. delete the comma after **anxiety**
G. delete the comma after **research**
H. delete the comma after **nervousness**

5. Read this paragraph:

> (1) Jones, who often struggled with self-control and a compulsive personality, knew that he had to take drastic measures if he was to adhere to his diet. (2) First, he put his cookie jar high up on a hard-to-reach-shelf. (3) Then, he promised that he would allow himself just one cheat day – during which he could eat whatever he wanted – per week. (4) Finally, he told his roommate about his diet plans and asked to be kept accountable.

Which sentence should be revised to eliminate unnecessary punctuation?

A. sentence 1
B. sentence 2
C. sentence 3
D. sentence 4

6. Read this paragraph:

> (1) It's not possible to understand geography simply by reading a map, looking at a globe, or watching a television show. (2) To truly understand geography, one must get out into the real world and explore. (3) For example, it's one thing to read about Aruba, but another thing entirely to stand on its shores and see, on a clear, sunny day, all the way to the South American continent. (4) It is difficult, to feel the awe, the sense of smallness that the real world inspires without setting foot outside.

Which sentence should be revised to eliminate unnecessary punctuation?

E. sentence 1
F. sentence 2
G. sentence 3
H. sentence 4

7. Read this paragraph:

> (1) Though, on the surface, there appear to be many differences between Eastern and Western philosophy, closer examination of these schools of thought reveals the fact that many core principles are, in fact, very similar. (2) Many philosophers in both the East and the West believe that morality – the idea of good versus bad – is something that is innate. (3) In addition, many of these philosophers, agree upon the purpose of human existence, which is to seek truth and improve the self. (4) These similarities prove, if nothing else, that people around the world experience life in similar ways, with similar goals, hopes, and dreams.

Which sentence should be revised to eliminate unnecessary punctuation?

A. sentence 1
B. sentence 2
C. sentence 3
D. sentence 4

The Tutorverse

Passage-Based Revising/Editing Skills

Overview

The Passage-Based Revising/Editing Skills section of the test asks students to read a short passage. Students must then identify errors in the passage and choose the best revision/edit to correct those errors. These questions assess a student's understanding of standard conventions used in the English language, as they do in the Stand-Alone Revising/Editing Skills section. In addition, the Passage-Based Revising/Editing Skills section tests students' ability to properly organize a paragraph and craft a coherent and logical piece of writing.

On the Actual Test

Students will likely see a passage in this section of the test that will be followed by several questions. As with the Stand-Alone Revising/Editing Skills section, the student must find an error, then answer the question to fix the error. These errors have to do with violations of standard writing conventions used in the English language. However, the Passage-Based Revising/Editing Skills section will include questions asking students to improve the organization and coherence of the passage.

In This Practice Book

This section contains several passages, each of which is accompanied by 7 questions. Unlike in the Stand-Alone Revising/Editing Skills section of this book, the grammar/convention topic of each question will not be known in advance. This is an opportunity for students to practice what they learned in the Stand-Alone Revising/Editing Skills section of this book and to demonstrate logical reasoning skills.

How to Use This Section

We recommend that students practice at least one passage per week in preparing for the test. This includes reading the answer explanations carefully to understand the reason why answer choices are correct or incorrect. It is extremely important to understand *why* a sentence or paragraph is written incorrectly, and what can be done to correct it. Perhaps most importantly, it is necessary for students to be able to recognize why certain revisions correct an error, while others do not.

As you work your way through this section, you may come across new words and phrases, especially those that describe the grammar or writing convention topics being tested. There are many online and in-print resources that can help students further develop proficiency in revising and editing skills. In addition, be sure to reach out to a trusted educator (like those at www.thetutorverse.com) for help learning new or confusing words or concepts.

Tutorverse Tips!

Remember that on the SHSAT, there is no penalty for guessing. If you don't know the answer to a question, take your best guess. In addition to never leaving an answer choice blank, remember to read the entire passage first. Take note of any errors you may catch along the way (or things that don't make sense), as this will help you save time when you review the questions and refer back to the passage.

The Tutorverse

Choosing a Chooser

(1) In a monarchy, only a king or queen has the authority to create laws and regulations that his or her subjects must follow. (2) In an aristocracy, this power is instead held by a small group of people. (3) In a democratic government, however, the power to rule over people is held by the people themselves.

(4) There are many types of democracies, though they can all be classified as either a direct democracy or a representative democracy. (5) In the former, each person votes on every law or regulation that needs to be decided. (6) In the latter, individuals don't vote directly on these laws or regulations; instead, they elect representatives to vote for them. (7) There are many benefits to a representative democracy.

(8) Many people do not have the time to research and vote on all of the laws or regulations that must be made. (9) Imagine everyone having to take the time to learn about things like international tax or public health policy, for example. (10) The people in a representative democracy choose to elect trusted representatives to make decisions for them. (11) These representatives can consult with experts and devote all of their time to researching a decision before voting on it. (12) The perfect elected representative would not only be an intelligent and charismatic leader, but would also be someone who is also free from conflicts of interest.

(13) A representative democracy also helps to better protect minorities. (14) In a direct democracy, people that belong to bigger groups could choose to make things happen that are good for them, but not good for smaller ones. (15) In a representative democracy, however, the government is more likely to work to protect all its citizens, including smaller groups. (16) This is important because all people, even those belonging to smaller groups, deserve to be represented and protected in a society.

(17) Representative democracy leads to more educated and careful decision making. (18) These decisions tend to protect all of a society's citizens, not just those with the most number of people. (19) Though representative democracy also have its challenges, its benefits outweigh its drawbacks.

1. Which sentence would best follow and support sentence 3?

   A. In a democracy, money is shared equally among all of its people.
   B. In some democracies, power is concentrated in a few well-established families.
   C. In fact, the word "democracy" comes from a Greek word meaning "rule of the commoners."
   D. In some nominal democracies, only the rich have the power to influence the lawmaking process.

2. What is the best way to combine sentences 5 and 6 to clarify the relationship between ideas?

   E. People in the former neither vote on every law or regulation that needs to be decided, nor do people in the latter elect representatives to vote for them.
   F. Unlike in the former, where each person votes on every law or regulation that needs to be decided, individuals in the latter elect representatives to vote for them.
   G. Because each person in the former votes on every law or regulation that needs to be decided, in the latter, individuals don't vote directly on these laws or regulations; instead, they elect representatives to vote for them.
   H. In the former, each person votes on every law or regulation that needs to be decided, despite that in the latter, individuals don't vote directly on these laws or regulations, instead electing representatives to vote for them.

The Tutorverse

3. Which sentence would best follow and support sentence 8?

   A. Some elected officials not only serve in the government, but also hold part-time jobs.
   B. Most people would rather serve as elected officials than be doctors, teachers, or athletes.
   C. Given the chance, most people would be able to eventually learn about the details of passing laws and regulations.
   D. People are busy with their jobs, friends, and family, and don't have time to learn the intricacies involved with passing new laws and regulations.

4. Which transition should be added to the beginning of sentence 10?

   E. Likewise,
   F. Regardless,
   G. To illustrate,
   H. With this in mind,

5. Which revision of sentence 14 uses the most precise language?

   A. In a direct democracy, larger groups could vote for policies that are good for them, but detrimental to smaller groups.
   B. In a direct democracy, people can choose to make things happen that are good for them but not everyone else in the place.
   C. In a direct democracy, making things happen depends on which group someone is in, if that group is big or small, for example.
   D. In a direct democracy, people belong to big groups and small groups, and each of these has a different ability to make things happen.

6. Which edit is needed to correct sentence 19?

   E. change **have** to **has**
   F. change **outweigh** to **outweighs**
   G. delete the comma after **challenges**
   H. change **its benefits** to **it's benefits**

7. Which sentence is irrelevant to the argument presented in the passage and should be deleted?

   A. sentence 9
   B. sentence 12
   C. sentence 17
   D. sentence 18

The Tutorverse

Sweet But Deadly

(1) There are a lot of different things said about nutrition, and it is hard to know what is true and what is not true. (2) One day, one might read in a magazine that too much coffee is bad because it can cause illnesses, like heart disease. (3) The next day, one might hear on television that a cup of coffee a day helps prevent cancer. (4) It's often hard to know which foods to avoid and which to seek out. (5) In most cases, moderation is key. (6) However, there is one food that should not be consumed except in very minimal amounts: refined sugar.

(7) Refined sugar is a type of carbohydrate. (8) The body uses carbohydrates to perform a number of important functions. (9) If carbohydrates are so critical, then why are refined sugars so bad?

(10) One way that refined sugars are bad for health is because they make a person's blood sugar level rise very quickly. (11) People feel an immediate burst of energy after eating or drinking refined sugars. (12) This energy doesn't last very long. (13) People often feel very tired, or even sleepy, after consuming a lot of refined sugars. (14) Children who eat a lot of candy on Halloween, for example, are often exhausted after eating fistfuls of candy. (15) A diet filled with refined sugars has been proven to lead to illnesses, like diabetes.

(16) While refined sugars provide people with energy, they don't provide people with other important substances, like vitamins and minerals. (17) This is another reason why refined sugar is bad for people's health. (18) People eat food because they need energy for their bodies to perform work. (19) But people's bodies also need vitamins and minerals. (20) Eating foods with too much refined sugar often make people feel too full to eat the foods that contain both energy and beneficial nutrients.

(21) Though refined sugars taste good, they should generally be eaten sparingly, if at all. (22) Protein, on the other hand, is something that should be eaten by almost everyone. (23) Even the healthiest person would do well to stay away from eating or drinking refined sugars.

1. Which revision to sentence 1 uses the most precise language?

    A. The media often writes about nutrition.
    B. Most of what is written about nutrition is false.
    C. Articles and stories about nutrition are plentiful, but sometimes confusing.
    D. They say many things about nutrition, some of which are true and some of which aren't.

2. Which transition should be added to the beginning of sentence 4?

    E. As a result,
    F. Conversely,
    G. Nonetheless,
    H. To illustrate,

The Tutorverse

3. Which sentence would best follow and support sentence 8?

    A. Many recent diets, however, have advised their followers to avoid carbohydrates entirely.
    B. Carbohydrates provide the fuel that helps the brain to think, and the energy that enables muscles to push and pull.
    C. Some people crave refined sugar because they were raised eating foods that contain high amounts of carbohydrates.
    D. As long as people eat enough protein and fat, the body can adapt to a complete lack of carbohydrates and enter a state known as ketosis.

4. What is the best way to combine sentences 11 and 12 to clarify the relationship between ideas?

    E. People feel an immediate but fleeting burst of energy after eating or drinking refined sugars.
    F. People feel an immediate burst of energy after eating or drinking refined sugars that don't last very long.
    G. After eating or drinking refined sugars that don't last very long, people feel an immediate burst of energy.
    H. People feel an immediate burst of energy after eating or drinking refined sugars, therefore this energy doesn't last very long.

5. Which sentence would best follow sentence 14 to support the argument presented in the paragraph?

    A. Adults are not as susceptible to the effects of sugars, and can eat as much candy as they like without feeling tired.
    B. Even adults who drink sodas, which are also filled with refined sugars, often feel tired after having a can or a glassful.
    C. Children tire quickly, however, so extra sugar may have little to do with the fact that they feel tired after having a lot of sugar.
    D. Since some people do not have access to healthier options, they often have no alternative but to eat candy, or other sugar-rich foods.

6. Which edit is needed to correct sentence 20?

    E. change **much** to **many**
    F. change **people** to **them**
    G. change **make** to **makes**
    H. add a comma after **foods**

7. Which sentence presents information that shifts away from the main topic and should be deleted?

    A. sentence 6
    B. sentence 15
    C. sentence 20
    D. sentence 22

The Tutorverse

A Lasting Monument

(1) The Parthenon is a building that survives from Ancient Greece. (2) It is one of the most well-known buildings from the ancient world. (3) The well-preserved structure has a long and storied history and still has relevance today.

(4) To understand the importance of the Parthenon, one must first understand why it was built. (5) Pericles, a prominent politician in Athens, wanted to build the Parthenon to replace an older temple that was destroyed by Persian invaders. (6) Like the ancient Greeks, the ancient Persians also left behind many important structures that shed light on their civilization. (7) Construction on the new building has begun around 2,500 years ago in the year 447 BCE and was completed approximately fifteen years later. (8) Decorated with extraordinarily detailed marble sculptures, the temple showed appreciation to Athena, the most important goddess of the city of Athens. (9) Time has not been kind to the proud monument. (10) No life-like statues remain standing within its hallowed halls.

(11) The Parthenon has also changed in other ways over the centuries. (12) While today the Parthenon is famous for its beautiful white marble, the building may have been much more colorful when it was first raised. (13) Many ancient buildings were partially painted and while no one knows what specific colors the Parthenon was painted, some scholars think it was originally painted in different colors, including red and blue.

(14) Not only has the appearance of the building changed over the years, but its purpose has changed, as well. (15) While it may have originally served as a Greek temple, it would later function as a treasury, a fortress, a mosque, and a church. (16) Today it overlooks the modern city of Athens, and functions primarily as a popular tourist attraction. (17) In addition to being popular with tourists, it is an important symbol of the modern country of Greece. (18) Today, the Greek government works with the European Union to document the artifacts of the Parthenon, transfer fragile artifacts to museums, and preserve what remains of the site for future generations. (19) There are much to be learned about ancient Greek civilization from the historic ruins of the Parthenon.

1. What is the best way to combine sentences 1 and 2 to clarify the relationship between ideas?

    A. The Parthenon is a building that survives from Ancient Greece, it is one of the most well-known buildings from the ancient world.
    B. The Parthenon is a building that survives from Ancient Greece, but is one of the most well-known buildings from the ancient world.
    C. The Parthenon is a building that survives from Ancient Greece, yet is one of the most well-known buildings from the ancient world.
    D. The Parthenon is a building that survives from Ancient Greece, and is one of the most well-known buildings from the ancient world.

2. Which edit is needed to correct sentence 7?

    E. change **has begun** to **began**
    F. change **has begun** to **will begin**
    G. add a comma after **approximately**
    H. change **was completed** to **has been completed**

The Tutorverse

3. Which transition should be added to the beginning of sentence 10?

    A. Although,
    B. Still,
    C. Furthermore,
    D. As a result,

4. Which revision of sentence 13 uses the most precise language?

    E. Like other ancient buildings that were painted, some scholars think the Parthenon may have originally been painted red and blue.
    F. Was the Parthenon painted, maybe red and blue, like so many other ancient buildings were or will we never know the specific colors?
    G. Some scholars think the Parthenon might have originally been painted red and blue and other scholars may disagree, but many ancient buildings were partially painted.
    H. Many ancient buildings were partially painted and while no one knows what specific colors the Parthenon was painted, some scholars think it was originally painted in different colors, including red and blue, although this is just an educated guess.

5. Which sentence would best follow and support sentence 16?

    A. Millions of people visit the Parthenon every year.
    B. Everything must be done to restore the Parthenon to its former glory.
    C. Athena was revered by the Ancient Greeks as the goddess of wisdom.
    D. When the Parthenon served as a mosque, a tall tower called a minaret was added to the structure.

6. Which edit is needed to correct sentence 19?

    E. change **are** to **is**
    F. change **are** to **were**
    G. change **much** to **many**
    H. change **to be** to **will be**

7. Which sentence is irrelevant to the argument presented in the passage and should be deleted?

    A. Sentence 3
    B. Sentence 6
    C. Sentence 10
    D. Sentence 11

The Tutorverse

Building Tomorrow

(1) A society's infrastructure – its roads, bridges, airports, power plants, railways, and ports – is often taken for granted. (2) Without a strong infrastructure network, today's interconnected society would be unable to function. (3) The flow of goods – like food, clothing, building materials, and even money – from place to place would come to a grinding halt. (4) It is important, therefore, that society continue to invest in infrastructure.

(5) This investment takes on many forms. (6) Generally, it refers to maintaining, improving, or expanding the reach or performance of different infrastructures. (7) This could include, for example, paving new roads, expanding the power grid by laying new wires, repairing ailing bridges, or building new air and sea ports. (8) These investments cost a lot of money and require a lot of time, but can create thousands upon thousands of well-paying jobs. (9) Infrastructure development can create opportunities in a wide range of industries, including in engineering, construction, equipment manufacturing and maintenance, energy, raw materials, and even accounting.

(10) Linked to job creation is what economists call "the multiplier effect." (11) A dollar spent on infrastructure development leads to a benefit of more than two dollars for the broader economy. (12) This is because the people who work on, say, a new power plant, need places to live, food to eat, and things to do. (13) As a result, investments in the local community begins to grow as people spend money on homes, transportation, food, and entertainment.

(14) Investing in infrastructure not only creates jobs and helps secure the future, but it also helps people save time and money, as well. (15) According to a study conducted by the National Economic Council (NEC), the second-highest expense Americans have are related to transportation. (16) The highest expense is related to the cost of housing and shelter. (17) A joint study between the NEC and the President's Council of Economic Advisers found that "the average motorist in the U.S. pays $377 each year in additional vehicle operating costs as a result of driving on roads in need of repair." (18) People were able to spend less time and money on transportation. (19) They would be able to spend more of their time and money on more productive things, like building business, attending to family, or simply resting and relaxing.

1. Which transition should be added to the beginning of sentence 2?

    A. Yet,
    B. Hence,
    C. Likewise,
    D. Specifically,

2. Which sentence would best follow and support sentence 9?

    E. The U.S. Department of Transportation estimates that highway fatalities have decreased in the last 50 years.
    F. According to the U.S. Department of Transportation, the value of transportation assets is more than $8 trillion.
    G. The U.S. Department of Transportation has estimated that every $1 billion invested in infrastructure could create some 35,000 new jobs.
    H. According to the U.S. Department of Transportation, the U.S. freight transportation system moves over 18 billion tons of goods each year.

The Tutorverse

3. Which edit is needed to correct sentence 13?

    A. add a colon after **on**
    B. change **begins** to **begin**
    C. add a semicolon after **grow**
    D. delete the comma after **result**

4. Which sentence would best follow sentence 13 to support the argument presented in the paragraph?

    E. The multiplier effect can also be seen in other types of economic and social investment.
    F. This leads to lower tax revenue that local, state, and federal governments can collect.
    G. The ultimate goal, after all, is to create non-infrastructure jobs, since they tend to last longer and pay more than infrastructure jobs.
    H. In this case, the power plant not only provides people with electricity and infrastructure jobs, but also generates non-infrastructure jobs, as well.

5. Which edit is needed to correct sentence 15?

    A. change **are** to **is**
    B. change **have** to **has**
    C. change **related** to **relates**
    D. change **conducted** to **conducts**

6. What is the best way to combine sentences 18 and 19 to clarify the relationship between ideas?

    E. People were able to spend less time and money on transportation and were able to spend more of their time and money on more productive things, like building business, attending to family, or simply resting and relaxing.
    F. If people were able to spend less time and money on transportation, they would be able to spend more of their time and money on more productive things, like building business, attending to family, or simply resting and relaxing.
    G. People were able to spend less time and money on transportation but need to be able to spend more of their time and money on more productive things, like building business, attending to family, or simply resting and relaxing.
    H. If people were able to spend less time and money on transportation, they would not be able to spend more of their time and money on more productive things, like building business, attending to family, or simply resting and relaxing.

7. Which sentence presents information that shifts away from the main topic and should be deleted?

    A. sentence 4
    B. sentence 7
    C. sentence 10
    D. sentence 16

The Tutorverse

Hammer, Feather, Vacuum

(1) Modern science is founded on theories that are proven or disproven by repeatable and observable experiments. (2) For example, if Jim, a scientist, has a theory about, say, how two chemicals will interact, he can conduct an experiment to prove or disprove his theory. (3) Sally, also a scientist, can then perform a similar experiment to see if Jim's theory holds true. (4) After enough time, and after enough people have verified through experimentation whether or not the theory is true, it ceased to be a theory and becomes fact.

(5) As an example of this, think about the thing that we now call gravity. (6) Hundreds of years ago, the phenomenon was taken for granted, and poorly understood. (7) At the time, people believed that heavier objects fall faster than lighter objects. (8) This was supported by normal, everyday observations. (9) An apple, for example, would fall from a tree faster than a feather would. (10) At the time, people did not realize that what caused the feather to fall more slowly was air resistance, and not gravity itself.

(11) Galileo Galilei, a famous thinker, sought to better understand gravity. (12) He would later be punished for his work as a scientist. (13) According to Vincenzo Viviani, one of Galileo's students, Galileo climbed to the top of the Leaning Tower of Pisa with two heavy cannonballs. (14) These cannonballs had a similar shape and similar size, but one cannonball had a greater mass and weight than the other. (15) Once at the top of the Tower, Galileo dropped both cannonballs at the same time, from the same height. (16) According to conventional wisdom, the heavier cannonball should have hit the ground first. (17) What Galileo found was that both cannonballs hit the ground at the exact same time. (18) This led Galileo to conclude that some force – what we know of today as gravity – acts upon objects with the same rate of acceleration, regardless of the object's mass or weight.

(19) Hundreds of years later, scientists at NASA conducted a similar experiment. (20) In a cavernous chamber, the scientists suspended a hammer and a feather at the same height above the chambers floor. (21) Then, they sucked out all of the air from the chamber, creating a vacuum. (22) The scientists then released the hammer and feather, letting them fall to the ground. (23) What resulted confirmed Galileo's theory from so long ago.

1. Which edit is needed to correct sentence 4?

    A. delete all commas
    B. change **ceased** to **ceases**
    C. change **whether** to **weather**
    D. add a semicolon after **theory**

2. Which revision of sentence 5 uses the most precise language?

    E. Take, for example, the phenomenon we now call gravity.
    F. The force that people today refer to as gravity is a perfect example of this.
    G. Some instance of this is called gravity by scientists and common people alike.
    H. A perfect example of this is the seemingly magical occurrence of what is today called by the name of gravity.

The Tutorverse

3. What is the best way to combine sentences 7 and 8 to clarify the relationship between ideas?

    A. At the time, people believed that heavier objects fall faster than lighter ones.
    B. While daily observation seemed to support it, people believed that heavier objects fall faster than lighter ones, at the time.
    C. People believed, at the time, that heavier objects fall faster than lighter ones, though this was supported by normal, everyday observation.
    D. At the time, people believed that heavier objects fall faster than lighter ones, a theory supported by daily observation.

4. Which transition should be added to the beginning of sentence 17?

    E. Instead,
    F. As a result,
    G. Accordingly,
    H. Undoubtedly,

5. Which edit is needed to correct sentence 20?

    A. change **chambers floor** to **chambers' floor**
    B. change **chambers floor** to **chamber's floor**
    C. change **scientists** to **scientists'**
    D. change **scientists** to **scientist's**

6. Which sentence would best follow sentence 23 to support the theory presented in the paragraph?

    E. As a force, air resistance is more powerful than gravity.
    F. There was no surprise when the hammer hit the ground first, followed a while later by the feather.
    G. The heavier object was the first to land on the ground, followed some time later by the lighter object.
    H. Without air molecules to slow down the feather, both the hammer and the feather landed on the ground at the same time.

7. Which sentence is irrelevant to the information presented in the passage and should be deleted?

    A. sentence 9
    B. sentence 10
    C. sentence 12
    D. sentence 19

The Tutorverse

Plastic, Plastic, Everywhere

(1) Few among us think about the amount of plastic we use each day, in part because we believe that so much of it is recycled. (2) According to the Environmental Protection Agency, only about seven percent of all of the plastic waste in the U.S. was recycled in 2009. (3) In many places, recycling involves collecting, sorting, and selling waste materials to manufacturers for reuse. (4) Thus, a great deal of plastic actually gets thrown away.

(5) Much of this plastic waste makes its way to the ocean. (6) The Great Pacific Garbage Patch is a swirling continent-sized vortex of debris between the coasts of California and Japan. (7) A plastic bottle tossed into the ocean by a careless beachgoer in California gets caught in oceanic currents and eventually winds up swirling around the Garbage Patch, where instead of biodegrading, it breaks up into tiny fragments and poisons the entire ecosystem.

(8) Some plastics leach toxic chemicals into the water, which makes its way up the food chain and all the way into people's homes. (9) One such chemical, bisphenol A (BPA), is extremely poisonous to animals. (10) Animals that are lucky enough to avoid choking on or becoming tangled in larger pieces of plastic unwittingly consume the tiny pieces of plastic that leach chemicals like BPA into the water. (11) Over time, these chemicals build up in the food chain. (12) Smaller animals are consumed by larger ones, in a food chain. (13) The ocean's apex predators often contain toxic amounts of plastic and chemicals.

(14) The good news is that there is much that we can do to reduce the amount of plastic waste in the world.

(15) One of the most helpful things to do to shrink plastic waste is to lessen our initial use of plastic. (16) Plastic water bottles are among the worst offenders. (17) Instead of reaching for a new water bottle every time we're thirsty, we can instead invest in reusable and refillable bottles. (18) Many conveniences that we accept without much thought – like the plastic utensils we receive when taking food to go, or the plastic sandwich bags we use to pack our lunches – can be replaced by reusable versions of the same.

(19) It's important that we become more informed and self-aware of the environmental consequences of our collective actions. (20) If nothing else, it is in our own self-interest to protect the environment from the deleterious effects of plastic waste.

1. Which transition should be added to the beginning of sentence 2?

   A. After all,
   B. In addition,
   C. Despite this fact,
   D. Because of this fact,

2. Which edit is needed to correct sentence 6?

   E. change **is** to **was**
   F. change **coasts** to **coast**
   G. add a comma after **swirling**
   H. delete the hyphen in **continent-sized**

The Tutorverse

3. Which edit is needed to correct sentence 8?

    A. change **its** to **their**
    B. change **leach** to **leech**
    C. change **makes** to **make**
    D. change **makes its** to **make their**

4. What is the best way to combine sentences 11 and 12 to clarify the relationship between ideas?

    E. Over time, these chemicals build up in the food chain, as smaller animals are consumed by larger ones.
    F. Over time, these chemicals build up in the food chain, thus smaller animals are consumed by larger ones.
    G. Over time, these chemicals build up in the food chain, despite smaller animals are consumed by larger ones.
    H. Over time, these chemicals build up in the food chain, and yet smaller animals are consumed by larger ones.

5. Which sentence would best follow 13 to support the argument presented in the paragraph?

    A. Without top predators like tuna, for example, there would be nowhere for chemicals like BPA to go.
    B. Many of the ocean's top predators – like tuna, for example – are on dinner menus around the world.
    C. Small pieces of plastic are not as harmful to large animals – like tuna, for example – as they are to smaller animals.
    D. Thankfully, by the time people consume top predators like tuna, for example, the chemicals are no longer a health concern.

6. Which revision of sentence 15 uses the most precise language?

    E. Decreasing plastic waste will have many positive outcomes.
    F. Among the helpful things to do to minimize and shrink plastic waste is to use less of it.
    G. To reduce, minimize, and decrease the amount of plastic waste, people must use less plastic.
    H. One of the best ways to reduce the amount of plastic waste is to reduce the amount of plastic used in the first place.

7. Which sentence presents information that shifts away from the main topic and should be deleted?

    A. sentence 3
    B. sentence 9
    C. sentence 18
    D. sentence 20

The Tutorverse

Scary Money

(1) In business, return on investment (ROI) refers to the ratio of profit made by the business to the amount of money people have put into the business. (2) ROI is often shown in percentage form; the higher the percentage the better, as this indicates a proportionally larger amount of profit than money risked in the investment. (3) Return on investment is a measure of profitability that can be used to analyze any business venture – including the business of making movies.

(4) Some of the most profitable movies – those with the highest ROIs – are horror movies. (5) This is because horror movies are relatively inexpensive to shoot compared with other movies. (6) Recently, a horror movie with a budget of only $0.5 million made a profit of nearly $89 million – an ROI of nearly 18,000%! (7) What is it about scary movies that captivates audiences to such a degree that a movie can profit 180 times its investment?

(8) The answer to this question has to do with hormones called dopamine and adrenaline. (9) They have been shown to have a significant impact on people's feelings of happiness and excitement. (10) If a person's expectations are exceeded or surprised, dopamine contributes to the sense of elation at the positive outcome. (11) In the face of danger, adrenaline will pump through the body, causing a person to feel energizing.

(12) Research suggests that horror movies triggers the body to produce these two hormones. (13) A particularly suspenseful or thrilling scene, for example, is thought to elicit a flood of dopamine and adrenaline. (14) For many, this is followed by a feeling of excitement and giddiness. (15) Though, the person may also be feeling fear and dread at the same time. (16) Essentially, horror movies encourage the release of dopamine and adrenaline in the body, which keeps audiences engaged and coming back for more. (17) At the same time, action/adventure movies need to keep coming up with flashier effects and more outlandish stories to keep audiences interested.

(18) It's no wonder, then, that there are die-hard fans of horror movies. (19) Horror movies do not necessarily need the best visual or sound effects to hold their own at the box office, as action/adventure movies typically do. (20) Horror movies need only penetrate the human psyche – to shock or scare their audiences to producing more and more dopamine and adrenaline. (21) They accomplish this on a budget a fraction of the size of their action/adventure counterparts.

1. Which revision of sentence 1 uses the most precise language?

   A. The amount of money made by a business is called the profit, whereas the amount of money put into the business is called the investment.
   B. A return on investment (ROI) is expressed as the ratio of money made by a business to the amount of money invested into that business.
   C. How much money a company makes divided by the amount of money put into a business is called return on investment, or ROI, an acronym, for short.
   D. In businesses, businessmen consider return on investment (ROI) to be the ratio of money made by businesses to the amount of money invested into businesses.

2. Which sentence would best follow and support sentence 5?

    E. The top ten highest-grossing films (by ticket sales) of all time have collectively generated more than $15 billion.

    F. Action/adventure films are very expensive to make because of all of the bells and whistles that go along with a big, blockbuster film.

    G. Ticket sales are another way to measure the success of movies, though in this regard, action/adventure movies exceed horror movies by a wide margin.

    H. Case in point: the most expensive action/adventure movie ever made cost $425 million, compared with the most expensive horror movie, which cost just $170 million.

3. Which edit is needed to correct sentence 11?

    A. change **body** to **bodies**
    B. remove the comma after **body**
    C. remove the comma after **danger**
    D. change **energizing** to **energized**

4. Which edit is needed to correct sentence 12?

    E. change **triggers** to **trigger**
    F. change **suggest** to **suggests**
    G. change **produce** to **produces**
    H. change **hormones** to **hormone**

5. What is the best way to combine sentences 14 and 15 to clarify the relationship between ideas?

    A. Instead of fear and dread, this leads to feelings of excitement and giddiness.

    B. Instead of feeling excited or giddy, people end up feeling mostly fear and dread.

    C. This is how a person can simultaneously feel fearful, yet excited – dreadful, yet giddy.

    D. For many, this is followed by a feeling of excitement and giddiness, however the person may also be feeling, including fear and dread.

6. Which transition should be added to the beginning of sentence 20?

    E. Besides,
    F. After all,
    G. Certainly,
    H. Consequently,

7. Which sentence is irrelevant to the argument presented in the passage and should be deleted?

    A. sentence 6
    B. sentence 8
    C. sentence 17
    D. sentence 19

The Gambler's Fallacy

(1) In psychology, a cognitive bias refers to any type of reasoning that departs from a purely rational line of thinking. (2) To understand one of the most subtle cognitive biases, we must travel back in time to a 1913 Monte Carlo casino.

(3) Players had gathered to play a game called European roulette. (4) There were many other games as well, including poker and blackjack. (5) In this game, a slotted wheel is spun in one direction. (6) At the same time, a ball is spun in the other direction, on a track along the edge of the wheel, just above the slots. (7) Each slot is alternatingly colored red or black, with the exception of one slot which is colored green. (8) Eventually, the ball falls out of the track into one of the colored slots on the wheel.

(9) One way to play the game is to bet on the color of the slot that the ball will fall into. (10) There is an almost fifty-percent chance that the ball will fall into a black slot, just as there is an almost fifty-percent chance that the ball will fall into a red slot. (11) This suggests that, as the game is played over time, the number of times the ball falls into red slots should be roughly equal to black slots.

(12) Players at one roulette table saw the ball fall into a black slot fifteen times in a row. (13) This was highly unlikely, since over fifteen spins, the ball should have fallen into a red slot about fifty-percent of the time. (14) Seeing that this had not happened, players began betting that after the next spin, the ball would land in a red slot. (15) Incredibly, the wheel was spun another eleven times before the ball finally came to land in a red slot.

(16) The players who assumed that there was a greater than fifty-percent chance of the ball falling into a red slot fell prey to The Gambler's Fallacy. (17) This cognitive bias causes people to disregard what they know to be true. (18) They believe what they want to be true. (19) In this case, the gamblers felt that the sixteenth spin was sure to see the ball land in a red slot, since it had fallen into a black slot fifteen times in a row. (20) Some do not acknowledge the fact that any time someone spins the wheel, there is most always a close-to-fifty-percent chance that the ball will stop spinning and fall into a black slot.

1. Which edit is needed to correct sentence 7?

   A. change **is** to **are**
   B. change **is** to **were**
   C. add a comma after **one slot**
   D. delete the comma after **black**

2. Which edit is needed to correct sentence 11?

   E. change **is** to **are**
   F. change **falls** into **fallen**
   G. change **suggests** to **suggest**
   H. add **the number of times the ball falls into** after **equal to**

3. Which transition should be added to the beginning of sentence 12?

    A. Afterward,
    B. However,
    C. Similarly,
    D. Hence,

4. Which sentence would best follow and support sentence 13?

    E. Though unusual, such an occurrence has happened before, and could happen again in the future.
    F. In fifteen spins, one would expect that the ball fall into the black slot only seven or eight times.
    G. Many of the patrons were not surprised, however, and never expected the ball to land in a red or green slot.
    H. Since there are more black slots than red or green slots, these results were as expected of a European roulette wheel.

5. What is the best way to combine sentences 17 and 18 to clarify the relationship between ideas?

    A. This cognitive bias causes people to abandon what they know to be true for what they want to be true.
    B. This cognitive bias causes people to abandon what they know to be true or instead believe what they want to be true.
    C. This cognitive bias causes people to abandon what they know to be true neither believing what they want to be true.
    D. This cognitive bias results in people abandoning what they know to be true but not believing what they want to be true.

6. Which revision of sentence 20 uses the most precise language?

    E. There is fifty-percent chance that the ball will end up in a black slot.
    F. Gamblers never fail to remember what the odds are of a ball spinning and coming to rest in a black slot.
    G. Some feel that when the wheel is spun, there is usually a fifty-percent chance that the ball will end up in a black spot.
    H. They ignored the fact that on any given spin, there is always a close-to-fifty-percent chance that the ball will land in a black slot.

7. Which sentence presents information that shifts away from the main topic and should be deleted?

    A. sentence 3
    B. sentence 4
    C. sentence 9
    D. sentence 10

The Tutorverse

State of Confusion

(1) The small island of Taiwan has been making big waves in international relations for decades. (2) To understand why, one must first understand the history of Taiwan's complicated relationships with its Asian neighbors.

(3) Taiwan was originally settled by the ancestors of today's Taiwanese aborigines. (4) By the 17th century, the ethnic Chinese had taken control of the island, integrating the island into the Qing dynasty's empire on continental Asia. (5) Following a war with Japan in the late 19th century China ceded Taiwan to Japan. (6) Taiwan would again change hands following the conclusion of the Second World War, with Japan's agreement to return Taiwan to China as part of its terms of surrender.

(7) The Chinese Civil War complicated the matter of Taiwan's return. (8) From 1927 to 1937, forces loyal to the nationalist party of China clashed with those loyal to the communist party of China. (9) The two adversaries suspended hostilities in 1937. (10) They united to repel a Japanese invasion as part of the Second World War. (11) Once they accomplished their goal, however, the two temporary allies resumed their fighting. (12) Though Japan had officially surrendered control of Taiwan, a new, more vexing question arose; which China would control Taiwan?

(13) Fighting in the Chinese Civil War effectively stopped in late 1949, whereupon the communist forces proclaimed Beijing, on continental Asia, to be the capital of the newly founded People's Republic of China (PRC). (14) The nationalist forces left mainland China for the island of Taiwan, proclaiming Taipei to be the capital of the Republic of China (ROC). (15) Ever since (and as of the date of this publication), the PRC and ROC have operated as independent countries. (16) The relationship between the PRC and the ROC are, at best, complicated – especially when it comes to the topic of the island, the people, and the government. (17) Nevertheless, the ROC, with its unique cuisine and tropical climate, is a popular tourist destination.

(18) Even today, the PRC maintains that it is the only legitimate Chinese state. (19) It tells everyone that the ROC has done things as a false and fake government ever since the 1949 founding of the PRC. (20) It asserts, furthermore, that because the Chinese Civil War was never legally concluded – with a peace treaty or armistice – both the PRC and ROC belong to the same sovereign entity, which is controlled by the PRC. (21) In Taiwan, the ROC disagrees. (22) It argues that it meets all requirements of statehood, and should therefore be recognized as an independent state.

1. Which edit is needed to correct sentence 5?

    A. change **ceded** to **gives**
    B. add a comma after **war**
    C. add a comma after **century**
    D. add a semicolon after **century**

2. Which transition should be added to the beginning of sentence 7?

    E. Yet,
    F. Surely,
    G. Therefore,
    H. Accordingly,

The Tutorverse

3. What is the best way to combine sentences 9 and 10 to clarify the relationship between ideas?

   A. The two adversaries suspended hostilities in 1937; they united during the Second World War.
   B. In 1937, the two adversaries suspended hostilities and united to repel Japan's Second World War invasion.
   C. During the Second World War, the two adversaries suspended hostilities but united in 1937 in order to repel a Japanese invasion.
   D. The two adversaries suspended hostilities in 1937, neither uniting nor repelling a Japanese invasion as part of the Second World War.

4. Which edit is needed to correct sentence 12?

   E. delete the semicolon
   F. delete the comma after **Taiwan**
   G. change the semicolon to a colon
   H. change the question mark to a period

5. Which revision of sentence 19 uses the most precise language?

   A. It tells people that the ROC has falsely run an illegitimate government ever since the 1949 founding of the PRC.
   B. It believes that the ROC has illegitimately done things as false government that has no credibility ever since 1949.
   C. The PRC tells everyone who will listen that the ROC has run an illegitimate government ever since its own founding.
   D. It argues that, ever since the 1949 founding of the PRC, the ROC has continued to operate as an illegitimate government.

6. Which sentence would best follow and support sentence 22?

   E. There is no way to determine whether or not the ROC is part of the PRC.
   F. Unlike most other sovereign states, Taiwan has not been recognized by most members of the United Nations.
   G. Whether Taiwan is an independent state or is part of the PRC is something that depends on a person's point of view.
   H. After all, Taiwan meets most of the criteria for statehood according to the Montevideo Convention, a widely accepted international treaty.

7. Which sentence is irrelevant to the argument presented in the passage and should be deleted?

   A. sentence 2
   B. sentence 7
   C. sentence 15
   D. sentence 17

<u>Bad Risks</u>

(1) The financial crisis of 2007-2009 is widely regarded as being the worst since the Great Depression of the 1930s. (2) A 2013 estimate by the Government Accountability Office suggested that the crisis cost the United States more than $22 trillion. (3) The superficial cause of the crisis was the bursting of the housing bubble. (4) At its core was a system riddled with perverse incentives that enabled reckless and consequence-free risk-taking.

(5) A home is often the biggest purchase a person can make during his or her lifetime. (6) Banks and other financial institutions help people do this by lending them money based on the value of those homes. (7) In the years leading up to 2007, the value of homes rose rapidly. (8) Virtually anyone who wanted to borrow money for the purposes of buying a house was allowed to do so, sometimes even despite his or her ability to repay the loan.

(9) Eventually, many people were not able to repay their loans, and the value of their homes rapidly lost value. (10) What had been worth billions the day before was suddenly worth nothing. (11) The entire financial infrastructure of the United States was shaken to its foundation as banks and other financial institutions went out of business. (12) Eventually, those people who had lost their homes were able to find new ones.

(13) According to many academics, industry insiders, and regulators, human behavior was ultimately to blame. (14) After all, any business – including those financial institutions that lent money to anyone who asked for it – are made up of people. (15) In a business, groups of people make decisions together. (16) How could – or, why would – groups of otherwise rational, intelligent people purposefully risk not only their own businesses, but also the health and welfare of the broader society?

(17) Many of the people responsible for the financial crisis were incentivized to pursue risky investments. (18) Asset managers, for example, are often compensated based on the value of their portfolio of assets. (19) This meant that the more valuable the homes, the more the loans on those homes would be worth, and the more money the manager could make. (20) In order to increase the value of their portfolios, managers would instruct their teams to lend as much money as possible, regardless of whether or not it seemed that the borrowers would be able to repay.

(21) In addition, many of the people responsible for the financial crisis were able to avoid responsibility for the negative consequences of their risk-taking behavior. (22) The asset managers, for example, were not risking their own money, but were instead risking the money of their company and their company's shareholders.

1. What is the best way to combine sentences 3 and 4 to clarify the relationship between ideas?

    A. The superficial cause of the crisis was the bursting of the housing bubble, though at its core was a system riddled with perverse incentives that enabled reckless and consequence-free risk-taking.
    B. The superficial cause of the crisis was the bursting of the housing bubble, and at its core was a system riddled with perverse incentives that enabled reckless and consequence-free risk-taking.
    C. The superficial cause of the crisis was the bursting of the housing bubble; still, at its core was a system riddled with perverse incentives that enabled reckless and consequence-free risk-taking.
    D. The superficial cause of the crisis was the bursting of the housing bubble; similarly, at its core was a system riddled with perverse incentives that enabled reckless and consequence-free risk-taking.

The Tutorverse

2. Which revision of sentence 8 uses the most precise language?

    E. People who wanted to borrow money for a house were allowed to do so.

    F. Almost anyone who wanted to borrow money for a house was allowed to do so, regardless of his or her ability to repay.

    G. If a bank determined that someone was not going to be able to repay a loan, they still lent him or her the money anyway as long as it was to buy a house.

    H. The vast majority of people who applied for a loan from a bank to buy a house was allowed to do so, even if it was determined that they would have a hard time repaying it.

3. Which edit is needed to correct sentence 14?

    A. change **are** to **is**
    B. change **lent** to **lends**
    C. remove the comma after **all**
    D. change the dashes to commas

4. Which transition should be added to the beginning of sentence 20?

    E. Otherwise,
    F. Besides,
    G. Yet,
    H. So,

5. Which concluding sentence should be added after sentence 22 to support the argument presented in the passage?

    A. As a result, shareholders were able to hold those managers answerable for their actions.

    B. In the past, the government had held those responsible accountable for their actions, as it did again after the 2007-2009 crisis.

    C. Furthermore, the government had previously – as it did again after the 2007-2009 crisis – allowed responsible parties to walk free without penalty.

    D. Thankfully, the government was able to force financial institutions and their employees to compensate the rest of the country as a punishment for their role in the crisis.

6. Which sentence is irrelevant to the argument presented in the passage and should be deleted?

    E. sentence 6
    F. sentence 7
    G. sentence 12
    H. sentence 17

7. Which sentence, if added to the end of the passage, would best summarize the main idea of the passage?

    A. A repeat of the financial crisis cannot be avoided.

    B. Therefore, borrowing money to purchase a house is not only unwise, but must also be avoided.

    C. Together, the strong incentives to take risks and the ability to avoid the consequences of those risks proved disastrous.

    D. If the government had done more to hold people accountable for the choices they made, the financial crisis could have been avoided.

The Tutorverse

Reading Comprehension

Overview

In the Reading section, students must read a passage and answer several reading comprehension-based questions. These questions will be based on what is either stated explicitly in or implicitly by the passage.

On the Actual Test

In the Reading section of the SHSAT, students will encounter 6 reading passages. The passages will vary by genre, topic, purpose, and length. 3-4 of these passages will be non-fiction, and will discuss topics in history, science, culture, or other areas of interest. Some passages will be persuasive in nature, while others will seek only to explain an event or idea. In addition to these non-fiction passages, there will always be a few works of fiction. There will always be 1 poem and between 1-2 excerpts from a work of literature.

Each passage is followed by 6-10 questions, each of which have 4 possible answer choices. In general, the questions you may see relate to:

- Determining Main Idea
  For non-fiction passages, one question (generally the first) in each set following a passage will pertain to identifying the main idea of the passage. For fiction passages, at least one question will pertain to the central theme of the passage.

- Making Inferences
  Another type of question that may be encountered pertains to inferences. This type of question asks the student to think about what is implied by the passage. For example, a question of this type might ask that the student think about what the author would or would not agree with, or what might have happened if certain facts described in the passage were different. For fiction passages, these questions may ask about an author's intention, the mood or tone being established, or the effect of a literary element on the central idea of the passage.

- Identifying Supporting Information
  The remaining questions in each set may ask the student to identify details from the passage. These questions include those that ask students to:

  - find something that is stated explicitly, like what happened, when, or why;
  - determine how a particular sentence or paragraph fits into the passage;
  - review a dataset (graph, chart, table, etc.) and determine how the information presented in that dataset relates to the central idea of the passage (non-fiction);
  - understand how certain elements (like structure or literary devices) contribute to the plot, character development, or theme of the passage (fiction & poetry)

In This Practice Book

The passages in this workbook are indicative of the length of passages you will likely see on the actual test, and, like the actual SHSAT, vary by length, topic, and purpose. Some passages are more challenging than others in order to help students develop their reading comprehension skills.

To facilitate practice, non-fiction and fiction passages are separated into two different units. Each passage is followed by 6-10 questions.

The Tutorverse

How to Use This Section

We recommend that you practice at least passages per week in preparing for the test.

As you work your way through this section, you may come across new words and phrases. Don't be surprised if you need to look up many of the words that you encounter in this section! We encourage you to make a list of words that give you trouble, whether they appear in the passage, question, or answer explanation. Write down the definition of each word as well as a sentence using the word. This is a good way to build a strong vocabulary. Reach out to a trusted educator for help learning new or confusing words or concepts.

Tutorverse Tips!

Remember that on the SHSAT, there is no penalty for guessing. If you don't know the answer to a question, take your best guess. In addition to never leaving an answer choice blank, consider the following:

🐦 Take Notes
As you read through the passage, it is important to take note of important information. Underline or circle key words or phrases. Jot down, in the margins of your test booklet, the main ideas of each paragraph, and how they relate to the paragraphs before or after them. This will help you understand the overall structure of the passage as well as determine the main idea of the passage (which you know will always be asked in a question set). Also pay attention to how main ideas of each paragraph (or the passage in general) are supported by the details given.

🐦 Use Process of Elimination
Sometimes, one or two answer choices can be eliminated outright. When this is the case, look more closely at the remaining answer choices and consult the passage. In this way, it's possible to use the answer choices themselves to help determine the correct answer.

Non-Fiction

Befriend the Sandman or Beware

1 Have you ever spent a restless night chasing sleep, only to have it elude you until morning? Have you ever then tried, the next day, to take a long and difficult test? If so, then you know exactly just how important sleep can be.

2 Without sleep, the human body begins to fall apart. Sleep is critical to everything that we do. It affects how well we process information, learn new things, socialize, and respond to physical stimuli. There is much that science still does not understand about sleep. What it does know, however, is that sleep is a necessary aspect of cognition. The brain forms new neural pathways while sleeping. This refreshes our ability to perform both mental and physical duties, like reading a book or flying an airplane.

3 But what happens in everyday life when a person gets less sleep than necessary? Even losing an hour or two of sleep per night can have negative consequences. One of the more dangerous consequences of lack of sleep can be found on America's roads and highways. According to the National Heart, Lung, and Blood Institute, drowsiness is implicated in roughly 100,000 car accidents a year. About 1.5% of these accidents prove fatal.

4 The issue of driving while fatigued is so important that it has made headlines. A 2014 New York Times article describes how a truck driver drove his tractor-trailer for nearly 11 hours before plowing into cars stopped on the highway, killing ten people. That same article described another incident, where a tractor-trailer slammed into a van, critically injuring one passenger and killing another. In both instances, though there were other factors, lack of sleep was implicated as the primary reason for the accidents. In all likelihood, both of these accidents – and many of the 100,000 accidents likely caused by drowsiness – were preventable.

5 The government has begun to take the necessary steps to help reduce the number of fatigue-related incidents, at least as it relates to drivers of trucks. Effective 2012, the Federal Motor Carrier Safety Administration ruled that the upper limit of the number of hours a trucker can legally work each week be reduced from 82 hours to 70 hours. It also ruled that a driver cannot drive for longer than 11 hours a day. Many critics argue that these hours are still too long, especially considering that an average workweek is around 40-50 hours long, spread across 5 days. Proponents, however, believe that such rules are a step in the right direction, especially considering how important trucking is to the overall economy.

Hours Driven with No Break	Increased Risk of Accident Relative to Average Driving Hours
8	1.09
9	1.44
10	1.89
11	2.46

Source: Federal Motor Carrier Safety Administration, *Regulatory Impact and Small Business Analysis*, 2005.

1. Which of the following choices best describes what the passage is about?

A. the importance of sleep in performing mental activities like reading
B. how lack of sleep impacts learning and socializing
C. the dangers of driving while sleep deprived
D. explaining what sleep is and how it works

The Tutorverse

2. According to the passage, all of the following reasons are mentioned as reasons why sleep is important **except** that sleep affects

   E. how people socialize.
   F. how well people process information.
   G. how people respond to physical stimuli.
   H. how well people's immune systems function.

3. The New York Times article about two particular accidents is included in order to

   A. support the idea that sleep is important to cognition.
   B. provide specific examples of how lack of sleep is dangerous to drivers.
   C. justify the Federal Motor Carrier Safety Administration's ruling.
   D. illustrate what happens when someone loses an hour or two of sleep.

4. What is the most likely reason why the author of the passage begins the passage with a series of questions?

   E. to address possible objections to the author's argument
   F. to refute commonly held beliefs about sleep
   G. to attract the reader's attention while also introducing the topic of passage
   H. to explain how sleep is little understood by science

5. According to the passage, some people believe that the Federal Motor Carrier Safety Administration's ruling is insufficient because

   A. truckers are required by their employers to work at least 11 hours a day.
   B. tired truckers contribute to 100,000 car accidents per year.
   C. the number of hours truckers are allowed to work is still higher than those of the average work week.
   D. the trucking industry is integral to the economy, providing jobs and moving goods across the country.

6. When did the number of hours a trucker can legally drive get reduced to 70 hours per week?

   E. 2012
   F. 2013
   G. 2014
   H. 2015

7. Which statement about sleep and traffic safety is best supported by the passage?

   A. The amount of sleep that people need to drive safely varies greatly.
   B. Sleep is not fully understood, but it is extremely important to safe driving.
   C. There are other factors that are as important to traffic accidents as lack of sleep.
   D. Sleep is important to human health, but its connection to traffic safety has not been proven.

8. Paragraph 5 contributes to the development of the central idea of the passage by

   E. describing the problem of driving while tired.
   F. taking a specific stance on the problem stated earlier in the passage.
   G. describing a potential solution to the problem stated earlier in the passage.
   H. providing statistical information about the magnitude of the problem of driving while tired.

9. The table contributes to the development of the central idea of the passage by

   A. determining the ideal number of hours to drive per day.
   B. providing evidence of the number of people killed by tired drivers.
   C. showing that long hours driving without a break increases the chances of an accident.
   D. illustrating the amount of sleep needed in order to overcome the effect of a day of driving.

Jack the Dripper

1 For students of abstract expressionist art, perhaps no artist is as influential and famous as Jackson Pollock.

2 Pollock was born in 1912 in Wyoming and was the youngest of five brothers. He grew up in various places throughout the American West, including Arizona and California. Pollock did not fare well in school and was expelled from two different high schools.

3 Pollock followed one of his older brothers to New York City in 1930, at the age of 18. There, despite his lack of success in traditional academic settings, he studied art under Thomas Benton. While Pollock did not identify strongly with his mentor's artistic interests, many of Pollock's biographers agree that some of Benton's artistic stylings and philosophies had a great influence on Pollock. Many art historians believe that Pollock's artistic departure from tradition derives from Benton's strong sense of independence.

4 It was difficult to be an artist during the late 1930s and early 1940s. The effects of the Great Depression[1] were at their worst. Yet, thanks to the federal government's Works Progress Administration, artists – including Pollock – were able to find work in the Federal Art Project.

5 Pollock barely managed to keep his head above water until 1943, when he signed a contract with Peggy Guggenheim, who became one of his primary paying patrons. Pollock was commissioned to produce a massive work for Guggenheim, measuring 8 feet tall by 20 feet long. This work helped to launch his career and propelled him toward artistic stardom.

6 With help from Guggenheim, Pollock bought a home and art studio on Long Island, New York, and began working on his now-famous "drip" technique of painting. Pollock would lay a canvas on the floor of his studio and would use flinging, pouring, splattering, and dripping motions to apply paint to the canvas. This was a technique previously unseen in Western art and earned Pollock critical acclaim. Pollock, and the iconic paintings he created, were, to the art community, one and the same. *Time* magazine even gave Pollock the moniker "Jack the Dripper."

7 Then, as suddenly as it began, Pollock stopped using the drip style in his work. By the 1950s, Pollock had moved on to experimenting with new artistic styles and methods. These works did not sell as well as his drip paintings. Pollock's iconic style was so popular that it limited the appeal of his later works. Art collectors were not interested in Pollock's departure from his now-famous drip paintings.

8 Tragically, Pollock died in a car crash in 1956 at only 44 years old. Though Pollock's life was cut short, his paintings and bold artistic integrity live on even today. Many of Pollock's most famous drip paintings can be viewed in famous museums, including the Metropolitan Museum of Art in New York City.

---

[1] **the Great Depression** – a period of great economic crisis where many people were unemployed

1. The passage is organized in which of the following ways?

   A. It describes events in chronological order.
   B. It tells a story from different points of view.
   C. It states a problem and recommends a solution.
   D. It presents an argument and supports it with facts.

2. Which of the following choices best describes the central idea of the passage?

   E. the art industry
   F. different New York City artists
   G. the biography of a famous painter
   H. the benefits of the Works Progress Administration

3. The passage suggests that Pollock's unique sense of style came from

   A. Peggy Guggenheim.
   B. one of his older brothers.
   C. his early life in Wyoming.
   D. his time with Thomas Benton.

4. How was Pollock able to support himself during the Great Depression?

   E. He taught art classes.
   F. He was paid by Thomas Benton to be an assistant.
   G. Peggy Guggenheim commissioned works of art.
   H. He worked for the Works Progress Administration.

5. According to the passage, Pollock's most celebrated works were

   A. created for Peggy Guggenheim.
   B. only recognized after his death.
   C. the works that earned him the nickname "Jack the Dripper."
   D. all donated to the Metropolitan Museum of Art in New York City.

6. Based on the passage, the reason why Pollock stopped producing drip style works

   E. is unknown.
   F. is due to a lack of interest.
   G. is at the Metropolitan Museum of Art's request.
   H. is because of negative feedback from critics.

7. Read this sentence from paragraph 5.

Pollock barely managed to keep his head above water until 1943, when he signed a contract with Peggy Guggenheim, who became one of his primary paying patrons.

What does the phrase "keep his head above water" imply about Pollock?

   A. His art was inspired by water.
   B. He had a steady job that paid him a salary.
   C. He stayed out of trouble and was never arrested.
   D. He was struggling to support himself financially.

8. With which statement would the author most likely agree?

   E. Pollock's preference for staying anonymous is justified by the craze for his work.
   F. For a collector of abstract expressionist art, works by Pollock are worth the money.
   G. The government should not consider funding public art projects like the Federal Art Project.
   H. Pollock would have developed his "drip" technique even had he not met Guggenheim and Benton.

9. Which excerpt from the passage supports the idea that Pollock had a non-traditional upbringing?

   A. "He grew up in various places throughout the American West, including Arizona and California." (par. 2)
   B. "Pollock was commissioned to produce a massive work for Guggenheim, measuring 8 feet tall by 20 feet long." (par. 5)
   C. "These works did not sell as well as his drip paintings." (par. 7)
   D. "Though Pollock's life was cut short, his paintings and bold artistic integrity live on even today." (par. 8)

The Tutorverse

The Lost City

1 Indiana Jones: fedora[1]-wearing, whip-wielding, satchel-bearing professor, archaeologist, explorer, and treasure-hunter.

2 The famous fictional character has captured the hearts of millions around the world. Though many have daydreamed about finding long-lost treasures and outsmarting cadres of ill-tempered thugs, few have come close to living out the fictional life of Jones.

3 Yet few is more than none, and Hiram Bingham III is one of those lucky few.

4 Like Jones, Bingham was a dedicated academic. Bingham received degrees from several distinguished institutions. At the University of California, he took one of the first courses on Latin American history offered in the U.S., and he continued this interest in his Ph.D. research at Harvard. He was as prolific a teacher as he was a learner, and went on to hold teaching positions at Harvard, Princeton, and Yale.

5 Over the years, Bingham held many positions that allowed him to further develop his interest in South and Latin America. From 1907-1910, he was a lecturer of South American History and Geography. From 1908-1930, he was a curator of South American History. From 1915-1924, he was professor of Latin American History. Yet Bingham was most famous not for rousing lectures, but for his 1911 expedition to South America. His expedition would result in one of the greatest archaeological rediscoveries of the century: the ruins of Machu Picchu.

6 Bingham's first trip to the Peruvian town of Cuzco, in 1909, left him yearning to see more of what the Incas had built. During that trip, he visited the ruins of Choqquequirau. These ruins were widely believed to be the last capital of the native Inca civilization. However, based on his studies, Bingham believed differently. He believed that the last capital of the Incas still remained to be found. Though not a trained archaeologist, Bingham was determined to prove his theory. He organized another expedition to do so, and embarked on a second adventure in 1911.

7 From Cuzco, Bingham and the rest of the expedition began their exploration. They traveled first to Urubamba, then to Ollantaytambo. On the sixth day after leaving Cuzco, they arrived at a small, isolated plantation called Mandorpampa. According to Bingham's 1913 account of the expedition, the owner of Mandorpampa, Melchor Arteaga, made a living selling "grass and pasturage to passing travelers."

8 Upon meeting Melchor, Bingham inquired as to the location of any nearby ruins. Through his interpreter, Bingham learned that there were indeed ruins very close by. He learned that Melchor would be happy to lead the way there.

9 The rest is, as they say, history.

10 Melchor did indeed lead Bingham to the ruins of Machu Picchu, as well as several other major ruins. After securing financial support from Yale and the National Geographic Society, Bingham would go on to orchestrate several more expeditions to excavate, catalogue, and preserve the now-famous ruins, which feature the royal palaces of some of the last rulers of the Incas.

11 Though Bingham didn't find a long-lost biblical relic or recover any sacred stones from a murderous cult as Jones did in his famous adventures, Bingham and Jones have more in common than most people realize.

---

[1] **fedora**: a low, soft felt hat with a curled brim and the crown creased lengthwise

The Tutorverse

1. Why does the author mention Indiana Jones in paragraphs 1-3?

   A. to highlight the outward appearances of famous archeologists
   B. to emphasize the main focus of the passage, which is Indiana Jones' sense of adventure
   C. to introduce Hiram Bingham III through references to a familiar and engaging character
   D. to compare the achievements of Hiram Bingham III to those of a more famous colleague in the same field of study

2. Which of the following best tells what the passage is about?

   E. Bingham's contributions as an educator
   F. the process of organizing an archaeological expedition
   G. a comparison between Bingham and Jones
   H. the story leading up to a major archaeological discovery

3. Which sentence is the best summary of the events that led to Bingham's famous 1911 expedition?

   A. Before visiting Cuzco, Bingham had done extensive research on the Inca civilization, which helped him find Machu Picchu on his first visit to Peru.
   B. When visiting Cuzco, Bingham saw a city of ruins, which inspired him to return for a more in-depth expedition exploring that ruin.
   C. During his visit to Cuzco, Bingham explored a city of ruins that was thought to be the last Inca city, and his suspicions that it was not led to a second expedition.
   D. After visiting Cuzco, Bingham was inspired to do further research, and his studies led him to organize an expedition to Peru to find the last city of the ancient Inca civilization.

4. The author most likely included the information in paragraph 5 to

   E. highlight Bingham's superior intelligence and academic achievement compared to other expeditioners.
   F. give a chronological overview of Bingham's life, from childhood influences to adult accomplishments.
   G. show that Bingham's interest in Latin American civilizations was an ongoing passion.
   H. list Bingham's impressive credentials, which gave him access to financial resources that were necessary for the expedition.

5. Which conclusion is best supported by the information in paragraphs 7 through 10?

   A. Bingham had known the way to Machu Picchu from his research, prior to reaching Peru.
   B. Bingham was initially unsuccessful in finding the ruins, and needed to make multiple expeditions.
   C. Bingham's expedition would not have been successful without help from locals.
   D. Bingham met many dangerous obstacles on his expedition, and discovered Machu Picchu due to his perseverance.

6. Read this sentence from paragraph 9.

   The rest is, as they say, history.

   What is the most likely reason the author includes this sentence?

   E. to show that Bingham's expedition was the most important discovery in Latin America
   F. to create a playful tone that references the story-telling style of the adventures of Indiana Jones
   G. to emphasize a shift from a formal, fact-based tone to a more narrative style
   H. to highlight how unimportant the events after the initial discovery were

The Tutorverse

7. Which sentence best describes the author's perspective on Hiram Bingham III's life?

    A. Hiram Bingham III was fortunate to have had such exciting and fantastical life experiences.

    B. Hiram Bingham III deserved all his academic awards given his accomplishments.

    C. Hiram Bingham III was a thoughtless archeologist who plundered the treasures of an ancient civilization.

    D. Hiram Bingham III's discovery was a reward for his kindness to the local people.

8. Which statement best supports the idea that Bingham had much in common with Indiana Jones?

    E. "Though many have daydreamed about finding long-lost treasures and outsmarting cadres of ill-tempered thugs, few have come close to living out the fictional life of Jones." (par. 2)

    F. "Like Jones, Bingham was a dedicated academic. Bingham received degrees from several distinguished institutions." (par. 4)

    G. "Through his interpreter, Bingham learned that there were indeed ruins very close by. He learned that Melchor would be happy to lead the way there." (par. 8)

    H. "…Bingham didn't find a long-lost biblical relic or recover any sacred stones from a murderous cult, as Jones did in his famous adventures…" (par. 11)

A Labor of Love

1 It hasn't always been easy to be a scientist. Though today's scientists are often held in high esteem, this wasn't always the case. In the not-too-distant past, many scientists were persecuted for their theories. These scientists were ridiculed or worse for making conclusions that were unpopular with the rest of society.

2 Take, for example, the work of Gregor Mendel. Today, Mendel is hailed as the father of genetics. He studied the characteristics of pea plants – their height, shape, color, and other physical traits. In doing so, Mendel realized that if plants with certain features were bred together, the next generation of pea plant would display certain qualities. Over time, he realized that there was something at work that controlled these characteristics of pea plants. Though he did not know precisely what those forces were, he knew that some forces were recessive and others dominant. Today, we know those forces as genes. We use the term "genes" without giving it much thought. But it was not until many years after his discovery – and, unfortunately, after his death – that the significance of Mendel's work was fully appreciated. In fact, his findings were initially rejected by his peers.

3 Mere rejection, however unfortunate, pales in comparison to persecution at the hands of the Inquisition. In 1615, Galileo Galilei's theories on heliocentrism[1] were submitted to the Roman Inquisition by Father Niccolo Lorini. Galileo believed that the bodies in the solar system revolved around the sun, not the earth. In Lorini's point of view, Galileo was reinterpreting the Bible, an activity that was prohibited by the Roman Catholic Church's Council of Trent. This was, unfortunately for Galileo, not his first run-in with the Church. Just years prior, he had needed to answer to the Grand Duchess of Florence for unrelated scientific claims. Galileo was ordered by the Inquisition to cease his work on heliocentrism.

4 Galileo obeyed – at least superficially. He began writing a book, which he submitted formally to the Inquisition and Pope for approval. Permission for Galileo to publish the book was granted, and the book

---

[1] **heliocentrism**: the idea that the sun is the center of the solar system

The Tutorverse

Dialogue Concerning the Two Chief World Systems was published in 1632. Despite the permission obtained from the Church, Galileo was summoned before inquisitor Vincenzo Maculani and charged with heresy for publishing the book. The Church formally condemned him for his ideas in 1633. In addition, the Church banned his book and included it in the infamous *Index of Forbidden Books*.

5 Ultimately, Galileo avoided a far more horrible fate than many of his contemporaries. He was sentenced to house arrest for the rest of his life. Still, Galileo was able to work. While under arrest, Galileo completed *Two New Sciences* – his seminal work.

6 Galileo did not live to see his work truly appreciated; he died in 1642 in his villa. It took over 200 years – until 1835 – for the Church to remove his 1632 book from the *Index of Forbidden Books*. It was not until 1992 – almost 160 years after his 1632 book was officially unbanned – that the Church finally agreed with Galileo's theories and admitted that Galileo had been wrongfully condemned.

1. Which statement best describes the central idea of the passage?

   A. Galileo's scientific work on the earth's position in the solar system drew heavy persecution from leaders of the Roman Inquisition.
   B. In the history of scientific discovery, scientists have been repeatedly punished, and some have died defending their beliefs.
   C. Throughout history, the early findings of scientists have often been rejected, only to be discovered true many years later.
   D. Scientists face many challenges, particularly when technology cannot keep up with the demands of their experiments.

2. Read this sentence from paragraph 2.

   Today, Mendel is hailed as the father of genetics.

   How does this sentence fit into the overall structure of the paragraph?

   E. It poses a contrast to the reaction that Mendel received from his peers during his lifetime.
   F. It illustrates a modern solution to the problem that Mendel was trying to solve during his lifetime.
   G. It details an example of Mendel's career success when he was still alive.
   H. It confirms how Mendel was viewed by scientists from his time.

3. The Inquisition found Galileo's work problematic because

   A. they had a grudge against him because he followed a different faith.
   B. they saw his work as a rethinking of their religious beliefs.
   C. they required him to seek approval from the Church before publishing his work, and he did not.
   D. they did not think that his findings were supported enough by provable information.

4. What is the most likely reason the author uses the word "persecution" in paragraph 3?

   E. to show that it was once very difficult for scientists, like Galileo, to spread their ideas
   F. to emphasize the severity of the negative treatment that scientists like Galileo had faced
   G. to argue that Mendel had received worse treatment than Galileo for the publication of his works
   H. to prove that the Inquisition was justified in its treatment of scientists such as Galileo

5. In paragraph 4, the phrase "at least superficially" is used to highlight how

(A.) Galileo continued to follow his scientific interests despite appearing to follow the demands of the Church.

B. Galileo verbally accepted the commands of the Inquisition, but internally fumed at their restrictions.

C. Galileo's personal faith was insincere in nature, and his true passion lay in scientific inquiry.

D. Galileo's scientific work was shallow in nature, and he needed to delve deeper to make true progress.

6. Which excerpt from the passage best conveys the author's perspective regarding the Inquisition's actions towards Galileo?

E. "Just years prior, he had needed to answer to the Grand Duchess of Florence for unrelated scientific claims. Galileo was ordered by the Inquisition to cease his work on heliocentrism." (par. 3)

F. "The Church formally condemned him for his ideas in 1633. In addition, the Church banned his book and included it in the infamous Index of Forbidden Books." (par. 4)

G. "Ultimately, Galileo avoided a far more horrible fate than many of his contemporaries. He was sentenced to house arrest for the rest of his life. Still, Galileo was able to work." (par. 5)

(H.) "It was not until 1992 – almost 160 years after his 1632 book was officially unbanned – that the Church finally agreed with Galileo's theories and admitted that Galileo had been wrongfully condemned." (par. 6)

7. With which statement would the author of the passage most likely agree?

A. Mendel and Galileo worked in very similar fields of scientific study.

B. Mendel and Galileo were treated in equally negative ways by their contemporaries.

(C.) Mendel and Galileo represent examples in which scientists were historically underappreciated.

D. Mendel and Galileo were both renowned for their work during their lifetimes.

8. Paragraph 6 contributes to the central idea of the passage by

E. reinforcing the satisfaction that scientists felt about their own work, despite a lack of recognition.

F. emphasizing how badly scientists were treated during their lifetimes for their most important works.

G. highlighting how many popular and influential titles were once on banned books lists.

(H.) conveying how people changed their minds about the value of scientific works over time.

The Tutorverse

Cellular Solutions

Big Punch, Tiny Package

1 Stem cells are unspecialized cells that are capable of undergoing cellular division to replicate themselves. In addition, stem cells can sometimes transform from unspecialized cells into specialized cells like muscle or nerve cells. Because of these two characteristics, stem cells have many practical applications. This has encouraged scientists to study stem cells for their potential medicinal benefits.

Leaps and Bounds

2 Before scientists could use stem cells in medicine, however, they first had to learn figure out a way to find or create them. For years, this remained an elusive goal. Finally, in 1981, scientists made a breakthrough when they discovered how to isolate embryonic stem cells from mouse embryos[1]. Once scientists unlocked the ability to isolate embryonic stem cells from small mammals, it didn't take them long to figure out how to do so in humans. In 1998, scientists reached this milestone. Though this was a big advance in science, many believed that harvesting stem cells from embryos was immoral.

3 Though scientists were finally able to work with human stem cells, progress was slow, and opposition fierce. It wasn't until 2006 that scientists made another discovery – one that would solve the twin issues of stem cell supply and morality. Scientists learned that under special circumstances, certain specialized adult cells could be "reprogrammed" to become like embryonic stem cells. With a steady supply of stem cells, scientists could finally focus on the next phase of research: finding ways to use stem cells to heal.

A Silver Bullet?

4 Over the years, research has shown that one of the most significant medical benefits of stem cells is their ability to repair damaged cells. Many cells in the human body replenish themselves over time. However, some cells, like the nerve cells that make up the brain, do not; when these cells are lost to injury, disease, or age, they don't come back. A recent discovery suggests that it may be possible for stem cells to replace previously irreplaceable cells, like those found in the brain. Scientists believe that stem cells can play a significant role in curing certain diseases caused by the loss of cells. Perhaps one day a person suffering from Alzheimer's disease will again be able to recognize her son. Perhaps one day someone paralyzed from a spinal cord injury will again be able to walk on his own.

5 Stem cell research continues to advance both our understanding of cellular replication and our ability to treat devastating medical conditions. With all that has already been discovered in just a few short decades, the possibilities seem limitless. If we continue to invest in stem cell research, who knows what the future will hold?

---

[1] **embryo**: an unborn or unhatched offspring in the process of developing

1. Which of the following choices best describes the central idea of the passage?

   A. Stem cell research is a divisive issue that has not been resolved.
   B. Stem cell research may result in many scientific and medical benefits.
   C. Stem cell research takes a long time to perform and costs a lot of money.
   D. There exist many diseases and medical conditions which researchers do not understand.

2. Read this sentence from paragraph 1.

> **Because of these two characteristics, stem cells have many practical applications.**

The "applications" mentioned refer to

   E. complicated paperwork.
   F. beneficial uses.
   G. scientific facts.
   H. medical questions.

3. According to the passage, cells in the brain

   A. are easily damaged but easily regrown.
   B. do not naturally grow back when damaged.
   C. are similar to most other cells in other parts of the body.
   D. can be "reprogrammed" to become like embryonic stem cells.

4. All of the following are supported by the passage **except** for which statement?

   E. Stem cells can become like other cells.
   F. Stem cells are medically useful.
   G. Stem cells require a great deal of study.
   H. Stem cells are guaranteed to cure all medical conditions.

5. According to the passage, in what year did scientists first begin to work with human stem cells?

   A. 1981
   B. 1989
   C. 1998
   D. 2006

6. The embryos mentioned in paragraph 2 most likely contain

   E. only unspecialized cells.
   F. a mix of cells that cannot regenerate.
   G. a mix of unspecialized and specialized cells.
   H. a mix of cells that cannot undergo cellular division.

That's Not Music!

1   What is music? Why is it that we think of some sounds as "music" but consider others to be just noise?

2   Music theory is an area of study that focuses on understanding how different qualities of sound make what we call music. One of the most important things in music is called melody. "The true goal of music," Johann Kirnberger, a student of the German composer Johann Bach, said in 1771, "is melody."

3   The dictionary definition of the word "melody" (a sequence of single notes or sounds that is musically pleasing) is not very useful in helping us understand what makes a melody good. Just what is it about a specific melody that leaves us humming it for days on end? After all, few would agree that just *any* random series of notes will *always* be musically pleasing.

4   As it turns out, what makes a sequence of notes or sounds musically satisfying is the pitch (the highness or lowness of a sound), rhythm, tempo (musical speed), duration, and tonal color (the mood or feeling of a melody) of those notes. To qualify as a melody, all of these elements must be tied together in such a way that the sounds make the listener have a positive reaction.

5   People's reactions to a certain order of notes can differ greatly. The same melody can inspire different feelings and emotions in different people. This is due primarily to differences in the way people's brains process the sounds they hear. Because of these differences, one sequence of notes can be musically satisfying to a listener, while that same sequence of notes can sound discordant to someone else.

The Tutorverse

6 Often, however, what we find appealing in music is also a matter of what we are used to. Genres and styles of music change over time, and what is popular to one generation may be unappealing to another. Take for instance, what kind of music your grandparents listen to. To you, music of their era may sound boring. To them, the pop that you enjoy may seem like mere noise. This lack of agreement on what makes good music is partly the result of generational differences in style – 1950s doo-wop and jazz can sound quite different from songs by Drake and Taylor Swift. But this disagreement is also in part due to how often you listen to the same songs, and what you've become accustomed to. According to one theory, the more exposure one has to a particular stimulus (like sound), the more positively one will feel about it. Repeatedly playing a song can, in that sense, alter a person's response to a particular melody or musical style. Simply playing a song on the radio over and over again can cause an entire generation to like a song! As a result, the short-term popularity of a song may not be the best way to judge the quality of its melody.

7 Despite these subjective differences, there are some songs that seem universally beloved. Underneath the superficial differences of genre, instrumentation, and recording technologies, most popular tunes actually share certain characteristics. Many of these most memorable melodies – many of which have also stood the test of time – tend to build up to a climactic point, which generally (but not always) contains the melody's highest pitch and strongest rhythm. The catchiest and most long-lived melodies often utilize repetition to reinforce the overall structure and theme of the piece. Such melodies often contain repeating rhythms, beats, or progressions of notes. From the repetition and emotional crescendo of the still-popular *Für Elise* to the iconic opening refrain and chorus of Michael Jackson's *Thriller,* musicians have been making their mark with unforgettable melodies for hundreds of years.

8 Ask the average person why he or she likes a particular song and one will often be told simply that "the song is catchy," or that it gets easily "stuck in the head." What this shows us is that an appealing melody is extremely important to a song – so much so that people often forgive a song for other offenses (like, for example, bad lyrics) as long as the song has a good melody.

1. The author includes questions in the first paragraph most likely to

   A. suggest that music is pleasing for unknown reasons.
   B. challenge preconceived notions about music and sound.
   C. introduce personal experiences with music.
   D. state a problem that has no solution.

2. Which of the following choices best tells what the passage is about?

   E. the stylistic changes of music through multiple generations
   F. the process of creating music and the way it evolved through music history
   G. an explanation of how and why a melody is important to music
   H. a comparison of one element of music with others

3. Read this sentence from paragraph 2.

   "The true goal of music," Johann Kirnberger, a student of the German composer Johann Bach, said in 1771, "is melody."

   What is the most likely reason the author included this quote?

   A. to support the claim that melody is the most important musical element
   B. to describe a specific branch of musical theory
   C. to compare the differences between two famous composers' opinions about music
   D. to show that only professional composers place a great emphasis on melodies

4. Which statement best supports the idea that melodies should be carefully designed?

   E. "Why is it that we think of some sounds as 'music' but consider others to be just noise?" (par. 1)
   F. "After all, few would agree that just *any* random series of notes will *always* be musically pleasing." (par. 3)
   G. "Because of these differences, one sequence of notes can be musically satisfying to a listener, while that same sequence of notes can sound discordant to someone else." (par. 5)
   H. "Ask the average person why he or she likes a particular song and one will often be told simply that 'the song is catchy,' or that it gets easily 'stuck in the head.'" (par. 8)

5. What role does paragraph 4 play in the overall structure of the paragraph?

   A. It contrasts a new perspective with the one described in paragraph 2.
   B. It offers an explanation in response to the question posed in paragraph 3.
   C. It introduces a subtopic which will be elaborated in paragraph 5.
   D. It summarizes the information from the rest of the passage.

6. According to the passage, how does exposure to a sound affect whether a person likes or dislikes a melody?

   E. A person who repeatedly listens to a melody will be guaranteed to eventually like it.
   F. The melodies that have been around for hundreds of years are perfect, and everyone likes them.
   G. Repeated exposure to a song or melody increases the chances that a person will have a positive response to it.
   H. Since people either like a melody or don't, repeated exposure to a sound has nothing to do with liking or not liking a melody.

7. Which conclusion is best supported by the information in paragraph 5?

   A. Scientists should alter the brain chemistry of listeners to create catchy melodies.
   B. It is difficult to compose a melody that appeals to all individuals.
   C. There are scintifically proven reasons why some songs have better melodies than others.
   D. One sequence of notes sounds objectively the same to any listener.

8. Read this sentence from paragraph 7.

   ...musicians have been making their mark with unforgettable melodies for hundreds of years.

   How does this sentence support the development of the central idea?

   E. It reinforces the idea that popular melodies do not require a great deal of education to enjoy.
   F. It highlights how the principles of a catchy melody have evolved through musical history.
   G. It shows how popular melodies from different genres and generations have certain characteristics in common.
   H. It emphasizes how the same melody can be greatly beloved by one generation, and disliked by a later generation.

9. With which of the following statements would the author most likely agree?

   A. The doo-wop and jazz from the 1950s is superior to music by modern artists.
   B. The best melodies are the ones composed in your youth.
   C. The length of time a melody is remembered for is a good way to determine its quality.
   D. The lyrics of a song are equally important to the melody in determining how successful a song will be.

Bridging the Gap

1 Sometimes, getting from one place to another is as simple as moving there in a straight line. But other times, there can be something in the way. Rocks, mountains, rivers, and other geological features often bar the way to a destination, forcing a detour. While it's usually a small matter to walk around a rock that's in one's way, crossing a large river or a deep chasm or gorge is another thing entirely. Many rivers and chasms extend for many miles, making a detour impractical, if not impossible. To overcome these challenges, people invented bridges.

2 At its most simple, a bridge can be nothing more than a piece of wood or a length of rope. Nature made the first bridges, when aged trees fell and lay across a stream; early humans refined this idea by making bridges out of simple logs or planks. These bridges help make small obstacles and short distances, like streams or brooks, easier and safer to cross.

3 As technology advanced over the ages, people developed new ideas for building bridges. Each development allowed people to span ever greater distances. Where wood was ineffective, people used stone. Eventually, people even learned to make beautiful bridges out of metal.

4 People also discovered that the manner in which a bridge is built is as important as the type of material used to build it. As humanity's access to different materials changed over time, so too did people's understanding of the science behind bridges. The forces of tension, compression, torsion, and shear all play a critical role in determining whether a bridge will stand or fall. Over time, people's understanding of these forces helped them to create different types of bridge structures.

5 The simplest type of bridge is the beam bridge: a horizontal beam placed across an obstacle, creating a path. Think of footbridges that you see on a hike, spanning streams and narrow rivers. This type of bridge is effective for spanning short distances, but fails at supporting heavier loads in the middle of the path or spanning longer distances. To solve this problem, builders of antiquity eventually learned to use the strength of the arch, creating what is known as the arch bridge. In this type of bridge, a path is formed by an arch, which helps to distribute the weight of the load on the bridge, especially in the middle of the span. These bridges are sturdy and long lasting. Indeed, some of the earliest arch bridges built in ancient Greece – like the Arkadiko Bridge – are still in use today. Still, the arch bridge had its limits. A single arch, or even a series of arches, can only support so much weight and span a certain distance. Over time, engineers realized that suspension bridges could be a possible solution to the problems of weight and distance. These bridges, which are some of the most scientifically challenging to design and build, are suspended from cables or ropes. Those cables and ropes, in turn, hang from towers along the length of the bridge. This new way of distributing weight increases the efficiency of the bridge, and allows for greater length and weight loads.

6 Civil engineers are the ones tasked with designing public infrastructure like bridges. They must consider a myriad of factors, from climate, traffic, to bridge load. In wintry climates, bridges must be able to withstand heavy snow and ice. Some bridges are located in densely populated areas while others carry loads of cars, trucks, or trains. Engineers must take into account fatigue, or how likely the material will break under stress. They learned this the hard way: the Quebec Bridge, for example, collapsed twice before it was stabilized, as a result of inaccurate engineering estimates. After three decades of careful engineering and construction work, the bridge finally opened in 1919, and now holds the record for the longest bridge of its kind in the world.

7 Nowadays, modern bridges are both stable and beautiful. In San Francisco, the Golden Gate Bridge has become an iconic symbol. In the 1930s, when it was first opened to the public, the Golden Gate Bridge was one of the longest and tallest bridges in the world. On the other side of the country, the Brooklyn Bridge is

similarly famous, appearing in movies, television shows, and literature. Conceived by German immigrant John Roebling, the Brooklyn Bridge opened in 1883 over the East River. As the world's first steel-wire suspension bridge, it was a true feat of engineering. It's gorgeous gothic revival style also led it to become a beloved part of the New York City skyline.

8 Though it was not a swift or straightforward journey, the design of bridges has come a long way. Our early ancestors would be astonished if they could see what scientists and engineers have accomplished today.

Bridge	Year Built	Length (in feet)
Arkadiko Bridge	c. 1300-1190 BC	72
Caravan Bridge	850 BC	28
Maria Pia Bridge	1877	1158
Brooklyn Bridge	1883	5989
Golden Gate Bridge	1937	8981

1. Which statement best describes the central idea of the passage?

   A. Bridges are made of many different types of building materials, and come in diverse forms.
   B. Bridges have become more complex and ambitious with the progression of human technology.
   C. Bridges are designed differently in response to the specific geographical obstacles that they are meant to span.
   D. Civil engineers must consider many factors, including loads, climate and traffic, when designing bridges.

2. Why did people transition into building suspension bridges?

   E. They were more beautiful visually than arch bridges.
   F. They are the most challenging bridges to design and build.
   G. They are longer lasting than arch bridges, which tend to crumble over time.
   H. They allowed for greater weight and distance than arch and beam bridges.

3. Read this sentence from paragraph 2.

   Nature made the first bridges, when aged trees fell and lay across a stream; early humans refined this idea by making bridges out of simple logs or planks.

   How does this sentence fit into the overall structure of the passage?

   A. It describes the recent history of bridges, in a sequential overview of bridge designs.
   B. It shows Nature's place amongst the historical innovators of bridge design.
   C. It emphasizes the sturdiness of wood as an example of high-quality bridge materials.
   D. It reveals the simplicity of early bridges in contrast to the complexity of modern bridge designs mentioned later in the passage.

4. Which statement best describes the role of paragraph 3 in the overall structure of the passage?

   E. It summarizes the information found in paragraphs 1-2.
   F. It offers a counterargument to the main points of paragraph 4-5.
   G. It mentions topics that are further explained in paragraphs 7-8
   H. It introduces the central idea of the entire passage.

The Tutorverse

5. Which sentence best supports the idea that scientific discoveries were essential to innovation in designing bridges?

    A. "These bridges help make small obstacles and short distances, like streams or brooks, easier and safer to cross." (par. 2)

    B. "The forces of tension, compression, torsion, and shear all play a critical role in determining whether a bridge will stand or fall." (par. 4)

    C. "Indeed, some of the earliest arch bridges built in ancient Greece – like the Arkadiko Bridge – are still in use today." (par. 5)

    D. "It's gorgeous gothic revival style also led it to become a beloved part of the New York City skyline." (par. 7)

6. Paragraph 6 contributes to the development of the central idea of the passage by

    E. revealing the inspiration behind the world's first bridges.

    F. detailing several examples of famous engineers and bridges throughout human history.

    G. emphasizing how difficult engineering has been in the quest for better bridge designs.

    H. demonstrating how bridges have ultimately failed due to natural disasters.

7. In paragraph 7, the word "feat" is used to highlight

    A. how difficult it is to travel across the full distance of many modern bridges.

    B. how complex the engineering process was in creating a modern bridge.

    C. how big hybrid cable suspension bridges and steel-wire suspension bridges can be.

    D. how heroic people were when the Quebec Bridge collapsed.

8. The table contributes to the development of the topic of the passage mainly by

    E. showing that there are many different types of bridges all over the world.

    F. emphasizing that Quebec Bridge is the longest bridge of its kind in the world.

    G. demonstrating how bridges became longer as technology improved over time.

    H. revealing how some of the oldest bridges were not technologically sound.

Pop, Pop!

1 It used to be that one needed to consult the music industry sales charts to grasp the magnitude of pop music's appeal. *Thriller*, by the "King of Pop" Michael Jackson, was one of the most commercially successful albums of its time – as evidenced by how it spent over two years on Billboard's charts[1] and occupied the number one spot for over 35 weeks. According to the Recording Industry Association of America, Epic Records, and Legacy Records, *Thriller* has sold over 100 million copies worldwide. Other pop albums that have sold at least 40 million copies or more worldwide include Pink Floyd's *The Dark Side of the Moon*, Whitney Houston's *The Bodyguard*, and Shania Twain's *Come on Over*. The diversity of musical styles reflected in these albums shows just how all-encompassing the pop genre once was. In fact, the word "pop" simply means popular. It is a category based purely on popularity. Historically, it has drawn inspiration from many musical styles.

2 But what, exactly, made these songs so popular?

---

[1] **Billboard's charts**: the magazine *Billboard*'s record of the popular songs during a period of time

3 Over the decades, a handful of songwriters have discovered the answer – and profited. As the rise of technology created new modes of production, these songwriters have distilled the key components of popular music down to a basic formula. Pop songs are no longer mostly written by their performers. A handful of writers are responsible for the lion's share of pop hits. Karl Martin Sandberg, Mikkel Eriksen, and Lukasz Gottwald are responsible for some of the most popular songs of recent years – songs performed by famous boybands and pop divas alike. This cabal of songwriters, guided by a keen ear and enabled by technology, has created music's version of the Golden Goose – one that lays multi-platinum colored, sonic eggs. Popular songs are carefully dissected to determine exactly what qualities make them so appealing. Everything from the chords to structure to choruses, beats, and hooks are carefully mapped out and often replicated. Indeed, careful listening will show that many pop songs share beats so similar that they are virtually identical.

4 This musical evolution is also due, in part, to how listener tastes have changed in this new internet age. Gone are the days when music listeners had to patiently wait for the record needle to move to the next vinyl groove to hear their favorite song. Our digital world has made it easier for people to simply click, swipe, or fast-forward their way to what they want to hear, and share or delete entire albums in seconds. It has created shorter attention spans for music enthusiasts across the globe. In the past, a pop song would only need one musical hook – that part of a song that is so catchy that they get stuck in people's heads – but today, a song typically has multiple hooks to ensure that a listener will not immediately find a different song to play.

5 Despite the stiff competition, those that manage to harness the power of pop can now reach new heights of success. Forget Billboard charts – today we need look no further than social media and online media outlets to determine the popularity of a singer or their songs. As of March 2016, pop stars Katy Perry, Justin Bieber, and Taylor Swift occupied the top three slots on the social network Twitter, with 84.1 million, 76.8 million, and 72.5 million followers, respectively. By comparison, then-president Barack Obama commanded only 70.9 million followers. The most viewed videos of all time on video-sharing website YouTube? As of March 2016, the top ten featured pop stars. Psy, a Korean pop star, appears in the number one slot with 2.5 billion views. Together, all ten videos account for just shy of 15 billion views.

6 Pop stars have leveraged their influence and following to create corporate partnerships, and directly sell products to their customers. From iTunes downloads to online t-shirt sales, pop musicians have developed new sources of revenue. Like many superstars, Rihanna has launched her own perfume and cosmetic companies. Between 2015 and 2016 alone, she earned $75 million – and not all of it from music sales. Similarly, Taylor Swift, who also has her own perfume line and active online store, earned $44 million in 2016. Compare this to Michael Jackson's earnings in 1982 (the year of *Thriller*'s release), including an adjustment for inflation: $15 million.

7 Clearly, the masters of the pop universe have found something that people like. With millions of dollars on the line, why fix, as the saying goes, what isn't broken? After all, 15 billion views can't be wrong –right?

Top 5 Best-Selling Artists on 2018 Billboard Charts

Billboard Ranking	Name	Latest Album	Instagram Following (as of January 31st, 2019)
1	Drake	Scorpion	53,400,000
2	Post Malone	Stoney	14,900,000
3	Ed Sheeran	÷	27,200,000
4	Taylor Swift	Reputation	114,000,000
5	Cardi B	Invasion of Privacy	40,600,000

Source: Billboard.com & Instagram

The Tutorverse

1. What is the most likely reason the author refers to Michael Jackson's album *Thriller* in paragraph 1?

   A. to establish the musical style of what makes a song "pop"
   B. to give an example of how musicians in the past measured success subjectively
   C. to cite an album that exemplifies success in the era of social media
   D. to establish the author's credibility as an expert on major pop music figures

2. Read this excerpt from paragraph 1.

   The diversity of musical styles reflected in these albums shows just how all-encompassing the pop genre once was. In fact, the word "pop" simply means popular... Historically, it has drawn inspiration from many musical styles.

   This excerpt supports the development of the central idea of the passage by

   E. introducing the "pop" genre and how it was created in the past.
   F. defining the musical elements that make a song qualify as a "pop" song.
   G. highlighting the biggest artists that have shaped pop music.
   H. emphasizing the author's preference for popular music over other genres.

3. What role does paragraph 2 play in the overall structure of the passage?

   A. It reinforces the author's confusion about the phenomenon of music popularity.
   B. It questions whether the direction pop music evolution has taken is truly a good one.
   C. It summarizes the main claim of the passage, that popular music has always had a significant impact on society.
   D. It demonstrates a shift from discussing the history of popular music to the change in its musical qualities.

4. How did the measures of success for pop music change from the past to modern day?

   E. In the past, pop musicians were successful if their albums sold well; now they are judged by the number of awards they win.
   F. In the past, pop musicians were recognized for their success by official industry statistics, while modern day success is more determined by social media following.
   G. The success of pop musicians was once determined by mass appeal, and is now determined by individual music professionals.
   H. The success of pop musicians has always been dependent on radio play, both in the past and now.

5. According to the passage, pop songs today include more than one musical hook because

   A. the more hooks there are, the more likely a listener will keep listening to a particular song.
   B. followers on Twitter requested more musical hooks from their favorite pop stars.
   C. *Thriller* was famous for its multiple musical hooks, which is emulated by most songs.
   D. songs with multiple musical hooks are easier and quicker to write.

6. Read this sentence from paragraph 3.

   As the rise of technology created new modes of production, these songwriters have distilled the key components of popular music down to a basic formula.

   The author uses the word "formula" to convey how

   E. brilliant and scientific these songwriters were.
   F. foolish audiences are for demanding low-quality music.
   G. repetitive and unoriginal pop music has become.
   H. similar composing is to mathematical proofs.

The Tutorverse

7. In paragraph 5, what is the most likely reason the author refers to "then-president Barack Obama"?

   A. to show how even national leaders were held in the sway of pop musicians and their online presence
   B. to highlight the decline of political interest and activism in recent years
   C. to emphasize the extent of influence that pop musicians now have through online followings
   D. to compare the political impact that pop musicians have relative to political leaders

8. The table contributes to the development of the ideas in paragraph 5 by

   E. revealing the discrepancy between Billboards chart rankings and social media influence of modern pop musicians.
   F. emphasizing how the top 10 best-selling musicians also have the greatest social media following.
   G. providing a comparison between the social media influence of pop musicians and notable politicians.
   H. suggesting that technology has also changed the language that pop artists use to title their albums.

9. How does paragraph 6 support the development of the central idea?

   A. It highlights the artistic decline of pop music as a result of increasing profits.
   B. It shows another aspect of the pop music industry that changed as a result of technology.
   C. It emphasizes the cultural and political impact of pop stars on social media.
   D. It reveals how modern pop stars are multi-talented and business savvy.

10. The author includes a series of questions at the end of the last paragraph most likely to

   E. encourage further study of pop music history.
   F. suggest uncertainty about the wisdom of the current direction of pop music.
   G. reflect a personal curiosity about how pop music will continue to evolve.
   H. emphasize that the phenomenon of popular music has not yet been fully explained.

The Legacy of Impressionism

1 People have expressed themselves through music for thousands of years. These forms and styles of music were as varied as the cultures that produced them. Even within a given culture, music changed from one time period to another.

2 As in other cultural traditions, the Western classical music tradition in Europe evolved over time. It can, consequently, be divided into many different styles or eras. For example, the Renaissance era of music blossomed between the 1400s and 1600s. It focused on humanist themes, such as love and romance. The Renaissance era of music was a contrast to the Medieval era of music, which focused on religious themes, such as prayer and sacrifice.

3 The Impressionist era emerged in the late 1800s. The main objective of the Impressionist era was to paint emotional pictures through unique musical arrangements. Impressionist musicians accomplished this by manipulating timbre. Timbre is often described as the "color of a sound." It is the quality of a sound that distinguishes one source from another. Timbre is what makes a middle C note sound different on a piano than on a guitar. It helps stimulate the visual senses of the audience.

The Tutorverse

4   Impressionist composers relied heavily on the use of timbre within their orchestras. Made up of many different instruments, orchestras allowed for a diversity of sounds. Composers like Claude Debussy and Maurice Ravel experimented with new orchestral chord combinations. They wanted to paint unique pictures for their audiences. The emotional result was much like an Impressionist painting – the calm evoked by light dancing on still waters; the tranquility of sunlight filtering through treetops.

5   The popularity of Impressionism waxed and waned in later decades. Nevertheless, Impressionism still managed to have a lasting impact on the history of modern music. Some music critics even argue that the Impressionist style helped sparked the advent of American jazz. They are able to find Impressionist sounds reverberating subtly in the vibrant compositions of early jazz musicians. These critics argue that jazz pianists, such as Bill Evans, borrowed from the colorful genius of Debussy and Ravel. According to this school of thought, Impressionism simply found a new, manic form in the 1920s jazz joints of New Orleans and Harlem.

6   Other music historians link the Impressionist tradition to the revolutionary sounds of rock and roll in the 1960s. They claim that, without Impressionism, rock and roll guitarists and organists would have never had the opportunity to experiment with their complex musical arrangements. Impressionism, according to this school of thought, was an example of how rejecting prior tradition could lead to innovation. Prior to the Impressionist era, music remained relatively structured and cerebral. Some even describe pre-Impressionist music as colorless or stoic. Impressionism allowed musicians to freely experiment with the relationships that exist between sounds, colors, and feelings, and opened the gates to new sound.

7   Impressionist concepts have affected other artistic fields as well. Due to shared creative goals, different disciplines began to innovate, blend, and collaborate. Paintings began invoking auditory senses, much like musical compositions. Novelists and poets began composing literary works that stimulate all human senses. Beyond jazz and other experimental musical forms, Impressionism helped birth a multitude of modern artistic movements. Impressionism helped create an entirely new paradigm – or historical framework – for music, art, and literature. As a historical force, it was so powerful that its beauty inevitably bled into other artistic disciplines.

8   The wide-reaching effects of the Impressionist era should not be understated. To an average listener, Impressionism may sound similar to other forms of classical music. But to informed listeners, the Impressionist musical tradition has a distinctive sound. This unique sound has not only had a lasting impact on music, but also on history at large.

1. Which statement best describes the central idea of the passage?

    A. "People have expressed themselves through music for thousands of years." (par. 1)
    B. "Impressionist composers relied heavily on the use of timbre within their orchestras." (par. 4)
    C. "Other music historians link the Impressionist tradition to the revolutionary sounds of rock and roll in the 1960s." (par. 6)
    D. "The wide-reaching effects of the Impressionist era should not be understated." (par. 8)

2. Which statement would the author of the excerpt most likely agree with?

    E. Other creative forms, such as visual art and literature, have much to learn from all genres of music.
    F. Music and other creative forms are more powerful when they collaborate and interact with each other.
    G. Music and other creative forms should be held strictly separate, and focus on improving within their own disciplines.
    H. Music is a superior art form to all other creative disciplines.

The Tutorverse

3. Read this sentence from paragraph 4.

   They wanted to paint unique pictures for their audiences.

   Which excerpt best reflects the idea implied in this sentence?

   A. "Made up of many different instruments, orchestras allowed for a diversity of sounds." (par. 4)
   B. "The popularity of Impressionism waxed and waned in later decades." (par. 5)
   C. "Nevertheless, Impressionism still managed to have a lasting impact on the history of modern music." (par. 5)
   D. "Impressionism allowed musicians to freely experiment with the relationships that exist between sounds, colors, and feelings, and opened the gates to new sound." (par. 6)

4. Read this excerpt from paragraph 3.

   Timbre is often described as the "color of a sound." It is the quality of a sound that distinguishes one source from another. Timbre is what makes a middle C note sound different on a piano than on a guitar. It helps stimulate the visual senses of the audience.

   What statement best describes how the excerpt fits into the overall structure of the paragraph?

   E. It indicates the shift in Impressionist composers' perspectives to the instruments rather than performers.
   F. It emphasizes the subtle continuity between Impressionist and Renaissance musical styles.
   G. It introduces the popular use of painters and sculptors in the composition process.
   H. It provides an example of a technique used by Impressionist musicians to achieve their goals.

5. What does the figurative language in paragraph 4 emphasize?

   A. the calm emotional tone of Impressionist musicians when they perform
   B. the poetic colors and images that inspired the titles of Impressionist compositions
   C. the heavy impact that visual beauty had on composing Impressionist music
   D. the gorgeous settings in which Ravel and Debussy did their best work

6. What is the most likely reason that the author uses the word "manipulating" in paragraph 3?

   E. to show how sly and manipulative the composers of Impressionist music could be in order to accomplish their goals
   F. to emphasize the complexity of the choices that Impressionist composers made about timbre
   G. to demonstrate the simplicity and power of the use of timbre in Impressionist compositions
   H. to prove that Impressionist composers did not have a good technical grasp of using timbre

7. How does the relationship between paragraphs 5 and 6 contribute to the structure of the overall passage?

   A. They contrast the aesthetic and cultural differences between Impressionist music in America versus Europe.
   B. They show the effects of the Impressionist era on the development of later musical styles and genres.
   C. They provide examples of famous composers of Impressionist music, and how their most famous works demonstrate the central concepts of the era.
   D. They introduce a transition to the idea that Impressionist concepts affected other kinds of art.

The Tutorverse

8. Read this sentence from paragraph 7.

> **As a historical force, it was so powerful that its beauty inevitably bled into other artistic disciplines.**

What role does this sentence play in the structure of the paragraph?

E. It signals the shift from the isolation that characterized Impressionist music to how it began to influence other disciplines.

F. It provides an example of how the qualities of Impressionism affected people working in other creative fields.

G. It highlights the ways in which Impressionism drew inspiration from many other artistic disciplines.

H. It reinforces the idea that Impressionism's historical impact went beyond the field of music.

A Different Lens

1 The plots of many science-fiction novels are often set in far-away lands and alien environments. Despite this, the themes discussed in science-fiction literature are usually relevant to the everyday. Science-fiction authors often dare to explore the unknown. They challenge preconceived notions and often test traditional values in exotic settings. In doing so, they tell us more about ourselves.

2 There are many science-fiction authors, but perhaps none are more famous than the "Big Three." These three authors – Robert Heinlein, Isaac Asimov, and Arthur Clarke – have written some of the most influential science-fiction novels in history. Many of the works created by these authors are paragons of the science-fiction style and perfectly embody science-fiction themes.

3 Asimov focused on themes of human society and the human condition. His 1941 short story "Nightfall" concerns a planet named Lagath, which is bathed in constant illumination by six suns. In "Nightfall" Lagath is soon threatened by the coming of darkness, a result of an eclipse of one of its suns. Asimov uses this setting to address pressing social and cultural issues. He focuses on chaos and turmoil brought about by society's reaction to a cataclysmic event.

4 Heinlein's 1961 novel *Stranger in a Strange Land* is considered to be one of the most popular works of science-fiction ever written. On the surface, the story considers the effects that space travel would have on humans. However, there is much more to the novel than just space travel. Threading throughout the novel are themes touching on such topics as religion, government, and the idea of cultural diversity. All the while, Heinlein weaves a tale of a Martian come to Earth and explores the meaning of being human.

5 Clarke is most widely known for the 1968 novel *2001: A Space Odyssey*. This novel has often been described as eerily prophetic. In his work, Clarke touches on a wide range of themes. Most notably, however, he explores technology and how it has many potentially negative effects on humanity. Clarke points out the dangers of poorly-understood technology run amok.

6 Though many of the Big Three's works were written decades ago, their work remains influential even today. We can see the influence of science-fiction literature in popular culture. Some of the most successful and well-liked films today, such as *The Matrix* and *Gravity*, are of the science-fiction genre. There is something about science-fiction that captures our imaginations and speaks to us.

The Tutorverse

1. The main idea of paragraph 1 is that science-fiction

   A. is both challenging to write and to read.
   B. appeals to readers because of the exotic settings.
   C. is the most relevant genre to everyday audiences.
   D. uses imagination to reveal more about what it means to be human.

2. Which of the following choices best describes what the passage is about?

   E. why Isaac Asimov addresses pressing social and cultural issues
   F. why Robert Heinlein wrote the most popular work of science fiction
   G. describing examples of different science-fiction themes
   H. describing the plots of famous science-fiction novels

3. Why was the planet Lagath unaccustomed to darkness?

   A. The light of six suns kept it constantly bright.
   B. Technology had gotten out of control.
   C. A cataclysmic event caused a sun to eclipse.
   D. The inhabitants of Lagath used light to power its buildings.

4. The "Big Three" mentioned in paragraph 6 refers to

   E. publications.
   F. authors.
   G. themes.
   H. genres.

5. Read these sentences from paragraph 5.

   Clarke is most widely known for the 1968 novel *2001: A Space Odyssey*. This novel has often been described as eerily prophetic.

   Which of the following is implied by these sentences?

   A. Before 1968, technology was more beneficial to people than harmful.
   B. Without technology, people would be much safer.
   C. Since 1968, technology has proven to have some negative effects on people.
   D. Technological innovation is important to people.

6. What was most probably true of the Martian who comes to Earth, as described in the paragraph 4?

   E. The Martian lacked a thorough understanding of human culture.
   F. The Martian was a powerful representative from Mars.
   G. The Martian was eager to return to Lagath.
   H. The Martian provided humans with a great deal of new technology.

7. Which of the following best summarizes paragraph 6?

   A. Science-fiction movies sell the most tickets.
   B. *The Matrix* was inspired by the novel *Stranger in a Strange Land*.
   C. Science-fiction authors often dare to explore the unknown.
   D. Science-fiction remains highly relevant and is widely enjoyed.

Paved with Good Intentions

A New Kind of Tourist

1 Who hasn't looked at a friend's travel photos and sighed in envy? But these images of adventures in exotic, far-off places often come with invisible, sinister consequences: the damage that tourism inflicts on native wildlife. Zoom out of that snapshot of cute monkeys dangling from overhead trees, and you'll see wild

monkeys eating human garbage. Endangered turtles are interrupted in their migrations by selfie-taking tourists. Rather than helping endangered species, profits from tourism goes into the pockets of travel agencies and purveyors.

2 In response to this damage, the tourism industry has developed a new offering: ecotourism. The idea is to visit nature to support, not damage, conservation. To make the trip fully guilt-free, the profits go towards preserving local ecosystems. Yet, the destinations are still exotic, featuring places like Costa Rica, Kenya, and the Amazon Rainforest. The United Nations Food and Agriculture Organization declares that ecotourism is nature-based and sustainable.

3 Sounds great, doesn't it?

4 The sad reality is that while ecotourism may seem like a noble pursuit, its practice does not always align with theory. Tourist flights contribute to air traffic and global climate change. Profits become the main priority, not ecological conservation. The result is that these exotic habitats are still suffering, despite many people choosing to be ethical "ecotourists."

Illusion of Safety

5 Ecotourism attempts to protect biodiversity[1], but often causes unintentional harm. Daniel Blumstein, chair of ecology and evolutionary biology at the University of California, Los Angeles, says that ecotourists are unaware of the consequences of their actions. People cannot go into an area and have no impact. Even hiking into an area has an impact on an ecosystem, though it does far less damage than other forms of recreation. Hikers often leave litter behind that, in the best scenario, takes time to decompose. In the worst scenario, travelers can leave behind plastic snack wrappers and water bottles that will virtually never disappear.

6 Another unintended effect is the domestication of wildlife. Animals become more accustomed to seeing humans after repeated exposure. In some cases, the latter can grow dependent on the former. One example of this can be found in the elk that roam Grand Teton National Park. Scientists have found that the elk move in less alert postures because they feel safe around humans. This has made the elk more vulnerable to predators. As a result, the ecosystem's food chain has been disrupted. Another tragic example is the famous African lion, Cecil. As a tourist attraction, Cecil was used to being photographed in his home in the Hwange National Park. A hunter was able to lure him out of his environment and kill him because he trusted humans.

7 Human visitors also impact wild animals in more direct ways. Many tourists are worried about the risks of catching diseases from wildlife, like malaria and yellow fever. Anthropologist Michael Muehlenbein of Baylor University instead asks: how does exposure to human diseases from tourists affect the health of animals? Many diseases can jump from species to species. The odds are worse yet for primates, genetic relatives of humans, since they are susceptible to the same kinds of illnesses as people.

Behind the Buzzwords

8 Since the early 1990s, Costa Rica has been considered the poster child of ecotourism. However, it is also an example of ecotourism gone wrong. In Costa Rica, protecting nature is no longer as important as making money. For one, the sheer number of visitors is threatening the environment. Though the government designates specific areas for ecotourism, these national parks are deteriorating from the overwhelming human traffic. Native species like the jaguar, sloth, and howler monkey are also suffering because of

---

[1] **biodiversity**: the variety of species of animals and plants in a particular habitat

development. Another issue is that regulations meant to protect and conserve nature are not enforced. This is often because there are limited resources to properly regulate the high standard of environmental protection put in place.

9 Tourism ultimately leads to development and loss of protected natural spaces. It means rising demands for hotels, excursions, and other tourist activities. Trees are cut down to make room for new buildings. Furthermore, not all tourist organizations are truly driven to protect the local environment. Words like "eco" and "green" have largely become marketing-only buzzwords.

10 On the other side of the planet, in Kenya, the Maasai Mara reserve has become one of the world's top safari destinations. In the 1980s, there were only spaces for 300 beds for visitors. Now, there are over 3,000. Many Kenyan safari lodges call themselves eco-friendly if they simply recycle their plastic and use ecofriendly cleaning supplies. Their tours continue to be delivered on minibuses, which trample over native vegetation, spew fumes into the air, and cause soil erosion. The delineation of land borders, with fences and walls, has blocked migration routes for many animals. This indifference to their local wildlife, combined with the influx of visitors, is negatively impacting Kenya's ecology.

11 There are many stakeholders in the ecotourism industry. It is a pity that they do not do more for the ones they most benefit from: the animals and plant life that live on those lands.

Tourism in Costa Rica

Year	Total Tourism Profit (in millions)	Number of International Tourists
1995	$336	785,000
2000	$545	1,088,000
2005	$591	1,679,000
2010	$629	2,100,000
2015	$898	2,660,000

Source: The World Bank – Dataset CRI_DS2

1. Which of the following best describes the definition of ecotourism according to the author?

A. a type of tourism that promotes exotic destinations that look good on social media
B. a type of tourism that is just another scheme to make money
C. a type of tourism that doesn't benefit the ecosystem as much as it claims to
D. a type of tourism that results in large donations to nature conservation groups

2. Read paragraph 3.

Sounds great, doesn't it?

How does this paragraph contribute to the tone of the passage?

E. It conveys enthusiasm for ecotourism as being beneficial to local ecosystems and economies.
F. It shows a sense of approval at how ecotourism is superior to traditional tourism.
G. It shows ambivalence about ecotourism, which has a neutral effect on the ecosystem.
H. It creates a sense of skepticism about the idea that ecotourism might be too good to be true.

The Tutorverse

3. Read this sentence from paragraph 2.

   **The United Nations Food and
   Agriculture Organization declares that
   ecotourism is nature-based and
   sustainable.**

   Which statement best describes the author's
   perspective about the statement made by the
   United Nations Food and Agriculture
   Organization?

   A. The statement is inaccurate because it fails
   to address the negative impacts of
   ecotourism.
   B. The statement is justified because it has
   helped improve the populations of
   endangered turtles.
   C. This statement accurately reflects how
   ecotourism helps grow local businesses.
   D. Ecotourism is nature-based but it is not
   long-lasting because of the high costs of
   building eco-friendly attractions.

4. Which excerpt from the passage best supports
   Daniel Blumstein's ideas about ecotourism in
   paragraph 5?

   E. "The idea is to visit nature to support, not
   damage, conservation." (par. 2).
   F. "Profits become the main priority, not
   ecological conservation." (par. 4).
   G. "A hunter was able to lure him out of his
   environment and kill him because he
   trusted humans." (par. 6).
   H. "Words like "eco" and "green" have
   largely become marketing-only
   buzzwords." (par. 9).

5. What role does paragraph 8 play in the overall
   structure of the passage?

   A. It describes an experiment that proves the
   central idea.
   B. It supports the general claims of the
   passage with a concrete example.
   C. It summarizes information found in the rest
   of the passage.
   D. It offers historical background knowledge
   for the main problem in the passage.

6. Which conclusion is best supported by the
   information in paragraph 6?

   E. Hunting for sport poses a serious threat to
   endangered species and needs to be
   regulated.
   F. Ecotourism does not account for the fact
   that animals adapt to the presence of
   humans.
   G. Humans are purposefully disrupting animal
   food chains.
   H. Domestication happens when wild animals
   gradually become safe to keep as pets.

7. How does the table support the ideas in
   paragraph 8?

   A. It supports the claim that the number of
   tourists visiting Costa Rica has been
   steadily rising.
   B. It illustrates how Costa Rica is an example
   of increasing profits in traditional tourism
   leading to environmental devastation.
   C. It emphasizes that the majority of profits
   from tourism do not go towards protecting
   indigenous species or national parks.
   D. It reinforces the idea that national parks in
   Costa Rica are deteriorating due to rising
   amounts of air traffic.

8. What is the most likely reason the author
   mentions "buzzwords" in paragraph 9?

   E. Ecotourism fulfills its promises of
   promoting more eco-friendly excursions.
   F. Buzzwords draw tourists to exotic
   destinations in hopes of seeing native
   wildlife.
   G. It is impossible to enforce the claims of
   these buzzwords in tourist areas.
   H. Buzzwords help tourists avoid thinking
   about the damaging side effects of their
   travels.

A Critical Point of View

1. On July 15, 1979, President Jimmy Carter addressed the nation from the Oval Office. In this address, known as the "Crisis of Confidence" speech, Carter discussed different issues facing Americans. Carter began by mentioning such common topics as energy use and America's reliance on foreign oil. However, he went on to discuss a far more unusual subject: an internal threat to American democracy. This crisis did not threaten America's standing with other nations or the civil rights of its citizens. Instead, it struck at the "heart and soul and spirit" of America's national will and spirit. In particular, Carter was concerned with America's obsession with material possessions and the citizenry's detachment from society.

2. Carter was the first president since the end of World War II to bring up the subject of America's spirit. Carter began his speech by reading excerpts from letters sent to him by concerned Americans. Many of these letters included comments that questioned the American Dream. From reading these personal appeals, Carter began to see a "crisis of confidence" looming on the American horizon. For Carter, this crisis was due to a shift from valuing family, faith, hard work, and community to worshipping self-indulgence and consumption. Americans were obsessing over what they could buy and consume. Carter believed that this crisis was an existential one – a crisis that took away people's sense of meaning and belonging.

3. Carter saw the symptoms of this crisis all across America. He pointed out how both voter turnout and worker productivity had dropped. He noted that people were spending more money to enjoy the current moment, and saving less for the future. He lamented that fewer and fewer people believed that the future would bring progress and better times.

4. In his speech, he declared that this crisis could not be solved by politicians alone. Carter believed it would take a concerted effort by Americans themselves and urged his fellow citizens to think of the greater good. Most importantly, he asked his audience to put an end to the age of American excess. Carter wanted people to put aside their selfish ways and focus on contributing positively to society. He believed that Americans had the strength to rise to the occasion.

5. At the time, his nationally televised speech was met with mixed reactions. Some publications praised it as an accurate diagnosis of the country. These publications believed Carter was being realistic and honest about the cultural, political, and economic crises facing the nation. Others were less impressed by his efforts, dubbing his address the "Malaise Speech." Critics in this camp believed that Carter was painting an apocalyptic portrait of the United States. They felt that he unfairly characterized a great country as sick and dying. Many believed Carter's statements were nothing more than hyperbole.

6. Nevertheless, the themes that Carter covered – consumption, identity, and unity – are issues that still resonate today. Looking back, it seems almost as if Carter had a crystal ball with which he glimpsed the future – a future where Americans care more for shiny gadgets and selfies than for their own health and for their neighbors. Indeed, when comparing the concerns expressed in the "Crisis of Confidence" speech to current issues, many find that there are more bridges than gaps. In 2009, President Barack Obama identified the same "profound…sapping of confidence" in America during his inaugural speech. The economic downturn of 2008, caused by years of over-ambitious spending and mortgage debt, echoed the high unemployment rates of Carter's era. The unchecked use of fossil fuels has led to staggering pollution and deadly climate change.

7. Perhaps the essence of Carter's speech was less apocalyptic and more visionary than many have claimed.

The Tutorverse

1. Which statement best describes the central idea of the passage?

   A. Carter's presidency was troubled by many economic, political and cultural problems.
   B. Carter's 1979 speech identified spiritual and cultural problems that continue to affect the American public.
   C. Carter's "Malaise Speech" wrongly diagnosed the American people with problems that they did not have.
   D. Carter's "Crisis of Confidence" speech helped fix Americans' problems in the 1970s.

2. Which statement best describes why Carter's speech was significant?

   E. "In this address, known as the 'Crisis of Confidence' speech, Carter discussed different issues facing Americans." (par. 1)
   F. "Instead, it struck at the 'heart and soul and spirit' of our national will..." (par. 1)
   G. "He lamented that fewer and fewer people believed that the future would bring progress and better times." (par. 3)
   H. "In his speech, he declared that this crisis could not be solved by politicians alone." (par. 4)

3. According to the passage, Carter was inspired to write his speech by

   A. observing the behavior of citizens and reading reports on national trends.
   B. suggestions from his team of dedicated speechwriters.
   C. direct communications from individual American citizens.
   D. news reports of the economic and environmental issues plaguing the country.

4. Paragraph 3 contributes to the development of the central idea of the passage by

   E. illustrating relatable examples of American citizens behaving in a concerning way.
   F. conveying Carter's personal dislike of the way most Americans behaved.
   G. proposes a solution to a political problem described earlier in the passage.
   H. connecting problems from the past with problems of today.

5. Which statement best describes how the author's use of problem-and-solution in paragraph 4 contributes to the development of ideas in the passage?

   A. Explaining how the problem cannot be resolved by politicians shows that Carter did not take responsibility for the issue.
   B. Describing the difficulty of proposed solutions highlights Carter's personal crisis of faith in the future.
   C. Illustrating the severity of the problem demonstrates Carter's intention to blame Americans for their own failings.
   D. Detailing the actions that American citizens need to take highlights how Carter wanted people to take responsibility for themselves.

6. Which sentence from paragraph 5 best describes the author's perspective on Carter's speech?

   E. "Critics in this camp believed that Carter was painting an apocalyptic portrait of the United States."
   F. "They felt that he unfairly characterized a great country as sick and dying."
   G. "These publications believed Carter was being realistic and honest about the cultural, political, and economic crises facing the nation."
   H. "Many believed Carter's statements were nothing more than hyperbole."

The Tutorverse

7. Read this sentence from paragraph 6.

Indeed, when comparing the concerns expressed in the "Crisis of Confidence" speech to current issues, many find that there are more bridges than gaps.

What is the most likely reason the author uses the word "bridges"?

A. to describe a potential solution to national unemployment
B. to reinforce the idea that connections still exist between past and present issues
C. to emphasize how much time has passed since Carter's presidency
D. to highlight how difficult it is to find similarities between the 1970s and now

8. In paragraph 7, how does the phrase "less apocalyptic and more visionary" contribute to the overall arguments of the passage?

E. It sheds light on the fact that Carter's concerns were out of touch with reality.
F. It reinforces the argument that Carter's speech was based on exaggerated information.
G. It counters the idea that Carter's speech focused too much on negative aspects of society.
H. It supports claims that Carter's speech reflected a unique kind of foresight.

Linguistically Speaking

1 Most people take for granted the fact that we can communicate clearly with one another. Yet it's nothing short of amazing that we're able to make ourselves understood – to convey complicated thoughts and ideas – to one another at all. It's thanks in part to languages that we have become the dominant species on our planet.

2 But what exactly is language, and how does it work? How was language created, and how did it change over time? Why is it still a challenge to communicate with those who speak different languages? Why is it, exactly, that the word "dog" refers to a furry, four-legged creature that barks and bites? And why is "dog" represented by *chien* in French, *perro* in Spanish, and *inu* in Japanese? These questions and more are the focus of linguists, or those who study language.

3 One might ask: "How can there be a whole field of study devoted to language? There's nothing more to it than reading, writing, speaking, and listening, right?" In reality, languages are as complex and nuanced as the way we use them. Thus, the field of linguistics is focused on learning about languages. Though the field of linguistics is actually quite broad, it can be thought of in two parts: studying the structure of a language, and observing how language is used.

4 There are many parts to a language. The most basic components of languages are words. Morphology refers to the study of words themselves, and how they are structured. In morphology, word parts are called "morphemes." Simple words are made up of a single morpheme that carries all of its meaning in a single unit, such as "teach," "push," and "kind." (The Greek and Latin roots that are used to form many English words are also considered morphemes, and many of them are simple.) Complex words have two or more morphemes, such as "teacher," "pushing," and "kindness." In the latter examples, notice how the suffixes "-er," "-ing," and "-ness" need to be attached to another morpheme to give them meaning. Although the rules are often quite different from language to language, every language has its own morphology.

5 If words are the building blocks of a language, then sentences are the buildings and skyscrapers. Syntax refers to the study of those buildings – the way in which words are arranged to make meaning. Each

language has its own rules of syntax, which govern such things as the placement of nouns, verbs, and adjectives. For example, in English we say, "She wore the black suit." The adjective "black" goes before the noun it describes, "suit." In Spanish, however, adjectives frequently follow the nouns they describe: instead of "the black suit," it's *el traje negro*. Translated directly into English by word order, "el traje negro" reads "the suit black."

6 Then, of course, there are the ways words are spoken – the way they sound, and how that relates to what they mean. This study of meaning is called semantics. Semantics can quickly become complicated, but people often use it without thinking. For example, the word "rose" can refer to a flower, or it can be the past tense of "rise." Native speakers often understand which meaning is appropriate intuitively, by noticing the position of the word within the syntax of the sentence.

7 Phonology refers to the way speech sounds create words and make up a language. For example, the letters "C" and "H" make specific sounds, which are called "phonemes." But when the two letters are put together as "CH," they create a third phoneme that sounds different from each letter individually. Pragmatics refers to how the meaning of a word depends on order and context. For example, imagine that it's a warm day and someone asks you to "crack a window." The pragmatics of that phrase indicates to you that you should open the window a little bit, and not that you should put a crack in the window glass.

8 Unlike the study of the structure of a language, the study of language usage focuses more on how people utilize languages. In historical linguistics, linguists are focused on how and why languages change over time. For example, many of the world's languages are derived from a single ancient language known as Indo-European. Historical linguistics study things such as how languages as different as English and Sanskrit both evolved from Indo-European.

9 Psycholinguistics, on the other hand, is primarily concerned with studying the psychological and neurological factors that allow people to develop linguistic skills. Psycholinguists study everything from how people learn a language to how they are able to draw on a language to convey their ideas. Much of the research psycholinguists do involves language learning in children. Every language is complex, and each has nuances that are sometimes difficult for adult language learners to grasp. Children, however, learn their respective languages with relative ease. By breaking down the process by which children acquire language, psycholinguists can gain broader insights into how people of all ages learn.

10 No matter which language you use, its history and development has been traced back thousands of years by historical linguists. You learned how to communicate through principles investigated by psycholinguists. You use words made of morphemes. The meaning of your words is affected by syntax, semantics, and pragmatics. Did you ever imagine that a simple conversation with a friend could be so complex?

1. Which sentence best describes the central idea of this passage?

    A. "Most people take for granted the fact that we can communicate clearly with one another." (par. 1)
    B. "Why is it still a challenge to communicate with those who speak different languages?" (par. 2)
    C. "In reality, languages are as complex and nuanced as the way we use them. Thus, the field of linguistics is focused on learning about languages." (par. 3)
    D. "Unlike the study of the structure of a language, the study of language usage focuses more on how people utilize languages." (par. 8)

The Tutorverse

2. What is the most likely reason the author uses the phrase "for granted" in paragraph 1?

   E. to contrast the common social perceptions of language with how it is viewed by linguistics scholars
   F. to emphasize how intuitive and simple language is to young children and native speakers
   G. to reinforce the importance of investing in further linguistics research and study
   H. to illustrate how people can communicate clearly with each other

3. What role does paragraph 2 play in the overall structure of the passage?

   A. It explains problems that are resolved later in the passage.
   B. It lists the subtopics that will be expanded upon in paragraph 9.
   C. It summarizes the information found in the rest of the passage.
   D. It introduces the topic of the passage through relatable examples.

4. Read this sentence from paragraph 5.

   If words are the building blocks of a language, then sentences are the buildings and skyscrapers.

   What is the effect of comparing sentences to "buildings and skyscrapers"?

   E. It demonstrates how written instructions are essential to constructing buildings.
   F. It shows how language enabled people to build an advanced civilization.
   G. It emphasizes the complexity of the relationships between words in a sentence.
   H. It illustrates how linguists construct sentences in the same way workers build skyscrapers.

5. Which conclusion is best supported by the information in paragraph 4?

   A. Morphemes have similar meanings regardless of the specific language.
   B. Knowing English is equivalent to being proficient in Greek and Latin.
   C. Knowing the meaning of many morphemes can help expand a person's vocabulary.
   D. Learning morphemes is more difficult than learning words.

6. Read this sentence from paragraph 7.

   Phonology refers to the way speech sounds create words and make up a language.

   Based on this definition, which sentence best describes an example of phonology?

   E. The word "pound" has multiple meanings that depend on the context in which the word is used.
   F. The idiom "raining cats and dogs" has a meaning completely different from that of the individual words making up the phrase.
   G. Adding the prefix "-un" to "wind," or "happy" creates new words with opposite meanings.
   H. The "Z" sounds in "cheese" and "zebra" are the same, but are represented by different combinations of letters.

7. The author includes a question at the end of the last paragraph most likely to

   A. restate the "what," "how," and "why" questions asked in paragraph 2.
   B. quiz the reader about his or her knowledge of the subjects discussed within the passage.
   C. point out to the reader that common interactions are more complicated than they seem.
   D. interest the reader in doing further research into historical linguistics and psycholinguistics.

The Tutorverse

8.   Based on paragraph 9, why does psycholinguistics place more emphasis on children's language learning than on that of adults?

   E.   Understanding the ways in which children learn a language intuitively may lead to ideas that support adult learning of languages.
   F.   Adults are less likely to cooperate with psycholinguists because language learning seems difficult and challenging to them.
   G.   Because time has passed between childhood and adulthood, the study of adult language learning is more properly a task for historical linguists.
   H.   The discipline of neurology, which is the study of brain functions, is more concerned with children than with adults.

Plastic Addiction

1   Look into any lunchbox, toy box, car, train or airplane cabin and you'll see it: plastic. Versatile, durable and inexpensive to manufacture, plastic has become a cornerstone of modern industry. Nearly every object encountered in our daily lives is made of plastic. As such, we live in a virtual sea of plastic, which, unfortunately for our environment, is choking our actual seas with some five billion tons of stagnant, stolid plastic waste.

2   In 2009, the Environmental Protection Agency estimated that a mere seven percent of all plastic waste in America is recycled. In 2015, scientists calculated that up to 14 million tons of plastic waste is whooshed into our oceans every year from coastal regions alone. Some of that trash originates from ships at sea. However, most of it comes from garbage that has been dumped alongside rivers and coastlines and is washed or blown out into deeper waters. How long will it take that plastic waste to biodegrade[1]? In terms of the most environmentally-friendly plastics that have only recently started to trickle into the market (think: the extra-thin and crinkly water bottles in supermarkets), scientists guess the process will take about 450 years. In terms of the rest: forever.

3   Even the plastic that will eventually break down (the allegedly "good" plastic) wreaks havoc with sea life and, hence, the entire ecosystem. Millions of marine animals – roughly 700 different species – are threatened by plastic. Some animals are maimed or killed externally – strangled by carelessly discarded six-pack rings or fishing nets. Many more, however, will be negatively affected by plastic internally. In 2004, scientists discovered that a species of common amphipods (a tiny shrimp-like crustacean) in search of its usual diet of microbial slime, was diligently gnawing away at plastic bags and bottles which were coated with that slime. The amphipods would then excrete the digested plastic bits in the form of dots of plastic less than one-fifth of an inch wide – dots that were subsequently dubbed "microplastics." Have you ever walked on a beach and felt a slight crunch underfoot? That crunch comes from microplastics grinding together. Some beaches contain sand that is up to 15 percent microplastic.

4   Worse than polluted beaches, however, is the fact that the world's fish and other assorted sea life are eating, drinking and breathing these plastic dots. Microplastics often contain toxins such as Bisphenol A (or BPA). These are passed up through the marine food chain, as common amphipods are eaten by fish, and fish are eaten by larger fish, and *those* fish are eaten by people. The higher up a fish is on the food chain, the greater the saturation of toxins. Two years ago, marine biologists in Massachusetts discovered that a third of the fish caught by fishermen in Plymouth Sound housed microplastics in their guts. And while fish guts can be

---

[1] **biodegrade**: the process of decomposition by bacteria or other living organisms.

removed before we eat the fish, medical experts worry that nanoplastics – microscopic bits of plastic – can be absorbed into the rest of a fish's body, and thus, into our bodies.

5   Plastic also threatens the ecosystem by disrupting the food chain at its beginning. Plastic waste blocks sunlight, reducing the amount of energy available to algae and plankton, which are the building blocks of the entire oceanic ecosystem. As these tiny creatures die off, populations of small animals that feed on algae and plankton begin to shrink. So too do the larger animals that feed on the small animals. The negative impact of plastics on the ocean's tiniest creatures have a profound impact on the largest – and most intelligent and sentient – marine beasts. If the movie "Free Willy[2]" were made today, the main characters would have to think twice before setting their beloved whale free in such dangerous waters.

6   The good news is that, despite the staggering statistics, ocean pollution isn't a lost cause. For starters, no politicians are claiming that ocean pollution is a hoax. In 2014, when Malaysia Airlines flight 307 disappeared at sea, television viewers around the world witnessed a raft of satellite images, all of which confirmed the fact that our oceans have become a global dump. More importantly, we already have the technology to pick up, dispose of, and recycle plastic. Environmentalists are calling for the simple addition of more garbage trucks, more landfills and more coastal cleanups. Big companies like Coca-Cola – which manufactures 128 billion plastic bottles a year – have to commit to clearing and recycling their product waste. More nations, like Kenya, need to ban plastic bags; more countries, like France, need to ban plastic cups and plates. In short, when it comes to plastic waste, we know how to do the right thing – we just need to *want* to do it.

Plastic Waste Management
United States, 1960-2015

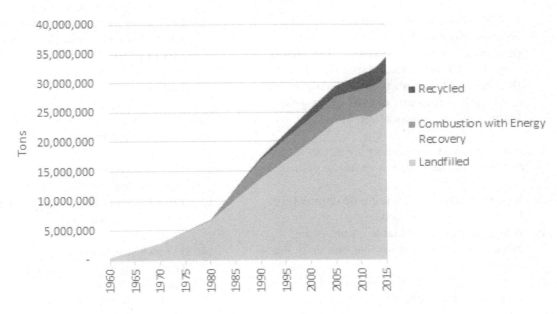

Source: United States Environmental Protection Agency

---

[2] **Free Willy**: a 1993 movie where a boy releases a whale from captivity

1. Which statement best describes the central idea of the passage?

   A. "As such, we live in a virtual sea of plastic, which, unfortunately for our environment, is choking our actual seas with some five billion tons of stagnant, stolid plastic waste." (par. 1)

   B. "In terms of the most environmentally-friendly plastics that have only recently started to trickle into the market (think: the extra-thin and crinkly water bottles in supermarkets), scientists guess the process will take about 450 years." (par. 2)

   C. "Even the plastic that will eventually break down (the allegedly "good" plastic) wreaks havoc with sea life and, hence, the entire ecosystem." (par. 3)

   D. "In short, when it comes to plastic waste, we know how to do the right thing – we just need to *want* to do it." (par. 6)

2. Read this excerpt from paragraph 2.

   In 2009, the Environmental Protection Agency estimated that a mere seven percent of all plastic waste in America is recycled. In 2015, scientists calculated that up to 14 million tons of plastic waste is whooshed into our oceans every year from coastal regions alone.

   What role do these sentences play in the development of the central idea of the passage?

   E. It proves that plastic should be completely banned from being used.

   F. It highlights the avoidable nature of the large quantity of plastics that end up in the ocean.

   G. It demonstrates the way plastic pollution is increasing exponentially on an annual basis.

   H. It shows the number of years it takes to decompose plastic, and subsequently how long it affects marine life.

3. Which sentence best supports the idea that plastic waste affects a variety of marine life?

   A. "The amphipods would then excrete the digested plastic bits in the form of dots of plastic less than one-fifth of an inch wide – dots that were subsequently dubbed 'microplastics'." (par. 3)

   B. "Millions of marine animals – roughly 700 different species – are threatened by plastic." (par. 3)

   C. "In 2014, when Malaysia Airlines flight 307 disappeared at sea, television viewers around the world witnessed a raft of satellite images, all of which confirmed the fact that our oceans have become a global dump." (par. 6)

   D. "The good news is that, despite the staggering statistics, ocean pollution isn't a lost cause." (par. 6)

4. Read this sentence from paragraph 4.

   And while fish guts can be removed before we eat the fish, medical experts worry that nanoplastics – microscopic bits of plastic – can be absorbed into the rest of a fish's body, and thus, into our bodies.

   What role does this excerpt play in the overall structure of the passage?

   E. It appeals to the reader's sense of empathy to inspire a change in perspectives.

   F. It presents and deconstructs an alternate view, to eliminate possible reader misgivings.

   G. It demonstrates the values of the author and why the author is a credible speaker on the topic.

   H. It appeals to the reader's self interest in an attempt to make a convincing argument.

5. Which statement would the author most likely agree with?

   A. Plastic pollution harms our ecosystem and, therefore, ourselves.
   B. Environmentally friendly plastic does not pose a threat to the ecosystem.
   C. Plastic should be eliminated entirely, as it has deadly consequences for the entire world.
   D. Plastic pollution negatively affects marine animals mainly through outward damages, like getting caught in a net.

6. What role does paragraph 6 play in the overall structure of the passage?

   E. It describes the scientific reasons for why plastic damages life on the planet.
   F. It summarizes the human factors that caused the overall conflict.
   G. It describes large changes that would need to be made to help resolve the problem.
   H. It indicates a course of action for how readers could personally participate in efforts to resolve the problem.

7. Which statement describes how the author's use of problem-and-solution in paragraph 6 contributes to the development of the central idea?

   A. It details the events that have increased public concern about the issue of ocean pollution.
   B. It shows how politicians' refusal to accept the reality of the pollution contributes to the problem.
   C. It describes the new technologies that would be needed to undo the damages caused by plastic pollution.
   D. It gives evidence that there are existing methods to solve the problem of plastic pollution, if people would choose to implement them.

8. How does the graphic contribute to the development of the central idea of the passage?

   E. It confirms that a large amount of plastic waste ends up in the oceans.
   F. It implies that the government should be passing laws to make plastic illegal.
   G. It illustrates that plastic use has both increased dramatically and is largely not recycled.
   H. It shows that worries about plastic pollution are overblown, as a large portion of plastic is recycled.

Two Treatises

1 John Locke, the son of an English lawyer, was born in 1632. The English Civil War erupted when John was ten. His father served on the side of the Parliamentary forces, which supported the Commonwealth and opposed the monarchy. While Locke studied at Oxford University to become a doctor, Oliver Cromwell, who had led the young Commonwealth, passed away. His death resulted in the restoration of the English monarchy. At that point, Charles II ascended the throne as king. Locke eventually became the personal physician of Lord Shaftesbury, one of the king's political opponents in the new Parliament.

2 Around this time Locke wrote a highly regarded book titled *Two Treatises of Government*. In this book, Locke set forth a view of government as a contract, of sorts, between subjects and rulers. The essence of the book was as follows: by participating in a society, people voluntarily relinquish certain rights so that the laws of the state can ensure impartial justice and protection for all.

3 Perhaps most importantly, Locke believed that the powers of government should be divided. This, he argued, would prevent a ruler from exercising absolute power. "Nobody can desire to have me in his absolute power unless it be to compel me by force to that which is against the right of my freedom – that is, to make me a slave," he wrote. If such a ruler did seize power, Locke advocated for the right of the citizens

The Tutorverse

to rebel: "It is lawful for me to treat him as one who has put himself into a state of war with me – that is, [defeat] him if I can."

4 Such ideas were dangerous during the restoration of the monarchy. Locke was forced to flee to the Netherlands. Many years later, the popularity of the monarchy began to wane again. Charles II's successor, James II, was removed from power. This time, the English Parliament left no doubt that it held the ultimate power. Parliament passed lasting laws that restricted the power of the monarchy.

5 Almost a century later, Locke's ideas engendered a new revolution. This revolution was likely very different from one that he might have imagined. Thomas Jefferson, Alexander Hamilton, and James Madison cited Locke as their inspiration when they wrote the Declaration of Independence that separated the American colonies from England. Locke had declared that among the natural rights of people were "life, liberty, and property" – echoes of which can be found in the Declaration: "All men are created…with certain unalienable rights, that among these are life, liberty, and the pursuit of happiness."

1. With which statement would Locke most likely agree?

   A. Freedom of religion is a person's most important right.
   B. People must always war against a monarchy.
   C. Too much power in the hands of any one person is dangerous.
   D. Because Parliament represents the people, it cannot pass unjust laws.

2. Which of the following choices best describes what the passage is about?

   E. Locke's childhood and adult life
   F. the advantages of a monarchy
   G. a philosophical idea
   H. comparisons between England and America

3. Locke believed that people should

   A. be governed by a single person.
   B. never rebel against their rulers.
   C. consent to a monarchy.
   D. overthrow an oppressive ruler.

4. According to the passage, Oliver Cromwell passed away

   E. after Locke fled to the Netherlands.
   F. after James II took the throne.
   G. before the English Civil War.
   H. while Locke was a student.

5. The monarchy under Charles II and James II most likely

   A. disagreed with Locke's philosophy.
   B. supported Locke financially as he wrote his *Treatise*.
   C. cooperated with Parliament to rule the country.
   D. understood why the American colonies wanted to separate from England.

6. As described in the passage, all of the following facts support the idea that Locke's upbringing influenced his philosophical views **except** that

   E. he served Lord Shaftesbury.
   F. he was a supporter of Charles II.
   G. his father opposed the monarchy.
   H. his father fought in service of Parliamentary forces.

7. What is the most likely reason that the author quotes the Declaration of Independence in paragraph 5?

   A. to show that Locke's ideas had a far-reaching influence
   B. to compare one type of government with another
   C. to explain why America wanted to separate from England
   D. to justify Locke's theories

Dear Evan Hansen

1   Boy meets national high school musical theater contest. Boy wins national high school musical theater contest. Boy gets lead in hit Broadway musical.

2   Does this sound like the unbelievable plot of some Off-Off-Broadway play? Well, it's real life for Andrew Barth Feldman, a 16-year-old junior at Woodmere Academy in Long Island. In June of 2017, Andrew competed in the National High School Musical Theater Awards, nicknamed the Jimmy Awards, against over 100,000 competitors from all over the country. Eighty of those participants were nominated by regional panels of judges to go to New York City. There, they had to compete in a week-long session of performances, where they were mentored by professional actors, singers, dancers, choreographers and directors. Eight teens qualified as finalists; each finalist sang in one final, Glee-style medley – aka mashup – round. One boy and one girl were chosen as winners. Last year, Andrew was that one boy.

3   As it happened, during that pivotal medley round, a group of producers for *Dear Evan Hansen*, a Tony award-winning musical with a teenage protagonist, was sitting in the audience. Before Andrew had even completed the first verse of his song, the lead producer turned to her colleagues and mouthed, "I think that's our next Evan Hansen."

4   Two days later, Andrew met with the show's casting director and, subsequently, auditioned in front of the creative team. Shortly thereafter, Andrew's mother received a phone call, offering her son his dream role. In November, the show announced that he would step into the role of Evan at the end of January, 2019.

5   While this may sound like a made-for-Disney overnight success story, a lot of grit and elbow grease went into Becoming Andrew. Andrew's lifelong love affair with musical theater began when he was three years old, after he saw a Broadway production of *Beauty and the Beast*. At the age of 8, he was in a community theater production of Annie; at 9, he began organizing flash mobs at assemblies. When he was 12, he founded his own theater company, Zneefrock Productions, which stages annual cabaret nights and musicals to benefit a charity for autism. In between, he managed to visit Disney World, Disneyland and Paris Disney about 20 times combined, watch and re-watch the Star Wars movies and go to three Broadway fan conventions. Along the way, he attended theater summer camps, starred in school plays and community theater musicals and learned to play the piano, guitar, bass, drums, and ukulele and write his own music. With determination and single-mindedness, Andrew arguably worked his entire life to get his first professional theater role.

6   And what a role it is. The part of Evan Hansen is an emotionally intense one. The play tells the story of a 17-year-old teenager who perpetually feels like he is on the outside looking in. Evan is the proverbial nose-pressed-up-against-the-cafeteria-window kid; the show portrays his often-misguided quest to find someone or something to prove to him that, somewhere, he belongs. The part is so demanding that, originally, the producers only auditioned actors in their 20s or older. In fact, the first actor who played Evan was 23.

7   To protect their young investment, the producers are breaking Andrew in semi-gently, with five performances a week, instead of eight (with the role's understudy performing the remaining three). He has started taking singing lessons and, in time, will gradually build up stamina, until he can shoulder the entire week's worth of shows. In the meantime, his life has been turned topsy-turvy: he rehearses five hours a day, attends vocal classes and is home-schooled by a tutor for 15 hours a week.

8   When Andrew announced to his friends and family that he had won – or rather, *earned* – the part of Evan Hansen, he posted on Instagram, "I got the email that they wanted me to audition. 'This is what you've been waiting for,' I said to myself. 'You've thought a lot about this, and you've figured out what to do.'" Indeed he has.

The Tutorverse

1. Which statement best supports the central idea of the passage?

   A. "Boy wins national high school musical theater contest." (par. 1)
   B. "With determination and single-mindedness, Andrew arguably worked his entire life to get his first professional theater role." (par. 5)
   C. "In between, he managed to visit Disney World, Disneyland and Paris Disney about 20 times combined, watch and re-watch the Star Wars movies and go to three Broadway fan conventions." (par. 5)
   D. "The play tells the story of a 17-year-old teenager who perpetually feels like he is on the outside looking in." (par. 6)

2. Read paragraph 1.

   Boy meets national high school musical theater contest. Boy wins national high school musical theater contest. Boy gets lead in hit Broadway musical.

   What is the effect of the repetition used in this paragraph?

   E. It emphasizes how many attempts Andrew made before his success.
   F. It highlights how the events of Andrew's life resemble those in a work of fiction.
   G. It creates an engaging rhythm that mimics the songs that Andrew sang in the contest.
   H. It suggests that not many boys make it to Broadway.

3. What role does paragraph 2 play in the overall structure of the passage?

   A. It provides a course of action for how potential teen actors can actively advance their skills.
   B. It describes how Andrew's life became inspiration for a hit Broadway play.
   C. It emphasizes the extent of Andrew's accomplishment in winning the competition.
   D. It summarizes the events of Andrew's childhood that were crucial to his win.

4. Read this sentence from paragraph 3.

   Before Andrew had even completed the first verse of his song, the lead producer turned to her colleagues and mouthed, "I think that's our next Evan Hansen."

   What role does this sentence play in the development of the central idea of the passage?

   E. It illustrates the moment that all of Andrew's hard work and determination were recognized.
   F. It highlights the fact that actors like Andrew are born and not made.
   G. It demonstrates the complex processes that Andrew undertook to reach success.
   H. It shows the amount of practice and skill it took for Andrew to sing a medley.

5. What conclusion is best supported by the information in paragraph 6?

   A. The role of Evan Hansen is emotionally straightforward for Andrew, as it describes a teenage boy.
   B. Andrew is the first actor to successfully play the role of Evan Hansen.
   C. Evan Hansen is a role that is better played by adult men, who have a more mature perspective on adolescence.
   D. Andrew's success in being cast as Evan Hansen is a testimony to his talent, and not a consequence of his age.

6. How does the word choice "earned" in paragraph 8 contribute to the meaning of the passage?

   E. It emphasizes how it was more than luck that led to Andrew's role.
   F. It reveals Andrew's preoccupation with his reputation on social media.
   G. It highlights Andrew's focus on his earnings for portraying Ethan Hansen.
   H. It shows the many hours Andrew's audition for Ethan Hansen lasted.

7. What sentence in the passage best supports the idea that Andrew is continuing to show a strong work ethic?

A. "With determination and single-mindedness, Andrew arguably worked his entire life to get his first professional theater role." (par. 5)

B. "To protect their young investment, the producers are breaking Andrew in semi-gently, with five performances a week, instead of eight…. (par. 7)

C. "In fact, the first actor who played Evan was 23." (par. 6)

D. "In the meantime, his life has been turned topsy-turvy: he rehearses five hours a day, attends vocal classes and is home-schooled by a tutor for 15 hours a week. (par. 7)

8. The author would most likely agree with which statement?

E. Determination is a guaranteed path to professional success.

F. Aspiring actors should compete in various competitions in order to be discovered.

G. Following your passion can yield unexpected results.

H. Young actors are valuable assets in professional theatre productions.

Masterminds of the Sea

1 Behold, the mighty octopus: it has six legs, three hearts, two arms, one venomous beak, no backbone – and a very impressive brain. Nine brains, to be more precise. The central brain that controls the nervous system is located in the octopus's head, and each of the tentacles houses another small brain. This ennead[1] is of particular interest to scientists, because the brainpower of an octopus breaks most of the rules of intelligence in the animal kingdom. As such, octopus intelligence has begun to redefine the very boundaries of intelligence, for both animals and humans.

2 Among animal vertebrates[2], high intelligence is usually found among those who share three common traits. First, they tend to have brains that are large in size. Second, they live relatively long lives – after all, the longer you live, the more time you have to learn. Third, they tend to form strong social bonds with members of their own and other species, and learn from working and cooperating with them. Think of herds of elephants, troops of chimpanzees, packs of wolves, pods of dolphins and how they live and work as a team. Think, too, of how elephants, monkeys and dogs are willing – even eager – to work with and for humans. These factors have combined, during the course of evolution, to form brains that are more powerful than before.

3 Octopuses, on the other hand, break the cerebral mold. While these cephalopods do boast the largest brains in the mollusk world – the common octopus has roughly a half-billion neurons[3], about as many as a house cat or a small monkey – they are surprisingly short-lived. In fact, their lifespans run anywhere from a few months to two years, which gives them little time for life lessons. What's more, they're habitual loners. Unlike their smart vertebrate counterparts, octopuses learn nothing from their parents or other octopuses; they are largely self-taught.

---

[1] **ennead:** a group of nine
[2] **vertebrate:** an animal that possesses a backbone or spinal column
[3] **neuron:** a specialized cell in the nervous system that transmits nerve impulses

The Tutorverse

4   Because the octopus is such an outlier in the area of animal intelligence, scientists have to ask: What classifies intelligence in cephalopods? Generally, experts agree that the ability to acquire information, and apply and adapt it to daily life, is a cornerstone of animal cleverness. Octopuses have this ability in spades. There are videos of octopuses in the sea finding coconut shells or sea shells, using them to hide from predators and, when the coast is clear, carrying the shells with them like luggage, to use later. This shows that octopuses see the shells as tools, which are not only useful now but may prove useful in the future.

5   The ability to acquire information becomes even more sophisticated when the animal uses it to make decisions. In one experiment, scientists presented octopuses in captivity the choice between clams and mussels to eat; the octopuses chose the mussels, because they were easier to open. When the researchers opened the clams for them, the octopuses chose the clams. In other words, they chose the most easily accessible food. The scientists also noticed that the octopuses had several methods of opening the shells: They wrenched them apart, broke them with their beaks or drilled holes into them – and they selectively switched methods according to the species of the food. When experimenters wired the easier mussels shut, the octopuses would change tactics until they succeeded. Any simple animal like a pigeon can peck mindlessly at a lever for hours in the hopes of getting food. Only more complex-minded animals like the octopus can make decisions on the spot.

6   Bear in mind, of course, that no self-respecting octopus would pull a food lever for hours anyway, because its lively mind would grow bored. More likely, an octopus would pull the lever once or twice and then use its nimble arms to take the entire apparatus apart, perhaps attempt to break the lever in two and then squirt the experimenter with water. Like other smart animals, octopuses are curious and like to play. Give an octopus in captivity an empty jar, and it will figure out how to ricochet it against the jet stream of the tank's intake valve and then catch it, much the way you might bounce a ball. The key point here is that the octopus is not merely interested in the jar because it may contain food; rather, it is trying to figure out how to do something interesting – dare we say, fun – with the jar itself.

7   And here lies a central part of octopus intelligence: octopuses can be fun. They can also be shy or naughty, quiet or emotional, passive or aggressive. They have personalities and preferences, and this is a hallmark of intelligence. Octopuses in captivity even demonstrated preferences among different caretakers and scientists. At an aquarium in New Zealand, researchers noticed that an octopus took a dislike to a certain caretaker – each time she passed his tank, he would squirt a half-gallon of water down her back. At other aquariums, cephalopods would squirt only the new staff members, while leaving the more familiar ones alone. Despite the fact that all the staffers were dressed identically, the octopuses were able to differentiate, catalogue and have opinions about them.

8   To be sure, many scientists would argue that the octopus's so-called intelligence is merely an evolutionary necessity. When cephalopods lost their shells some 275 million years ago, they were left extremely vulnerable to predators. They required canny and cunning and the ability to think on the fly in order to survive. Still, this should not dim the importance of the impressive octopus brain. By breaking the rules of animal cognition, octopuses show us that there are different roads to and reasons for intelligence. Humans ponder these different roads every day. How can a genius child be born from two parents of average intelligence? Why is a twin better in school than his or her identical sibling? One day, the mighty octopus may help us understand why.

Animal	Average Number of Total Neurons (million)
House Mouse	71
Southern Red Octopus	500
Cat	760
Chimpanzee	28,000
Adult Human	86,000

The Tutorverse

1. Which statement best describes the central idea of the passage?

   A. "These factors have combined, during the course of evolution, to form brains that are more powerful than before." (par. 2)
   B. "And here lies a central part of octopus intelligence: octopuses can be fun." (par. 7)
   C. "When cephalopods lost their shells some 275 million years ago, they were left extremely vulnerable to predators." (par. 8)
   D. "By breaking the rules of animal cognition, octopuses show us that there are different roads to and reasons for intelligence." (par. 8)

2. How does paragraph 2 support the development of the central idea?

   E. It illustrates the methodology that scientists use to identify the most powerful animal brain.
   F. It shows how animals that collaborate are more likely to be intelligent than solitary animals.
   G. It reinforces how vertebrates are generally more intelligent than cephalopods.
   H. It highlights the qualities shared by animals with high intelligence.

3. Read this sentence from paragraph 3.

   Octopuses, on the other hand, break the cerebral mold.

   The author uses the phrase "break the cerebral mold" to convey

   A. how octopuses have the strength and intelligence to escape any containment.
   B. how octopuses defy the stereotypes of animal intelligence.
   C. the violent and aggressive nature of octopuses.
   D. the rigidity and consistency of octopus brain structures.

4. What role does paragraph 4 play in the overall structure of the passage?

   E. It identifies the ways in which different cephalopods display intelligence.
   F. It gives behavioral examples of octopus intelligence observed in captivity.
   G. It explains how experts viewed and recorded intelligence of the octopuses at aquariums.
   H. It details specific scenarios that demonstrate how octopuses exhibit intelligence in daily life.

5. Read this sentence from paragraph 5.

   The ability to acquire information becomes even more sophisticated when the animal uses it to make decisions.

   How does this sentence fit in the overall structure of the passage?

   A. It introduces a measure for a more challenging type of intelligence than previously mentioned, which octopuses also demonstrate.
   B. It highlights a reason why octopus intelligence is inferior to that of humans, despite being more intelligent than most other animals.
   C. It emphasizes the amount of energy used when an animal's brain switches to decision making.
   D. It indicates a shift from higher measures of intelligence in animals to more basic measures.

6. What is the most likely reason the author uses the words "shy," "naughty," "aggressive," and "emotional" in paragraph 7?

   E. to emphasize the emotional volatility that characterizes octopuses as a species
   F. to highlight the variation in personality, and therefore intelligence, in individual octopuses
   G. to compare behaviors that show octopus intelligence to those of young children
   H. to reinforce the idea that octopuses can be enjoyable to observe

The Tutorverse

7. Which sentence from the passage best supports the idea that an octopus mind needs to receive stimulation?

   A. "This shows that octopuses see the shells as tools, which are not only useful now but may prove useful in the future." (par. 4)
   B. "In one experiment, scientists presented octopuses in captivity the choice between clams and mussels to eat; the octopuses chose the mussels, because they were easier to open." (par. 5)
   C. "The key point here is that the octopus is not merely interested in the jar because it may contain food; rather, it is trying to figure out how to do something interesting..." (par. 6)
   D. "By breaking the rules of animal cognition, octopuses show us that there are different roads to and reasons for intelligence." (par. 8)

8. Read this excerpt from paragraph 8:

   By breaking the rules of animal cognition, octopuses show us that there are different roads to and reasons for intelligence. Humans ponder these different roads every day.

   What is the most likely reason the author uses the word "roads" in this paragraph?

   E. to highlight the great distances that octopuses may travel in the wild
   F. to show the solid genetic construction behind octopus intelligence
   G. to argue that there is no single correct path to higher intelligence
   H. to illustrate the visual manifestation of intelligence in human and octopus intelligence

9. How does the graphic support the idea that octopus intelligence is unusual?

   A. It contrasts the small size of the octopus nervous system to the much more complex nervous systems of mammals.
   B. It reveals that octopus intelligence is comparable to that of certain mammals, despite being a cephalopod.
   C. It proves that the total number of neurons is the most important indicator of intelligence.
   D. It highlights the ways in which octopuses and cats demonstrate similar behaviors.

The Cost of Convenience

1 It seems as if every transaction these days includes a plastic bag. Shopping for groceries at a supermarket? Buying new clothes? Have leftovers at a restaurant, or ordering takeout? Why not make carrying things home a little bit easier by using free plastic bags from the store?

2 Since time immemorial, people have used objects to help carry things from one place to another. Baskets, pots, and other containers were, for millennia, the standard vessel used by people around the world. These containers were typically used repeatedly. After all, it took time, energy, and resources to weave a basket or sculpt a pot. Because of this, containers were valuable to the people that used them. As a result, bringing one's own bags or containers to a store to carry goods home, for example, was a commonly accepted fact of life.

3 In the never-ending quest to make life easier and more convenient, humanity stumbled upon a way to challenge that fact of life. The industrial revolution made it possible to produce virtually any good – including bags and other containers – on a massive scale. Now, suddenly, it became relatively inexpensive for everyone to have a bag – or to have as many bags as they wanted. This led people to value not the bag or container itself, but the convenience it represented. If it was so easy and inexpensive to get a new bag, why not just get a new bag every time it's needed, rather than having to bother with carrying and reusing an old bag?

4 In many parts of the world – including all across the United States – using plastic bags only one time or for only one purpose has become the norm. People's prioritizing of convenience has come at a steep price. After all, what happens to single-use plastic bags when groceries are emptied out, clothes put away, and leftovers stored in the fridge?

5 The New York City Sanitation Department indicated that it collects some 10 billion single-use plastic bags every year. Though some of these plastic bags are repurposed – for example, to line trash-cans – the vast majority are simply thrown away. Too often, these plastic bags end up in landfills or, even worse, blowing in the wind where they end up in rivers, lakes, and trees. It can take a single plastic bag hundreds of years to decompose. In the meantime, plastic bags leech chemicals into groundwater and have a destructive impact on the food chain by killing marine life.

6 It's no wonder, then, that cities around the country – and many nations around the world – are taking steps to reduce the number of plastic bags used by consumers. New York City is just one of the latest major municipalities to propose a tax on plastic bags, following examples set in California and Washington D.C. The goal of the tax, which will require shoppers to pay for each plastic bag – is simply to incentivize shoppers to think before reaching for another bag. Reusing plastic bags – or using reusable cloth or fiber bags, for example – reduces waste and helps to save the environment.

Plastics Generation and Recovery (Recycling), 1960 to 2010

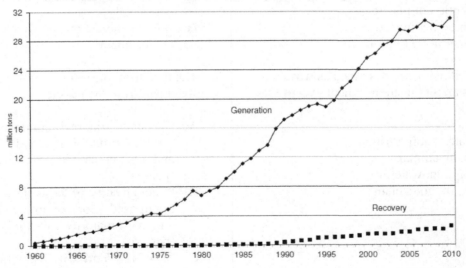

Source: EPA 2010 Municipal Solid Waste Fact Sheet

The Tutorverse

1. Which of the following choices best describes what the passage is about?

   A. the history of bags and containers
   B. the reason for a problem and how a tax can help fix it
   C. ways in which plastic bags are bad for the environment
   D. why the environment is more important than convenience

2. Compared with the present, why, for much of history, did people used to carry their own containers?

   E. Containers were more valuable then than they are now.
   F. People only bought what they could carry in their hands.
   G. People valued convenience more than they do now.
   H. There were no such things as supermarkets in the past.

3. What led people today to prioritize convenience over the value of containers?

   A. more money
   B. the invention of plastic
   C. taxes and other incentives
   D. the industrial revolution

4. All of the following are described as ways that plastic bags affect the environment **except** that they

   E. contribute to soil erosion.
   F. kill aquatic animals.
   G. pollute groundwater.
   H. interrupt the food chain.

5. Read this sentence from paragraph 3.

   If it was so easy and inexpensive to get a new bag, why not just get a new bag every time it's needed, rather than having to bother with carrying and reusing an old bag?

   What purpose does the above question serve for the rest of the passage?

   A. It describes a question that cannot be answered.
   B. It provides theoretical examples of how people use plastic bags every day.
   C. It suggests that there is a cost to earlier examples of conveniences.
   D. It describes the specific uses of plastic bags to be taxed by New York City.

6. In what way might a bag tax help the environment?

   E. Fewer people will be interested in buying a reusable bag.
   F. Some people will value convenience less than before the tax.
   G. People will stop using plastic bags completely.
   H. It will generate money for cleaning up the environment.

7. The data from the graphic best supports which statement from the passage?

   A. "The industrial revolution made it possible to produce virtually any good – including bags and other containers – on a massive scale." (par. 3)
   B. "Though some of these plastic bags are repurposed – for example, to line trash-cans – the vast majority are simply thrown away." (par. 5)
   C. "The New York City Sanitation Department indicated that it collects some 10 billion single-use plastic bags every year." (par. 5)
   D. "The goal of the tax, which will require shoppers to pay for each plastic bag – is simply to incentivize shoppers to think before reaching for another bag." (par. 6)

Fiction & Poetry

Night

by Hilda Doolittle

The night has cut
each from each
and curled the petals
back from the stalk
5   and under it in crisp rows;

under at an unfaltering pace,
under till the rinds break,
back till each bent leaf
is parted from its stalk;

10   under at a grave pace,
under till the leaves
are bent back
till they drop upon earth,
back till they are all broken.

15   O night,
you take the petals
of the roses in your hand,
but leave the stark core
of the rose
20   to perish on the branch.

---

1. Read lines 6 and 10 from the poem.

   under at an unfaltering pace

   under at a grave pace

   The parallel structure of the two lines helps convey a central idea of the poem by

   A. reinforcing the beauty of the flower during the day.
   B. stressing the negative effects of night on the flower.
   C. revealing the direction in which night acts on the flower.
   D. emphasizing the merciless and unavoidable effect of time.

2. Read lines 8 and 9 from the poem.

   back till each bent leaf
   is parted from its stalk

   Which of the following supports what is implied in these lines?

   E. "and curled the petals / back from the stalk" (lines 3-4)
   F. "under at a grave pace, / under till the leaves" (lines 10-11)
   G. "you take the petals / of the roses in your hand" (lines 16-17)
   H. "but leave the stark core / of the rose" (lines 18-19)

3. How does isolating the phrase "O night," (line 15) affect the meaning of the poem?

    A. by creating a sense of hopefulness
    B. by contrasting the night with the flower
    C. by highlighting the painfulness of aging
    D. by emphasizing the despair of the speaker

4. The use of commas and semicolons in the first three stanzas (lines 1-14) mirrors which of the following ideas?

    E. "each from each" (line 2)
    F. "crisp rows" (line 5)
    G. "grave pace" (line 10)
    H. "you take the petals" (line 16)

5. How does the last stanza (lines 15-20) convey a central idea of the poem?

    A. by showing that roses have both beautiful and painful qualities
    B. by explaining that one must find something positive to look for in life
    C. by demonstrating that one loses many precious things as one grows old
    D. by illustrating how difficult experiences in life help make a person stronger

---

When You Are Old

by William Butler Yeats

When you are old and grey and full of sleep,
And nodding by the fire, take down this book,
And slowly read, and dream of the soft look
Your eyes had once, and of their shadows deep;

5   How many loved your moments of glad grace,
And loved your beauty with love false or true,
But one man loved the pilgrim soul in you,
And loved the sorrows of your changing face;

And bending down beside the glowing bars,
10 Murmur, a little sadly, how Love fled
And paced upon the mountains overhead
And hid his face amid a crowd of stars.

1. The metaphor of taking down a book and reading it (lines 2-3) most likely refers to

    A. reading an interesting novel to pass the time during retirement.
    B. reflecting on one's past experiences, both positive and negative.
    C. writing an autobiography so people can learn from life experiences.
    D. making note of mistakes made and what has been learned from them.

2. How do the words "you" and "your" contribute to the central idea of the poem?

    E. They emphasize the conversational style of the poem.
    F. The speaker could be addressing anyone, expanding relevance of the poem's meaning.
    G. The speaker gives relationship advice to the reader.
    H. The speaker addresses an unknown person in her life, blaming that person for what has happened.

The Tutorverse

3. Read line 9 from the poem.

And bending down beside the glowing bars

How does this line contribute to the development of ideas in the stanza?

A. It represents youthful beauty and love.
B. It drives the speaker deep into a daydream filled with thoughts.
C. It brings the speaker back to the present and leads to a final conclusion.
D. It mirrors the shining of the stars mentioned in the last line of the poem.

4. Read lines 3-4 from the poem.

And slowly read, and dream of the soft look
Your eyes had once, and of their shadows
deep

Which of the following supports what is implied by the "soft look" referred to in these lines?

E. "old and grey and full of sleep" (line 1)
F. "moments of glad grace" (line 5)
G. "sorrows of your changing face" (line 8)
H. "face amid a crowd of stars" (line 12)

5. How does the second stanza (lines 5-8) contribute to the development of a central idea of the poem?

A. It illustrates the effect of a lost love.
B. It proves that people cannot be trusted.
C. It gives examples of the process of growing older.
D. It describes the difference between superficial love and true love.

6. How does the capitalization of "Love" (line 10) contribute to the central idea of the poem?

E. It shows that love has helped the speaker conquer her sadness.
F. It identifies the specific person to whom the speaker addresses.
G. It is an example of apostrophe, where the speaker addresses an abstract idea.
H. It emphasizes the fact that there was only ever one person who truly loved the speaker.

Leisure

by Amy Lowell

Leisure, thou goddess of a bygone age,
   When hours were long and days sufficed to hold
   Wide-eyed delights and pleasures uncontrolled
By shortening moments, when no gaunt presage
5 Of undone duties, modern heritage,
   Haunted our happy minds; must thou withhold
   Thy presence from this over-busy world,
And bearing silence with thee disengage
   Our twined[1] fortunes? Deeps of unhewn woods
10   Alone can cherish thee, alone possess
Thy quiet, teeming vigor. This our crime:
   Not to have worshipped, marred by alien moods
   That sole condition of all loveliness,
The dreaming lapse of slow, unmeasured time.

---

[1] **twined**: interwoven

The Tutorverse

1. How does line 1 contribute to the development of the central idea of the poem?

    A. It confirms that the speaker is returning from a vacation.
    B. It shows that the speaker believes Leisure to be a goddess.
    C. It suggests that the speaker regrets the lack of free time.
    D. It gives examples of how people could spend their free time.

2. By addressing Leisure directly, the author creates the effect of a

    E. powerful emotional sense of regret and remorse.
    F. feeling of comic relief for an otherwise serious topic.
    G. sense of confusion as to who the speaker is addressing.
    H. dialogue between the speaker and the person who represents Leisure.

3. Read lines 4-6 from the poem.

    By shortening moments, when no gaunt presage
    Of undone duties, modern heritage,
    Haunted our happy minds; must thou withhold

    These lines help develop the theme of the poem by suggesting that

    A. busy people have a rich tradition of customs and beliefs.
    B. haunts people because they no longer respect her as a goddess.
    C. people must always be aware of the time and date and what they must do.
    D. people feel that there is not enough time in the day because they have so many things to do.

4. Read lines 9-11 from the poem.

    Deeps of unhewn woods
    Alone can cherish thee, alone possess
    Thy quiet, teeming vigor.

    How do these lines reflect the speaker's point of view?

    E. People must search energetically for leisure.
    F. Leisure hides from people and does not wish to be found.
    G. People can only find leisure by themselves because others are a distraction.
    H. Leisure is so rare now that one can only find it in the solitude of unspoiled nature.

5. The most appropriate example of the "crime" mentioned in line 11 is most likely

    A. never going to church to worship.
    B. always wasting time walking in the woods.
    C. taking too much time for oneself despite responsibilities.
    D. constantly rushing from one appointment to another.

6. How does the rhythm of lines 1-9 relate to the central idea of the poem?

    E. It is swift yet leisurely, like the author's childhood.
    F. It is rushed and continuous, like the demands of modern life.
    G. It is unhurried and uninterrupted, mirroring the idea of leisure.
    H. It is calm and frequently interrupted, like a vacation in a bygone age.

The Tutorverse

Song

by John Rollin Ridge

I saw her once—her eye's deep light
Fell on my spirit's deeper night,
   The only beam that e'er illumed
Its shadows drear. The glance was slight,
5   But oh, what softness it assumed!

I saw her twice—her glance again
Lit up its fire within my brain;
   My thoughts leaped up, like lightning warm,
And felt a sweetness mixed with pain,
10   While gath'ring wildly round her form.

I saw her thrice—she was alone,
And her deep glance more deeply shone
   Upon my heart with rapture chained,
The thrill was a meteor thrown
15   Athwart some sky where darkness reigned!

I saw her yet again—and clear,
But low, her rich tones met my ear;
   They wandered thro' my bosom[1] sad,
As waters thro' a woodland sere[2],
20   That make decay itself seem glad.

The fifth time I saw her—and still
She taught my quiv'ring heart to thrill,
   Like some wild hand upon a lyre[3],

That's borne along, without its will,
25   Across the strings of magic fire!

I saw her oft again—, each hour
Enhanced o'er me her conquering power;
   Her image in my thought became
A spirit-planted, fadeless flower;
30   And all my music was her name!

I loved the earth on which she trod—
More beautiful than if a God
   Had placed immortal foot-prints there!
I loved the world, though dark its load
35   Of ills, because she breathed its air!

I loved her slightest careless word—
More sweet than matin[4] of the bird
   That scales the Heaven on mounting wing!
It through my maddened pulses stirred,
40   As though it were a living thing.

Oh, that 'rapt heart's forever gone,
That boweth once to Beauty's throne,
   And feels the bliss her looks inspire;
For, oh, the seeds of death are sown,
45   When love assumes its mad empire!

[1] **bosom**: the heart, or seat of emotions
[2] **sere**: dry or withered

[3] **lyre**: an stringed instrument
[4] **matin**: a bird's morning song

1. Which lines from the poem best illustrate how the speaker feels before meeting the woman?

   A. "Fell on my spirit's deeper night, / The only beam that e'er illumed / Its shadows drear." (lines 2-4)
   B. "My thoughts leaped up, like lightning warm, / And felt a sweetness mixed with pain" (lines 8-9)
   C. "And all my music was her name!" (line 30)
   D. "I loved her slightest careless word - /More sweet than matin of the bird" (lines 36-37)

2. How do stanzas 2-5 (lines 6-25) contribute to the central idea of the poem?

   E. They describe the woman's appearance and behaviors.
   F. They tell about how the speaker came to meet the woman.
   G. They illustrate how the woman and the speaker are similar.
   H. They emphasize the effect that the woman has on the speaker.

3. Read lines 22-23 from the poem.

   She taught my quiv'ring heart to thrill,
   Like some wild hand upon a lyre

   The simile in these lines suggests that

   A. the woman stills the speaker's wildly beating heart.
   B. the woman is playing him like an instrument, making him do what she wants.
   C. the woman is a musician who has captured the speaker's heart by playing beautifully.
   D. the woman has an energizing effect on the speaker, making him feel excited.

4. Which of the following supports the idea that the speaker is unable to forget the woman's image?

   E. "I saw her thrice—she was alone, / And her deep glance more deeply shone" (lines 11-12)
   F. "I saw her yet again—and clear, / But low, her rich tones met my ear" (lines 16-17)
   G. "Her image in my thought became / A spirit-planted, fadeless flower" (lines 28-29)
   H. "For, oh, the seeds of death are sown, / When love assumes its mad empire!" (lines 44-45)

5. Which of the following best supports the central ideas of stanzas 7 and 8 (lines 31-40)?

   A. "The glance was slight, / But oh, what softness it assumed!" (lines 4-5)
   B. "The thrill was a meteor thrown / Athwart some sky where darkness reigned!" (lines 14-15)
   C. "As waters thro' a woodland sere, / That make decay itself seem glad." (lines 19-20)
   D. "I saw her oft again—, each hour / Enhanced o'er me her conquering power" (lines 26-27)

6. The rhyme scheme of the individual stanzas has which effect on the poem in general?

   E. The rhyme scheme repeats, while the general ideas change.
   F. The rhyme scheme changes, while the general ideas stay the same.
   G. Both the rhyme scheme and general idea of each stanza repeat.
   H. Both the rhyme scheme and general idea of each stanza change.

7. Which of the following supports the idea that, to the speaker, the woman could do nothing wrong?

   A. "I saw her twice—her glance again / Lit up its fire within my brain" (lines 6-7)
   B. "I loved her slightest careless word— / More sweet than matin of the bird" (lines 36-37)
   C. "Oh, that 'rapt heart's forever gone, / That boweth once to Beauty's throne" (lines 41-42)
   D. "For, oh, the seeds of death are sown, / When love assumes its mad empire!" (lines 44-45)

Adapted from *A Modern Tomboy*

by L. T. Meade

1 It was Rosamund who proposed that the rugs should be rolled back and that they should have a dance.

2 Lucy's eyes widened. Nobody before had ever dared to make such a suggestion. Lucy, it is true, had dancing lessons from a teacher who came once a week to instruct her and other girls, and she had occasionally gone to a children's party. But beyond that, she never danced.

3 Lucy heard Rosamund, in a clear voice, say, "Let us push back the sofas. This is a splendid room. We can roll up the rugs in a twinkling. Where is Mrs. Merriman? She will play the dance music. Oh, there are seven of us – one too many. Perhaps you will play for us, Lucy?"

4 "But I don't know any dance music," said Lucy; "and then mother would not like the rugs being disturbed. The room is arranged just as father and mother wish it to be. I think perhaps – "

5 She colored painfully.

6 "We will do nothing without leave, of course," said Phyllis Flower. "I'll just run and find Mrs. Merriman and ask her." Before Lucy could prevent her, Phyllis had darted out of the room, returning in a minute or two with the required permission.

7 "It's all right, girls," she said; "we can trip it on the light fantastic toe as long as ever we please, and the rugs may go to Hong Kong for all Mrs. Merriman cares."

8 Lucy colored with rage. Rosamund gave a quiet smile – a smile which seemed to denote power. Phyllis's dancing eyes lit for a moment on Lucy's face. Those eyes said in the most provoking manner, "I told you so." And then someone went to the piano, and a minute or two later all the girls, Lucy included, were dancing round and round the room in a merry waltz.

9 The dance lasted for over an hour; and just in the midst of it, when Lucy was really laughing in quite a heart-whole manner, she raised her eyes and saw no less a person than Mr. Merriman himself standing in the doorway. He was smiling, and his eyes were fixed on Rosamund's face.

10 The moment Rosamund saw him she stopped at once, and said to Lucy, "Is that your father, the great professor?"

11 "Yes," said Lucy.

12 "Please introduce him to me."

13 Lucy longed to give any sort of excuse, but none would come to her lips. She was forced to take Rosamund up to Mr. Merriman.

14 "This is Rosamund Cunliffe," she said, "and she wants to meet you, Father."

15 Lucy went back and tried to keep dancing. But she could not help straining her ears and trying to catch the subject of Rosamund's conversation. The Professor, who was generally so grave and quiet, was laughing also. What did it all mean?

The Tutorverse

16 "Father, aren't you tired? – Miss Cunliffe, you are tiring father," said Lucy at last, running up to the door and trying to speak calmly.

17 "No, my dear," said her father. "On the contrary, I am intensely interested – you must tell me that story again, Miss Cunliffe. Would you like to come and see my library?"

18 The two went off together, and Lucy felt almost as though she must burst into tears. Phyllis's eyes again met her face, and she had to restrain her feelings. The "I told you so" look was too maddening to bear.

1. Read this sentence from paragraph 3.

   We can roll up the rugs in a twinkling.

   "twinkling" refers to

   A. an amount of time.
   B. a style of organizing.
   C. the appearance of the rugs.
   D. a method of rolling up rugs.

2. Read paragraph 5.

   She colored painfully.

   This sentence suggests that

   E. Lucy's mother expressed her disapproval.
   F. Rosamund was humiliated by Lucy's harsh scolding.
   G. Lucy wishes she had come up with Rosamund's idea.
   H. Lucy was flustered by and does not support Rosamund's suggestion.

3. Read paragraph 7.

   "It's all right, girls," she said; "we can trip it on the light fantastic toe as long as ever we please, and the rugs may go to Hong Kong for all Mrs. Merriman cares."

   These sentences are most likely spoken in what tone?

   A. direct
   B. animated
   C. dignified
   D. impartial

4. The fact that Mrs. Merriman says the rugs can "go to Hong Kong" (paragraph 7) suggests that

   E. Phyllis lied about what Mrs. Merriman said.
   F. Lucy is actually interested in having a dance party.
   G. Lucy was incorrect about upsetting her mother.
   H. Lucy's mother cares deeply for the valuable rugs.

5. Which of Rosamund's traits is most central to her relationship with Lucy?

   A. her physical beauty
   B. her skill at dancing
   C. her talent for influencing others
   D. her ability to carry a conversation

6. Based on the passage, all of the following might be something Lucy thinks to herself EXCEPT

   E. "I wish father had stayed in his library all night!"
   F. "I wish Rosamund had tripped while dancing."
   G. "I wish I had more practice playing dance music."
   H. "I wish Phyllis had never asked my parents for permission to dance."

The Tutorverse

7. According to the passage, why does Lucy need to "restrain her feelings" (paragraph 18)?

   A. She blames Phyllis for bringing Rosamund.
   B. Her parents never let her do as she wishes.
   C. Rosamund controlled the entire night's activities.
   D. She hates dancing and never wanted to participate.

8. The "I told you so" look mentioned in paragraph 8 and paragraph 18 most likely suggests that

   E. Lucy did not believe Phyllis's secret warning about Rosamund's love of dancing.
   F. Phyllis did not believe Lucy's secret warning about Rosamund's love of dancing.
   G. Lucy did not believe Phyllis's secret warning about Rosamund's personality.
   H. Phyllis did not believe Lucy's secret warning about Rosamund's personality.

Adapted from *The Jolliest School of All*

by Angela Brazil

1 "David Beverley," he gasped. "David Beverley! Lorna! Great Heavens! By all that's sacred, where did you get this?"

2 "Why, Dad! What's the matter? Irene lent me the book. It belongs to her father."

3 "Her father! You don't mean to tell me your friend's father is David Beverley?"

4 "Why not, Dad," whispered Lorna, looking with apprehension into his haggard, excited face.

5 She guessed even before he spoke what the answer was going to be.

6 "David Beverley is the man who ruined my life!"

7 The blow which had fallen was utterly overwhelming. For a moment Lorna fought against the knowledge like a drowning man battling with the waters.

8 "Oh, Dad! Surely there's some mistake. It can't be! Isn't it some other Beverley perhaps?"

9 "I know his writing only too well. There's no possibility of a mistake. Besides, I saw him in Naples – at the end of February. I haven't forgotten the shock it gave me. Why," turning almost fiercely upon Lorna, "didn't you tell me your schoolfellow's name before? Have you all this time been making friends with your father's enemy?"

10 "I thought I'd often talked about Renie," faltered poor Lorna. "Perhaps I never mentioned her last name. Oh, Dad! Dad! Is it really true? It's too horrible to be believed."

11 Lying in the soft Capri[1] grass, with the pink cistus flowers brushing her hot cheeks, Lorna raged impotently against the tragedy of a fate which was changing the dearest friendship of her life into a feud. Irene! – the only one at school who had sympathized and understood her, who had behaved with a delicacy and kindness such as no other person had ever shown her, who had taken her into her home circle and given her the happiest time she had ever had in her shadowed girlhood; Irene with her merry

gray eyes and her bright sunny hair, the very incarnation of warm-hearted genuine affection – Irene, her roommate, her buddy, her chosen confidante. How was it possible ever to regard her as an enemy? Yet had she not vowed a solemn oath to hate all belonging to the man who had so desperately injured them? Oh! The world seemed turning upside down. Loyalty to her father and love for her friend dragged different ways, and in the bitter conflict her heart was torn in two.

12 She was ready to humor her father's every whim, for in the blackness of her trouble nothing seemed at present to really matter. The whirling eddies of her thoughts rushed through her brain in a perpetual series of questions and answers. Must hate strike the death knell of love? Surely the only thing to do with an injury is to forgive it. Would revenge wipe out the wrong or in any way solve anything? No, there would only be one more wrong done in the world, to go on in ever-widening circles of hatred and misery. Curses, like chickens, come home to roost, and "getting even" may bring its own punishment.

---

[1] **Capri**: an Italian island known for its beauty

1. Which sentence best describes Lorna's struggle against a realization?

   A. "'By all that's sacred, where did you get this?'" (par. 1)
   B. "For a moment Lorna fought against the knowledge like a drowning man battling with the waters." (par. 7)
   C. "'I haven't forgotten the shock it gave me.'" (par. 9)
   D. "'I thought I'd often talked about Renie.'" (par. 10)

2. Based on the passage, a reader can conclude that David Beverley was a

   E. writer.
   F. teacher.
   G. student.
   H. relative.

3. According to the passage, Lorna's friendship with Irene was characterized by all of the following EXCEPT

   A. mutual kindness and respect
   B. the feud between their fathers
   C. Irene made Lorna feel accepted
   D. Lorna shared deep feelings with Irene

4. The passage suggests that Lorna

   E. was jealous of Irene.
   F. was popular at school.
   G. is part of a wealthy family.
   H. had trouble making friends.

5. The main conflict that Lorna experiences throughout the passage is

   A. between her loyalty to her family and to her friend.
   B. whether or not she should tell her father about Irene's family.
   C. whether or not she should return the book borrowed from Irene.
   D. between her love for Irene and her allegiance to David Beverley.

6. Read these sentences from paragraph 12.

   Must hate strike the death knell of love? Surely the only thing to do with an injury is to forgive it. Would revenge wipe out the wrong or in any way solve anything?

   How do these questions contribute to the development of ideas in the paragraph?

   E. They demonstrate that David Beverley is very forgiving.
   F. They show that Lorna is obsessed with retaliating against Irene.
   G. They illustrate that complicated questions have no answer.
   H. They indicate that Lorna is forgiving despite an initial desire for revenge.

The Tutorverse

7. The author's main purpose in this passage is to cause the reader to

   A. empathize with Lorna.
   B. dislike David Beverley.
   C. agree with Irene's point of view.
   D. question Lorna's loyalty as a friend.

8. According to paragraph 12, what stops Lorna from siding with her father completely?

   E. the memory of sharing happy experiences with Irene
   F. the belief that love will conquer hatred and her father will forgive
   G. the understanding that her friendship with Irene is more important
   H. the idea that retaliating will bring more suffering to everyone involved

---

Adapted from *Ride Proud, Rebel!*

by Andre Norton

1 The stocky roan switched its tail angrily against a persistent fly and lipped water, dripping big drops back to the surface of the brook. His rider moved swiftly, with an economy of action, to unsaddle, wipe the sweaty back with a wisp of last year's dried grass, and wash down each mud-spattered leg with stream water. Always care for the mount first – when a man's life, as well as the safety of his mission, depended on four subordinate legs more than on his own two.

2 Though he had little claim to a thoroughbred's points, the roan was as much a veteran of the forces as his groom, with all a veteran's ability to accept and enjoy small favors of the immediate present without speculating too much concerning the future. He blew gustily in pleasure under the attention and began to sample a convenient stand of spring green.

3 His mount cared for, Drew Rennie swung up saddle, blanket, and the meager possessions which he had brought out of Virginia two weeks ago, to the platform in a crooked tree overhanging the brook. He settled beside them on the well-seasoned timbers of the old tree house to rummage through his saddlebags.

4 The platform had been there a long time – before Chickamauga and the Ohio Raid, before the first roll of drums in '61. Drew pulled a creased shirt out of the bags and sat with it draped over one knee, remembering...

5 Sheldon Barrett and he – they had built it together one hot week in summer – had named it Boone's Fort. And it was the only thing at Red Springs Drew had really ever owned. His dark eyes were fixed now on something more than the branches about him, and his mouth tightened until his face was not quite sullen, only shuttered.

6 Five years ago – only five years? Yes, five years next month! But the past two years of his own personal freedom – and war – those seemed to equal ten. Now there was no one left to remember the fort's existence, which made it perfect for his present purpose.

7 The warmth of the sun, beating down through yet young leaves, made Drew brush his battered slouch hat to the flooring and luxuriate in the heat. Sometimes he didn't think he'd ever get the bite of last winter's cold out of his bones. The light pointed up every angle of jaw and cheekbone, making it clear that experience – hard experience – and not years had melted away boyish roundness of chin line, narrowed the watchful eyes ever alert to his surroundings. A cavalry scout was wary, or he ceased to be a scout, or maybe even alive.

The Tutorverse

8 Shirt in hand, Drew dropped lightly to the ground and with the same dispatch as he had cared for his horse, made his own toilet, scrubbing his too-thin body with a sigh of content as heartfelt as that the roan had earlier voiced.

9 The fresh shirt was a dark brown-gray, but the patched breeches were Yankee blue, and the boots he pulled on when he had bathed were also the enemy's gift, good stout leather he'd been lucky enough to find in a supply wagon they had captured a month ago. Butternut shirt, Union pants and boots – the unofficial standard uniform of most any trooper of the Army of the Tennessee in this month of May, 1864. And he had garments which were practically intact. What was one patch on the seat nowadays?

10 For the first time Drew grinned at his reflection in the small mirror he had been using, when he scraped a half week's accumulation of soft beard from his face. Sure, he was all spruced up now, ready to make a polite courtesy call at the big house. The grin did not fade, but was gone in a flash, leaving no hint of softness now about his gaunt features, no light in the intent, measuring depths of his dark gray eyes.

1. The roan mentioned in paragraph 1 is most likely

    A. a cat.
    B. a dog.
    C. a cow.
    D. a horse.

2. From the passage, it can be inferred that Drew has

    E. a home in Virginia.
    F. few responsibilities.
    G. a job taking care of animals.
    H. experienced much beyond his years.

3. Read this sentence from paragraph 1.

    His rider moved swiftly, with an economy of action, to unsaddle, wipe the sweaty back with a wisp of last year's dried grass, and wash down each mud-spattered leg with stream water.

    What does the phrase "economy of action" tell us about the person in the first paragraph?

    A. The person is inexperienced.
    B. The person is hesitant and reluctant.
    C. The person has had a lot of practice.
    D. The person is a careful manager of resources.

4. Boone's Fort (paragraph 5) is most likely

    E. a military base.
    F. the roan's home.
    G. a childhood retreat.
    H. Drew's final destination.

5. Read this sentence from paragraph 5.

    His dark eyes were fixed now on something more than the branches about him, and his mouth tightened until his face was not quite sullen, only shuttered.

    The "something more" refers to

    A. Drew's memories.
    B. Drew's traveling companion.
    C. the warmth of the summer sun.
    D. Drew's hopes and desires for the future.

6. Drew's "present purpose" (paragraph 6) is to

    E. perform a secret task.
    F. rebuild Boone's Fort.
    G. enjoy the beauty of Red Springs
    H. join up with people at Chickamauga.

7. From the last sentence in the excerpt, Drew's grin is

    A. practiced and insincere.
    B. one of genuine happiness.
    C. the result of hearing a funny joke.
    D. caused by his memories of Sheldon Barret.

8. Read this sentence from paragraph 6.

> **Five years ago – only five years? Yes, five years next month!**

The author accomplishes all of the following with the use of the above excerpts EXCEPT

E. emphasize the amount of time that has passed.

F. share details about the author's personal history.

G. describe the character's reaction and feelings toward a realization.

H. show how much of an impact the events of that time have had on a character.

9. Read this sentence from paragraph 7.

> **Sometimes he didn't think he'd ever get the bite of last winter's cold out of his bones.**

What does the figurative language in this sentence emphasize?

A. a feeling of regret about Boone's Fort

B. a sense of gladness that Drew has found new purpose in life

C. a sense of pride and confidence in Drew's skills and abilities

D. a feeling of exhaustion and wariness as Drew considers his life

---

Adapted from *The Most Dangerous Game*

by Richard Connell

1 "After the debacle in Russia I left the country, for it was imprudent for an officer of the Czar[1] to stay there. Many noble Russians lost everything. I, luckily, had invested heavily in American assets, so I shall never have to open a tearoom in Monte Carlo or drive a taxi in Paris. Naturally, I continued to hunt – grizzlies in your Rockies, crocodiles in the Ganges, rhinoceroses in East Africa. It was in Africa that the Cape buffalo hit me and laid me up for six months. As soon as I recovered I started for the Amazon to hunt jaguars, for I had heard they were unusually cunning. They weren't." The Cossack sighed. "They were no match at all for a hunter with his wits about him, and a high-powered rifle. I was bitterly disappointed. I was lying in my tent with a splitting headache one night when a terrible thought pushed its way into my mind. Hunting was beginning to bore me! And hunting, remember, had been my life. I have heard that in America businessmen often go to pieces when they give up the business that has been their life."

2 "Yes, that's so," said Rainsford.

3 The general smiled. "I had no wish to go to pieces," he said. "I must do something. Now, mine is an analytical mind, Mr. Rainsford. Doubtless that is why I enjoy the problems of the chase."

4 "No doubt, General Zaroff."

5 "So," continued the general, "I asked myself why the hunt no longer fascinated me. You are much younger than I am, Mr. Rainsford, and have not hunted as much, but you perhaps can guess the answer."

6 "What was it?"

---

[1] **Czar:** supreme ruler, especially in Russia

The Tutorverse

7 "Simply this: hunting had ceased to be what you call 'a sporting proposition.' It had become too easy. I always got my quarry. Always. There is no greater bore than perfection."

8 The general lit a fresh cigarette.

9 "No animal had a chance with me anymore. That is no boast; it is a mathematical certainty. The animal had nothing but his legs and his instinct. Instinct is no match for reason. When I thought of this it was a tragic moment for me, I can tell you."

10 Rainsford leaned across the table, absorbed in what his host was saying.

11 "It came to me as an inspiration what I must do," the general went on.

12 "And that was?"

13 The general smiled the quiet smile of one who has faced an obstacle and surmounted it with success. "I had to invent a new animal to hunt," he said.

14 "A new animal? You're joking."

15 "Not at all," said the general. "I never joke about hunting. I needed a new animal. I found one. So I bought this island, built this house, and here I do my hunting. The island is perfect for my purposes – there are jungles with a maze of traits in them, hills, swamps – "

16 "But the animal, General Zaroff?"

17 "Oh," said the general, "it supplies me with the most exciting hunting in the world. No other hunting compares with it for an instant. Every day I hunt, and I never grow bored now, for I have a quarry with which I can match my wits."

18 "But you can't mean –" gasped Rainsford.

1. Read these sentences from paragraph 1.

   I, luckily, had invested heavily in American assets, so I shall never have to open a tearoom in Monte Carlo or drive a taxi in Paris.

   The speaker's attitude in these sentences is one of

   A. respect.
   B. contempt.
   C. reverence.
   D. acceptance.

2. General Zaroff states that he has hunted all of the following EXCEPT for

   E. lions.
   F. bears.
   G. jaguars.
   H. buffalos.

3. According to the passage, General Zaroff is also

   A. Rainsford.
   B. the narrator.
   C. the Cossack.
   D. the Russian Czar.

4. To General Zaroff, the act of hunting is

    E. a way to obtain food.
    F. an important rite of passage.
    G. about the challenge of the chase.
    H. for acquiring impressive trophies.

5. The speaker of the first paragraph would most likely agree with which of the following statements?

    A. Perfection is desirable, since there can be nothing better than it.
    B. The idea of perfection is a lie, since nothing can be perfect.
    C. Perfection is undesirable, since there is nothing left to achieve after it.
    D. The idea of perfection is an illusion, since it can never be obtained.

6. Based on the passage, which of the following is most likely an example of a "sporting proposition" (paragraph 7)?

    E. shooting fish in a barrel
    F. a game of chess with a peer
    G. predicting the direction of the sunrise
    H. an expert challenging a novice to a game

7. According to General Zaroff, which of the following would be the most challenging animal to hunt?

    A. a highly intelligent gorilla
    B. a fast-flying bird with sharp claws
    C. a giant snake with powerful venom
    D. a rhinoceros with a long, sharp horn

8. How does Rainsford's tone change over the course of the passage?

    E. from familiar to polite
    F. from casual to concerned
    G. from anxious to apprehensive
    H. from admiring to respectful

Adapted from *The Cruise of the Dazzler*

by Jack London

1 "Hello! Where have you been?" he said.

2 "To sea," Joe answered demurely, not sure of just what kind of a reception he was to get and fiddling with his hat nervously.

3 "Short trip, eh? How did you make out?"

4 "Oh, so-so." He had caught the twinkle in his father's eye and knew that it was all clear sailing. "Not so bad – er – that is, considering."

5 "Considering?"

6 "Well, not exactly that; rather, it might have been worse, while it couldn't have been better."

7 "That's interesting. Sit down."

8 It was all Joe could do to keep from crying, so kindly and naturally had his father received him, making him feel at once as if not the slightest thing uncommon had occurred. It seemed as if he had just returned from a vacation.

The Tutorverse

9 "Now go ahead, Joe."

10 Joe sat down and told what had happened – all that had happened – from Monday night to that very moment. Each little incident he related – every detail – not forgetting his conversations with 'Frisco Kid nor his plans concerning him. His face flushed and he was carried away with the excitement of the narrative, while Mr. Bronson was almost as eager, urging him on whenever he slackened his pace, but otherwise remaining silent.

11 "So you see," Joe concluded, "it couldn't possibly have turned out any better."

12 "Ah, well," Mr. Bronson deliberated judiciously, "it may be so, and then again it may not."

13 "I don't see it." Joe felt sharp disappointment at his father's qualified approval. It seemed to him that the return of the safe merited something stronger.

14 Mr. Bronson clearly understood the way Joe felt about it, for he went on: "As to the matter of the safe, all hail to you, Joe! Credit, and plenty of it, is yours. Mr. Tate and myself had already spent five hundred dollars in attempting to recover it. So important was it that we had also offered five thousand dollars reward, and this very morning were considering the advisability of increasing the amount. But, my son," – Mr. Bronson stood up, resting a hand affectionately on his boy's shoulder – "there are certain things in this world which are of still greater importance than the gold, or papers which represent what the gold may buy. How about yourself? That's the point. Will you sell the best possibilities of your life right now for a million dollars?"

15 Joe shook his head.

16 "As I said, that's the point. A human life the money of the world cannot buy; nor can it redeem one which is misspent; nor can it make full and complete and beautiful a life which is dwarfed and warped and ugly. How about yourself? What is to be the effect of all these strange adventures on your life – your life, Joe? Are you going to pick yourself up tomorrow and try it over again? Or the next day? Or the day after? Do you understand? Why, Joe, do you think for one moment that I would place against the best value of my son's life the paltry value of a safe? And can I say, until time has told me, whether this trip of yours could not possibly have been better? Such an experience is as potent for evil as for good. One dollar is exactly like another – there are many in the world: but no Joe is like my Joe, nor can there be any others in the world to take his place. Don't you see, Joe? Don't you understand?"

1. Based on the passage, it can be inferred that Joe expected his father to be all of the following EXCEPT

A. patient.
B. critical.
C. furious.
D. disappointed.

2. The passage provides an answer to all of the following questions EXCEPT

E. What was in the safe?
F. Who is the 'Frisco Kid?
G. Has the safe been found?
H. What was the outcome of Joe's trip?

3. Read this sentence from paragraph 13.

Joe felt sharp disappointment at his father's qualified approval.

Joe feels this way because

A. 'Frisco Kid had been relying on him.
B. Mr. Tate trusted Joe to bring back the safe.
C. he had done the best he could and thought he would be recognized for it.
D. he knows he could have done more to be successful and should have tried harder.

4. The word "qualified" (paragraph 13) most nearly means

   E. expert.
   F. absolute.
   G. reserved.
   H. competent.

5. The passage provides evidence to suggest that the safe

   A. belonged to Joe.
   B. belonged to Mr. Bronson.
   C. contained a million dollars.
   D. contained five thousand dollars.

6. The lesson that Mr. Bronson attempts to teach Joe is that

   E. one must be responsible with one's money.
   F. the only risks worth taking are those that can result in making money.
   G. living a full life, even one with mistakes, is more valuable than money.
   H. one must live up to one's potential but must also be careful to avoid taking risks that can lose money.

7. Mr. Bronson most likely speaks to Joe in paragraph 16 in what tone?

   A. humor
   B. outrage
   C. frustration
   D. tenderness

8. What does Mr. Bronson mean when he says that Joe's experience "is as potent for evil as for good" (paragraph 16)?

   E. It is too soon to tell how the experience will affect Joe.
   F. The experience will have both negative and positive effects on Joe.
   G. The experience was mostly negative, since it put Joe's life in danger.
   H. The experience was mostly positive, since it resulted in the return of the safe.

Adapted from *The Innocents Abroad*

by Mark Twain

1 All day Sunday at anchor. The storm had gone down a great deal, but the sea had not. It was still piling its frothy hills high in air "outside," as we could plainly see with the glasses. We could not properly begin a pleasure excursion on Sunday; we could not offer untried stomachs to so pitiless a sea as that. We must lie still till Monday. And we did. But we had repetitions of church and prayer-meetings; and so, of course, we were just as eligibly situated as we could have been anywhere.

2 I was up early that Sunday morning and was early to breakfast. I felt a perfectly natural desire to have a good, long, unprejudiced look at the passengers at a time when they should be free from self-consciousness – which is at breakfast, when such a moment occurs in the lives of human beings at all.

3 I was greatly surprised to see so many elderly people – I might almost say, so many venerable people. A glance at the long lines of heads was apt to make one think it was all gray. But it was not. There was a tolerably fair sprinkling of young folks, and another fair sprinkling of gentlemen and ladies who were non-committal as to age, being neither actually old or absolutely young.

4 The next morning, we weighed anchor and went to sea. It was a great happiness to get away after this dragging, dispiriting delay. I thought there never was such gladness in the air before, such brightness in the sun, such beauty in the sea. I was satisfied with the picnic then and with all its belongings. All my malicious instincts were dead within me; and as America faded out of sight, I think a spirit of charity rose up in their place that was as boundless, for the time being, as the broad ocean that was heaving its billows about us. I wished to express my feelings – I wished to lift up my voice and sing; but I did not know anything to sing, and so I was obliged to give up the idea. It was no loss to the ship, though, perhaps.

5 It was breezy and pleasant, but the sea was still very rough. One could not promenade without risking his neck; at one moment the bowsprit[1] was taking a deadly aim at the sun in midheaven, and at the next it was trying to harpoon a shark in the bottom of the ocean. What a weird sensation it is to feel the stern[2] of a ship sinking swiftly from under you and see the bow[3] climbing high away among the clouds! One's safest course that day was to clasp a railing and hang on; walking was too precarious a pastime.

6 By some happy fortune I was not seasick – that was a thing to be proud of. I had not always escaped before. If there is one thing in the world that will make a man peculiarly and insufferably self-conceited, it is to have his stomach behave itself, the first day at sea, when nearly all his comrades are seasick. Soon a venerable fossil, shawled to the chin and bandaged like a mummy, appeared at the door of the cabin, and the next lurch of the ship shot him into my arms. I said:

7 "Good-morning, Sir. It is a fine day."

8 He put his hand on his stomach and said, "Oh, my!" and then staggered away and tripped over a skylight.

9 Presently another old gentleman was projected from the same door with great violence. I said:

10 "Calm yourself, Sir – There is no hurry. It is a fine day, Sir."

11 He, also, put his hand on his stomach and said "Oh, my!" and reeled away.

12 In a little while another veteran was discharged abruptly from the same door, clawing at the air for a saving support. I said:

13 "Good morning, Sir. It is a fine day for pleasuring. You were about to say –"

14 "Oh, my!"

15 I thought so. I anticipated him, anyhow. I stayed there and was bombarded with old gentlemen for an hour, perhaps; and all I got out of any of them was "Oh, my!"

16 I went away then in a thoughtful mood. I said, this is a good pleasure excursion. I like it. The passengers are not garrulous, but still they are sociable. I like those old people, but somehow they all seem to have the "Oh, my" rather bad.

17 I knew what was the matter with them. They were seasick. And I was glad of it. We all like to see people seasick when we are not, ourselves. Playing cards by the cabin lamps when it is storming outside

---

[1] **bowsprit**: a long beam extending forward from the front point of a ship or boat
[2] **stern**: the rearmost part of a ship or boat
[3] **bow**: the front end of a ship or boat

is pleasant; walking the quarterdeck in the moonlight is pleasant; smoking in the breezy foretop is pleasant when one is not afraid to go up there; but these are all feeble and commonplace compared with the joy of seeing people suffering the miseries of seasickness.

1. The phrase "piling its frothy hills high in air" in paragraph 1 refers to

    A. the rough seas.
    B. passengers playing a game.
    C. the feeling of being seasick.
    D. the excitement of sailing on the ocean.

2. Read this sentence from paragraph 1.

    But we had repetitions of church and prayer-meetings; and so, of course, we were just as eligibly situated as we could have been anywhere.

    How does this sentence contribute to the plot of the excerpt?

    E. It shows that the narrator is impatient and demanding.
    F. It demonstrates that the narrator is a very religious and pious person.
    G. It illustrates that the weather conditions were favorable to having meetings.
    H. It emphasizes the boredom experienced by the narrator during a delay in the trip.

3. From paragraph 2, it can most reasonably be inferred that the narrator

    A. wishes that he had more time to sit and observe his fellow travelers.
    B. prefers the company of older people, who he believes are more honorable.
    C. believes that during the day, most people's true selves are usually masked.
    D. thinks that breakfast is the most important meal of the day and should never be skipped.

4. Read this sentence from paragraph 4.

    … as America faded out of sight, I think a spirit of charity rose up in their place that was as boundless, for the time being, as the broad ocean that was heaving its billows about us.

    The simile used in the sentence affects the tone of the paragraph by emphasizing a

    E. sense of dread at the sight of land fading from view.
    F. sense of selflessness to help as many passengers as he can.
    G. feeling of nervousness as he looks out onto the broad ocean.
    H. feeling of optimism as the narrator embarks on the next phase of his trip.

5. The tone of the last sentence in paragraph 4 is best described as

    A. bitter.
    B. certain.
    C. boastful.
    D. humorous.

6. It can be inferred from the passage that the narrator

    E. is immune to seasickness.
    F. is a wealthy businessperson.
    G. is an American going on a vacation at sea.
    H. is more self-centered than considerate of others.

The Tutorverse

7. In what way does "this is a good pleasure excursion" (paragraph 16) contribute to the development of the narrator's character?

   A. It demonstrates that the narrator has a great passion for traveling by boat.
   B. It shows that the narrator is a very sociable person who enjoys the company of others.
   C. It contrasts the narrator's positive thoughts with the negative experiences of his fellow travelers.
   D. It illustrates how the narrator's opinion of other people changes over the course of the excerpt.

8. Read this sentence from paragraph 5.

   One could not promenade without risking his neck; at one moment the bowsprit was taking a deadly aim at the sun in midheaven, and at the next it was trying to harpoon a shark in the bottom of the ocean.

   The imagery in this sentence helps establish

   E. the purpose of the trip.
   F. a sense of the surrounding conditions.
   G. the aspects of the trip that the narrator likes most.
   H. the narrator's feelings toward his fellow passengers.

9. Read this sentence from paragraph 6.

   If there is one thing in the world that will make a man peculiarly and insufferably self-conceited, it is to have his stomach behave itself, the first day at sea, when nearly all his comrades are seasick.

   Which quote from the excerpt best supports the central idea of the above sentence?

   A. "We could not properly begin a pleasure excursion on Sunday; we could not offer untried stomachs to so pitiless a sea as that." (par. 1)
   B. "A glance at the long lines of heads was apt to make one think it was all gray. But it was not." (par. 3)
   C. "I knew what was the matter with them." (par. 17)
   D. "And I was glad of it. We all like to see people seasick when we are not, ourselves." (par. 17)

10. How do the details in paragraphs 7-15 help support a central idea of the excerpt?

   E. They show that the narrator is a bold and fearless traveler.
   F. They demonstrate that the narrator is very polite and is a friendly traveling companion.
   G. They establish that the ship conditions affect the narrator in a different way than others.
   H. They illustrate how the author greatly enjoys taking walks and playing games with others.

Adapted from *The Luckiest Girl in the School*

by Angela Brazil

1 "Well, I don't know, Winona!" wavered Mrs. Woodward. "We must look at it from all sides, and perhaps Aunt Harriet's right, and it really would be for the best. Miss Harmon's a poor teacher, and I'm sure your music, at any rate, is not a credit to her. You know you said yourself that you were getting beyond Miss Harmon!"

2 Whatever critiques Winona may have brought against her teacher, she was certainly not prepared to admit them now. She rejected the project of the Seaton High School with the utmost energy and determination, bringing into the fray all that force of character which her mother lacked. Poor Mrs. Woodward vacillated[1] feebly—she was generally swayed by whoever was nearest at the moment—and I verily believe Winona's arguments would have prevailed, and the whole scheme would have been abandoned, had not Mr. Joynson opportunely happened to turn up.

3 Mr. Joynson was a solicitor, and the trustee of Mrs. Woodward's property. He managed most of her business affairs, and some of her private ones as well. She had confidence in his judgment, and she at once thankfully submitted the question of Winona's future to his decision.

4 "The very thing for her!" he declared. "Do her a world of good to go to a proper school. She's frittering her time away here. Send her to Seaton by all means. What are you to do without her? Nonsense! Nobody's indispensable—especially a girl of fifteen! Pack her off as soon as you can. Doesn't want to go? Oh, she'll sing a different song when once she gets there, you'll see!"

5 Thus supported by an authority, Mrs. Woodward settled the question in the affirmative, and replied to her aunt by return of post.

6 Naturally such a stupendous event as the exodus of Winona made a sensation in the household.

7 "It's atrocious!" groaned Winona. "I'm a victim sacrificed for the good of the family. Oh! why couldn't mother have thought of some other way of economizing? I don't want to win scholarships and go in for a career!"

8 "Buck up! Perhaps you won't win! There'll be others in for the exam., you bet! You'll probably fail, and come whining home like a whipped puppy with its tail between its legs!"

9 "Indeed I shan't!" flared Winona indignantly. "I've a little more spirit than that, thank you! And why should you imagine I'm going to fail? I suppose I've as much brains as most people!"

10 "That's right! I was only trying to comfort you!" teased Percy. "In my opinion you'll be returned like a piece of spoiled fruit, or one of those articles 'of no use to anybody except the owner.' Aunt Harriet will be cheated of her prey after all!"

11 "If Win goes away, I shall be the eldest daughter at home," said Letty airily, shaking out her short skirts. "I'll sit at the end of the table, and pour out tea if mother has a headache, and unlock the apple room, and use the best inkpot if I like, and have first innings at the piano."

12 "You forget about the nursery governess," retorted Winona. "If I go, she comes, and you'll find you've exchanged King Log for King Stork[2]. Oh, very well, just wait and see! It won't be as idyllic as you imagine. I shall be saved the trouble of looking after you, at any rate."

13 "What I'm trying to ascertain, madam," said Percy blandly, "is whether your ladyship wishes to take up your residence in Seaton or not. With your perversity you pursue a pig policy. When I venture to picture

---

[1] **vacillate** – to go back and forth; wobble.
[2] In Aesop's fable, *The Frogs Who Desired a King*, a group of frogs asked the gods for a king. The gods threw down a log, which initially terrified and impressed the frogs. Eventually, the frogs realized that the log was passive and unresponsive. When they asked for another king, the gods sent down a stork, which began to eat them.

The Tutorverse

you seated at the board of your venerable aunt, you protest you are a sacrifice; when, on the other hand, I suggest your return to the bosom of your family, you revile me equally."

14 "You're the most unsympathetic *beast* I've ever met!" declared Winona aggrievedly.

15 When she analyzed her feelings, however, she was obliged to allow that they were mixed. Though the prospect of settling down at Seaton filled her with dismay, Percy's gibe at her probable failure touched her pride. Winona had always been counted as the clever member of the family. It would be too ignominious to be sent home labeled unfit. She set her teeth and clenched her fists at the bare notion.

16 "I'll show them all what I can do if I take a thing up!" she resolved.

1. Read this sentence from paragraph 2.

   I verily believe Winona's arguments would have prevailed, and the whole scheme would have been abandoned, had not Mr. Joynson opportunely happened to turn up.

   How does the sentence contribute to the development of the plot?

   A. It reveals how Ms. Woodward's lack of knowledge makes it difficult for her to make decisions.
   B. It shows how Ms. Woodward's dependence on the opinion of others alters her decisions.
   C. It highlights how Ms. Woodward's indecision results in the external conflict being prolonged.
   D. It illustrates how Ms. Woodward's determination helps resolve the external conflict.

2. Which statement best describes Percy's tone in paragraphs 8 and 10?

   E. He uses an accusatory tone by suggesting that Winona wants to abandon the family.
   F. He speaks with a mocking tone as he predicts the ways in which her adventures will end in failure.
   G. He uses an encouraging tone to convince Winona that going away for school will be better than her expectations.
   H. He uses a joking tone by suggesting that the letter is a prank and Winona will remain at home.

3. Which sentence from the excerpt best supports the idea that Winona's family will not be upset to see her go away to school?

   A. "'The very thing for her!' he declared. 'Do her a world of good to go to a proper school. She's frittering her time away here. Send her to Seaton by all means.'" (par. 4)
   B. "'You'll probably fail, and come whining home like a whipped puppy with its tail between its legs!'" (par. 8)
   C. "'If Win goes away, I shall be the eldest daughter at home…I'll sit at the end of the table…and use the best inkpot if I like, and have first innings at the piano.'" (par. 11)
   D. "'What I'm trying to ascertain, madam,' said Percy blandly, 'is whether your ladyship wishes to take up your residence in Seaton or not.'" (par. 13)

4. Read this sentence from paragraph 12.

If I go, she comes, and you'll find you've exchanged King Log for King Stork.

The author reference "King Log" and "King Stork" in order to

E. show the condescension in Winona's interactions with her younger siblings, as she speaks about things she knows they won't understand.
F. highlight the vulnerability that Winona feels when she realizes her siblings are eager for her departure.
G. emphasize Winona's feeling of nostalgia as she imagines living away for the first time.
H. capture Winona's sense of irritation as she tells her sister that her absence won't actually be a good thing.

5. How does paragraph 9 contribute to the overall structure of the excerpt?

A. It reinforces Winona's loving relationship with the rest of her family.
B. It foreshadows the events that will occur after Winona leaves for school.
C. It indicates the moment when Winona's reaction to going away for school changes.
D. It shows the resolution of the argument between Winona and her siblings.

6. Read this sentence from paragraph 15.

It would be too ignominious to be sent home labeled unfit. She set her teeth and clenched her fists at the bare notion.

The descriptions in this sentence conveys the

E. deep hurt and sorrow that Winona feels at Percy's insulting comments.
F. determination to prove everyone wrong and show her intellectual worth.
G. affection and attachment to her younger siblings, whom she does not want to leave behind.
H. anger at the adults in her life for not allowing her to make her own choices.

7. Read paragraph 16 below.

"I'll show them all what I can do if I take a thing up!" she resolved.

How does it compare to Winona's reaction to her situation in paragraph 7?

A. It shows that Winona's feelings have changed from her original reaction to the main conflict.
B. It reinforces the consistency of Winona's negative reaction to the main conflict.
C. It shows how Winona handles the conflict with greater maturity and poise than when she was younger.
D. It highlights how Winona's relationship with her sister impacts how she reacts to her situation.

The Tutorverse

Mathematics

On the Actual Test

The Mathematics section on the SHSAT covers a wide range of topics. These topics include:

- ☞ Numbers & Operations
- ☞ Algebra
- ☞ Probability & Statistics
- ☞ Geometry & Measurements

There are 57 questions on the actual Mathematics section of the test (though 10 of these will not be scored on the actual test). There is no specific time limit during which students must finish the Mathematics section. Instead, students have 180 minutes to complete both the English Language Arts and Mathematics sections of the test. Generally, students should spend approximately 90 minutes on each section. However, this guideline should be adjusted based on a student's strengths.

Of the 57 questions, 52 will be multiple choice. There are 4 answer choices for each multiple-choice question. Most answer choices will be ordered from least to greatest. The remaining 5 questions will be "grid-in," requiring students to produce their own response. Students must write their answers into the provided grid, and bubble in the corresponding value beneath the grid <u>from left to right</u>. Students should <u>not</u> leave a box blank in the middle of an answer and should <u>not</u> fill in a circle under an unused part of the grid.

Students may *not* use calculators on the Mathematics section of the SHSAT.

In This Practice Book

This workbook further divides each of the above-listed topics into sub-topics. This way, students can hone in on areas that require more practice. This differs from the actual test, where questions covering various topics are mixed together. We have divided the main topics in the following manner:

- ☞ Numbers & Operations
    - ☞ Numbers
    - ☞ Operations
    - ☞ Percents
    - ☞ Fractions
    - ☞ Word Problems
    - ☞ Ratios & Proportions
    - ☞ Factors, Multiples, Exponents, & Radicals
    - ☞ Absolute Value
    - ☞ Scientific Notation
    - ☞ Counting Principle
    - ☞ Imaginary Operations

- ☞ Algebra
    - ☞ Algebraic Expressions & Equations
    - ☞ Algebra in Context
    - ☞ Plugins
    - ☞ Inequalities

- ☞ Probability & Statistics
    - ☞ Probability
    - ☞ Averages

- ☞ Geometry & Measurements
    - ☞ Area & Perimeter
    - ☞ Volume
    - ☞ Triangles
    - ☞ Circles
    - ☞ Angles
    - ☞ Measurements
    - ☞ Coordinates

How to Use This Section

As determined by your study plan, including the results of your practice test, we encourage you to focus on the topics that are most challenging to you. Because there may be material on this test that you may be unfamiliar with, we encourage you to seek additional help from trusted educators or tutors. Bring these materials to your tutor or teacher if you need additional reinforcement in any given topic.

The questions in each section are progressive. This means that they start out easier, but then become more and more difficult as they build on more nuanced concepts related to that topic. Don't get discouraged if you find some questions difficult. Instead, consider asking a trusted educator to help you better understand the material.

Note that grid-in questions are included at the end of each section.

Tutorverse Tips!

Remember that on the SHSAT, there is no penalty for guessing. If you don't know the answer to a question, take your best guess. In addition to never leaving an answer choice blank, consider the following:

- Memorize Basic Terms & Formulas
  The meaning of mathematical terms (like "similar") and operators (like "≥") are *not* given. Therefore, you *must* be familiar with the meaning of these things before taking the actual exam (this is part of the reason why you are practicing ahead of time!). The terms and operators used will all be grade-level appropriate. Similarly, formulas (like that used to determine the area of a circle) must also be committed to memory. Developing a strong command of mathematical terms, operators, and formulas is critical on this test. Memorizing this kind of information will make it easier to solve questions quickly and accurately.

- Do Math on Paper
  Students often try to do math in their heads and end up making careless mistakes. Many of the answer choices to questions are designed to take advantage of this fact, leading students to choose the incorrect answer. Spending 60 seconds doing math on paper to answer a question correctly is usually more valuable than wasting 30 seconds doing math in your head only to answer a question incorrectly. Translate word problems into equations. Solve equations on paper. Check your answers by plugging them back into the equation.

- Simplify
  Answer choices should always be simplified to the lowest possible term. For example, if your calculations lead you to an answer of $\frac{2}{4}$, remember that this is also equivalent to $\frac{1}{2}$, 0.50, or 50%. Check the answer choices to see which is offered as an option. There will always only be one correct answer choice.

The Tutorverse

Numbers & Operations

Numbers

1. Which of the following numbers is between $\frac{1}{4}$ and $\frac{1}{3}$?

    A. 0.14
    B. 0.31
    C. 0.34
    D. 0.41

2. Which of the following sums can be expressed as a non-repeating decimal?

    E. $\frac{1}{3} + \frac{1}{6}$ → $\frac{3}{6}$ → 0.5
    F. $\frac{1}{3} + \frac{1}{3}$
    G. $\frac{1}{2} + \frac{1}{3}$
    H. $\frac{1}{2} + \frac{1}{6}$

3. If $x \times m = x$ for all values of x, what is the value of m?

    A. $-x$
    B. 0
    C. 1
    D. x

4. If 7 more than p is a negative number and if 9 more than p is a positive number, which of the following could be the value of p?

    $-9 + 7 = -2$
    $-9 + 9$

    E. -9
    F. -8
    G. -7
    H. 6

5. The product of 3 different positive integers is 15. What is their sum?

    $3 \cdot 5 \cdot 1$
    9

    A. 8
    B. 9
    C. 15
    D. 45

6. If x and y are consecutive positive integers and $x^2 - y^2 = 11$, what is the value of y?

    E. 1
    F. 3
    G. 5
    H. 6

7. Alice, Bob, and Carol were riding their bikes along the same path at different speeds. Alice's speed was twice Bob's speed, and Carols' speed was one-third that of Alice's. What was Carol's speed if Bob's speed was 9 miles per hour?

    A. 6 miles per hour
    B. 9 miles per hour
    C. 13.5 miles per hour
    D. 54 miles per hour

    $6 \times 18 \cdot \frac{1}{3} = 6$

8. A certain editor can review between 25 and 40 words per minute, inclusive. The editor's rate varies between $18 and $33 per hour, inclusive. What is the least amount that an author would need to pay the editor in order to have her 10,000-word manuscript reviewed by the editor?

    E. $75
    F. $120
    G. $220
    H. $4,500

9. The table below shows the distribution of seed and flower color for 72 pea plants.

    DISTRIBUTION OF SEED AND FLOWER COLOR FOR 72 PEA PLANTS

    | | | Seed Color | | |
		Green	Yellow	Total
Flower Color	Purple	17	23	40
	White	13	19	32

    How many of these pea plants have a white flower, a yellow seed, or both?

    A. 32
    B. 36
    C. 55
    D. 74

10.

PEA POD AND FLOWER OBSERVATIONS

	Yellow Pod	Green Pod	Total
Purple Flower	k	m	n
White Flower	p	q	r
Total	x	y	z

The table above shows the results of a biology class experiment. Each variable represents the number of peas in that category. Which of the following must be equal to z?

E. $y + r$
F. $p + q + r$
G. $k + m + p + q$
H. $x + y + n + r$

11.

HIGH SCHOOL FRESHMAN

	Latin	Mandarin	Total
Algebra	72,000		
Geometry			12,500
Total	84,000		101,500

The table above is partially filled in. Based on the information in the table, how many freshman who take Mandarin are also taking Geometry?

A. 500
B. 12,000
C. 17,000
D. 17,500

12. How many integers are there from 10 to 20, inclusive?

E. 9
F. 10
G. 11
H. 12

13. How many integers are between $-\frac{7}{3}$ and $\frac{7}{3}$?

A. 6
B. 5
C. 4
D. 3

14. Set A contains all integers from 50 to 100, inclusive, and Set B contains all integers from 69 to 138, exclusive. How many integers are included in both Set A and Set B?

E. 29
F. 30
G. 31
H. 32

15. How many positive integers under 50 are multiples of <u>neither</u> 4 nor 6?

A. 16
B. 20
C. 33
D. 34

16. How many positive three-digit integers have the hundreds digit equal to 7 and the units (ones) digit equal to 1?

E. 10
F. 19
G. 20
H. 190

17. Dimitri wants to make 17 cents using only pennies, nickels, and dimes. How many different combinations can he make using only these three types of coins?

A. 3
B. 4
C. 5
D. 6

18. The price of a share of a company's stock has been decreasing at a constant rate of $0.50 per share every half hour. If the price of the share of stock is now $25, for how many <u>hours</u> has the price been below $30 per share?

E. 3.5 hours
F. 4.0 hours
G. 4.5 hours
H. 5.0 hours

The Tutorverse

19. If $x = \dfrac{1}{y}$ and y is any positive integer under 5, what is the greatest possible value of x?

  A. 0.2
  B. 0.4
  C. 0.6
  D. 1.0

20. If x is a positive integer, what is the least value of x for which $\sqrt{\dfrac{7x}{4}}$ is an integer?

  E. 4
  F. 7
  G. 28
  H. 112

21. If $p = -1$, which of the following has the greatest value?

  A. $4p^2$
  B. $6p^3$
  C. $8p^4$
  D. $10p^5$

22. If $a = b^2$ and $b = \left(-\dfrac{1}{2}\right)^c$ for $c = 1$, 2, or 3, what is the greatest possible value of a?

  E. $\dfrac{1}{4}$
  F. $\dfrac{1}{8}$
  G. $\dfrac{1}{16}$
  H. $\dfrac{1}{32}$

23.

If x, x^2, and x^3 lie on a number line in the order shown above, which of the following could be the value of x?

  A. $-\dfrac{1}{3}$
  B. $\dfrac{2}{3}$
  C. 1
  D. $\dfrac{4}{3}$

24.

x	0	1	2	3
y	1	2	5	10

Which of the following rules describes the table above?

  E. $y = x^2 + 1$
  F. $y = x^2 + 2$
  G. $y = 2x^2 - 2$
  H. $y = 2x^2 - 1$

25. The table below shows two rows of integers, Row X and Row Y, and the relationship between them.

RELATIONSHIP BETWEEN ROW X & ROW Y

Row X	1	2	3	4	5	6
Row Y	1	4	9	16	25	36

Assume each row continues in the pattern shown. When the number 100 appears in Row Y, what is the corresponding number that will appear in Row X?

  A. 10
  B. 20
  C. 40
  D. 60

26. 9, 21, 45, 93...
The first term in the sequence is 9, and each term after the first is determined by multiplying the preceding term by x and then adding y. What is the value of x if y is an integer > 0?

  E. 1
  F. 2
  G. 3
  H. 4

27. In an 8th grade homeroom, 16 students take Biology, 8 students take Chemistry, 4 students take both Biology and Chemistry, and 2 students take neither Biology nor Chemistry. How many students are in the homeroom?

  A. 18
  B. 22
  C. 24
  D. 30

The Tutorverse

28. If z is an integer and 3 is the remainder when $2z + 7$ is divided by 5, then z could be

   E. 11
   F. 12
   G. 13
   H. 14

29. A piggy bank contains only pennies and nickels. If there are 2 nickels for every 1 penny in the piggy bank, each of the following could be the number of coins in the piggy bank EXCEPT

   A. 30
   B. 33
   C. 55
   D. 66

30. Stanley noticed that he is both the 10th tallest and the 10th shortest student in his class. If everyone in the class is a different height, how many students are in the class?

   E. 19
   F. 20
   G. 21
   H. 22

31. A computer program randomly selects a positive three-digit integer. If the integer selected is even, half that integer is printed onto a piece of paper. If the integer selected is odd, the integer itself is printed onto a piece of paper. If the integer that was printed onto a piece of paper is 102, which of the following could have been the integer selected?

   A. 51
   B. 102
   C. 204
   D. Any of the above

32. Tina's locker combination consists of 3 two-digit numbers. The combination satisfies the three conditions below:

   One number is odd
   One number is a factor of 24
   One number is the month of Tina's birthday

   If each number satisfies exactly one of the conditions, which of the following could be the combination to Tina's locker?

   E. 11-14-24
   F. 10-15-24
   G. 1-12-24
   H. 3-8-11

Grid-In Questions (Open-Ended Questions)

33. What is the sum of all the positive integers from 1 to 100, inclusive?

34. How many positive integer values of x satisfy the inequality $7 < \sqrt{x} < 8$?

35. How many distinct positive integer factors does 60 have?

36. n is divisible by 3, 4, and 5. If $n > 100$, what is the smallest possible value of n?

37. How many perfect squares are between 1,600 and 3,600?

The Tutorverse

Operations

1. $\dfrac{1}{2} \times \dfrac{3}{4} + \dfrac{1}{6} =$

   A. $\dfrac{5}{12}$

   B. $\dfrac{4}{13}$

   C. $\dfrac{11}{24}$

   D. $\dfrac{13}{24}$

2. $\dfrac{1}{2} + \dfrac{3}{4} \div \dfrac{1}{6} =$

   E. $\dfrac{5}{8}$

   F. $\dfrac{5}{4}$

   G. 5

   H. 7.5

3. $2.34 \div 1.2 =$

   A. 0.195
   B. 1.95
   C. 19.5
   D. 195

4. $73 \div 0.365 =$

   E. 0.002
   F. 0.02
   G. 20
   H. 200

5. $2.4 \div \dfrac{1}{6} =$

   A. 0.4
   B. 4.4
   C. 12.4
   D. 14.4

6. $\dfrac{2.02}{0.01} \times 0.03 =$

   E. 0.606
   F. 6.06
   G. 60.6
   H. 66.0

7. $100(3 + 0.2)^2 - 24 =$

   A. $-1{,}376$
   B. 280
   C. $1{,}000$
   D. $43{,}264$

8. The value of $\sqrt{50} + \sqrt{60}$ is between which pair of integers?

   E. 5 and 6
   F. 14 and 15
   G. 16 and 17
   H. 27 and 28

9. The value of which expression is between the consecutive positive integers 7 and 8?

   A. $\sqrt{5+6}^{\,2}$

   B. $\sqrt{(5+6)^2}$

   C. $\sqrt{5^2 + 6^2}$

   D. $\sqrt{5^2} + \sqrt{6^2}$

Grid-In Questions (Open-Ended Questions)

---

10. $-27, -8, -1, 0, 1, 8, 27, \ldots$

    What is the next number in the sequence?

11. $x = 14 - 4y$
    $x = y - 1$
    What is the value of x?

The Tutorverse

12. $\dfrac{4}{5} - 1.2 \div \dfrac{3}{4} + 2.5 \times \dfrac{3}{10} =$

13. What is the value of the expression
$0.1 + 0.2 - 0.3 \times 0.4 \div 0.5$?

14. $(4 - 0.8)^2 - 15.36 =$

15. $4.2 \times \dfrac{5}{6} \div 10 + \dfrac{3}{20} =$

Percents

1. Which of the following is equivalent to $\dfrac{1}{3}$ of 35% of 924?

A. 35% of 308
B. 35% of $\dfrac{308}{3}$
C. $\dfrac{35}{3}$% of 308
D. $\dfrac{35}{3} \times 924$

$\dfrac{35}{200} \cdot \dfrac{1}{3} = \dfrac{35}{300}$

$\dfrac{35}{300} \cdot \dfrac{924}{1} \quad 308$

$\dfrac{100}$

2. 3,000 students at Regional High School were surveyed about their favorite color. The chart below shows the result of this survey.

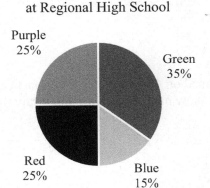

Student Favorite Colors
at Regional High School

Purple 25%
Green 35%
Blue 15%
Red 25%

Green is the favorite color of how many students at Regional High School?

E. 350
F. 1,050
G. 1,500
H. 10,500

$\dfrac{35}{100} \cdot \dfrac{3,000}{1} = 1050$

$\begin{array}{r} 35 \\ \times\ 30 \\ \hline 1050 \end{array}$

3. In a class of 30 students, there are 12 boys. What percent of the class is girls?

A. 18%
B. 40%
C. 54%
D. 60%

$\dfrac{18}{30} \rightarrow \dfrac{6}{10}$

4. If there are 200 pencils in a case and 75 are sharpened, what percentage of pencils are not sharpened?

E. 25.5%
F. 60.0%
G. 62.5%
H. 80.0%

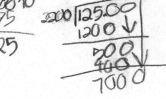

5.

VIDEO GAMES OWNED

# of Video Games	# of Students
0	1.5x
1	x
2	2x
3	3x
4	0.5x

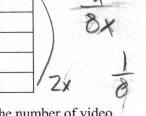

The table above shows the number of video games owned by students in a school. What percent of the student body owns 1 video game?

A. 6.25%
B. 12.50%
C. 18.75%
D. Cannot be determined from the given information.

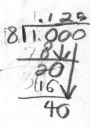

The Tutorverse

6.

Apartment Building Age Profile

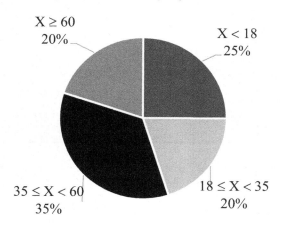

A census taker recorded the ages of all 1,000 people living in a certain apartment building. Each person's age is represented by X. How many people living in the apartment building are under the age of 35?

E. 200
F. 250
G. 450
H. 800

7.

Students Studying Spanish, French, Both, or Neither

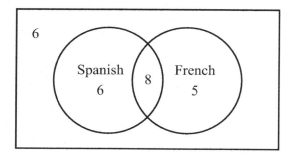

The Venn diagram above shows the distribution of 25 eighth grade students who studied Spanish, French, both, or neither. What percent of the students studied French?

A. 5%
B. 13%
C. 52%
D. 60%

8. A school took a survey of all its students to see how many pets each student owned.

PET OWNERSHIP

Number of Pets	Percent of Student Body
0	30%
1	35%
2	25%
3	8%
4 or more	2%

The table above shows the percent distribution for the school's 2,400 students. How many students own at least 2 pets?

E. 240
F. 600
G. 720
H. 840

9. A survey showed that between 20% and 30% of university graduates go on to pursue a master's degree. If 4,000 students graduate from a certain college, what is the minimum number of graduates who will **not** continue on to a master's degree program?

A.   800
B. 1,200
C. 2,800
D. 3,200

10. It rained on 40% of the 365 days last year. Last year, how many more days did it rain than not?

E.   20
F.   73
G. 146
H. 219

11. A high school held an election for class president. Exactly 1,000 votes were cast and they were all for either Gillian or Clive. Gillian received 100 more votes than Clive. What percent of the 1,000 votes were for Gillian?

A. 45%
B. 55%
C. 60%
D. 65%

12. Bruce and Betty recycled a total of 600 bottles. Bruce recycled twice as many bottles as Betty. What percent of the 600 bottles did Bruce recycle?

E. 33.3%
F. 50.0%
G. 66.7%
H. 75.0%

13. A rectangle is 50 feet long and 40 feet wide. The length is decreased by 40% and the width is increased by 20%. What is the percent decrease in the area?

A. 10%
B. 14%
C. 20%
D. 28%

14. The price of a laptop was first increased by 10% and then the new price was decreased by 20%. The final price was what percent of the initial price?

E. 10%
F. 80%
G. 88%
H. 90%

15. Kevin watched 2 hours of TV on Saturday. On Sunday, he watched 100% as many hours of TV as he did on Saturday. How many hours of TV did he watch on Sunday?

A. 2
B. 3
C. 4
D. 5

16. A clothing company charges a 15% shipping fee on orders under $50 and a 12.5% shipping charge on orders of $50 or more. How much more would the company charge for shipping on a $49 order than on a $50 order?

E. $1.10
F. $2.50
G. $6.25
H. $7.35

17.

Smartphone Sales by Brand

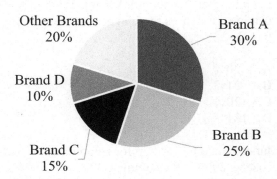

The circle graph above represents all the smartphones, sorted by their brands, that were sold by an electronics store last month. If the store sold 700 smartphones other than brands A, B, C, and D, how many smartphones did it sell altogether?

A. 2,000
B. 2,400
C. 2,800
D. 3,500

18. John ran 8 miles on Tuesday. On Wednesday, he ran 150% farther than he ran on Tuesday. How far did he run on Wednesday?

E. $5\frac{1}{3}$
F. 12
G. 16
H. 20

19. X is 80% of Y, and Y is 20% of 100. What is the value of X?

A. 16
B. 40
C. 80
D. 100

20. Fermium-253 decays at a rate of 50% every 3 days. By how much will some amount of fermium-253 decrease after 9 days?

E. 6.25%
F. 12.5%
G. 15.5%
H. 87.5%

21. A certain savings account increases in such a way that the amount in the account at the end of each month is 10% more than the amount at the beginning of that month. What percent of the original amount is there in account after two months?

  A.   20%
  B.   21%
  C.   120%
  D.   121%

22. Janet signed her son up for summer camp, which cost $1,200 for the summer. 30% was due at signup. Of the remaining balance, 75% was due the week before camp started. The rest was due on the first day of camp. How much was due on the first day of camp?

  E. $210
  F. $270
  G. $300
  H. $630

23. A farmer is planning on picking 1,000 bell peppers on the first day of the harvest. After picking the first 600, he finds that 70 percent of them are green and 30 percent of them are red. How many of the remaining peppers he must pick must be red in order for exactly half of the total number of peppers picked to be red?

  A.   80
  B.   180
  C.   320
  D.   420

24. By 9pm Friday night, a restaurant had sold 200 entrées, 50 of which were steak. The restaurant makes a greater profit on steak than on any other entrée, so they want steak to represent at least 50% of their total number of entrées sold. If they sell no additional other types of entrées, what is the minimum number of steak entrees that the restaurant must sell in order to reach their goal?

  E.   75
  F.   100
  G.   150
  H.   300

25. A store buys coffee beans at $5.50 per pound. If they charge 80% more than their purchase price when they sell the beans to customers, what is the price per pound of the beans they sell?

  A. $4.40
  B. $6.30
  C. $9.90
  D. $13.50

26. A furniture store charges $52 for a certain lamp. This price is 30% more than the amount it costs the store to buy one of these lamps. Once the following year's models arrive, store employees can purchase any remaining lamps at 40% off the store's cost. How much would it cost an employee to purchase one of these lamps at this discount?

  E. $6.24
  F. $21.84
  G. $24.00
  H. $40.00

Grid-In Questions (Open-Ended Questions)

27. 100 chickens were on Billings Farm. 20% of the chickens were sold to neighboring Brockport farm, and 20% of the remaining chickens were sold to Luscious Farm. How many chickens are on Billings Farm now?

28. In the wild dogs' section of the zoo, there are 16 wolves, 12 coyotes, and 8 dingoes. This represents 45% of all the animals in the zoo. How many animals does the zoo have in total?

29. 24% of the students in a class are left-handed. What's the minimum number of students that could be in the class?

30. 1,000 students are polled. 30% of the students list the Turkish Angora as their favorite cat breed. Of the other students, 10% list the Scottish Fold as their favorite cat breed. How many students' favorite cat breed is neither the Turkish Angora nor Scottish Fold?

The Tutorverse

Fractions

1. $6 \times 6\frac{2}{3} =$ $\frac{2\cancel{0}}{1} \cdot \frac{20}{\cancel{3}_1} = 40$

   A. $12\frac{2}{3}$

   B. 18

   C. $36\frac{2}{3}$

   D. 40

2. $4\frac{1}{2} \times 3\frac{3}{5} =$ $\frac{9}{\cancel{2}} \cdot \frac{\cancel{18}^9}{5} = \frac{81}{5}$

   E. 12.3 $\frac{162}{10}$

   F. 14.1

   G. 14.85

   H. 16.2 $\frac{81}{16.2}$

3. What is $\frac{44}{64}$ in decimal form?

   A. 0.68

   B. 0.68875

   C. 0.687

   D. 0.6875

4. What is $\frac{25}{32}$ in decimal form?

   E. 0.78

   F. 0.781

   G. 0.781125

   H. 0.78125

5. What is $\frac{1}{3}$ of Q if $\frac{2}{3}$ of Q is 36?

   A. 9

   B. 18

   C. 36

   D. 54

6. A jar was filled with 35 teaspoons of oil and 15 teaspoons of vinegar. A chef poured more vinegar into the jar until the vinegar represented $\frac{1}{2}$ of the jar's liquid. How many teaspoons of vinegar were added to the jar?

   E. 15 tsp

   F. 20 tsp

   G. 25 tsp

   H. 30 tsp

   $\frac{15+x}{50+x} = \frac{1}{2}$

   $50+2x = 50+x$
   $2x = 20+x$
   $x = 20$

7. A truck leaves a construction site with its cargo hold $\frac{1}{4}$ full of sand. On the way, the truck stops at a depot, where 9 tons of sand is added to the cargo hold, making it $\frac{5}{8}$ full. How many tons of sand could the cargo hold contain if completely full?

   A. 12

   B. 24

   C. 36

   D. 48

   $\frac{1}{4}x + 9 = \frac{5}{8}x$

   $2x + 72 = 5x$

   $72 = 3x$
   $24 = x$

8. The table below shows the price per piece of certain fabrics.

   Prices for Fabric

Size	Price
$\frac{1}{3}$ square yard	$150
$\frac{2}{3}$ square yard	$275
Full square yard	$500

   A tailor purchased one-third, two-third, and full square yard pieces of fabric in equal numbers, spending $5,550 in total. What was the total amount of fabric, in square yards, that the tailor purchased?

   E. 4

   F. 6

   G. 8

   H. 12

   $150x + 275x + 500x = 5550$

   $925x = 5550$

9. $X_1X_2 + X_2X_3 - X_3X_4 - X_4X_5$

Let k be a positive integer. If $X_k = \dfrac{2}{k}$ for any positive value of k, what is the value of the above expression?

A. $\dfrac{64}{25}$

B. $\dfrac{32}{15}$

C. $\dfrac{16}{8}$

D. $\dfrac{8}{3}$

10. In Pleasantburg, 2,850 people pay taxes. Of these taxpayers, $\dfrac{1}{6}$ pay between \$10,000 and \$20,000 in taxes per year, inclusive. How many taxpayers pay either **more** than \$20,000 or **less** than \$10,000 in taxes per year?

E. 475
F. 950
G. 1,900
H. 2,375

11. A submarine sandwich created for a party is measured to be 63 inches long. This sandwich is cut into thirds. One of the resulting pieces is again cut into thirds. Before serving it, one of these pieces is cut in half. Of the final 6 pieces, what is the difference in length between **one** of the two longest pieces and **one** of the two smallest pieces?

A. 3.5 in.
B. 10.5 in.
C. 17.5 in.
D. 21.0 in.

12. Jennifer finds a rare painting while shopping at a thrift store. She convinces the manager to put the painting on hold with a deposit of \$600 toward the purchase price. If the price of the painting is \$2,000, what fraction of the price of the painting is represented by Jennifer's deposit?

E. $\dfrac{1}{6}$

F. $\dfrac{3}{10}$

G. $\dfrac{7}{10}$

H. $\dfrac{5}{6}$

13. Tiffany drove from New York to California over the course of 8 days. Each day, she took a one-hour lunch break and a two-hour dinner break. What fraction of the total number of hours in these eight days did she spent breaking for lunch and dinner?

A. $\dfrac{1}{8}$

B. $\dfrac{1}{6}$

C. $\dfrac{1}{4}$

D. $\dfrac{3}{8}$

14. The numerator of a certain fraction is 4 less than the denominator. If the fraction is equal to $\dfrac{2}{3}$, what is the denominator of this fraction?

E. 8
F. 12
G. 15
H. 18

Grid-In Questions (Open-Ended Questions)

15. What is $600 \times \left(\dfrac{1}{2}\right)\left(\dfrac{2}{3}\right)\left(\dfrac{3}{4}\right)\left(\dfrac{4}{5}\right)$?

16. What is the value of x in the equation $\dfrac{x}{3} - \dfrac{x}{6} = 1 + \dfrac{x}{9}$?

The Tutorverse

17. What is the decimal value of $\dfrac{(1 \times 2 \times 3)}{(4 \times 5 \times 6)}$?

18. What is the smallest possible positive integer value for n if $\dfrac{1}{n} < 0.3$?

19. 12 people can wash 40 cars in 12 days. How many days would it take 4 people to wash 30 cars?

Word Problems

1. Alan makes cuckoo clocks. He then sells the cuckoo clocks for $500 each. It costs Alan $275 to make each cuckoo clock. Every month, Alan spends $2,500 to rent his workshop. If, in a month, Alan sells 30 clocks, how much <u>profit</u> will he have made in that month?

   A. $4,250
   B. $6,750
   C. $10,750
   D. $12,500

2. A summer camp counselor is given $45 to spend on snacks for her campers. The counselor wants to provide his campers with s'mores, each of which requires 2 graham crackers, 1 marshmallow, and 2 bars of chocolate. Graham crackers cost $0.50 each, marshmallows cost $0.75 each, and bars of chocolate cost $1.25 each. How many completed s'mores can the counselor make for her campers?

   E. 10
   F. 11
   G. 12
   H. 18

3. The surface temperature of Mercury changes drastically. On a certain day, surface temperatures reached 869°F during the daytime. At night, the surface temperature dropped to −299°F. On this particular day, what was the total change in temperature on the surface of Mercury?

   A. 570°F
   B. 869°F
   C. 1,168°F
   D. 1,439°F

4. There are 271 guests at a wedding. Each table at the wedding reception can seat 8 guests. The bride and groom will fill a table with as many guests as possible before adding another table to the reception. How many guests will be seated at the last table added to the reception?

   E. 1
   F. 5
   G. 6
   H. 7

5. A department store is having a sale where a pocketbook is on sale for $\dfrac{1}{4}$ off the retail price. Jacquie brings with her a coupon entitling her to an additional 30% off the sale price. The pocketbook's retail price is $800. What will Jacquie have to pay in sales tax if the tax is 9% of the final price of the pocketbook?

   A. $5.40
   B. $21.60
   C. $37.80
   D. $54.00

6. There are between 25 and 49 monkeys living at a particular zoo. Exactly 20% of the monkeys are Langur monkeys, while exactly $\dfrac{1}{4}$ of the monkeys are Colobus monkeys. How many monkeys are there in this zoo?

   E. 25
   F. 30
   G. 40
   H. 45

The Tutorverse

7. Bao makes $25 per hour. In one week, he works for a total of 4 days. On each day of that week, Bao worked for 8.5 hours. How much did Bao make that week?

   A. $200.00
   B. $212.50
   C. $850.00
   D. $1,487.50

8. On days that Ashley goes to the gym, she drinks three 11-ounce glasses of juice. On days that Ashley does not go to the gym, she drinks one 11-ounce glass of juice. During one particular week, the price per ounce of juice that Ashley buys from her convenience store is higher than normal by $0.02 per ounce. How much more did Ashley pay for her juice over the course of a normal seven-day week, to the nearest cent, if she went to the gym three days that week?

   E. $4.62
   F. $2.86
   G. $1.98
   H. $1.54

Grid-In Questions (Open-Ended Questions)

11. 3 eggs and 4 strips of bacon cost $3.10. 5 eggs and 1 strip of bacon cost $4.90. If a family orders 16 eggs and 10 strips of bacon, how much, in dollars, do they pay?

12. Dan can wash a car in one hour. His older brother Dave can wash a car in half an hour. How many minutes would it take to wash one car if they worked together?

13. Daphne and Josephine earn commission on the sales they each make. Daphne earned $80 in commission on a sale of $1,600. Josephine earns twice the commission percentage as Daphne. If the commission Josephine earns is $150, how much were her sales, in dollars?

9. A new delivery person is required to make 36 deliveries per day, 365 days per year. The deliveries will take place along a circular route, with each stop being labeled 1 through 36, consecutively. The first stop is labeled 1, the second stop is labeled 2, and so on. At which stop will the delivery person make his or her 546th delivery?

   A.   stop number 5
   B.   stop number 6
   C.   stop number 15
   D.   stop number 18

10. In the morning, a buoy in a certain tidal bay shows that the water beneath it is 24 feet deep. The depth of the water beneath the buoy decreased by 6 inches each hour for the next 12 hours. What was the depth of the water beneath the buoy 12 hours later?

    E.   12 ft.
    F.   18 ft.
    G.   24 ft.
    H.   30 ft.

14. Train A leaves a train station at noon, traveling at a constant speed of 80 miles per hour. Train B leaves the same station on a parallel track at 1 PM, traveling a constant speed, and catches up with Train A at 5 PM. How fast, in miles per hour, is Train B going?

15. In Frank's piggy bank, there are only quarters and dimes. He has 37 coins, and has a total of $5.50. How many quarters does he have?

16. In Mrs. Wiggins' class of 32 students, $\frac{3}{8}$ of the students are taking French, and $\frac{1}{2}$ of the students are taking Latin. If 6 students are taking both, how many students are taking neither?

The Tutorverse

Ratios & Proportions

1. A supermarket is selling a chicken that has a mass of 2,000,000 milligrams. What is the chicken's mass in kilograms?

   A. 2 kg
   B. 20 kg
   C. 200 kg
   D. 2,000 kg

2. The scale on a blueprint of a building states that 20 feet is represented by 0.5 inches. If a wall is 60 yards long, how many inches long will it be on the blueprint?

   E. 1.5
   F. 3.0
   G. 4.5
   H. 6.0

   handwritten: 20 ft → 0.5 .075
   10 ft → 0.25 × 60
   1 ft → 0.025 4.500
   1 yd → .075

3. A recipe for salad dressing uses 5 ounces of oil for every 2 ounces of vinegar. If a restaurant needs to make exactly 35 ounces of salad dressing, how many ounces of oil will it need?

   A. 10
   B. 14
   C. 15
   D. 25

   handwritten: 5:2   25:10

4. A newspaper editor can proofread an average of 300 words every 9 minutes. At this rate, how long will it take the editor to proofread 1,000 words?

   E. 30 minutes
   F. 33 minutes
   G. 35 minutes
   H. 40 minutes

   handwritten: 100:3   1000:30

5. A man that weighs 76 kilograms on Mars would weigh 228 kilograms on Neptune. If a certain object weighs 57 grams on Neptune, how much would it weigh on Mars?

   A. 1.9 grams
   B. 19 grams
   C. 1,900 grams
   D. 19,000 grams

   handwritten: 1:3 $\frac{1}{3} \cdot \frac{57}{1}$ 3)57 = 19

6. At a zoo, the ratio of tigers to lions is 7:4. What is the total number of tigers and lions if there are 28 tigers?

   E. 16
   F. 44
   G. 49
   H. 77

   handwritten: 7:4 28:16   28 + 16 = 44

7. On Monday, Cheyenne drove the 1,000 miles from Denver to Chicago in 25 hours. On Tuesday, he drove the 800 miles from Chicago to New York City in 16 hours. How much greater was his average speed, in miles per hour, on Tuesday than on Monday?

   A. 0 mph
   B. 10 mph
   C. 20 mph
   D. 40 mph

   handwritten: 40 mph 50 mph $\frac{816}{\times 5} = 80$

8. Brenda must deliver 100 newspapers by bicycle on Sunday. It took her 25 minutes to deliver the first 40 newspapers. At this rate, how much time will it take her to deliver the remaining papers?

   E. $\frac{1}{4}$ hr
   F. $\frac{1}{3}$ hr
   G. $\frac{5}{8}$ hr
   H. $\frac{3}{5}$ hr

   handwritten: $\frac{25}{60} = \frac{5}{12}$ $\frac{840}{1} \cdot \frac{12}{5} = \frac{96}{1}$
   $\frac{96x}{96} = \frac{60}{96} = \frac{30}{48} = \frac{15}{24}$ $\frac{5}{8}$

9. 1 terp = 5 plogs
   1 terp = 0.2 hucks
   Una has 200 plogs and 40 hucks. If she exchanges the plogs and hucks for terps according to the rates above, how many terps will she receive?

   A. 60 terps
   B. 200 terps
   C. 240 terps
   D. 280 terps

   handwritten: 200 ÷ 5 = 40   40 ÷ 0.2 = 200

10. In a bowl, the ratio of red marbles to yellow marbles is 4:5. The ratio of yellow marbles to blue marbles is 3:7. If there are 35 blue marbles in the bowl, how many red marbles are there?

E. 12
F. 20
G. 28
H. 35

$\frac{4}{5} \cdot \frac{3}{7} = \frac{12}{35}$

11. A container of mixed nuts contains 75 ounces of peanuts, almonds, and walnuts only. The ratio of the weights of peanuts and almonds is 5:7, and the ratio of the weights of almonds to walnuts is 7:3. If all the peanuts were removed, what would be the new weight of the container?

A. 40 oz.
B. 50 oz.
C. 60 oz.
D. 70 oz.

5:7:3
25:35:15
$\frac{3/5}{5}$

12. During lunch, kids are trading snacks. 5 potato chips are worth 9 jelly beans. 2 potato chips are worth 9 carrots. How many carrots are needed to trade for a dozen jelly beans?

E. 12
F. 24
G. 30
H. 60

$\frac{5}{7} \cdot \frac{9}{2} = \frac{5}{2}$ 5×6 30

13. On a bookshelf, the ratio of fiction to nonfiction books is 4:1. What percent of the books are fiction?

80:20

A. 20%
B. 25%
C. 75%
D. 80%

14. A spring stretches 8 cm when a load of 20 pounds is hung on it. If the weight required to stretch a spring is proportional to how far the spring is stretched, how far will the spring stretch in all if an additional load of 30 pounds is added to the spring?

E. 12 cm
F. 18 cm
G. 20 cm
H. 24 cm

15.

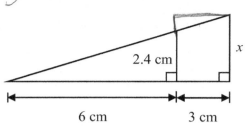

In the figure above, what is the value of *x*?

A. 1.2 cm
B. 1.6 cm
C. 3.6 cm
D. 4.8 cm

16.

Number of Students by Gender

School	Boys	Girls
Washington	1,500	4,000
Lincoln	1,200	3,500
Kennedy	1,020	3,456
Martin Luther King, Jr.	1,357	4,000
Roosevelt	429	1,200

The table above shows the number of boys and girls in five different high schools. For which of the five schools is the ratio of girls to boys the greatest?

W: 15:40 → 3:8
L: 12:35
K: 510:1728 → 255:864
85:288

E. Lincoln
F. Kennedy
G. Washington
H. Martin Luther King, Jr.   R: 143:400

17. If $\frac{m}{8} = \frac{2m}{z}$, and $z \neq 0$, what is the value of *z*?

A. 16
B. 8
C. 4
D. 0.25

$\frac{mz}{m} = \frac{16m}{m}$ z = 16

18. Ingrid usually runs 12 miles in 2 hours. If she only has 40 minutes to run today, how many miles can she run going at the same rate?

E. 2.4 miles
F. 3 miles
G. 4 miles
H. $6\frac{2}{3}$ miles

12mi : 120mins
1mi : 10mins
4mi : 40mins

19. If $\frac{3}{4} = \frac{5}{x}$, what is the value of x?

A. $\frac{3}{20}$

B. $3\frac{3}{4}$

C. 6

D. $6\frac{2}{3}$

(handwritten: $\frac{3x}{3} = \frac{20}{3}$ $x = \frac{20}{3}$ $x = 6\frac{2}{3}$*)*

20. Brandon is 6 feet tall. At 4pm, his shadow is 20 feet long, as shown in the diagram.

6 ft

20 ft

At the same time, the shadow of a flagpole is 120 feet long. What is the height of the flagpole?

E. 20 feet

F. 36 feet

G. 134 feet

H. 400 feet

(handwritten: 6:20 36:120*)*

21. Triangle *LMN* (not shown) is similar to triangle *PQR* (not shown). The length of $\overline{LM}$ is 8 cm, and the length of $\overline{PQ}$ is 4 cm. If the length of $\overline{MN}$ is 6 cm, what is the length of $\overline{QR}$?

A. 2 cm

B. 3 cm

C. $5\frac{1}{3}$ cm

D. 12 cm

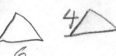

22. Two hoses can fill a bucket in 5 hours. How long will it take 5 of the same hoses to fill the bucket?

E. 2 hours

F. 5 hours

G. 8 hours

H. 12.5 hours

(handwritten: 2.5 22.5 *5 12.5*)*

23. At an arcade game, for every 16 points June scores, she earns 3 tickets that she can redeem for prizes. If June earned 48 tickets, how many points did she score?

A. 61

B. 144

C. 240

D. 256

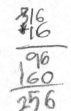

(handwritten: 16:3 :48 ; 816 ×16 96 160 256 *)*

24.

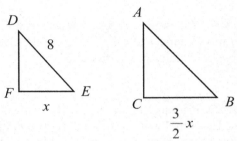

Triangle *ABC* is similar to Triangle *DEF*.

What is the length of side *AB*?

E. 6 units

F. 12 units

G. 16 units

H. 18 units

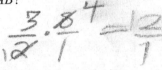

(handwritten: $\frac{3}{12} \cdot \frac{8}{1} = \frac{12}{1}$ *)*

25. A high-speed train can travel an average of 500 km in 2 hours. If it left its station at noon and traveled nonstop, how many kilometers had it traveled by midnight?

A. 1,500 km

B. 3,000 km

C. 6,000 km

D. 12,000 km

(handwritten: *500 6 3000 *)*

26. A farmer has 4 cows that can eat all the grass in a field in 10 days. If the farmer buys 1 more cow, how many days would it take the cows to eat all the grass in that same field? *(Assume that all cows eat the same amount at the same rate.)*

E. 8

F. 10

G. 12

H. 12.5

The Tutorverse

Grid-In Questions (Open-Ended Questions)

27. 1 rint = 0.2 drins
1 rint = 0.5 vungs

Mila has 500 drins and 200 vungs. If she exchanges the drins and vungs for rints according to the rates above, how many rints will she receive?

28. In a vase, the ratio of roses to daisies is 3:4, and the ratio of daisies to tulips is 5:6. If there are 48 tulips, how many roses are there?

29. Matthew is taking a math test with 80 questions on it. He completed the first 60 questions in 75 minutes. At this rate, how much additional time, in minutes, will it take him to complete the remaining questions?

30.

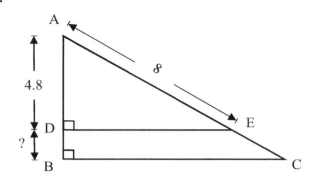

In the figure above, AE is 8 inches, and AD is 4.8 inches. If AC is 10 inches, what is the length of DB, in inches?

Factors, Multiples, Exponents & Radicals

1. What is the least common multiple of 450 and 675?

A. 225
B. 1,125
C. 1,350
D. 303,750

2. What is the least common multiple of 135 and 180?

E. 45
F. 270
G. 360
H. 540

3. What is the greatest common factor of 450 and 675?

A. 25
B. 225
C. 450
D. 1,350

4. What is the greatest prime factor of 48?

E. 2
F. 3
G. 7
H. 24

5. How many integers greater than 30 and less than 40 are each the product of two distinct prime factors?

A. 1
B. 3
C. 4
D. 5

6. If x is the greatest prime factor of 39 and y is the greatest prime factor of 20, what is the value of $x + y$?

E. 5
F. 18
G. 23
H. 59

The Tutorverse

7. A = 2 × 3 × 3 × 5
B = 2 × 2 × 3 × 3

What is the least common multiple of A and B?

A. 2 × 3 × 3
B. 2 × 3 × 5
C. 2 × 2 × 3 × 3 × 5
D. 2 × 2 × 2 × 3 × 3 × 3 × 3 × 5

8. A certain bell rings every 60 minutes. Another bell rings every 90 minutes. Both bells begin ringing at midnight (12:00 A.M.). How many more times will both bells ring by 1 PM?

E. 4
F. 5
G. 8
H. 12

9. If $3^x = 27$, then $x =$

A. $\dfrac{1}{9}$
B. 3
C. 9
D. 24

10. If $2^x = 32$, what is x?

E. 4
F. 5
G. 16
H. 64

11. If $2^x \times 5^y = 80$, what is $x - y$?

A. 2
B. 3
C. 8
D. 10

12. If $3^x \times 5^y = 225$, what is xy?

E. 4
F. 9
G. 15
H. 25

13. If $2^x \times 3^y \times 5^z = 900$, what is $x + y + z$?

A. 6
B. 8
C. 11
D. 30

14. If x and y are different positive integers and $5^x \times 5^y = 125$, what is the value of xy?

E. 2
F. 3
G. 6
H. 9

15. If a, b, and c are different positive integers and $2^a \times 2^b \times 2^c = 64$, then $abc =$

A. 3
B. 6
C. 8
D. 12

16. Which of the following represents 25^4 in terms of 5?

E. 5^6
F. 5^8
G. 5^{10}
H. 5^{20}

17. If $x^a \times x^6 = x^{24}$ and $(y^4)^b = y^{20}$, what is the value of $a + b$?

A. 9
B. 10
C. 23
D. 34

18. What is the value of the expression $\dfrac{(5^3)(2^5)}{(5^2)(2^3)}$?

E. 10
F. 20
G. 25
H. 10^{10}

19. $\dfrac{100^5}{50^5} =$

A. 2
B. 32
C. 40,000,000
D. 312,500,000

20. $\dfrac{7^4 \times 2^2}{28^3} =$

    E. $\dfrac{1}{112}$

    F. $\dfrac{7}{16}$

    G. $\dfrac{4}{3}$

    H. $\dfrac{7}{4}$

21. What is the value of $\sqrt{100 - 36}$?

    A. 8
    B. 10
    C. 12
    D. 16

22. $\sqrt{\dfrac{100}{25}} =$

    E. $\dfrac{1}{4}$

    F. $\dfrac{10}{25}$
    G. 2
    H. 4

23. What is the value of $\sqrt{\dfrac{144}{81}}$?

    A. $\dfrac{\sqrt{12}}{9}$

    B. $\dfrac{\sqrt{16}}{9}$

    C. $\dfrac{3}{4}$

    D. $\dfrac{4}{3}$

24. If $\sqrt{5} = x + 3$, what is the value of $(x + 3)^2$?

    E. 5
    F. 6
    G. 7
    H. 8

25. If $7 + \sqrt{x} = 16$, then which of the following could equal x?

    A. 9
    B. 32
    C. 49
    D. 81

Grid-In Questions (Open-Ended Questions)

26. What is the greatest prime factor of 64?

27. Edina and Patsy are in different math classes. Edina's math tests always have exactly 30 questions on them, while Patsy's math tests always have exactly 24 questions on them. By the end of the year, Edina and Patsy have had the same total number of questions on all their math tests. What is the minimum number of questions they each could have gotten during the year?

28. If $\sqrt{x - 40} = 9$, and $x > 0$, what is the value of x?

29. If $2^x \times 5^y \times 7^z = 1{,}400$, what is $x + y + z$?

30. If $x^2 \times y^3 = 500$, what is $x - y$?

The Tutorverse

Absolute Value

1. $|(-5) - 1 + (-3)| + |2 - 7| =$

   A. −12
   B. 12
   C. 14
   D. 18

2. What is the value of $5|x - y|$ if $x = 3$ and $y = 9$?

   E. −30
   F. 11
   G. 30
   H. 60

3. What is the value of $|x - y| - |x + y|$ if $x = -5$ and $y = -15$?

   A. −10
   B. 0
   C. 10
   D. 30

4. What is the value of $|-9| + |9| - |9| \times |-\frac{1}{9}|$?

   E. 3
   F. 1
   G. 17
   H. 19

5. $|240 - 420| - |24 - 42| + a = 200$

   In the equation above, what is the value of a?

   A. 2
   B. 38
   C. 162
   D. 394

6. $|180 - 225| + p^2 - |-3 \times 12| = 90$.

   What is the value of p?

   E. 6
   F. 9
   G. 18
   H. 21

7. Let K $= -(-|-3| - |6| - |-9|)$.

   What is the value of $-|-K|$?

   A. −18
   B. −6
   C. 6
   D. 18

8. $|x - 5| = 7$
   $|y + 9| = 21$

   In the equations above, $x < 0$ and $y < 0$. What is the value of $x + y$?

   E. −32
   F. − 8
   G. 10
   H. 24

Grid-In Questions (Open-Ended Questions)

9. What is the value of $-|a - b| - |b + a|$ if $a = -10$ and $b = -20$?

10. Let J $= -|-5| - |5| + |-5| \times \left|\frac{1}{5}\right|$.

    What is the value of $-|-J|$?

11. $|m - 8| = 12$
    $|n + 4| = 11$

    In the equations above, $m < 0$ and $n > 0$. What is the value of mn?

12. What is the smallest integer value that satisfies the inequality $|v - 7| < 17$?

The Tutorverse

Scientific Notation

1. Express 51,000 in scientific notation.

    A. 5.1×10^4
    B. 5.1×10^3
    C. 0.51×10^4
    D. 51.0×10^4

2. What is the value of 0.513 in scientific notation?

    E. 5.13×10^{-3}
    F. 5.13×10^{-1}
    G. 51.3×10^{-1}
    H. 513×10^{-1}

3. What is the value of 0.0002088 in scientific notation?

    A. 2.088×10^{-4}
    B. 2.088×10^{-3}
    C. 2.88×10^{-4}
    D. 2.88×10^{-3}

4. Express $513,700 \times 1,000$ in scientific notation.

    513,700,000

    E. 5.137×10^3
    F. 5.137×10^5
    G. 5.137×10^8
    H. $5.137 \times 10^5 + 10^3$

5. Express $952.65 \times 1,000$ in scientific notation.

    952650

    A. 9.5265×10^2
    B. 9.5265×10^3
    C. 9.5265×10^5
    D. 95.265×10^5

6. Write 5×10^{-3} in standard form.

    E. 0.00005
    F. 0.0005
    G. 0.005
    H. 0.05

7. Write 3.695×10^{-7} in standard form.

    A. 0.00000003695
    B. 0.0000003695
    C. 0.000003695
    D. 0.0003695

8. The distance between two cities is 4×10^3 kilometers. What is the distance between the two cities, in meters?

    E. 4,000
    F. 40,000
    G. 400,000
    H. 4,000,000

9. On a blueprint, 1 meter is represented by 1 millimeter. If the building has a length of 370 m, what is the length on the blueprint, in meters?

    .370

    A. 3.7×10^{-1} m
    B. 3.7×10^1 m
    C. 3.7×10^2 m
    D. 3.7×10^4 m

10. The distance from Earth to the moon is approximately 2.4×10^5 miles, and the distance from Earth to Mars is approximately 6.0×10^7. How many times farther is Mars than the moon from Earth?

    E. 2.5×10^1
    F. 2.5×10^2
    G. 2.5×10^3
    H. 2.5×10^4

11. What is the value of the numerical expression $(5 \times 10^3)(3 \times 10^5)$ in scientific notation?

    A. 15×10^{15}
    B. 1.5×10^{15}
    C. 1.5×10^9
    D. 15×10^8

12. What is the value of the numerical expression $(5 \times 10^4)(6 \times 10^4)$ in scientific notation?

    $30 * 10^8$
    $3.0 * 10^9$

    E. 3.0×10^9
    F. 3.0×10^8
    G. 30×10^9
    H. 30×10^8

13. What is the value of the numerical expression $(3 \times 10^3)(2 \times 10^2)$ in scientific notation?

   A. 6.0×10^5
   B. 6.0×10^6
   C. 5.0×10^5
   D. 5.0×10^6

Grid-In Questions (Open-Ended Questions)

14. What is the value of 7.56×10^3 in standard form?

15. What is the value of 6.8×10^{-1} in standard form?

16. What is the value of the expression $(1.2 \times 10^{-3})(6 \times 10^5)$ in standard form?

17. What is the value of the expression $\dfrac{3 \times 10^5}{6 \times 10^2}$ in standard form?

18. The distance from Ben's house to school is 4.6×10^3 meters, and the distance from Ben's house to the library is 6.4×10^2 meters. How much farther is Ben's house from school than the library?

Counting Principle

1. Alex, Bea, Cindy, and Dave are cleaning a storage room. If they take turns working in teams of 2, how many different teams can they make?

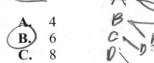

   A. 4
   B. 6
   C. 8
   D. 12

2. Tonya has 6 cards lying on a table with the numbers 1, 1, 1, 2, 2, and 3 written on them. How many different two-digit numbers can be made by placing a pair of cards side by side?

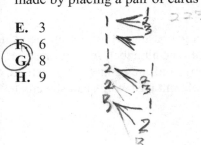

   E. 3
   F. 6
   G. 8
   H. 9

3. Sam is baking a three-layer cake. She has three choices for each layer — red, yellow, and blue — and each layer must be a different color. How many different ways are there to layer the cake?

   A. 3
   B. 6
   C. 9
   D. 27

4. A teacher is lining up 5 students in a row for a class photo. The shortest student will stand in the middle, the next 2 taller on his left, and the 2 tallest on his right. In how many different ways can the 5 students be lined up?

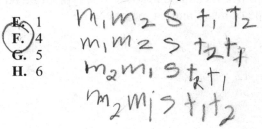

   E. 1
   F. 4
   G. 5
   H. 6

5. Ashton's wardrobe consists of 10 different shirts and 4 different pairs of pants. How many different outfits consisting of one shirt and one pair of pants can he make from his wardrobe?

   A. 14
   B. 20
   C. 40
   D. 60

   $p^1 \to 10$
   $p^2 \to 70$
   $p^3 \to 10$
   $p^4 \to 10$

6. The menu at a fast-casual restaurant offers 9 different soups and 6 different salads. How many different soup-and-a-salad combinations are possible from this menu?

   E. 9
   F. 15
   G. 30
   H. 54

7. Chet must create a code for his locker. It must be 3 characters long. For each character, he may choose from all ten digits (0-9), and he may repeat digits. How many different codes can he create?

   A. 30
   B. 720
   C. 729
   D. 1,000

   10^3
   if not C

8. Deepak is choosing a password for his phone using letters from the alphabet, A-Z. The password must be four letters long, and he can repeat letters. How many different passwords can he create?

   E. 4^{26}
   F. 26^4
   G. 26×4
   H. $26 \times 25 \times 24 \times 23$

   if not E

9. A deli offers 3 kinds of bread, 4 kinds of deli meat, and 3 types of cheese. How many different sandwiches can be made from 1 type of bread, 1 type of meat, and 1 type of cheese?

   A. 3
   B. 10
   C. 12
   D. 36

   B_1 — 4 deli → 3 cheese
   B_2 — 4 meat → 3 cheese
   B_3 — 4 meat → 3 cheese

10. A multiple-choice quiz has only 3 questions, each one with answer choices A, B, C, and D. Assuming a student answers every question, in how many ways could he fill in the answers?

    E. 12
    F. 24
    G. 64
    H. 256

    $4 \cdot 4 \cdot 4$
    $16 \cdot 4$

11. Ephram is ordering a custom license plate. It must be 6 characters long. For each of the first three characters, he may choose any letter A through Z, and for each of the last three characters, he may choose any digit 0 through 9. How many different license plates can Ephram choose from?

    A. $26^3 \times 10^3$
    B. $26^3 + 10^3$
    C. $26 \times 3 \times 10 \times 3$
    D. $26^3 \times 26^3 \times 26^3 \times 10^3 \times 10^3 \times 10^3$

12. Lewis must create a code for his locker. It must be 3 characters long. For each character, he may choose from all ten digits (0-9), and he may NOT repeat digits. How many different codes can he create?

    E. 27
    F. 30
    G. 720
    H. 1,000

    $10 * 9 * 8$

13. Five swimmers (Al, Bob, Chet, Dave, and Ed) are competing for the gold, silver, and bronze medals. In how many different ways can they place?

    A. 15
    B. 60
    C. 120
    D. 125

    $5 \cdot 4 \cdot 3$
    $20 \cdot 3$

14. Gail is choosing a password for her phone using any letters from the alphabet, A-Z. It must be four letters long, and she cannot repeat letters. How many different passwords can she create?

    E. 26^4
    F. 26×4
    G. $26 + 25 + 24 + 23$
    H. $26 \times 25 \times 24 \times 23$

15. Qurashi is ordering a custom license plate. It must be 6 characters long. For each of the first three characters he may choose any letter A through Z and for each of the last three characters he may choose any digit 0 through 9, but no letter or digit can be repeated. How many different license plates can Qurashi choose from?

A. $26^3 \times 10^3$
B. $26 \times 3 \times 10 \times 3$
C. $26 + 25 + 24 + 10 + 9 + 8$
D. $26 \times 25 \times 24 \times 10 \times 9 \times 8$

16. Partha has 7 different books. She is going to arrange three of them on the shelf above her desk. In how many different ways can she arrange three books?

E. 21
F. 210
G. 343
H. 441

Grid-In Questions (Open-Ended Questions)

17. A deli offers 3 kinds of bread, 5 kinds of meat, and 3 kinds of condiments. If a sandwich is made from one type of bread, one type of meat and one condiment, how many different sandwiches are possible?

18. In a math competition, the first place winner receives $100, the second place winner receives $50, and the third place winner receives $25. If ten people compete, in how many ways can the first, second and third place finishers be decided?

19. Simone has 3 shirts (red, yellow and blue), 3 skirts (red, yellow and blue), and 3 belts (red, yellow and blue). How many different outfits can she create, if she doesn't want all three items to be the same color?

20. A social studies class imagines that the United States creates a 51st state and needs a two-letter state abbreviation (like CA for California). The class can use any letter in the alphabet (A-Z), and they can repeat letters, but they cannot use an abbreviation that is already being used by one of the 50 existing states. How many different abbreviations can the class create?

Imaginary Operations

For questions 1-3, use the following operation:

$\square b = 6b - 12$

1. What is the value of $\square 4$?

A. −24
B. 12
C. 24
D. 52

2. What is the value of $\square 7 - \square 3$?

E. 4
F. 12
G. 24
H. 30

3. What is the value of b if $\square b = 42$?

A. 5
B. 9
C. 180
D. 240

The Tutorverse

For questions 4–6, use the following operation:

$^\wedge x^\wedge = x^2 + 6x + 9$

4. What is the value of $^\wedge 2^\wedge$?

    E. 1
    F. 13
    G. 25
    H. 75

5. What is the value of $^\wedge(-3)^\wedge$?

    A. 0
    B. 18
    C. 24
    D. 26

6. For which of the following values of x does $^\wedge x^\wedge = 64$?

    E. 4
    F. 5
    G. 8
    H. 11

For questions 7–9, use the following operation:

$x@y = 2x - 3y$

7. What is the value of $5@3$?

    A. −8
    B. 1
    C. 9
    D. 21

8. What is the value of $x@7$?

    E. $21 - 3x$
    F. $14 - 3x$
    G. $2x - 21$
    H. $2x - 14$

9. What is the value of $7@y$?

    A. −7
    B. $14 - 3y$
    C. $14 - y$
    D. $21 - 3y$

For questions 10–12, use the following operation:

$c\#d = c^2 + cd + 16$

10. What is the value of $4\#d$?

    E. $4d$
    F. $4d + 32$
    G. $d + 8$
    H. $d^2 + 16$

11. What is the value of $2\#3$?

    A. 17
    B. 20
    C. 24
    D. 26

12. What is the value of $10\#4 - 4\#10$?

    E. −116
    F. 0
    G. 84
    H. 116

For questions 13–15, use the following operation:

$p\sim = \dfrac{1}{p} + p^2$

13. What is the value of $(-5)\sim$?

    A. $-25\frac{1}{5}$
    B. $-24\frac{4}{5}$
    C. $24\frac{4}{5}$
    D. $25\frac{1}{5}$

14. What is the value of p if $p\sim = 0$?

    E. −1
    F. $-\frac{1}{2}$
    G. 0
    H. $\frac{1}{2}$

15. Which value of p would NOT result in an integer?

    A. −1
    B. 0
    C. 1
    D. All real number values of p will result in an integer.

For questions 16–18, use the following operation:

$$\left(\!x\!\right) = \frac{x}{4} + x^2$$

16. What is the value of $\left(\!-2\!\right)$?

    E. −4.5
    F. −3.5
    G. 3.5
    H. 4.5

17. What is the value of $\left(\!1\!\right)$?

    A. $\dfrac{1}{4}$
    B. $\dfrac{1}{2}$
    C. $\dfrac{3}{4}$
    D. $\dfrac{5}{4}$

18. What is the value of x if $\left(\!x\!\right) = 17$?

    E. −6
    F. −4
    G. 4
    H. 6

Grid-In Questions (Open-Ended Questions)

19. If $^\wedge p^\wedge = p^2 - 10p + 24$, what is the value of $^\wedge(-2)^\wedge$?

20. $\underline{/x\backslash} = 9x - 7$

    What is the value of x if $\underline{/x\backslash} = 110$?

21. If $m@ = m + \dfrac{10}{4}$, what is the value of $10@ - 2@$?

22. If $x\,\blacksquare\,y = \dfrac{x}{y} - xy$, what is the value of $4\,\blacksquare\,5$?

23. $//ab\backslash\backslash = 5a + 3b$

    If $b = 6$, for what value of a would $//ab\backslash\backslash = 63$?

Algebra

Algebraic Expressions & Equations

1. If $\dfrac{a}{b} = 4$ and $b = 3$, what is the value of $a^2 - 5b$?

    A. 1
    B. 9
    C. 91
    D. 129

2. For what value of x is $x - \dfrac{1}{5}x = 8$?

    E. 5
    F. 8
    G. 10
    H. 40

The Tutorverse

3. What is the value of x in the equation:
$4x - (5 - 3x) = 16$?

A. $\dfrac{11}{7}$

B. 3

C. 11

D. 21

$4x - 5 + 3x$
$7x - 5 = 16$
$+5 \quad +5$
$7x = 21$

4. If $(3 - x) - (x - 3) = x$, then which of the following is equivalent to x?

E. 2

F. 0

G. 2

H. 6

$(3-2)-2+3$
$1+2+3$
$-1+3$
2

5. $10 - (-3y - 8) = 4y - (2 - 9y)$

Which of the following statements will make the above equation true?

$\dfrac{20 = 10y}{10 \quad 10}$

$2 = y$

A. $y = -\dfrac{1}{2}$

B. $y = 0$

C. $y = \dfrac{1}{2}$

D. $y = 2$

$10 + 3y + 8 = 4y - 2 + 9y$
$18 + 3y = 13y - 2$
$-3y \quad -3y$
$18 = 10y - 2$
$+2$

6. If $x = 6$, which of the following is the greatest in value?

E. $(x + 1)(x + 3)$ $\quad 7 \cdot 9 = 63$

F. $(x + 1)(x - 1)$ $\quad 7 \cdot 5 = 35$

G. $(x + 3)(x - 3)$ $\quad 9 \cdot 3 = 27$

H. $(x - 3)(x + 1)$ $\quad 3 \cdot 7 = 21$

7. If $2x + 3y = y$, which of the following must be equivalent to $12x + 12y$?

A. 0

B. 6

C. $9y$

D. $24y$

$12x + 12(2x + 3y)$
$12x + 24x + 36y$
$36x + 36y$?

8. If $a = 5$, which of the following is equal to $ax^2 + ax + a$?

E. $5(x^3 + 1)$

F. $5(x + 1)^2$

G. $5(x^2 + x + 1)$

H. $5(5x^2 + x + 1)$

$5x^2 + 5x + 5$
$5(x^2 + x + 1)$

9. If $(x - 5)^2 = 36$ and $x < 0$, what is the value of x?

A. -31

B. -6

C. -1

D. 11

10. If $x = y - 9$ and $23x - 12x = 11$, what is the value of y?

E. 2

F. 8

G. 10

H. 20

$23(y - 9) - 12(y - 9) = 11$
$23y - 207 - 12y + 108 = 11$
$11y - 99 = 11$
$\quad +99 \quad +99$
$11y = 110$

11. If $9x + 7 = 11$, what is the value of $9x - 3$?

A. $\dfrac{5}{9}$

B. 1

C. 8

D. 4

$9x + 7 = 11$
$\quad -7 \quad -7$
$\dfrac{9x}{9} = \dfrac{4}{9}$
$9\left(\dfrac{4}{9}\right) - 3$
$\dfrac{36}{9} - 3$
$4 - 3$

12. $\dfrac{5 + @}{2} = 5\dfrac{1}{2}$

What number, when used in place of the @ above, makes the statement true?

E. $\dfrac{1}{2}$

F. 1

G. 6

H. 11

$\dfrac{11}{2} = 5\dfrac{1}{2}$

13. If 8 more than twice a number is 14, what is 8 times the number?

A. 3

B. 16

C. 24

D. 112

14. If $\dfrac{2}{3}$ of a number is 32, what is $\dfrac{3}{4}$ of the number?

E. 8

F. 12

G. 24

H. 36

$32 = \dfrac{2}{3}x$

$*3 \quad *3$

$\dfrac{96}{2} = \dfrac{2x}{2}$

$48 = x$

$\dfrac{48 \cdot 3}{1 \quad 4} = \dfrac{144}{4}$

36

The Tutorverse

15. If $\dfrac{3}{5}$ of a is 30, what is $\dfrac{4}{5}$ of a?

A. 14.4
B. 18
C. 24
D. 40

(handwritten work: $\dfrac{3}{5}a = 30$ $a = 50$ $*5$ $*5$ $\dfrac{4}{5} \cdot \dfrac{50}{1} = \dfrac{200}{5}$ $3a = 150$ 40)

16. When the number c is multiplied by 5, the result is the same as when 5 is added to c. What is the value of $4c$?

E. $\dfrac{4}{5}$
F. 0
G. 4
H. 5

(handwritten work: $5c = c + 5$ $-c \quad -c$ $4c = 5$)

17. If $y = \dfrac{1}{2}$, what is the value of $\dfrac{1}{y} + \dfrac{1}{(y-1)}$?

A. -4
B. 0
C. 1
D. 2

18. If $a - b = 10$, $b = 4c$, and $c = 3$, what is the value of a?

E. 2
F. 12
G. 22
H. 24

19. If $mn = 10$, what is the value of $2 \times \dfrac{m}{n} \times n^2$?

A. 8
B. 10
C. 12
D. 20

20. What is the value of x in the equation $\dfrac{0.16}{0.40} = \dfrac{2.5}{x}$?

E. 0.84
F. 1.16
G. 6.25
H. 6.41

21. "The sum of x and the square root of y is equal to the square root of the sum of x and y."

Which of the following is an expression for the statement above?

A. $x + \sqrt{y} = \sqrt{x + y}$
B. $\sqrt{x + y} = \sqrt{x + y}$
C. $x + \sqrt{y} = \sqrt{x + y}^2$
D. $x + \sqrt{y} = (x + y)^2$

22. 7, 15, 23, 31, 39,…
The first five terms of a sequence are shown above. Each term after the first is found by adding 8 to the term immediately preceding it. Which term in this sequence is equal to $8(25) - 1$?

E. The 8th term
F. The 24th term
G. The 25th term
H. The 26th term

23. If $3{,}838 = 38(x + 1)$, then $x =$

A. 10
B. 11
C. 100
D. 101

24.

Position	Value
1	0
2	3
3	6
4	9
5	12
1,000	?

Certain values in a list of multiples of 3 are shown in the table above. What will the 1,000th number in the list be?

E. 2,991
F. 2,994
G. 2,997
H. 3,000

The Tutorverse

25. If $x(a + b) = 28$ and $ax = 7$, what is the value of bx?

    A. 4
    B. 14
    C. 21
    D. 35

26. The sum of three consecutive even integers is 84. If s represents the least of the three integers, which of the following equations represents the statement above?

$$\left(\frac{s+y}{2}\right)3 = 84$$

    E. $3s = 84$
    F. $3s + 3 = 84$
    G. $3s + 4 = 84$
    H. $3s + 6 = 84$

27. If $\dfrac{x}{x-4} = \dfrac{43}{39}$, then $x =$

    A. 37
    B. 39
    C. 41
    D. 43

28. If $73{,}000 = 1{,}000(7p + 3)$, then $p =$

    E. $\dfrac{1}{10}$
    F. 1
    G. 10
    H. 100

$$73000 = 7000p + 3000$$
$$-3000 \qquad -3000$$
$$\frac{70000}{7000} = \frac{7000p}{7000}$$
$$10 = p$$

29. If $5a + b = a + 5$, what is b in terms of a?

    A. $6a + 5$
    B. $4a + 5$
    C. $5 - 4a$
    D. $5 - 6a$

30. Which of the following equations represents the statement "the product of x and $\dfrac{2}{5}$ is equal to the sum of $5x$ and 2"?

    E. $\dfrac{2}{5}x + 2 = 5x$
    F. $x + \dfrac{2}{5} = 2(5x)$
    G. $\dfrac{2}{5}x = 5(x + 2)$
    H. $\dfrac{2}{5}x = 5x + 2$

$$\frac{2}{5}x = 5x + 2$$

Grid-In Questions (Open-Ended Questions)

31. If $\dfrac{x}{y^2} = 5$ and $y = 3$, what is the value of $\dfrac{x}{3 + 2y}$?

$$\frac{x}{9} = \frac{5}{1} \qquad x = 45$$
$$\frac{45}{9} = \boxed{5}$$

32. If $ab = 12$, what is the value of $4a \times 3b$?

33. When 12 less than twice x is doubled, the result is the same as when x is subtracted from 10. What is the value of $5x$?

34. $\dfrac{3}{8} = \dfrac{x + 10}{x + 30}$

What is the value of x in the equation above?

$$\frac{3}{8} = \frac{x + 10}{x + 30}$$
$$3x + 90 = 8x + 80$$
$$-80 \qquad\qquad -80$$
$$3x + 10 = 8x + 10$$

The Tutorverse

Algebra in Context

1. Yannis and Malcolm have a total of 60 books. If Yannis has 8 more books than Malcolm, how many books does Yannis have?

   A. 22
   B. 26
   C. 34
   D. 38

2. Michael is 3 more than twice Leon's age. If Michael is 35 years old, how old is Leon?

   E. 7
   F. 12
   G. 16
   H. 19

3. A machine can weld 10 times as many car bumpers as a human can in any given amount of time. In one day, a machine and a human can weld a combined 550 car bumpers. How many did the machine weld?

   A. 450
   B. 495
   C. 500
   D. 540

4. Sue read 12 more than twice as many pages as Tom did last week. If Sue read 90 pages, how many pages did Tom read?

   E. 33
   F. 39
   G. 168
   H. 192

5. In right triangle ABC, angle C is a right angle, and angle B is 18 less than twice angle A. How many degrees is angle B?

   A. 27
   B. 36
   C. 54
   D. 63

6. If the degree measures of a triangle are in the ratio 1:2:3, what is the degree measure of the largest angle?

   E. 30
   F. 36
   G. 90
   H. 108

7. If the degree measures of a triangle are in the ratio 3:4:5, what is the degree measure of the smallest angle?

   A. 15
   B. 36
   C. 45
   D. 75

8. Shonda is currently one-third of Ronan's age. 10 years from now, she will be one-half of Ronan's age. How old is Ronan now?

   E. 6
   F. 10
   G. 16
   H. 30

9. A sneaker factory's old machine makes 60 sneakers per minute. Its new machine makes 90 sneakers per minute. If both machines begin running at the same time, how many minutes will it take the two machines to make a total of 5,400 sneakers?

   A. 36
   B. 60
   C. 75
   D. 90

10. At a car wash, Sherman is paid $4 for each car he washes, plus a flat rate of $60 per week. Which of the following expressions represents the total dollar amount Sherman receives for a week in which he has washed c cars?

    E. $(60 + 4)c$
    F. $60c + 4$
    G. $60 + 4c$
    H. $(60 + c)4$

11. A biology student is growing fruit flies in a lab for an experiment. The population, P, of the fruit flies t days after the experiment began is modeled by the function $p(t) = 5{,}000 \times 2^{\left(\frac{t}{3}\right)}$. By how many fruit flies does the population grow from $t = 3$ to $t = 9$?

A. 10,000
B. 30,000
C. 40,000
D. 50,000

12. A telephone call between two countries costs 30 cents for the first minute and 12 cents for each additional minute or portion thereof. Which of the following equations represents the cost, C, in dollars, of a phone call between these two countries that lasts for m minutes, if m is a positive integer?

E. $C = 0.42m$
F. $C = 0.30 + 0.12m$
G. $C = 0.30 + 0.12(m - 1)$
H. $C = 0.30m + 0.12(m - 1)$

Grid-In Questions (Open-Ended Questions)

13. The width of a door is w feet. The length of the door is 4 feet longer than the width. If the length of the door is 10 feet, what is w?

14. In one minute, Luke can do 3 times as many pushups as his brother. If they can do a total of 60 pushups, how many can Luke do?

15. Pam's age is 10 less than twice Ed's age. If the sum of their ages is 32, what is Pam's age?

16. An isosceles triangle has a perimeter of 46 inches. The base is 6 less than twice each of the congruent legs. What is the sum of the lengths of the two congruent legs?

17. If the degree measures of a quadrilateral are in the ratio 1:2:4:5, what is the degree measure of the largest angle?

18. James has 8 more dimes than nickels. If the total value of all his coins is $2.15, how many dimes does he have?

19. If $24 - 3x$ is 8 more than $5x$, what is the value of $3x$?

20. TubeMusic costs $8.75 per month plus $0.75 per downloaded song. In one month, Harrison's total TubeMusic expense was $17. How many songs did Harrison download?

21. When 7 times the number y is added to 21, the result is 14. What is the result when 3 times y is added to 3?

22. One pound of cherries normally costs $8. Exactly how many pounds of cherries can someone buy with $48 if cherries go on sale for 25% off?

23. In January, Caleb worked 13 hours more than Rai. If they worked a combined total of 73 hours, how many hours did Rai work in January?

Plugins

1. $x, 3x, 9x, 27x$

If $x < 0$, which of the four values above is the greatest?

A. x
B. $3x$
C. $9x$
D. $27x$

2. If m represents an odd integer, which of the following expressions represents an even integer?

E. $m + 2$
F. $2m - 1$
G. $3m - 2$
H. $5m + 1$

The Tutorverse

3. If $a = \dfrac{b}{5}$ and $b \neq 0$, what does $4b$ equal in terms of a?

   A. $\dfrac{4a}{5}$

   B. $20a$

   C. $\dfrac{a}{20}$

   D. $\dfrac{a}{4}$

4. If A, B, and C are digits in the positive three-digit integer ABC, what is the decimal equivalent of $ABC \times 10^{-3}$?

   E. 0.00ABC
   F. 0.ABC
   G. A,BC0
   H. ABC,000

5. If $a + b < a$, which of the following must be true?

   A. $a < 0$
   B. $a = 0$
   C. $b > 0$
   D. $b < 0$

6. If $ab = c$, $c = kb$, and $bc \neq 0$, which of the following is equal to k?

   E. $\dfrac{1}{a}$

   F. $a - 1$

   G. a

   H. $a + 1$

7. Mr. Thompson has been teaching math for 8 years less than twice as long as Mrs. Simmons. If Mrs. Simmons has been teaching math for x years, which of the following expressions represents the number of years that Mr. Thompson has been teaching math?

   A. $x - 8$
   B. $2x - 8$
   C. $2x + 8$
   D. $8 - 2x$

8. If a represents an even integer, which of the following represents the next even integer greater than a?

   E. $a + 1$
   F. $a + 2$
   G. $a + 3$
   H. $2a - 1$

9. If $a > b$, how much greater is the sum of c and a than the sum of c and b?

   A. $c - a$
   B. $2c - b$
   C. $a - b$
   D. $a + b$

10. If x and y are odd integers, which of the following must also be odd?

    E. $x - 1$
    F. $(x - 1)y$
    G. $(x + 1)y$
    H. $(x + 1) + y$

11. A phone company's international calling plan costs \$1.30 per day of usage, plus an additional charge of \$0.13 per minute of talk time. Which of the following represents the total charge, in dollars, of having this international phone plan and talking x minutes in one day?

    A. $1.43x$
    B. $1.30 + 13x$
    C. $1.30 + 0.13x$
    D. $1.30 + 0.13 + x$

12. If $q - \dfrac{1}{4}p = 0$, what is p when $q = 1$?

    E. -4
    F. -1
    G. 1
    H. 4

The Tutorverse

13.

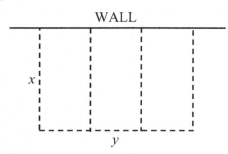

In a classroom, a dance teacher places colored tape on the floor to mark off three rectangular areas where students should sit, as shown in the diagram above. Three of the outer edges of the area will be marked by tape, with the fourth side bound by the classroom wall. The overall dimensions of the marked off area are x and y and the total area of the marked off area is 600 square feet. What is the total length of tape that is needed to mark the three outer edges of the area as well as divide it into three sections?

A. $x + \dfrac{600}{x}$

B. $3x + \dfrac{2,400}{3x}$

C. $4x + \dfrac{1,800}{3x}$

D. $4x + \dfrac{2,400}{3x}$

14. During a sale, a customer can buy one book for b dollars. Each additional book costs d dollars less than the first book. For example, the cost of the second book is $b - d$ dollars. Which of the following represents the total cost, in dollars, of 5 books during the sale?

E. $2b - 5d$
F. $2b - d$
G. $5b - 5d$
H. $5b - 4d$

15. If $2a = 5b$ and $5b = 6c$, what does a equal in terms of c?

A. $\dfrac{6}{5}c$

B. $3c$

C. $15c$

D. $30c$

16. A movie ticket costs m dollars. During a sale, if a customer buys one ticket for m dollars, each additional ticket he buys costs n dollars less than the first ticket. For example, the cost of the second ticket is $m - n$ dollars. Which of the following represents the total cost, in dollars, of x tickets during the sale?

E. $m + (x - 1)(m - n)$
F. $m + x(m - n)$

G. $m + \dfrac{(m - n)}{x}$

H. $(m - n) + \dfrac{(m - n)}{x}$

17. There are 25% more girls than boys enrolled at Hilcrest High. If there are b boys enrolled, then, in terms of b, what percent of those enrolled are boys?

A. $\dfrac{b}{b + 25}$ %

B. $\dfrac{b}{2.25b}$ %

C. $\dfrac{100b}{b + 25}$ %

D. $\dfrac{100b}{2.25b}$ %

18. A total of g eggs were transported to the market. Each of the c crates that were used to transport the eggs could hold a maximum of m eggs. If one crate had 5 empty slots and the remaining crates were all filled, which of the following expresses the relationship among, g, c, and m?

E. $cm - 5 = g$
F. $cm + 5 = g$
G. $cg = m + 5$
H. $cg = m - 5$

19. If x and y are positive consecutive odd integers, where $x > y$, which of the following is equal to $x^2 - y^2$?

A. $4y$
B. $2y + 2$
C. $2y + 4$
D. $4y + 4$

20. If the average of a and b is z, which of the following is the average of a, b, and c?

E. $2z + \dfrac{c}{3}$

F. $2z + \dfrac{c}{2}$

G. $z + \dfrac{c}{2}$

H. $\dfrac{2z + c}{3}$

21. If $m + 5 = z$, then $2m + 10 =$

A. $z + 5$
B. $2z$
C. $2z + 5$
D. $2z + 10$

22. How old was Kim 1 year ago if m years ago she was n years old?

E. $n - m - 1$
F. $m - n - 1$
G. $n + m + 1$
H. $n + m - 1$

23. After the first term, each term in a sequence is 2 greater than $\dfrac{1}{2}$ of the preceding term. If x is the first term of the sequence and $x \neq 0$, what is the ratio of the second term to the first term?

A. $\dfrac{x + 4}{2}$

B. $\dfrac{x + 2}{2}$

C. $\dfrac{x + 4}{2x}$

D. $\dfrac{x + 2}{2x}$

24. If $(m + 2)^2 - n = 0$, and $n = 9$, what is the value of m?

E. 1
F. 3
G. 16
H. 79

25. The sum of two numbers that differ by 1 is x. In terms of x, what is the value of the greater of the two numbers?

A. $\dfrac{x - 1}{2}$

B. $\dfrac{x + 1}{2}$

C. $\dfrac{x}{2} + 1$

D. $\dfrac{2x - 1}{2}$

26. The price of tea leaves is x dollars for 10 ounces and each ounce makes y cups of brewed tea. In terms of x and y, what is the dollar cost of the tea leaves required to make 1 cup of brewed tea?

E. $\dfrac{x}{10y}$

F. $\dfrac{xy}{10}$

G. $\dfrac{10y}{x}$

H. $\dfrac{10x}{y}$

27. One end of a spring is attached to a hook on the ceiling. A basket of apples is attached to the other end of the spring, stretching it to a length of 27 inches. The length in inches, l, that the spring is stretched is given by the equation $l = 12 + 2.5m$. What is m?

A. 6.0
B. 12.5
C. 15.6
D. 36.5

The Tutorverse

28. A class trip costs a total of d dollars, which is supposed to be divided equally amongst the s students in a class. If n students decide not to go on the trip and do not chip in for the expense of the trip, which of the following represents the <u>additional</u> amount, in dollars, that each of the remaining students must contribute to pay for the trip?

E. $\dfrac{d}{s-n}$

F. $\dfrac{dn}{s-n}$

G. $\dfrac{d(s-n)}{s}$

H. $\dfrac{dn}{s(s-n)}$

Inequalities

1. $2x + 4 < 30$
What is the solution to the inequality shown above?

    A. $x < 13$
    B. $x > 11$
    C. $x < 19$
    D. $x > 17$

2. $6 - 2x < 28$
What is the solution to the inequality shown above?

    E. $x < 17$
    F. $x > -17$
    G. $x < 11$
    H. $x > -11$

3. $9 > 8 + 7x$
What is the solution to the inequality shown above?

    A. $x < \dfrac{1}{4}$

    B. $x < \dfrac{1}{7}$

    C. $x > \dfrac{1}{7}$

    D. $x > \dfrac{17}{7}$

4. $11 > 8 - 5x$
What is the solution to the inequality shown above?

    E. $x < -\dfrac{3}{5}$

    F. $x > -\dfrac{3}{5}$

    G. $x < \dfrac{19}{5}$

    H. $x > \dfrac{19}{5}$

5. If $10 - 3z > 20$, which of the following is a possible value of z?

    A. -4
    B. -3
    C. 1
    D. 3

6. If $4m + 8 < 20$

Which of the following CANNOT be the value of m?

    E. -1
    F. 1
    G. 2
    H. 3

The Tutorverse

7. $-2(x-6) < 18$

What is the solution to the inequality shown above?

A. $x < -3$
B. $x < -15$
C. $x > 15$
D. $x > -3$

8. $3x + 16 > 5x - 28$

What is the solution to the inequality shown above?

E. $x < 6$
F. $x > 6$
G. $x < 22$
H. $x > 22$

9. $-(7x + 8) \leq 9$

What is the solution to the inequality shown above?

A. $x \leq -\dfrac{17}{7}$

B. $x \geq -\dfrac{17}{7}$

C. $x \leq -\dfrac{1}{7}$

D. $x \geq -\dfrac{1}{7}$

10. $-12x - 46 \geq 21x + 64$

What is the solution to the inequality shown above?

E. $x \geq \dfrac{6}{11}$

F. $x \leq \dfrac{6}{11}$

G. $x \leq -\dfrac{10}{3}$

H. $x \leq \dfrac{110}{9}$

11. At the entrance to a roller coaster is a sign that reads:

"All riders must be at least 54 inches tall."

If r represents the height of a rider in inches, which of the following represents the statement on the sign?

A. $r < 54$
B. $r > 54$
C. $r \geq 54$
D. $54 > r$

12. All of the students in a class measured their heights, h, in inches. The shortest student was 44 inches tall and the tallest student was 72 inches tall. Which of the following inequalities represents the range of all the heights in the class?

E. $44 < h < 72$
F. $44 \leq h \leq 72$
G. $44 \leq h > 72$
H. $44 \geq h \geq 72$

13. Which of the following represents "twelve is greater than five less than twice a number x"?

A. $12 > 5 - 2x$
B. $12 > 2x - 5$
C. $12 > 2 - 5x$
D. $12 < 5 - 2x$

14. Which of the following indicates that x is less than or equal to twice the value of y and that y is less than zero?

E. $x \leq 2y < 0$
F. $x \leq \dfrac{1}{2}y > 0$
G. $x < 2y \leq 0$
H. $x \geq \dfrac{1}{2}y < 0$

15. Which graph represents the solution set for $x \geq 4$?

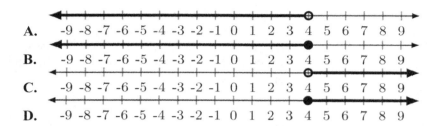

A. -9 -8 -7 -6 -5 -4 -3 -2 -1 0 1 2 3 4 5 6 7 8 9

B. -9 -8 -7 -6 -5 -4 -3 -2 -1 0 1 2 3 4 5 6 7 8 9

C. -9 -8 -7 -6 -5 -4 -3 -2 -1 0 1 2 3 4 5 6 7 8 9

D. -9 -8 -7 -6 -5 -4 -3 -2 -1 0 1 2 3 4 5 6 7 8 9

16. Which graph represents the solution set for $a < -6$?

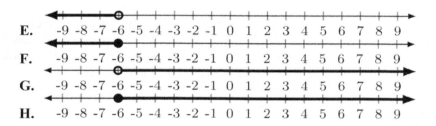

E. -9 -8 -7 -6 -5 -4 -3 -2 -1 0 1 2 3 4 5 6 7 8 9

F. -9 -8 -7 -6 -5 -4 -3 -2 -1 0 1 2 3 4 5 6 7 8 9

G. -9 -8 -7 -6 -5 -4 -3 -2 -1 0 1 2 3 4 5 6 7 8 9

H. -9 -8 -7 -6 -5 -4 -3 -2 -1 0 1 2 3 4 5 6 7 8 9

17. What is the solution set for $3x + 3 \geq 6$?

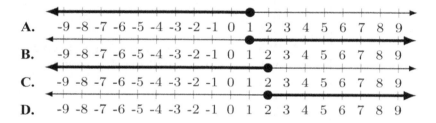

A. -9 -8 -7 -6 -5 -4 -3 -2 -1 0 1 2 3 4 5 6 7 8 9

B. -9 -8 -7 -6 -5 -4 -3 -2 -1 0 1 2 3 4 5 6 7 8 9

C. -9 -8 -7 -6 -5 -4 -3 -2 -1 0 1 2 3 4 5 6 7 8 9

D. -9 -8 -7 -6 -5 -4 -3 -2 -1 0 1 2 3 4 5 6 7 8 9

18. What is the solution set for $-3a + 5 \geq -7$?

E. -6 -5 -4 -3 -2 -1 0 1 2 3 4 5 6

F. -6 -5 -4 -3 -2 -1 0 1 2 3 4 5 6

G. -6 -5 -4 -3 -2 -1 0 1 2 3 4 5 6

H. -6 -5 -4 -3 -2 -1 0 1 2 3 4 5 6

19. What is the solution set for $-9 \leq 3h + 3 \leq 6$?

A. -9 -8 -7 -6 -5 -4 -3 -2 -1 0 1 2 3 4 5 6 7 8 9

B. -9 -8 -7 -6 -5 -4 -3 -2 -1 0 1 2 3 4 5 6 7 8 9

C. -9 -8 -7 -6 -5 -4 -3 -2 -1 0 1 2 3 4 5 6 7 8 9

D. -9 -8 -7 -6 -5 -4 -3 -2 -1 0 1 2 3 4 5 6 7 8 9

The Tutorverse

Grid-In Questions (Open-Ended Questions)

20. The range of temperatures on a particular day could be described as $|x - 68| \leq 9$. How many integer values are included in this range?

21. $|x + 4| < 8$
$|x - 5| < 3$
What integer value of x that satisfies both inequalities shown above?

22. What is an integer value that satisfies the inequality $15 < -2x + 9 < 19$?

23. If $x = 6$, what is the least integer value of y that satisfies the inequality $5x - 4y < 3$?

24. The cost, in dollars, of producing x books is $500 + 4x$. The books sell for 10 dollars each. What number of books would need to be sold so that the revenue received is greater than the cost of producing them?

Probability & Statistics

Probability

1. A bowl contains 3 red marbles, 4 white marbles, and 5 blue marbles. If one marble is chosen at random, what is the probability that it will be white?

A. $\dfrac{1}{12}$

B. $\dfrac{1}{4}$

C. $\dfrac{1}{3}$

D. $\dfrac{2}{3}$

2. A plastic cylinder contains 12 dice. 5 of them are red, 4 of them are white, and the rest are blue. If one die is drawn at random from the cylinder, what is the probability that the die will be blue?

E. $\dfrac{1}{12}$

F. $\dfrac{1}{4}$

G. $\dfrac{1}{3}$

H. $\dfrac{3}{4}$

3. An office worker is allowed to take three 10-minute coffee breaks over the course a normal work day, which lasts from 9 a.m. to 5 p.m, at randomly chosen times. If someone tries to call this office worker at a random time during the work day, what is the probability that the worker will be on a coffee break?

A. $\dfrac{1}{16}$

B. $\dfrac{1}{8}$

C. $\dfrac{1}{4}$

D. $\dfrac{3}{8}$

4. A television station airs 8 minutes of commercials during each half hour. If someone turns the television on to that station, what is the probability that a commercial will be airing at that moment?

E. $\dfrac{2}{15}$

F. $\dfrac{4}{11}$

G. $\dfrac{4}{15}$

H. $\dfrac{1}{3}$

The Tutorverse

5. A car company created a 90-second commercial and purchased enough air time for it to be played at 4 random times during prime-time hours of 8 p.m. to 11 p.m. If a viewer turns their television on at a random time during prime-time hours, what is the probability that the car commercial will be playing at that time?

A. $\dfrac{1}{120}$

B. $\dfrac{1}{30}$

C. $\dfrac{1}{45}$

D. $\dfrac{1}{2}$

6. A lollipop is chosen at random from a bucket of lollipops. The probability that the lollipop chosen will be grape-flavored is $\dfrac{3}{4}$. Which of the following could NOT be the number of lollipops in the bucket?

E. 16
F. 28
G. 49
H. 144

7.

6	3
5	2
4	1

The figure above shows a diagram of six classrooms. The classrooms labelled 4, 5, and 6 each have an area twice that of the classrooms labelled 1, 2, and 3. If a student is blindfolded and told to randomly point at one of the classrooms on the diagram, what is the probability that she will point at classroom 4?

A. $\dfrac{1}{9}$

B. $\dfrac{1}{6}$

C. $\dfrac{2}{9}$

D. $\dfrac{2}{3}$

8. A bowl contains orange and green candies. The probability of randomly selecting an orange candy is $\dfrac{1}{4}$, and the probability of randomly selecting a green candy is $\dfrac{1}{6}$. Which of the following could be the total number of candies in the bowl?

E. 10
F. 12
G. 18
H. 30

9. A bowl contains a apples and b bananas and no other fruit. If a piece of fruit is picked at random from this bowl, the probability that an apple is picked is $\dfrac{3}{7}$. What is the value of $\dfrac{a}{b}$?

A. $\dfrac{3}{10}$

B. $\dfrac{3}{7}$

C. $\dfrac{4}{3}$

D. $\dfrac{3}{4}$

10. When an animated film is shown on network television, it requires a 90-minute block of time. Of that block of time, the movie itself is 63 minutes, credits take an additional 7 minutes, and commercials take 20 minutes. At a randomly chosen time, what is the probability that a commercial will <u>not</u> be airing?

E. $\dfrac{5}{7}$

F. $\dfrac{2}{9}$

G. $\dfrac{2}{7}$

H. $\dfrac{7}{9}$

11. At a state fair, a game involves throwing a ring onto one of 60 bottles. If it is equally likely that the bottle will land on any of the bottles, and 36 of these bottles are green, what is the probability that a ring will <u>not</u> land on a green bottle?

    A. $\dfrac{1}{36}$

    B. $\dfrac{2}{5}$

    C. $\dfrac{3}{5}$

    D. $\dfrac{5}{6}$

12. Leo's pencil case contains 8 black pens, 6 blue pens, and 2 red pens. He loses 4 pens, 2 of which are blue. If he then picks one pen out of the pencil case at random, what is the probability that it will be blue?

    E. $\dfrac{1}{3}$

    F. $\dfrac{1}{4}$

    G. $\dfrac{1}{6}$

    H. $\dfrac{1}{8}$

13. In a bucket of 20 apples, 12 were green and the rest were red. 2 green apples are removed from the bucket. If one more apple is removed from the bucket, what is the probability that it is a red apple?

    A. $\dfrac{2}{5}$

    B. $\dfrac{4}{9}$

    C. $\dfrac{5}{9}$

    D. $\dfrac{3}{5}$

14. From a bookshelf containing 12 fiction and 15 non-fiction books, 5 books are removed, 1 of which is non-fiction. If one more book is removed, what is the probability that it will be fiction?

    E. $\dfrac{1}{22}$

    F. $\dfrac{1}{11}$

    G. $\dfrac{4}{11}$

    H. $\dfrac{1}{2}$

15. A box initially contained 30 chess pawns, all either black or white. The probability of drawing a white pawn was $\dfrac{2}{5}$. Some more white pawns were added to the box so that the probability of picking out a white pawn was raised to $\dfrac{1}{2}$. How many white pawns were added to the box?

    A. 2
    B. 3
    C. 6
    D. 18

16. A box contains 24 pieces of fruit: 7 cherry, 8 orange, and 9 lemon. If no cherries are sold, what is the minimum number of lemons that can be sold in order to increase the probability of picking out a cherry to 50%?

    E. 0
    F. 1
    G. 2
    H. 3

17. In a crate of 20 orange and yellow peppers, the probability of picking out a yellow pepper is $\dfrac{3}{4}$.

    If 2 peppers are picked from this bucket, without replacement, what is the probability that they are both orange?

    A. 1/19
    B. 1/16
    C. 3/16
    D. 9/16

The Tutorverse

Grid-In Questions (Open-Ended Questions)

18. A bowl contains a total of 60 Bartlett, Bosc, and Anjou pears. The probability of randomly picking out a Bartlett pear is $\frac{2}{5}$, and the probability of picking out a Bosc pear is $\frac{7}{12}$. If all the Bosc pears are removed, what is the probability of randomly picking an Anjou pear?

19. A store sells only apple, orange, and grape juice in its refrigerated case. The case contains 48 bottles of juice, $\frac{1}{3}$ of which are apple. If there are 3 times as many bottles of orange juice as grape juice, what is the probability of reaching into the case and randomly picking out a bottle of orange juice?

20. A box of chocolates contains only milk, dark, and white chocolates. The probability of picking out a milk chocolate is $\frac{3}{8}$. If there are 24 dark chocolates and 6 white chocolates, how many milk chocolates are there?

21. Shonda is picking a movie to watch from her streaming queue of 18 dramas and 10 comedies. She decides she's not interested in some of the movies anymore, so she removes 8 of them, 2 of which are dramas. If she picks a movie at random from the remaining list, what is the probability that she will pick a comedy?

22. Harold's phone contains 36 apps, $\frac{4}{9}$ of which are games. He downloads more games (and no other apps) so that $\frac{2}{3}$ of the apps on his phone are now games. How many games did he download?

23. A container holds several different types of equally-sized cookies. The probability of picking an oatmeal cookie out of the container is $\frac{1}{5}$. The probability of picking an oatmeal cookie out of a container, putting it back into the container, and then picking a chocolate chip cookie out of a container, is 3/20. What is the probability of picking a chocolate chip cookie out of the container?

Averages

The following three questions refer to the chart below:

BIRDS SPOTTED PER DAY

Number of Birds	Number of Days During Which That Number of Birds Was Spotted
1	3
2	3
3	5
4	8
5	11

The frequency chart above shows the number of birds observed by a bird watcher over several days.

1. What is the mean number of birds spotted during all the days tracked?

   A. 3.0
   B. 3.7
   C. 4.4
   D. 6.0

2. What was the median number of birds spotted during all the days tracked?

   E. 2
   F. 3
   G. 4
   H. 5

The Tutorverse

3. What was the range of the number of birds spotted during all the days tracked?

A. 4
B. 6
C. 8
D. 10

The following three questions refer to the line plot below:

QUIZ SCORES FOR 20 STUDENTS

```
                        x
                        x
                        x                   x
         x      x       x       x       x
         x      x       x       x       x
  x      x      x       x       x       x
◄──┼──────┼──────┼──────┼──────┼──────┼──────┼──►
   4      5      6      7      8      9      10
```

4. According to the line plot above, what was the median score for the test?

E. 6
F. 7
G. 8
H. 9

5. According to the line plot above, what was the mode score for the test?

A. 7.5
B. 7.9
C. 8.0
D. 10.0

6. According to the line plot above, what was the mean score for the test?

E. 7.0
F. 7.5
G. 7.9
H. 8.0

7. If the mean of x, $4x$, and $5x$ is 90, what is the value of the largest of the three numbers?

A. 27
B. 45
C. 108
D. 135

8.

MATH QUIZ SCORES

Score	Number of Students
10	1
9	2
8	3
7	4
6	5
5	3
4	1
3	1
2	0
1	0

20 students took a math quiz yesterday. The results are shown in the table above. If one more student takes the quiz tomorrow and scores an 8, what will be the median quiz score?

E. 8.0
F. 7.5
G. 7.0
H. 6.5

9. 2, 3, 4, 8, 9, 13, 15, 17
The number a is to be added to the list above. If a is an integer, which of the following could be the median of the new list of 9 numbers?

A. 8.5
B. 9
C. 10
D. 11

10. If the mean of 6, x, and y is 10, what is the value of $x + y$?

E. 18
F. 24
G. 30
H. 36

11. Jack, Chrissy, and Janet own a total of 345 books. If Chrissy owns 135 of them, what is the mean number of books owned by Jack and Janet?

A. 70
B. 105
C. 115
D. 210

The Tutorverse

12. When the mean of a series of values is multiplied by the number of values in the series, the result is

    E. half the mean of the values in the series.
    F. the difference of the values in the series.
    G. the median of the values in the series.
    H. the sum of the values in the series.

13. Brenda was trying to calculate the mean of her four test scores. She forgot what she had scored on each of the first 3 tests but knew that the sum of those three scores was 252. If Brenda's scored a 96 on her fourth test, then what was the mean of all 4 scores?

    A. 63
    B. 84
    C. 87
    D. 174

14. Ellen will take 6 tests this semester. If she wants to end her semester with a mean test grade of 95, what must the sum of all her tests be?

    E. 101
    F. 190
    G. 550
    H. 570

15. After three tests, Brandon had a mean test grade of 90. After his fourth test, his mean dropped to an 85. What did he score on his fourth test?

    A. 70.0
    B. 80.0
    C. 82.0
    D. 87.5

16. A set of 8 numbers has a mean of 20. What additional number must be included in this set to create a new set with a mean that is 4 less than the mean of the original set?

    E. −16
    F. −11
    G. 11
    H. 16

17.

NUMBER OF PETS PER STUDENT IN A CLASS

Number of Pets	Number of Students
0	3
1	6
2	2
3	1

The table above shows how many students in a class of 12 students had 0, 1, 2, or 3 pets. Later, a new student joined the class, and the mean number of pets per student became equal to the median number of pets per student. How many pets did the new student have?

    A. 0
    B. 1
    C. 2
    D. 3

18. Daniel scored at least one point during each of 5 games. If the mean number of points he scored is 10, what is the greatest possible number of points he could have scored in one game?

    E. 10
    F. 40
    G. 46
    H. 50

19. The average of three consecutive integers is −54. What is 45 less than the least of these integers?

    A. −53
    B. −98
    C. −100
    D. 9

20. A class has 6 girls and 4 boys. On the last math test, the girls scored a mean of 92 and the boys scored a mean of 82. What was the mean of all 10 students?

    E. 87
    F. 88
    G. 89
    H. 90

The Tutorverse

21. The set M consists of all multiples of 5 greater than 10 and less than 35. What is the median of the numbers in M?

A. 12.5
B. 20.0
C. 22.5
D. 25.0

22. Trang spent 8 days studying for a science test. On each of the last three days, she studied 1 hour more than the mean number of hours she studied per day during the first 5 days. If she studied 27 hours in all, how many hours in total did she study during the last 3 days?

E. 3
F. 4
G. 9
H. 12

23. X is a set of three numbers whose mean is 5. Y is a set that is created by tripling each number in X. What is the sum of the numbers in set Y?

A. 5
B. 9
C. 15
D. 45

24. Markus took 5 tests and has an average test score of 86. If Markus' goal is to raise his average test score to 87, and there is only one more test in the semester, what score does he need to receive on the last test in order to reach his goal?

E. 87
F. 88
G. 92
H. 100

Grid-In Questions (Open-Ended Questions)

The following three questions refer to the chart below:

ITEMS PURCHASED

Number of Items	Number of Customers Who Bought That Many Items
5	3
4	5
3	8
2	9
1	12
0	13

25. How much larger is the range of the data than the mode of the data?

26. If one more customer comes in and buys 4 items, what will be the median number of items bought by all the customers who came in that day?

27. What is the mean number of items bought by all the customers who came in that day?

Geometry & Measurements

Area & Perimeter

1. A rectangle has a perimeter of 28 feet. If the length is 4 feet, what is the area?

A. 22 sq. ft.
B. 28 sq. ft.
C. 40 sq. ft.
D. 96 sq. ft.

2. A square has an area of 25 square inches. What is its perimeter?

E. 5 in.
F. 10 in.
G. 20 in.
H. 25 in.

The Tutorverse

3. A triangle has an area of 24 square centimeters. If the base is 6 centimeters long, then the height is

    A. 5 cm
    B. 6 cm
    C. 8 cm
    D. 12 cm

4.

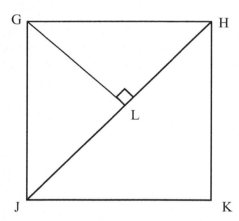

The area of the square above is 72 square centimeters. GL is half the length of HJ, which divides the square exactly in half. What is the length of GL?

    E. 6 cm
    F. 8 cm
    G. 18 cm
    H. 36 cm

5.

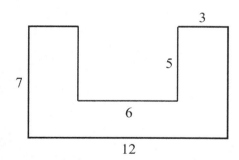

In the figure above, all angles appearing to be right angles are right angles. The area of the figure is

    A. 30 units^2
    B. 54 units^2
    C. 60 units^2
    D. 108 units^2

6.

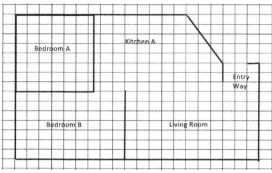

The floor plan above is drawn on a grid made of 1-inch squares. Each square represents 9 square feet. About how many square yards of carpet are needed to cover Bedroom A?

    E.   52 sq. yds.
    F.   156 sq. yds.
    G.   468 sq. yds.
    H. 1,404 sq. yds.

7. The length of a rectangular room is 9 less than twice its width, and the width is 18 feet. If square porcelain tiles 3 feet long are used to cover the floor, how many tiles are needed?

    A.   27
    B.   54
    C.   81
    D. 162

8.

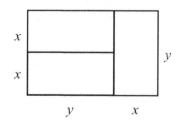

Tiles come prefabricated in rectangular sets of three, in the orientation shown above. These sets are used to tile a rectangular area measuring $8y$ by $9x$. How many sets are needed to tile this area?

    E. 12
    F. 24
    G. 36
    H. 48

9. The diagram below represents a kitchen that will be covered in square marble tiles, which are indicated by the dotted lines.

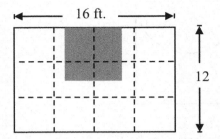

The shaded region represents a counter that will be placed in the kitchen. About how many square feet of marble will not be covered by the counter?

A. 64
B. 128
C. 160
D. 176

10. Two triangles share the same base, with length 5 mm. One triangle's height is twice the other's. The combined area of both triangles is 60 mm. What is the height of the larger triangle?

E. 4
F. 8
G. 16
H. 20

11.

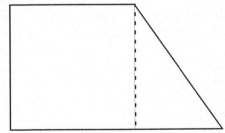

In the above figure, the square has an area of 16. The perimeter of the triangle is 12. What is the perimeter of the trapezoid outlined by the solid line?

A. 20
B. 24
C. 26
D. 28

12.

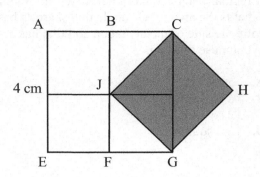

ACGE and JCHG are squares. BJF is a straight line segment that passes through point J, bisecting ACGE. What is the area of the shaded region?

E. 4 sq. cm
F. 8 sq. cm
G. 16 sq. cm
H. 24 sq. cm

13. A hexagon has 2 sides of length x inches each, 2 sides of length $3x$ inches each, one side of length $4x$ inches, and one side of length 6 inches. If the perimeter of the hexagon is 54 inches, what is the value of x?

A. 4
B. 4.5
C. 8
D. 9

14. A square (not shown) has the same perimeter as the regular hexagon shown below.

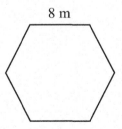

8 m

What is the area of the square?

E. 36 sq. m
F. 48 sq. m
G. 64 sq. m
H. 144 sq. m

15. A regular pentagon has a perimeter of 15 mm. What is the area of a triangle that shares a base with one side of the pentagon and that has a hypotenuse of 5 mm?

    A.   5 sq. mm
    B.   6 sq. mm
    C. 12 sq. mm
    D. 12.5 sq mm

16.

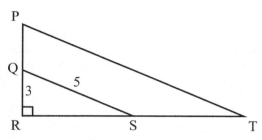

In the above figure, Q bisects $\overline{PR}$, and S bisects $\overline{RT}$. What is the perimeter of quadrilateral PQST?

    E. 21
    F. 22
    G. 23
    H. 24

17. A gallon of paint can cover 30 square feet. If a circular swimming pool has a radius of 10 feet, how many gallons of paint are needed to paint the entire floor of the pool?

    A.   7
    B.   8
    C. 10
    D. 11

18.

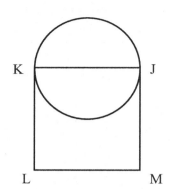

The figure shows square JKLM. The circle has endpoints at J and K. If the square has a perimeter of 16 cm, what is the circumference of the circle?

    E. 2π
    F. 4π
    G. 6π
    H. 8π

19. In the diagram below, A is the center of the circle, the area of which is 36π inches.

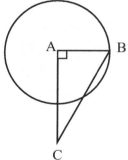

If point B is on the circle, and $\overline{AC} = 2\overline{AB}$, what is the area of triangle ABC?

    A. 12 in^2
    B. 18 in^2
    C. 36 in^2
    D. 72 in^2

20.

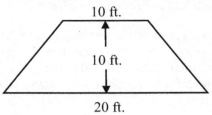

A circle is inscribed in a square, as shown above. If the area of the circle is 64π sq. cm., what is the area of the square?

E. 32 sq. cm
F. 64 sq. cm
G. 128 sq. cm
H. 256 sq. cm

21. A painter is calculating how much paint he will need to cover a cylindrical foam roller (including both ends of the roller). The roller is 10 inches long and has a diameter of 4 inches. What is the surface area of the foam roller?

A. 40π sq. in.
B. 48π sq. in.
C. 64π sq. in.
D. 96π sq. in.

22. What is the area of the trapezoid shown below?

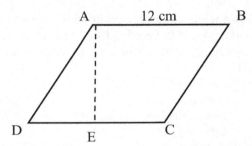

E. 75 sq. ft.
F. 100 sq. ft.
G. 150 sq. ft.
H. 300 sq. ft.

23.

If the area of triangle ADE is 24 cm^2, and E is the midpoint of DC, what is the area of parallelogram ABCD?

A. 48 cm^2
B. 96 cm^2
C. 120 cm^2
D. 144 cm^2

Grid-In Questions (Open-Ended Questions)

24. The perimeter of a rectangle is 22 in. If the length is one more than the width, what is the area of the rectangle, in square inches?

25. A regular pentagon has a side length of 8 inches. A square has the same perimeter as the pentagon. What is the area of the square?

26. A rectangle has an area of 24 square inches. If all four side lengths are integers, how many possible different perimeters could this rectangle have?

27. A circle is inscribed in a square. If the area of the circle is 36π sq. in, what is the perimeter of the square in inches?

28. A square is inscribed in a circle. If the area of the circle is 25π sq. mm, what is the area of the square?

29. Two circles share the same center. The larger circle has a radius twice that of the smaller circle. How many times bigger is the area of the larger circle?

30. A parallelogram has vertices at (4, 2), (10, 2), (8, 9), and (14, 9). What is the area of the parallelogram?

The Tutorverse

Volume

1. The floor of a rectangular swimming pool has an area of 350 sq. meters, and every point on the floor is of equal depth. If 4,200 cubic meters of water is poured into the pool, how deep will the water level be?

   A. 6 m
   B. 12 m
   C. 24 m
   D. 36 m

2. A rectangular swimming pool is 20 feet long and 40 feet wide, and every point on the floor is of equal depth. If the pool is filled to a depth of 6 inches, what is the volume of the water in the pool?

   E.   66 cubic feet
   F.   400 cubic feet
   G.   480 cubic feet
   H. 4,800 cubic feet

3. At a packaging and shipping warehouse, packages that await shipment are stored in a storage area measuring 16 feet long, 24 feet wide, and 4 feet high. All packages in this warehouse are cubical, measuring 2 feet on all sides. How many packages can be stored in the storage area?

   A.   96
   B.   192
   C.   768
   D. 1,536

4. On top of a cube that has a measure of 3 inches on one of its sides sits a pyramid. All sides are perfectly aligned such that the pyramid sits perfectly atop the cube. The pyramid is 1 inch high. What is the total volume of the combined figure?

   E. 30 in.^{3}
   F. 33 in.^{3}
   G. 36 in.^{3}
   H. 39 in.^{3}

5. What is the radius of a sphere with volume 36π cubic inches?

   A. 3 inches
   B. 4 inches
   C. 9 inches
   D. 27 inches

6. A perfect sphere with a volume of 288π cubic inches is flattened into a perfect circle. What is the circumference of the resulting circle?

   E. 6π in.
   F. 12π in.
   G. $24\ \pi$ in.
   H. 36π in.

7. Professional sandcastle-builders create a pyramid with a square base. The pyramid's volume is 128 cubic feet, and stands 6 feet high. What is the length of one side of the pyramid's base?

   A. 4.6 ft.
   B. 6 ft.
   C. 7 ft.
   D. 8 ft.

8. A pyramid has a triangular base. Its volume is 36 cubic inches. The base is an equilateral triangle with an area of 12 square inches. What is the height of the pyramid?

   E.   3 in.
   F.   6 in.
   G.   9 in.
   H. 12 in.

9. Fancy Cakes bakery has been asked to create a customized cake in the shape of a rectangular pyramid. The volume of the cake must contain 144 cubic inches of cake. The customer specified that the cake must be exactly 9 inches high. Which of the following could be the dimensions of the rectangular base of the cake?

   A. 4 in. by 4 in.
   B. 5 in. by 6 in.
   C. 6 in. by 7 in.
   D. 6 in. by 8 in.

The Tutorverse

10. The base of the rectangular prism shown below has an area of 24 in².

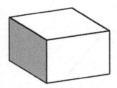

If the volume of the prism is 84 in³, what is the height of the prism?

E. 3.5 in.
F. 4.0 in.
G. 4.5 in.
H. 7.0 in.

11. What is the volume of the trapezoidal prism shown below, if it has a height of 5?

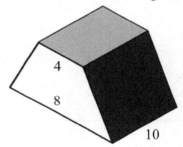

A.   280 cubic units
B.   300 cubic units
C.   320 cubic units
D.   1,600 cubic units

Grid-In Questions (Open-Ended Questions)

12. A rectangular prism sits atop a larger rectangular prism, as shown.

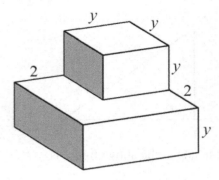

Which expression represents the total volume of both rectangular prisms?

E. $y^3 + 4y$
F. $y^3 + 4y^3$
G. $y^3 + y(y+2)(y+2)$
H. $y^3 + y(y^2+2)(y^2+2)$

13. A flat beachball has an area of 9π square inches. What is the amount of air the beachball can hold when inflated?

A. 3π in³
B. 6π in³
C. 12π in³
D. 36π in³

---

14. A box measures 24 inches long, 20 inches deep, and 16 inches high. How many cubes with side length of 2 inches can fit in the box?

15. The base of a cone is a circle with radius 4 mm. If the volume is 16π mm³, what is the height, in millimeters?

16. A cylindrical container has a radius of 2 inches and a volume of 48π cubic inches. If the container is $\dfrac{2}{3}$ filled with water, how many inches deep does the water fill the container?

17. An empty rectangular swimming pool is 12 ft long and 50 ft wide, and every point on the floor is of equal depth. The pool is filled at a rate of 20 ft³ per minute. After how many minutes will the water in the pool have a depth of 3 feet?

18. A square pyramid has a height of 6 meters and a volume of 32 meters³. What is the side length of its base?

19. A filled beachball has a volume of 36π cm³. How many times bigger is the volume than the circumference when flattened into a perfect circle?

The Tutorverse

Triangles

1.

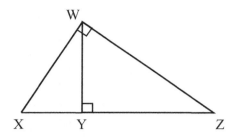

The longest side in the above figure is

A. WZ
B. XZ
C. YZ
D. WX

2.

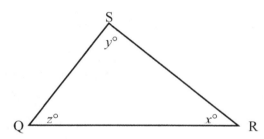

In terms of z, what is the value of $x + y$ in the figure above?

E. $2z$
F. $2(90 - z)$
G. $180 - z$
H. $360 - z$

3.

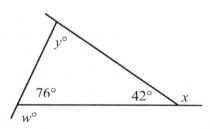

In the above figure, what is the value of $w° + x° + y°$?

A. $118°$
B. $180°$
C. $298°$
D. $304°$

4.

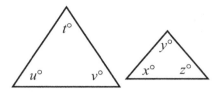

In the triangles above, which of the following must be true?

E. $u = x$
F. $t + u + v = 3z$
G. $3v = x + y + z$
H. $t + u + v = x + y + z$

5.

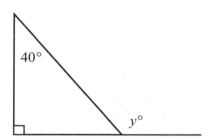

What is the value of y?

A. 40
B. 50
C. 130
D. 145

6.

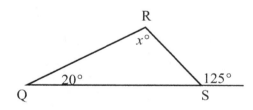

The value of x is

E. 35
F. 105
G. 115
H. 125

The Tutorverse

7.

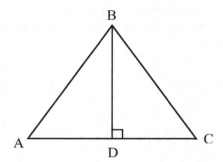

In the diagram above, D is the midpoint on side AC of equilateral triangle ABC. What is the measure of ∠DBC?

A. 15°
B. 30°
C. 45°
D. 60°

8.

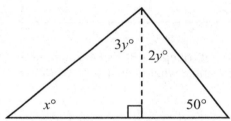

In the above figure, what is the value of x?

E. 20°
F. 30°
G. 40°
H. 60°

9.

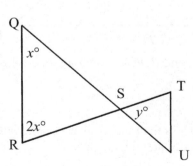

If $x = 35$ what is the value of y?

A. 70
B. 75
C. 105
D. 145

10.

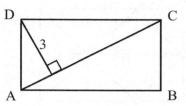

The area of the rectangle is 15 cm. The area of triangle ACD and triangle ABC are equal. What is the length of AC?

E. 1.5 cm
F. 5.0 cm
G. 7.5 cm
H. 15 cm

11.

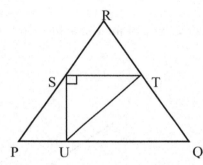

In the figure shown above, PQ = QR = PR. If the measure of ∠RST = 60°, and ST = SU, what must be the measure of ∠UTQ ?

A. 45°
B. 60°
C. 75°
D. 105°

12.

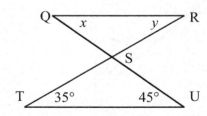

What is $x + y$ if QR and TU are parallel?

E. 45
F. 70
G. 80
H. 100

The Tutorverse

13.

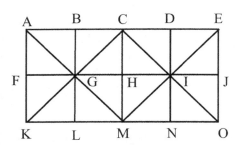

The figure to the left is made up of 16 small right triangles. How many triangles are congruent to triangle AKM? (Do not count AKM itself.)

A. 3
B. 7
C. 16
D. 19

Grid-In Questions (Open-Ended Questions)

14.

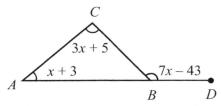

What is the measure of interior angle *ABC*, in degrees?

15.

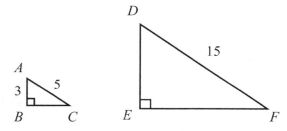

Triangles *ABC* and *DEF* are similar. How many units long is *EF*?

16.

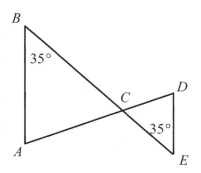

In the figure above, *AB* is parallel to *ED*. If angle *CDE* is 39°, and angle *CAB* is 8x + 7 degrees, what is the value of *x*?

17.

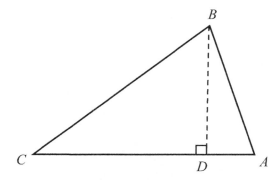

The area of triangle *ABC* is 84 square units. If *AC* = 14 units, what is the length of *BD*, in units?

18.

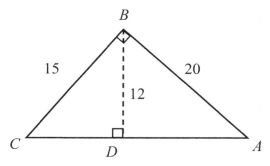

Angles *ABC* and *BDC* are right angles. What is the length of *AC*?

19. What is 180 less than the measure of one interior angle in an equilateral triangle?

20. In an isosceles triangle, the measure of the smallest angle is 28. What is the measure of one of the other angles?

The Tutorverse

Circles

1. If there are 120 degrees of arc in $\frac{1}{3}$ of a circle, how many more degrees of arc are there in $\frac{5}{6}$ of a circle?

   A. 120°
   B. 180°
   C. 240°
   D. 300°

2. What is the diameter of a circle that has an area of 4π?

   E. 2
   F. 4
   G. 2π
   H. 4π

3. A circle has a circumference of q square feet. If the radius of the circle is 4, what is the value of q?

   A. 2π
   B. 4π
   C. 8
   D. 8π

4. The radius of circle Q is 4 times the diameter of circle R. What is the ratio of the diameter of circle Q to the diameter of circle R?

   E. 16 : 1
   F. 8 : 1
   G. 4 : 1
   H. 2 : 1

5. The tire of a tractor is 4 feet in diameter. Approximately how many feet does the tire move in a single revolution?

   A. 4.0 ft.
   B. 8.0 ft.
   C. 12.5 ft.
   D. 16.0 ft.

6. The penny-farthing bicycle is a type of bicycle with one large front wheel and one small rear wheel. On a particular penny-farthing bicycle, the radius of the front wheel is three times larger than the radius of the rear wheel. For every one time the front wheel completes a revolution, how many times will the rear wheel complete a revolution?

   E. 9
   F. 3
   G. $\frac{1}{3}$
   H. $\frac{1}{9}$

7.

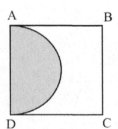

   In square ABCD above, arc AD represents a half circle. Each side of square ABCD has a length of 2. What is the area of the shaded region?

   A. π
   B. $\frac{\pi}{4}$
   C. $\frac{\pi}{2}$
   D. 2 + π

8. Circle A has a circumference of 8π. The radius of circle B is twice the radius of circle A. What is the area of circle B?

   E. 8π
   F. 32π
   G. 64π
   H. 256π

The Tutorverse

9.

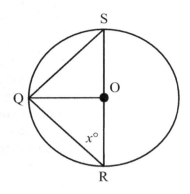

O is the center of the circle above. QS = QR. What is the value of *x*?

A. 30
B. 45
C. 60
D. 75

10.

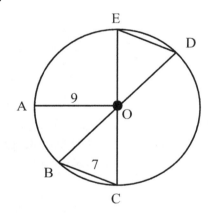

In the above figure, O is the center of the circle. Segments $\overline{EC}$ and $\overline{BD}$ are diameters of the circle, and $\overline{AO}$ represents the radius. Which of the following statements is true?

E. $\overline{EC}$ = 9
F. $\overline{ED}$ = 9
G. $2\,\overline{AO} = \overline{ED} + \overline{BC}$
H. $2\,\overline{AO} = \overline{EC} = \overline{BD}$

11.

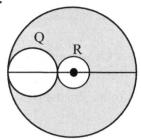

In the above figure, circle Q has a radius of 5, and circle R has a radius of 3. The center of circle R is also the center of the largest circle. Circle Q is tangent to circle R as well as the largest circle. What is the diameter of the largest circle?

A. 8
B. 13
C. 16
D. 26

12. Circle X has a radius of $\frac{1}{3}$ meter. Circle Y has a radius of 1 meter. What is the ratio of the area of circle X to the area of circle Y?

E. 1 : 9
F. 9 : 1
G. 1 : 3
H. 3 : 1

13.

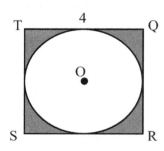

A circle with center O is inscribed inside of square QRST. What is the area of the shaded portion of the square?

A. $1 - \pi$
B. $4 - \pi$
C. $16 - 4\pi$
D. $16 - 16\pi$

The Tutorverse

Grid-In Questions (Open-Ended Questions)

14. To the nearest integer, what is the circumference of a circle that has an area of 16π?

15. Square ABCD has a side length of 4 units. A circle of radius 2 units is centered at point D. Rounded to the nearest hundredth, what is the area of the section of the circle that is inside the square?

16.

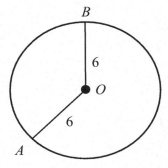

Arc *AB* has a measure of 4π units. What is the measure of angle *AOB*, in degrees?

17. Circle O (not shown) has an area of 81π square units. Circle P has a radius that is 2 units shorter than the radius of circle O. What is the diameter of circle P, in units?

18.

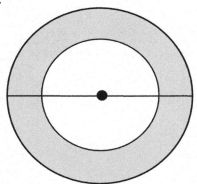

The outer circle and the inner are concentric, as shown in the figure above. The outer circle has a radius of 6 units. The area of the shaded region is 20π units squared. What is the radius of the inner circle, in units?

Angles

1. G is a point on line *l*. How many lines can be drawn through G that form a 90° angle with line *l*?

A. 0
B. 1
C. 2
D. The number varies.

2.

What is the degree measure of angle MNL?

E. 45°
F. 90°
G. 135°
H. 180°

3.

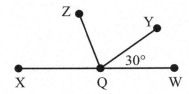

In the above figure, Q is on segment XW. ∠XQY is bisected by segment QZ. What is the measure of ∠ZQY ?

A. 30°
B. 45°
C. 60°
D. 75°

The Tutorverse

4.

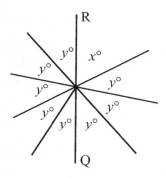

In the above figure, QR is a line. What is the value of x?

E. 36
F. 40
G. 45
H. 72

5.

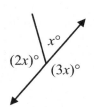

In the above figure, a line segment intersects with a line, forming three angles, as shown. What is the value of x?

A. 30°
B. 45°
C. 60°
D. 75°

6.

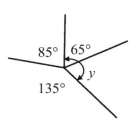

In the above figure, what is the degree measure of arc y?

E. 75°
F. 135°
G. 140°
H. 150°

7.

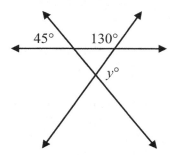

What is the value of y in the above figure?

A. 85°
B. 95°
C. 115°
D. 175°

8.

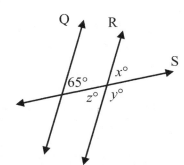

In the above figure, lines Q and R are parallel. What is the sum of $x + y + z$?

E. 195°
F. 245°
G. 295°
H. 345°

9.

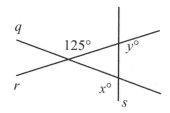

In the figure above, $x + y =$

A. 55
B. 110
C. 125
D. 235

The Tutorverse

10.

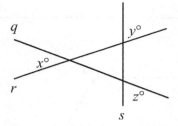

In the above figure, if $x = 40$, what is the value of $y + z$?

E. 40°
F. 80°
G. 120°
H. 140°

11.

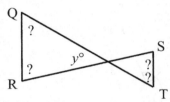

In the figure above, QT and RS are straight lines. In terms of y, what is the sum of the four angles indicated by question marks?

A. $180 - y$
B. $180 - 2y$
C. $360 - 2y$
D. $360 - 4y$

12.

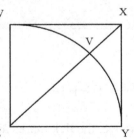

In the diagram above, WXYZ is a square. WVY is an arc of a circle centered at Z. XZ is a line segment that intersects the arc at point V. Find the measure of $\angle ZWV$ (not shown).

E. 45°
F. 60°
G. 67.5°
H. 84.5°

13.

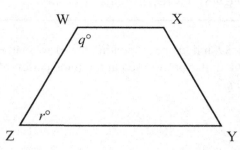

In isosceles trapezoid WXYZ shown above, sides WX and YZ are parallel. What is the value of $2(q° + r°)$?

A. 180°
B. 270°
C. 360°
D. 720°

14. What is the sum measurement of all interior angles in a regular octagon?

E. 720°
F. 900°
G. 1,080°
H. 1,440°

15. What is the measure of one angle in a regular pentagon?

A. 108°
B. 180°
C. 360°
D. 540°

16.

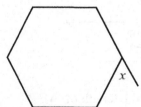

If the above figure is a regular hexagon, then $x =$

E. 45°
F. 60°
G. 72°
H. 120°

Grid-In Questions (Open-Ended Questions)

17. Lines *l* and *m* are perpendicular. How many right angles are formed at the intersection of *l* and *m*?

18. What is the average measure, in degrees, of each angle in a hexagon?

19.

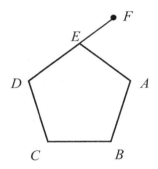

ABCDE is a regular pentagon. *DE* is extended outside the pentagon, as shown by *EF* in the figure above. What is the measure of angle *AEF*, in degrees?

20.

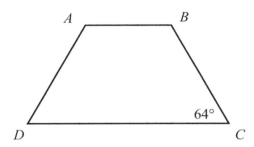

ABCD is an isosceles trapezoid. What is the sum of *ABCD*'s two largest angles, in degrees?

21.

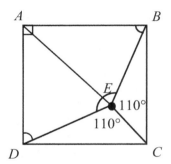

In square *ABCD*, one line from each vertex converges on point *E*. Angles *BEC* and *DEC* each have measures of 110°, as shown in the figure above. What is the sum of the degree measures of angles *ADE* and *ABE*?

Measurements

1.

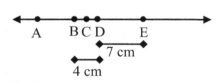

If $\overline{AB} = \overline{BD}$, what is the length of $\overline{AE}$?

A. 7 cm
B. 11 cm
C. 15 cm
D. 18 cm

2.

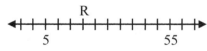

On the number line above, the tick marks are spaced apart equally. What is the value of R?

E. 8
F. 11
G. 20
H. 38

The Tutorverse

3.

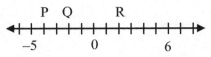

The letters P, Q, and R represent numbers as shown on the above number line. Which of the following expressions has the least value?

A. P + R
B. P – R
C. Q + R
D. Q – R

4.

$\overline{AB}$ is divided into 4 equal parts by points L, M, and N (not shown), and L < M < N. What position will point N fall on?

E. –2
F. –1
G. 3
H. 4

5.

Point C (not shown) is located between A and B such that $\overline{AC}$ is 3 times as long as $\overline{CB}$. What is the location of point C?

A. 8
B. 9
C. 11
D. 14

6.

What are the locations of points A and B?

E. A is located at 0.6; B is located at 1.4
F. A is located at 0.6; B is located at 1.2
G. A is located at 0.2; B is located at 1.4
H. A is located at 0.2; B is located at 1.2

7.

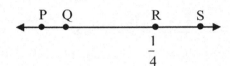

On the number line above, the length of $\overline{WZ}$ is 23, the length of $\overline{YZ}$ is 6, and the length of $\overline{WX}$ is 4. What is the position of point Y?

A. 13
B. 17
C. 19
D. 20

8.

On the number line below, the length of $\overline{PQ}$ is 2.5, the length of $\overline{PS}$ is 9.25, and the length of $\overline{RS}$ is 4.75. What is the position of point Q?

E. –2.25
F. –1.75
G. 2.75
H. 4.5

9.

In the above line segment, the midpoint of $\overline{AB}$ is C (not shown). Point A is located at 0. $\overline{AC}$ = 17. What is the value of $\overline{BC}$?

A. 4.25
B. 8.5
C. 17
D. 34

10. If Q is the midpoint of $\overline{RS}$, which of the following must be true?

E. 2RS = QS
F. 2QS = RS
G. $\frac{1}{2}$RQ = RS
H. $\frac{1}{2}$RS = 2RQ

11. On a number line, what is the midpoint of a line segment beginning at –4 and ending at $\frac{3}{4}$?

A. $2\frac{3}{8}$

B. $-1\frac{5}{8}$

C. $-2\frac{3}{8}$

D. $-3\frac{1}{4}$

12.

Point X (not shown) is the midpoint of $\overline{AB}$. If point M (not shown) is the midpoint of $\overline{XB}$, what is $\overline{XB}$ in terms of $\overline{AB}$?

E. $\frac{1}{4}\overline{AB}$

F. $\frac{1}{2}\overline{AB}$

G. $\frac{2}{3}\overline{AB}$

H. $\frac{3}{4}\overline{AB}$

13.

In the above figure, QS = 36 and 2QR = RS. Point T (not shown) is on the line between R and S such that RT = TS. What does QT equal?

A. 9

B. 12

C. 24

D. 27

14.

On the above number line, the length of $\overline{WZ}$ is 16. Point X is the midpoint of $\overline{WY}$, and is located at –1 on the number line. Which number below is the midpoint of $\overline{YZ}$?

E. 5

F. 6

G. 7

H. 8

15. A machine glazes donuts at the rate of one donut per second. How many hours will it take the machine to glaze 36,000 donuts?

A. 1

B. 10

C. 100

D. 1,000

16. Every day, to avoid traffic during her morning commute, Yunru takes the backroads from her home to her workplace. There is less traffic during the afternoon commute home from her workplace, so she always takes the highway instead of the backroads. Taking the backroads is 7 miles longer than taking the highway, and her total commute distance is 57 miles long. How many miles long is her morning commute?

E. 25 miles

F. 32 miles

G. 39 miles

H. 43 miles

17. If 1 gallon of paint covers 300 sq. feet of wall, what is the fewest number of 1-gallon cans of paint that are needed to cover all 4 walls of a 10-foot by 12-foot bedroom that has 8 foot high ceilings (assume there are no windows or doors)?

A. 1

B. 2

C. 3

D. 4

18.

Figure X   Figure Y

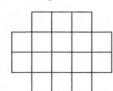

The individual squares in Figures X and Y are equally sized. If the area of Figure X is 48 square inches, what is the area of Figure Y?

E. 24 sq. in.
F. 36 sq. in.
G. 48 sq. in.
H. 60 sq. in.

19. To decorate for the holidays, Jolie wants to cover a wall in her home with wrapping paper, which is sold by the square yard. What is the minimum amount of wrapping paper, in square yards, she will need in order to cover the wall if the wall measures 18 feet by 24 feet?

A. 48 sq. yds.
B. 96 sq. yds.
C. 144 sq. yds.
D. 432 sq. yds.

20. Packing foam weighs 0.4 kg per cubic meter. If a box that measures 2 m by 3 m by 5 m is filled with packing foam, how much foam will be used?

E. 4 kg
F. 6 kg
G. 10 kg
H. 12 kg

21. A square swimming pool is 10 m long on each side and has a level depth of 3 m. It is being filled with water at a rate of 3 cubic meters per minute. At the same time, a hose is draining water from the pool at a rate of 8 cubic meters per minute. If the pool started $\frac{2}{3}$ full at noon, at what time will it be empty?

A. 12:25 pm
B. 12:40 pm
C. 12:55 pm
D. 1:00 pm

22. How many minutes are in 3.65 hours?

E. 215 min.
F. 219 min.
G. 245 min.
H. 339 min.

23. Samson is running a marathon. He will try to finish the marathon by first running for 45 minutes, then walking for 45 minutes, and repeating that pattern until he reaches the finish line. If Samson began running at 9:00 a.m., what time will be begin his fourth period of walking?

A. 12:00 p.m.
B. 1:30 p.m.
C. 2:15 p.m.
D. 3:00 p.m.

24. What time will it be 70 hours after 12:30 p.m. on Monday?

E. 12:30 a.m. on Thursday
F. 10:30 a.m. on Thursday
G. 2:30 p.m. on Thursday
H. 10:30 p.m. on Thursday

25. Amanda biked 22 miles in 3 hours. Byron biked three times farther than Amanda, in twice the amount of time. What was Byron's average speed in miles per hour?

A. 7
B. 11
C. 14
D. 44

26. When it is 1:00 P.M. eastern standard time (EST) in Newark, it is 8:00 A.M. Hawaiian-Aleutian standard time (HAST) in Honolulu. A plane departs from Newark at 12:00 P.M EST and lands in Honolulu at 6:00 P.M HAST that same day. A second plane departs from Honolulu at 7:00 A.M. HAST and travels for the same amount of time as the first plane. When did the second plane land in Newark?

E. 1:00 P.M. EST
F. 7:00 P.M. EST
G. 8:00 P.M. EST
H. 11:00 P.M. EST

Grid-In Questions (Open-Ended Questions)

27. On a number line, point X is located at –12, point Y is located at –5, and point Z is located at 8. A is the midpoint of XY, and B is the midpoint of YZ. What is the midpoint of AB?

28.

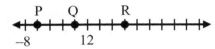

How many units is it from the midpoint of PQ to the midpoint of PR?

29.

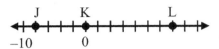

In the figure above, point A is to be placed on the number line one-fourth of the way from point J to point K. What number will be at the midpoint of AL?

30. Kathryn is tiling her bathroom, which is a rectangle with dimensions 2 yards by 3 yards. If each tile is a square with side length 4 inches, and there is no space between tiles, how many tiles will she need to completely cover her bathroom floor?

Coordinates

1.

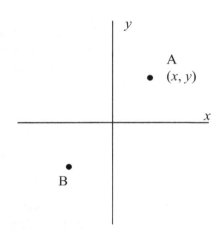

In the above figure, A and B are equidistant from the origin. Which of the following could be the coordinates of point B?

A. $(-x, -y)$
B. $(x, -y)$
C. $(-x, y)$
D. (y, x)

2.

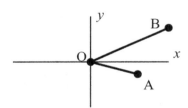

In the coordinate plane above, point O is the origin, and point A lies at (12, –5). Segment OA is half the length of segment OB. What is the length of segment OB?

E. 10
F. 12
G. 13
H. 26

3. On an *xy*-plane, what is the area of a rectangle with points at (3, 3), (3, 1), (0, 1), and (0, 3)?

A. 2
B. 4
C. 6
D. 9

The Tutorverse

4. Which of the following graphs satisfies the criteria that no points on that graph share the same *y*-coordinate?

   E.

   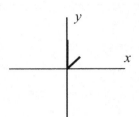

   F.

   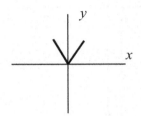

   G.

   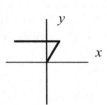

   H.

   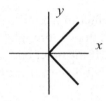

5. In the *xy* coordinate plane, how many points have a distance of exactly 2 units from the origin?

   A. Two
   B. Three
   C. Four
   D. More than four

6. On an *xy*-coordinate grid, the coordinate point (*j*,*k*) is located at (–7,3). Which of the following represents (–*k*,*j*)?

   E. (–3, 7)
   F. (–3, –7)
   G. (–7, –3)
   H. (7, –3)

7. A triangle has two vertices at (4,5) and (10,5). Which of the following could NOT be the perimeter of the triangle?

   A. 12
   B. 13
   C. 14
   D. 15

8. Line MN represents a proportional relationship. If point N lies at (18,9), which ordered pair could represent the coordinates of point M?

   E. (9, 18)
   F. (13, 4)
   G. (14, 7)
   H. (27, 18)

9. On an *xy*-coordinate grid, three vertices of a square are (2,3), (7,3), and (2,–2). Which of the following could be the fourth vertex of the square?

   A. (7, –2)
   B. (4, –2)
   C. (–1, 3)
   D. (7, 1)

10. One side of a square is 5 units long and lies on the *y*-axis of a coordinate grid. If one vertex of the square lies at (0,10), the coordinates of another corner of this square could be any of the following EXCEPT

    E. (5, 5)
    F. (-5, 5)
    G. (0, 5)
    H. (5, 0)

The Tutorverse

Grid-In Questions (Open-Ended Questions)

11. What is the area, in square units, of a right triangle on an *xy*-plane with vertices at (–3, –2), (–3, 5) and (4, 5)?

12. On an *xy*-plane, the center of a circle is located at (1, 1). A diameter is drawn through the center, with one at end (4, 5). If the other end of the diameter is at (*p,q*), what is the value of *q*?

13. On an *xy*-plane, what is the area of a triangle with vertices at (–2, –2), (3, –2), and (1, 4)?

14. On an *xy*-plane, point *A* is located at (4, –2). If it is reflected over the *x*-axis, then the *y*-axis, what its new *y*-coordinate?

15. On an *xy*-plane, what is the area of an isosceles trapezoid with vertices at (–3, –1), (–1, 3), (3, – 1), and (1, 3)?

16.

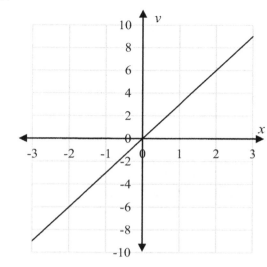

What is the value of *y* when *x* is equal to –2?

17.

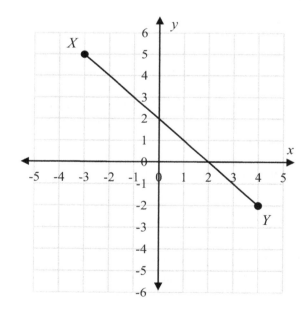

Point *Z* (not shown) is the midpoint of *XY*. What is the *y*-coordinate of point *Z*?

Practice Test 2

Overview

The practice test is designed to assess your understanding of key skills and concepts. The number of questions, content, time limit, and format mirror the actual test closely. It is important to take the final practice test after completing Practice Test 1 and after you have spent time studying and practicing.

The practice test is scored differently from how the actual test is scored. To replicate an actual test-taking scenario, the practice test includes all 114 questions students will see on the actual test. Note that 20 of these (10 from each section) will <u>not</u> be scored on the actual test. The results from this practice test should be used to gauge your mastery over skills and concepts, <u>not</u> as a gauge of how you will necessarily score on the test.

Format

The practice test includes the following sections:

Practice Test Section	Questions	Time Limit
English Language Arts	57	90 minutes *suggested
Mathematics	57	90 minutes *suggested
Total	**114**	**180 minutes**

* The time limits indicated above are recommendations only. The entire test must be completed in 180 minutes. Students are not required to finish the test in any particular order, nor are they limited to a certain amount of time for each section. How students choose to allocate their time between sections is entirely discretionary.

Answering

Use the answer sheets provided on the following pages to record your answers. You may wish to tear this page out of the workbook.

The Tutorverse

Practice Test Answer Sheet

Section 1: English Language Arts

1. Ⓐ Ⓑ Ⓒ Ⓓ	13. Ⓐ Ⓑ Ⓒ Ⓓ	25. Ⓐ Ⓑ Ⓒ Ⓓ	37. Ⓐ Ⓑ Ⓒ Ⓓ	49. Ⓐ Ⓑ Ⓒ Ⓓ
2. Ⓔ Ⓕ Ⓖ Ⓗ	14. Ⓔ Ⓕ Ⓖ Ⓗ	26. Ⓔ Ⓕ Ⓖ Ⓗ	38. Ⓔ Ⓕ Ⓖ Ⓗ	50. Ⓔ Ⓕ Ⓖ Ⓗ
3. Ⓐ Ⓑ Ⓒ Ⓓ	15. Ⓐ Ⓑ Ⓒ Ⓓ	27. Ⓐ Ⓑ Ⓒ Ⓓ	39. Ⓐ Ⓑ Ⓒ Ⓓ	51. Ⓐ Ⓑ Ⓒ Ⓓ
4. Ⓔ Ⓕ Ⓖ Ⓗ	16. Ⓔ Ⓕ Ⓖ Ⓗ	28. Ⓔ Ⓕ Ⓖ Ⓗ	40. Ⓔ Ⓕ Ⓖ Ⓗ	52. Ⓔ Ⓕ Ⓖ Ⓗ
5. Ⓐ Ⓑ Ⓒ Ⓓ	17. Ⓐ Ⓑ Ⓒ Ⓓ	29. Ⓐ Ⓑ Ⓒ Ⓓ	41. Ⓐ Ⓑ Ⓒ Ⓓ	53. Ⓐ Ⓑ Ⓒ Ⓓ
6. Ⓔ Ⓕ Ⓖ Ⓗ	18. Ⓔ Ⓕ Ⓖ Ⓗ	30. Ⓔ Ⓕ Ⓖ Ⓗ	42. Ⓔ Ⓕ Ⓖ Ⓗ	54. Ⓔ Ⓕ Ⓖ Ⓗ
7. Ⓐ Ⓑ Ⓒ Ⓓ	19. Ⓐ Ⓑ Ⓒ Ⓓ	31. Ⓐ Ⓑ Ⓒ Ⓓ	43. Ⓐ Ⓑ Ⓒ Ⓓ	55. Ⓐ Ⓑ Ⓒ Ⓓ
8. Ⓔ Ⓕ Ⓖ Ⓗ	20. Ⓔ Ⓕ Ⓖ Ⓗ	32. Ⓔ Ⓕ Ⓖ Ⓗ	44. Ⓔ Ⓕ Ⓖ Ⓗ	56. Ⓔ Ⓕ Ⓖ Ⓗ
9. Ⓐ Ⓑ Ⓒ Ⓓ	21. Ⓐ Ⓑ Ⓒ Ⓓ	33. Ⓐ Ⓑ Ⓒ Ⓓ	45. Ⓐ Ⓑ Ⓒ Ⓓ	57. Ⓐ Ⓑ Ⓒ Ⓓ
10. Ⓔ Ⓕ Ⓖ Ⓗ	22. Ⓔ Ⓕ Ⓖ Ⓗ	34. Ⓔ Ⓕ Ⓖ Ⓗ	46. Ⓔ Ⓕ Ⓖ Ⓗ	
11. Ⓐ Ⓑ Ⓒ Ⓓ	23. Ⓐ Ⓑ Ⓒ Ⓓ	35. Ⓐ Ⓑ Ⓒ Ⓓ	47. Ⓐ Ⓑ Ⓒ Ⓓ	
12. Ⓔ Ⓕ Ⓖ Ⓗ	24. Ⓔ Ⓕ Ⓖ Ⓗ	36. Ⓔ Ⓕ Ⓖ Ⓗ	48. Ⓔ Ⓕ Ⓖ Ⓗ	

Section 2: Mathematics

58.   59.   60.   61.   62.

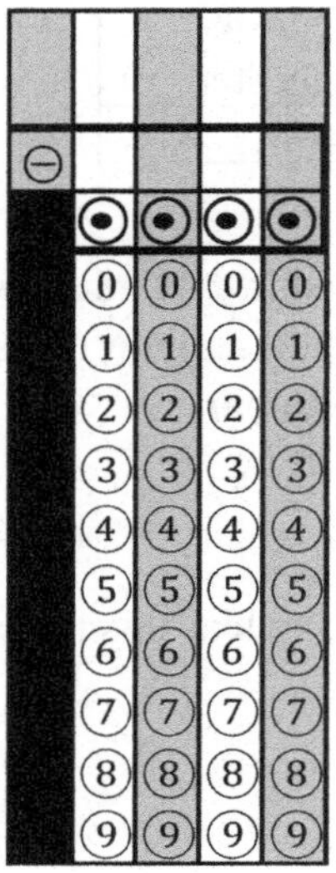

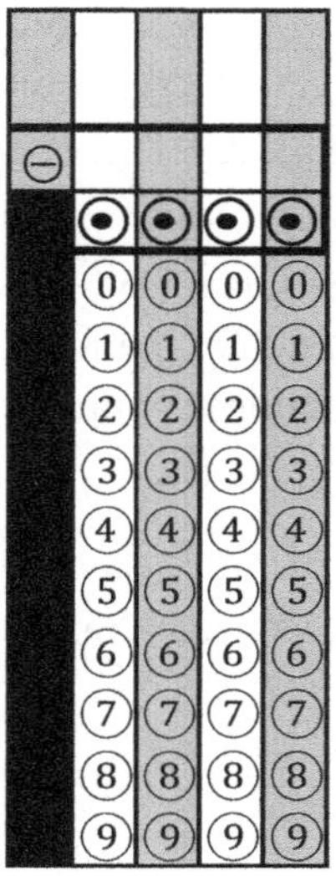

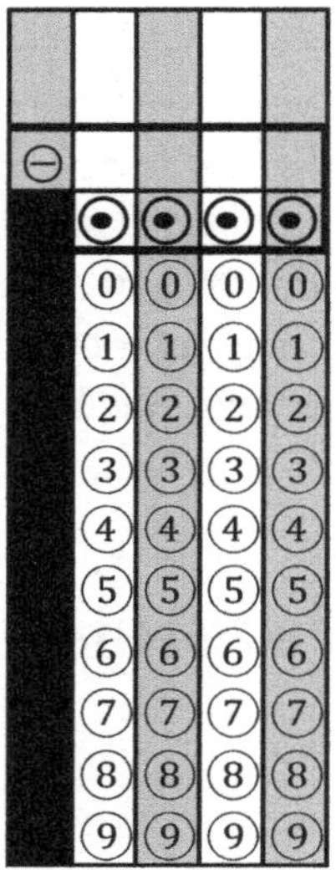

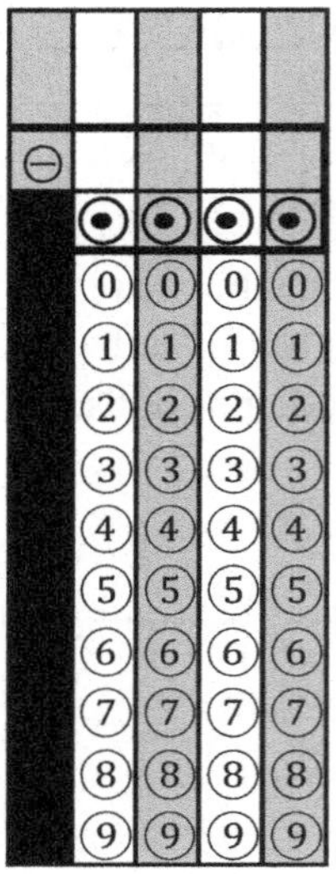

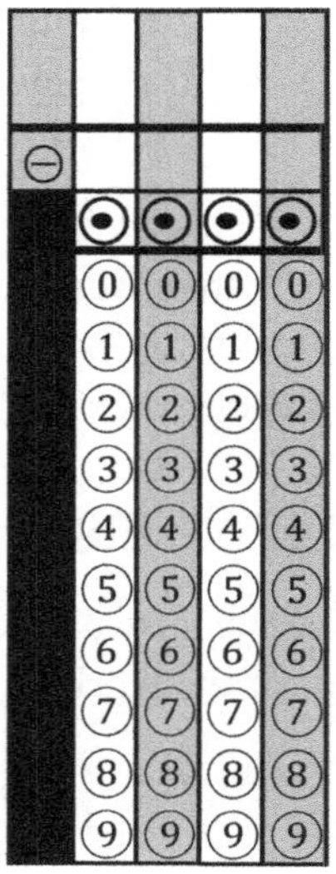

(Grid-in answer bubbles for questions 58–62, each with columns of digits 0–9)

63. Ⓐ Ⓑ Ⓒ Ⓓ	73. Ⓐ Ⓑ Ⓒ Ⓓ	84. Ⓔ Ⓕ Ⓖ Ⓗ	95. Ⓐ Ⓑ Ⓒ Ⓓ	106. Ⓔ Ⓕ Ⓖ Ⓗ
	74. Ⓔ Ⓕ Ⓖ Ⓗ	85. Ⓐ Ⓑ Ⓒ Ⓓ	96. Ⓔ Ⓕ Ⓖ Ⓗ	107. Ⓐ Ⓑ Ⓒ Ⓓ
64. Ⓔ Ⓕ Ⓖ Ⓗ	75. Ⓐ Ⓑ Ⓒ Ⓓ	86. Ⓔ Ⓕ Ⓖ Ⓗ	97. Ⓐ Ⓑ Ⓒ Ⓓ	108. Ⓔ Ⓕ Ⓖ Ⓗ
65. Ⓐ Ⓑ Ⓒ Ⓓ	76. Ⓔ Ⓕ Ⓖ Ⓗ	87. Ⓐ Ⓑ Ⓒ Ⓓ	98. Ⓔ Ⓕ Ⓖ Ⓗ	109. Ⓐ Ⓑ Ⓒ Ⓓ
66. Ⓔ Ⓕ Ⓖ Ⓗ	77. Ⓐ Ⓑ Ⓒ Ⓓ	88. Ⓔ Ⓕ Ⓖ Ⓗ	99. Ⓐ Ⓑ Ⓒ Ⓓ	110. Ⓔ Ⓕ Ⓖ Ⓗ
67. Ⓐ Ⓑ Ⓒ Ⓓ	78. Ⓔ Ⓕ Ⓖ Ⓗ	89. Ⓐ Ⓑ Ⓒ Ⓓ	100. Ⓔ Ⓕ Ⓖ Ⓗ	111. Ⓐ Ⓑ Ⓒ Ⓓ
68. Ⓔ Ⓕ Ⓖ Ⓗ	79. Ⓐ Ⓑ Ⓒ Ⓓ	90. Ⓔ Ⓕ Ⓖ Ⓗ	101. Ⓐ Ⓑ Ⓒ Ⓓ	112. Ⓔ Ⓕ Ⓖ Ⓗ
69. Ⓐ Ⓑ Ⓒ Ⓓ	80. Ⓔ Ⓕ Ⓖ Ⓗ	91. Ⓐ Ⓑ Ⓒ Ⓓ	102. Ⓔ Ⓕ Ⓖ Ⓗ	113. Ⓐ Ⓑ Ⓒ Ⓓ
70. Ⓔ Ⓕ Ⓖ Ⓗ	81. Ⓐ Ⓑ Ⓒ Ⓓ	92. Ⓔ Ⓕ Ⓖ Ⓗ	103. Ⓐ Ⓑ Ⓒ Ⓓ	114. Ⓔ Ⓕ Ⓖ Ⓗ
71. Ⓐ Ⓑ Ⓒ Ⓓ	82. Ⓔ Ⓕ Ⓖ Ⓗ	93. Ⓐ Ⓑ Ⓒ Ⓓ	104. Ⓔ Ⓕ Ⓖ Ⓗ	
72. Ⓔ Ⓕ Ⓖ Ⓗ	83. Ⓐ Ⓑ Ⓒ Ⓓ	94. Ⓔ Ⓕ Ⓖ Ⓗ	105. Ⓐ Ⓑ Ⓒ Ⓓ	

The Tutorverse

Practice Test 2

Section One: English Language Arts

Recommended Time Limit: 90 minutes

Revising/Editing

Questions 1-10

The Revising/Editing section is in two parts: Part A and Part B

Revising/Editing Part A

Directions: Read and answer each of the following questions. You must recognize and correct errors in conventions of standard written English in sentences or short paragraphs. Mark the best answer for each question on the answer sheet.

1. Read this sentence:

> Jessica was very excited to ride the extreme rollercoaster at the theme park, since she was deathly afraid of heights and was prone to motion sickness.

Which edit should be made to correct this sentence?

    A. change **since** to **even though**
    B. change **since** to **because**
    C. change **since** to **unless**
    D. change **since** to **if**

2. Read this sentence:

> When the cold, rainy, season sets in, many of the city's residents believe that they suffer from Seasonal Affective Disorder, a type of depression that is related to changes in general weather patterns.

Which edit should be made to correct this sentence?

    E. delete the comma after **in**
    F. delete the comma after **cold**
    G. delete the comma after **rainy**
    H. delete the comma after **Disorder**

3. Read these sentences:

> (1) When Floyd goes grocery shopping, he always buys grapefruits, which are his favorite fruit.
>
> (2) When Floyd goes grocery shopping, he always buys carrots, which are his favorite vegetable.

What is the best way to combine these sentences?

    A. When Floyd goes grocery shopping, he always buys grapefruits and carrots.
    B. When Floyd goes grocery shopping, he always buys his favorite fruit and vegetable.
    C. When Floyd goes grocery shopping, he always buys grapefruits and carrots, which are his favorite fruit and vegetable, respectively.
    D. When Floyd goes grocery shopping, he always buys carrots and grapefruits, which are his favorite fruit and vegetable, respectively.

CONTINUE TO THE NEXT PAGE

The Tutorverse

Revising/Editing Part B

Directions: Read the passage below and answer the questions following it. Each question asks how best to improve the writing quality of the passage and to correct errors so that the passage follows the conventions of standard written English. You may reread the passage if you need to. Mark the **best** answer for each question.

Frankenstein Corn

(1) Short for "genetically modified organism," GMOs have been making headlines recently for the role they play in the global food chain.

(2) In principle, genetically modifying the genes of a plant or animal in a laboratory is similar to doing so naturally, through a process called selective breeding. (3) In it, people identify the things that they like about a plant or animal, and allow the plants or animals with those things to multiply. (4) Thus, over time, organisms with qualities that people prefer become more and more prevalent.

(5) Thanks to modern science, people can quickly modify the traits of an organism. (6) It has unlocked the ability to combine genes across entirely different biological domains of life. (7) To grasp the enormity of this concept, consider that plants, animals, and fungi are all part of the domain eukarya. (8) Thanks to science, it is now possible to combine genes from plants with genes from the domains bacteria and archaea. (9) Bacteria and archaea are among the oldest living things on the planet.

(10) A famous example of this kind of genetic modification is Bt corn. (11) Bt, short for *Bacillus thuringiensis*, is a bacterium that produces toxins lethal to insects. (12) Bt has, since 1928, been used as a pesticide to kill insects and improve the yield of produce. (13) But it was not until 1995 that the genes responsible for the insect-killing toxins was isolated and combined with the genes of corn. (14) Bt corn proved so successful at staving off insects that the Bt genes were subsequently introduced into other plants, like cotton and potatoes.

(15) Proponents of GMOs point to the many meaningful ways that GMOs contribute to quality of life. (16) These supporters argue that GMOs like Bt organisms increase the productivity of farms, reduce the amount of chemical pesticides used on farms, have no material impact on the overall environment, and can even offer higher nutritional value than unmodified organisms.

(17) Opponents of GMOs maintain that GMOs are damaging to the body and to the environment. (18) They argue that that despite testing and oversight by government agencies, the long-term influence of GMOs on complex things – like the human body, or the global ecosystem – cannot be fully understood.

4.   Which revision of sentence 3 uses the most precise language?

    E. People multiply the organisms that have things that they like.
    F. In it, they enable those organisms to thrive when they have traits or qualities that they like.
    G. In the latter, people identify an organism's desirable traits, and encourage the organisms with those traits to reproduce.
    H. Some people discover certain things that they enjoy about a plant or animal, and help those things become part of the plant in the future.

5.   Which transition should be added to the beginning of sentence 17?

    A. Nevertheless,
    B. Accordingly,
    C. Specifically,
    D. Likewise,

CONTINUE TO THE NEXT PAGE

The Tutorverse

6. Which sentence can follow sentence 4 to help develop the ideas in the second paragraph (sentences 2-4)?

    E. Sometimes, despite our best efforts, nature prevails, failing to produce the type of organism that we want.

    F. There is little need to genetically modify plants or animals in a laboratory, since the same effect takes place naturally.

    G. Since we no longer need to rely on selective breeding, the practice is quickly becoming a lost art, replaced instead by laboratory science.

    H. This is how we came to have the large, sweet apples everyone loves; over many years, farmers continuously reserved the seeds of the largest, sweetest apples to plant the next season.

7. What is the best way to combine sentences 5 and 6 to clarify the relationship between ideas?

    A. Science allows people to change the traits of an organism no matter its biological domain.

    B. Modern science has not only enabled people to quickly modify the traits of an organism, but to combine traits from entirely different biological domains of life, as well.

    C. People can quickly modify the traits of an organism in a laboratory thanks to science, but they can unlock the ability to combine genes across entirely different biological domains of life.

    D. Though people can quickly modify the traits of an organism in a laboratory thanks to science, they can unlock the ability to combine genes across entirely different biological domains of life.

8. Which edit is needed to correct sentence 13?

    E. add a comma after **1995**

    F. change **was not** to **is not**

    G. delete the hyphen in **insect-killing**

    H. change **was isolated** to **were isolated**

9. Which sentence would best follow sentence 16 to support the argument presented in the paragraph?

    A. Though the use of pesticides may have decreased, the use of herbicides has not.

    B. The genes from Bt corn are spreading to other species of corn, with potentially dangerous consequences for the environment.

    C. The decreased use of chemical pesticides has not been shown to be the direct result of the increased popularity of Bt organisms.

    D. Engineered in the early 2000s, Golden Rice, another result of the mixing of plant and bacteria genes, provides four to five times more Vitamin A than regular white rice.

10. Which sentence is irrelevant to the argument presented in the passage and should be deleted?

    E. sentence 9

    F. sentence 11

    G. sentence 14

    H. sentence 18

CONTINUE TO THE NEXT PAGE

Reading Comprehension

Questions 11-57

Directions: Read each passage below and answer the questions following it. Base your answers only on information contained in the passage. You may reread a passage if you need to. Mark the best answer for each question.

Mary Oliver

1 Mary Oliver, who died in January, 2019, was one of the best-selling poets of our time. Her poetry – which was singular in its plainness of language and overall brevity – focused primarily on nature. In her hands, plants and animals became symbols for the grief and gift of everyday life.

2 Some critics snubbed her work for being too commercial, too pandering. Other critics raved about her glowing meditations on nature, comparing her to Ralph Waldo Emerson, Walt Whitman or Robert Frost. Either way, Ms. Oliver was one of the most-read poets of the century. Unlike other poets, who were often considered the scribes of the intellectual elite, she reached a broad audience, from pro-football players to college professors. Celebrities as diverse as Gwyneth Paltrow and Hillary Clinton celebrated her work. Numerous composers set her words to music. Oprah Winfrey created a special poetry issue of O Magazine in order to highlight a rare interview that Ms. Oliver gave to the journalist, Maria Shriver. In an all-too-rare achievement for poets, several of her books made the best-seller lists. Here, at last, was a poet who could speak to the masses – and this ability earned her both praise and rebuke.

3 And indeed, Ms. Oliver enjoyed a long and illustrious poetic career. Her first book, "No Voyage and Other Poems," was published when she was 28 years old, in 1963. In 1984, her fourth book, "American Primitive," won the Pulitzer prize. In 1992, "New and Selected Poems" won the National Book Award. She was a poet-in-residence at Bucknell University, Sweet Briar College and Bennington College. For the large part of 40 years, though, Ms. Oliver lived in Provincetown, MA, with her partner, the photographer Molly Malone Cook, and several dogs. Most days, even in old age, she could be found walking through the woods, a dog by her side, and a pen and notebook in her hand.

4 Her fame never led to an inflated ego, nor did she mind the criticisms of others. Poetry was, for her, not so much a means of self-expression as much as self-exploration, and eventually self-realization: "I did not think of language as the means to self-description. I thought of it as the door – a thousand opening doors! – past myself. I thought of it as the means to notice, to contemplate, to praise, and, thus, to come into power."

5 This desire to escape to another world was due, in part, to her upbringing. Born in Maple Heights, Ohio, in 1935, she was the product of an unhappy home. "It was a very dark and broken house that I came from," she said in a radio interview. "To this day, I don't care for the enclosure of buildings." To escape the unhappiness, Ms. Oliver fled for some neighboring woods, where she would walk for hours and observe the sights around her – and thusly scribble down those observations in a notebook. The trees were her cathedral; venturing forth under the shelter of branches and leaves, she would find physical and spiritual renewal. Her home life, she said, made her want to be invisible; she took to the woods to disappear. But a funny thing happened on the way through the forest. Amongst the trees, she appeared to herself. She discovered that she had a voice. "I made a world out of words," she said to Maria Shriver in her O Magazine interview. "It was my salvation."

CONTINUE TO THE NEXT PAGE

The Tutorverse

6 In the woods, Ms. Oliver also found faith. In the endless life and death cycles of nature, she found spiritual fervor: the birth of a new moon, the death of a snake in the road, were equal sources of inspiration. In her poem, "The Swan," Ms. Oliver recounts the sight of a swan, drifting on a river and then taking flight, "an armful of white blossoms." The description concludes with the bird, aloft in the air, "And did you feel it, in your heart" she asks with some urgency, "how it pertained to everything? / And have you too finally figured out what beauty is for?/ And have you changed your life?" In the swoop and grace of a single swan, Ms. Oliver found deeper meaning; from her personal pain and confusion, she found a beautiful perspective to share with the world.

11. Which statement best describes the central idea of the passage?

   A. Mary Oliver was an obscure poet who wrote darkly emotional poems.
   B. Mary Oliver was an influential poet who was inspired by nature and her childhood memories.
   C. Mary Oliver was a well-known poet who wrote for the sake of popular appeal.
   D. Mary Oliver was a famous poet who built her career out of writing poems to please critics.

12. Read this sentence from paragraph 3.

   Most days, even in old age, she could be found walking through the woods, a dog by her side, and a pen and notebook in her hand.

   What role does this sentence play in the overall structure of the passage?

   E. It highlights how her love of animals is equal to her passion for writing.
   F. It goes into detail about the process Oliver uses to create beautiful poetry.
   G. It indicates a transition from discussing Oliver's professional career to her personal relationship to poetry.
   H. It contrasts her daily life in old age against the activities of her youth.

13. Why does Oliver compare poetry to "a thousand opening doors" in paragraph 4?

   A. It highlights how Oliver saw poetry as a way to explore the world.
   B. It demonstrates how Oliver's style of poetry worked their way into her everyday conversations.
   C. It emphasizes the numerous interpretations that a single poem can inspire.
   D. It shows how Oliver saw poetry as a way meet new people in her neighborhood.

14. Read this sentence from paragraph 4.

   Poetry was, for her, not so much a means of self-expression as much as self-exploration, and eventually self-realization

   Which excerpt from paragraph 5 best supports the ideas in this sentence?

   E. "This desire to escape to another world was due, in part, to her upbringing."
   F. "'It was a very dark and broken house that I came from,' she said in a radio interview."
   G. "Her home life, she said, made her want to be invisible; she took to the woods to disappear."
   H. "Amongst the trees, she appeared to herself. She discovered that she had a voice."

CONTINUE TO THE NEXT PAGE

The Tutorverse

15. Read this sentence from paragraph 5.

   The trees were her cathedral; venturing forth under the shelter of branches and leaves, she would find physical and spiritual renewal.

   How does the metaphor "the trees were her cathedral" affect the tone of the passage?

   A. by creating a sense of familiarity as she saw the shape of her church in the tree branches
   B. by highlighting her desperation to find a spiritual place of protection
   C. by emphasizing the sense of comfort, safety, and wonder that she discovered in nature
   D. by demonstrating her sorrow at the way her parents neglected her

16. Which sentence from paragraph 6 best supports the central idea of the passage?

   E. "In the swoop and grace of a single swan, Ms. Oliver found deeper meaning; from her personal pain and confusion, she found a beautiful perspective to share with the world."
   F. "Ms. Oliver recounts the sight of a swan, drifting on a river and then taking flight, 'an armful of white blossoms.'"
   G. "The description concludes with the bird, aloft in the air, 'And did you feel it, in your heart'"
   H. "In the woods, Ms. Oliver also found faith."

17. The author would most likely agree with which statement?

   A. Poets can be inspirational and successful regardless of their age.
   B. Writing every day is a guaranteed path to a successful poetic career.
   C. The opinion of critics is not as important as the reaction of the majority of society.
   D. A poet should follow personal interests and not be influenced by the expectations of others.

CONTINUE TO THE NEXT PAGE

The Tutorverse

Adapted from *The Youngest Girl in the Fifth*

by Angela Brazil

1 "I don't want your lockets or your pencil cases," said Netta, "I've heaps of my own. I know one thing I do want, though, and if you like to trade, you can."

2 "Done! Only name it, and it's yours with my blessing."

3 "Well, I want your essay—"

4 "My essay! What do you mean?" exclaimed Gwen, as she snatched back her exercise book like a mother clutching her first-born.

5 "I mean what I say. If you like to hand over 'Thomas Carlyle' to me, I'll take my money back instead, and call us quits. It would be a new experience to win a prize. How amazed everyone would be!"

6 "You surely wouldn't pass it off as your own?"

7 "Why not?"

8 "Netta! That would be bold, even for you!"

9 "I told you long ago I was no saint. Besides, what's the harm? It's a business arrangement. You offered to repay me, and this happens to be the 'pound of flesh,' I want. It's perfectly fair."

10 "I don't quite see the fairness myself."

11 "But it is!" protested Netta rather huffily. "I believe lots of popular authors don't do all their own writing themselves. They engage secretaries to help them. I've even heard of clergymen buying their sermons."

12 "Oh, oh! Father doesn't!" Gwen face felt warm.

13 "Well, I didn't say he did, but I believe it's done all the same. And if it's alright for a vicar to read somebody else's sermon in the pulpit as if it were his own, I can hand in somebody else's essay. Don't you see?"

14 "No, I don't see!" grunted Gwen.

15 "Look here, Gwen Gascoyne, you've got to see it! I've been uncommonly patient with you, but I don't quite appreciate the joke of being cheated out of that money. I must either have the money or its equivalent. You can choose yourself which."

16 Netta's eyes were flashing, and her mouth was twitching ominously. She was a jolly enough fair-weather comrade, but she could be uncommonly nasty if things went wrong.

17 "Don't you think it's unfair to keep me waiting all this time?" she added scathingly.

18 Gwen kicked the desk and groaned.

19 "Well, it just amounts to this: if you don't choose, I'll tell Miss Roscoe. Yes, I will! I don't care a bit that I went into her room too. You broke the china, and you'd get into the worst trouble. It wouldn't be pleasant for you. I think you'd better hand over Mr. Thomas Carlyle to me, my dear."

20 "And what am I to do about my own submission, exactly?"

21 "Write another on a different author."

22 "There's no time."

23 "Yes there is, heaps! I don't want it to be as good as this, of course. Well, are you going to trade, or are you not? I can't wait here all day!"

CONTINUE TO THE NEXT PAGE

The Tutorverse

24 For answer, Gwen held out the exercise book. She was in a desperately tight corner; everything seemed to have conspired against her. She knew Netta and her crazy, reckless moods quite well enough to appreciate the fact that her threat to tell Miss Roscoe was no idle one. When her temper was roused, Netta was capable of anything.

25 "Oh! Glad you've come to your senses at last!" sneered Netta, as she clutched the precious manuscript and stalked away, slamming the door behind her. Gwen laid her head down on the desk. Her essay – her cherished essay, over which she had taken such superhuman pains, to be torn away from her like this! It was to have brought her such credit from Miss Roscoe, for even if it did not win the prize, it would surely be highly praised.

26 Netta in the meantime had put the essay away in her locker with the utmost satisfaction. She felt she had decidedly scored. Neither brilliant nor a hard worker, she had no opportunity of distinguishing herself in the class under ordinary circumstances: here chance had flung into her hand the very thing she wanted. It would not take long to copy the sixteen pages of rather sprawling writing, then "Thomas Carlyle" would be her own.

27 To Gwen, not the lightest part of the business was that she was faced with the horrible necessity of writing another essay. Only two days remained. It was impossible to look up any subject adequately, so she chose Dickens, as being an author whose books she knew fairly well, and by way of much brain wracking and real hard labor contrived to give some slight sketch of his life and an appreciation of his genius. She was painfully conscious, however, that the result was poor, the style slipshod, and the general composition lacking both in unity and finish. She pulled a long face as she signed her name to it.

28 She felt sicker still on the day when Miss Roscoe returned the essays.

29 "I had hoped the average results would be higher," commented the Principal. "Very few girls have treated the subject with any real effort. There is only one paper worthy of notice – that on Thomas Carlyle by Netta Goodwin, and it is so excellent that it stands head and shoulders above all the others. You thoroughly deserve the prize which I offered, and I have written your name in the book."

30 The class gasped as Netta, with a smile of infinite triumph, marched jauntily up the room to receive her copy of *Browning's Poems*. Each girl looked at her neighbor in almost incredulous astonishment. Netta Goodwin, of all people in the world, to have won such praise!

31 Gwen drew her breath hard and clenched her fists till her nails hurt her palms.

18. Read paragraph 4 from the excerpt.

> **"My essay! What do you mean?" exclaimed Gwen, as she snatched back her exercise book like a mother clutching her first-born.**

The simile used in the sentence contributes to the development of the plot by

   E. revealing Gwen's motivation for writing the essay.
   F. showing how deeply Gwen is emotionally invested in her essay.
   G. illustrating the quality of Gwen's essay through the envy it inspired in others.
   H. Demonstrating the fragility of Gwen's confidence in herself as a writer.

CONTINUE TO THE NEXT PAGE

The Tutorverse

19. What conclusion is best supported by the dialogue in paragraph 13?

    A. Netta will say anything to get her way.
    B. Netta has cheated in the past in order to win.
    C. Netta is insecure about her own academic abilities.
    D. Netta has a strong sense of fairness and wants to do the right thing.

20. How does paragraph 24 contribute to the development of the plot?

    E. It reveals that Gwen and Netta were never friends, and will never be friends again.
    F. It demonstrates that Netta would rather cheat than work hard at getting a good grade on the essay.
    G. It marks the moment where Gwen makes a difficult decision which leads to misery.
    H. It shows that Gwen would rather get in trouble with Miss Roscoe than let Netta win a prized possession.

21. Which sentence best supports the idea that Gwen cares deeply about how others perceive her?

    A. "'I don't quite see the fairness myself.'" (paragraph 10)
    B. "'Yes, I will! I don't care a bit that I went into her room too. You broke the china, and you'd get into the worst trouble. It wouldn't be pleasant for you.'" (paragraph 19)
    C. "It was to have brought her such credit from Miss Roscoe, for even if it did not win the prize, it would surely be highly praised." (paragraph 25)
    D. "To Gwen, not the lightest part of the business was that she was faced with the horrible necessity of writing another essay." (paragraph 27)

22. All of the following are reasons why Gwen cooperates with Netta EXCEPT

    E. "'I've been uncommonly patient with you, but I don't quite appreciate the joke of being cheated out of that money. I must either have the money or its equivalent.'" (paragraph 15)
    F. "She was a jolly enough fair-weather comrade, but she could be uncommonly nasty if things went wrong." (paragraph 16)
    G. "'Well, it just amounts to this: if you don't choose, I'll tell Miss Roscoe.'" (paragraph 19)
    H. "Neither brilliant nor a hard worker, she had no opportunity of distinguishing herself in the class under ordinary circumstances: here chance had flung into her hand the very thing she wanted." (paragraph 26)

23. How do the consequences of Gwen's agreement with Netta show the theme of the excerpt?

    A. It reveals the downsides of dishonesty, as Gwen had to do twice as much work as a result of not telling the truth.
    B. It highlights the importance of not leaving things to the last minute, as Gwen didn't have time to do a good job on her second essay.
    C. It shows how wishes can be dangerous, Gwen's desire for attention led to her punishment by the Principal.
    D. It emphasizes the strength of friendship, as Netta eventually returns the essay to a distraught Gwen.

CONTINUE TO THE NEXT PAGE

The Tutorverse

24. Which of the following sentences best supports the narrator's description of Netta from paragraph 26?

    E. "'I had hoped the average results would be higher,' commented the Principal. 'Very few girls have treated the subject with any real effort.'" (paragraph 29)
    F. "You thoroughly deserve the prize which I offered, and I have written your name in the book." (paragraph 29)
    G. "Each girl looked at her neighbor in almost incredulous astonishment." (paragraph 30)
    H. "Gwen drew her breath hard and clenched her fists till her nails hurt her palms." (paragraph 31)

25. Read paragraph 31 from the excerpt.

    Gwen drew her breath hard and clenched her fists till her nails hurt her palms.

How does this sentence contribute to the tone of the end of the excerpt?

    A. It shows a sorrowful tone, as Gwen realizes her actions would have disappointed her father.
    B. It creates a righteous tone, as Gwen sacrificed her chance to receive praise so that someone else could experience it.
    C. It highlights a fearful tone, as Gwen is worries someone will find out about her arrangement with Netta.
    D. It reinforces a frustrated tone, as Gwen is unable to claim authorship to her winning essay.

CONTINUE TO THE NEXT PAGE

The Tutorverse

The Big One

1   San Francisco, one of the most populous cities in the United States, stands atop one of the world's most active tectonic faults. The San Andreas Fault is formed by the meeting of the Pacific Tectonic Plate and the North American Tectonic Plate. These two giant landmasses often bump into or brush up against each other, resulting in earthquakes.

2   One of the most powerful earthquakes ever recorded in the area struck San Francisco at 5:12 a.m. of April 18, 1906, beginning with an initial foreshock. No more than 30 seconds later, violent shocks began, lasting 45 to 60 seconds altogether. Though the shocks lasted barely a minute, they were felt from southern Oregon to south of Los Angeles, rupturing 296 miles of the 800-mile San Andreas Fault. The depth of the shift between the plates was approximately a 24 feet slip, about the size of a two-story building. According to Mr. Bacigalupi, a resident of San Francisco, he was startled awake "by a terrific trembling, which acted in the same manner as would a bucking bronco[1]." He added, "My bed was going up and down in all four directions at once, while all about me I heard screams, wails, and crashing of breaking china-ware and nick-knacks."

3   The quake happened decades before the development of the Richter scale used to measure the strength of earthquakes. Today, many estimates suggest that the quake likely registered a magnitude between 7.7 and 8.3. This estimate is based on the damage done to the city as well as the changes to the geography of the surrounding area itself. In the city itself, some 3,000 people perished. Between the quake and the resulting fires, over 75% of San Francisco was destroyed.

4   Some estimates suggest that approximately 90% of the damage done to San Francisco was due to the fires that resulted from the shocks. When the quake struck, it ruptured gas lines, causing them to explode or catch fire. The fires – over 30 in all – burned through tens of thousands of buildings and hundreds of blocks. Though many of the fires were started as a direct result of the earthquake, many more happened days after the first rumblings. In an attempt to stop fires from spreading from one building to the next, firefighters attempted to create firebreaks by demolishing buildings. The hope was that by sacrificing some buildings, they could stop the fire from consuming thousands more. However, many firefighters were not well trained. In the course of demolishing buildings, some firefighters accidentally started new fires.

5   Fire took many important buildings from the city of San Francisco. The Palace Hotel, for example, was a city landmark, and was completely consumed by the blaze. The Metropolitan Opera Company, at the time in San Francisco on tour from New York, lost many sets and costumes to the fires. The fire did not discriminate, taking from the city even knowledge; the California Academy of Science, which housed a large botanical collection, went up in flames.

6   Though technically less than a minute long, the quake devastated a vast number of lives. Of the 400,000 San Francisco residents, the quake left about 225,000 homeless. Then-mayor E. E. Schmitz called in 2,500 Army personnel to assist with the aftermath. After helping to douse the fires, they began supplying the newly homeless with clothing. However, after large quantities of Army clothing was passed out, they quickly saw that food and shelter were the main concerns.

7   The U.S. House and Senate Appropriations committee quickly sent funds to supply residents with food, water, tents, blankets, and medical supplies. They also offered people daily rations of bread, vegetables and meat. Referred to as "bread lines," residents would wait in long lines that were several blocks long to obtain their ration. However, because of the destruction, chimneys were deemed unsafe and people

---

[1] **bronco**: a wild or half-tamed horse

CONTINUE TO THE NEXT PAGE

had to transport their wood stoves to the streets for cooking. Homeless people established neighborhoods of tents in city parks such as the Golden Gate Park. Some of these tent neighborhoods lasted for years after the quake.

8   It's hard to fathom that a minute could change lives, infrastructures, and even geography. Though the fires died out and the smoke cleared within a few days, it took several months for San Francisco to reorganize and begin reconstruction of lives and buildings. The city was not fully restored for another few years. In the end, insurance companies estimated losses at over $200 million, the equivalent of $6 billion today.

9   Eventually, San Francisco recovered from the devastation of 1906, going on to enjoy decades of geological peace.

San Andreas Fault – CA

Source: United States Geological Survey

CONTINUE TO THE NEXT PAGE

The Tutorverse

26. Which statement best describes the central idea of the passage?

    E. "One of the most powerful earthquakes ever recorded in the area struck San Francisco at 5:12 a.m. of April 18, 1906." (paragraph 2)
    F. "Though many of the fires were started as a direct result of the earthquake, many more happened days after the first rumblings." (paragraph 4)
    G. "The U.S. House and Senate Appropriations committee quickly sent funds to supply residents with food, water, tents, blankets, and medical supplies." (paragraph 7)
    H. "Eventually, San Francisco recovered from the devastation of 1906, going on to enjoy decades of geological peace." (paragraph 9)

27. The map supports a central idea of paragraphs 1-2 by

    A. indicating the extent of the damage caused by the quake to the west coast of Canada and the United States.
    B. proving that the earthquake of San Francisco was caused by man-made factors.
    C. showing the population decreases by geographical location after the quake.
    D. demonstrating how San Francisco was located squarely on top of the San Andreas fault line.

28. With which statement would the author of this excerpt most likely agree?

    E. The geography around San Francisco returned to its original form in the span of several months.
    F. The earthquake of San Francisco caused great damage due to its sustained length.
    G. The damages caused by the earthquake to the city of San Francisco have become exaggerated over time.
    H. The recorded strength of the earthquake may not be precisely accurate due to less advanced technology at the time.

29. How did the author's use of sequencing in paragraph 2 contribute to the mood of the paragraph?

    A. It shows the atmosphere of confusion as people attempted to identify what caused the quake.
    B. It highlights the feeling of terror that people must have felt during the quake, as it wreaked devastation extremely quickly.
    C. It reveals the sense of efficiency that characterized how government officials planned their response to the quake.
    D. It creates a sense of boredom as it gives an in-depth scientific overview of the geological aspects of the quake.

30. Which statement best describes the firefighters' experience in putting out the flames caused by the quake?

    E. They were extremely efficient and experienced in how they approached the problem.
    F. They lacked organization and as a result failed to solve the problem.
    G. They caused additional damage to the city in their efforts to solve the problem.
    H. They educated local people on ways to prevent a repeat of the problem.

CONTINUE TO THE NEXT PAGE

The Tutorverse

31. Read this sentence from paragraph 5.

> **The fire did not discriminate, taking from the city even knowledge; the California Academy of Science, which housed a large botanical collection, went up in flames.**

How does the word choice in this sentence contribute to the overall meaning of the excerpt?

    A. It personifies the fire as relentlessly burning through the city's treasures.
    B. It creates a chaotic atmosphere, mimicking the experience of city inhabitants during the initial shocks.
    C. It shows that trees and wood-based infrastructures were particularly vulnerable to the fire.
    D. It highlights how the fire intentionally targeted places of learning and knowledge.

32. Which statement best supports the idea that the government effectively responded to people's needs after the quake?

    E. "However, after large quantities of Army clothing was passed out, they quickly saw that food and shelter were the main concerns." (paragraph 6)
    F. "The U.S. House and Senate Appropriations committee quickly sent funds to supply residents with food, water, tents, blankets, and medical supplies." (paragraph 7)
    G. "Though the fires died out and the smoke cleared within a few days, it took several months for San Francisco to reorganize and begin reconstruction of lives and buildings." (paragraph 8)
    H. "In the end, insurance companies estimated losses at over $200 million, the equivalent of $6 billion today." (paragraph 8)

33. What role does paragraph 9 play in the structure of the overall passage?

    A. It describes the experiences of San Francisco with repeated earthquakes in subsequent years.
    B. It emphasizes the long reaching impact of the earthquake on San Francisco's infrastructures and geography.
    C. It provides a sense of closure to the narrative style of the events that happened during the earthquake.
    D. It critiques the way city officials of San Francisco responded to the emergency, and offered suggestions for future improvements.

CONTINUE TO THE NEXT PAGE

The Tutorverse

Learning Differently

1   Students are often told that they must memorize information. They are told that certain information is essential to their education. As a consequence, many students believe that memorizing information is the only way to learn it.

2   But studies have shown that memorization is not always an effective way to learn. Having to memorize something simply for the sake of memorizing it is ineffective because it lacks context. Ask a typical middle schooler how to find the missing side of a right triangle, and he or she will hopefully recite the Pythagorean Theorem. But go one step further and ask the reason why it works, and most students will fumble for an explanation. Many students will simply say that they don't know – that they were told to memorize the formula and substitute values into an equation in a problem.

3   One can have a similar conversation with students across grade levels, from kindergarten all the way up through college. This is a fact that should worry students, parents, and teachers alike. The problem of rote memorization – that is, memorizing and recalling specific pieces of information – happens most in math and science. This might make sense, at first, because of the nature of these subjects. But this seemingly logical idea hides the more dangerous pitfalls of rote memorization itself.

4   Rote memorization encourages students to learn only tidbits of information. The recall of this information can be easily assessed by standardized tests. As a society, we record the results of these tests and look at them as an indicator of intelligence. But do standardized tests really measure intelligence? Some standardized tests certainly do. They are designed to measure a student's ability to reason critically and apply past learnings to new problems. But many more do not, requiring students to memorize facts and formulas that show only a surface understanding of the subject. This becomes an issue when students leave the school system and must face problems that are far more ambiguous and complex. In fact, research has shown that high test scores do not necessarily translate to overall success in life. In one study, the U.S. Department of Education analyzed achievement in nations throughout the world. The study looked at a number of indicators of a nation's success, such as national wealth, degree of democracy, economic growth and even happiness. There was no clear connection between high test scores – and the ability to memorize specific information to pass the tests – and the success of advanced countries.

5   We should not overemphasize rote memorization; it consumes a great deal of student study time while resulting in little real learning. Instead, we should be developing our students' conceptual understanding. This means focusing on critical thinking skills that, though more difficult to quantify, are arguably more important than the ability to remember out-of-context information. After all, the human brain is not designed like a computer. Where computers more effectively store and retrieve information, the human mind demonstrates a greater ability to reason and process complex information.

6   The development of critical thinking in students results in vital skills necessary to success in life. Critical thinkers use logic to help them to make decisions and choose belief systems that will guide later actions and behaviors. Critical thinking means being able to see connections between ideas, and spot flaws in arguments. It leads to effective problem solving because the thinker is able to foresee consequences of actions. These skills are much more necessary in the complexity of adult life than the ability to recite facts or formulas.

7   Teachers of every grade level across the curriculum can – and should – help their students become critical thinkers. This can seem like a difficult task to achieve, but there are many practical ways to accomplish this in the classroom. Regardless of the subject being taught, all teachers should provide opportunities for students to ask questions. This should take the place of much of the drill-like tasks and

CONTINUE TO THE NEXT PAGE

The Tutorverse

mimicry that happens in the classroom. Students should be encouraged to thoughtfully examine ideas and give their opinions. Teachers should challenge students to explain their perspectives and come up with alternate ways to solve problems, rather than focusing on the single correct answer. This requires students to both know the formulas (for example, that the Pythagorean Theorem can be written as $a^2 + b^2 = c^2$) and understand how to apply them.

8 Journaling is an effective tool in fostering critical thinking. Teachers can ask students to write about their reactions to a reading or a class discussion. Students can explain the way they arrived at a certain conclusion or solved a problem or make predictions about the outcome of a short story or a lab experiment. This is a focus on "thinking about thinking," or metacognition. Practicing metacognition makes students more self-aware of the ways in which they learn and how they can develop their own understanding. This will bring a host of benefits later in life.

9 Brainstorming and peer group work can also help students become critical thinkers. Brainstorming is a relaxed and fun way to come up with new solutions to problems. It encourages students to "think outside the box." It can reveal seemingly crazy but often creative and novel ways to tackle problems. Peer groups can brainstorm, or they can simply verbalize ideas they generated in their journaling. The sharing of ideas with peers helps students become open to new perspectives. It also fosters empathy and tolerance of different opinions. Discussing with peers also teaches students how to learn and work in a social setting, which most work places require.

10 Critical thinkers have never been more vital to the success of the individual and society. So, let's leave the memorizing to computers and instead teach our students to become better problem solvers. Let's teach our students to be better able to draw on their knowledge and experiences in order to tackle new problems of all kinds.

34. Which statement best describes the central idea of the passage?

E. Learning things by rote memorization is essential for high performance on standardized tests.
F. Learning things by rote memorization can be helpful on some standardized tests but does not lead to skills that are useful after leaving the school environment.
G. Learning things by rote memorization is more efficient than learning how to think critically.
H. Learning things by rote memorization will eventually lead to the development of critical thinking skills.

35. Read this excerpt from paragraph 2.

Ask a typical middle schooler how to find the missing side of a right triangle, and he or she will hopefully recite the Pythagorean Theorem. But go one step further and ask the reason why it works, and most students will fumble for an explanation.

What is the most likely reason the author included this example?

A. to illustrate a drawback to rote memorization of information by using a familiar example
B. to highlight students' lack of math knowledge by showing how they lack basic knowledge of formulas
C. to explain how critical thinking skills would help students remember math concepts
D. to give step-by-step directions of what can be done to improve test scores

CONTINUE TO THE NEXT PAGE

The Tutorverse

36. In paragraph 3, the word "pitfalls" is used to highlight

   E. how rote memorization is an obviously dangerous method of teaching and learning.
   F. how rote memorization can have unexpected drawbacks for students despite appearing beneficial.
   G. that students may trip and stumble if they are too focused on memorizing information while traveling.
   H. that critical thinking skills can trap students into a repetitive and rigid way of thinking.

37. The author most likely included the study by the U.S. Department of Education in paragraph 4 to

   A. offer evidence to support the main claim of the paragraph.
   B. explain that rote memorization can help students be more successful in life.
   C. provide a counterargument to common arguments against the claim.
   D. highlight the universal nature of the main problem identified in the passage.

38. Read this excerpt from paragraph 5.

   After all, the human brain is not designed like a computer. Where computers more effectively store and retrieve information, the human mind demonstrates a greater ability to reason and process complex information.

   What is the most likely reason the author compares human brains to computers?

   E. to introduce the similarities between human brain structure and circuitry paths in computers
   F. to conclude that computers are superior to human minds in their ability to reason and process information
   G. to emphasize the ways in which human brains are specialized and distinct from computers
   H. to provide an example of how rote memorization can make the human mind become computer-like in its processes

39. What role does paragraph 6 play in the overall structure of the passage?

   A. It contrasts the short-term benefits of critical thinking with those of rote memorization.
   B. It reinforces the long-term benefits of developing critical thinking skills in students.
   C. It highlights how rote memorization can help students become better critical thinkers.
   D. It explains various methods that instructors can use to foster the development of critical thinking skills.

CONTINUE TO THE NEXT PAGE

The Tutorverse

40. Which statement best supports the idea that the development of critical thinking skills will assist students in life beyond school?

    E. "The recall of this information can be easily assessed by standardized tests." (paragraph 4)
    F. "Instead, we should be developing our students' conceptual understanding." (paragraph 5)
    G. "Regardless of the subject being taught, all teachers should provide opportunities for students to ask questions." (paragraph 7)
    H. "The sharing of ideas with peers helps students become open to new perspectives. It also fosters empathy and tolerance of different opinions." (paragraph 9)

41. What is the most likely reason that the author uses the word "crazy" in paragraph 9?

    A. to point out one of the few negative aspects of brainstorming in the classroom
    B. to warn teachers about the problems associated with teaching critical thinking skills
    C. to acknowledge the often unconventional yet beneficial outcomes of critical thinking
    D. to question the overemphasis on rote memorization in traditional classroom teaching

CONTINUE TO THE NEXT PAGE

The Tutorverse

Summer

by Amy Lowell

Some men there are who find in nature all
Their inspiration, hers the sympathy
Which spurs them on to any great endeavor,
To them the fields and woods are closest friends,
5   And they hold dear communion[1] with the hills;
The voice of waters soothes them with its fall,
And the great winds bring healing in their sound.
To them a city is a prison house
Where pent up human forces labour and strive,
10   Where beauty dwells not, driven forth by man;
But where in winter they must live until
Summer gives back the spaces of the hills.
To me it is not so. I love the earth
And all the gifts of her so lavish hand:
15   Sunshine and flowers, rivers and rushing winds,
Thick branches swaying in a winter storm,
And moonlight playing in a boat's wide wake;
But more than these, and much, ah, how much more,
I love the very human heart of man.
20   Above me spreads the hot, blue mid-day sky,
Far down the hillside lies the sleeping lake
Lazily reflecting back the sun,
And scarcely ruffled by the little breeze
Which wanders idly through the nodding ferns.
25   The blue crest of the distant mountain, tops
The green crest of the hill on which I sit;
And it is summer, glorious, deep-toned summer,
The very crown of nature's changing year
When all her surging life is at its full.
30   To me alone it is a time of pause,
A void and silent space between two worlds,
When inspiration lags, and feeling sleeps,
Gathering strength for efforts yet to come.
For life alone is creator of life,
35   And closest contact with the human world
Is like a lantern shining in the night
To light me to a knowledge of myself.
I love the vivid life of winter months
In constant intercourse with human minds,
40   When every new experience is gain
And on all sides we feel the great world's heart;
The pulse and throb of life which makes us men!

---

[1] **communion**: sharing of intimate thoughts and feelings

CONTINUE TO THE NEXT PAGE

The Tutorverse

42. How do lines 1-5 contribute to the development of ideas in the poem?

    E. They show that everyone has things to learn from nature.
    F. They explain how nature can be both a blessing and a curse.
    G. They compare nature to a beautiful symphony which has no other parallel.
    H. They describe a particular point of view on the relationship between people and nature.

43. Read line 6 from the poem.

    The voice of waters soothes them with its fall

    The personification in these lines suggests that nature is

    A. a clumsy companion who can inadvertently cause harm.
    B. an ally who will help people overcome their weaknesses.
    C. a dear friend with whom people can find comfort and relief.
    D. a comrade who gives good advice and helps generate new ideas.

44. Read lines 8-9 from the poem.

    To them a city is a prison house
    Where pent up human forces labour and strive

    The metaphor contributes to the meaning of the poem by

    E. illustrating the need for more parks and greenspaces in cities.
    F. providing a perspective on how the city may be oppressive.
    G. demonstrating how the speaker hates living in the crowded conditions of towns and cities.
    H. showing how people do work in cities when they should instead be taking vacations in nature.

45. How does the imagery in lines 13-17 help to develop the central ideas of the poem?

    A. It shows how the author shares some aspects of other people's opinions about summer, but not all.
    B. It presents a picture that contrasts with the opinion that nature is a wild and untamable thing.
    C. It shows that nature alone can provide the inspiration and relief that people need to be creative and learn.
    D. It provides evidence of the point of view that people must conquer nature in order to fully achieve their goals.

46. Which detail from the poem demonstrates that the speaker's views differ from those of others?

    E. "But where in winter they must live until / Summer gives back the spaces of the hills." (lines 11-12)
    F. "But more than these, and much, ah, how much more, / I love the very human heart of man." (lines 18-19)
    G. "Above me spreads the hot, blue mid-day sky, / Far down the hillside lies the sleeping lake" (lines 20-21)
    H. "The blue crest of the distant mountain, tops / The green crest of the hill on which I sit" (lines 25-26)

CONTINUE TO THE NEXT PAGE

The Tutorverse

47. Read line 19 from the poem.

    I love the very human heart of man.

    Which of the following supports what is implied in this line?

    A. "Some men there are who find in nature all / Their inspiration, hers the sympathy" (lines 1-2)
    B. "But where in winter they must live until / Summer gives back the spaces of the hills." (lines 11-12)
    C. "When inspiration lags, and feeling sleeps, / Gathering strength for efforts yet to come." (lines 32-33)
    D. "And closest contact with the human world / Is like a lantern shining in the night" (lines 35-36)

48. Read lines 30-34.

    To me alone it is a time of pause,
    A void and silent space between two worlds,
    When inspiration lags, and feeling sleeps,
    Gathering strength for efforts yet to come.

    These lines contribute to the development of the central idea by

    E. emphasizing the poet's passion and celebration of the season of summer.
    F. showing how the poet actually likes winter more than summer.
    G. revealing the poet's unusual perspective on the season of summer.
    H. highlighting the poet's sense of loneliness when she is surrounded by nature.

49. Which detail from the poem best describes the speaker's point of view on summer?

    A. "And the great winds bring healing in their sound" (line 7)
    B. "Where beauty dwells not, driven forth by man" (line 10)
    C. "When inspiration lags, and feeling sleeps" (line 32)
    D. "When every new experience is gain" (line 40)

50. Read lines 38-39 from the poem.

    I love the vivid life of winter months
    In constant intercourse with human minds

    Which of the following offers a contrasting idea to those implied in these lines?

    E. "But where in winter they must live until / Summer gives back the spaces of the hills" (lines 11-12)
    F. "Thick branches swaying in a winter storm, / And moonlight playing in a boat's wide wake" (lines 16-17)
    G. "And closest contact with the human world / Is like a lantern shining in the night" (lines 35-36)
    H. "And on all sides we feel the great world's heart; / The pulse and throb of life which makes us men!" (lines 41-42)

CONTINUE TO THE NEXT PAGE

The Tutorverse

Superheated

1 The incomprehensibly hot ball of hydrogen and helium at the center of the solar system is known to us as the sun. The sun's diameter is more than 100 times greater than Earth's. A yellow dwarf star, the sun has a mass more than 300,000 times greater than Earth's, making it the most massive object in the solar system. The sun alone accounts for more than 99% of all matter in our solar system.

2 Scientists estimate that the sun was formed more than 4.5 billion years ago as the result of what is known as a gravitational collapse. The gravity where the sun is now became so strong that it continued to attract more and more matter to it. As the matter within the center of the collapse became increasingly dense, individual atoms began to fuse together in a process known as nuclear fusion. Nuclear fusion has sustained the sun ever since, resulting in the release of massive amounts of energy.

3 Life on earth owes its existence to this energy. This energy takes on many forms, one of which is light radiation. It takes light from the sun just over eight minutes to reach Earth, on average. Once here, sunlight supports virtually all life on Earth, powering photosynthesis, heating the surface of the earth, and influencing climate and weather patterns. Another form of this energy comes in the form of particle radiation, which influences unique properties in Earth's ionosphere – the topmost layers of the earth's atmosphere. Thanks to particle radiation from the sun, the ionosphere is electrically charged, allowing radio waves – and the ideas they carry – to bounce around the world.

4 The sun has been ejecting this radiation into space for quite some time, and will continue to do so for another 4-5 billion years. But this does not mean that the sun will remain the same forever.

5 The sun as we know it will exist for an estimated 10 billion years, sustained by the nuclear fusion of hydrogen at its core. But once this hydrogen has been completely exhausted, the sun will begin turning into what is known as a red giant star. Once the sun's core hydrogen reserves have been depleted, the sun will start to grow larger and brighter. Every 500 million years or so, the sun will double in size until it reaches a size more than 200 times larger than it is today. By then, the sun will be thousands of times brighter than it is today. During this process, Mercury, Venus, and most likely even Earth will be consumed by the swelling star.

6 During its red giant phase, with no hydrogen left, the sun will burn off all of its helium. Once this happens, the sun becomes unstable and constantly loses matter in powerful solar ejections. Eventually, after many more millions of years, the sun will begin to cool and shrink, eventually becoming a white dwarf star with approximately half the mass it had during its yellow dwarf stage.

Celestial Object	Mass (Relative to Earth)
Mercury	0.06
Mars	0.11
Venus	0.82
Earth	1.00
Neptune	17.15
Uranus	14.54
Saturn	95.16
Jupiter	317.83
Sun	332,889.71

CONTINUE TO THE NEXT PAGE

The Tutorverse

51. Which of the following tells what the passage is about?

    A. the life cycle of the sun
    B. how the sun benefits the earth
    C. explaining how nuclear fusion works
    D. the amount of energy given off by the sun

52. According to paragraph 2, which scientific process keeps the sun shining?

    E. light radiation
    F. particle radiation
    G. nuclear fusion
    H. photosynthesis

53. The passage provides evidence that the sun's energy

    A. is almost entirely absorbed by the Earth's atmosphere.
    B. is used to power long-distance communications from different locations on Earth.
    C. is far less than that of other stars – which are already red giants – in our galaxy.
    D. will double in size every 500 million years after the hydrogen runs out.

54. The passage indicates that the sun will become a red giant

    E. when it runs out of helium.
    F. when it runs out of hydrogen.
    G. when it undergoes gravitational collapse.
    H. when it emits light and particle radiation.

55. Once the sun becomes a red giant, all of the following will take place **except** that

    A. the sun will destroy Venus.
    B. the sun will grow brighter and brighter.
    C. the sun will begin burning off its supply of hydrogen.
    D. the sun will grow to be more than 200 times its current size.

56. In order from the present to the distant future, which of the following represents the stages in which the sun will progress?

    E. yellow dwarf, red giant, white dwarf
    F. yellow dwarf, white dwarf, red giant
    G. white dwarf, yellow dwarf, red giant
    H. red giant, white dwarf, yellow dwarf

57. Which sentence from the passage does the table best support?

    A. "The sun alone accounts for more than 99% of all matter in our solar system." (paragraph 1)
    B. "Scientists estimate that the sun was formed more than 4.5 billion years ago as the result of what is known as a gravitational collapse." (paragraph 2)
    C. "The sun has been ejecting this radiation into space for quite some time, and will continue to do so for another 4-5 billion years." (paragraph 4)
    D. "Every 500 million years or so, the sun will double in size until it reaches a size more than 200 times larger than it is today." (paragraph 5)

CONTINUE TO THE NEXT PAGE

The Tutorverse

Section Two: Mathematics

Recommended Time Limit: 90 minutes

IMPORTANT NOTES: (1) Formulas and definitions of mathematical terms and symbols are not provided. (2) Diagrams other than graphs are not necessarily drawn to scale. Do not assume any relationship in a diagram unless it is specifically stated or can be figured out from the information given. (3) Assume that a diagram is in one plane unless the problem specifically states that it is not. (4) Graphs are drawn to scale. Unless stated otherwise, you can assume relationships according to appearance. For example, (on a graph) lines that appear to be parallel can be assumed to be parallel; likewise for concurrent lines, straight lines, collinear points, right angles, etc. (5) Reduce all fractions to lowest terms.

Mathematics – Grid-In Questions
Questions 58-62

Directions Solve each problem. On the answer sheet, write your answer in the boxes at the top of the grid, starting *on the left side of each grid*. Print only one number or symbol in each box. *Do not leave a box blank in the middle of an answer.* Under each box, fill in the circle that matches the number or symbol you wrote above. *Do not fill in a circle under an unused box.*

58.
$$1 \text{ jorp} = 3 \text{ wims}$$
$$2 \text{ jorps} = 4 \text{ saffs}$$

Using the conversions above, how many wims are equivalent to one saff?

59. In how many ways can 5 students line up for lunch?

60.
$$-2 < x < 4$$
$$3 < x < 10$$

How many integer values of x satisfy both of the above statements?

61.

Point C (not shown) is the midpoint of AB. If point D (not shown) is the midpoint of CB, and the length of DB is 3, what is the value of B?

62. Egret buys 2 containers of orange candies, 4 containers of green candies, and 5 containers of purple candies. There are 35 orange candies in a container, and 15 green candies in a container. There are as many purple candies as orange and green candies combined. All of the candies are combined together and distributed among 65 party bags. How many candies are in each party bag?

CONTINUE TO THE NEXT PAGE

The Tutorverse

Mathematics – Multiple Choice

Questions 63-114

Directions Solve each problem. Select the best answer from the choices given. Mark the letter of your answer on the answer sheet. You can do your figuring in the test booklet or on paper provided by the proctor. DO NOT MAKE ANY MARKS ON YOUR ANSWER SHEET OTHER THAN FILLING IN YOUR ANSWER CHOICES.

63. $\sqrt{16+9} =$

   A. 5
   B. 7
   C. 12.5
   D. 25

64. Adina is older than Boaz but younger than Ezra. If a, b, and e represent their ages, respectively, which of the following is true?

   E. $b < a < e$
   F. $b < e < a$
   G. $a < b < e$
   H. $e < a < b$

65. $0.324 \div 72 =$

   A. 0.00045
   B. 0.0045
   C. 0.045
   D. 4.5

66. If $4m - 20 = 9$, then $2m - 10 =$

   E. −2.7
   F. 4.5
   G. 7.25
   H. 19

67.

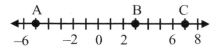

How many units is it from the midpoint of $\overline{AB}$ to the midpoint of $\overline{AC}$?

   A. 2
   B. 4
   C. 5
   D. 6

68. The total cost of 3 equally priced notebooks is $7.50. If the cost of each notebook is increased by $0.75, how much will 5 of the notebooks cost at the new rate?

   E. $8.25
   F. $9.75
   G. $12.50
   H. $16.25

69. $\dfrac{(4)^2 + (-3)^2}{(-2)^3 - (1)^5} =$

   A. $-\dfrac{25}{9}$
   B. $-\dfrac{5}{2}$
   C. $-\dfrac{7}{9}$
   D. $\dfrac{25}{7}$

70. Albert biked 3 times the number of miles Bob did yesterday. They biked 72 miles altogether. How many miles did Albert bike?

   E. 18
   F. 24
   G. 48
   H. 54

71. What is the greatest common factor of 420 and 1,155?

   A. 15
   B. 21
   C. 105
   D. 4,620

CONTINUE TO THE NEXT PAGE

72.

1 dollar = 1.2 euros
1 dollar = 102 yen

Using the conversions above, how many yen are equivalent to 1 euro?

E.   85.0 yen
F.   100.8 yen
G.   103.2 yen
H.   122.4 yen

73. An equilateral triangle and a regular pentagon have equal perimeters. One side of the triangle has length 5. What is the length of three sides of the pentagon?

A.   3
B.   5
C.   9
D.   15

74. If $3x + 4 - 5x = 6 - 7x + 8$, then $x =$

E. $-\dfrac{10}{9}$

F. $\dfrac{2}{5}$

G. $\dfrac{14}{9}$

H.   2

75. How many numbers between 50 and 100 are evenly divisible by 3?

A.   16
B.   17
C.   18
D.   33

76. A fast food restaurant sold 100 burgers and 100 hotdogs. If they want burgers to be 60% of their sales for the week, how many more burgers must they sell, if the number of hotdogs sold remains the same?

E.   20
F.   40
G.   50
H.   150

77. A box contains only blue and black glass beads. The probability of randomly choosing a blue bead out of the box is 3 times the probability of randomly choosing a black bead out of the box. If there are 12 beads in the box, how many are blue?

A.   3
B.   4
C.   6
D.   9

78. If $\dfrac{3}{7}$ of K is 210, what is $\dfrac{5}{7}$ of K?

E.   150
F.   294
G.   350
H.   1,050

79. A certain piece of candy weighs 90 milligrams. What is the candy's weight in grams?

A.   0.009 g
B.   0.09 g
C.   0.9 g
D.   9.0 g

80. A class trip costs a total of d dollars, which is supposed to be divided equally amongst the s students in a class. If n students decide not to go on the trip and therefore do not chip in for the expense of the trip, which of the following represents the new amount, in dollars, that each of the remaining students must pay to go on the trip?

E. $\dfrac{d}{s-n}$

F. $\dfrac{dn}{s-n}$

G. $\dfrac{d(s-n)}{s}$

H. $\dfrac{dn}{s(s-n)}$

CONTINUE TO THE NEXT PAGE

The Tutorverse

81. Carmen works at a bagel store, where her job is to fill trays with bagels that are to be baked. Each tray can hold 18 bagels. If Carmen has 163 bagels and fills each tray to capacity except for the last tray, how many bagels will be placed on the last tray?

    A. 1
    B. 3
    C. 5
    D. 7

82.

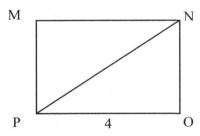

Figure MNOP is a rectangle. The area of triangles MNP and NOP are equal. If the perimeter is 14, what is the length of NP?

    E. 3
    F. 4
    G. 5
    H. $\sqrt{52}$

83. Line *m* and line *n* are parallel. At how many points will they intersect?

    A. 0
    B. 1
    C. 2
    D. The number varies.

84. If the mean of 5, 5, 8, 10, and *x* is equal to *x*, what is the value of *x*?

    E. 5
    F. 6
    G. 7
    H. 8

85.

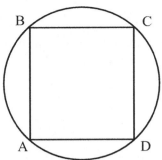

ABCD is a square that touches the circle at points A, B, C, and D. AC (not shown) has a length of 36 cm. What is the area of the circle?

    A. 36π sq. cm.
    B. 72π sq. cm.
    C. 324π sq. cm.
    D. $1,296\pi$ sq. cm.

86. When 20 is divided by the positive integer *x*, the remainder is 4. For how many different values of *x* is this true?

    E. One
    F. Two
    G. Three
    H. Four

87. Which of the following represents 2^6 in terms of 8?

    A. 8^2
    B. 8^3
    C. 8^{12}
    D. 8^{18}

88. A certain bucket can hold 7,500 milliliters of water when it is filled to the top. At the moment, the bucket is only $\frac{2}{5}$ full of water.

    Approximately many **liters** (L) of water must be added to fill the bucket to the top?

    E. 3.0 L
    F. 4.5 L
    G. 3,000.0 L
    H. 4,500.0 L

CONTINUE TO THE NEXT PAGE

The Tutorverse

89. If A is the set of all odd integers, B is the set of all positive integers, and C is the set of all integers less than 7, which of the following integers will be in all three sets?

A. 6
B. 4
C. 1
D. −1

90. The name of every student in a class is written on separate pieces of paper and put into a hat. The probability of randomly picking the name of a boy out of the hat is $\frac{2}{5}$. If there are 15 girls in the class, how many more girls are there than boys in the class?

E. 5
F. 6
G. 9
H. 10

91. If $\overset{\vee}{y} = \frac{y}{2}$, what is the value of $2 + \overset{\vee}{6}$?

A. 4
B. 5
C. 6
D. 8

92. One side of a 6-sided number cube is painted green, and the other sides are all painted red. The total surface area of the red sides is 45 square millimeters. What is the volume of the number cube in cubic millimeters?

E. 9 cu mm
F. 27 cu mm
G. 54 cu mm
H. 81 cu mm

93. A number is decreased by 20%, and then the new number is decreased by another 20%. What is the percent decrease from the original number?

A. 36%
B. 40%
C. 60%
D. 64%

94. What is the value of the numerical expression $\frac{4.8 \times 10^6}{1.2 \times 10^4}$ in scientific notation?

E. 4.0×10^1
F. 4.0×10^2
G. 4.0×10^3
H. 4.0×10^4

95. A 7-ounce bag of prunes sells for $3.50. At this rate, what would be the price of a 1-pound bag of prunes? (Note: 1 lb. = 16 oz.)

A. $7.00
B. $8.00
C. $8.50
D. $16.00

96. How many minutes are there in h hours and m minutes?

E. $60h + m$
F. $60(h + m)$
G. $\frac{(h + m)}{60}$
H. $\frac{h}{60} + m$

97. What is the solution set for $-5c + 10 > 15$?

A. (number line, open circle at 1, shaded left)
B. (number line, open circle at 1, shaded right)
C. (number line, open circle at −1, shaded left)
D. (number line, open circle at −1, shaded right)

CONTINUE TO THE NEXT PAGE

The Tutorverse

98. If $3x = 5y^2 = 45$, what is the value of xy^2?

    E.   15
    F.   135
    G.   405
    H.   1,215

---

99. Let $Q = (-|-2| - |-8|)$.

What is the value of $-|-Q|$?

    A. −10
    B. − 6
    C.   6
    D. 10

---

100. A set of 7 numbers has a mean of 12. What additional number must be included in this set to create a new set with a mean that is 3 more than the mean of the original set?

    E. 15
    F. 13.5
    G. 21
    H. 36

---

101. A rectangular bedroom is 10 feet by 12 feet. How many square tiles that are 4 inches on each side must be used to completely cover the floor?

    A.   7.5
    B.   720
    C. 1,080
    D. 1,920

---

102. In how many different ways can the letters MATH be arranged?

    E.   16
    F.   24
    G.   64
    H. 256

---

103. If $2^x \times 3^y = 72$, what is $x + y$?

    A. 5
    B. 6
    C. 7
    D. 12

104.

x	y
1	4
2	7
3	10
4	13
10	31

What is the pattern shown in the table above?

    E. $y = x + 3$
    F. $y = x + 21$
    G. $y = 3x + 1$
    H. $y = 4x$

---

105. Rectangle *ABCD* is similar to rectangle *WXYZ*.

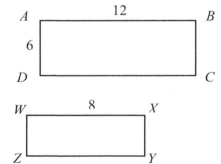

What is the length of side *XY*?

    A. 2
    B. 4
    C. 6
    D. 9

---

106. Kevin plans to hike up a certain mountain. His only drinking water will be that which he purifies himself using iodine tablets. Kevin has 20 packets of iodine tablets, each of which contain 5 iodine tablets. To have enough drinking water for the day, Kevin knows that he must use $\dfrac{3}{5}$ of a packet per day. For how many days can Kevin purify enough water to drink for the entire day?

    E.   33
    F.   34
    G.   60
    H. 166

CONTINUE TO THE NEXT PAGE

The Tutorverse

107.

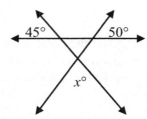

The figure above shows three intersecting straight lines. What is the value of x?

A. 50°
B. 85°
C. 95°
D. 130°

108.   5, 14, 32, 68, …
In the sequence above, the 1st term is 5. Each number after the first is obtained by adding 2 to the preceding number, then doubling the result. What is the 7th term in the sequence?

E. 278
F. 286
G. 558
H. 572

109. A real estate broker receives a 3% commission on all of his sales. If he made a total of $9,000 over the last 3 months, what was his average sales total for each of those three months?

A. $27,000
B. $100,000
C. $150,000
D. $300,000

110. A rectangle has a perimeter of 70 meters. Its length is 9 more than its width. What is the length of the rectangle?

E. 13.0
F. 22.0
G. 26.0
H. 30.5

111. If $y = a(a - 5)$, then $y - 1 =$

A. $a^2 - 6a$
B. $a^2 - 5a - 1$
C. $a^2 + 5a - 1$
D. $a^2 - 6$

112. The total daily profit, p, in dollars, from selling s shirts is given by the function $p = 25s - (12s + b)$, where b is a constant. If 50 shirts were sold yesterday for a total profit of $600, what is the value of b?

E. −50
F. 50
G. 550
H. 600

113. A model of a real ship is built at a scale of 1 inch represents 6 yards. If the model is 2.5 feet long, how long is the real ship? *(Note: 1 yard = 3 feet)*

A. 15 feet
B. 90 feet
C. 180 feet
D. 540 feet

114. A real estate agent's commission is p percent of the price of a house. Which of the following represents the commission, in dollars, on 2 houses that sold for $100,000 each?

E. $2,000p$
F. $50,000p$
G. $200,000p$
H. $200,000 + \dfrac{p}{100}$

THIS IS THE END OF THE TEST. IF THERE IS TIME REMAINING, YOU MAY CHECK YOUR ANSWERS TO BOTH PARTS 1 AND PART 2.

ENSURE THAT THERE ARE NO STRAY MARKS, PARTLY FILLED ANSWER CIRCLES, OR INCOMPLETE ERASURES ON THE ANSWER SHEET.

The Tutorverse

Scoring the Practice Test

Using your answer sheet and referring to the answer key at the end of the workbook, calculate the percentage of questions you answered correctly in each section by taking the number of questions you answered correctly in that section and dividing it by the number of questions in that section. Multiply this number by 100 to determine your percentage score. The higher the percentage, the stronger your performance in that section.

Note that the actual test will not directly evaluate your score based on percentage correct or incorrect. Instead, it will convert the raw number of questions answered correctly into a scaled score. This scaled score will be used to compare your score with the scores of other students.

Record your results here:

Section	Questions Correct	Total Questions	Percent Questions Correct
English Language Arts – Revising/Editing Skills	_____	10	_____%
English Language Arts – Reading Comprehension	_____	47	_____%
Mathematics	_____	57	_____%

Carefully consider the results from your practice test. If you're not happy with your performance on a certain section, don't worry! Use these results to determine where you should spend more studying. Revisit some of the practice materials, or complete practice materials that you may have skipped along the way.

If you're stuck, reach out to a trusted educator – a parent, teacher at school, or tutor – to help you improve in the areas that still need some more work.

The Tutorverse is home to many highly-experienced tutors. Get a parent's permission first, then send us an email at info@thetutorverse.com, or visit us online at www.thetutorverse.com.

The Tutorverse

Answer Explanations

This section provides the answer solutions and explanations to the practice tests, practice questions, and practice sections of the workbook.

Practice Test 1 (Diagnostic)

Part One: English Language Arts

1. C. *Modifiers*. Modifiers are words or phrases that describe (or modify) other parts of a sentence. Modifiers tell us more information and paint a more detailed picture about a sentence's primary nouns and verbs. Modifiers can be adjectives, adverbs, adjective or adverb clauses, and verb or prepositional phrases. In general, modifiers should be placed as closely as possible to the thing that it modifies. Confusion can arise when the modifiers are placed "far away" from the things they modify. In this case, the modifier is "with a bushy wagging tail," and it is misplaced. It doesn't make sense for this to modify the "soccer ball." Instead, it should modify the dog. This means we should put it close to "dog," and the only place that suits this is after "dog" and before "chased." The other arrangements confuse the meaning of the sentence. In some, it can be construed that the dog actually chased after the ball along with a bushy wagging tail (a strange image!).

2. F. *Logical Comparison*. The noun being compared is "temperature." In this case, we are comparing temperatures in Hawaii with temperatures in Antarctica. As written, the sentence compares the temperatures in Hawaii with Antarctica itself. This is the same for the other answer choices. Only by using "those in" is it clear that the comparisons being made are between the temperatures of two different locations (as opposed to the temperature of one location with another location itself).

3. A. *Possessive Nouns & Determiners*. We can split the first sentence into two smaller sentences: "Since chili was my sister favorite food, we decided to enter the chili contest at the county fair" and "Since chili was my favorite food, we decided to enter the chili contest at the county fair." Notice that "sister" is missing an " 's". We need the comma after "contest" and "food" because they are at the end of a subordinate clause (the respective sentences start with "since" and "during"). Therefore, we can eliminate B, C, and D. "Ours" is the appropriate way to signal possession of the collective "our".

4. F. The sentence in question states that King made references to "sources." Sources are listed in sentence 6, which also refers to "these." Without having "sources" immediately preceding it, we would not know that "these" refers to "sources."

5. C. The previous sentence describes how King thought that these allusions would have made the audience like his speech more. Sentence 8 describes how this did not actually happen. Therefore, the best transition word to use should signify a contrast, as "nonetheless" does.

6. E. Sentence 9 describes how King did not follow his speech, and improvised. However, it does so in a roundabout way, including redundancies ("departed from his carefully written speech" and "not following his prepared speech"; "improvising" and "making it up as he went along"). Improvising is itself the act of coming up with a speech on the spot, and the first choice expresses this most clearly. We do not need to also say that King stopped following his prepared speech, since we already know that he "began to improvise."

7. C. Sentence 16 describes the speaking tactic called anaphora. Sentence 17 says that "this" (referring to anaphora) is "the repetition of a phrase at the beginning of sentences." Sentence 18 goes on to describe that for King, this was the phrase "I have a dream." Therefore, we know that sentence 17 provides more information about sentence 16, so we should not use a conjunction like "not" or even "and," since this suggests that anaphora and repetition are not the same thing. Neither should we use "because," since there is no causal relationship here. Instead, we need simply

to connect the two sentences with a "which is" and a comma to describe more about "anaphora."

8. H. The paragraph describes specifically how King used various techniques to enhance his speech, making it memorable. The sentence states "these tactics," so it must refer to specific tactics, and must come after the other sentences. This sentence also describes an effect, which is best described after the causes (i.e. the varied use of volume).

9. A. Though it would be correct to say that "King moved the hearts and minds of an entire generation," the sentence uses the phrase "was able," which means we must use "move" in the present tense. This is because the phrase "to move...generation" is an infinitive phrase. The actual core of the sentence is "he was able." "Thanks to...speech" is a dependent clause (which needs to be separated from the rest of the sentence with a comma) that describes more about what he was able to do, just as the infinitive phrase does. Changing "was" to "has been" does not change this fact. The word "an" signifies a single entity, so "generations," which is plural, would be incorrect.

10. F. Sentence 11 describes some of King's biographical information, which is not the focus of the passage and is irrelevant given the context of the rest of the paragraph. The passage is concerned with one of King's speeches, and how it was effective. The other choices are all important aspects of this idea.

The Cold

11. D. Lines 1-2 are "In the city, the cold is / thin and vain", and lines 31-21, "In the country, the cold is / Soft. Soft" contrast how different the cold feels in the two places. Though it introduces the cold in the city and the cold in the country as the main characters of the poem, the poem is not a dialogue between them.

12. F. The comparison of the cold to a blade, or saber, shows how it penetrates protections: "shearing through feather and wool and bone." It is not a literal blade that disfigures people or shaves off their fur and feathers.

13. A. The city is known for being a busy, rushed place – attributes which the cold takes on – while the country is known for being lush and abundant. They show how the cold is different because it takes on the characteristics of its locale. Though later in the poem, it is revealed that the two meet, these two excerpts are not referring to them attempting to meet one another.

14. G. The descriptions of outer appearances of the cold of the city shows how sleek and sharp it is, as he wears a "suit of ice" and "granite topcoat." On the other hand, the descriptions of the cold of the country are soft and cozy: "her fleecy white coat/...her magnificent hoary cloak." These descriptions are metaphorical rather than literal, and not meant to show different degrees of cold.

15. D. This The stanza begins with "The buildings stand taller, sharper as he passes, / polished and menacing," while the two quoted lines show how the city can be beautiful as well. The "diamond necklace" is a simile of something beautiful, not a literal present.

16. F. At the end of the poem, the cold in the city and the cold in the country are revealed to be romantically connected. These two phrases hint at this connection, implying that each one is searching for the other. They are not directly addressing the reader, despite the use of "you."

17. A. The line "chill-y! chilly-chilly-chilly-chill-EE!—" is a play on the word "chilly," where the alternate spelling "chill-EE" mimics the literal sound of birdcalls, while the meaning of the word describes how cold it is. This supports an image of playfulness for the cold of the country, who is being contrasted as the opposite of

the serious and sharp cold of the city throughout the poem. The emphasis of this moment is not on the birds suffering in winter.

18. G. The description, "before the wind can take a breath, / swoops through" shows how quickly the cold in the country moves, out of eagerness to embrace the city-cold lingering on the visitors. The poem does not characterize the country cold as "reckless" anywhere else, so it is unlikely that that is the main point here.

19. C. The poem establishes the longing between the two colds at earlier points (lines 12, 15, 51, 53-56), and this last stanza ends on a somber note, as it emphasizes how rarely the two entities are able to meet despite their feelings.

A Garden Masterpiece

20. F. In paragraphs 1-2, the passage discusses how Monet and his series of paintings Water Lilies are some of the most influential Impressionist paintings. As discussed in paragraph 5, Impressionism focuses on perception rather than appearance. Though Impressionist artists challenged the conventions of established art institutions of the time, there is no evidence that Monet personally hated them. The idea that Monet escaped poverty is not discussed in the passage, and his near-blindness is a supporting detail rather than the central idea.

21. C. The author discusses the classical and realistic art in studios in the likes of École des Beaux in order to contextualize the artistic choices that Impressionists made as innovators. There is no mention of them once studying at these academies, or of art schools in the post-Impressionist eras.

22. H. "Idealized" means representing the most perfect, or typical, example. By using the word to describe the type of landscapes that artists during that time painted, the author implies that the landscapes were quintessential versions of nature rather than reality. This is also supported by the detail that they painted landscapes in their studios, and not outside. This particular sentence does not discuss the realism of the landscapes.

23. D. Paragraph 3 explains that Monet painted the same scene over and over again in order to capture how it looked at different times of day; we can infer that the changes he was observing were in appearance, light, and shadows as the sun moved in the sky. He was not a perfectionist, but an impressionist, and the passage does not connect his poor vision to painting scenes repeatedly (in fact, it says that the poor vision led to powerful and beautiful works).

24. E. Since Monet wanted to capture his perception of his garden rather than its realistic appearance, the paragraph describes how Monet's paintings embodied the artistic concepts of sensation that he valued. The passage discusses his renown for painting the series in paragraph 3, not 5. Similarly, Monet's high regard for his garden is mentioned in paragraph 4.

25. B. Since Monet was able to portray his perceptions of the garden despite not being able to see the details accurately, Monet truly embodied the value of perception over accuracy. The large size of his paintings does not prove anything about his style, and having two compositions could just as well be realistic as subjective.

26. G. Throughout the passage, the author describes how Impressionists were concerned with perception and feeling as opposed to details and made-up ideals. This rules out all other answer choices. One can use process of elimination here to note that the other choices describe things that are the same, and therefore cannot all be the correct choice.

27. A. Paragraph 7 explains why Monet used different sized canvases, specifically large ones. Monet wanted to give the illusion of a wave with no end point, no horizon or shore. This would evoke a sensation of peace. The two different styles of compositions are distinct and Monet might have experimented with different canvases with them. However, they do not explain Monet's reasoning behind choosing large canvases.

The Rule of Law

28. H. The passage shows the progression of rule of law from being a theory in ancient China and Greece, to becoming realized through the Magna Carta and American Constitution, and eventually

popularized. Though rule of law is used in the Constitution, the idea was not invented by Americans.

29. A. The text states that, under the rule of law, "everyone is bound by the same rules and laws that govern society." This shows an inherent equality in the law, whereby everyone is held equally accountable. Therefore, being a political leader does not make one exempt from codified law under any circumstances.

30. E. The paragraph highlights the stratocracies, monarchies, and plutocracies that existed prior to the rule of law's general acceptance within the global community, though there is no mention of them being more or less successful. The next paragraph focuses on the birth of the rule of law in ancient society, but paragraph 3 focuses mainly on the governments that created power structures that were antithetical to the rule of law.

31. D. The author makes no comparisons between Aristotle and Han Fei, instead describing how they shared a similar idea. Rule by the strongest is a stratocracy, and rule by a single person is a monarchy; neither is a type of rule that the author thinks highly of. We only know for certain that the U.S. Constitution was heavily influenced by a similar document in medieval England, the Magna Carta.

32. H. The text implies that Han Fei and Aristotle had a high regard for the equalizing power of the rule of law. Conceptually, they believed nobody could rule above the law, so they would have frowned upon the consolidation and abuse of power described in options F and G.

33. D. According to the text, the signing of the Magna Carta is what allowed the theoretical concept of the rule of law to be implemented. The rule of law allowed for a kind of legal equality that was not reflected in monarchies or plutocracies.

34. E. Other nations tried to replicate, or imitate, the U.S. Constitution because it showed them that the rule of law was possible to implement, and lead to a successful and powerful society. These nations did not fear the Constitution or try to undermine it.

Prove It!

35. D. Although the first paragraph discusses how, in the past, "people used myths and fantastical tales to explain the world around them," the rest of the passage describes how the scientific method has helped people better understand natural phenomena more accurately. Galileo's experiment is only referenced as a detail to support this central idea. Additionally, while gravity (i.e., falling objects) is referenced as one kind of natural phenomenon that has been studied over time using the scientific method, the passage is about how perceptions of all-natural phenomena have changed over time, due to the scientific method.

36. G. The entire passage discusses how scientific knowledge has become more accurate and objective thanks to the modern employment of the scientific method. However, paragraph 1 sets the stage for this larger discussion by explaining how early understandings of science were simplistic and fanciful, with examples like earthquakes being caused by giant catfish. This purpose of this paragraph is neither to highlight the role of nature in inspiring myths, nor to defend the accuracy of these myths. Its sole purpose is to transition the text into a larger discussion on the utility of the scientific method. Likewise, paragraph 1 does not reference gravity like the other paragraphs.

37. A. The words "repeatable" and "observable" are used in paragraph 2 to argue that there is a certain dependability and validity that emerges from the scientific method due to its repetitious character and its objective intent. The paragraph does not imply that only scientists can use the scientific method.

38. F. The word "suspected" means "thought of with suspicion," which implies that Galileo's active skepticism, or thought process, was necessary to the development of his experiment. This is a part of the scientific method, where scientists observe and research, then come up with a claim about how the phenomenon works. Galileo was not being paranoid, as his suspicions were then supported by

evidence. It is implied that this reaction was different from the ideas of other scientists at the time, not similar.

39. B. The fifth paragraph describes Galileo's gravity experiment at the Leaning Tower of Pisa – a historical example of using the scientific method – and how it led Galileo "to conclude – rightly" an important scientific concept. There is no indication in the text that the scientific findings of the experimenter were not supported by later re-enactments.

40. E. Paragraph 6 discusses how air resistance causes objects to fall to the ground at different rates. In a vacuum, there is no air resistance; therefore, a feather and a hammer would fall at the same rate in a vacuum. A feather and hammer do not fall at different speeds due to their mass (which Galileo proves is not the cause behind different speeds of free fall) or the materials that they are made of.

41. C. Paragraph 7 discusses how modern-day scientists have reproduced Galileo's experiments in space, where they would be more accurate (due to air resistance). The last sentence, "Their results confirmed Galileo's findings – and demonstrate how the scientific method can illuminate truth," shows that this information was included to show how Galileo's experiment is an example of the scientific method, due to this reproducibility.

Adapted from *The Scarlet Plague*

42. E. Following this phrase, Granser goes on to detail all the ways in which the world before the Scarlet Plague were vastly different from now (restaurants and airships, instead of bears). Given his audience are boys who had never seen that past world, we can in infer that he is using a marveling tone. There is no evidence that he feels his loss is unjust, and his nostalgia is for the world that has changed, not his individual body.

43. D. Granser refers to things like restaurants and ships, which are associated with present times, as being from the far past. Therefore, the setting of the story must be in a hypothetical future, after the Scarlet Plague. It is not a realistic fiction story, nor is there evidence that it takes place on another planet.

44. G. In this answer option, Edwin is demonstrating his confusion by asking about the meaning of a word which Granser uses freely. Option F is an example of the boys correcting each other's crude speech, but does not show that they cannot understand Granser's words.

45. B. "Garrulous" means overly talkative, or talking often of trivial and unimportant things. The boys are shown to ignore Granser, but not to be frustrated or annoyed by him. In fact, later they request one of his stories. Though talkative, Granser is never shown as irritable or grumpy.

46. H. Paragraph 4 offers the only detail throughout the story that shows the new world in a positive light as opposed to a negative one, in comparison to the past. However, Granser does not appear to be arguing that the current world is superior or fundamentally similar to the past, and seems to be saying it as a random aside.

47. B. The story poses a contrast throughout of Granser's educated thinking and the uneducated, more "primitive" nature of the boys. The scene with the wolves shows how much the boys fit in with this current, wilder world, and the Biblical reference to David and Goliath emphasizes this. The boys show no terror of the wolves, since they react to it by laughing and lying back in the sand. Also, the story itself of David and the Goliath does not describe David as being "confident in dealing with dangerous predators" (instead, he is the underdog), so that cannot be why the author included the simile.

48. E. The metaphor connecting human progress to foam supports the idea that all human labor eventually disappears: as foam dries out in the sand, so too did the markings of civilization disappear after the plague. The reference to 'foam' is not a literal one, and there is no mention in any other part of the story of sea levels rising or tidal patterns.

49. C. In paragraph 10, Hare-Lip speaks rudely to Granser. However, in paragraph 15, when the boys ask Granser a question, Granser exhibits great patience in teaching their number concepts and explaining the word. The boys tolerate Granser throughout the story, but are not particularly patient with him. While it is true that they have very different backgrounds, Granser does not argue constantly with the boys.

Helping Others Pays Off

50. F. Prior to this excerpt, the author states "it is hard to find a job that has all the desired qualities" (paragraph 1), and the two quoted sentences are examples to support this idea. As such, though the specific drawbacks (stressful versus not satisfying) and benefits (pays well) may be different, the parallel structure is emphasizing the imperfect nature of jobs. It is not discussing the nursing industry specifically, as that is introduced in paragraph 2.

51. C. Over the course of the passage, the author describes the various benefits of being an RN. She mentions in passing how to become an RN, as well as different specializations, but those are subtopics addressed by individual paragraphs and not the entire passage. Although drawbacks are mentioned in paragraph 4, paragraph 5 immediately follows up with a counterexample, and the tone of the whole passage is favorable to the nursing career.

52. H. The central idea of paragraph 2 is stated in its last sentence: "Because there are so many options for specialization, RNs can choose to work in different environments and roles that best suit their interests and strengths" (paragraph 2). The diverse settings that they work in, and their various duties, are details to support this idea.

53. B. In the third paragraph, the author discusses how the career has a positive outlook primarily because the world's population "continues to grow" and "demand for healthcare professions" is also expected to grow. The author explicitly states that compensation is predicted to grow along with the number of open positions. There is no mention of staff turnover, or funding from the Department of Labor.

54. G. Paragraph 4 is the only one that lists negative aspects, or counterarguments to becoming an RN. Paragraph 5 then challenges this counterargument by showing how nurses are generally happy with their jobs despite the challenges. Paragraph 4 is not related to the ideas introduced in paragraph 3 (the growth of the job), or paragraph 6 (degrees necessary to become an RN).

55. D. The quotes in paragraph 5 are specific anecdotes for why individual nurses love their job, and follow the statistics describing overall job satisfaction in the industry. They are not particularly dramatic, and do not offer a new argument to support the overall claim.

56. H. The graph shows that the job growth from 2006-2016 for RNs has far exceeded those of other healthcare jobs. The chart does not provide information about length of age, compensation, or the length of illnesses.

57. A. The last sentence of the passage states: "Many find that these requirements are a small price to pay to be a part of such a well-respected and well-compensated profession" (paragraph 7), implying that the effort needed to get the necessary degrees for nursing are well worth it (in job satisfaction, career opportunities, and compensation). Given the information in paragraph 4, the passage does not argue that nursing is an occupation with zero drawbacks.

Part Two: Math

58. –424. *Numbers & Operations – Absolute Value.* $|150 – 510| = |–360| = 360$, and $|15 – 51| = |–36| = 36$, so the equation simplifies to $36 – 360 – q = 100$. Combine like terms, and isolate the variable for $–q = 424$, and finally $q = –424$.

59. 0.4. *Algebra – Algebraic Expressions & Equations.* Simplify the equation by distributing to get rid of parentheses: $9 – 2x – 10 = 3x – 5 + 5x$. Then combine like terms: $–1 – 2x = 8x – 5$. Adding $2x$ and 5 to both sides results in $4 = 10x$. Therefore, $x = 4/10$, which can be gridded in as 0.4 or .4.

60. 92. *Probability & Statistics – Averages.* If Janelle's final average from 6 tests is to be 90, then the sum of her scores must be 540. If she already has 4 test scores that average 87, then the sum of those

four tests is 348, so she still needs 192 points. If the she scores the maximum 100 points on one test, then she can afford to score as low as 92 on the other test.

61. 48. *Geometry & Measurements – Area & Perimeter*. If we let x = the length, then the width is $3x$. The area can then be represented as $3x^2 = 108$, which simplifies to $x^2 = 36$, so $x = 6$. This means the length is 6 and the width is 18, so the perimeter is $2(6) + 2(18) = 12 + 36 = 48$.

62. 54. *Geometry & Measurements – Triangles*. This is a variation on the classic 3-4-5 right triangle where each side of the triangle is multiplied by 3. Since $3 \times 3 = 9$, and $5 \times 3 = 15$, we know that $4 \times 3 = 12$. Once we have this, simply apply the formula for area of a triangle: $\frac{1}{2}bh$, or $0.5(12)(9) = 54$.

63. A. *Algebra – Inequalities*. To isolate the variable, we subtract 1 from all three sides, giving us $-2 \leq -2f \leq 8$, and then divide all three sides by -2, resulting in $1 \geq f \geq -4$. That means that f can be any value less than or equal to 1 and greater than or equal to -4. On a graph, this is closed circles over -4 and 1 and the number line shaded in between them.

64. H. *Algebra – Algebra in Context*. There are two different expressions provided, each of which describe how much a phone plan will cost, depending on the number of minutes spent talking, x. Set the two expressions equal to each other: $50 + 3x = 60 + 2x$. Combine like terms, and isolate the variable to one side of the equation: $x = 10$. Note that x represents the number of minutes spent talking. We can plug this back into either expression to determine the cost of a 10-minute conversation: $50 + 3(10) = 80$; similarly, $60 + 2(10) = 80$. The companies charge the same amount of \$80.

65. C. *Numbers & Operations – Counting Principle*. Since there are four possible positions, and four different runners, there are $4 \times 3 \times 2 \times 1 = 24$ different ways for the four runners to finish. We can abbreviate the runners with the letter of their first names and see that this is true. If William finishes first, then there are 6 possible ways for the other runners to finish in second, third, and fourth place. WXYZ, WXZY, WYXZ, WYZX, WZXY, WZYX. We could repeat the same thing to see what would happen if Xing Mei, Yuki, and Zack each finish in first place, but we can intuit that the results would be similar. No matter who finishes first, there are 6 ways for the other three runners to finish the race.

66. F. *Probability & Statistics – Averages*. Let the variable x represent Olu's score on the final exam. Her mean can then be represented as $\frac{94 + 100 + 88 + 80 + x + x}{6}$. We are adding up all the scores, with the final exam counted twice, and dividing be the number of scores. This expression can be simplified as $\frac{362 + 2x}{6}$. Olu wants her mean to be no less than 92, so we can make an inequality $\frac{362 + 2x}{6} \geq 92$. To solve this inequality, the first step is multiplying both sides by 6. We get $(362 + 2x) \geq 552$. Next, subtract 362 from both sides to get $2x \geq 190$. Finally, divide both sides by 2 to get $x \geq 95$. The lowest score she can get is 95.

67. B. *Numbers & Operations – Ratios & Proportions*. $\frac{0.25}{24} = \frac{x}{60}$ so $24x = 15$ and $x = \frac{5}{8}$.

68. E. *Geometry & Measurements – Circles*. Since Q is the center of the circle on the left, then PR represents the diameter, which we know to be 8. The radius, represented by PQ or QR, is half of this,

or 4. The area of the circle with center $Q = \pi(4)^2 = 16\pi$. If this is 4 times larger than the area of the circle with center S, then the latter must be $16\pi \div 4 = 4\pi$. This means that the radius of the circle with center S can be determined by solving for r in the equation of the area of a circle: $4\pi = \pi r^2$. Therefore, $4 = r^2$, and $r = 2$, which is represented as RS or ST. Since the question asks for QS, and the circles are tangent (meeting exactly and only at point R), and we know that QR = 4 and RS = 2, then QR + RS = QS, and $4 + 2 = 6$.

69. D. *Numbers & Operations – Word Problems*. We can represent the information provided algebraically. Let x equal the number of times Ezekiel ran around the track. In terms of x, Darius ran $\frac{1}{6}x$ around the track. We know that this is equal to $2\frac{2}{3}$, because the question tells us that Darius actually ran around the track this many times. So, we have an equation and solve for x: $\frac{1}{6}x = 2\frac{2}{3}$. We can rewrite both sides of the equation as follows: $\frac{x}{6} = \frac{8}{3}$. Simply cross multiply and solve for x: $(8)(6) = 3x$ becomes $48 = 3x$, and $x = 16$.

70. F. *Geometry & Measurements – Angles*. Since the question asks for the average number of degrees in each interior angle of a decagon, we can use the formula for finding the degree measure of a regular polygon. Plugging in 10 for n in $\frac{180(n - 2)}{n}$, we arrive at $180(8) \div 10 = 144$.

71. C. *Algebra – Algebraic Expressions & Equations*. To find the correct answer, try each answer choice by choosing any x-value and plugging it into each answer choice to see which results in the correct corresponding y-value. If we start by plugging in 0 for x, we find that $y = x + 1$ and $y = 2x + 1$ both work, but we can eliminate the other choices. If we move on and plug in 2 for x, $y = x + 1$ does not work, leaving us with $y = 2x + 1$.

72. H. *Numbers & Operations – Absolute Value*. If $|9 - y + 6| = 21$, then $9 - y + 6 = \pm 21$. Solving both equations gives us $y = -6$ or $y = 36$. Since $y < 0$, then $y = -6$. Plug y into $|x - 3 \times 5| = 6 + y$ and simplify to $|x - 15| = 0$. Thus, $x = 15$.

73. B. *Probability & Statistics – Probability*. Since it is not possible to pick out a part of a piece of chocolate, the probability of picking a piece of dark chocolate out of a bowl of candy must be a multiple of 6. If there were 11 pieces of candy in the bowl, and the probability of picking a piece of dark chocolate out of a bowl is $\frac{5}{6}$, then there would need to be $5 \times 11 \div 6 = 9.16$ pieces of dark chocolate in the bowl of candy.

74. F. *Geometry & Measurements – Volume*. Use the formula for a pyramid to determine the volume of the glued-together figure. $\frac{1}{3}25(3) + \frac{1}{3}25(6) = 25 + 50$. In total, this becomes 75 cu in.

75. D. *Algebra – Plugins*. If b is doubled, then b^3 is doubled 3 times, resulting in $2 \times 8b^3$. If c is doubled, we get $\frac{2 \times 8b^3}{2c}$, which

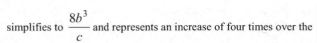

simplifies to $\dfrac{8b^3}{c}$ and represents an increase of four times over the

original $\dfrac{2b^3}{c}$.

76. E. *Numbers & Operations – Fractions.* The total number of students polled is 24 + 15 + 1 = 40. This means that 24 ÷ 40 students chose pizza. We can reduce this fraction by finding the greatest common factor for both the numerator and the denominator. This would be 8, since 8 × 3 = 24, and 8 × 5 = 40.

Dividing both parts of the fraction by 8, we get $\dfrac{3}{5}$.

77. A. *Numbers & Operations – Factors, Multiples, Exponents, & Radicals.* Observe the proper order of operations. First, simplify the expression inside the parenthesis, which gives us 4 + 3 = 7. Then, simplify $\sqrt{16 + 9}$ to be $\sqrt{25} = 5$. Then, take the difference: 5 − 7 = −2.

78. E. *Geometry & Measurements – Triangles.* Since points S and T are midpoints, triangle RST is also equilateral, and line segment PT creates two right angles – angle PRT and angle PTQ. This means that angles STP and TPS must each be 30°. Therefore, angle PST must be 180 − (30 + 30) = 120°.

79. A. *Numbers & Operations – Numbers.* If Bradley increased his speed by 2 miles per hour every minute for 15 minutes, then he increased his speed by a total of 30 miles per hour. If his starting speed was 40 miles per hour, then his speed at 12:15 p.m. was 70 miles per hour. If he was going 15 mph over the speed limit, then the speed limit was 55 mph.

80. G. *Numbers & Operations – Operations.* First calculate the value of the expression as it is, observing proper order of operations (PEMDAS). We first resolve the terms inside parenthesis so the formula becomes 5 × 2². We then resolve exponents: 5 × 4. Finally, we multiply to arrive at 20. Next, calculate the value of expressions without parenthesis. This expression would read: 2 + 3 × 4 − 2². We resolve exponents first: 2 + 3 × 4 − 4. Then we multiply: 2 + 12 − 4. Then we add and subtract to arrive at 10. The difference between 20 and 10 is 10.

81. C. *Numbers & Operations – Percents.* Since Pete's total living expenses are $1,200, and he spends 30% of it on rent, then his total rent expenses are $1,200 × 0.3 = $360. Since he has 2 other roommates, there are 3 people in total who share the rent equally. Therefore, Pete's rent expense represents 1 of 3 or $\dfrac{1}{3}$ of the total rent. Thus, the total rent is 3 × $360 = $1,080.

82. H. *Geometry & Measurements – Area & Perimeter.* The area of the piece of paper can be determined by the formula $A = 2\pi rh$, since this is the area of the cylinder without including the area of the top or bottom bases. We know that $h = 8$ in. and $r = 1.5$ in. Substituting these values into the formula, we find that $A = 2(\pi)(8)(1.5)$. This equals 24π.

83. B. *Numbers & Operations – Percents.* Let x represent the original number. We can represent the fact that x was increased by 30% in two different ways: $x + 0.3(x)$, or simply $1.3x$. If from this point, the new number is increased further by another 30%. We repeat the calculations just performed, replacing x with $1.3x$ instead: $1.3x + 0.3(1.3x)$, or simply $(1.3)(1.3)(x)$. Both simplify to $1.69x$, which means that compared to the original number x, the final number is 69% more.

84. G. *Geometry & Measurements – Coordinates.* We can use the midpoint formula to find the coordinates of point C. The formula is $M = \left(\dfrac{x_2 + x_1}{2}, \dfrac{y_2 + y_1}{2} \right)$. Substituting the coordinates of A

and B into the equation: $M = \left(\dfrac{2 + (-1)}{2}, \dfrac{2 + (-2)}{2} \right)$ and simplifying, we end up with $M = \left(\dfrac{1}{2}, \dfrac{0}{2} \right)$, or (0.5, 0).

85. A. *Geometry & Measurements – Area & Perimeter.* To find the length of a side of a square, take the square root of the area. Since the area of $WXYZ = 9$, $\sqrt{9} = 3$, and each of the four sides of the square has length 3. Since the area of square $ABCD$ is 4 times larger than the area of square $WXYZ$, it must have a total area of 4 × 9 = 36. Thus, the length of a side in square $ABCD = \sqrt{36} = 6$. The difference between the length of sides in each square is 6 − 3 = 3.

86. E. *Numbers & Operations – Imaginary Operations.* Substitute the values provided into the operation. Then, determine the value of each notation separately. We can express the first notation as ((2 × 6) + 4) ÷ 8. This simplifies to 12 + 4 = 16, which we divide by 8 to get 2. The second notation can be expressed as ((4 × 7) + 2) ÷ 6. This simplifies to 28 + 2 = 30, which we divide by 6 to get 5. The sum of 2 and 5 is 7.

87. D. *Numbers & Operations – Numbers.* If $0 < y < 1$, then y must be a positive fraction less than 1 whole. Going through each answer choice, we see that $y^2 > y^3$ is true because every time you multiply a positive fraction by itself the value gets smaller. $Y > 0.5y$ is also true because any positive value is always greater than half of its own value. Lastly, $y > y^3$ is true for the same reason $y^2 > y^3$ is true, meaning that all three inequalities are all true. We can prove this by substituting an example (i.e., a simple fraction like $\dfrac{1}{2}$).

88. H. *Probability & Statistics – Averages.* A mean is simply the sum of all numbers in a range (list), divided by the total count of the numbers in that range (list). The question already describes the "sum of a list of integers" and the "mean of the integers." The only other piece of information missing is the "count of numbers in that range." We can use a simple example to prove this: if a range consists of the numbers 1, 2, and 3, then the sum of that range is 6, and the average of that range is 6 ÷ 3 = 2. If we divide the sum (6) by the average (2), we arrive at 3, the count of numbers in the range.

89. A. *Numbers & Operations – Scientific Notation.* 10 raised to a negative power, like 10^{-5}, lets us know that we need to move the decimal point "over" to the left a certain number of times. So, we move the decimal point to the left 5 times.

90. F. *Geometry & Measurements – Measurements.* Start by writing down the information provided, labeling the number line if needed. We must first determine the location of M and N. Since M is the midpoint of $\overline{XY}$, and since X and Y are located at −10 and −2, respectively, we know that the midpoint of $\overline{XY}$ is (−10 + (−2)) ÷ 2 = −6, so M is located at −6. Since N is the midpoint of $\overline{YZ}$, and since Y and Z are located at −2 and 8, respectively, we know that the midpoint of $\overline{YZ}$ is (8 + (−2)) ÷ 2 = 3, so N is located at 3. Therefore, the midpoint between M and N is ((−6) + 3) ÷ 2 = −1.5.

91. C. *Geometry & Measurements – Measurements.* Since we start with Wesley's shift at 6:00 a.m., we know that he must drive two more times after that to complete his third shift. If W stands for Wesley's shift, and F stands for Wesley's friends' shifts, then the order of shifts will be WFFWFFW. If each shift is 7 hours long, and there are a total of 7 shifts, then Wesley's third shift will be over 49 hours later. Since 48 hours is 2 full days, 49 hours is 1 hour more than 2 full days. Wesley's third shift is over at 7:00 a.m.

92. H. *Numbers & Operations – Ratios & Proportions.* Since x is already being used, we'll assign side JK another variable, y.

$\dfrac{3/4x}{12} = \dfrac{x}{y}$. Cross multiply to get $\dfrac{3}{4}xy = 12x$. Divide both sides

by $\dfrac{3}{4}x$ to get $y = 16$.

93. C. *Numbers & Operations – Numbers.* If we set each of the answer choices equal to $x^2 + 1$, we can see which results in a nonzero integer value of x. For example, if $x^2 + 1 = 16$, then $x^2 = 15$ in which case x is not an integer because 15 is not a square number. Going through each answer choice we find that only 82 works because if $x^2 + 1 = 82$, then $x^2 = 81$ in which case $x = 9$.

94. F. *Geometry & Measurements – Measurements.* Using the formula for a midpoint, we take the sum of the two points and divide by two: $(-17 + (-3.5)) \div 2 = -10.25$.

95. D. *Numbers & Operations – Ratios & Proportions.* The ratio of the real tree to the painting is $1 : \dfrac{2}{9}$ for the trees. Therefore, our proportion is $\dfrac{1}{2/9} = \dfrac{x}{16}$. Solving gives us $16 = \dfrac{2}{9}x$, and $x = 72$.

96. H. *Geometry & Measurements – Triangles.* The figure is divided into two right triangles: one on the left of the dotted line, and one on the right. On the right, we know the value of two of the three angles: 30° and 90°. Therefore, $3y = 180 - 90 - 30$, and $y = 20°$. We can use this to solve for the measurement of x in the triangle on the left: $x = 180 - 90 - 20$. Therefore, $x = 70°$.

97. B. *Numbers & Operations – Operations.* Resolve each exponential term so that the equation becomes $\dfrac{-27 + 32}{16 - 1}$. This simplifies to $\dfrac{5}{15}$, or $\dfrac{1}{3}$.

98. H. *Numbers & Operations – Percents.* The sales tax was $6 and that was 8% of the original cost. Let x represent the original cost of the textbook. We can set this up using the proportion $\dfrac{6}{x} = \dfrac{8}{100}$. If we cross multiply this, we get $8x = 6 \times 100$. Dividing both sides by 8, we get $x = 75$.

99. D. *Algebra – Algebraic Expressions & Equations.* Solve for x by isolating it to one side of the equation, remembering order of operations, and the fact that what is done to one side of an equation must be done to the other side. First, divide both sides of the equation by 4 to remove the 4 in front of the factor $x - 5$. This gives us $x - 5 = 7$. Then add 5 to both sides, giving us $x = 12$.

100. G. *Numbers & Operations – Fractions.* After the first day of reading, the number of pages remaining is $1 - \dfrac{1}{4} = \dfrac{3}{4}$. The whole number 1 represents the total number of pages, whatever that is. We don't actually need to know how many pages there are, only that 1 represents the entire number of pages of the book, since we don't need to know how many pages remain to be read. After the second day, Latonya reads $\dfrac{1}{3}$ of the $\dfrac{3}{4}$ pages, meaning $\dfrac{2}{3}$ of the $\dfrac{3}{4}$ pages remain to be read. Multiply across the numerator and denominator for $\dfrac{6}{12}$ and simplify to $\dfrac{1}{2}$.

101. B. *Geometry & Measurements – Angles.* Because lines W and X are parallel, and lines Y and Z are parallel, all angles formed by the intersection of the vertical and horizontal lines are corresponding. This means that the angles formed at each of the four intersections have the same relative angle measurements. For example, the top-left angle at each intersection shares the same degree measurement as q. In addition, the opposite angle (the bottom-right angle at each intersection) also shares the same degree measurement as q because they are vertical angles. Similarly, the bottom-left and top-right angles at each intersection share the same degree measurement as r. Therefore, q and r are supplementary angles adding up to 180°.

102. E. *Numbers & Operations – Word Problems.* First, determine the amount of money taken out of the piggy bank. $12 \times \$0.25 + 9 \times \$0.1 + 6 \times \$0.05 + 5 \times \$0.01 = \$4.25$. So, from the original \$4.31, we subtract the amount taken out (\$4.25) to be left with \$0.06 in the piggy bank. Of the given choices, the only way to do this is with 1 nickel and 1 penny.

103. C. *Geometry & Measurements – Circles.* A tire is a circle that rotates along its circumference. The circumference of a circle is $C = 2\pi r$. In this case, we know that the radius is 1 foot. Thus, $C = 2\pi(1)$, or 2π, which is approximately 6.3 ft. In 2 minutes, the motorcycle will travel $6,300 \times 2 = 12,600$ ft. $12,600$ ft. $\div 6.3$ ft. $= 2,000$.

104. E. *Numbers & Operations – Scientific Notation.* Divide the coefficients: $9 \div 3 = 3$. Divide the exponents and bases: $10^6 \div 10^4 = 10^2$. The resulting expression is 3.0×10^2.

105. D. *Algebra – Inequalities.* We first want to get rid of parentheses by distributing, so we get $7 - 3x + 5 < 9x - 6 + 3x$. Then we can combine like terms, resulting in $12 - 3x < 12x - 6$. We only want the variable on one side of the inequality, so we will cancel out the smaller variable by adding $3x$ to both sides, giving us $12 < 15x - 6$. Now isolate the variable by adding 6 to both sides, getting us $18 < 15x$, and dividing both sides by 15, resulting in $\dfrac{18}{15} < x$, which simplifies to $x > \dfrac{6}{5}$.

106. F. *Geometry & Measurements – Coordinates.* The given coordinates of $(2, -3)$ are in the fourth quadrant, where x values are positive and y values are negative. The other end of the line segment must be in the second quadrant, where all x values are negative and y values are positive, since the line must pass through the origin (the center of the circle). The only coordinates that fit this criteria are $(-2, 3)$ and $(-3, 2)$. If we were to plot these points on a graph, we would see that a line connecting $(2, -3)$ with $(-3, 2)$ does not pass through the origin.

107. A. *Algebra – Plugins.* To find out whether a proportion is true or not, you can cross multiply. If we do that to all four answer choices, we see that they all equal $xy = wz$ except for the first choice.

108. F. *Numbers & Operations – Ratios & Proportions.* We can solve algebraically: $2x + 3x + 4x = 180$. Therefore, $9x = 180$ and $x = 20$. But 20 is not the final answer because we are looking for the degree measure of the largest angle, which is $4x = 4(20) = 80$.

109. A. *Probability & Statistics – Probability.* If there are 21 marbles originally, and 5 are removed, then 16 remain. The question states that after the 5 marbles are removed, the probability of picking out a brown marble is 50%. This means that the total number of brown marbles must be exactly half of the total number of marbles that remain. Since 16 remain, the number of brown marbles must be 8, which is the same as the original. Thus, no brown marbles were removed.

110. F. *Geometry & Measurements – Measurements.* If Maritza always reads at a rate of 1 page per minute, then in 15 minutes, she will have read 15 pages. Since the total number of pages in the

magazine is 25, then 25 – 15 = 10 pages remain. As a fraction, this is $\dfrac{10}{25}$, which simplifies to $\dfrac{2}{5}$.

111. D. *Probability & Statistics – Averages.* If we put the nine given numerical values in order, we have 1, 5, 5, 5, 9, 9, 9, 9, 11. Including the tenth value, the only way for the median to be 7 is if the two middle values are 5 and 9. However, x cannot be 5 because then the mode would be 5 and 9 instead of just 9.

112. F. *Geometry & Measurements – Area & Perimeter.* The area of a parallelogram is equal to $A = bh$. So the area is equal to $A = 12 \times 18 = 216$.

113. A. *Geometry & Measurements – Angles.* The total degree measure of the interior angles of any polygon with n sides can be found using the formula $180(n - 2)$. Since we are given the total degree measure, we can set the formula equal to the known amount. $1{,}800 = 180(n - 2)$. Isolate and solve for n by dividing both sides by 180, then adding 2 to both sides. This gives us $10 = n - 2$, then $12 = n$.

114. G. *Algebra – Algebraic Expressions & Equations.* Like the above problem, we can find the smallest integer in the group by setting up an equation: $x + x + 2 + x + 4 + x + 6 + x + 8 = 110$, which simplifies to $5x + 20 = 110$, resulting in $5x = 90$ and finally $x = 18$. However, that is not the final answer because we are looking not just for the smallest integer but the sum of the three smallest integers, which is therefore $18 + 20 + 22 = 60$.

Stand-Alone Revising/Editing Skills

Grammar Glossary

The explanations in this section make frequent reference to elements of grammar. To maximize the efficacy of the answer explanations, we have included the following Grammar Glossary.

- 🐢 Sentence – a sentence must have a predicate (most generally, a verb) and a subject (of that predicate/verb). It may also have other words that help to form a complete thought.
    - 🐢 Subject – usually a noun or pronoun; the person, place, or thing that the sentence is actually about
    - 🐢 Predicate – what the subject of the sentence is doing
- 🐢 Clause – a group of words that has a predicate and subject
    - 🐢 Independent clause – a clause that can also stand alone as a sentence (a clause that also contains a complete thought)
    - 🐢 Dependent (subordinated) clause – a clause that cannot stand alone as a sentence (a clause that does not contain a complete thought)
- 🐢 Phrase – a group of words that does not contain the sentence's verb or subject
    - 🐢 Prepositional phrase – a group of words beginning with a preposition but ends with a noun (acts like an adjective, or adverb)
    - 🐢 Participial phrase – phrase beginning with a participle (a verb that ends in "–ing", which acts like an adjective or adverb)
- 🐢 Fragment – a group of words that lacks any one or more of the three elements that form a sentence; sometimes a dependent clause written as if it was an independent clause.
- 🐢 Run-on – two independent clauses joined together without appropriate or sufficient punctuation and/or conjunctions
    - 🐢 Fused sentence – a run-on sentence resulting from the lack of any punctuation
    - 🐢 Spliced comma – a run-on sentence resulting from the inappropriate use of a comma to join two independent clauses
- 🐢 Compound sentence – two independent clauses joined together with appropriate or sufficient punctuation and/or conjunctions
    - 🐢 Conjunction – a word that joins two clauses together; frequently preceded by punctuation
        - 🐢 Coordinating conjunction – connects two clauses of equal importance (i.e. two independent clauses); *and, but, or, so, for, nor, yet*
        - 🐢 Subordinating conjunction – connects a dependent clause to an independent clause; *after, before, if, since, while, etc.*
        - 🐢 Correlative conjunction – pairs of words that signal a relationship between two elements in a clause (i.e. either/or, both/and, neither/nor)
- 🐢 Verb Tense – at its most basic, the different forms of a verb that indicate when an action takes place (i.e. in the past, present, or future; whether something continues to happen)
- 🐢 Verb Mood – indicate the author's attitude in terms of what the intention is: to show a statement of fact (indicative), issue a command (imperative), or propose a statement contrary to fact (subjunctive)
- 🐢 Number (verb, noun) – indicates whether a verb or noun is singular or plural
- 🐢 Preposition – a word that links a noun to another word, often describes the position of that noun (i.e. in, etc.)
- 🐢 Voice – refers to the way a sentence is written where the subject performs the action indicated by the verb (active) or where the verb acts upon the subject (passive)

Pronoun Clarity

1. A. As written, "her" could refer to either the manager or the employee; so too could "his" refer to both the employee and the manager, since we do not know either's gender. Using "a" helps to clarify the ownership of the bonus. This question is an example of a pronoun with more than one possible antecedent. We do not refer to people as "it." Remember that "its" is possessive, and "it's" is not (it's a contraction for "it is").

2. H. In this sentence, the word "they" could refer to the people who do the shopping, the actual after-dinner sales, or even the dinners themselves – another example of a pronoun with more than one possible antecedent. "These," "those," and "some" do not clarify the sentence any more than "they." Only by repeating "the sales" in the dependent clause after the second comma in the sentence does the sentence become clear. Alternatively, "the former."

3. D. The pronoun "he" is unclear: is the sentence referring to the stranger, or to the agoraphobic man? In order to clarify, the best choice is "the former," as "anyone" and "it" are as vague or inappropriate. Pronouns must have a clear antecedent to which they refer. In this case, "former" refers to "stranger," letting the reader know who spoke the sentence. "Him" results in the improper use of the pronoun.

4. G. The pronoun "she" could apply to either Sarah or Melissa, so the sentence must clarify who had made the bigger mess. In this case, the word "bigger" means that one person made a mess larger than the other, so "they" does not work to replace "she." "Melissa's" is possessive, not a contraction for "Melissa has".

5. A. An antecedent need not always precede the pronoun. In this sentence, the pronoun "it" refers to the extra water, which needs to be pumped out of the ship. "He," "they," and "those" are not appropriate pronouns to refer to the water. In this case, "it" clearly refers to "extra water," since we don't refer to people as "it."

6. H. There is no pronoun in sentence 1. The "he" and "his" used in sentence 2 clearly refer to Jordan, a proper noun (particular person). Similarly, in sentence 3, though we now have Jake, another proper noun (particular person), the "he" clearly refers to Jordan. It is not until sentence 4 that we have an unclear pronoun; we are unsure who "he" is – is the pronoun's antecedent Jake or Jordan? Is Jake suggesting that Jordan go to the doctor, or is Jordan himself making that suggestion?

The Tutorverse

7.   B. Clyde and Billy are mentioned in sentence 1, but sentence 2 begins with "he," so we are unsure of who made the suggestion to | jackhammer through the vault. It is clear from sentence 3 that "they" refers to Clyde and Billy.

Modifiers

1.   D. The word "quickly" is a squinting modifier (a modifier placed in such a way as to be able to modify multiple ideas in the sentence). As written, we can interpret the sentence in two different ways: either "reading at a greater speed" improves one's vocabulary, or "reading a greater quantity" improves one's vocabulary at a greater speed. Only by moving "quickly" to the end of the sentence does the sentence become clear: that reading a greater quantity ("reading more") can improve one's vocabulary more rapidly. The other revisions do not address the issue of ambiguity.

2.   F. As written, the sentence begins with a dangling modifier – one that modifies nothing in the sentence as written. In this case, the modifier is "While playing the lead in *Hamlet*". Without it, the sentence is grammatically correct, yet with it, the sentence is confusing and ambiguous: was the audience groaning as the actor played the lead in *Hamlet*, or was the audience – for some reason – playing the lead in *Hamlet* and groaning simultaneously? This choice correctly places the modifier close to the modified thing (the actor) and clarifies the sentence.

3.   C. The dangling modifier "shining from a new coat of car polish" inappropriately modifies Jeremy, but should modify car. Therefore, we should move it after "his car" and offset the modifier with two commas, one before it, and one after it. The other choices do not clarify the ambiguity, as moving the modifier to the end of the sentence or directly after "Jeremy" results in an equally nonsensical sentence.

4.   H. The modifier "dripping with anticipation" could be deleted and still result in a grammatically correct sentence. However, deleting or switching the other modifiers in the sentence would still leave the sentence ambiguous: is it Corey or the kitten that is "dripping with anticipation"?

5.   D. There are many modifiers in the paragraph ("on the last day of February"; "which he had received for his birthday"; "nearby"). However, it is not until "collecting into tiny pools" that we find a modifier out of place. As written, it sounds like Forrest himself is "collecting into tiny pools" when from context we find that the modifier should actually apply to the melting icicles. One way to correct this would be to write "Forrest watched the icicles hanging from the trees slowly melt onto the sidewalk, collecting into tiny pools."

6.   F. There are modifiers throughout the paragraph, but only in the second sentence is the modifier misplaced. In sentence 2, "with a grudge" describes how Amber signed the agreement. Instead, as written, it suggests that Amber signed an agreement literally with the other party being "a grudge." One way of clarifying this would be to write "As a result, Amber grudgingly signed the unfavorable agreement."

7.   A. To find a modifier, remove a word or phrase that describes how, when, why, or what happened to something else in the sentence, and see if the sentence can stand alone as a complete thought. In this case, the phrase "after the science lesson" describes when something happened. However, we don't know what this applies to: is it when Ms. Cortez said something, or when the students would be able to enjoy a break? Depending on the intended meaning, the sentence could read "Ms. Cortez said that the students would be able to enjoy a break after the science lesson." Or, it could read "After the science lesson, Ms. Cortez said that the students would be able to enjoy a break."

Tenses, Mood, & Number

1.   A. Verbs must agree in tense, and tenses relate to time. The three main verb tenses relate to the past (something that happened in the past), present (something that is happening now), and future (something that will happen in the future). Each of these three tenses are further divided into the simple, progressive, perfect, and perfect progressive tenses, which each indicate when something has been (or is being or will be) done. In this sentence, the verbs "realized" and "searched" are written in the past simple tense. Therefore, the verb "jump" should also be written in the past simple tense as "jumped." The other forms of the verb "jump" are written in various forms of the present or future tense.

2.   H. The sentence suggests that the counselors had already found Tanya, which means that Tanya must have already hidden after hearing the scary story and subsequently been found by the counselors. Since this is the case, neither the future simple tense "will hide" nor the future perfect tense "will have hidden" make sense; neither does the present perfect progressive form "has been hiding." Notice that "is hidden" works like an adjective, not a verb. Only the past perfect progressive form "had been hiding" makes sense, as the hiding has already taken place and describes how Tanya had hidden for some extended period of time.

3.   A. In addition to tenses, verbs can also be classified by mood. There are three moods: the indicative, the imperative, and the subjunctive. The vast majority of verbs are used in the indicative mood, which states a fact or indicates a state of being. The imperative mood is used to indicate a request or a command. The subjunctive mood is used to express a wish or state something contrary to fact. In this sentence, the verb "call" is written in the imperative mood, telling someone (the "your" in the sentence) to make a phone call. "Tell" expresses the verb "tell" in the imperative mood. The other choices are written in the indicative mood, including "you tell."

4.   G. The subjunctive mood (only used with the verbs "be" and "were [to be]") are used to show something contrary to a fact or to express a wish or request. Since the author is not likely to be a fictional character in reality, the person the author addresses is not likely a billionaire. The indicative verbs "was," "is," and "are" are not appropriate to use. The phrase "would be" is often a clue that the verb in question should be in the subjunctive mood.

5.   D. It may appear that no sentence is affected by a verb in the wrong mood. Upon closer inspection, sentence 4 describes a state of being that currently is not the case (i.e. that all teachers and students should attend the assembly). Notice that what is described calls for the subjunctive mood, as it describes a situation "as it should be." This means the verb "are" should be changed to "be." "Are," "is," and "being" are all indicative moods, and are inappropriate for this type of sentence.

6.   E. When an action is being performed by the subject on objects, then that is called active voice. When the sentence is written so that the objects are being performed on by the subject, then that is called passive voice. Along with choices C and D, the subordinated clause ("as…him") is written in the passive voice where the independent clause ("Brent…routine") is written in the active voice. To correct this, this choice uses the present simple tense of "treat" (which is congruent with the present simple tense of "make") to show that the action is being performed on the beans, water, and implements by Brent.

7.   C. In every sentence but number 3, the verbs all use the appropriate tenses to describe the ideas in the sentence. In sentence 3, we are told that Dominic "will have been continuing" to invest based on the fact that he "had been receiving" high returns. The sentence tells us that what happened in the past will affect the future. However, "will have been continuing" is written in the future perfect progressive form, where it requires the future progressive form.

The Tutorverse

Possessive Nouns & Determiners

1. C. In the case of nouns referring to more than one person, place, or thing (nouns with a number greater than one), it is important to add an apostrophe after the pluralized ending of the noun or proper noun. In this case, "waitress" refers to a single person, while "waitresses" refers to a group of people. Generally, an "-'s" is added to a noun to indicate possession. However, in the case that the noun ends in an "s", the extra "s" is omitted. The possessive form of "waitress" is "waitress'" (note the apostrophe, but no additional 's'), and the possessive form of "waitresses" is "waitresses'" (again, the same rule for the apostrophe). We know that we are talking about more than one person because the sentence says "they" earlier on.

2. G. Though we generally add an "-'s" at the end of a noun or proper noun to indicate possession, some pronouns are understood to indicate possession. The word "his" is the possessive form for the pronoun "him" and does not require an apostrophe to indicate possession. There is no such word as "his'" or "his's". In this case, "its" is inappropriate because we are referring to a person, not a thing. "Their" is the possessive form for "they," or more than one person, though we are only talking about Dexter in this case.

3. A. The possessive form of the pronoun "she" is "hers" and similarly does not require an apostrophe to indicate possession. There is no such word as "her's". "She's" is a contraction for "she is." Note that "her" is also possessive, but is a possessive adjective, not a pronoun.

4. E. The word "its" is the possessive form of the pronoun "it." Remember that "it's" is a contraction (an abbreviated form) of "it is". The apostrophe DOES NOT indicate possession.

5. D. As with pronouns that represent a single noun or proper noun, pronouns that represent more than one noun or proper noun do not require an "-'s". The sentence compares one person's responsibility with some unknown number of other people's responsibility. The pronoun for "other people" would be "them/they." The possessive form of this is "their/theirs" (depending on whether or not the object is left out of the sentence).

6. E. Sentence 2 uses the possessive pronoun "hers" to tell us that it is Camilla's closet that is filled to overflowing. This is the possessive form for "she," which as a pronoun, refers to Camilla, in this case. "She" is a different pronoun which refers to Camilla. Notice that sentence 3 uses the possessive adjective "her" to tell us whose favorite item was the beret. Sentence 1 simply omits a "-'s" to indicate possession. Instead, the sentence should be begin with "Camilla's preference...". This tells us that it is Camilla who has the preference

7. C. We can see several examples of the possessive form of plural nouns and pronouns being used. In sentence 1, "people" is the noun representing more than one person, and "people's" is the possessive of this noun. "Those" in sentence 2 tells us that it is the homes' value that have recovered. In sentence 4, "their" refers to Cassidy and Kaleb. The subject of sentence 3 requires an apostrophe to show that it is their home that lost 50% of its value. The subject, in this case, is two proper nouns: Cassidy and Kaleb. We're told that the two of them purchased the house together. Therefore, they have joint possession, and the "-'s" should come after the last of the nouns. The sentence should begin with "Cassidy and Kaleb's home...". As written, the sentence tells us that the home is "Cassidy's," not Kaleb's.

Subject-Verb Agreement

1. A. Singular subjects must be matched with singular verbs, as plural subjects must be used with plural verbs. The matching of singular subjects with singular verbs and plural subjects with plural verbs is the act of ensuring subject-verb agreement, or ensuring that the subject and verb numbers agree. Identifying the subject is critical. The boys, the lake, the time, and the town are all nouns, but only the camp is the subject. The prepositional phrase "for girls" describes "camp" while the entire phrase "some five hours away from the closest town" describes the general location. The subject, therefore, is "camp." The verb "are" is plural, and the subject "camp" is singular. Therefore, the only correct choice is to use the verb "is."

2. F. The verb "was" must be congruent and match in number with the subject ("Doris"), which is singular in number (there is only one Doris). Therefore, the only singular verb of "be" is the past tense verb "was"; "have been" and "were" are both plural (i.e. "they were" or "they have"). "Is" and "will be" are also singular, but in the wrong tense.

3. B. Whenever the word "every" appears in front of a word or group of words, the verb associated with those words should be singular. "Was" is the only singular answer choice. Changing "participate" to "participates" does not fix the problem of agreeing the verb "to be" with the subject "every member."

4. E. Certain indefinite pronouns such as "everybody" may seem like they should be plural (since it does talk about more than one person), but they are actually singular. Therefore, only the singular verb "was" is appropriate here (think of "everybody" as a single unit).

5. D. Compound subjects (in this case, "financial functions and operational functions") that are joined by the word "and" take a plural verb (in this case, "are").

6. G. Some compound subjects that are joined by the word "and" are actually treated as singular if they are thought of as a single unit. In this case, the friend is also the coworker, and should be accompanied by a singular verb such as "schedules." We know this because the following sentence tells us that there are only two people involved.

7. A. When a plural subject and a singular subject ("Grace's three daughters" and "her son," respectively) are joined by "or" or "nor," the number of the verb follows the number of the subject closest to it. In this case, "Grace's son" is closest to the verb of being, "is/are/was/were," etc. Thus, we should choose the singular verb of being: "was." We could write the sentences out separately to prove this. 1) "Even though it was bedtime, Grace's three daughters **were** not ready for bed." 2) "Even though it was bedtime, her son **was** not ready for bed." So, "are" should change to "is."

Frequently Confused Words

1. C. To "meddle" is to interfere with something. "Medal" (an award or commendation) and "metal" (a hard, material made of certain minerals) are tangible objects; only "mettle" refers to the intangible resolve of the team. All three of these words are homophones. Note that "muddle" means to confuse something.

2. H. There are three homophones in this question: "whether," "weather," and "wether." Only the former expresses doubt about the students' ability to pass the test. "Wether" is not a real word, and "weather" refers to the atmosphere in a particular place. "Solely" means "only," and is far from the meaning of "soulfully," which means to do something with passion or emotion.

3. D. "Bare" and "bear" are homophones. To "bare" something means to uncover it, whereas to "bear" something means to carry, support, or endure something (unless, of course, we're talking about the large, furry mammal; context dictates the meaning). Note that another homophone is used in the sentence: "accept" and "except". To "accept" something means to consent or believe it, where "except" specifies that something should not be included. In this case, Jamie could not believe, she was going to "actually" jump out of a plane.

4. G. "Off" is an adverb/preposition that describes how something is removed or separate from something else. "Of" is a preposition that describes the relationship between some part of a whole. In this

case, "off" is used to describe how one might move away from a route. The homophones "course" and "coarse" have different meanings. The first describes a path or route, while the second describes somethings that is rough. Similarly, "threw" is the past tense of "throw," where "through" describes the action or motion of going from one side of something to another.

5. **A.** The word "new" refers to something that is novel or not seen or experienced before. The word "knew" is the past tense used to describe how something was understood. There are other homophones in the other sentences ("real" and "reel"; "flower" and "flour"), but they are all used correctly in context.

6. **F.** There are many homophones used through the paragraph ("week" and "weak"; "horse" and "hoarse"; "suite" and "sweet"; "vein" and "vain"). However, all of the context-appropriate words are used except for "horse," which is a noun referring to the four-legged animal. Instead, the word should be "hoarse," which is used to describe a person's voice which sounds rough or scratchy.

7. **D.** Sentence 2 requires a revision. "There" and "their" are used correctly, but "wave" (the motion) is not. Instead, "wave" should be written as "waive," which is a verb that describes the refraining from enforcing a rule. In sentence 4, "their" should be "there."

Logical Comparison

1. **D.** The noun being compared is "weight." The other answer choices all compare the dire wolf's weight to domesticated lapdogs themselves, not the weight of the domesticated lapdogs. Only by using "that of a" is it clear that we are comparing weights, and not an attribute of an object with an object itself.

2. **H.** The noun being compared is "taste" or "quality" (of pizzas), though this is not made explicitly clear in the sentence. Simply adding an " –'s" to "Chicago" does not help clarify that this is the case, since the sentence could be read to compare NYC's pizzas with NYC's pizzas "that belong to Chicago." This is clearly nonsensical. Instead, we are talking about pizzas made in NYC as compared with pizzas ("those") made in Chicago.

3. **B.** The noun being compared is "ability"(or skill, to make delicious sauces). The sentence as written compares one person's ability with "anyone else," not the skill or ability of "anyone else." Only by saying "anyone else's skill" is this clear. The other choices make a similarly erroneous comparison, comparing skill (the attribute of a person) with a person itself.

4. **G.** The noun being compared is the day's newspaper (yesterday's versus today's). The only choice that makes this clear explicitly says "yesterday's cover." The first two choices change the meaning of the sentence, but also compare the cover of today's paper with the other day itself.

5. **D.** The comparison made in sentence 4 is illogical, since it compares the noun "amount" with "everyday glassware." The true comparison being made is between the amount in one thing versus the amount in another, not the amount in one thing versus another thing itself. Note that this is the only sentence in which a comparison is being made.

6. **G.** In this paragraph, sentences 2 and 3 both contain logical comparisons. In sentence 2, the quality of "bagels" at "one shop" are compared to the quality of "bagels" at "another [shop]". This is a logical comparison. In sentence 3, however, a comparison is made between "the West Side" (a place) and "living on the East Side" (an action). This is illogical, as the comparison should be between "the West Side" or "the East Side" (or alternatively, "living on the East Side" versus "living on the West Side").

7. **B.** The paragraph is concerned with comparing the amount of potassium in a variety of different foods. Sentence 2 compares "the amount of potassium" in kiwis with "bananas." This doesn't make sense. Instead, it should compare "the amount of potassium" in one food with "the amount of potassium" in another, which is the case in sentences 3 and 4.

Subordination & Coordination

1. **C.** Conjunctions are used to join two related ideas together to form a complete, logical thought. There are two different types of conjunctions: coordinating conjunctions and subordinating conjunctions. The first refers to conjunctions that typically connect two independent clauses/sentences that are related in idea. The second refers to conjunctions that connect an independent clause with a dependent (subordinated) clause (an idea that cannot stand alone as a sentence). There are two separate but related ideas in this sentence. The first is a statement that products with more reviews sell more than those with fewer reviews. The second is that retailers desire that shoppers leave reviews. These ideas are related – they have to do with product reviews. So, we can connect the two with an appropriate coordinating conjunction: but, or, yet, so, for, and, nor. Of these choices, only "so" indicates a cause/effect relationship. In this case, it makes sense that stores would want to have shoppers leave reviews for products, since those products sell more than those without reviews.

2. **H.** There are two independent clauses ("The car...yesterday" and "It nevertheless...supermarket") that discuss the same idea – a broken car needing repairs. The clauses are joined by the coordinating conjunction "for," which is similar to "because" in that it shows a positive cause/effect relationship (one thing led to another thing). However, this is illogical, since the sentence as written states that it was taken to the mechanics to be repaired yesterday *because* (for) it broke down today. Since a car that had just been fixed should not break down again the next day, the appropriate conjunction to use is "yet," which describes a situation contrary to expectations.

3. **D.** A sentence must express a complete thought. In this case, the sentence is made up of two parts: an independent clause and a dependent (subordinated) clause. Dependent clauses are "dependent" on something else – they tell about things elsewhere in the sentence; for example, when, how, or why something

happens. In this sentence, "The street performer...tourists" is an independent clause because it is a complete thought by itself. The phrase "during juggling six bowling pins and a sword" is a subordinated clause because it tells more about something in the independent clause, and cannot stand alone as a sentence on its own. In this case, we can tell that the dependent clause describes when something happened. However, "during" is used to describe a noun (for example, during the juggling <u>act</u>). In this case, no noun is described (an action – juggling – is described), and the appropriate conjunction to use to show subordination is "while." "Whether," "whenever," and "because" require another noun (for example, "Whenever he juggled six bowling pins and a sword...").

4. **E.** A special type of conjunction is called a correlative conjunction, and is always used in pairs. These are "both/and," "either/or," "neither/nor," "not only/also," and "not only/but also." They show a relationship between different clauses. In this case, the sentence describes a choice between two things, so we must use "either" and "or" not "either" and "and."

5. **B.** There are many conjunctions used throughout the paragraph ("and," "though," "for,"). In sentence 3, "for" is used incorrectly, as it is similar to "because' in that it describes how one thing was the result of another. It doesn't make sense to say that her parents were more concerned than upset as a result of Amie's expecting them to be very angry. Instead, since the parents' reaction was not as Amie expected, the right word to use would be "but" or "yet." These conjunctions are coordinating conjunctions. In sentence 2, "though" is used incorrectly. It doesn't make sense that her parents cared about her grades "though" they always asked..." In this case, "since" would make more sense.

6. **H.** The subordinating conjunctions "whenever," "as soon as," "so that," and "though" are used in the paragraph. However, "though" is used incorrectly because sentence 4 describes two similar situations where not having a clear storyline would negatively

impact other departments. In this case, we're told that the casting department might pick the wrong actors, and the costume department might pick the wrong styles of clothing. Since these two are related (and are joined by "so too,") we know they must be logically equivalent. This means we must change "though," which

implies a contradiction of some kind, to be something else (like "just as").

7. B. Every sentence uses a correlative conjunction. Sentence 1 uses "both/and," sentence 3 uses "neither/nor," and sentence 4 uses "either/or." Sentence 2 tries to use "not only/but also," but inappropriately uses "not only/and to also."

Within-Sentence Punctuation

1. B. Commas are used to separate a series of items, to separate adjectives, to help conjunctions join two independent clauses, to signal quoted material (along with quotation marks), and to otherwise set apart clauses and phrases. Colons do not function like commas, and are used to signal a list. A semicolon is used to join two logically connected independent clauses together. In this case, "friends and family" is not an independent clause (it is incapable of standing alone as a sentence), so a semicolon is inappropriate. The sentence indicates that there are two things needed for Jordan to be happy, and a colon is best used to signal that a list of these things follows.

2. F. Commas are used at the end of an introductory adverb clause, in this case "Because she had recently moved to a new town." Adverb clauses are a group of words with their own subject and verb that together act like an adverb, describing a verb, adjective, or another adverb. A semicolon is inappropriate, as the adverb clause cannot stand alone as a sentence. Neither is a colon appropriate, since the phrase after it is not a list of items. There is no need to offset "recently" since it gives important information about when Melissa moved.

3. D. There are two independent but illogically related clauses in this sentence. Droughts in the American Southwest have little to do with umbrellas in India. Because these ideas are unrelated, they cannot be joined with a semicolon. Using a comma results in a comma splice. A colon is also inappropriate to use given the content of the two clauses. Thus, only by splitting the sentence in two can the sentences be properly punctuated.

4. E. Commas are used to separate two or more adjectives that describe the same noun. In this case, "sleek" and "stealthy" describe the cat and should be separated by a comma. This is not accomplished by adding a comma in any other suggested locations.

5. C. One of the ways a hyphen (not a dash) is used is to denote a compound adjective, which is a situation where two or more

adjectives form a single image or thought that describes a noun. In this case, "sixteenth-century" is used as a compound adjective to describe the type of scientist that Galileo was. If we were simply referring to the "sixteenth century," no hyphen would be needed, because "sixteenth century" is a noun (a period of time).

6. H. "If they could get a ride" is not an independent clause, so neither the semicolon nor a period are appropriate. A dash is used to introduce an interruption to the original thought, to emphasize a previously mentioned thought, or to expand further on something mentioned in the sentence. The main purpose of the sentence is to tell about how Seth wants to go out with Travis. A dash is used to provide additional information that complements the main purpose of the sentence – namely, a condition that must be met. A compound adjective, such as "three-day", is used to describe a noun ("weekend"), and must be hyphenated. No commas are needed in sentence 2, as "he" (Seth) is the subject that does both actions: "stay" and "play" (this is a compound sentence where one subject does two actions). A comma is always needed after a subordinate clause ("however") as well as to separate extra information ("Travis") from the rest of the sentence.

7. B. Commas are only necessary in certain circumstances. The comma in sentence 4 is necessary since it connects the conjunction "now" with the rest of the independent clause. The commas in sentence 3 are similarly necessary, since they offset clauses that tell more about why the investigators drew the conclusion that they did (the sentence is a compound sentence and includes a subordinated clause "Since…area"). Similarly, the comma in sentence 1 is used to offset the subordinated clause "after…extinguished" from the independent clause "the firefighters…happened." In sentence 2, however, it is not used correctly, and should be removed. This is because "The investigators…corner" is not an independent clause – it can't stand alone as a sentence. It needs the verb "caught" in order to work.

End-of-Sentence Punctuation

1. D. The sentence is an interrogative sentence (that asks a question) and should be punctuated with a question mark. Many interrogative sentences begin with similar phrases that use words such as: "who, what, where, when, why, how, do." Exclamation points are used to punctuate exclamatory sentences (that express strong emotion). Periods are used to punctuate declarative sentences (that make a statement) or imperative sentences (that give commands). It is never appropriate to use two forms of punctuation to end a sentence.

2. F. The sentence is a declarative sentence and should be punctuated with a period. A question mark is used to punctuate an interrogative sentence. It is never appropriate to use two forms of punctuation to end a sentence.

3. C. The sentence is not a question and should not be punctuated with a question mark. The sentence could either be declarative or exclamatory, but only one option is presented (the one using an exclamation point). It is never appropriate to use two forms of punctuation to end a sentence.

4. F. While declarative and imperative sentences (punctuated with a period) are always included before the closing quotation marks, question marks and exclamation points can either be included before or after the closing quotation marks, depending on the

content being quoted. If the quoted material asks a question or is itself exclamatory, the question mark and exclamation point go before the closing quotation marks. If the sentence itself (not the quoted material) is a question or an exclamation, the punctuation goes after the closing quotation marks. In this case, the quoted material is a question – the sentence itself is not a question. When concluding a sentence with a question mark or exclamation point, no other punctuation is necessary.

5. C. This sentence is actually a question, quoting a statement (not a question) made by Allison. Because of this, the question mark does not go inside the quotation marks, but after it. No other punctuation is necessary.

6. F. Sentence 2 is actually a question, asking "Who knew…". Therefore, it requires a question mark, not an exclamation point.

7. C. Sentence 3 talks about questions, but is a statement of fact. Since it is a declarative statement, it should be punctuated with a period. Note that in sentence 4, it is appropriate and permitted to use question marks to punctuate fragments if there is a series of questions. No capitalizing of the fragments are necessary, since they are understood to be extensions of the same "base question" (which in this case is "What should the students pack…").

Punctuating a Series

1. D. As it is written, the only acceptable choice uses a comma. A semicolon or period results in a fragmented second-half of the sentence. A colon is not used appropriately since the items in a

series are already denoted as such with the use of the phrase "such as the."

2. G. Semicolons are often used to separate items in a list (as signaled by the use of a colon in "places: Seattle") that are already punctuated with commas. By leaving a comma between "Washington" and "Chicago," it would be unclear if the author meant that he or she lived in four places as opposed to three. By using a semicolon after each location, it becomes clear that the author had lived in three places only. A city and state are properly separated by a comma (as in "Seattle, Washington").

3. D. We cannot leave the semicolon or colon in the sentence. The semicolon creates two fragments. Leaving the colon and changing the semicolon into a comma creates a list of four things: three names, and the rest of the sentence (which doesn't make sense to include in the list). We can't change the colon and semicolon to commas, because what results is a confusing sentence (did Cheryl, Blake, and Daniel argue with three coworkers, or were Cheryl, Blake, and Daniel the three coworkers themselves?). Instead, by using dashes, we know that Cheryl, Blake, and Daniel are the three coworkers themselves.

4. F. As written, the sentence incorrectly employs dashes, offsetting "set the alarm" as a parenthetical when it is in fact an important part of the sentence. The comma and colon surrounding "remember" are appropriate, but we need commas to separate the individual items in the list. Changing the colon to a semicolon would create fragments that are not designated as part of a list. In a simple list like this, commas are sufficient.

5. A. Though the first part of this sentence ("When...factors.") is an independent clause that could stand alone should a period separate it from the rest of the sentence, the rest of the sentence would not be able to stand alone, so the semicolon after "factors" must change. Velocity, acceleration, and the impact of gravity are all items in a series that describe the factors important to determining the path of a projectile. Thus, a colon is needed. And because the factors described are complicated and already separated by commas, semicolons are used to separate each factor rather than commas.

6. H. Lists are used in sentences 1, 3, and 4. However, the simple lists in sentences 1 and 3 do not require revision. In sentence 4, however, the sentence is very long and describes the opportunities mentioned in sentence 3. These are time with family, donating, or relaxing. However, the sentence describes "donating" in greater detail, offering examples like "time, money, or goods." Instead, the ideas of spending time with loved ones, donating, and relaxing should be separated by semicolons.

7. D. Lists are used in sentences 1, 2, and 4. However, in sentence 4, the independent clause "Cooking is...pastimes" needs to be followed by a colon, since the items following it describe reasons why this is the case. As written, the sentence is a run on, since the comma between "pastimes" and "it" is inappropriate.

Parenthetical Expression & Nonrestrictive Clauses

1. A. The phrase "that was docked at the end of the pier" is restrictive, as without it the sentence is unclear (To which boat are residents referring? Where is the boat?) and the meaning lost. In general, a comma does not precede the word "that," as the phrase that follows "that" generally restricts or limits the thing that it modifies. In such a case, the clause is restrictive and does not need to be punctuated with commas, parentheses, or dashes.

2. H. The nonrestrictive clause "which is sometimes known as 'mini golf'" should be punctuated with commas before it and after it. Generally, the word "which," when used to precede an explanation or provide more information about something already mentioned (in this case, telling us another name for "miniature golf") should be preceded by a comma. The clause should generally also end with a comma (when included as an interruption within a sentence). In this case, reading the sentence aloud can help determine where commas are necessary. The nonrestrictive clause only serves to provide more information about what "miniature golf" is, and doesn't change the meaning of the sentence (that the game is popular with children and adults).

3. B. The phrase "who...offenders" is a nonrestrictive clause. Without it, we still know that Judge Lemon surprised the courtroom with an uncharacteristic action (her leniency is the opposite of "throwing the book"). The nonrestrictive clause simply tells more about Judge Lemon. Without it, we still know that she is usually more strict, since the courtroom was surprised by her leniency.

4. F. The extra information provided within the parentheses is not necessary to the basic meaning of the sentence – it simply provides more detail. Without it, the sentence still needs a comma to separate the dependent clause ("Unable...walls") from the independent clause ("The client...coin"). Thus, the comma should go after "warming)". Changing the parentheses to commas does not

solve the problem of adding a comma between the dependent and independent clauses, and actually confuses the sentence further with too many commas. We should not offset "which...walls" because this is not a restrictive clause. In this case, "which" is used as a determiner, not a pronoun, and describes a choice, not additional information about something else.

5. A. Nonrestrictive clauses and parenthetical expressions add richness and detail to writing. However, it must be properly offset with punctuation. Sentence 2 uses commas to properly offset "giving...family," which describes more about "abruptly." Sentence 4 is missing a comma between "trunk" and "which." "Which...*Mayflower*" provides nonessential information to the sentence. The family was still amazed at the antique trunk in good condition. The additional information only adds the richness and detail to the sentence. The word "that" always signifies a restrictive clause, and should never be preceded by a comma.

6. E. In sentence 1, the clause "Frank was under the mistaken impression that the food on display was free" can stand alone as a sentence. By introducing additional information about why, we learn that Frank was unfamiliar with the local culture. This is a parenthetical expression, and needs to be offset with punctuation. There is one dash already at the beginning of the expression, but another one needs to be included at the end.

7. C. The expressions offset by dashes in sentence 2 and 4 are done so appropriately, since they provide additional, clarifying information to the sentence, but do not change the sentences' fundamental meanings. However, in sentence 3, the clause "that confuse...most" is restrictive; it is necessary to the meaning of the sentence. Without it, we don't know what questions the sentence is referring to. So, no dash is necessary.

Unnecessary Punctuation

1. D. It is important to understand the rules for commas. In this sentence, there is an independent clause ("Cheetahs are one of nature's most effective hunters") and a dependent clause ("possessing both stealth and speed"). The latter cannot stand alone, and needs to be separated from the independent clause with a comma. Without it, there would be a run-on sentence. It is not appropriate to separate "cheetahs" from the rest of the sentence, because as written, there is no independent clause. The fact that cheetahs possess two qualities (stealth and speed) does not need to be separated by a comma, since it is a simple description.

2. F. The phrase "over the roar of the crowd" describes when Curtis yelled something. It cannot stand alone, and therefore must be separated from the rest of the sentence with a comma. However, no comma is needed to separate "roar" from "of," since it is the roar of the crowd that Curtis is yelling over.

3. A. There are no commas required in this sentence. The sentence is long and complicated, but does not require additional punctuation beyond the period at the end. The sentence is not just about investment, investment in science, or investment in medical advancement, individually. Instead, it is about "investment in

The Tutorverse

scientific and medical advancement." The rest of the sentence describes this, saying that experts on all sides of the political spectrum agree on this statement. Adding extra commas results in a confusing sentence – on what sides are the experts on? What does the political spectrum have to do with anything?

4. E. There are no commas required in this sentence. The sentence is long and complicated, but does not require additional punctuation beyond the period at the end. There is no reason to separate "research" from what that research is. The sentence is about research studying the impact of news stations on the elderly. That impact is nervousness and anxiety, so no commas are necessary.

5. B. Punctuation in each sentence is used correctly except in sentence 2. "hard-to-reach" is punctuated correctly since it is a compound adjective that describes "shelf." However, no hyphen should be included between the compound adjective and the noun itself. Notice in sentences 1 and 3 that the parenthetical expressions

"who often…personality" and "during which…wanted" (respectively) are properly offset by dashes.

6. H. The last sentence should be written: "It is difficult to feel the awe – the sense of smallness – that the real world inspires without setting foot outside." The parenthetical description of "awe" (sense of smallness) must be offset by punctuation, and there is no need for a comma after "difficult" because the clause is "it is difficult to feel the awe."

7. C. The sentences in this paragraph are very complex, so it is important to identify the different parts of each sentence. In sentence 3, an extra comma after "philosophers" is unnecessary. The core sentence is "many of these philosophers agree upon the purpose of human existence." The "in addition" at the beginning is a conjunctive adverb, and requires a comma after it. The phrase "which is…self" is dependent on the core sentence, and cannot stand alone. Therefore, it requires a comma before it to connect it to the rest of the sentence.

Passage-Based/Editing Skills

Choosing a Chooser

1. C. Sentence 3 discusses only the "power to rule over people," not the distribution of money. It emphasizes that the people are the ones with the power to rule themselves. It would not support this idea to say that some democracies are like aristocracies ("a few well-established families"), which are described in sentence 2. Neither would it make sense to say that only the rich have the power to influence the lawmaking process. Instead, the fact that the word itself derives from a Greek word meaning "rule of the commoners" provides the best support.

2. F. Sentences 5 and 6 describe how each type of democracy works. "Former" refers to "direct democracy," and "latter" refers to "representative democracy." The first choice combines both sentences, but rewrites it with a meaning that is the opposite of the original. The second choice properly uses the word "unlike" to draw a comparison between the two ideas. The third choice uses the phrase "despite that" while the fourth choice uses the word "because"; neither of these is appropriate given the fact that there are two very different ways of operating a democracy being described, and one does not happen as a result of the other.

3. D. Sentence 8 describes how people don't have the time to learn about all of the details when voting on new laws or regulations, as would be the case in direct democracies. Instead, they're busy, and elect others in a representative democracy. To support this idea, the author could include the last choice, since it reinforces this idea and provides examples of how people are busy. The other choices describe the opposite of the idea put forth in sentence 8, describing how people could "eventually learn" or would "rather serve" as elected officials.

4. H. Sentence 10 describes how people elect officials to make decisions for them. This is not an example of sentence 9 (sentence 9 itself is an example of why people choose to elect officials), as "to illustrate" would suggest. There are no similarities between sentences 9 and 10, so "likewise" would not be appropriate. Instead, sentence 9 provides an example of why sentence 10 is true, so the best phrase is "with this in mind." "Regardless" would be used to signify a contrast between ideas, instead of the cause/effect relationship of "with this in mind."

5. A. Sentence 14 attempts to describe how bigger groups have more power and could do things that do not benefit smaller groups. This is neatly summed up in the first choice. The other choices include vague phrases ("make things happen") or wordy/redundant construction ("that group"; "each of these").

6. E. The subject ("representative democracy") is singular, so the verb "to be" must also be singular in the form of "has" ("have" is plural). "Benefits" is plural, as is "outweigh." The dependent clause "though…challenges" must be separated from the independent clause "its benefits…drawbacks." "Its" shows proper possession, while "it's" is a contraction for "it is" that is inappropriate in this case.

7. B. Sentence 12 mentions qualities of a "perfect" elected representative. This is not the focus of the passage. Instead, the passage is concerned with describing the benefits of a representative democracy only. The other choices mention key examples of or summarize this.

Sweet But Deadly

1. C. The sentence describes how there are "a lot of different things said," which is vague by itself (said where? By whom?). If something is "hard to know" or difficult to determine if it is true or false, then it is confusing. The first and second choices do not capture the idea that what is stated is often confusing. The last choice uses a vague pronoun "they."

2. E. Sentences 2 and 3 describe specific instances where nutrition can be confusing, which is first put forth in sentence 1. Sentence 4 reconfirms the idea put forth in sentence 1, so the appropriate transition is "as a result," which conveys the idea that the sentence is a conclusion, or effect of what was described previously. It doesn't make sense to use contrasting transitions ("conversely" and "nonetheless"). Neither does it make sense to say "to illustrate," since the examples were provided in sentences 2 and 3, not in sentence 4.

3. B. Sentence 8 discusses how the body uses carbohydrates. Sentence 9 describes carbohydrates as "critical." Therefore, we can infer a sentence inserted between the two should discuss carbohydrate's importance, and give examples of how the body uses carbohydrates. The first choice does not address either of

these points, instead conflicting with sentence 9. The third choice describes a theory about why some people crave refined sugar; this too does not refer to the ideas in sentences 8 and 9.

4. E. The point of sentence 11 is to explain how sugar leads to a quick burst of energy. Sentence 12 describes how the energy doesn't last. An immediate rush of energy doesn't necessarily mean that it is lasting, so the best way to connect the two ideas is to show a contrast or qualification. Thus, the word "but" can connect the two adjectives that describe the "burst of energy": "immediate" and "fleeting." It's not the drinking or eating of refined sugars that doesn't last long, but the energy that comes from that action.

5. B. The purpose of the paragraph, including the preceding sentence, is to describe the immediate negative effects of eating refined sugars: that they make blood sugar levels rise, and make people feel tired. This is echoed in the second choice, while the other choices mention off-topic ideas (as in the last choice) or make statements that contradict the main idea of the paragraph.

6. G. It may appear that the verb "make" should agree with "foods," but the subject of the sentence is actually "eating," which is a gerund (verb ending in "–ing" that functions like a noun). This is

The Tutorverse

tricky, but if we remove the information "foods with…often," we are left with "Eating make[s] people feel too full…"

7. D. The passage is focused with describing why refined sugars are bad for health, not with describing other things that people should

be eating. The other choices describe important parts of the author's main idea.

A Lasting Monument

1. D. The correct choice combines the sentences using the word "and." The choice that combines the sentences with a comma is a run-on sentence. The choices that combine the sentences with "but" and "yet" are incorrect because these ideas are consistent with each other, not in opposition to each other. Therefore "and" is the best conjunction to use.

2. E. The correct choice changes "has begun" to "began," as the verb needs to just be in the simple past tense here. "Has begun" represents the present perfect which is used to describe an action that began in the past and continues into the present. Since the sentence makes clear this was an action started in the past and completed in the past, the past tense is necessary. The future tense is also not appropriate. Adding a comma after "approximately" is incorrect because the entire amount of time was "approximately fifteen years." Changing "was completed" to "has been completed" is not correct because this verb also needs to be in the past tense, not the present perfect.

3. D. Sentence 10 is true because of Sentence 9. Thus, the correct answer is "As a result," meaning "for that reason" or "consequently." The other words do not convey the correct relationship. "Although" and would make this sentence into a fragment and are therefore incorrect. "Still" implies that sentence 10 should be true in spite of what was said in sentence 9. "Furthermore" would mean sentence 10 provides additional information to sentence 9, but does not convey the cause-effect relationship between these two sentences.

4. E. This choice is the most concise version of the sentence without losing any pertinent information. The other choices all further complicate an already unnecessarily wordy sentence, or include redundant information.

5. A. This choice is related to the idea of tourists visiting the Parthenon, which is the topic of sentence 16 and also mentioned at the beginning of sentence 17. The other choices describe other aspects of the Parthenon which do not relate directly to the fact that it is now primarily a tourist attraction.

6. E. The verb "are" needs to be changed to a singular present tense verb because this sentence has a singular subject. While the sentence starts with the word "there," the subject of this sentence actually is found after the verb. This is the case for sentences that begin with "there" or "here," in which one needs to look after the form of the verb "to be" to find the subject. In this case, the subject is the word "much." Changing the verb to "were" (plural, past) is not grammatically correct, since the verb must agree in number with the word "much." Changes to "much" or "to be" are not necessary, as these parts of the sentence are correct as they are written.

7. B. The correct sentence provides unrelated information about the Ancient Persians whereas the rest of the passage is about the Ancient Greeks and the Parthenon. The other choices discuss key ideas that are central to the Parthenon and how it has changed over time.

Building Tomorrow

1. A. Sentence 1 describes how infrastructure is "taken for granted." Sentence 2 describes how without infrastructure, society would be "unable to function." It is not because of sentence 1 that sentence 2 happens, as "hence" would suggest. The two are not equivalent, as "likewise" would suggest. Sentence 2 is not an example of sentence 1. Instead, sentence 2 shows a contrast to sentence 1 in that what is taken for granted is actually very important.

2. G. The paragraph containing sentence 9 discusses how investment can create jobs. The only statistic that includes information about jobs is choice C. The other choices describe other statistics that are related to transportation infrastructure, but do not have to do specifically with job creation.

3. B. The subject of the sentence is "investments" ("in the local community" is a prepositional phrase that tells us more about the type of "investments"), which is plural. The verb "begins" is singular (think "he begins to…") whereas the verb "begin" is plural (think "they begin to…"). All of the commas are appropriately included in the sentence.

4. H. The paragraph describes how spending on infrastructure leads to positive effects for the "broader economy." The preceding sentences describe how this happens. There's no evidence to suggest that this phenomenon can be seen in other types of

investment, that it leads to lower taxes, or that one type of job is better than another type.

5. A. The subject of the sentence is "expense," which is singular. Therefore, the verb must also be singular. In this case, the form of the verb "to be" is "are," which is plural. We must change this to "is." Be careful not to confuse the subject and verb with other parts of the sentence. "According to…(NEC)" is an adverbial phrase that tells more about the rest of the sentence. Similarly, "second-highest" is an compound adjective describing "expense." "[that] Americans have" also describes "expense."

6. F. The last paragraph describes how investing in infrastructure can help save money and time. The preceding sentences describe how there is an additional cost associated with driving on roads in need of repairs. So, it makes logical sense that sentences 18 and 19 should describe how this could translate to savings. Only choice B describes the hypothetical situation where people could save more money and do more with their time.

7. D. The passage is not primarily focused on describing the expenses that Americans have. It mentions transportation expense only in context of the fact that infrastructure development could help lower the cost of transportation. The fact that housing and shelter costs are the highest cost is irrelevant to the main idea of the paragraph, let alone the passage.

Hammer, Feather, Vacuum

1. B. The sentence describes something that happens after experiments are proven true or false. The word "becomes" is written in the present tense, so "cease" should also be written in the present tense as "ceases." "Weather" is the word to describe the short-term climate of a place. Deleting all of the commas results in a run-on sentence, where adding a semicolon after "theory" results in a fragment.

2. E. The sentence seeks simply to provide an example of how a theory became a fact, or to transition from the previous paragraph to the current paragraph. There is no need to write "think about," since "take" is a shorter and more direct imperative. Similarly, "the thing that" is better referred to as "the phenomenon," since a

"thing" could be any number of things. The other choices use more words to describe less clear ideas – the opposite of precise writing.

3. D. There is a distinction between when people believed in a theory, and why they do. This is confused in the other choices. To say "while" observations support the reason why people believe in the theory is incorrect, since the reason and the theory are related. This is the same by using the word "though" to join the ideas in the sentence.

4. E. Sentence 16 describes what "conventional wisdom" would have suggested would happen. This is the opposite of what Galileo found according to sentence 17. Therefore, only a transition that highlights this difference should be added to the beginning of

sentence 17. "As a result" and "accordingly" show a cause and effect relationship; it is not "because of" the conventional wisdom that Galileo found the opposite to have happened. Neither is there a concession about the relationship between these ideas, as "undoubtedly" suggests.

5. B. There is only one chamber, and it is the chamber's floor that the hammer and feather are suspended above. Therefore, the proper way to show possession for "chamber" would be to write "chamber's".

6. H. Sentence 23 describes how the result confirmed Galileo's theory. His theory had nothing to do with stating that air resistance

is stronger than gravity. It also said that it was not heavier things that fall faster than lighter ones. Instead, it simply said that gravity acts on everything equally, which is implied by the fact that the hammer and feather landed on the ground simultaneously without the influence of air resistance.

7. C. Sentence 12 describes nothing about Galileo's theory, nor anything about how experiments help confirm theories into facts, but instead talks about how Galileo was punished for his work. This is not the focus of the rest of the passage, unlike the other sentences, which detail or transition between ideas of how experiments influence theories and facts.

Plastic, Plastic, Everywhere

1. C. Sentence 1 describes how people believe that so much plastic is recycled, but sentence 2 describes how very little is actually recycled. This shows a contrast, so we must use a transition like "despite" to show this contrast. "Because" shows a cause and effect relationship, which is not valid in this case. "In addition" means that the following sentence should be another related point, with a similar idea, which is clearly not the case in this case. "After all" is used to signal a conclusion of some kind; again, this is not appropriate, since the two sentences present contrasting information.

2. G. When multiple adjectives are used to describe a single noun, we must put commas between those adjectives. In this case, "swirling" is an adjective, as is "continent-sized." Both of these describe "vortex." To change tense (from "is" to "was") would be incorrect, since the rest of the sentence paragraph is written in the present tense. The adjective "continent-sized" is a compound adjective, and must be hyphenated. To change "coasts" to "coast" is incorrect, since we are talking about two different coasts (California and Japan).

3. D. The sentence fails to agree in number. The first part of the sentence ("Some…chemicals") can stand alone as an independent clause, and describes "toxic chemicals," which is plural. The second part of the sentence describes more about "toxic chemicals" (that they make their way up the entire food chain). The problem is that "makes" is singular (think "he makes"), as is "its" (which is the possessive form of "it," referring to a singular object). The plural form of these words is "make" and "their." "Leech" is a noun, referring to the animal, or a verb, referring to the habitual reliance on something.

4. E. Sentence 11 describes how chemicals travel up the food chain. Sentence 12 describes the food chain as a situation where smaller

animals are consumed by bigger ones. The two are related logically, so the word "as" is the only conjunction that makes sense. "Thus" suggests that because chemicals build up in the food chain, animals are consumed by others. The opposite is suggested by "despite" and "and yet."

5. B. The main purpose of the paragraph is to describe how chemicals travel up the food chain and affect people. Only the second choice describes this as happening after presenting the reader with information about the food chain and how chemicals can travel up the food chain. This is the opposite of the statements made in the third and last choice. The first choice is illogical given the information presented in the rest of the paragraph.

6. H. We must be clear that we are referring to "the amount of plastic waste" and "the amount of plastic used," which is different than referring to "plastic waste" and "plastic used." We can do many things to "plastic waste" – we can burn it, eat it, etc., but we cannot do those things to "the amount of plastic waste." "Minimize and shrink plastic waste" is confusing, since the sentence and paragraph conveys the idea of generating less plastic waste, not "shrinking plastic waste" (which could be construed as literally making plastic waste smaller in size). Saying "reduce, minimize, and decrease the amount of" is redundant.

7. A. Sentence 3 describes the process of recycling. While this may be interesting, it is only tangentially related to the main idea of the passage, which is about the prevalence and danger of plastic, and what can be done about it. It has little to do with the sentence that follows it, and is not by itself a reason for the information provided in sentence 2. The other sentences provide important examples or statements that are central the author's main ideas.

Scary Money

1. B. The sentence seeks to explain and define what ROI means. The first choice simply gives us the definition of profit and investment, but not ROI. The third choice uses redundant phrases like "an acronym" and "for short." The last choice also uses redundant phrases like "in businesses" and "businessmen" and "made by businesses" or "invested into businesses". Only the second choice defines ROI in the most economical way.

2. H. Sentence 5 discusses how horror movies are inexpensive to make compared with other movies. Only this choice discusses the cost of making movies. The other choices do not continue this train of thought, instead diverting to different topics or contradicting the preceding sentence entirely.

3. D. "Energizing" describes how something gives energy to something else. "Energized" is the feeling of being supplied with energy. The commas are necessary to separate the different parts of the sentence, including the prepositional phrase "in the face of danger."

4. E. The subject of the sentence is "movies," which is plural. Therefore, the verbs that apply to "movies" must agree. In this case, the verb "triggers" is singular ("he triggers") and should instead be plural ("they trigger"). The phrase "Research suggests

that" tells us more about the core of the sentence, which is "Horror movies trigger the body [to produce…]").

5. C. The main idea of the two sentences is that excitement and giddiness can also happen "at the same time" as fear and dread." The other choices do not properly capture this nuance.

6. F. This sentence summarizes what horror movies do to the minds of its viewers, which is described throughout the passage. "After all" is a concluding transition, which can also show a contrast with the preceding sentence. This makes sense, given that the preceding sentence discusses what horror movies do not need to do. "Besides" tells us that there should be more, new information (there is not), "certainly" adds emphasis which is not the case here, and "consequently" shows how something the result of something else (in this case, it is not because of what horror movies do not do that causes what they do).

7. C. Sentence 17 describes what action/adventure movies do to keep audiences interested. This is not the focus of the passage, which instead describes how and why horror movies make a lot of money without spending much money. The other sentences are important transitions or main ideas of the passage.

The Gambler's Fallacy

1. C. The nonrestrictive clause "which is colored green" describes more about the slot that isn't colored red or black. When a clause is nonrestrictive, and begins with "which," it requires a comma before it. The other choices make the sentence incorrect, changing the tense and number of the verb "to be." We know the clause is nonrestrictive because the sentence still makes sense without it.

2. H. To ensure that the comparison between nouns is appropriate, we must add the words in the answer choice. The sentence describes how the chance of the ball falling into each colored slot is nearly fifty-percent. As written, however, the sentence compares "the number of times the ball falls into red slots" with "black slots" themselves. The other choices change the tense or number of the verb inappropriately.

3. B. Sentence 11 tells us that the ball should fall into the red slots and black slots a roughly equal number of times. Sentence 12 describes how, over a period of time, the ball fell into only black-colored slots. "Afterward" describes a period of time, which does not make sense given the context. "Similarly" doesn't make sense, since the two sentences describe different things. Neither does "hence."

4. F. The preceding sentence describes how there should have been more times the ball landed in green and red slots. This is because the chance of a ball falling into a black slot is only about fifty-percent. The other choices contradict the information we are given in the preceding sentence or earlier in the passage.

5. A. Both sentences describe what happens when people fall prey to The Gambler's Fallacy. If a conjunction is to be used, then it should connect the two ideas together. The conjunctions "or" and "neither" do not; neither does "but not." The first choice describes giving up one set up beliefs for another set.

6. H. The first choice omits the fact that people forget the odds of something happening. The sentence is not about forgetting, as the second choice suggests, but is about ignoring, or falling victim to, the bias. The third choice uses vague language (who is "some," and what does "end up" mean?).

7. B. The passage does not delve into the different games that are offered at the casino. Instead, it is focused on using roulette as an example of The Gambler's Fallacy. The other choices represent important supporting or main ideas of the passage.

State of Confusion

1. C. The clause "China ceded Taiwan to Japan" is an independent clause, meaning it can stand alone. The phrase that comes before it, "Following...century," tells us more about the action of ceding Taiwan. Specifically, it tells us when it took place. It cannot stand alone as a sentence, and so therefore needs to be joined with the independent clause with a comma.

2. E. Both "accordingly" and "therefore" show a cause and effect relationship. However, it is not because of the preceding sentence, where Japan agreed to return Taiwan to China, that causes the current sentence, where Taiwan's return is complicated. Instead, it is everything else after sentence 7 that describes why it was complicated. This shows a contrast, so "yet" is the appropriate choice.

3. B. Sentence 9 is primarily concerned with describing how the nationalists and communists stopped fighting. Sentence 10 describes why. The first choice loses this nuance. The third and last use incorrect conjunctions like "but" and "neither/nor." Instead, it is possible to combine the sentence by saying that the two adversaries stopped fighting "[in order] to" repel the Japanese.

4. G. The sentence could end at "arose." However, "which...Taiwan" is additional information that explains more about the question mentioned in the preceding sentence. It should not be separated from the rest of the sentence by a semicolon. Instead, we can use a colon to signify that there is a particular piece of information that needs to be introduced.

5. D. The first choice, though shorter than the other choices, provides nonsensical information (that the ROC has "falsely run" an "illegitimate government"? Does this mean the government is actually legitimate?). Similarly, in the second choice, we see redundancy in "illegitimately done" and "false government." The third choice is verbose, saying "tells everyone who will listen" and uses vague words ("its own founding"). The last choice succinctly uses "argues" (instead of "tells people"), "illegitimate government" (instead of "false and fake") and conveys the intended meaning of the sentence.

6. H. Sentence 22 describes Taiwan's point of view. The last choice supports the ROC's point of view, while the second choice directly counters it. The first and third choices are neutral.

7. D. Sentence 17 describes how Taiwan is a popular tourist destination. This is irrelevant, as the rest of the passage is concerned with describing the dispute between the ROC and PRC in terms of historical context.

Bad Risks

1. A. The two sentences convey different ideas. Sentence 3 describes how there was a "superficial" cause – or something that appears to be so on the surface. Sentence 4 describes how there was another reason but that this reason was "at its core." The idea of something superficial is the opposite of something that is deep and meaningful. Therefore, the best combination of the sentences highlights this with the word "though." "And" and "similarly" express congruency of ideas, where "still" conveys an idea that something is the case notwithstanding something else.

2. F. We must be careful not to delete too much of the sentence when editing for precision. Sentence 8 describes how loans were given to almost everyone even if they could not repay. Choice A fails to capture the fact about the inability to repay the loan – an important part of the original sentence. Choices C and D use roundabout ways of saying things. For example, it is implied that the loans are from banks or other financial institutions, so it is unnecessary to mention that the loans are from a bank. Similarly, "if it was determined that they would have a hard time repaying it" is a longer and less direct way of saying that the loans were given "regardless of their ability to repay." Similarly, we do not need to know that it is the inability to repay a loan, since the fact that it is a loan is understood.

3. A. In this sentence, there is nothing wrong with offsetting the parenthetical expression "including those...it" with dashes. It would also be correct to offset the expression with commas, though doing so does not correct for anything wrong with the sentence. Instead, we have a problem with subject-verb agreement. The subject "any business" is treated as a singular subject, so the verb to be must reflect that number. "Is" is singular, where "are" is plural (think "he is" versus "they are"). We must keep the comma after "after all" since it is a connecting phrase which helps us to understand what follows it in relation to what precedes it. We cannot change "lent" to "lends" because the other verb in the sentence ("asked") is already written in the past tense.

4. H. "So" indicates the appropriate cause/effect relationship between sentence 19, which describes an idea generally, and sentence 20, which describes specifically how that idea applies to the topic being discussed. "Yet" and "otherwise" are used to show a contrast, and "besides" is used to show something additional.

5. C. The other choices describe situations where managers and those responsible for the crisis are held "answerable" or "accountable" for their actions. Another way of describing this is to say that they were "punished" for their actions and forced to make things right with the rest of the country. This runs contrary to the main thesis of the passage, and indeed, the paragraph, which describes how the people responsible "were able to avoid responsibility for the negative consequences of their risk-taking behavior."

6. G. Sentence 12 describes how people who had lost their homes found new ones. The passage focuses on how the crisis was caused, and why it happened. It does not focus primarily on what happened to people as a result of the crisis.

7. C. The passage never discusses whether or not the crisis could have been avoided. Though the passage does mention how borrowing money to buy a house contributed to the crisis, it stops short of claiming that it is "unwise" or to be "avoided." Instead, the passage is focused primarily on describing how risk taking and a lack of accountability enabled the financial crisis.

Reading Comprehension

Non-Fiction

Befriend the Sandman or Beware

1. C. The passage is primarily concerned with explaining why sleep is important and how a lack of sleep is dangerous for drivers. Choices A and B describe aspects of sleep's importance, but omit the information provided in the rest of the passage about how sleep affects driving. The author does not advocate for the reading of headlines and newspapers, only using an example cited from a newspaper to support his explanation. The author does not explain what, precisely, sleep is, or how it works.

2. H. The passage does not mention sleep's impact on people's immune systems. The 2nd paragraph describes all of the other choices.

3. B. Use of the article supports the author's main idea, connecting the idea of sleep's importance and the dangers associated with driving while fatigued. The inclusion of the examples from the article precedes mention of the ruling by the Federal Motor Carrier Safety Administration. There is no evidence to suggest that the two incidents described in the article occurred as a result of losing an hour or two of sleep. The article is included to show how the main idea is relevant to everyday life. While sleep is important to cognition, the examples provided by the article would more likely support the idea that sleep is important to responding to physical stimuli (i.e. driving).

4. G. The questions address the reader directly and are a stylistic way of writing to capture a reader's attention. The topic of the questions is related to the main idea of the passage; that is, the importance of sleep and the dangers of driving while tired. The passage does not address objections or refute commonly held beliefs about sleep. While the author writes that some aspects of sleep are not well understood, the questions posed at the beginning of the passage do not relate to what about sleep is or is not understood.

5. C. According to the last paragraph, critics (i.e. those people who do not agree with the Federal Motor Carrier Safety Administration's ruling) often cite that the hours are "still too long," and compare those hours with average workweek hours (40-50 hours long). The passage does not support the idea that truckers must work at least 11 hours per day or that the 100,000 car accidents are all due to tired truckers.

6. E. The last paragraph states that the Federal Motor Carrier Safety Administration ruling took place in 2012 and reduced the upper limit of hours truckers can drive from 82 to 70.

7. B. The passage never describes the diversity of people's sleeping habits and how that factors into driving safely. However, the passage does describe how sleep is not completely understood, but that it is still very important to traffic safety. Lack of sleep is singled out as the most important factor that contributes to traffic accidents; the passage doesn't dive into any other factors that are as important.

8. G. Paragraph 5 describes the government's new laws aimed at helping reduce the number of traffic accidents caused by fatigue. This can be viewed as a solution to the problem of driving with a lack of sleep. The information about the magnitude of the problem was stated in paragraph 4. The figures in paragraph 5 describe more about how the changes can help reduce the magnitude of the problem.

9. C. The table presents data that shows the number of hours driven with no break and the increased chances of an accident. The risk increases more per 0.5 hours, showing that not every half hour of driving is equally "dangerous." This table doesn't show the number of people killed by drivers, or the ideal amount of sleep or driving per day.

Jack the Dripper

1. A. The passage follows Pollock from the beginning to the end of his life. There is only one point of view offered (the narrator's). There is no problem stated, nor is there an argument being advanced. Facts are stated simply in a chronological order.

2. G. The passage describes Jackson Pollock's life and work and describes him as a famous artist. While some parts of the passage discuss the art industry (Guggenheim's patronage of Pollock), other artists (Benton), and even the Works Progress Administration, they are all done so in context of describing Pollock's life in biographical form.

3. D. The third paragraph tells us that Benton's influence on Pollock was significant, and states that "many art historians believe that Pollock's artistic departure from tradition derives from Benton's strong sense of independence." The other answer choices are unsupported by the passage, as there is no indication that any of the other choices happened.

4. H. The Works Progress Administration employed many artists to work in the Federal Art Project during the Great Depression. We know this from the fourth paragraph. There is no evidence offered to support the other answer choices.

5. C. The sixth paragraph tells us more about how Pollock's drip technique earned "critical acclaim" and was "iconic." "Jack the Dripper" was a name given to him by *Time* magazine because of his drip painting. The passage does not indicate that these works were created for Guggenheim, nor does it mention that all the works were donated. We know that Pollock's most celebrated works happened while he was still alive based on the sixth paragraph.

6. E. The passage never describes why Pollock stopped using drip style, only that it stopped "as suddenly as it began." There's no mention of negative feedback, and there is the opposite of a lack of interest.

7. D. We can infer from the third and fourth paragraphs that working as an artist during the Great Depression was difficult. The first sentence of the fourth paragraph tells us that Pollock "barely" got by until Guggenheim became a "paying patron." This phrasing lets us know that "keeping his head above water" has to do with money. We can infer the meaning from context clues. The fact that the art was inspired by water, that he had a paying job or had previously been in trouble with the law, are unsupported.

8. F. The author begins the passage by saying that Pollock's works are among the most influential and famous in the world. This, coupled with the statements about his success in paragraphs 6 and 7, suggest that buying his works might be well worth the expense. There's no mention of Pollock being reclusive. Since the WPA helped Pollock survive, and the author has a positive opinion on Pollock, we can infer that the author would be in support of government funded art projects. Pollock's drip technique was developed as a result of many factors, but we cannot make inferences about its development.

9. A. Part of his non-traditional upbringing was that he was raised in many different places and had exposure to many different

experiences. The only statement that supports this idea is the first. The rest do not deal with his upbringing.

The Lost City

1. C. Indiana Jones is a fictional character that would be more likely to be familiar to readers than Hiram Bingham III. The author uses this reference to engage the readers, and introduce Bingham, who is the main focus of the piece. Indiana Jones is only mentioned later in reference to Bingham, and the passage overall is not about Jones.

2. H. The passage focuses on how Bingham discovered Machu Picchu. Though Bingham's contributions as an academic are mentioned, they are background details rather than the central idea.

3. C. Paragraph 6 describes how Bingham saw the ruins of Choqquequirau on his first visit to Peru in 1909, and how "he believed differently" from the commonly held assumption that it was the last capital. His theory then leads him to organize the second expedition in 1911. He did not find Machu Picchu on his first visit; nor was his second visit a return to Choqquequirau. There is no mention of him doing research after returning from Cuzco; it was his experience of Choqquequirau, and not studies from America, that inspired him to return.

4. G. Paragraph 5 shows how Bingham's interest in Latin American history was consistent through his various academic positions. There is no mention of his childhood, financial resources, or other expeditioners in this paragraph.

5. C. Paragraphs 7 to 9 how Bingham meets a local man, Melchor Arteaga, who leads him directly to Machu Picchu. We can infer that without local help, in an unfamiliar terrain, Bingham would have been unlikely to find the ruins. There is no mention of dangerous obstacles, or of Bingham knowing the way himself prior to reaching Peru.

6. F. From the beginning of the story of how Bingham finds Machu Picchu, the author is comparing Bingham to Indiana Jones. The playful tone of this sentence mirrors the thrilling adventure-story style that Indiana Jones stories are told in.

7. A. In paragraph 3, the author calls Hiram Bingham "one of those lucky few" for coming "close to living out the fictional life of Jones." At no point in the passage does the author describe Bingham's discovery in a negative light.

8. F. Although academics are not necessarily the first thing that people think of when they hear the name Indiana Jones, this quote starts with "Like Jones, Bingham was…," and therefore highlights a commonality. The quote from paragraph 2 does not explicitly mention Bingham, and the quote from paragraph 11 discusses a difference, not a commonality.

A Labor of Love

1. C. The passage describes two scientists – Mendel and Galileo – whose work was rejected during their lifetimes, but later found to be essential foundations for modern science. Though much of the passage focuses on Galileo, he is being used as an example to support the central idea, and the passage as a whole is not solely focused on his conflicts with the Roman Inquisition. None of the examples describe scientists dying for their beliefs; Galileo was only sentenced to house arrest.

2. E. The word "hail" means "celebrate," and "father of genetics" shows how important Mendel's work is now considered to be. After this sentence, the paragraph goes on to detail Mendel's ideas and how "his findings were initially rejected by his peers" (paragraph 2). As such, this sentence poses a contrast to the reaction that Mendel received during his peers. While it does show how modern scientists view him, the question is asking about structure and not simply meaning.

3. B. In paragraph 3, the author explains that "In Lorini's point of view, Galileo was reinterpreting the Bible, an activity that was prohibited by the Roman Catholic Church's Council of Trent," and that is the reason why the Church forbade his studies. There is no mention of Galileo's personal faith, and paragraph 4 goes on to show that he did in fact ask for permission to publish his work.

4. F. The word "persecution" means "ill-treatment," and the statement that "mere rejection, however unfortunate, pales in comparison to persecution" (paragraph 3) emphasizes how severe, or unpleasant, "persecution" feels. The examples of how the Inquisition treated Galileo (house arrest, being ordered to stop his studies) are more focused on how badly he was treated, rather than how difficult it was for him to spread his ideas. In fact, the author does not mention whether Galileo prioritized spreading his findings, so

much as his perseverance in conducting his research despite opposition.

5. A. In the sentence "Galileo obeyed – at least superficially" (paragraph 4), "superficially" or "only in appearance" is used to describe Galileo's obedience to the commands of the Church. The passage then goes on to detail how he wrote a book on his studies; the Church's negative reaction to its contents implies that he did not modify his ideas to please them, despite following technicalities by asking for permission to publish. There is no mention of Galileo's emotional state about these events, or of his faith.

6. H. Earlier in the paragraph, the author states that "Galileo did not live to see his work truly appreciated," implying that Galileo's work deserved appreciation, and that the author did not agree with the way the Inquisition treated him. This answer option is the best match, since it declares that "Galileo had been wrongfully condemned."

7. C. The author makes a distinction between the "mere rejection" that Mendel received, versus the "prosecution" that Galileo faced, so they are different examples of ways in which scientists were historically underappreciated. Mendel worked on genetics and Galileo on solar systems, so they did not work in similar disciplines.

8. H. Paragraph 6 is about how Galileo's worth as a scientist was eventually recognized many years after his death, which shows a change of mind from how he was treated in his present day. "Emphasizing how badly scientists were treated during their lifetimes" was discussed at other points in the passage, and not in paragraph 6.

Cellular Solutions

1. B. The passage as a whole is arguing in favor of stem cell researching, citing its scientific and medical benefits (paragraph 4-5). Though it discusses how stem cell research was once controversial, that is in the past (when the cells were taken from embryos), and scientists have already figured out a way around that issue, by using adult stem cells (paragraph 3).

2. F. The word "applications" means "uses." In the context of this sentence, is it referring to the beneficial uses of stem cells. Although in other contexts "applications" can also refer to paperwork, that meaning does not apply here.

3. B. Paragraph 4 discusses how brain cells were "previously irreplaceable" before the discovery of stem cells, which implies that they do not naturally regenerate when damaged. Hence the example of a person with Alzheimer's: without stem cell treatment, the disease cannot be reversed.

4. H. Although the passage discusses many uses for stem cells, it does not claim that stem cells are guaranteed to cure all medical conditions. The research is still ongoing, and many of the proposed uses are not fully developed yet.

5. C. In paragraph 2, the passage describes how scientists figured out how to isolate human stem cells in 1998. The year 1981

refers to when they first discovered how to isolate stem cells in small mammals.

6. G. Since paragraph 2 describes how complicated it was for scientists to "isolate," or separate, specialized stem cells, we can infer that the embryos contained more than just that type – in other words, a mix of unspecialized and specialized cells. The embryos cannot contain only unspecialized cells, since that would defeat the purpose of searching for stem cells in embryos.

That's Not Music!

1. B. The author is challenging readers to think more deeply about what makes music. The passage later contrasts the views of an average person (paragraph 8) with music theory (paragraph 2), and is mostly about how complex the melodies we take for granted actually are. The questions are not part of the author's personal exploration of music theory.

2. G. The passage focuses on the most important element that makes music: melody. Stylistic changes in music and the composition process over time are mentioned but neither are the main focus of the passage.

3. A. The importance of melody in qualifying sounds as music is the central claim of the passage, and this quote supports that idea. Though the statement came from the student of a great composer, neither their ideological differences nor the idea that only great composers are concerned with melody are likely purposes for including the quote.

4. F. The idea that random notes in any order do not necessarily result in something nice to listen to suggests that there is a deliberate design process that must take place to create what can be called a melody. The quote from paragraph 1 hints at this idea, but pointing out a difference between music and noise does not necessarily imply that that difference arises from design.

5. B. In paragraph 3, the author asks the reader to consider what it is about melody that makes music pleasing to the ear. Paragraph 4

provides an answer to this question by discussing the technical aspects of a good melody.

6. G. The author discusses repeated exposure in paragraph 6, stating that repeatedly listening to a song can change the way people respond to it. This is not guaranteed, as the author uses the word "can".

7. B. In paragraph 5, the author states that different people have different reactions to the same melodies due to variations in brain chemistry. This implies that it would be difficult to create one melody which many different individuals would like. However, the author is not implying that brain chemistry should be changed to guarantee a positive reaction.

8. G. The main point of the passage is that all good melodies share the same qualities that make them musically pleasing to listen to. This quote illustrates that these qualities have not changed throughout history, even though musical styles may have changed.

9. C. The author discusses the elements of memorable music that have stood the test of time, so he would likely agree that the length of time a melody is remembered and enjoyed by future generations would be a way to determine its quality. Though it is a skill to create a melody that is universally liked by all, the author would not say that this is impossible, given the examples of *Thriller* and *Für Elise*.

Bridging the Gap

1. B. Paragraphs 2-5 show how bridges have become more structurally and technologically advanced with time. The central idea is not simply that there are different types of bridges, but that bridge designs grew more complex and ambitious over time.

2. H. The author discusses in paragraph 4 that suspension bridges solved the problem of weight and distance that arch bridges could not. It also discusses how some of the oldest bridges in history are arch bridges, so there is no evidence that they tend to crumble. Even though suspension bridges are aesthetically beautiful and challenging to build, these are not the reasons given for why people transitioned to using them. The quote is also not claiming the Nature was an "innovator" of bridges, since that would imply sentient intention.

3. D. This sentence establishes the idea that early humans built bridges from simple logs, which is a big contrast from the complex suspension bridges detailed later in the passage. It does not show the *recent* history of bridges, nor is the passage an overview of the historical innovators of bridge design.

4. H. Paragraph 3 states the central idea of the whole passage: "As technology advanced over the ages, people developed new ideas for building bridges. Each development allowed people to span ever greater distances." There is no argument or counterargument in paragraphs 4-5, and paragraph 7 is about bridges in modernity.

5. B. Paragraph 4 explicitly states the types of scientific principles at work in building a bridge. The other choices describe bridges, but not how science was necessary to the development of bridges.

6. G. Paragraph 5 emphasizes the role of engineers in bridge construction, and how difficult their work is, from the many different factors they must take into account, to the dire consequences of their miscalculations. The paragraph does not discuss multiple famous engineers, or the impact of natural disasters on bridges.

7. B. A "feat" is an accomplishment that was difficult to achieve. By using the word "feat" to describe the engineering process behind the Brooklyn Bridge, an example of a modern bridge, the author implies that it is an impressive construction. Though "feat" implies something difficult occurred, there is no reference in the text to the difficulty of traveling over these bridges. Nor is there any mention of how big the cables are, or the heroism displayed during the Quebec Bridge collapse.

8. G. The table supports the ideas outlined in the passage by suggesting that bridges became longer through human history, since it gives the lengths of bridges from 1310 B.C. to 1937 A.D., and the lengths increase. This supports the claim in the passage, that longer bridges were possible due to improvements in technology and engineering. The table does not highlight the different types of bridges. This chart alone does not reveal that the Quebec bridge is the longest of its kind nor how sound the technology of the oldest bridges was.

Pop, Pop!

1. D. Referencing Michael Jackson, an iconic pop figure, as well as providing statistical details about his sales history, helps establish the author's credibility as an expert on pop music history. The entire premise of the first paragraph is to establish how success was established *prior* to social media, in the era of Billboard charts. Paragraph 1 also claims that pop music of that era did not have one universal style or sound.

2. E. The major claim of this excerpt is that pop music was historically characterized by diversity of musical styles, and is

defined as an all-encompassing category based on popularity. Later on, the passage goes on to lament the lack of diversity in pop music now, so diversity does not still characterize pop music.

3. D. The first paragraph introduces pop music and its history. The third paragraph discusses how the musical qualities of pop music is now different in the present. The third paragraph beckons a question – "But what makes pop music so popular, anyway?" – that bridges these two larger discussions in the passage. This question is presented not to analyze or criticize the digitalization of pop music, but rather to dive deeper into how the music changed as a result of technological advances.

4. F. In the past, the success of pop music was predicated on album sales statistics and Billboard chart rankings. But, as paragraph 5 states, "Forget Billboard charts – today we need look no further than social media and online media outlets to determine the popularity of a singer or their songs." Mass appeal still determines the success of pop music, as evidenced by the importance of online followings. Radio play is not specifically mentioned for either the past or present.

5. A. Paragraphs 4 and 5 argue that shortened attention spans, caused by digital changes, have forced many musical artists to rely on multiple hooks, which help maintain the attention of listeners. People have not requested these hooks, and there is no indication that they are easier to write.

6. G. The word "formula" refers to the widespread uniformity of music and formulaic composition of hooks, which the author openly laments later in the passage. The author is not impressed by the work of the songwriters, and does not describe them as "scientific." Though the passage attributes part of this problem to listener tastes, which have been changed by technology, there is no direct blame for audiences.

7. C. The reference to Barack Obama emphasizes that some pop musicians have a greater social media following than the president at the time, which is a testament to their widespread impact. It does

8. E. The numbers in the "Instagram Follower" column do not match the ranking order of the Billboard charts (especially in the case of Taylor Swift, whose social media following would rank her higher than the Billboard charts do). The social media followings and album sales do not match, so not all best-selling artists have the greatest social media impact.

9. B. Paragraph 6 highlights how, due to technology, pop stars are now able to generate profits through more than just album sales. With the internet, they are able to sell different products directly to fans, and are making more money than stars in the time of Michael Jackson. Though the examples may show how these stars are multi-talented and business savvy, that does not tie in to the central idea of the passage, which is about how technology changed the pop music industry.

10. F. The final question, "After all, 15 billion views can't be wrong – right?" incorporates a hyphen in order to create an explicit of hesitation or pause. There is an inherent contradiction that is being conveyed through the juxtaposition of the words wrong and right, which are separated by this explicit hesitation. This creates a sense of ambiguity. The author is not encouraging further research or highlighting the inability to explain pop music. Instead, the author is suggesting that the line between wrong and right when it comes to the current direction of pop music may be ambiguous or blurred.

The Legacy of Impressionism

1. D. The passage is primarily concerned with describing the wide-reaching effects Impressionism had on history and other musical genres. While Impressionism can be linked "to the revolutionary sounds of rock and roll in the 1960s," it can also be linked to other artistic movements and musical styles, such as American jazz, so that is a detail rather than the main idea. The passage does not give an overview of all of music history for thousands of years, and the use of timbre is another detail.

2. F. The author states that music impacted other fields, but also that it drew inspiration from fields like visual arts. He/she never describes Impressionism as a "strictly separate" or "superior" art form. Instead, the entire article focuses on how Impressionism became more powerful because of its collaborative capacities.

3. D. The sentence from paragraph 4 captures the idea that Impressionist music drew inspiration from visual art, which is reinforced by the quote from paragraph 6, which highlights how Impressionists "experiment with the relationships…between sounds, colors, and feelings." Diversity of sound, innovation, and change in popularity are all other ideas about Impressionism, and are not addressed by this particular sentence.

4. H. The third paragraph is mostly about how the "main objective of the Impressionist era was to paint emotional pictures through unique musical arrangements." They did this by using a technique known as timbre, which the excerpt describes as a means to "stimulate the visual senses of the audience." Therefore, it is an example of a technique. While timbre is utilized to paint emotional pictures, this is metaphorical language, and timbre has nothing to do with actual sculptors or painters.

5. C. Impressionist musicians wanted to capture visual beauty in their orchestral arrangements. When the passage describes "the calm evoked by light dancing on still waters" and "the tranquility of sunlight filtering through treetops," it is directly referencing the impact visual beauty had on composing Impressionist music. These descriptions are not reflective of the settings in which Impressionists composed their music, but rather the mental images they tried to create for their audiences.

6. F. The word "manipulate" implies a task involving skill and delicacy. Its usage supports the idea that timbre was not easy to use, and that the composers used it skillfully. Though the words sound similar, there is no evidence to conclude the composers were manipulative – or sly, devious individuals.

7. B. Paragraphs 5 and 6 highlight the ways in which Impressionism influenced later musical styles and genres, such as American jazz and rock and roll. Paragraph 7 is the one that transitions into the idea that Impressionist concepts affected many people beyond the field of classical music.

8. H. The phrase "its beauty inevitably bled into other artistic disciplines" is used to describe the historical impact of Impressionist concepts blending with, or bleeding into, other art forms. Though other parts of the passage discuss how Impressionist music is influenced by visual art, this statement does not show evidence of that. It is also a general statement, and does not give an example of specifically how Impressionist music influenced other fields. The passage does not indicate anywhere that Impressionism lived in isolation from other disciplines.

A Different Lens

1. D. Paragraph 1 sets forth the claim that science fiction is more than just exotic settings and far-fetched technological premises. At its heart, it "tell[s] us more about ourselves." Though the passage praises the relevance of science fiction, it does not compare it to other genres, so it cannot be said to be the most relevant genre. The main idea of paragraph 1 is that science-fiction is relevant to the everyday.

2. G. The central idea of the passage is that science fiction deals with human themes. This claim is supported by various examples (paragraphs 3-5), written by "the Big Three," Though it briefly touches upon the plots of these books, that is in service to the central idea previously mentioned.

3. A. According to paragraph 3, "Lagath…is bathed in constant illumination by six suns." The eclipse is an unanticipated and rare event, and not the reason why Lagath is unaccustomed to darkness.

4. F. The "Big Three" mentioned in paragraph 6 refers to Heinlein, Clarke and Asimov, who are all science fiction authors.

5. C. "Prophetic" means accurately predicted, so we can infer that the sentence implies that the issues described in the novel later became true in real life. As the book is about "technology and how it has many potentially negative effects on humanity," that is most likely what has proven true since 1968. We cannot assume the inverse, that technology was beneficial to people before 1968.

6. E. As the Martian "explores the meaning of being human" in the book, we can infer that the Martian did not have a thorough

understanding of human culture prior to contact. We cannot tell, from paragraph 4, whether the Martian was a powerful representative or provided humans with new technology. Lagath is the setting of a different novel.

7. D. The passage concludes by noting to prevailing popularity of the science fiction genre, in movies as well as books. That science fiction movies sell well is a supporting detail, and not the central idea of the paragraph.

Paved with Good Intentions

1. C. Paragraphs 2-4 describes that ecotourism is a type of tourism that attempts to support conservation, but is actually quite limited in making the impact it claims to. Although the article discusses tourism for social media self-promotion in paragraph 1, this is the type of tourism that ecotourism tries to prevent. The passage does not claim that ecotourism is illegal nor that it generates donations for conservation non-profits (in fact, it criticizes ecotourism for not sharing sufficient profits with conservation causes).

2. H. "Skepticism" means thinking that something is too good to be true. The tone of the question casts doubts on the idea of ecotourism because its premises are not realized in practice (for example, foot traffic not being zero impact). Paragraph 2 establishes the positive intentions of ecotourism and Paragraph 4 exposes that the reality of ecotourism, so paragraph 3 offers a transition to the more skeptical tone of paragraph 4. The tone is not neutral or ambivalent because the author makes a clear stance against ecotourism.

3. A. Even though the United Nations Food and Agriculture Organization claims that ecotourism is nature-based and sustainable, the author most likely does not agree with this perspective, as the passage focuses on the unintended negative impacts of ecotourism (domestication of wild animals, loss of resources due to development, spreading human diseases, etc). There is no mention of the relationship between ecotourism and the high cost of living.

4. G. In paragraph 5, Daniel Blumstein "says that ecotourism is unaware of its consequences." The example of the lion dying at the hands of hunters, because he felt safe around tourists, shows an

unintended consequence. Blumstein's quote does not discuss marketing or how the profits are used.

5. B. Paragraph 8 uses Costa Rica as a specific example of ecotourism gone wrong, where ecotourism is harming wildlife through sheer numbers of tourists arriving. There are no scientific claims in the paragraph nor does the paragraph summarize the entire passage. Even though the paragraph gives the historical context of ecotourism in Costa Rica, it does not discuss the history of ecotourism at large, which is the main problem in the passage.

6. F. Paragraph 6 discusses the phenomenon of domestication where animals adapt to the presence of humans and are therefore more vulnerable to danger, as an example of an unintended consequence of ecotourism. The passage does not suggest that this effect is intentional, nor does it discuss hunting regulations. Though the word "domestication" can, in other contexts, refer to the process of wild animals becoming pets, that is not how it is being used in this passage.

7. A. Paragraph 8 discusses how the rising number of tourists in Costa Rica has led to increased development, which has negatively impacted the local wildlife. This chart gives statistical support for the claim that there have been a rising number of tourists in Costa Rica between 1995 and 2015. The chart does not specify where the profits from ecotourism are going.

8. H. The author most likely mentions the ecotourism "buzzwords" – like "eco" and "green" – because they draw tourists into thinking they are making a positive impact while it actually makes a negative one. The author does not imply that the buzzwords are about native wildlife. The question of enforcing ecotourism practices is mentioned in a different paragraph.

A Critical Point of View

1. B. Paragraph 6 states: "Nevertheless, the themes that Carter covered – consumption, identity, and unity – are issues that still resonate today." The paragraph then goes on to cite several examples of how the issues he described manifest in modern times (how climate change has escalated, how over-spending led to economic downturns), so it is not accurate to say that the central idea is only about the problems during Carter's presidency, or that his speech helped fix the issues he discussed.

2. F. In paragraph 2, the author points out how remarkable it was for Carter to discuss spiritual problems in his speech, being the first U.S. president since World War II to do so. The other answer options mention aspects of his speech that would likely have occurred in other presidential speeches as well, or are supporting details.

3. C. The second paragraph states that "Carter began his speech by reading excerpts from letters sent to him by concerned Americans." These letters can be categorized as a form of direct communication. While Carter also referred to national trends and news reports, it was the letters by American citizens that inspired his speech, not the advice of his speechwriters or other sources.

4. E. Paragraph 3 detailed some of the concerning human behaviors that support Carter's claim of an American spiritual crisis. His tone does not convey dislike of American citizens so much as worry for America's future. The comparison of the problems of the past with those of today occurs in paragraph 6, not 3.

5. D. His words call the American public to action, explaining that the "crisis could not be solved by politicians alone." This is not a

reference to his "lack of personal accountability" or his "personal crisis of faith" but rather a focus on collective action to "focus on contributing positively to society." In this paragraph, Carter's words are not antagonistic toward the American public; he is not blaming them.

6. G. The author's perspective on Carter's speech is largely positive, and he only references the fact that others believe Carter was being apocalyptic, unfair, and hyperbolic in order to offer a balanced historical assessment of American responses to the speech. Overall, however, the author seems to think highly of Carter's justified concerns.

7. B. The word "bridges" is used here to show how the present connects to the past, and how the issues that Carter described have their equivalents in current times (i.e. global warming, economic depressions). These connections are not difficult to find, according to the passage, but rather are quite relevant, even though a lot of time has passed.

8. H. To be "visionary" means "to have foresight." The author argues that Carter's speech was not only accurate, but also predictive of future issues, as evidenced by how there is still a "crisis of confidence" by the time of Obama's presidency. This statement counters critics' claims about the apocalyptic and hyperbolic nature of Carter's speech. Carter's background as a Christian is mentioned to explain the spiritual focus of his concerns, and they are cohesive rather than competitive elements.

Linguistically Speaking

1. C. The passage describes the many different ways in which linguists study language—from individual sounds and collections of sounds (phonology and morphology) to the way meaning is constructed and used (syntax, semantics, pragmatics), to historical

and psychological aspects of language. This discussion reveals the complexity and nuance involved in language. Though the passage mentions the intuitive ease with which native speakers use language (paragraph 6), that is a detail and not the central idea.

2. E. The phrase "for granted" is an idiom, meaning that something is assumed and/or unquestioned. So, the passage is saying that we do not question the fact that we can communicate with each other. But as the passage goes on to suggest, communication as viewed by linguists is a far more complex process than is commonly perceived. There is no mention in paragraph 1 of young children.

3. D. The purpose of paragraph 2 is to present examples of some of the aspects of language that are studied by linguists, and it is the first paragraph to define the topic of linguistics. Some questions are presented in the paragraph, but not all of them are answered by the passage. Paragraph 9 is the conclusion, and does not elaborate on paragraph 2.

4. G. The passage compares words to the building blocks of a language. In keeping with this metaphor, groups of words like phrases and sentences would be buildings and skyscrapers, since they are each made up of many individual components. Just as individual words make up a phrase or sentence, so too are buildings and skyscrapers made up of different individual pieces, and are therefore complex. There is no reference to construction workers.

5. C. Morphemes include root words, prefixes, and suffixes, and the paragraph discusses how the meaning of a multi-syllabic word can be formed by combining the meanings of its morphemes. Therefore, we can infer that the more morphemes a person knows, the easier it will be for that person to determine the meaning of unknown words.

6. H. Phonology refers to the sounds that make up words. The only one of the choices that refers to sound is the one that mentions the similarity in sound between "cheese" and "zebra."

7. C. The passage begins by stating that we take for granted the way we are able to communicate with one another, but then discusses the complexity of language that lies beneath the simple fact of our communication. The question at the end of the last paragraph is rhetorical, and reinforces both the way communication seems simple to us and the reality of how complicated it really is.

8. E. The last sentence of paragraph 8 says, "By breaking down the process by which children acquire language, psycholinguists can gain broader insights into how people of all ages learn." While it may be more difficult for adults to learn a new language, there is no reference to adults being uncooperative.

Plastic Addiction

1. A. The passage focuses on the massive amounts of plastic in seas and how it effects our marine ecosystems, so this answer option, which cites that we are "choking our...seas with 6.3 tons of...plastic waste," is the best fit. In paragraph 6, the author closes the passage with "we just need to *want* to do it," but this call to action is only mentioned in the conclusion, and not throughout the passage as a whole

2. E. The excerpt points out "a mere seven percent" of plastic is recycled and "14 million tons[...] is whooshed into our oceans," which implies that the majority of the plastics in the ocean could have been recycled and therefore diverted. This particular excerpt does not mention that "plastic pollution" is increasing.

3. B. By stating that "700 different species" are threatened by plastic, this option supports the idea that a "variety of marine life" are affected. Though one option mentions that "a third of the fish caught [...] housed microplastics," and addresses the number of animals affected, it does not discuss the variety of species affected.

4. H. The author writes that the nanoplastics can be absorbed into "our own bodies." The use of first person "our," and the fact that many readers probably consume fish, show that the author is appealing to the reader's self-interest. Although the excerpt may appeal to a reader's empathy, it is not focused on the harm to the fish so much as the eventual impact on humans from consumption.

5. A. The complaint that it takes "environmentally friendly plastic" 450 years to decompose (paragraph 2) shows that the author does not want any kind of plastic, biodegradable or not, to be in the

ocean. The passage also says only "seven percent" of plastic is recycled (paragraph 2), and "we have technology to pick up, dispose of, and recycle plastic" (paragraph 6), which shows that the author believes it is realistic and possible to eliminate plastic waste in the ocean. The author states that plastic is damaging to the planet, but never says that it should be completely banned, only that it should be cleaned up properly.

6. G. The final paragraph discusses systematic changes (more garbage trucks, big companies committing to recycling product waste, countries putting plastic bans into effect) rather than individual changes, so it is not a call to action for readers to personally attempt to solve the problem. Paragraph 6 also does not summarize "human factors that caused the overall conflict."

7. D. The author says "we have the technology" to recycle better, if we *want* to do it." This paragraph both re-frames the problem as one of human choice, and offers a solution. The technologies mentioned are real, not hypothetical, and "no politicians are claiming that ocean pollution is a hoax" (paragraph 6).

8. G. The graphic shows a trend over time. The amount of plastic is given in the y-axis, and the year on the x-axis. We can see an explosive growth in the amount of plastic waste generated, and that only a small portion of this is being recycled. We do not have any evidence that laws are being passed or that plastic is ending up in the ocean.

Two Treatises

1. C. The author describes how Locke believed "the powers of government should be divided" (paragraph 3), so we can infer that he would also believe the inverse, that no one person should hold too much power. His resistance of the monarchy also supports this. Though he disliked the monarchy, there is no mention of how Locke felt about the Parliament.

2. G. The passage as a whole is focused on Locke's ideas about governance (paragraphs 2-3) and how they influenced others (paragraph 5). Though there is information about Locke's life, the passage does not mention Locke's childhood, and only discusses the aspects of Locke's life that are relevant to his philosophical idea.

3. D. In paragraph 3, the author quotes Locke advocating "for the right of the citizens to rebel," if the ruler is unfair and attempting to "compel...by force." Though paragraph 2 discusses Locke's idea that governments require the consent of their subjects to be

ruled over, he does not imply that that government should take the form of a monarchy.

4. H. Paragraph 1 explicitly states that Cromwell passed away when Locke was studying at Oxford to become a doctor.

5. A. Since Locke's philosophy was in opposition to monarchies, most likely Charles II and James II would disagree with it.

6. F. Locke was an antagonist to Charles II, and not supporter. However, he did serve Lord Shaftesbury, who was an opponent of the monarchy on the Parliament, and his father's experiences in the Parliamentary forces most likely influenced his political views as well.

7. A. As paragraph 5 states, "Almost a century later, Locke's ideas engendered a new revolution." The purpose of this paragraph is to show how Locke's ideas remained influential long after his death, and in lands far away from his own. Though America's separation from England is mentioned in this paragraph, that is a supporting detail and not the main point.

Dear Evan Hanson

1. B. The passage is specifically focused on Andrew's hard work and passion toward pursuing a theatrical career when he "competed in

the National School Musical," "starred in school and community theater," learned musical instruments, and wrote music. Winning the high school musical theater contest is only the first part of the passage, which also goes on to discuss his childhood and his role of Evan Hansen in great detail. Being an outsider looking in describes the character of Evan Hansen, and not Andrew himself.

2. F. Winning a national competition is a great exhilaration, but then to obtain not just a part in a Broadway production but the lead—that is an astonishing feat at 16, and sounds more like events from a fiction story than reality. The story-like use of repetition in these opening sentences reinforce that feeling of surrealism. The events described are not common/typical.

3. C. Paragraph 2 describes Andrew's journey at the National High School Musical Theater Awards, and specifically tells the multiple challenges that Andrew had to overcome, which demonstrates the extent of his accomplishment when he does win the contest. Even though the passage summarizes Andrew's childhood, that happens later, in paragraph 5.

4. E. The sentence shows the moment that all of Andrew's prior preparation culminated in, when he is finally rewarded for his efforts by being noticed by industry professionals. Although we can infer that it took a great deal of skill and practice for Andrew to sing his medley, this particular sentence addresses the reward and not the process.

5. D. The paragraph educates the reader on the character Evan Hansen—a 17-year old that is always trying to belong—and, that the role is an "emotionally intense one," usually cast by actors in

their 20s. This fact is a testimony to Andrew's talent, since he is much younger than all previously casted actors. Even though "adult men" had previously played Evan Hansen, the paragraph never indicates that the role should only be played by them, since Andrew, a teenager, was also selected.

6. E. Paragraph 8 first uses the term "win" then changes it to "earned," which has the connotation of something you worked for, or deserve. Andrew won the competition due to his hard work and dedication, not luck. Even though Andrew will likely earn money while on Broadway, the word "earn" here is not being used to describe financial earnings.

7. D. The sentence says his current schedule is "topsy-turvy" and lists his weekly tasks, which illustrates his continued strong work ethic. The quote from paragraph 5 describes his work ethic prior to the win, and not after. And although the statement about giving "five performances" may seem difficult, it goes on to say that producers are wary of asking him to give eight, which does not indicate a strong work ethic so much as the idea that he is still young and needs to be protected.

8. G. The author's upbeat tone about Andrew's success in the opening of paragraph 2 and the illustration of Andrew's passion for performing (paragraph 5) shows us the author believes one should follow his or her passion. Even though the passage demonstrates the need for determination, it never guarantees success.

Masterminds of the Sea

1. D. The passage details how intelligence has been categorized in mammals (paragraph 2) then it goes into how octopuses, a cephalopod, contradicts those norms (paragraph 3). While the topic is octopus intelligence, the central idea is specifically how octopuses demonstrate intelligence even though many of their traits do not match scientists' conceptions for intelligent animals. Being "fun" animals is a supporting detail, not the central idea.

2. H. Paragraph 2 "highlights the three most common traits" that indicate high intelligence: large brains, long lives, and social skills. The paragraph does not illustrate the methodology (technical step by step process) scientists use to identify the most powerful brain.

3. B. In paragraph 2, the author talks about scientists' observations about high intelligence animals. In paragraph 3, the author's use of "on the other hand" conveys how octopuses are a contradiction to these ideas. "Breaking the mold" is a phrase that also generally means to be an exception. Even though the passage demonstrates their activity in containment (paragraph 7), these details reinforce an octopus's intelligence and personality, and not a desire to escape. Also, while aggression may be seen in individual octopuses – a fact that the author mentions to support the idea that octopuses have different personalities – it does not characterize the species as a whole.

4. H. Paragraph 4 illustrates examples of octopuses adapting to situations in ways that demonstrate intelligence (ex: tool use, problem solving) in their daily lives. Even though the passage explains how "experts viewed and recorded intelligence of the octopus," the octopus mentioned were in the sea and not aquariums.

5. A. In paragraph 5, the author explains how an octopus shows the ability to make decisions, which is an "even more sophisticated,"

or challenging, type of intelligence. The paragraph then goes on to detail specific experiments where octopuses showed clear decision-making skills.

6. F. In paragraph 7, the author lists various octopuses' personalities (naughty, aggressive, emotional), and supports this claim with examples of ways octopuses demonstrated preferences among caregivers. Though we may correlate those behaviors with young children, the passage does not.

7. C. In paragraph 6, the author says an octopus is not just interested in food but wants "to do something interesting." Throwing a jar repeatedly does not satisfy any basic survival needs (food, breeding, etc), but rather shows a need for mental stimulation. The example of tool use shows intelligence generally, but not that octopuses specifically need mental stimuli.

8. G. The word "road" here is used to describe metaphorical pathways to intelligence. To say that there are "different roads to…intelligence" means that there are different ways animals can develop high intelligence, as evidenced by the octopus, which is an outlier to conventional expectations. "Road" is not being used as a literal reference to travel.

9. B. The graphic compares the average total number of neurons among various mammals and the lone cephalopod, the octopus. It shows that the octopus has neurons that number as many as a cat, which is a mammal, showing that it is more intelligent than people may expect for a cephalopod. It does not prove that this is the only indicator of intelligence, or show that the nervous systems are similar. There is no mention of cat behaviors, or how those might compare to octopus behaviors.

The Cost of Convenience

1. B. The passage describes the environmental problem caused by plastic bags, as well as how this problem arose: the industrial revolution led to people being able to cheaply produce many types of different things, including containers and bags. The tax is designed to take away the appeal of using these bags all the time, in order to reduce waste. A history of containers and an explanation for why plastic bags are bad for the environment are provided, though they are all offered to advance a greater point, and are not described in detail throughout the passage. There is no explanation offered as to why the environment is more important than convenience.

2. E. The first two paragraphs describe why carrying one's own container "was a commonly accepted fact of life." The reason for this, the passage states, is that the "containers were valuable." There's no indication that people only bought what they could carry in their hands (if anything, people only did that because they couldn't carry more containers with them). We don't know if people in the past valued convenience more or less than they do today.

3. D. The third paragraph highlights how, with the industrial revolution, suddenly things like bags became cheap to produce. Because of this, everyone could have a bag or "as many bags as

they wanted." This does not mean there is more money, just that things like containers cost less than they did before. The invention of plastic and taxes are not cited as reasons for why people valued convenience over the containers themselves.

4. E. In the second-to-last paragraph, various environmental effects are listed. Soil erosion is not among these, but the rest of the answer choices are.

5. C. The question comes at a point in the passage where the focus shifts from explaining how bags became ubiquitous to why that is a problem. The question goes on to be answered in the next

paragraph and describes more than just theoretical examples of how people use plastic bags.

6. F. The passage never indicates that the money generated from the tax will be used to clean up the environment, nor does it suggest that people will stop using plastic bags completely. Instead, people can be expected to value the convenience less, thereby generating less waste. This will help the environment in turn.

7. B. The graphic shows the amount of plastic generated vs. the amount recovered or recycled. This supports the fact that the "vast majority" of plastic is "simply thrown away."

Fiction & Poetry

"Night"

1. D. The repetition of "under" and the reference to "pace" emphasizes the unrelenting effect of the night, which in this case, is interpreted to be old age, or time. The "under" does refer to a direction, but this is not the a central idea of the poem. This does not emphasize beauty.

2. E. Lines 8 and 9 describe a specific effect of night: that it peels back a leaf from the stalk. This is echoed in what night does to the petals. This is more than just taking the petals in hand, and is the opposite of leaving something behind.

3. D. By using apostrophe here to speak directly to "night," (which is not night, but age, or time), the speaker makes a powerful emotional plea. The fact that it is alone emphasizes the speaker's loneliness and despair – that she is left with nothing more than the

core of her person. This is the opposite of hopefulness. There is no contrast made with the flower, as the speaker appeals directly to night regarding what it has done to the flower.

4. G. The use of commas and semicolons don't let the reader pause, as a period would. Instead, it mirrors the relentless (grave) pace of night as it has its effects on the petals and leaves. There is a lack of punctuation that gives pause to the ideas, just as nothing can give pause to the march of "night."

5. C. The final stanza summarizes the speaker's lament: that night is cruel by taking away everything but the core of the person. There isn't anything here about hope, nor does the speaker show that there are pros as well as cons. The stanza doesn't describe how these trials make a person better in any way.

"When You Are Old"

1. B. The act of reading is one of reflection – a person reads words on a page but processes them through his or her own experiences and knowledge. This is similar to reflecting on the past. We don't know that the speaker is in retirement, and that this is what the metaphor represents. Instead, from context with the rest of the passage, we know that this is a time for reflection, not a time to literally read a book. There's no mention of writing an autobiography, or sharing lessons learned from life with others.

2. F. The word "you" can be directed toward a specific person, or to a group of people. In this case, we don't know who the speaker is addressing. This is deliberate on the speaker's part, as a central idea of the passage, then, can apply to anyone. In this case, the speaker can be addressing herself directly, or can be telling someone (or some group of people) what to do. The speech is more of an internal dialogue that we are privileged to, as opposed to a conversation.

3. C. The glowing bars recall back to the earlier image of a fireplace. This is in the last stanza of the poem in which the speaker reflects on the loss of that true love. The glowing bars are the flames in the fireplace, which hasn't been compared with youthful beauty and

love before (those were described in the second stanza). It is in the first stanza where the speaker falls deep into her thoughts.

4. F. The "soft look" describes the look of the person's eyes, and represents youth or innocence. This is echoed by the line "moments of glad grace," as opposed to "sorrows of your changing face." The former describes youthful grace (remember to read the lines before and after the ones in question), while the latter describes the pains of growing old (as does "old and grey and full of sleep").

5. D. The second stanza describes how the speaker was beautiful, and had many loves, but these loves were "false or true." This suggests that physical beauty can cause a superficial love, which is only skin deep, and may or may not have been true love. However, one person loved the speaker's soul, and the "sorrows of your changing face." This is true love – love that stays with a person through the ups and downs, no matter the outward beauty.

6. H. The fact that "Love" is capitalized is significant and intentional. The speaker is still very sad, and it is not thanks to love that she has recovered (she hasn't), but because of it that she is sad. The specific person that was her love has not been identified, and here, the speaker does not speak directly to the concept of love, as apostrophe would suggest.

"Leisure"

1. C. The speaker addresses Leisure herself with a strong desire, wishing that she would bless the over-busy-world today with her presence. She may be frustrated by the lack of leisure in the present, but there is a desire and longing in her writing that extends beyond just frustration.

2. E. Apostrophe is the impassioned, direct address made by someone to an abstract idea or inanimate object (or an absent person). This creates a conversational tone where emotions are revealed. The speaker does not address a person, nor does this addressing of Leisure directly cause confusion or comic relief.

3. D. These lines tell us that nowadays, people are haunted by the reminder of things undone, and so they feel they have no time to enjoy life. The word heritage does mean customs and beliefs, but not in the sense of tradition. Instead, it means that the customs of daily life are too arduous and keep people too busy, leading to "shortening moments."

4. H. After telling us that leisure is withheld from "this over-busy world," the speaker tells us that leisure can still be found, but only

in the "unhewn woods" – or nature. While this could be construed to mean that this is alone and without other people, we don't know for sure whether or not the speaker means that leisure can only be found by oneself. Instead, we can take this to mean that the speaker believes leisure can be found away from society, in nature.

5. D. The crime here is to constantly be rushing around – not to have "worshipped" leisure. The speaker doesn't mean that we must literally go to a church, nor does the speaker refer to spending *too* much time on one's self. She would view walking in the woods as time well-spent.

6. G. When reading anything, we read commas as short pauses, and periods as stops. In the first 9 lines, there is no end-of-sentence punctuation. Indeed, the longest pause is a semicolon, which is not quite as "strong" of a stop as a period. The effect of this lack of punctuation is that the poem reads uninterruptedly. The many commas cause us to pause, and slow down – ideas reflected in the actual words and ideas of the passage.

The Tutorverse

"Song"

1. A. The speaker consistently describes how he feels. In the first stanza, he describes the first time he saw her, and the effect it had on him. This effect gives us a glimpse into how he feels – that his spirit was a "deeper night" and that the only thing that had ever shone on "its shadows drear" was her light. The other choices describe his reactions, but don't give an insight into his frame of mind.

2. H. All of these stanzas begin with a different time that the speaker sees the woman. The fact that the speaker counts these times is significant, almost obsessive. The stanzas describe how the woman has had positive effects on the speaker, making the speaker more excited, happy, and glad.

3. D. The simile compares the woman's effect on thrilling the speaker's heart to a "wild hand" (active hand) playing a stringed instrument (lyre). This is not meant to be taken literally. We don't know that the woman is a musician. This is the opposite of being calmed by the woman.

4. G. The comparison to the woman as a "fadeless flower" suggests that in the speaker's mind, the woman's image is indelibly ingrained. Note the lines that precede these: "I saw her oft again—, each hour / Enhanced o'er me her conquering power". The other lines describe her appearance or sound, as well as the ultimate effect the woman has on the speaker.

5. A. The 7th and 8th stanzas focus on describing the woman's beauty in more detail. This echoes back to the first line, where the woman's beauty is first mentioned. The other lines describe the effects the beauty has on the speaker.

6. G. The stanzas follow the pattern: AABAB, which repeats throughout the entire poem. Like this, the general idea of each stanza is the same in that they describe a quality of the woman and its effect on the speaker.

7. B. The fact that nothing the woman could say would be less beautiful than the sweet song of a bird suggests that the woman is perfect, to the speaker. Note the context: the stanza immediately preceding this one describes how even her footsteps are "More beautiful than if a God / Had placed immortal foot-prints there".

Adapted from *A Modern Tomboy*

1. A. From context, we can tell that the word is describing the amount of time in which the rugs can be rolled up.

2. H. Lucy turns red because she dislikes Rosamund's suggestion, not because she was jealous of Rosamund's ideas. There's no evidence that Rosamund was humiliated, since shortly thereafter, she gives a "smile which seemed to denote power." Instead, Rosamund has usurped (seized control over) Lucy's party, and is giving orders even to Lucy, the apparent host.

3. B. The tone, which is clearly not a phrase meant to be taken literally, is positive. In context, we can tell that Phyllis had gone off to find permission, and just returned to find out that it has been granted. This means that she was likely animated, not direct (in which case she would not have used such a long phrase), particularly dignified, or impartial. She wanted to dance, otherwise, she would not have gone to get permission. The phrase is colloquial, not formal or dignified.

4. G. The expression "go to Hong Kong" is used to mean that Lucy's mother doesn't care about the rugs at all. We can infer this because Lucy becomes enraged, as this was the opposite of what she expected, and now she has no reason not to let Rosamund have her way and dance.

5. C. We don't know much about Rosamund and Lucy except for what is shown in this passage. However, we do know that at the center of the conflict in this passage is Rosamund's ability to get her way: once with the dancing, which Lucy objects to, and another time with Lucy's father, the professor, which Lucy also objects to. There are no allusions to the fact that Rosamund's appearance, dancing, or conversations are the object of Lucy's rage (though the latter is part of what makes Lucy angry toward the end of the passage).

6. G. Lucy clearly did not want Rosamund to meet or talk to her father, as she "longed to give any sort of excuse, but none would come to her lips." She resented Rosamund for making everyone dance, and may well have wished she would trip to embarrass her and decrease her influence over the other girls. She would definitely have wished that Phyllis never asked permission to dance, since then Lucy would have gotten her way, and Rosamund would not have. However, she would not have wished to practice more dance music, since she would not have wanted to help Rosamund in any way.

7. C. Lucy is boiling with rage at the fact that Rosamund has gotten her way the entire night. Lucy opposed the dancing, but Rosamund made it happen. Lucy didn't want Rosamund to talk to her father, but couldn't stop Rosamund.

8. G. It appears that Phyllis had an idea that something like this would happen, because the secret looks that she gives to Lucy drive Lucy mad with rage.

Adapted from *The Jolliest School of All*

1. B. The only sentence which describes Lorna's internal struggle are in this choice, where the narrator describes the realization as a "blow" that was "overwhelming." A drowning man battling the waters is as vivid an image of a struggle as one can imagine!

2. E. Paragraph 9 tells us that Lorna's father knows "his [Beverley's] writing only too well," all of which was prompted by the revelation that Lorna had been reading a book written by him.

3. B. Lorna likes Irene and describes this friendship in paragraph 11. This includes statements that Irene was kind, loving, accepting, and could be trusted. The feud between the fathers had not affected the girls (this is the first that Lorna has realized that her friend's father is her father's enemy).

4. H. The passage only shows us that Lorna and Irene were friends, never that Irene was the object of Lorna's jealousy. The passage states that Irene was "the only one at school who had sympathized and understood her." This shows that Lorna was clearly not popular, and in fact, had difficulties making friends.

5. A. The issue in the passage is the fact that Lorna and Irene are friends, but that this friend is related to her father's enemy. Thus, there is tension between family and friend.

6. H. These questions are asked in the last paragraph of the excerpt. In this paragraph, the reader is shown how Lorna has confusion ("whirling eddies of her thoughts") about how to respond but ultimately concludes that forgiveness is the only solution ("Curses, like chickens, come home to roost").

7. A. The desired purpose of the passage is to help the reader to empathize with Lorna. We aren't told why David Beverley and Lorna's father are feuding. Instead, we are given a glimpse into Lorna's feelings, and thus, are asked to feel for her.

8. H. The understanding that revenge will only make things worse (the last line in the passage) prevents Lorna from following her father unconditionally.

Excerpt from *"Ride Proud, Rebel!"*

1. D. The author gives us clues as to what the "roan" is. It has a tail, which is not helpful since all of the choices have tails. However, we know that it is big enough to have a "rider" and that it is saddled (since it was unsaddled). The author also writes about how it is a "mount." Thus, it is most likely a horse.

2. H. The passage gives us many clues about Drew's experiences. The fact that there is an "economy of action" is one such clue. However, the bigger clue is from paragraph 7, which describes his "boyish roundness" as being melted only through "hard experience."

3. C. The word "economy" has many definitions, one of which has to do with saving, or carefully using something (think: economy class, which is no-frills, the opposite of first class luxury). When used to describe action, it means that the action wastes no energy, and is very efficient (think of a talented athlete who relies on muscle memory). Thus, the person is not inexperienced, but experienced (or has had lots of practice). The person is not necessarily a manager of resources, since in this case, the word is being used to describe an action.

4. G. We can infer that Drew is currently at Boone's Fort, and that because nobody knows about it (paragraph 6), it was a retreat that he had built with his friend, Sheldon.

5. A. Reading the paragraph in context, we know that Drew is "remembering" and that he is recalling his friend, Sheldon, and how they built "it" (Boone's Fort), and how this was his only piece of property. He looks out onto the scene, but is looking vacantly, as

he recalls the passage of time, and his memories.

6. E. We are not told what his present purpose is, but there is no evidence to suggest that he is there to simply enjoy Red Springs, or even to join up with people at Chickamauga. Instead, we can infer that Drew is working on some unknown task.

7. A. Since the sentence tells us that it was "gone in a flash" and left "no hint of softness," we can tell that Drew was faking the smile. His features are described as "gaunt" and "dark" – two very negative descriptors.

8. F. The fact that it has been five years is almost unbelievable to Drew. This emphasizes the amount of time that has passed, and also shows us how Drew feels about this passage. It also lends gravity to the fact that during those years, a great deal has transpired. This doesn't tell us anything about the author.

9. D. The "bite of last winter's cold" feels permanent to Drew, and is a negative emotion. The fact that he doesn't think he'll ever warm up again is strongly negative, so we can rule out "gladness" and "pride." Though there may be regret about Boone's Fort, this paragraph deals primarily with Drew's difficult and challenging life experiences.

Adapted from *The Most Dangerous Game*

1. B. The speaker does not have a positive view of the alternatives offered to him after the "debacle in Russia." He says he is "lucky" to have alternatives so he would "never have to" open a tearoom.

2. E. In the first paragraph, the speaker states that he has hunted grizzlies, jaguars, and buffalos, but not lions.

3. C. In the passage, General Zaroff is the same person as "the Cossack." This is the same speaker in the first paragraph, and is the person we learn that Rainsford addresses.

4. G. General Zaroff does not hunt for food, or for trophies. Instead, he is a hunter to chase the animals. He states that he enjoys "the problems of the chase."

5. C. The speaker of the first paragraph is the Cossack, or General Zaroff. He detests perfection, since it is boring. This is confirmed when he says that it was "a tragic moment" because "there is no greater bore than perfection."

6. F. A "sporting proposition" is something that is fair and challenging and conducted for the enjoyment and experience, not a "bore" or a "sure thing." The other choices describe examples of a "sure thing" or something unfair.

7. A. For the general, the problem with most animals is that animal instincts are "no match for reason." In this case, "reason" is used to mean intelligence, or sentience. Therefore, the general would want to hunt something that is not just fast, powerful, or dangerous, but intelligent.

8. F. Rainsford, listening to the general, is at first just a listener, occasionally chiming in to ask Rainsford a question. However, as the general reveals that he has invented a new animal to hunt, Rainsford becomes more and more intrigued. Rainsford insists that the general tell him more about the animal, and eventually gasps. The author uses this to suggest that Rainsford is shocked and no longer just a casual listener, but actively concerned, or worried.

Adapted from *The Cruise of the Dazzler*

1. A. Joe is described as being "demure" (shy) and "nervous" (since he was fiddling). This means that he was expecting his father to be something negative, like critical, furious, or disappointed. One would not be shy or nervous if one knew that someone was going to react patiently.

2. F. The passage tells us that "the gold" was recovered, implying that the contents of the safe included gold. Joe's father gives him "credit, and plenty of it" to Joe for recovering the safe. We know that Joe was successful in his trip, and recovered the safe, but don't know who the 'Frisco Kid is.

3. C. Joe said that the outcome "couldn't possibly have turned out any better," implying that he thought he had done his best. However, his father's reaction was deliberate and judicious, as well as reserved. This leads Joe to be disappointed, since he was hoping his father would agree and share in the triumph.

4. G. In some cases, "qualified" means "experienced" and "capable." In this case, however, we can tell that the word is negative. This rules out "expert" and "competent." "Absolute" doesn't work, because we know that Joe felt disappointment, and therefore, he

did not receive "absolute approval." Instead, his father was reserved, and offered partial, or incomplete, approval.

5. B. The most likely choice is that the safe belong to Joe's father, since he was the one spending money (in the form of an award) to recover it. We are not told the amount of money contained in the safe.

6. G. Mr. Bronson, Joe's father, launches into a big speech in the second half of the passage, telling Joe that life and experiences are invaluable; one would not trade one's life for a million dollars. This is to say that even if an outcome is not as good as hoped for, that this doesn't mean the experience was pointless.

7. D. In the aforementioned lines, Mr. Bronson speaks with a great deal of care. Otherwise, he would not go to such lengths to explain himself, ask rhetorical questions, or demonstrate his care about Joe's safety and life experiences.

8. E. The phrase "potent for evil as for good" suggests that it is too early to tell whether Joe's experience was good or bad. This is supported further when he says "until time has told me, whether…"

Excerpt from *The Innocents Abroad*

1. A. The phrase refers to the waves in the ocean and is explicitly discussing the rough seas that are keeping the boat from traveling.

2. H. "Repetitions" and the fact that the passengers were "just as eligibly situated as we could have been anywhere" means they had nowhere to go, and nothing to do. Thus, this describes the author's boredom. The fact that he indicates that he is "just as eligibly situated as we could have been anywhere" suggests that he is patient, not impatient.

3. C. Paragraph 2 describes the narrator's musings on breakfast, which is a time, he believes, when people can be vulnerable. During this time, people are more relaxed, if they ever are, and their true nature can be observed. This implies that normally, people are guarded, or masked, covering up their true nature or selves.

4. H. The simile in question is "a spirit of charity rose up in their place that was as boundless…as the broad ocean". Here, the comparison is made between the amount of charity and the

vastness of the ocean. This represents a very positive, or optimistic, point of view. We can rule out "dread" and "nervousness," which are negative feelings that have disappeared. The narrator is selfless, but not because he wants to help passengers (there's no indication of that at all); remember that we must read paragraph 4 in its entirety to determine context.

5. D. The narrator is so happy he could sing, except he doesn't. He may be certain about this fact, but it's certainly not something he boasts of. Instead, the sentence should be read as tongue-in-cheek – a self-deprecating comment about how he is sparing his fellow passengers his singing.

6. H. The author is not selfless or particularly considerate of others. He greets them, but he cares more about the fact that their seasickness makes him feel better about himself. He acknowledges this fact, but this doesn't make him any less self-involved.

7. C. The "good pleasure" the narrator feels is mentioned right after the experience of interacting with many miserable people. The contrast between how he feels (positively) and what he experiences (other people's negative feelings) tells us more about the narrator's

character.

8. F. The sentence is an excellent example of imagery that describes the violence of the seas. The quote describes the front and back of the ship pitching and yawing in the rough waters. The phrase "taking a deadly aim at the sun in midheaven" suggests that the front of the boat is nearly vertical one moment, while the next it is "trying to harpoon a shark in the bottom of the ocean" suggests that it is nearly vertical the opposite way.

9. D. The central idea of the sentence is that a person will feel proud if he or she is not seasick when others around them are. There is a feeling of superiority that is inherent in such a belief. This is echoed in the last choice, which describes how the narrator is glad that others felt badly because he liked it. It made him feel better than others.

10. G. These paragraphs describe the narrator's interaction with others. Time after time, he meets other people who say "Oh my" as they feel sick from the roiling waters. This makes the narrator gleeful, ultimately, that he is superior to others and does not succumb to seasickness.

Adapted from *The Luckiest Girl in the School*

1. B. The argument at the center of the passage is about where Winona will attend school, and Ms. Woodward is on the edge of capitulating to Winona's demands. The excerpt shows that it took Mr. Joynson's reassurances to convince Ms. Woodward to stick to her intention; hence, she is depending on others to make a decision. Although it is true that Ms. Woodward's indecision prolongs the debate, this excerpt specifically is not addressing that.

2. F. As Percy goads Winona about how she will do terribly at school, he uses many mocking words, calling her a "pig," and a "whipped puppy with its tail between its legs." Though it is possible that he is doing this "to comfort" her (paragraph 10), his tone cannot be described as "encouraging."

3. C. In this moment, Winona's little sister, Letty, is listing all the things she is looking forward to in Winona's absence, and she seems happy that Winona will be leaving. Percy's comments from paragraph 8 show no reluctance to let Winona leave, even if he does not think she will succeed while away.

4. H. The Aesop's story that she references, according to the footnote, is an example of a fulfilled request not turning out as positively as

the requester expected. In this context, Winona is using it to say that her absence may not be a good thing, since the younger children will then have to obey a governess/teacher. She is expressing irritation at Letty's pleasure at her departure.

5. C. In paragraph 9, Winona's feelings about going away for school change from fully negative to mixed, since she now wants to prove to Percy that she won't be a failure. The argument between the siblings continued, and is not resolved. The excerpt ends before Winona goes away for school, so we cannot tell if her words were a correct prediction/foreshadowing.

6. F. Since she "set her teeth and clenched her fists," Winona's emotions cannot be characterized as "sorrowful;" instead, they show determination. Her reaction is to her siblings' comments, and not the adults in her life.

7. A. In paragraph 7, Winona is still complaining about having to go away. Paragraph 16 shows her resolved to succeed. Not enough time has passed for the comparison between the two moments to show how Winona has "matured" from a younger self.

Numbers & Operations

Numbers

1. B. $\frac{1}{4} = 0.25$. $\frac{1}{3} = 0.33$. Therefore, only $0.33 > 0.31 > 0.25$.

2. E. A repeating decimal never ends. We know that $\frac{1}{3} + \frac{1}{6}$ is equal to $0.\overline{33} + 0.1\overline{66}$, which equals 0.5. If we were to add the fractions, we would arrive at $\frac{2}{6} + \frac{1}{6} = \frac{3}{6} = 0.5$. If we add any of the other fractions together, we end up with a non-terminating fraction.

3. C. The only way for the product of one number and another number to equal one of those numbers is for one of the numbers to be equal to 1. We can prove this by using examples. Let $x = 10$ and substitute into the equation: $10m = 10$. By dividing both sides by 10, we can see that $m = 1$.

4. F. We can express these inequalities as follows: $p + 7 < 0 < p + 9$. Try each answer choice to find that only -8 makes a true statement.

5. B. If the three different numbers are multiplied together to get 15, the only way to do this is to multiply 5 by 3 by 1. This is because 15 only has the following factors: 1, 3, 5, and 15. If we have to use 3 different numbers, the only way to do so is to use 1, 3, and 5. The sum, then, is $1 + 3 + 5 = 9$.

6. G. We are looking for two square numbers that have a difference of 11. Going through the square numbers (1, 4, 9, 16, 25, 49, 64, etc.)

we see that only 36 and 25 have a difference of 11, meaning $x^2 = 36$ and $y^2 = 25$, so $x = 6$ and $y = 5$.

7. A. We know that Alice's speed is twice Bob's speed, which is 9 mph. This means Alice is biking at 18 mph. If Carol's speed is one-third of Alice's, then her speed is 6 mph.

8. E. Since the question asks for the least amount the author could pay the editor, we can assume that the editor is reviewing as many words per minute as possible, at the lowest rate possible. The editor will take 10,000 words ÷ 40 words per minute = 250 minutes to review the manuscript at his fastest possible speed. This translates to 250 minutes ÷ 60 minutes = 4 hours and 10 minutes. If the editor is paid the lowest rate of $18 per hour, then the editor will make $18 per hour × 4 hours = $72 plus $18 per hour × 10 minutes (or $\frac{1}{6}$ of an hour) = $3. So, a total of $75.

9. C. Consulting the chart, we see that there are a total of 32 plants with white flowers, 19 of which already contain yellow seeds. There are 23 plants with yellow seeds. Thus, $32 + 23 = 55$.

10. G. z represents the total of all flowers in the experiment, which can be found by adding all mutually exclusive values. We can add $x + y$, or we can add $n + r$, or we can add $k + m + p + q$. They will all add up to z. As shown in the Plugins section, you can also solve this by replacing the variables with numbers and seeing which answer choice works with your chosen values.

11. A. We can start filling out the rest of the chart by filling in any row or column in which there is only one blank space. The intersection of Latin and Geometry is 12,000 (84,000 − 72,000), and the total number of mandarin students is 17,500 (101,500 − 84,000). We can already now see that, if the total number of Geometry students is 12,500 and 12,000 of them are taking Latin, then that mean only 500 Geometry students are taking Mandarin.

12. G. An integer is a whole number. The word "inclusive" means to include the numbers in the range itself. So, we have 10, 11, 12, 13, 14, 15, 16, 17, 18, 19, 20: 11 integers. A rule for determining the number of items in an inclusive range is to take the difference of the upper and lower bounds of the range and add 1.

13. B. Convert the fractions provided in the question into standard form: $7 \div 3 = 2.33$ (−2.33 for the negative fraction). From this, we know that there are 5 whole numbers (integers) between (greater than) (−2.33) and (less than) 2.33: −2, −1, 0, 1, and 2. Note that both fractions result in non-terminating (repeating) decimals, but we don't need to worry about those since we are concerned with integers.

14. G. When describing a range, the word "inclusive" means to include the end numbers in the range itself. The word "exclusive" means to exclude the end numbers in the range itself. Set A contains all whole numbers from 50 to 100 (including 50 and 100), and Set B contains all whole numbers from 69 to 138 (excluding 69 and 138). Another way of saying this is that Set B includes all whole numbers from 70 to 137, inclusive. We know that all numbers from 70 to 100 inclusive are in both Set A and B. $100 − 70 + 1 = 31$.

15. C. There are 49 positive integers under 50 (1 through 49). To find out how many are <u>not</u> multiples of 4 or 6, we must find out how many integers <u>are</u> multiples of 4 or 6. There are twelve multiples of 4 under 50 and 8 multiples of 6 under 50. That would make a total of twenty, but there are overlaps, namely 12, 24, 36, and 48. Making sure those numbers are not counted twice, that leaves us with sixteen multiples to take out. We are left with 33 integers.

16. E. A three-digit integer is any number from 100-999 inclusive. The question tells us to consider only numbers in the 700 range, from 700-799 inclusive. It also tells us to consider only integers where the units digit equals 1. This can only happen once in every set of 10: 701, 711, etc. Therefore, there are a total of 10 integers fitting the criteria described by the question.

17. D. If the values of the coins Dimitri has are 1, 5, and 10 cents, we need to list out different ways for the sum to equal 17. Using the dime, there are 2 ways to make 17 cents: $10 + 5 + (2)1$, or $10 + (7)1$. If we don't use the dime, we can use just nickels and pennies: $3(5) + 2(1)$ or $2(5) + 7(1)$ or $5 + 12(1)$. If we don't use the nickels or dimes, and just use pennies, we can use $17(1)$. Therefore, there are 6 different ways to solve the question.

18. H. We must work backwards from the current share price of $25 up to the price of $30. The price has been dropping at a rate of $0.50 per half hour, or $1 per hour. Since there is a difference of $5 between the price now and the price before the price began dropping, and since we know that the price drops $1 per hour, then we know that it has taken 5 hours for the price to have dropped $5.

19. D. Since the numerator in the fraction is 1, we know that the larger the denominator, the smaller the value of the fraction. Since there is a finite range for y (between 1 and 5, inclusive), we know that the smallest value for the denominator will give us the largest value of the fraction. Thus, $1 \div 1 = 1$ (as opposed to $1 \div 5 = 0.2$).

20. G. Substitute the values of the answer choices and simplify. $7(4) \div 4 = 7$, and the square root of 7 is not an integer. Similarly, $7(7) \div 4 = 12.25$, which is not an integer, so its square root will not be an integer. $28 \div 4 = 7 \times 7 = 49$, which does simplify to an integer when you take the square root ($7 \times 7 = 49$).

21. C. Remember to resolve terms raised to an exponent before multiplying terms. In this case, this means to substitute −1 in for p and raising it to the power indicated in each answer choice before multiplying by the coefficient in front of p. A negative number that is raised to an even number will always result in a positive number

(while a negative number that is raised to an odd number will always result in a negative number). This is because a negative number times a negative number (in this case, itself), will always be a positive number, but a positive number times a negative number will always be negative. Thus, $8(1)$ is greater than all other answer choices.

22. E. Use substitution to try each possible value of c. If we substitute 1, we arrive at $b = \left(-\dfrac{1}{2}\right)^1 = -\dfrac{1}{2}$. If we square b, we arrive at $\left(-\dfrac{1}{2}\right)^2 = \dfrac{1}{4} = a$. If we substitute in 3, we arrive at $b = \left(-\dfrac{1}{2}\right)^3 = -\dfrac{1}{8}$. If we square b, we arrive at $\left(-\dfrac{1}{8}\right)^2 = \dfrac{1}{64} = a$. Since $\dfrac{1}{4} > \dfrac{1}{64}$, then the greatest value for a must be when $c = 1$. Remember also that the more times we multiply a fraction by a fraction, the smaller the resulting value. Since the exponent means to multiply a fraction by itself, we know that if we keep doing this, the resulting value will be smaller and smaller.

23. B. When a negative number is squared (raised to the second power), the result is positive, making it larger than the original number. Since the number line shows that x is greater than x^2, the negative answer choice will not work. We know that x cannot equal 1, because then $x = x^2 = x^3$. We can test out both remaining fractions. If we square $\dfrac{4}{3}$, we will get $\dfrac{16}{9}$, which is greater than $\dfrac{4}{3}$. This means that $x^2 > x$, which we know cannot be the case given the number line. Therefore, only $\dfrac{2}{3}$ works, as the square of $\dfrac{2}{3}$ will be $\dfrac{4}{9}$ making $x > x^2$.

24. E. Substitute the values of x into the different answer choices. Be sure to test at least two values of x. 0 is the simplest to test. We see, if we test 0, that both $x^2 + 1$ and $2x^2 + 1$ are valid, leaving us with a y value of 1. 1 is an easy value to test also. If we test 1, we see that only $x^2 + 1$ is valid.

25. A. Test the relationship between Y and X at various points in the table. By doing so, we can see that Y represents the square of the X value. For example, $2^2 = 4$, and $6^2 = 36$. Therefore, if 100 appears in Y, the X value must be 10, since $\sqrt{100} = 10$.

26. F. Since y is a positive integer, we can automatically rule out $x = 3$ or 4 because the product of each term times these numbers would exceed the value of the next term (for example, $9 \times 3 = 27$, which is greater than 21; this might work if y were allowed to be negative). We can test out 1 or 2. If we plug in 1 for x, then y would have to be 12 if the first term is 9 and the second term is 21 ($21 = 9(1) + y$). However, if we do this for the second term, we see that the equation doesn't work: $21(1) + 12 = 33$, which is not 45. Trying $x = 2$, we see that $9(2) + y = 21$, and $y = 3$. For the second term, $21(2) + 3 = 45$, which works.

27. B. We must add together the sum of students who are taking Biology or Chemistry, as well as those who take neither Biology nor Chemistry. This is $16 + 8 + 2 = 26$. Then, we should subtract the number of students who take both Biology and Chemistry. This is because they are also counted in the number of students who take

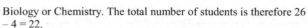

Biology or Chemistry. The total number of students is therefore $26 - 4 = 22$.

28. G. Substitute values in for each value of z. When we do this, we see that only when we plug in 13 for z is this true:

$2(13) + 7 = 33$, and $33 \div 5 = 6\dfrac{3}{5}$. The numerator tells us that the remainder is 3.

29. C. If there are 2 nickels for every 1 penny in the piggy bank, then $\dfrac{1}{3}$ of all coins in the piggy bank are pennies, and $\dfrac{2}{3}$ are nickels. Since this is the case, we know that the total number of coins must be evenly divisible by 3, otherwise, we would have a remainder/partial coin, which would be impossible. All choices are evenly divisible by 3 except for 55.

30. E. If Stanley is the 10th tallest and 10th shortest student in the class, then he represents the median height of his class. This is because there are 9 students who are taller than him, and 9 students who are shorter than him. This is a total of 18, plus Stanley himself, which makes 19.

31. C. If the program selected 51, then 51 would be printed, not 102. If 102 was selected, then 51 would be printed. Only selecting 204 would result in printing 102.

32. F. There can only be one number between 1 and 12 in the combination, as that represents the month of Tina's birthday. Therefore, we can rule out the other choices immediately. The last choice is incorrect because 11 is both the only odd number and the only number that could represent Tina's birthday month. 10 represents the month of Tina's birth, 15 the odd number, and 24 the factor of 24.

33. 210. There are 10 pairs equal to 21. $1 + 20 = 21$, $2 + 19 + 21$, and so on, up to $10 + 11 = 21$. $21(10) = 210$.

34. 14. Square all three parts of the inequality: $49 < x < 64$. All integers from 50 to 63 are acceptable values of x. There are 14 solutions.

35. 12. Either list them out as 1, 2, 3, 4, 5, 6, 10, 12, 15, 20, 30, 60, or do a prime factorization tree to see that $60 = 2^2(3)(5)$. Adding one to each exponent and multiplying these new numbers yields $3(2)(2) = 12$.

36. 120. If n is divisible by 3, 4, and 5, it must have 3, 4, and 5 as factors. The least common multiple of these numbers is 60. Since the question states that n must be greater than 100, the next common multiple greater than 60 is 120.

37. 19. $1,600 = 40^2$. $3,600 = 60^2$. In between, there are the squares of the positive integers from 41 through 59. There are 19 perfect squares in total.

Operations

1. D. Observe proper order of operations (PEMDAS). Multiply fractions first, and do so by multiplying across the numerators and denominators. This gets us to $\dfrac{3}{8} + \dfrac{1}{6}$. To add, we find equivalent fractions that have common denominators, so $\dfrac{3}{8} + \dfrac{1}{6} = \dfrac{9}{24} + \dfrac{4}{24}$. Now, we can simply add across the numerators since the denominators are the same: $\dfrac{9}{24} + \dfrac{4}{24} = \dfrac{13}{24}$.

2. G. Following the correct order of operations, we must divide $\dfrac{3}{4}$ by $\dfrac{1}{6}$ first, which we can rewrite as $\dfrac{3}{4} \times 6$, which equals $\dfrac{18}{4}$, or $\dfrac{9}{2}$. Adding $\dfrac{1}{2}$ to that results in $\dfrac{10}{2} = 5$.

3. B. Notice that all answer choices use the same digits, and only the decimal place changes. Since $2 \div 1 = 2$, we know that the answer must be close to 2. Thus, 1.95.

4. H. Notice that all answer choices use the same digits, and only the decimal place changes. We can use logical reasoning to know that $73 \div 2 = 36.5$. Since the decimal in 36.5 is two places from where it should be, we know we must move the decimal in 2 two places to the right, giving us 200.

5. D. When dividing a number by a fraction, we can multiply that number by the fraction's denominator then divide by the fraction's numerator. In this case, $2.4 \times 6 \div 1 = 14.4$.

6. F. Following order of operations, we divide 2.02 by 0.01 first. We can move both decimal points over two places, meaning we are now dividing 202 by 1, which is 202. Multiplying that by 0.03 gives us 6.06.

7. C. Remember proper order of operations: PEMDAS. Resolve terms inside of parenthesis, then exponents, then multiplication and division before addition and subtraction.

8. F. We know that $\sqrt{49} = 7$ and $\sqrt{64} = 8$, so $\sqrt{50}$ and $\sqrt{60}$ are both between 7 and 8. Therefore, the sum must be greater than 14 and less than 16. The only reasonable range is between 14 and 15.

9. C. The most efficient way to solve is to go through each answer choice, observing the correct order of operations. For choice A, solve the operation inside the radical first, giving you $\sqrt{11}^2$, which is equal to 11. For choice B, solving the operations inside the radical results in $\sqrt{121}$, which also equals 11. For choice C, the operations inside the radical result in $\sqrt{25 + 36}$ which equals $\sqrt{61}$. We may not know the exact value of $\sqrt{61}$, but we know that $\sqrt{49} = 7$ and $\sqrt{64} = 8$ so $\sqrt{61}$ must be between 7 and 8.

10. 64. The sequence is made of cubes of integers. $0^3 = 0$, $2^3 = 8$, etc. Since $3^3 = 27$, the next term is $4^3 = 64$.

11. 2. Set the two equations for x to equal each other. $14 - 4y = y - 1$. This means, upon adding $4y$ and 1 to both sides of the equation, $15 = 5y$, so $y = 3$. Substituting this value into either original equation yields $x = 2$.

12. -0.05. Remembering PEMDAS, we know that multiplication and division go first, so $1.2 \div .25 = 1.6$, and $2.5 \times 0.3 = 0.75$, giving us $0.8 - 1.6 + 0.75 = -0.05$.

13. 0.06. First, evaluate all multiplication and division operations. So, the equation becomes $0.1 + 0.2 - 0.12 \div 0.5$, and then $0.1 + 0.2 - 0.24$. Then, evaluate from left to right: $0.3 - 0.24 = 0.06$.

14. −5.12. Observe PEMDAS. Simplify inside the parenthesis for $3.2^2 - 15.36$. This simplifies to $10.24 - 15.36$, or -5.12.

15. 0.5. Observe PEMDAS. Converting to improper fractions may help. $4.2 = 4\dfrac{1}{5}$, or $\dfrac{21}{5}$. Multiplying by $\dfrac{5}{6}$ gives us $\dfrac{105}{30}$. Dividing a fraction by an integer is the same as multiplying that fraction by the integer's reciprocal, or $\dfrac{105}{30} \times \dfrac{1}{10} = \dfrac{105}{300}$. Simply multiply both the numerator and denominator of $\dfrac{3}{20}$ by 15 to end up with $\dfrac{45}{300}$, which we can add to $\dfrac{105}{300}$ and end up with $\dfrac{150}{300} = 0.5$.

Percents

1. A. The first thing to notice is that you do NOT have to actually find the numerical value of the expression. The answer choices tell you to simplify, not solve. It's easier to find $\frac{1}{3}$ of 924 rather than 35% of 924. Simple division tells us that $924 \div 3 = 308$. The equivalent of the statement is 35% of 308.

2. F. Green was the favorite color for 35% of the students and there were 3,000 students total, so we must find 35% of 3,000. This is $0.35 \times 3,000 = 1,050$.

3. D. If there are 12 boys, then the number of girls is $30 - 12 = 18$. To figure out what percent this is, take the number of girls and divide by the total number of students: $18 \div 30 = 0.6 = 60\%$.

4. G. If there are 200 pencils in a case, and 75 are sharpened, then 125 pencils are not sharpened. $125 \div 200 = 62.5\%$

5. B. In total, there are $1.5x + x + 2x + 3x + 0.5x = 8x$ students in the school. Of this, x number of students own 1 video game. This is $1 \div 8 = 0.125$, or 12.5%.

6. G. By interpreting the chart, we can see that people under the age of 35 consists of 20% + 25% of the building population. 45% of 1,000 = 450.

7. C. The overlapping circles with a value of 8 tells us that 8 students studied both Spanish and French. Since the question asks the number of students studying French (not exclusively French), then this is $5 + 8 = 13$. Since there are 25 students in total, $13 \div 25 = 0.52 = 52\%$.

8. H. We want to find the number of students who own 2 pets or more. 25% of the students own 2 pets, 8% own 3 pets, and 2% own 4 or more pets. In total, this makes 35%. We must calculate 35% of 2,400 which is $0.35 \times 2,400 = 840$.

9. C. If 20% to 30% of the students go on to a master's program, then 70% to 80% will not go on to a master's program. Therefore, the minimum that will not go on to a master's program is 70%. Calculate 70% of 4,000 students, which is $0.70 \times 4,000 = 2,800$.

10. F. It rained on 40% of the days which is $0.40 \times 365 = 146$ days. The number of days when it did not rain was $365 - 146 = 219$, or 0.6×365. The question asks: on how many more days did it rain than not? We must subtract the days when it rained from the days when it did not rain: $219 - 146 = 73$ days.

11. B. We can probably intuitively determine that the number of votes that Gillian received was 550, and the number of votes that Clive received was 450. However, let's solve this algebraically. Let x equal the number of votes that Clive received. In terms of x, Gillian received $x + 100$. So, $x + x + 100 = 1,000$. Simplify so that $2x = 900$, and $x = 450$. Thus, Clive received 450 votes, and if Gillian received 100 more, then she received 550. The percentage is simply $550 \div 1,000$, or 55%. We can just eliminate a zero from both numbers to see that the remaining fraction is $55 \div 100$, or 55%.

12. G. Let x represent the number of bottles that Betty recycled. In terms of x, Bruce recycled $2x$ bottles. In total, the number of bottles recycled by both Betty and Bruce was 600, so $600 = x + 2x$, or $600 = 3x$. Solving for x, we find that Betty recycled 200 bottles, and Bruce recycled $200(2) = 400$ bottles. This represents $4 \div 6 = 0.667$, or 66.7%.

13. D. The initial area is $50 \times 40 = 2,000$ ft². A decrease of 40% to the length of 50 ft. results in a new length of $50 \times 0.6 = 30$ ft. An increase of 20% to the width of 40 ft. results in a new width of $40 \times 1.2 = 48$ ft. The new area is 30 ft. $\times$ 48 ft. $= 1,440$ ft². This represents a total decrease of $2,000 - 1,440 = 560$ ft², or $560 \div 2,000 = 28\%$.

14. G. Let x equal the original price of the laptop. If it was first increased by 10%, this can be represented as $1.1x$. If it was then decreased by 20%, we can represent this as $0.8(1.1x)$. Simply

multiplying tells us that the final price is $0.88x$, or, in other words, 88% of the original price.

15. A. If Kevin watched 2 hours of TV on Saturday, and he watched 100% <u>as many</u> hours on Sunday, there is no increase or decrease. Thus, he also watched for 2 hours on Sunday.

16. E. The charge for shipping a $49 order would be 15% of $49, which is equal to $0.15 \times \$49 = \$7.35$. The charge for shipping a $50 order would be 12.5% of $50, which is equal to $0.125 \times \$50 = \$6.25$. The difference in the shipping charges is $\$7.35 - \$6.25 = \$1.10$

17. D. We are asked to find the total number of smartphones sold. Since 700 smartphones were sold other than Brands A, B, C, and D, the 700 smartphones that were sold were of Other Brands. Since Other Brands represents 20% of the total, then $700 \div 20\% = 700 \div 0.2 = 3,500$. We can check this by calculating 20% of 3,500 total sales: $3,500 \times 0.2 = 700$.

18. H. A 150% increase is the same as multiplying by 2.5. If the baseline was 8 miles, then John ran $8 \times 2.5 = 20$ miles on Wednesday.

19. A. Starting with the second piece of information, we know that Y is 20% of 100, so $Y = 20$. X is 80% of Y, so $X = 0.80 \times 20 = 16$.

20. H. The half-life of fermium-253 is 3 days, meaning 50% of any amount of it decreases by 50% every 3 days. There are 3 such periods in 9 days. This means there is $x(0.5)(0.5)(0.5)$ remaining after 9 days. This is a total decrease to 0.125, or 12.5% of the original amount. This means there was a $100\% - 12.5\% = 87.5\%$ decrease. Use an easy number, like 100, to prove it out.

21. D. When there are no concrete numbers given, use a number that is easy to work with. Let's say it is 100. At the end of one month, there will be $100 \times 1.1 = \$110$ in the account. This is because 1 represents the entire value of the original amount (or 100%), and the 0.1 represents the 10% increase. After the second month, there will be $110 \times 1.1 = \$121$. This represents an increase of 21%, but the question asks for the percent of the original amount that is there, or 121%.

22. E. 30% of the cost was due at signup, or $0.30 \times \$1,200 = \$360$. The amount that was left to pay after that was $\$1,200 - 360 = 840$. Then, 75% of this remaining balance was due the week before camp, or $0.75 \times \$840 = \$630$. Finally, the amount left to pay on the first day of camp was $840 - 630 = 210$.

23. C. Of the first 600, if 30% are red, then $600 \times 0.3 = 180$ are red. If the total number of red peppers must be 50% of the total, which is 1,000, then the red peppers must number at $1,000 \times 0.5 = 500$. Since there are already 180, then $500 - 180 = 320$, which is the number of peppers remaining that must be red.

24. F. If the restaurant sold 50 steak entrées out of a total of 200, that means they sold 150 "other" entrées. If steak must represent a minimum of 50% of their total sales, they must have a minimum of 150 steaks entrées sold as well. If they've already sold 50, they need to sell another 100 to reach their goal.

25. C. 80% of $5.50 can be calculated as $0.80 \times \$5.50 = \$4.40$. The company charges 80% more than the original cost so we must add $4.40 to $5.50. The answer is $9.90.

26. G. Percent problems can be solved using proportions. Here, $52 represents 130% of the amount the store paid to acquire the lamp, so we can set up the proportion $\frac{130}{100} = \frac{52}{x}$. Cross multiplying gives us $130x = 5,200$, so $x = 40$. If the employee discount is 40% off the this amount, then we can find 40% of $40, which is $16, and subtract that from the $40 cost, which leaves $24.

27. 64. 20% of 100 is 20, so at first 80 chickens remain. 20% of 80 is 16, so finally $80 - 16 = 64$ chickens are left.

28. 80. There are $16 + 12 + 8$ wild dogs in the zoo, or 36 wild dogs. Set up a proportion to determine the total number of animals in the

zoo. If $\dfrac{36}{x} = \dfrac{45}{100}$, where $16 + 12 + 8 = 36$ total wolves, coyotes, and dingoes, and x represent the total number of animals in the zoo, then we cross-multiply to get $3,600 = 45x$, or $x = 80$.

29. 25. As a fraction in lowest terms, $24\% = \dfrac{6}{25}$. Since the number of students must be an integer, there could be any integral multiple of 25 students in the class. 25 itself is the smallest of these multiples,

since multiplying 0.24 by any integer less than 25 will result in a decimal, or "partial" person (which doesn't make sense).

30. 630. 30% of 1,000 is 300 ($0.3 \times 1,000 = 300$) students who like the Scottish Fold. There are $1,000 - 300 = 700$ remaining students. 10% of this would be $0.1 \times 700 = 70$ students who like the Turkish Angora. This leaves $700 - 70 = 630$ other students who have a different favorite breed of cat.

Fractions

1. D. A whole number can be rewritten as a fraction by putting the number in the numerator and a 1 in the denominator. So, we can express 6 as $\dfrac{6}{1}$. Similarly, we can express $6\dfrac{2}{3}$ as $\dfrac{20}{3}$, by multiplying the integer 6 by the denominator 3 and adding it to the numerator 2. Now, we need to multiply across the numerator and denominator, and simplify: $\dfrac{6}{1} \times \dfrac{20}{3} = \dfrac{120}{3} = 40$.

2. H. We can solve by converting both mixed numbers to improper fractions, giving us $\dfrac{9}{2} \times \dfrac{18}{5} = \dfrac{162}{10}$. We can use division to figure out that this equals 16.2

3. D. A fraction can be represented as a decimal using division. Divide 44 by 64; we see that the fraction equals 0.6875.

4. H. A fraction can be represented as a decimal using division. Divide 25 by 32; we see that the fraction equals 0.78125.

5. B. We can solve this algebraically. We are told that $\dfrac{2}{3}Q = 36$. We can remove the denominator from the left side by multiplying both sides of the equation by 3. The equation then becomes $2Q = 108$. Dividing both sides by 2, we arrive at $Q = 54$. $\dfrac{1}{3}$ of this is the same as $54 \div 3 = 18$. We can also understand that $\dfrac{1}{3}$ is half of $\dfrac{2}{3}$.

6. F. For two amounts to each represent half of the total amount, they must be equal. In this case, no additional oil is added, so there must be $35 - 15 = 20$ tsp of vinegar added. This makes both amounts 35 tsp, which is 50% of the new total, 70 tsp.

7. B. Let x represent the maximum tons of sand that can be contained in the cargo hold of a truck. In terms of x, the truck leaves the construction site at $\dfrac{1}{4}x$ or $\dfrac{x}{4}$ capacity. To this is added 9 tons of sand, making the total capacity $\dfrac{5}{8}$ full. We can represent this as $\dfrac{x}{4} + 9 = \dfrac{5x}{8}$. We can combine like terms and solve for x. First, to subtract fractions, they must have the same denominator, so we multiply the fraction on the left by $\dfrac{2}{2}: \dfrac{2x}{8} + 9 = \dfrac{5x}{8}$. Then we arrive at $9 = \dfrac{3x}{8}$ and remove the denominator on the right by multiplying both sides by 8: $72 = 3x$. Dividing both sides by 3, we arrive at 24.

8. H. Since the tailor purchased each quantity of fabric in equal numbers, then we know that each lot of fabric cost him $500 + $275 + $150 = $925. We can divide his total purchase cost of $5,550 by $925 to determine that he purchased 6 lots in total. Since each lot contains 1 full square yard, $\dfrac{2}{3}$ square yard, and $\dfrac{1}{3}$ square yard, the total square yardage in each lot is $1 + \dfrac{2}{3} + \dfrac{1}{3} = 2$. 2 square yards per lot × 6 lots = 12 square yards.

9. B. Substitute the value of each subscript of X in for k. This becomes $\left(\dfrac{2}{1}\right)\left(\dfrac{2}{2}\right) + \left(\dfrac{2}{2}\right)\left(\dfrac{2}{3}\right) - \left(\dfrac{2}{3}\right)\left(\dfrac{2}{4}\right) - \left(\dfrac{2}{4}\right)\left(\dfrac{2}{5}\right)$. We can multiply across each pair of fractions and simplify to $\left(\dfrac{4}{2}\right) + \left(\dfrac{4}{6}\right) - \left(\dfrac{4}{12}\right) - \left(\dfrac{4}{20}\right)$, or $2 + \left(\dfrac{2}{3}\right) - \left(\dfrac{1}{3}\right) - \left(\dfrac{1}{5}\right)$. Multiply each term such that the denominator equals 15: $\dfrac{30}{15} + \dfrac{10}{15} - \dfrac{5}{15} - \dfrac{3}{15}$. Simplify across the numerators: $\dfrac{32}{15}$.

10. H. If $\dfrac{1}{6}$ of Pleasantburg taxpayers pay between $10,000 and $20,000 in taxes per year, then $\dfrac{5}{6}$ do not. $\dfrac{5}{6}$ of 2,850 = $2,850 \times 5 \div 6 = 2,375$. Alternatively, $\dfrac{1}{6}$ of 2,850 = $2,850 \times 1 \div 6 = 475$, and $2,850 - 475 = 2,375$.

11. C. A sandwich 63 inches long is cut into thirds, which means each piece is now 21 inches long. One of these is cut into thirds again, which makes each of the resulting pieces 7 inches long. One of these is cut in half, making the resulting pieces 3.5 in. long. The question asks the difference between this and the longest pieces, which are 21 in. long. The difference is $21 - 3.5 = 17.5$ in.

12. F. Jennifer's deposit of $600 out of a total cost of $2,000 is $600 \div $2,000 = 0.3$, or $\dfrac{3}{10}$.

13. A. There are 24 hours in each day. In total, Tiffany drove 8 days × 24 hours per day = 192 hours. If she took a break for a total of 3 hours on each day for lunch (1 hour) and dinner (2 hours), then she took a break for a total of 8 days × 3 hours per day = 24 hours. We don't need to divide 24 by 192 to realize that the answer is $\dfrac{1}{8}$. This is because the 24 hours is equal to 1 day. So, out of the 8 total days, she took a break for 1 day. Alternatively, since 3 out of 24

The Tutorverse

hours is equal to $\dfrac{1}{8}$ of the day, and Tiffany did the same thing each day, then $\dfrac{1}{8}$ of the entire trip was spent on break.

14. F. Let x equal the denominator. In terms of x, the numerator can be expressed as $x - 4$. We could substitute answer choices for x, but this could be time consuming. Instead, we can solve this algebraically. If $\dfrac{x-4}{x} = \dfrac{2}{3}$, then we can cross-multiply, arriving at $3x - 12 = 2x$. Solving for x, we find that it equals 12. Thus, the denominator is 12.

15. 120. Using simplification by cancelling similar numerators and denominators, we get $600(\dfrac{1}{5})$, or 600 divided by 5, which is 120.

16. 18. Multiply through by the common denominator 18 to obtain $6x - 3x = 18 + 2x$. Combining like terms, we get $x = 18$.

17. 0.05. Cancel out the entire numerator with the 6 in the denominator, and obtain $\dfrac{1}{20}$, which is also $\dfrac{5}{100}$, or 0.05.

18. 4. One-third is about 0.33, which is greater than 0.3. $\dfrac{1}{4}$ is equal to 0.25, less than 0.3. Therefore, n must be at least 4.

19. 27. 4 people will take 3 times as long to do something as 12 people, so it would take $12 \times 3 = 36$ days to wash 40 cars. Since 30 is only $\dfrac{3}{4}$ of 40, it will take $\dfrac{3}{4}$ of the time. So, $\dfrac{3}{4}(36) = 27$.

Word Problems

1. A. Profit can be defined as revenue minus expense. If Alan sells 30 clocks in one month at $500 each, then he generates $15,000 in revenue ($300 \times \$500$). In one month, Alan spends $2,500 on rent, which is an expense he would have to pay regardless of how many clocks he sells. However, it costs Alan $275 to make each clock. For 30 clocks, it will cost Alan $30 \times \$275 = \$8,250$ in total. Alan's total costs are $\$8,250 + \$2,500 = \$10,750$. We subtract this from his total revenue of $15,000 and arrive at $4,250.

2. E. First calculate the cost per completed s'more. If each graham cracker costs $0.50, and 2 graham crackers are needed, then $2 \times \$0.50 = \$1$. 1 marshmallow costs $0.75, and 2 bars of chocolate cost $2.50 ($2 \times \$1.25$). So, one completed s'more costs $\$1 + \$0.75 + \$2.50 = \$4.25$. Since the counselor only has $45, she can make 10 s'mores at a total cost of $42.50 ($10 \times \$42.5$). She can't make an 11th s'more because she only has $2.50 remaining, after making the 10th s'more, which is not enough to buy the ingredients for the 11th s'more.

3. C. The total change can be expressed as the difference between the two numbers. This means $869 - (-299)$. When we subtract by a negative, we add that number. So we can rewrite this as $869 + 299 = 1,168$.

4. H. This is another remainder problem. Since there are 271 guests, and each table can seat 8 guests, we can divide 271 by 8 to determine the number of tables needed. $271 \div 8 = 33$ remainder 7. This means that there will be 33 full tables and 7 guests seated at the last table.

5. C. The price of the pocketbook starts at $800. The sale price can be calculated as $\$800 \times 0.75$ (since the sale is 25% off). This means the sale price is $600. If Jacquie has a coupon for another 30% off the sale price, we can express the final price as $\$600 \times 0.70 = \$420$. If sales tax is calculated on this price, then $\$420 \times 0.09 = \$37.80$.

6. G. Since it is impossible to have a fractional part of a monkey, we know that the number of monkeys must be an integer. Therefore, we need an integer from which both 20% and $\dfrac{1}{4}$ will result in integers. Simply going through the answer choices shows that only 40 works. With the other answer choices, finding either 20% or $\dfrac{1}{4}$ results in an integer, but not both.

7. C. Bao works 8.5 hours per day each day for 4 days. This translates to a total of $8.5 \times 4 = 34$ hours. At $25 per hour, he makes $34 \times \$25 = \$850$ that week.

8. F. The incremental cost to Ashley is $0.02 per ounce. Since she drinks 11 ounces per glass, the incremental cost per glass is $0.02 \times 11 = \$0.22$. If she went to the gym 3 days that week, and she drank

3 glasses of juice per day, then the incremental cost is $3 \times 3 \times \$0.22 = \$1.98$. There are still 4 days where she did not go to the gym. On those days, she only drinks 1 glass of juice. So the incremental cost on those days is $4 \times 1 \times \$0.22 = \$0.88$. For the week, the incremental cost to Ashley was $\$1.98 + \$0.88 = \$2.86$.

9. B. This question is simply asking about remainders. If we divide 546 by 36, we get 15 remainder 6. That means the new delivery person's 546th stop will be stop number 6.

10. F. If the depth of the water beneath the buoy decreases 6 inches each hour, it decreases by 1 foot over the course of 2 hours. Over 12 hours, this will happen 6 times (12 hours ÷ 2 hours per foot = 6 feet) for a total decrease of 6 feet. If the depth starts at 24 feet, and decreases by 6, the depth 12 hours later is 18 ft.

11. 16. We could try to find out how much each egg and strip of bacon costs, but we don't need to. If we add up the amounts in the first two sentences, we get 8 eggs and 5 strips of bacon cost $8. The family ordered exactly twice as many eggs and twice as much bacon, so their cost will be $8 \times 2 = 16$.

12. 20. Dan can wash one car in one hour. His brother can wash two cars in one hour. Together, they can wash three cars in one hour. Therefore, they can wash one car in $\dfrac{1}{3}$ of an hour, or 20 minutes.

13. 1500. If Daphne earned $80 in commission on a sale of $1,600, then her percentage is $\dfrac{80}{1,600} = 0.05$, or 5%. Josephine earns twice the commission percentage as Daphne, or 10%. If her commission was $150, then her sales must have been $150 \div 0.1 = 1500$.

14. 100. By 5 PM, Train A has been traveling for 5 hours at 80 miles per hour, or $5 \times 80 = 400$ miles. Train B caught up to train A so it traveled the same distance, but it did so in 4 hours, so $400 \div 4 = 100$ mph.

15. 12. If we let x = the number of quarters Frank has, then the number of dimes = $37 - x$. Since each quarter has a value of 0.25 and each dime has a value of 0.10, we can create the equation $0.25x + 0.10(37 - x) = 5.50$, which simplifies to $0.25x + 3.7 - 0.10x = 5.50$. Combining like terms gives us $0.15x = 1.8$. Solving for x results in $x = 12$.

16. 10. $\dfrac{3}{8}$ of 32 is 12, and $\dfrac{1}{2}$ of 32 is 16, so 12 students take French and 16 students take Latin. However, that is not a total of 28 students because there is overlap, as 6 students are taking both. Therefore, only $28 - 6 = 22$ students are taking one or both of the languages, meaning $32 - 22 = 10$ students are taking neither.

The Tutorverse

Ratios & Proportions

1. A. Students must be familiar with the metric system. 1 kg = 1,000 g, and 1 g = 1,000 mg. Therefore, 1 kg = 1,000 g × 1,000 mg = 1,000,000 mg, and 2,000,000 mg = 2 kg.

2. G. Any scale problem can be solved with proportions. Here, we can also set up a proportion: $\dfrac{20\text{ ft.}}{0.5\text{ in.}} = \dfrac{60\text{ yds.}}{x\text{ in.}}$. However, the units must match, so we can convert yards to feet, giving us $\dfrac{20\text{ ft.}}{0.5\text{ in.}} = \dfrac{180\text{ ft.}}{x\text{ in.}}$. Now we can cross multiply and solve for x: $90 = 20x$, so $x = 4.5$.

3. D. If salad dressing is 2 oz. vinegar and 5 oz. oil, then in total 1 serving of dressing uses 7 oz. liquid. The restaurant needs a total of 35 oz. of dressing, which is 5 servings of dressing (35 oz. needed ÷ 7 oz. per serving). Since every 1 serving of dressing needs 5 oz. oil, we multiply 5 oz. oil per serving × 5 servings = 25 oz. oil.

4. E. We can represent the editor's proofreading rate in ratio form as 300 words : 9 minutes. The problem says he will proofread 1,000 words at the same rate. We can set up the proportion $\dfrac{300\text{ words}}{9\text{ min.}} = \dfrac{1,000\text{ words}}{x\text{ min.}}$. Cross multiply and solve: $9,000 = 300x$, so $x = 30$.

5. B. We can set up a proportion to solve this problem just like all the others in this section, but we don't have to. Notice that all the answer choices use the same two digits – 1 and 9 – with the only difference being the placement of the decimal point. Looking at the given ratio, we see that items weigh roughly three times what they weigh on Mars. Knowing that, we can tell that that we are looking for a number that is roughly $\dfrac{1}{3}$ that of 57. The only number that make sense is 19.

6. F. We can set up a proportion as follows: $\dfrac{7\text{ tigers}}{4\text{ lions}} = \dfrac{28\text{ tigers}}{x\text{ lions}}$. Cross multiply and solve for x: $112 = 7x$, so $x = 16$. However, 16 is not the answer because the question asks for the total number of lions and tigers, not just the number of lions. So, $16 + 28 = 44$.

7. B. The question asks us to compare the average speed in miles per hour (mph) from two different trips. Miles per hour can be calculated by dividing the number of miles driven by the number of hours it took to drive that distance. On Monday, $1,000 ÷ 25 = 40$ mph. On Tuesday, $800 ÷ 16 = 50$ mph. The difference between Tuesday's and Monday's speeds is 10 mph.

8. G. There are several ways to solve this question, but the most straightforward way is to set up a proportion: $\dfrac{40\text{ newspapers}}{25\text{ minutes}} = \dfrac{60\text{ newspapers}}{x\text{ minutes}}$. The first ratio is given, and the second represents what we are trying to determine. Note that the ratio does not use 100 newspapers as the numerator because the question asks us to determine the amount of time it will take to deliver the *remaining* newspapers. Cross multiply and solve for x: $1,500 = 40x$, so $x = 37.5$ mins.

9. C. We need only to divide the total number of plogs and hucks by the amount that they convert to in terms of terps. 200 plogs ÷ 5 plogs = 40 terps. 40 hucks ÷ 0.2 hucks = 200 terps. $200 + 40 = 240$.

10. E. We can set up multiple proportions to solve this question. Because we know how many blue marbles there are, we can first use this and the second ratio to determine the number of yellow marbles: $\dfrac{3\text{ yellow}}{7\text{ blue}} = \dfrac{x\text{ yellow}}{35\text{ blue}}$. Cross multiply and solve for x: $7x = 105$, so $x = 15$, the number of yellow marbles. Then use 15 in a second proportion: $\dfrac{4\text{ red}}{5\text{ yellow}} = \dfrac{x\text{ red}}{15\text{ yellow}}$. Cross multiply and solve for x: $5x = 60$, so $x = 12$.

11. B. Though we could set up proportions to solve this question, we can recognize immediately that, in both ratios, the number representing the weight of almonds is the same: 7. We can think of the ratio as telling us about how the whole container is split into parts. There are, then, 5 parts peanuts, 7 parts almonds, and 3 parts walnuts, for a total of 15 parts. The total weight of the container is 75 oz., which is 5 times larger than 15; this means there are 5 times the amount of each type of nut than the one part. The container contains $5 × 5 = 25$ oz. peanuts, $7 × 5 = 35$ oz. almonds, and $3 × 5 = 15$ oz. walnuts. If we remove the weight of the peanuts, which is 25 oz., we get 75 oz. total – 25 oz. peanuts = 50 oz. remaining.

12. G. We are given two ratios and another value. We will set up our first proportion using the first ratio as it includes jelly beans: $\dfrac{5}{9} = \dfrac{x}{12}$, so $9x = 60$ and $x = \dfrac{20}{3}$ potato chips. Now we use that in our second proportion: $\dfrac{2}{9} = \dfrac{20/3}{x}$, so $60 = 2x$ and $x = 30$ carrots.

13. D. Remember that a ratio tells us how many parts there are of some total. In this case, there are 4 "parts" fiction books and 1 "part" nonfiction book, meaning there are 5 "parts" of books in total. Even if the ratio is represented in a fraction, for example $\dfrac{4\text{ fiction}}{1\text{ non-fiction}}$, the denominator does not represent the "whole," as it does when working with non-ratio fractions. In this case, let's just assume there are 5 books in total. This means there are 4 fiction books, which means 4 out of the 5 books are fiction. $4 ÷ 5 = 0.8$, or 80%.

14. G. We can solve using a proportion: $\dfrac{8}{20} = \dfrac{x}{50}$. Note that we use 50 instead of 30 because the problem says an <u>additional</u> 30 pounds is used. Cross multiplying, we get $400 = 20x$, so $x = 20$.

15. C. We can think of the diagram as two separate triangles, a smaller one with sides 6 and 2.4, and a larger one with sides 9 (because $6 + 3 = 9$) and x. Since they share an angle and are both right triangles, they are similar triangles and therefore their sides are proportional: $\dfrac{6}{9} = \dfrac{2.4}{x}$. Cross multiplying results in $6x = 21.6$, so $x = 3.6$.

16. F. A ratio can normally be expressed as $x ÷ y$, in this case, girls ÷ boys. Since the number of girls is greater than the number of boys, this ratio will be greater than 1. We can use estimation to narrow down our choices. At Washington, Lincoln, Roosevelt, and Martin Luther King, Jr., the ratio of girls to boys is less than 3:1. We can tell this simply by multiplying the number of boys at each school by 3 to find that the number of girls there should be is greater than the number of girls that there actually are. For example, at Washington, a ratio of 3:1 girls to boys would mean that there should be 1,500 boys × 3 = 4,500 girls. In fact, however, there are only 4,000 girls. Only at Kennedy is the ratio more than 3:1 because $1,020 × 3 = 3,060$; since the actual number of girls at Kennedy is greater than this, Kennedy has the greatest ratio of girls to boys.

17. A. We can cross multiply, but we can also just notice that the numerator goes from m to $2m$, meaning the second ratio is double the first, so the value of $z = 2(8) = 16$.

18.　G. The words "at the same rate" describe the use of proportions. Note that two different units are given for time. We must use matching units, so we'll first convert 2 hours to 120 minutes:

$\dfrac{12}{120} = \dfrac{x}{40}$. Therefore, $120x = 480$ and $x = 4$.

19.　D. Using cross multiplication, we get $3x = 20$, so $x = \dfrac{20}{3}$, which equals $6\dfrac{2}{3}$.

20.　F. Any problem regarding the shadows of two objects in the same vicinity at the same time is referring to proportions. Here we can set up $\dfrac{6}{20} = \dfrac{x}{120}$. We cross multiply to get $20x = 720$, so $x = 36$.

21.　B. Any problem describing similar polygons can be solved using proportions. We must make sure to set up the proportion using corresponding sides. Polygons will always be named using corresponding vertices. Here, we get $\dfrac{8}{4} = \dfrac{6}{x}$. Therefore, $8x = 24$ and $x = 3$.

22.　E. This is more of a logic problem. We are told that 2 hoses can fill a bucket in 5 hours. Therefore, 5 hoses should be able to fill the bucket in less than 5 hours. 2 is the only answer choice that is less than 5.

23.　D. The words "for every" imply a rate is being given, so a proportion can be used to solve: $\dfrac{16}{3} = \dfrac{x}{48}$. We can cross multiply, but since 3 fits evenly into 48 exactly 16 times, we can simply multiply 16 by 16 to get 256.

24.　F. We can set up a proportion, but we can also just notice that side FE is x and side BC is $\dfrac{3}{2}x$, meaning the second triangle is 1.5 times the size of the first, so the length of side AB is $1.5(8) = 12$.

25.　B. We are looking for the distance, so in order to set up our proportion, we need to know the elapsed time. There are 12 hours from noon to midnight, so $\dfrac{500}{2} = \dfrac{x}{12}$, which we cross multiply to get $2x = 6{,}000$, or $x = 3{,}000$.

26.　E. This is more of a logic problem. We are told that 4 cows can eat all the grass in 10 days. If they add 1 more cow, then they should be able to eat all the grass in less than 10 days. 8 is the only answer choice that is less than 10.

27.　2900. 0.2 fits into 500 2,500 times ($500 \div 0.2$ or 500×5), so 500 drins = 2,500 rints. 0.5 fits into 200 400 times ($200 \div 0.5$ or 200×2), so 200 vungs = 400 rints, for a total of $2{,}500 + 400 = 2{,}900$ rints.

28.　30. If there are 48 tulips, then the 5:6 ratio of daisies to tulips can be multiplied to make 40:48, meaning there are 40 daisies. This means that the 3:4 ratio of roses to daisies must be multiplied by ten, resulting in 30 roses.

29.　25. First, determine amount of time it takes for Matthew to solve each question. We are told that he completed 60 questions in 75 minutes, or spent $75 \div 60 = 1.25$ minutes per question. If there are $80 - 60 = 20$ questions to go, he will spend an additional $20 \times 1.25 = 25$ minutes finishing the test.

30.　1.2. The image shows two similar triangles, so their sides are proportional. The ratio of AE to AC is equivalent to the ratio of AD to AB, so $\dfrac{8}{10} = \dfrac{4.8}{AB}$. Cross multiplication gives us $48 = 8(AB)$, so $AB = 6$. However, the question asks for DB, which is $6 - 4.8 = 1.2$.

Factors, Multiples, Exponents, & Radicals

1.　C. A multiple is the result when two numbers are multiplied together; a common multiple is one that is shared between different numbers. In this case, the multiples of 450 are 450 (450×1), 900 (450×2), 1,350 (450×3), etc. The multiples of 675 are 675 (675×1), 1,350 (675×2), 2,025 (675×3), etc. We see that 1,350 is the first number that appears in both lists, so it is the least common multiple. 5, 225, and 1,125 are not multiples of these numbers. 303,750 is a common multiple (which can be found by multiplying 450×675), but it is not the least common multiple.

2.　H. The multiples of 135 are 135, 270, 405, 540, etc. The multiples of 180 are 180, 360, 540, etc. We see that 540 is the first number that appears in both lists, so it is the least common multiple.

3.　B. A common factor is any number that divides two numbers evenly. The largest of these is called the greatest common factor. In this case, it is 225. 5 and 25 are common factors, but they are not the greatest. 450 is not a factor of 675. 1,350 is a common multiple, not a common factor.

4.　F. The only prime factors of 48 are 2 and 3, so 3 is the greatest prime factor. If we look at the other answer choices, 7 is prime but not a factor of 48 and 24 is a factor of 48, but is not prime.

5.　D. The integers between 30 and 40 are 31, 32, 33, 34, 35, 36, 37, 38, and 39. An additional criteria tells us that the integers must be the product of two distinct (different) prime factors. Test each integer. 31 and 37 do not fit this criteria because they are already prime and cannot be the product of two different prime factors (1 is not a prime number). 33, 34, 35, 38, and 39 fit this criteria because $3 \times 11 = 33$, $2 \times 17 = 34$, $5 \times 7 = 35$, $2 \times 19 = 38$, and $3 \times 13 = 39$. 32 and 36 have several factor pairs, but none of them are comprised of two distinct prime numbers.

6.　F. The factors of 39 are 1, 3, 13, and 39. Of these, only 3 and 13 are prime (1 is not prime, and 39 itself is divisible by numbers other than 1 and itself, so it is also not prime). The factors of 20 are 1, 2, 4, 5, 10, and 20. Of these, only 2 and 5 are prime. Thus, $x = 13$, and $y = 5$, and the sum is 18.

7.　C. The number of times that each factor occurs in the least common multiple is equal to the greatest number of times that it occurs in either of the original numbers. The least common multiple must have two 2's (because B has two 2's), it must have two 3's (because both A and B have two 3's), and it must have one 5 (because A has one 5). Another way to solve this problem is to multiply out the numbers: A = 90, B = 36. The least common multiple of these numbers is 180.

8.　E. The first bell will ring at 1:00, 2:00, **3:00**, 4:00, 5:00, **6:00**, 7:00, 8:00, **9:00**, 10:00, 11:00, **12:00**, 1:00. The second bell will ring at 1:30, **3:00**, 4:30, **6:00**, 7:30, **9:00**, 10:30, **12:00**, 1:30. The times when they both ring are underlined. There are 4 times in total when they both ring.

9.　B. Express 27 in prime factors. $27 = 3 \times 9$, and $9 = 3 \times 3$. Therefore, $27 = 3 \times 3 \times 3$. Since we multiply 3 by itself 3 times, this is equal to 3^3. Therefore, $x = 3$.

10.　F. In an exponential expression like 2^x, the base (which is 2) is multiplied by itself a certain number of times. The number of times the base is multiplied by itself is determined by the number in the exponent (in this case, x). So in this case, 2 is multiplied by itself a certain number of times until the value is 32. $2 \times 2 = 4$, $2 \times 2 \times 2 = 8$, etc. We can repeat this until we find that $32 = 2 \times 2 \times 2 \times 2 \times 2$. Since 2 is multiplied by itself 5 times over, the exponent is 5, or 2^5.

11.　B. Break down 80 into its prime factors. We know that $80 = 8 \times 10$. We can break this down further because $8 = 2 \times 2 \times 2$ and $10 = 2 \times 5$. Therefore, we get $80 = 2 \times 2 \times 2 \times 2 \times 5$. Now write this in exponent form. $80 = 2^4 \times 5^1$. This shows that $x = 4$ and $y = 1$. Therefore, $x - y = 3$.

12. E. Break down 225 into its prime factors. Since it ends in 5, we know it is divisible by 5. We get $225 = 5 \times 45$. Then we can break down 45 as $5 \times 9 = 5 \times 3 \times 3$. This gives the prime factorization $225 = 5 \times 5 \times 3 \times 3$. This can be expressed in exponential form as $3^2 \times 5^2$. Therefore, $x = 2$ and $y = 2$ so we get $xy = 4$.

13. A. Break down 900 into its prime factors. We get $900 = 9 \times 100$. This breaks down further to $3 \times 3 \times 10 \times 10$. The 10s can be broken down further, resulting in $3 \times 3 \times 2 \times 5 \times 2 \times 5$. In exponential form, this becomes $2^2 \times 3^2 \times 5^2$. Therefore $x = 2$ and $y = 2$ and $z = 2$, so we get $x + y + z = 6$.

14. E. Using prime factorization, we know that $125 = 5 \times 5 \times 5$, or 5^3. If the bases of the exponential terms are already 5, then we know that term must be 5^1 and the other must be 5^2, since if we multiply exponential terms, we add the exponents together. Therefore, x must be 1 or 2 (it doesn't matter which), and y must be the other. Therefore, $(1)(2) = 2$.

15. B. Using prime factorization, we know that 64 can be expressed as $2 \times 2 \times 2 \times 2 \times 2 \times 2$ or 2^6. In $2^a \times 2^b \times 2^c$, since we multiply each term, which has the same base, we are adding together the exponents. If $64 = 2^6$, then $2^{a+b+c} = 2^6$. But since each exponent must be different, they can't all be equal to 2. Instead, they are equal to 1, 2, and 3 (since $1 + 2 + 3 = 6$). Thus, $1 \times 2 \times 3 = 6$.

16. F. The question asks which expression is equal to 25^4. We know from prime factorization that 25 can be expressed as 5^2, or 5×5. This means 25^4 is equivalent to $\left(5^2\right)^4$. When we raise an exponential expression (like 5^2) to another power (in this case, 4), we multiply the exponents. In this case, we end up at 5^8.

17. C. Solve for a first. Since the bases are the same (all x), we know that we must add the exponents together. Therefore, $a + 6 = 24$, and $a = 18$. Solve for b next. Since we are raising one exponent to another, and the bases are the same, we know that we must multiply the exponents together. Therefore, $4b = 20$, and $b = 5$. The sum becomes $18 + 5 = 23$.

18. F. We could simplify the expression by multiplying out the individual exponential expressions, but there is an easier way. When the bases of an exponential expression are the same, and we divide the exponential expressions, we simply take the difference in the exponent. Therefore, $\frac{5^3}{5^2} = 5^1$ and $\frac{2^5}{2^3} = 2^2$. This becomes $5(4) = 20$.

19. B. There are several ways to solve this question. We could rewrite the expression so that the bases are the same, but it is perhaps simpler to write the expression in expanded form since the exponents share the same value (both 100 and 50 are raised to the 5th power). $\frac{100}{50} \times \frac{100}{50} \times \frac{100}{50} \times \frac{100}{50} \times \frac{100}{50}$ is equal to $2 \times 2 \times 2 \times 2 \times 2$, or 2^5, or 32.

20. F. There are several ways to solve this question, but again it is perhaps more simple to write the expression in expanded form using prime factorization. Notice that 7 and 2 are already prime, but that 28 can be expressed as $7 \times 2 \times 2$. This means that the expression given can be rewritten as $\frac{7 \times 7 \times 7 \times 7 \times 2 \times 2}{7 \times 2 \times 2 \times 7 \times 2 \times 2 \times 7 \times 2 \times 2}$. We can cancel out values in the numerator and denominator until we are left with $\frac{7}{2 \times 2 \times 2 \times 2} = \frac{7}{16}$.

21. A. Observe the proper order of operations. First, simplify under the radical, so that the expression is $\sqrt{64}$. The number that, when multiplied by itself gives you 64, is 8.

22. G. First simplify the fraction under the radical. $100 \div 25 = 4$. Then we take the square root of 4 which equals 2 because $2 \times 2 = 4$.

23. D. $\sqrt{\frac{144}{81}} = \frac{\sqrt{144}}{\sqrt{81}}$. $\sqrt{144} = 12$ and $\sqrt{81} = 9$. Therefore, $\frac{12}{9} = \frac{4}{3}$.

24. E. In this case, if we square $x + 3$ (multiply the term by itself), on the right side of the equation, we must also square the left side of the equation. Doing so would cancel out the radical (square root) sign and leave us with 5.

25. D. Solve for x first by subtracting 7 from both sides then squaring both sides to rid the left side of the radical. This becomes $\sqrt{x} = 9$ and then $x = 81$.

26. 2. In prime factorization, 64 can be represented as $2 \times 2 \times 2 \times 2 \times 2 \times 2$. It has no other prime factors except 2.

27. 120. If Edina's tests have 30 questions, her total number of test questions could be 30, 60, 90, 120, 150, 180, etc. Patsy's total number of questions could be 24, 48, 72, 96, 120, 144, 168, etc. The smallest number they could have each had (i.e. the least common multiple) is 120.

28. 121. If $\sqrt{x - 40} = 9$, then $x - 40 = 81$, so $x = 121$.

29. 6. The prime factorization of 1,400 is $2 \times 2 \times 2 \times 5 \times 5 \times 7$, which can be written as $2^3 \times 5^2 \times 7^1$, so x is 3, y is 2, and z is 1. Therefore, $x + y + z = 3 + 2 + 1 = 6$.

30. −3. The prime factorization of 500 is $2 \times 2 \times 5 \times 5 \times 5$, which can be written as $2^2 \times 5^3$, so x is 2 and y is 5. Therefore, $x - y$ can be expressed as $2 - 5$, which equals −3.

Absolute Value

1. C. In the first absolute value, $(-5) - 1 + (-3) = -9$, so the absolute value is positive 9. In the second absolute value, $2 - 7 = -5$, so the absolute value is positive 5. When we add these together, we get $9 + 5 = 14$.

2. G. If we plug in the values $x = 3$ and $y = 9$, we get $5 |3 - 9|$. For the numbers inside the absolute value, we get $3 - 9 = -6$, so the absolute value is positive 6. Finally, we multiply this by 5 and get $5 \times 6 = 30$.

3. A. If we plug in the values $x = -5$ and $y = -15$, we get $|(-5) - (-15)| - |(-5) + (-15)|$. Inside the first absolute value, we get $(-5) - (-15) = -5 + 15 = 10$. This is already positive, so the absolute value is still 10. In the second absolute value we get $(-5) + (-15) = -20$, so the absolute value is positive 20. Finally, we do $10 - 20$ and get −10. This subtraction is not inside of an absolute value, so the answer stays negative.

4. G. When we take the absolute value of each number, they all become positive and we get $9 + 9 - 9 \times \frac{1}{9}$. Following the order of operations, we do multiplication before addition and subtraction. $9 \times \left(\frac{1}{9}\right) = 1$, so the expression becomes $9 + 9 - 1 = 17$.

5. B. Inside the first absolute value we get $240 - 420 = -180$, so the absolute value is positive 180. Inside the second absolute value we get $24 - 42 = -18$, so the absolute value is positive 18. This means that the equation becomes $180 - 18 + a = 200$. When we subtract the numbers on the left side we get $162 + a = 200$. Finally, subtract 162 from both sides of the equation. The final answer is $a = 38$.

The Tutorverse

6. F. Observe order of operations and simplify the equation to $|-45| + p^2 - |-36| = 90$. This becomes $45 + p^2 - 36 = 90$, and eventually $p^2 = 81$. Take the square root of both sides and $p = 9$.

7. A. $|-3|$ is positive 3. $|6|$ is positive 6. $|-9|$ is positive 9. Therefore, the equation can be rewritten as K = − (−3 − 6 − 9). For the expression inside the parentheses, we get −18. However, there is another negative outside the parentheses, so it becomes positive: K = 18. Finally, the question asks for − |−K|. This becomes −|−18| = −18. The answer stays negative because there is a negative sign outside of the absolute value.

8. E. If $|x - 5| = 7$, then $x - 5 = 7$ or $x - 5 = -7$. Solving both equations results in $x = 12$ or -2. If $|y + 9| = 21$, then $y + 9 = 21$ or $y + 9 = -21$. Solving both equations results in $y = 12$ or -30. Since x and y must both be negative, $x = -2$ and $y = -30$. Therefore, $x + y = -2 + (-30) = -2 - 30 = -32$.

9. −40. Begin by plugging in −10 and −20, giving us −|(−10) − (−20)| − |(−20) + (−10)|. Simplifying the expressions inside the set of absolute value bars gives us −|10| − |−30|. At this point, we can solve the absolute values, giving us −10 − 30, which results in −40.

10. −9. Simplify for J, giving us $-5 - 5 + 5 \times \frac{1}{5}$, which equals −9.
Therefore, −|−J| = −|−(−9)|, which equals −9.

11. −28. Remember that absolute value equations have two solutions: $m - 8$ can equal 12 or −12, in which case $m = 20$ or −4. $n + 4$ can equal 11 or −11, in which case $n = 7$ or −15. The problem states $m < 0$ and $n > 0$; we use −4 for m and 7 for n, so $mn = (-4)(7) = -28$.

12. −9. $|v - 7| < 17$ can also be written as $-17 < v - 7 < 17$, which simplifies to $-10 < v < 24$. Since v must be greater than −10, the smallest integer value that satisfies the statement is −9.

Scientific Notation

1. A. Scientific notation expresses very large (or small) numbers by multiplying a number between 1 and 10 by 10 raised to some power. The exponent of 10 indicates the number of times the decimal point must be moved in order to produce a number in standard form. The sign of the exponent tells us which way to move the decimal point: positive means move the decimal to the right (increasing the number), and negative means move the decimal to the left (decreasing the number). In this case, 51,000 is written in standard form. In order to write this in scientific notation, we need to multiply a number between 1 and 10 by 10 raised to some power. In this case, we can use 5.1 as the number between 1 and 10, and multiply it by 10^4. This is because from 5.1, we can move the decimal place "over" to the right 4 times, each time inserting a 0, since 10 raised to some power means that we're multiplying by 10 over and over again. $5.1 \times 10^4 = 51,000$.

2. F. A number expressed in scientific notation is a number between 1 and 10 multiplied by 10 raised to a certain power (given by the exponent). In this case, the only number between 1 and 10 we can make from "0.513" is 5.13. From 5.13, we need to move the decimal place "over" to the left one place in order to make 0.513. Therefore, the exponent must be 10^{-1}.

3. A. A number expressed in scientific notation is a number between 1 and 10 multiplied by 10 raised to a certain power (given by the exponent). In this case, the only number between 1 and 10 we can make from "0.0002088" is 2.088. From 2.088, we need to move the decimal place "over" to the left four places in order to make 0.0002088. Therefore, the exponent must be 10^{-4}.

4. G. We know that the number between 1 and 10 should be 5.137. All we need to do is determine the number of times that we need to move the decimal place "over" to the right. Since $10 \times 10 = 100 = 10^2$, and $10 \times 10 \times 10 = 1,000 = 10^3$, etc., the number of times the decimal place needs to be moved depends on what number we need to multiply 5.137 by to get the number in standard form. To get 513,700, we would need to move the decimal point over 5 times, or multiply by 10^5. However, the expression tells us to multiply 513,700 by 1,000, which is adding another 3 zeros. Thus, we should multiply 5.137 by 10^{5+3}, or 10^8. We can also see this is true as follows: $513,700 \times 1,000 = 513,700,000$. Moving the decimal point 8 places to the left results in 5.137.

5. C. If we multiply $952.65 \times 1,000$, we get 952,650. In scientific notation, this would be 9.5265×10^5, since we would have to move the decimal point 5 places to the right from 9.5265 to arrive at 952,650.

6. G. 10 raised to a negative power, like 10^{-3}, lets us know that we need to move the decimal point "over" to the left a certain number of times. In this case, we move the decimal point over to the left 3 times. Since there is an implied decimal at the end of 5 (which can be written as 5.0), move the decimal place over 3 places, each time inserting a 0, arriving at 0.005.

7. B. 10 raised to a negative power, like 10^{-7}, lets us know that we need to move the decimal point "over" to the left a certain number

of times. In this case, we move the decimal point over to the left 7 times.

8. H. The distance between the two cities in km is 4×10^3 which is equivalent to 4,000 km. There are 1,000 meters in 1 km, so the distance in meters is $4,000 \times 1,000$ or 4,000,000 meters.

9. A. If the length of the building is 370 meters, it is represented on the blueprint by 370 mm. The question asks for the length in meters. To convert millimeters to meters, divide by 1,000, so $370 \div 1,000 = 0.37$, which is written in scientific notation as 3.7×10^{-1}.

10. F. If we needed to, we could write out both distances as 240,000 miles to the moon and 60,000,000 miles to Mars. We could then divide the distance to Mars by the distance to the moon and arrive at 250. An easier way is to divide both of the coefficients (the 2.4 and the 6.0) as well as the base and exponents (the 10 and their exponents). $6.0 \div 2.4 = 2.5$. $10^7 \div 10^5 = 10^2$; when dividing exponents, simply subtract the numbers in the exponents when the bases are the same. We end up with 2.5×10^2, or 250.

11. C. One way to solve arithmetic with scientific notation is to rewrite the numbers in standard form. $5 \times 10^3 = 5,000$ and $3 \times 10^5 = 300,000$, so their product is 1,500,000,000, which is equivalent to 1.5×10^9. If the problem involves multiplying or dividing of scientific notation, as this example does, another way is to use the factors to help you. Here, $5 \times 3 = 15$ and $10^3 \times 10^5 = 10^8$ (when multiplying exponents, simply add the exponents if the bases are the same), which gives you 15×10^8. However, the first factor of any number in scientific notation must be at least 1 but less than 10, so 15×10^8 becomes 1.5×10^9.

12. E. Multiply the coefficients 5 and 6 to get 30. Then, multiply the base 10 and exponents, adding the exponents 4 and 4 to get 10^8. Remember that the coefficient must be between 1 and 10, so we should express 30 as 3.0×10^1. Combined with the base and exponents of 10^8, we would have an expression of $3.0 \times 10^1 \times 10^8$, which can be expressed as 3.0×10^9.

13. A. The product of the coefficients is $3 \times 2 = 6$. The product of the base and exponents is $10^3 \times 10^2 = 10^5$. Thus, we have 6.0×10^5.

14. 7560. To convert scientific notation into standard form, simply move the decimal point the number of places noted by the exponent. The exponent tells us to move the decimal point three places to the right, turning 7.56 into 7,560, which should be gridded in without the comma.

15. 0.68. The exponent tells us to move the decimal point back one place, turning 6.8 into 0.68.

16. 720. $1.2 \times 10^{-3} = 0.0012$, and $6 \times 10^5 = 600,000$, so their product is 720. Or, multiply 1.2×6 and move the decimal over by two, since canceling exponential expressions with the same base leaves us with 10^2.

17. 500. $3 \times 10^5 = 30,000$, and $6 \times 10^2 = 600$, so 30,000 divided by 600 = 500. When we perform operations on exponential expressions with the same term (10^5 and 10^2), we are allowed to simply work with their exponents. Since we are dividing two exponential terms,

we subtract the value of the exponents. $5 - 2 = 3$, so the exponential term becomes 10^3. $3 \div 6 = 0.5$ and $0.5 \times 10^3 = 500$.

18. 3960. $4.6 \times 10^3 = 4,600$, and $6.4 \times 10^2 = 640$, so the difference between the two distances is $4,600 - 640 = 3,960$.

Counting Principle

1. B. We can list each different combination of different teams. The order is *not* important (that is, Alex and Bea is the same as Bea and Alex, so this would only count as one team). We'll abbreviate as follows: Alex = A, Bea = B, etc. So, the different combinations are AB, AC, AD, BC, BD, CD. There are 6 possible combinations.

2. G. Since there are only 3 different numbers (1, 2, and 3), the most efficient way to solve this is to list all the possible 3-digit numbers: 11, 12, 13, 21, 22, 23, 31, 32.

3. B. There are different possible orientations of the red (R), yellow (Y), and blue (B) layers. From top to bottom, she could have RYB, RBY, YRB, YBR, BRY, or BYR.

4. F. If we imagine that each student is numbered from 1-5, with 1 being the shortest and 5 being the tallest student, we can list the different combinations. 1 will always be in the middle, so the other combinations will only affect the orientation of 2-5. Since 2 and 3 (the next taller students) will always be on the left of 1, we can imagine either 231 or 321. For each of these, to the right of 1 could be 45 or 54. So, we could have 23145, 23154, 32145, or 32154. This is a total of 4 different combinations.

5. C. Once the numbers in a question start to get higher, listing out every possible combination becomes too time consuming and prone to error. Instead, we can use what is known as the counting principle to help us solve this question. Each pair of pants can be paired with 10 different shirts, making 10 outfits. Since there are 4 different pairs of pants, then there are $4 \times 10 = 40$ different outfits.

6. H. Since each of the 9 soups can be paired with each of the 6 salads, there are a total of $9 \times 6 = 54$ possible combinations.

7. D. We can use the counting principle to solve this question. Since we know that Chet may repeat digits, each of the 3 characters can be any one of 10 possible digits. So, $10 \times 10 \times 10 = 1,000$. If the first digit is 0, the next digit could be 0, and the last could also be 0. This represents one combination of a code. We could cycle through every possible combination until the first digit is 9, the next digit is 9, and the last is also 9. In total, this represents 1,000 different combinations.

8. F. We can use the counting principle to solve this question. The password must have four letters, each of which can repeat from each of 26 letters. If we started at the very beginning of the alphabet, we would have a password of AAAA. By changing just one of these letters at a time, we would eventually cycle through every possible combination (AAAB, AAAC, etc.) until we arrived at a password of ZZZZ. This would be a total of $26 \times 26 \times 26 \times 26 = 26^4$ different possible combinations.

9. D. There are $3 \times 4 \times 3 = 36$ different possible sandwiches that can be made with the different types of bread, meat, and cheese.

10. G. Each question has four different possible answer choices. The answer to each of the questions could be all A's, or all D's, etc., or some other combination of A, B, C, and D. The answers could be filled in as AAA, AAB, AAC, etc., all the way up to DDD. Since this is the case, we have $4 \times 4 \times 4 = 64$ different combinations.

11. A. Since the first 3 characters can be any letters from A-Z, each character can be any of the 26 letters (including the same letters). So for the first 3 characters, we have $26 \times 26 \times 26 = 26^3$ possible combinations. The last 3 characters can be any of 10 digits (0-9), including the same digits. So for the last 3 characters, we have $10 \times 10 \times 10 = 10^3$. Since we must pair these combinations together into a 6 digit long combination, we must multiply both values together.

12. G. If Lewis were allowed to repeat digits, he would be able to choose from 10 digits (0-9) for each of the 3 characters in his code. This would mean $10 \times 10 \times 10 = 1,000$ possibilities. However, he is not allowed to repeat digits in the 3 different character spaces. This means that though he can choose from any of the 10 digits for one character space, he can only choose from 9 digits for another character space and from 8 digits for another character space. This is because once a digit is chosen for a character space, it cannot be reused in another character space, thereby decreasing the total number of digits from which a number can be chosen. This means there are $10 \times 9 \times 8 = 720$ possibilities.

13. B. In this question, the order each swimmer places in matters (gold, silver, then bronze going to Al, Bob, then Chet is different than Chet, Bob, then Al). For gold, there are 5 swimmers to choose from. Once one of the swimmers wins gold, there are only 4 swimmers left to give the silver to. Once that swimmer gets the silver, there are only 3 swimmers left to give the bronze to. Using the counting principle, $5 \times 4 \times 3 = 60$.

14. H. Since Gail cannot repeat letters in each of the four characters of her password, she can only choose from 26 letters in one of the character spaces, from 25 in another character space, from 24 in yet another character space, and 23 in the final character space. This is because once a letter is chosen for a character space, it cannot be reused in another character space, thereby decreasing the total number of letters from which a letter can be chosen.

15. D. For each of the first three characters, he may choose from the alphabet consisting of 26 letters. However, after he makes his first choice, he will not be allowed to repeat a letter. This means that his second choice must be made from 25 letters, and his third choice from 24 letters. Thus, the total number of combinations is $26 \times 25 \times 24$. For each of the last three characters, he may choose from the digits 0-9, consisting of 10 different digits. However, as with the letters, once he makes a choice, he will have 1 fewer option to choose from. So, though his first choice will be from among 10 different digits, the second will be from 9 and the third will be from 8. Thus, $10 \times 9 \times 8$. Altogether, this makes $26 \times 25 \times 24 \times 10 \times 9 \times 8$.

16. F. Partha has 7 books to choose from for one of the positions above her desk. After she chooses that first book, it can't go in another one of the positions, so she only has 6 books to choose from. Once the second book is chosen, she only has 5 books to choose from for the last position above her desk. Therefore, she has $7 \times 6 \times 5 = 210$ different ways to arrange the books above her desk.

17. 45. For each type of bread, there are 5 choices of meat, creating 15 sandwiches. Each of the 15 sandwiches get 3 choices of condiment, so the answer is $3 \times 5 \times 3 = 45$.

18. 720. Since 10 people are competing, there are 10 options for first place. Once one person places first, there are 9 options left for second place. Once one of those people places second, there are 8 options left for third place. The answer is $10 \times 9 \times 8 = 720$.

19. 24. To find all the possible outfit combinations, multiply $3 \times 3 \times 3 = 27$. However, we must remove the outfits that are all red, all yellow, and all blue, leaving us with 24 possible outfits.

20. 626. With 26 options for the first letter and 26 options for the second letter, there are $26 \times 26 = 676$ different possible combinations, but 50 are already in use, so there are $676 - 50 = 626$ options left.

Imaginary Operations

1. B. We can substitute 4 for b in the equation, since the symbol □ appears before both b and 4. Doing so gives us $6(4) - 12 = 12$.

2. G. We must calculate the value of each □7 and □3 and subtract the latter from the former. □7 $= 6(7) - 12 = 30$. Similarly, □3 $= 6(3) - 12 = 6$. Therefore, $30 - 6 = 24$.

3. B. We are told that □$b = 42$, therefore $6b - 12 = 42$. Simply solve for b: $54 = 6b$, and $b = 9$.

4. G. Substitute the value in between the two carrots (^ ^) for x. In this case, we get to $2^2 + 6(2) + 9 = 25$.

5. A. Substitute the value in between the two carrots (^ ^) for x. In this case, we get to $-3^2 + 6(-3) + 9 = 0$.

The Tutorverse

6. F. Set the equation equal to 64 and solve for x. $64 = x^2 + 6x + 9$. Simplify and then try each answer choice in the equation $55 = x^2 + 6x$. We see that 5 works, as $55 = 25 + 30$.

7. B. Substitute the values provided into the operation. $x = 5$ and $y = 3$. Therefore, $5@3 = 2(5) - 3(3)$. This simplifies to $10 - 9 = 1$.

8. G. Substitute the value provided into the operation. $y = 7$. Therefore, $x@7 = 2x - 3(7)$. This simplifies to $2x - 21$.

9. B. Substitute the value provided into the operation. $x = 7$. Therefore, $7@y = 2(7) - 3(y)$. This simplifies to $14 - 3y$.

10. F. Substitute the value provided into the operation. $c = 4$. Therefore, $4\#d = 4^2 + 4(d) + 16$. This simplifies to $32 + 4d$.

11. D. Substitute the values provided into the operation. In this case, we are given the fact that $c = 2$ and $d = 3$. Therefore, $2\#3 = 2^2 + 2(3) + 16$. This simplifies to $4 + 6 + 16 = 26$.

12. G. Substitute the values provided into the operation and solve each operation separately. In the first case, we are given the fact that $c = 10$ and $d = 4$. Therefore, $10\#4 = 10^2 + 10(4) + 16$. This simplifies to $100 + 40 + 16 = 156$. In the second case, we are given the fact that $c = 4$ and $d = 10$. Therefore, $4\#10 = 4^2 + 4(10) + 16$. This simplifies to $16 + 40 + 16 = 72$. The difference is then $156 - 72 = 84$.

13. C. Substitute the value provided into the operation. In this case, we are given the fact that $p = -5$.
Therefore, $-5\sim = \frac{1}{-5} + (-5)^2$. This simplifies to $25 - \frac{1}{5} = 24\frac{4}{5}$.

14. E. Set the operation equal to 0, and we can solve for p. $0 = = \frac{1}{p} + p^2$. Subtract p^2 from both sides to get $-p^2 = \frac{1}{p}$. Multiply both sides by p to cancel the denominator: $-p^3 = 1$. Rid the variable of the negative by dividing both sides by -1 to get $p^3 = -1$. The cube root of both sides gives us $p = -1$.

15. B. A fraction cannot have 0 as its denominator, as the result would be undefined (you can't divide something by nothing).

16. G. Substitute the value provided into the operation. In this case, we are given the fact that $x = -2$. Therefore,
$-2 = \frac{-2}{4} + (-2)^2$, which simplifies to $4 - \frac{1}{2}$, or 3.5.

17. D. Substitute the value provided into the operation. In this case, we are given the fact that $x = 1$. Therefore,
$1 = \frac{1}{4} + 1^2$, which simplifies to $1\frac{1}{4}$, or $\frac{5}{4}$.

18. G. Set the operation equal to 17 and solve for x. $17 = \frac{x}{4} + x^2$. Since we have variables with different exponents, it is easiest to solve by trying each answer choice. By doing so, we find that 4 satisfies the equation, as $\frac{4}{4} + 4^2 = 1 + 16 = 7$.

19. 48. Plugging -2 into the operation gives us $(-2)^2 - 10(-2) + 24$, which simplifies to $4 + 20 + 24 = 48$.

20. 13. We've been told that the result of the operation must be 100, we set up the equation $9x - 7 = 110$ and solve for x, resulting in 13.

21. 8. Plugging in 10 and 2 gives us $(10 + \frac{10}{4}) - (2 + \frac{10}{4})$, which simplifies to $12.5 - 4.5 = 8$.

22. -19.2. Plugging 4 and 5 gives us $\frac{4}{5} - 4(5)$, which simplifies to $0.8 - 20 = -19.2$.

23. 9. Plugging in 6 for b and 63 for the result gives us $5a + 3(6) = 63$. Solving for a results in $a = 9$.

Algebra

Algebraic Expressions & Equations

1. D. If $b = 3$, then a must equal 12. Therefore, $a^2 - 5b = 12^2 - 5(3) = 144 - 15 = 129$.

2. G. To solve for x, start by simplifying the left side of the equation by combining like terms. If we subtract one-fifth of x from one x, we are left with fourth-fifths of x. The equation becomes $\frac{4}{5}x = 8$, which we can solve by dividing both sides of the equation by $\frac{4}{5}$. When we divide by a fraction, we actually multiply both sides by its reciprocal. This just means multiplying both sides by the "flipped" fraction, since doing so will cancel out the fraction on one side. In this case: $\left(\frac{5}{4}\right)\left(\frac{4}{5}\right)x = \left(\frac{5}{4}\right)8$ gives $x = \frac{40}{4} = 10$.

3. B. To solve for x, start by distributing to get rid of the parentheses: $4x - 5 + 3x = 16$. Combining like terms gives us $7x - 5 = 16$. Adding 5 to both sides and then dividing both sides by 7 results in $x = 3$.

4. G. Removing the parentheses by distributing, we get $3 - x - x + 3 = x$. Combining like terms results in $6 - 2x = x$. Adding $2x$ to both sides and then dividing both sides by 3 results in $x = 2$.

5. D. To begin solving any algebraic equation, distribute to remove parentheses. Here, you get $10 + 3y + 8 = 4y - 2 + 9y$. The next step is to combine like terms: $3y + 18 = 13y - 2$. Then we make sure the variable is only on one side of the equation by cancelling out the smaller variable: $18 = 10y - 2$. Finally, isolate the variable by cancelling out the constant and then dividing by the coefficient: $20 = 10y$ and $y = 2$.

6. E. The most efficient way to solve is to simply plug in 6 for each x value and multiply. The answer choices become 7×9, 7×5, 9×3, and 3×7. The first option results in 63, which is the greatest of all the products.

7. A. Whenever we see a single equation with two different variables, we know that we will not be able to solve for each variable individually, but we won't need to. We want to recognize a relationship between the given equation and the expression we're trying to find. If we subtract y from both sides, we get $2x + 2y = 0$. The goal is to recognize that $2x + 2y$ is a factor of $12x + 12y$. All we have to do is multiply both sides of the equation by 6, resulting in $12x + 12y = 0$.

8. G. Plugging in 5 for a gives $5x^2 + 5x + 5$. Looking at the answer choices, we see that the goal is to correctly factor out 5 from the expression. If we factor 5 out of each term, we are left with $5(x^2 + x + 1)$. This matches only one answer choice exactly, and since there can only be one correct answer, we can eliminate all other answers.

9. C. To solve for x, we first want to cancel out the exponent by finding the square root of both sides of the equation. The square root of $(x - 5)^2$ is $x - 5$ because square roots cancel out squares. The square root of 36 can be either 6 or -6, so we must solve for both options: $x - 5 = 6$ results in $x = 11$ while $x - 5 = -6$ results in $x = -1$. Since the problem specifies that x must be less than 0, the answer is -1.

10. G. We should recognize that we can only solve for a variable when there is only one variable in the equation. We cannot solve for either variable in the first equation yet, so we will solve for x in the

second equation. Combining like terms gives us $11x = 11$, so $x = 1$. Plugging that value into the first equation gives us $1 = y - 9$. Since there is now only one variable, we can solve for it: adding 9 to both sides results in $y = 10$.

11. B. Since we are asked to find the value of $9x - 3$, and since the equation $9x + 7 = 11$ already contains the term $9x$, we need only to subtract 10 from both sides of the provided equation to arrive at $9x - 3 = 1$. We could solve for x using $9x + 7 = 11$, then plug that value into $9x - 3$, but this is time consuming. We would first subtract 7 from both sides, then divide by 9. This would result in $\frac{4}{9}$, which we would plug into the x value of $9x - 3$ to arrive at $4 - 3 = 1$.

12. G. The @ symbol is a variable, just like x or y. To solve for @, we want to cancel out the other numbers on that side of the equation, namely the 5 and the 2. Because 5 and @ are both being divided by 2, we'll cancel out the 2 first by multiplying both sides of the equation by 2, leaving us with $5 + @ = 11$. Now simply subtract 5 from both sides, leaving us with $@ = 6$.

13. C. Create an equation to represent the information given. "Twice a number" can be represented as $2x$. If 8 more than this is equal to 14, then it can be expressed as $2x + 8 = 14$. Solve for x by subtracting 8 from both sides then dividing by 2 to get $2x = 6$ and then $x = 3$. Remember: the question is not asking us to find this number. We are trying to find 8 times the number, which is $8 \times 3 = 24$.

14. H. Express the information provided algebraically. Let x represent the unknown number. The first part of the question tells us that $\frac{2}{3}x = 32$. Divide both sides of the equation by $\frac{2}{3}$; this is the same as multiplying both sides by the reciprocal, or $\frac{3}{2}$. So, $32 \times \frac{3}{2} = 48 = x$. We are asked to find $\frac{3}{4}$ of x, which is $48 \times \frac{3}{4} = 36$.

15. D. There are several ways to solve this question. Algebraically, we can solve for a using $\frac{3}{5}a = 30$ and substitute the value of a into $\frac{4}{5}a$ to solve the question. Under this method, we would first multiply both sides of the equation by the reciprocal of the fraction: $\left(\frac{5}{3}\right)\left(\frac{3}{5}a\right) = \left(\frac{5}{3}\right)(30)$. This leaves us with $a = 50$. Then, substitute into $\frac{4}{5}a$: $\left(\frac{4}{5}\right)(50) = 40$. This is perfectly valid, but time consuming. We can intuit that because $\frac{3}{5}$ of a is equal to 30, then each $\frac{1}{5}$ portion of a must equal 10. Four $\frac{1}{5}$ portions of a must, then, equal 40.

16. H. We can set up an algebraic equation to represent the information provided. c multiplied by 5 can be represented as $5c$. 5 added to c can be represented as $c + 5$. If they are "the same," then they must be set equal to one another. Thus, $5c = c + 5$. Simplify by subtracting c from each side: $4c = 5$. We could simplify further, but we don't need to: we're asked to find $4c$, and the equation already tells us $4c = 5$.

17. B. When dividing a whole number by a fraction, we simply multiply the numerator by the reciprocal of the denominator (the fraction) and simplify. We can look at each term individually.

$\frac{1}{1/2} = 1 \times \frac{2}{1} = 2$. The next term can be expressed as follows:

$\frac{1}{\left(\frac{1}{2} - 1\right)} = \frac{1}{\left(-\frac{1}{2}\right)} = 1 \times -\frac{2}{1} = -2$. Therefore, $2 + (-2) = 0$.

18. G. We have been given the value for c, so we can just work our way backwards through each statement to solve for a. $b = 4(3) = 12$. Substitute 12 in for b in the first statement: $a - 12 = 10$. Add 12 to both sides; $a = 22$.

19. D. Simply if the expression by multiplying: $2 \times \frac{m}{n} \times n^2 = \frac{2mn^2}{n}$. Then simplify by cancelling one n from the numerator and denominator, leaving us with $2mn$. That is all we need to do. The problem is asking for the value of $2mn$, which is simply twice the value of mn. Since $mn = 10$, we know that $2mn = 20$.

20. G. To solve any algebraic equation that consists of two fractions set equal to each other, start by cross multiplying. Here, you get $0.16 \times x = 0.40 \times 2.5$, which simplifies to $0.16x = 1$. To isolate the variable, divide both sides by 0.16, which results in $x = 6.25$.

21. A. Concentrate on each statement separately. First, "the sum of x and the square root of y": this can be represented by $x + \sqrt{y}$. "Is equal to" is simply an "=" sign. "The square root of the sum of x and y," can be represented by $\sqrt{x + y}$. Thus, $x + \sqrt{y} = \sqrt{x + y}$.

22. G. As with other problems, this question tests students' abilities to figure out a function based on a numerical pattern. If we assign a variable, n, to any position in the sequence, we see that the value of the position can be multiplied by 8 and have 1 subtracted from it to produce the number in that position. Therefore, plugging in 25 will produce the 25th value in the sequence.

23. C. To solve for the variable we want to first cancel out the 38. If we divide both sides of the equation by 38, we are left with $101 = x + 1$, so $x = 100$.

24. G. The problem tells us that the list of values is made exclusively of multiples of 3, which we can see by looking down the list. However, we cannot simply multiply the Position number by 3. The 1,000th value will not be 3,000 because that would require starting the list with 3×1. Instead, every Value has 3 subtracted from it, so the 1,000th value will be 2,997.

25. C. Whenever we see parentheses in an equation, we want to think about whether we should start by distributing. Here, distributing would result in $ax + bx = 28$. The problem tells us what ax equals, and asks us to find bx, so this was the correct first step. We can now plug in 7 for ax, giving us $7 + bx = 28$. Now all we have to do is subtract 7 from both sides, leaving us with $bx = 21$. We do not have to find the value of b or x individually.

26. H. If s represents the smallest of three consecutive even integers, then the other two integers are $s + 2$ and $s + 4$. The sum would be $s + s + 2 + s + 4$, which simplifies to $3s + 6$.

27. D. We can solve any proportion by cross multiplying, but here we can also solve by recognizing that the denominator of the left-hand fraction is 4 less than the numerator. Likewise, in the right-hand fraction, 39 is 4 less than 43. Therefore, x must also be 43 for the two sides to be equal.

28. G. We can solve by cancelling out the 1,000 using division, leaving us with $73 = 7p + 3$, which results in $70 = 7p$ and finally $p = 10$.

The Tutorverse

29. C. Regardless of how many variables an equation has, we solve for the target variable by isolating it. Here, the questions is asking us to isolate the b, which we do by subtracting $5a$, resulting in $b = a + 5 - 5a$. Combining like terms gives us $b = 5 - 4a$.

30. H. To translate an equation from words to symbols, first find where the equal sign goes, represented by "is equal to". Now look at the words to the left, "the product of x and $\frac{2}{5}$," which becomes $\frac{2}{5}x$, and the words to the right, "the sum of $5x$ and 2" becomes $5x + 2$.

31. 5. We know what y equals, but we don't know yet what x equals, so we plug 3 in for y in the first equation to solve for x: $\frac{x}{3^2} = 5$.

This simplifies to $\frac{x}{9} = 5$, which results in $x = 45$. Now we can plug in 45 and 3 into the final equation: $\frac{45}{3 + 2(3)} = \frac{45}{9} = 5$.

32. 144. We don't know what a or b equals, only that their product is 12, but that is all we need to know. $4a \times 3b$ equals $12ab$. If we plug 12 in for ab, we get $12 \times 12 = 144$.

33. 34. The sentence describes an algebraic equation: $2(2x - 12) = 10 - x$, which can be simplified to $4x - 24 = 10 - x$. Adding x and 24 to both sides results in $5x = 34$. We don't need to solve for x because we are only asked to find the value of $5x$.

34. 2. To solve a proportion, cross multiply. That give us $3(x + 30) = 8(x + 10)$, which simplifies to $3x + 90 = 8x + 80$. Solving for x results in $x = 2$.

Algebra in Context

1. C. Let x = the number of books that Malcolm has. In terms of x, Yannis has $x + 8$ books. Together, they have 60 books. This can be represented as: $60 = x + x + 8$, or $60 = 2x + 8$. Solve for x. Subtract 8 from both sides: $52 = 2x$. Divide both sides by 2: $x = 26$. This represents Malcolm's books. Yannis has 8 more, or $26 + 8 = 34$.

2. G. Let x = Leon's age. In terms of x, Michael's age can be represented as $2x + 3$. Since we know Michael is 35, we set the equation for Michael's age equal to 35: $35 = 2x + 3$. Solve for x by subtracting both sides by 3 then dividing both sides by 2. So, $x = 16$.

3. C. Let x = the number of bumpers a human can make. A machine can therefore make $10x$ bumpers. Altogether, they can make $x + 10x$, or $11x$, bumpers. Since we know the total is 550, we can set up the equation $11x = 550$, so $x = 50$. But that number represents the number of bumpers a human can make. The question asks for the number a machine can make, which is $50(10) = 500$.

4. F. Let x = Tom's pages, in which case $2x + 12$ equals Sue's pages. We know Sue read 90 pages, so $2x + 12 = 90$, in which case $x = 39$, which represents Tom's pages.

5. C. We know that C is a right angle, so the sum of the degree measures of angles A and B is 90. If we let x = the degree measure of angle A, then angle $B = 2x - 18$, in which case their sum is $3x - 18$. We can set up the equation $3x - 18 = 90$, in which case $x = 36$. This is the degree measure of angle A, so angle B must be $2(36) - 18 = 54$.

6. G. The total degree measure of a triangle is 180, so the three angles of the given triangle can be represented as $x + 2x + 3x = 180$, which can be simplified to $6x = 180$, in which case $x = 30$. We are looking for the largest angle, which is $3x = 3(30) = 90$.

7. C. The total degree measure of a triangle is 180, so the three angles of the given triangle can be represented as $3x + 4x + 5x = 180$, which can be simplified to $12x = 180$, in which case $x = 15$. We are looking for the smallest angle, which is $3x = 3(15) = 45$.

8. H. Let x = Ronan's current age, in which case $\frac{1}{3}x$ will be Shonda's current age. The second sentence describes the equation: $\frac{1}{3}x + 10 = 0.5(x + 10)$. Using standard algebra we get $x = 30$.

9. A. You can set up an algebraic equation to solve, but you don't need to. The two machines together will make 150 sneakers per minute. To find out how many minutes it will take them to make 5,400 sneakers, divide 5,400 by 150, which results in 36.

10. G. The variable c represents the number of cars Sherman has washed, for which he is paid \$4 each, so the amount of money he makes is $4c$. To that we add the flat rate of \$60, which is not multiplied by c because he does not earn \$60 for each car he washes.

11. B. We can solve this question by substituting values of t into the equation provided. $p(t) = 5{,}000 \times 2^{\left(\frac{3}{3}\right)}$ is really just $p(t) = 5{,}000 \times 2^1$, which is $5{,}000 \times 2 = 10{,}000$. $p(t) = 5{,}000 \times 2^{\left(\frac{9}{3}\right)}$ simplifies to $p(t) = 5{,}000 \times 2^3$, which is $5{,}000 \times 8 = 40{,}000$. The difference is 30,000.

12. G. The phone company will charge 12 cents for every minute except the first minute because they charged 30 cents for that first minute. That means there would be a flat rate of \$0.30 and then \$0.12 for each minute minus the first minute, or $0.30 + 0.12(m - 1)$.

13. 6. If a door is 10 feet long, and this is 4 feet longer than the width, the width must be $10 - 4 = 6$.

14. 45. If we let x = the number of pushups Luke's brother can do, then Luke can do $3x$, and we can set up the equation $x + 3x = 60$, which simplifies to $4x = 60$, resulting in $x = 15$, so Luke can do $3(15) = 45$ pushups.

15. 18. To solve, set up an equation. Let x = Ed's age. Pam's age is therefore $2x - 10$. If the sum of their ages is 32, then $x + 2x - 10 = 32$. Solving for x results in $x = 14$, which is Ed's age. Pam's age is $2(14) - 10 = 18$.

16. 26. If we assign x for each of the two legs, we can set up the equation $x + x + 2x - 6 = 46$, which simplifies to $4x - 6 = 46$. Solving for x results in $x = 13$, so the sum of the two congruent legs is 26.

17. 150. The total degree measure of the 4 angles of any quadrilateral is 360, so the relationship can be represented as $x + 2x + 4x + 5x = 360$, which simplifies to $12x = 360$. Solving for x results in $x = 30$, so the largest angle is $5(30) = 150$.

18. 17. We can assign x for the number of nickels James has, so he has $x + 8$ dimes. The value of his coins will then be $0.05x$ and $0.10(x + 8)$, and we can set up the equation $0.05x + 0.10(x + 8) = 2.15$, which can be simplified to $0.05x + 0.10x + 0.80 = 2.15$. Combing like terms gives us $0.15x = 1.35$, which results in $x = 9$. Therefore, he has 9 nickels and 17 dimes.

19. 2. The word "is" denotes an equal sign, so $24 - 3x = 5x + 8$. Combine like terms for $16 = 8x$. Divide both sides by 8 for $x = 2$.

20. 11. The base cost for TubeMusic is \$8.75, which Harrison would incur no matter how many songs he downloaded. This means he spent \$17 - \$8.75 = \$8.25 on downloading songs. This is \$8.25 ÷ \$0.75 = 11 songs.

21. 0. Start by finding y: $7y + 21 = 14$. Combine like terms for $7y = -7$. Divide both sides by 7 to isolate the variable for $y = -1$. Then, multiply y by 3 for -3. Add this to 3 for 0.

22. 8. The normal cost of cherries is \$8. If cherries are on sale for 25% off, then they cost only \$6 (since $8 \times 0.75 = 6$). Create an equation for the cost of cherries: pounds of cherries × price per pound = total cost. If we know we only have \$20, then this is the total cost of the cherries. So, we have the following: pounds of cherries × 6 = 20. Divide both sides by 6 for 8 pounds total.

23. 30. The total number of hours worked can be expressed as follows: hours worked by Rai + hours worked by Caleb. Let's represent the former by r and the latter by c. So, we know $r + c = 73$. We know that Caleb worked 13 more hours than Rai. So, if the number of hours Rai worked is r, then we know $c = r + 13$. Substitute this into the original equation for $r + 13 + r = 73$. Combine like terms for $2r = 60$, and $r = 30$.

Plugins

1. A. If $x < 0$, it is a negative number. Any negative number multiplied by a positive number will also be a negative number. The smaller the negative number (the less negative it is), the greater the value it has. Thus, x will be greater than any of the other answer choices so long as x is negative.

2. H. If m represents an odd integer, then $m + 2$ also represents an odd integer. $2m$ represents an even integer, but $2m - 1$ represents an odd integer. $3m$ represents an odd integer, and $3m - 2$ and $3m + 2$ both also represent odd integers. $5m$ represents an odd integer, so $5m + 1$ represents an even integer. We can also solve this question by plugging in an easy-to-work-with odd number, like 1.

3. B. The problem is asking for the value of $4b$. This means we should solve for b first. Multiply both sides of the equation by 5, resulting in $b = 5a$. To then find the value of $4b$, multiply both sides by 4, resulting in $4b = 20a$.

4. F. Multiplying any integer by 10^{-3} means to simply move the decimal point three places to the left. Since there is no decimal shown in ABC, that means it is at the end (as in ABC.0). Therefore, ABC × 10^{-3} = 0.ABC.

5. D. $a + b < a$ means that we're taking some number a, adding another number b to it, and the answer is somehow less than the original number a that we started with. How is that possible? b has to be a negative number!

6. G. Since c equals both ab and kb, that means that $ab = kb$. Since b is the same in both equations, k must equal a.

7. B. If x represents the number of years Mrs. Simmons has been teaching, then twice that number of years would be $2x$. Mr. Thompson has been teaching 8 years less twice Mrs. Simmons, which would be $2x - 8$.

8. F. If 1 is added to a, which is an even integer, we will end up with an odd integer. For example, if $a = 2$, then $2 + 1 = 3$, which is odd. To get to the next even integer, we must add 2.

9. C. We can substitute values in for a, b, and c to see which answer choice is true. a must be greater than b, so we can let $a = 2$ and $b = 1$. Now we can add any number c – let's choose 0 for c – to both numbers. $a + c = 2$ and $b + c = 1$. The difference between these two sums is 1, which tells us that the sum of c and a is 1 greater than the sum of c and b. Then, we can plug in the same values for a, b, and c into the answer choices and see which choice gives us 1. Only $a - b$ gives us the same answer.

10. H. There are a few simple rules to help with these questions. The addition or subtraction of two even or two odd integers will always result in an even integer; the addition or subtraction of one even and one odd integer will always result in an odd integer. With multiplication, only when two odd numbers are multiplied will the result be odd; in all other circumstances, the multiplication of two integers will always result in an even number. In this case, increasing or decreasing x by 1 results in an even number.

11. C. There are two rates described in this question: a per day fee ($1.30) as well as a per minute fee ($0.13). To calculate the cost having this phone plan, we need to know two variables: the number of days, and the number of minutes. We are told to assume that the plan is active for one day, but are only told that the phone is used for x minutes of talking. Thus, $1.30 per day × 1 day + $0.13 × x, which simplifies to $1.30 + 0.13x$.

12. H. Substitute 1 into q for $1 - \dfrac{1}{4}p = 0$. Subtract 1 from both sides for $-\dfrac{1}{4}p = -1$. Divide both sides by $-\dfrac{1}{4}$ for $p = 4$. Prove this by resubstituting p into the equation.

13. C. The shape that's being described has 5 lengths, four of which are x and one of which is y. The means the total length of tape should be $4x + y$. However, none of the answer choices have y. Since the area of a rectangle is length times width, and we know that the area is 600, we can create the equation $xy = 600$, in which case y can be written as $\dfrac{600}{x}$, and the total length of tape is now $4x + \dfrac{600}{x}$. That is still not an answer choice, but if we simplify the fractions in the choices, we see that C simplifies to $4x + \dfrac{600}{x}$.

14. H. The first book costs b dollars. The remaining 4 books each cost $b - d$ dollars. The total amount would then be $b + 4(b - d)$, which simplifies to $b + 4b - 4d$, which equals $5b - 4d$.

15. B. We can substitute $6c$ in for $5b$ in the first equation and arrive at $2a = 6c$. Simplifying, $a = 3c$.

16. E. The first ticket is m dollars. Each ticket after that is $m - n$ dollars. We cannot multiply the total number of tickets x by $m - n$ because the first ticket was not at the rate; we can instead multiply $m - n$ by $x - 1$, and add that to the price of the first ticket, which was m.

17. D. The percentage of something can be expressed as "the part" ÷ "the whole." In this case, we know that b is the part: the number of boys enrolled at the school. To determine "the whole" (the total number of boys and girls enrolled at the school), we must use the information provided. We already know that b represents the number of boys. In terms of b, there are 1.25b girls enrolled at the school; this represents the fact that there are 25% more girls than boys at the school, since we multiply whatever the number of boys is by 1.25 to get the number of girls. The denominator becomes 2.25b, so the percent of the school that is boys is $\dfrac{b}{2.25b} \times 100$.

18. E. g represents the total number of eggs. We are told that all of the crates, c, are filled except for one, which had 5 empty slots. Each crate holds m eggs when filled. So, if there are c crates, each filled to m capacity except for 5 slots, then $g = c \times m - 5$.

19. D. Choose any two consecutive odd integers – say, 5 and 7. Plugging them into the expression $x^2 - y^2$ gives us $7^2 - 5^2 = 49 - 25 = 24$. All of the answer choices are in terms of the smaller of the two integers, y. Plugging 5 into each choice reveals that only one gives 24.

20. H. If the average of a and b is z, then $a + b = 2z$. Therefore, the average of a, b, and c equals $\dfrac{2z + c}{3}$.

21. B. We can see that simply multiplying $m + 5$ by 2 results in $2m + 10$. What is done to one side of an equation must be done to the other. Thus, $2m + 10 = 2z$.

22. H. If Kim was n years old m years ago, then she is $n + m$ years old now, so 1 year ago she must have been $n + m - 1$.

23. C. We can use substitution to help us find the correct answer choice. Since x can't be equal to 0, we can use any other number x to be the first term. Let $x = 2$. We know that the next term in the sequence must be 2 more than 0.5 of the first term. This is $2(0.5) + 2 = 3$, so the second term is 3. The ratio of the second term to the first term, then, is 3:2, or 1.5. We can substitute 2 in for x in the answer choices to see which gives us 1.5.

24. E. Plug in 9 for n to get $(m + 2)^2 - 9 = 0$. Isolate m first by adding 9 to both sides, giving us $(m + 2)^2 = 9$. Take the square root for $m + 2 = 3$. Subtract 2 for $m = 1$.

25. B. Using substitution can help us solve this question. We can use two easy-to-work-with numbers like 4 and 5, since they differ by 1. The sum of these two numbers is 9, so $x = 9$. We can plug in 9 for each instance of x in the answer choices and know that we want to end up with 5 (since that is the greater of the two numbers. Only $(9 + 1) \div 2 = 5$.

26. E. Pick any number for x – say, 20. That means each ounce costs 2 dollars. If we choose 2 for y, then 2 dollars' worth of tea leaves will make 2 cups of tea, so 1 cup of brewed tea will cost $1. Plugging 20 and 2 into each answer choice for x and y, we see that only this choice results in a value of 1.

27. A. The question tells us that the spring's length is given by the equation $l = 12 + 2.5m$. Since we know that $l = 27$, plug in: $27 = 12 + 2.5m$. Subtract 12 from both sides for $15 = 2.5m$. Divide both sides by 2.5 for $m = 6$.

28. H. Pick a number for the total cost of the trip – say, $100 – as well as a number for the total number of students in the class – say, 10 – and the number of students not going – say, 9. If everyone in the class went, each student would have to pay $10. With 9 students not going, that leaves only 1 student who is going, which means each student must now pay a total of $100, which is an additional $90. Plugging these values into each answer choice, only the last choice result in 90.

Inequalities

1. A. To solve an inequality, use the same rules as when solving algebraic equations. First cancel out the constant by subtracting 4 from both sides, resulting in $2x < 26$. Then cancel out the coefficient by dividing both sides by 2, resulting in $x < 13$.

2. H. First cancel out the constant by subtracting 6 from both sides, resulting in $-2x > 22$. Then cancel out the coefficient by dividing both sides by -2, resulting in $x > -11$. *Remember that, when working with inequalities, dividing both sides by a negative number causes the inequality to switch directions!

3. B. First cancel out the constant by subtracting 8 from both sides, resulting in $1 > 7x$. Then cancel out the coefficient by dividing both sides by 7, resulting in $\frac{1}{7} > x$, or $x < \frac{1}{7}$.

4. F. First cancel out the constant by subtracting 8 from both sides, resulting in $3 > -5x$. Then cancel out the coefficient by dividing both sides by -5, resulting in $-\frac{3}{5} < x$, or $x > -\frac{3}{5}$. *Remember that, when working with inequalities, dividing both sides by a negative number causes the inequality to switch directions!

5. A. This problem is not asking us to find all possible values of z, but rather to find which is the only one of the given four choices that is a possible value for z. One way is to solve the inequality algebraically (resulting in $z < -\frac{10}{3}$) and then see which answer choice falls within the given range (only -4 is less than $-\frac{10}{3}$). Another way to solve is to plug each answer choice into the given inequality and see which one results in a correct statement.

6. H. This problem is not asking us to find all possible values of m, but rather to find which is the only one of the given four choices that is not a possible value for m. One way is to solve the inequality algebraically (resulting in $m < 3$) and then see which answer choice does not fall within the given range (3 is the only value that is not less than 3). Another way to solve is to plug each answer choice into the given inequality and see which one results in a false statement.

7. D. We can distribute the -2, but we can also just cancel out the -2 by dividing both sides of the inequality by -2, giving us $x - 6 > -9$. (*Remember that, when working with inequalities, dividing both sides by a negative number causes the inequality to switch directions!) Lastly, cancel out the constant by adding 6 to both sides, resulting in $x > -3$.

8. G. We only want the variable on one side of the inequality, so we will cancel out the smaller variable by subtracting $3x$ from both sides, giving us $16 > 2x - 28$. Now we can isolate the variable by

adding 28 to both sides, giving us $44 > 2x$, and then dividing both sides by 2, resulting in $22 > x$, or $x < 22$.

9. B. We can distribute the negative sign, but we can also just cancel it out by dividing both sides of the inequality by -1, giving us $7x + 8 \geq -9$. (*Remember that, when working with inequalities, dividing both sides by a negative number causes the inequality to switch directions!). Subtract 8 from both sides, giving us $7x \geq -17$, and then divide both sides by 7, resulting in $x \geq -\frac{17}{7}$.

10. G. We only want the variable on one side of the inequality, so we will cancel out the smaller variable by adding $12x$ to both sides, giving us $-46 \geq 33x + 64$. Now we can isolate the variable by subtracting 64 from both sides, giving us $-110 \geq 33x$, and then dividing both sides by 33, resulting in $-\frac{10}{3} \geq x$, or $x \leq -\frac{10}{3}$.

11. C. If all riders must be at least 54 inches tall, then any value that is 54 or larger satisfies the inequality. $r > 54$ does not work because it says that a rider's height must be <u>greater than or equal to</u> 54.

12. F. The heights must all be greater than or equal to 44 because the shortest student is 44 inches tall. The heights must all be less than or equal to 72 because the tallest student is 72 inches tall. Only this choice satisfies both those requirements.

13. B. The expression starts with 12. The words "is greater than" translates to the greater than symbol, or $>$. "Five less than twice a number x" becomes $2x - 5$ (<u>not</u> $5 - 2x$) because whatever value precedes "less than" is the value to be subtracted.

14. E. "x is less than or equal to twice the value of y" can be written as $x \leq 2y$. "y is less than zero" can be written as $y < 0$. We need a matching variable, so we can multiply both sides by 2 to get $2y < 0$, in which case we can create the compound inequality $x \leq 2y < 0$.

15. D. $x \geq 4$ means any number 4 or larger satisfies the inequality so we shade in the number line above the 4. We want the circle over the 4 to be filled in because 4 itself also satisfies the inequality.

16. E. $a < -6$ means any number less than -6 satisfies the inequality so we shade in the number line to the left of -6. We want the circle over the -6 to be open because -6 itself does not satisfy the inequality.

17. B. To find the correct answer, we first need to solve the inequality algebraically. Subtracting 3 from both sides and then dividing both sides by 3, we get $x \geq 1$. That means we want a closed circle over 1 with a number line shaded to the right.

18. G. To solve the inequality algebraically, we subtract 5 from both sides, giving us $-3a \geq -12$, and then divide both sides by -3, resulting in $a \leq 4$. (*Remember that when you multiply or divide by a negative number, the inequality switches direction!) That

means we want a closed circle over 4 with the number line shaded to the left.

19. A. To solve this compound inequality algebraically, we want to isolate the variable by subtracting 3 from all three sides, giving us $-12 \leq 3h \leq 3$, and then dividing all three sides by 3, resulting in $-4 \leq h \leq 1$. That means that h can be any value greater than or equal to -4 and less than or equal to 1. We show this on a graph with closed circles over -4 and 1 and the number line shaded in between them.

20. 19. $|x - 68| \leq 9$ can also be written as $-9 \leq x - 68 \leq 9$ and simplified to $59 \leq x \leq 77$. This means the low temperature was 59 and the high temperature was 77. There are 19 integers from 59 to 77, inclusive.

21. 3. $|x + 4| < 8$ can be written as $-8 < x + 4 < 8$, in which case $-12 < x < 4$. $|x - 5| < 3$ can be written as $-3 < x - 5 < 3$, in which case $2 < x < 8$. The only integer that satisfies both inequalities is 3.

22. -4. First subtract 9 from all sides, giving us $6 < -2x < 10$. Then divide all sides by -2, giving us $-3 > x > -5$, or $-5 < x < -3$. There is only one integer that falls within this range, as -3 and -5 are both omitted.

23. 7. We can plug 6 in for x, giving us $5(6) - 4y < 3$, which simplifies to $30 - 4y < 3$. Solving for y results in $y > \dfrac{27}{4}$. The least integer value that satisfies this is 7.

24. 84. If books sell for 10 dollars each, then the total revenue could be called $10x$. If revenue must exceed production cost, then $10x > 500 + 4x$. Solving for x results in $x > \dfrac{500}{6}$, or $x > 83.3$. Therefore, 84 is the least number of books that must be sold.

Probability & Statistics

Probability

1. C. The probability of some specific event happening can be represented as a fraction or a percentage. In this case, the "whole" is the total number of marbles in the bag (12). This will be the denominator in our fraction. The numerator will be the number of white marbles in the bag (4), since we "want" to draw a white marble. Therefore, the probability of the thing that we "want" to happen (to draw a white marble) can be represented as $\dfrac{4}{12}$, which simplifies to $\dfrac{1}{3}$.

2. F. Since the plastic cylinder contains 12 dice, and 5 are red and 4 are white, we know that there must be 3 blue dice in the cylinder. Since there are 3 chances to draw a blue dice out of 12 possible dice, the probability is $\dfrac{3}{12} = \dfrac{1}{4}$.

3. A. The normal work day lasts for 8 hours (9:00 [9:00 a.m.] – 17:00 [5:00 p.m.]). The three 10-minute coffee breaks lasts for a total of 30 minutes, or 0.5 hours. Since the thing that we are trying to determine is the chance that the office worker will be on break, we can divide 0.5 hours (the total time during the day spent on break) by the total number of hours in the work day (8). This gives us. $\dfrac{0.5}{8} = \dfrac{1}{16}$

4. G. During any given 30-minute interval, we are told that there are 8 minutes of commercials. The question asks us to determine the chance that a commercial will be airing when the television is tuned to the station in question. This means we "want" the commercials to happen, so the numerator of our fraction is 8. The denominator is the total number of minutes, or 30. $\dfrac{8}{30} = \dfrac{4}{15}$.

5. B. There are a total of 3 hours between 8-11pm, or 180 minutes. The commercial is 1.5 minutes long, and will be played 4 times, for total air time of $1.5 \times 4 = 6$ minutes. 6 minutes out of a possible 180 minutes is $\dfrac{6}{180} = \dfrac{1}{30}$.

6. G. Since it is not possible to choose a part or piece of a lollipop, the total number of lollipops must be a multiple of 4. 49 is not evenly divisible by 4 (it will result in a remainder, or partial piece of a lollipop). If there were 49 lollipops in the bucket, then there would be $3 \times 49 \div 4 = 36.75$ grape-flavored lollipops in the bucket.

7. C. Let x represent the area of one of classrooms 1, 2, and 3. The total area of classrooms 1, 2, and 3 can be represented as $x + x + x = 3x$. In terms of x, the area of one of classrooms 4, 5, and 6 is $2x$.

The total area of classrooms 4, 5, and 6 can be represented as $2x + 2x + 2x = 6x$. The total area of all 6 classrooms can therefore be represented as $3x + 6x = 9x$. The thing that we "want" is to find out the chance of randomly pointing at classroom 4, which has area $2x$.

Thus, the probability is $\dfrac{2x}{9x} = \dfrac{2}{9}$.

8. F. Since the probabilities of selecting an orange and green candy are given, we know that the total number of candies must be a multiple of both denominators, in this case, 4 and 6. If the total number is not a multiple of both 4 and 6, we would be left with a remainder and would not know whether or not a piece of candy was a certain color. For example, if there are 30 total pieces of candy, there should be 7.5 pieces of orange candy, which is impossible. Thus, 12, the only multiple of 4 and 6.

9. D. The "value of $\dfrac{a}{b}$" is a ratio, telling us how many apples there are relative to bananas. Assume that there are only 7 pieces of fruit in the bowl, since the denominator of $\dfrac{3}{7}$ tells us the total number of fruit is 7 (or a multiple of 7). Since this is the case, a apples $+ b$ bananas $= 7$, the total number of pieces of fruit. Since we know that $a = 3$ (from the probability of picking an apple of $\dfrac{3}{7}$), we know that $7 - 3 = b = 4$. We know that the ratio of apples to bananas, then, is $\dfrac{3}{4}$. There may actually be more than 3 apples and 4 bananas, but they will always stay in this proportion.

10. H. The amount of time a commercial is not airing is $90 - 20 = 70$ minutes. Therefore, the probability of a commercial _not_ airing is 70 minutes of non-commercial time $\div$ 90 minutes total time, which simplifies to $\dfrac{7}{9}$.

11. B. If there are 36 green bottles, then there are $60 - 36 = 24$ bottles that are _not_ green. The question asks us what the probability is that a ring will not land on a green bottle; this means that the thing that we "want" to happen is for the ring to not land on a green bottle. Since there are 24 not-green bottles out of a total of 60 bottles, the probability is $\dfrac{24}{60} = \dfrac{2}{5}$.

12. E. Before Leo loses his pens, he has a total of $8 + 6 + 2 = 16$ pens. If he loses 4 pens in total, then he is left with only 12 pens. Since we know that 2 of the 4 lost pens are blue, then of the 12 remaining pens, only 4 are blue. Thus, Leo's chances of picking out a blue pen randomly are 4 out of 12, or $\frac{1}{3}$.

13. B. Initially, the bucket of 20 apples contained 8 red apples, since $20 - 12 = 8$. If 2 green apples are then removed from the bucket, that leaves the bucket with 18 apples, 8 of which are still red, and 10 of which are green. If one more apple is chosen at random (in this case, "removed from the bucket"), the chances of it being red are 8 out of 18 total apples. This simplifies to 4 out of 9.

14. G. Initially, the bookshelf holds a total of 12 fiction + 15 non-fiction = 27 books. 5 are removed, 1 of which is non-fiction, meaning the other 4 are fiction. The bookshelf now contains 8 fiction + 14 non-fiction books = 22 books. If one more book is removed, the chance of it being fiction is $\frac{8}{22} = \frac{4}{11}$.

15. C. Initially, there must have been $\frac{2}{5} \times 30 = 12$ white pawns in the box, which means $30 - 12 = 18$ black pawns in the box. If the probably of drawing a white and a black pawn from the box is exactly 50%, after adding in more white pawns, that must mean that the number of white and black pawns are equal, at 18. Therefore, $18 - 12 = 6$ white pawns were added to the box.

16. G. If no cherries are sold, then the number of cherries must remain at 7 even after other fruit are sold. If the probability of picking a cherry after other fruits are sold must be 50%, then we know that the total remaining number of fruit (including the 7 cherries) must be twice the number of cherries remaining. This means the total number of fruit after some are sold is 14, with 7 being cherry. Of the other 7, we don't know how many remaining are oranges or lemons; we only know that where there were 17 oranges and lemons before, now there are only 7. This means a total of 10 oranges or lemons were sold. Since the question asks what the fewest number of lemons sold was, we can assume that as many oranges as possible were sold. Since this is 8, and 10 were sold in total, that means the minimum number of lemons that could have been sold is 2.

17. A. If 75% of the 20 peppers are yellow, then there are 15 yellow and 5 orange. The probability of both peppers being orange (without replacement) is $5 \div 20 \times 4 \div 19 = 1/19$.

18. 0.04. If $\frac{2}{5}$ of the pears are Bartlett and $\frac{7}{12}$ are Bosc, then there are 24 Bartletts and 35 Boscs, meaning there is only 1 Anjou. If all the Boscs are removed, then there will be 25 pears remaining, and the probability of picking an Anjou will be 1 out of 25, or 0.04.

19. 0.5. If $\frac{1}{3}$ of the 48 bottles are apple, then there are 16 apple, and a total of 32 orange and grape. If there are 3 times as many orange as grape, then there must be 24 orange and 8 grape, meaning the probability of picking a bottle of orange is 24 out of 48, or 0.5.

20. 18. If $\frac{3}{8}$ of the box is milk, then $\frac{5}{8}$ of the box is dark and white. There is a total of 30 dark and milk, meaning the total number of chocolates is 48, so there must be 18 milk chocolates.

21. 0.2. If Shonda removed 8 movies, 2 of which are dramas, then she removed 6 comedies, leaving 16 dramas and 4 comedies, for a new total of 20 movies. The probability of picking a comedy is now 4 out of 20, or 0.2.

22. 24. If $\frac{4}{9}$ of Harold's 36 apps are games, then he has 16 games and 20 other apps. The same 20 other apps must eventually represent $\frac{1}{3}$ of all the apps on his phone, meaning there must be a total of 60 apps, so he needs 24 more games.

23. 0.75. This is a compound probability problem, meaning we set up a multiplication equation: $\frac{1}{5} \times x = \frac{3}{20}$. Using either basic algebra or our fact families, we know that $\frac{3}{20} \div \frac{1}{5} = \frac{3}{4}$, or 0.75.

Averages

1. B. To calculate the mean, we must add up the total number of birds spotted during all the days and then divide by the number of days. To get the total number of birds, multiply each number of birds by the number of days and add them together. $1 \times 3 + 2 \times 3 + 3 \times 5 + 4 \times 8 + 5 \times 11 = 3 + 6 + 1 5 + 3 2 + 35 = 111$ birds total. To get the number of days, add up the numbers in the second column. $3 + 3 + 5 + 8 + 11 = 30$ days. Finally, we divide the total birds by the number of days and we get $111 \div 30 = 3.7$.

2. G. There were 3 days when 1 bird was spotted, 3 days when 2 birds were spotted, 5 days when 3 birds were spotted, etc. We can list out the number of birds spotted each day as follows: 1,1,1,2,2,2,3,3,3,3,3,4,4,**4,4**,4,4,4,4,5,5,5,5,5,5,5,5,5,5,5. The list has 30 numbers in it, which is even so there are two middle numbers. Since both middle numbers are 4, the median is 4. Another way to solve this problem without writing out the entire list is to notice that there are a total of 30 days (get this by adding up the second column of the chart). Therefore, the middle numbers will be the 15th and 16th numbers. These must both be 4 (because there are 11 numbers that are 1's, 2's, and 3's, and 11 numbers that are 5's).

3. A. The range is the highest number of birds spotted minus the lowest number of birds spotted. $5 - 1 = 4$.

4. G. The median is the middle number. Cross off numbers from both sides until you reach the middle. There are two middle numbers, which are both 8, so the median is 8.

5. C. The mode is the number that appears the most often. The number 8 appears 6 times, which is more often than any other number, so 8 is the mode.

6. G. To find the mean, add up all the scores and divide by the number of scores. The total of the scores is 158 and the number of scores is 20. Therefore, the mean is $158 \div 20 = 7.9$.

7. D. A mean is simply the sum of all the values in a given set, divided by the total number of the values in that set. In this case, the set consists of 3 numbers: x, $4x$, and $5x$. Adding these together, we arrive at $10x$, and must divide by 3 (the total count of numbers in the range) to arrive at the mean, which we are told is 90. So, $10x \div 3 = 90$. Solving for x, we multiply both sides by 3 to arrive at $10x = 270$, and then divide both sides by 10 for $x = 27$. The question asks for the value of the largest of these, which is $5x$, so $5 \times 27 = 135$.

8. G. The median is the middle value in a set when all values are in order. If one more student takes the quiz, there will be 21 values, so the 11th value will be the median. If one student scores a 10, two students score a 9, and now four students score an 8, that accounts for seven values. The four 7's mean that the median is 7.

9. B. If a is any number 8 or smaller, then the new median will be 8. If it is 9 or larger, then the new median will be 9. 8 is not an answer choice, so the answer must be 9.

10. F. A mean is a sum of numbers in a range divided by the count of numbers in that range. In this case, the sum is $6 + x + y$, which, when divided by 3, equals 10. Simplify to $6 + x + y = 30$. Subtracting 6 from both sides, we arrive at $x + y = 24$.

11. B. If the total number of books is 345, and Chrissy owns 135, that means 210 remain between Jack and Janet. To find the mean, we divide their sum by 2: $210 \div 2 = 105$.

12. H. Since we can find a mean by dividing the sum of the values by the number of values in the set, we can therefore use our fact families to know that multiplying a mean by the number of values in the set results in the sum of the values.

13. C. The problem tells us that Brenda's first three scores add up to 252 and her fourth score is 96. Therefore, the total of all the scores is $252 + 96 = 348$. To calculate the mean, we divide the sum by the number of scores, which is 4. We get $348 \div 4 = 87$.

14. H. Ellen wants her test mean to be 95. In other words, when she adds up all her scores and divides by 6, she should get 95. Working backwards, this means that if we multiply 95 by 6, we will get the sum of all the scores. $95 \times 6 = 570$.

15. A. Let x represent Brandon's score on the fourth test. Then his mean for the four tests can be represented as $\dfrac{3 \times 90 + x}{4}$. We have to multiply 3 times 90 in the numerator because there were three tests with a mean of 90. We divide by 4 because there were 4 tests total. This expression simplifies to $\dfrac{270 + x}{4}$. Brandon's mean on the first four tests was 85, so we can make an equation $\dfrac{270 + x}{4} = 85$. To solve this equation, multiply both sides by 4. The equation becomes $270 + x = 340$. Then subtract 270 from both sides. Then answer is $x = 70$.

16. E. Let x represent the extra number that is being added to the set. The total of the new set is $8 \times 20 + x$ because there are 8 numbers with a mean of 20 and we are adding x to them. This total simplifies to become $160 + x$. In order to get the new mean, the total must be divided by 9 because there are 9 numbers including the new one. Therefore, the new mean is $\dfrac{160 + x}{9}$. The problem tells us that the new mean is 4 less than the old mean (which was 20) so the new mean is 16. Therefore, we get $\dfrac{160 + x}{9} = 16$. To solve this equation, first multiply both sides by 9 and then subtract 160 from both sides. The answer is $x = -16$.

17. A. No matter how many pets the new student has, the median will remain 1. This means that the new mean should also be 1. We can therefore find the unknown value by setting up an algebraic equation: $\dfrac{0+0+0+1+1+1+1+1+1+2+2+3+x}{13} = 1$. Combining like terms and cancelling out the denominator gives us $13 + x = 13$, so $x = 0$.

18. G. If Daniel scored a mean of 10 points in each of 5 games, then the total number of points he scored is $10 \times 5 = 50$. We know that he scored at least 1 point in each game. The highest number of points he could score in one game would be 46, because he could score 46 points in one game and then only 1 point in each of the other games. $46 + 1 + 1 + 1 + 1 = 50$, so the answer is 46.

19. C. If the average of 3 integers is -54, then three integers must be -55, -54, and -53. The least of these is -55 (it is further left on the number line). If we subtract 45 from it, we get $-55 - 45 = -100$.

20. F. To get the mean, we must add up the total scores of all the students and divide by the number of students. To get the total scores for all ten students we must multiply 92 by the number of girls, multiply 82 by the number of boys, and add these together. $92 \times 6 + 82 \times 4 = 552 + 328 = 880$ total points. Finally, we divide the total points by the number of students. $880 \div 10 = 88$.

21. C. The numbers in M are 15, 20, 25, 30. The median is the middle number, but in this case we have two middle numbers, which are 20 and 25. Therefore, we have to take the mean of 20 and 25, which is 22.5.

22. H. Let x represent the mean number of hours that Trang studied per day during the first 5 days. Then $x + 1$ represents the number of hours per day that she studied during the last 3 days. The total number of hours that she studied in the first 5 days is $5x$. The total number of hours that she studied during the last 3 days is $3(x + 1)$. Therefore, total number of hours that she studied during all 8 days is $5x + 3(x + 1)$. To simplify this expression, use the distributive property. We get $5x + 3x + 3$. Then combine like terms to get $8x + 3$. We know that she studied for a total of 27 hours, so we get the equation $8x + 3 = 27$. To solve this equation, subtract 3 from both sides and then divide both sides by 8. We get $x = 3$. This means that the mean number of hours she studied per day during the first 5 days was 3, so she must have studied $3 + 1 = 4$ hours per day during the last 3 days. Therefore, her total in the last 3 days was (3 days) $\times$ (4 hours per day) = 12 hours.

23. D. Set X contains three numbers whose mean is 5, which means the sum of the three numbers is 15. Set Y is made from those three numbers being tripled, so their sum is 45. It doesn't matter what the individual numbers are.

24. G. If Markus took 5 tests and has an average of 86, then he scored a total of $86 \times 5 = 430$ points on all 5 tests. If he wants an average of 87, and he can only take 1 more test, then he will need to have a total of $87 \times 6 = 552$ points on all 6 tests. This is a difference of $552 - 430 = 92$ points.

25. 5. The range is 5 (because the greatest number of items bought is 5 and the least is 0) and the mode is 0 (because more customers bought 0 items than any other number), so the range is 5 more than the mode.

26. 2. The median is the middle number. There were initially 50 customers, so one more would make 51 customers. The median would be the 26th number of items bought, which would be 2.

27. 1.78. Finding the mean requires finding the total number of items bought by everyone. 3 customers bought 5 items each (15 total), 5 customers bought 4 items each (20 total), 8 customers bought 3 items each (24 total), 9 customers bought 2 items each (18 total), 12 customers bought 1 item each (12 total), and 13 customers didn't buy anything. The final sum is 89 items. Dividing by the total number of customers (found by adding up the right column) gives us $89 \div 50 = 1.78$.

Geometry & Measurements

Area & Perimeter

1. C. If the perimeter is 28 feet, then 28 is equal to the sum of the sides of the rectangle. If the length, or one side, is 4 feet, then there is a second side that is 4 feet long, so the remaining side is equal to $28 - 8 = 20 \div 2 = 10$. So the width of this rectangle is 10 feet. Find the area by multiplying the width times the length: $10 \times 4 = 40$.

2. G. If the area of a square is 25 inches, then each side is equal to the square root of 25 inches, or 5 inches. The perimeter is the sum of all the sides, or 4 times the length of one side in a square, or 20 in.

3. C. The area of a triangle is given by the formula $A = \dfrac{1}{2}bh$, where b is the base of the triangle and h is the height of the triangle. The area is given as 24 square centimeters, so the equation is $24 = \dfrac{1}{2}$

The Tutorverse

bh, which simplifies to $48 = bh$. The base is given as 6, so we know that $h = 8$.

4. E. If the area of the square is 72 square centimeters, then triangle GLH has an area equal to $\frac{1}{4}$ of that, or 18 square centimeters. GL and LH are equal, and the area of a triangle is equal to $\frac{1}{2}bh$. So, $18 = \frac{1}{2}$(GL)(LH) and $36 = $(GL)(LH). Since GL = LH, both are equal to 6.

5. B. The easiest way to solve this question is to imagine a complete rectangle measuring 7 by 12, with an area of 84. Since a piece is missing, measuring 5 by 6 and having an area of 30, we simply subtract the square from the rectangle. $84 - 30 = 54$.

6. E. Bedroom A is 8 by 6.5 1-inch squares. If each 1-inch square is equal to 9 square feet, then each 1-inch square is equal to 1 square yard. Since there are 3 feet per yard, a 3 foot (or, 1 yard) by 3 foot (1 yard) square results in a 9 square foot (1 square yard) area. The area of Bedroom A is simply $8 \times 6.5 = 52$ square yards.

7. B. If the width of the rectangle is 18 feet, and the length is 9 less than twice that, then the length is $2(18) - 9 = 27$. Thus, the total area of the room is 18 ft. wide × 27 ft. long = 486 sq. ft. Each square porcelain tile measures 3 by 3 feet long, and has an area of 9 sq. ft. Therefore, it will take $486 \div 9 = 54$ tiles to cover the floor.

8. F. There are several ways to solve this question. We can start by finding the area of each smaller rectangle, which is *xy*, and the area of the larger rectangle, which is therefore $3xy$. If one is tiling a rectangular area $8y$ by $9x$, then the total area to be tiled is $72xy$. Divide to find how many sets of area $3xy$ will be needed to tiled an area of $72xy$, which is 24.

9. C. The total area of the kitchen is 16 ft. × 12 ft. = 192 sq. ft. We can tell that each square marble tile will measure 4 ft. by 4 ft., since we can divide the total length and width of the kitchen by the number of tiles that fit into that measurement. Each square marble tile therefore has an area of $4 \times 4 = 16$ sq. ft. The top two partially-shaded areas are $\frac{2}{3}$ of a full tile, or $\frac{32}{3}$ sq. ft. each. Both top shaded areas represent $\frac{64}{3}$ sq. ft. The bottom two partially-shaded areas are about half of the size of the top two partially-shaded areas, or $\frac{32}{3}$ sq. ft. Together, they represent $\frac{64}{3} + \frac{32}{3} = 32$ sq. ft. Subtracting that from the total area leaves $192 - 32 = 160$ sq. ft.

10. G. Draw these triangles to help visualize. They share a base, so the two shapes form a lopsided diamond. The shorter triangle has a height of *x*, and the larger triangle has a height of $2x$. We know that the area of one triangle is $A = \frac{1}{2}bh$. For the small triangle, this is $A = \frac{1}{2}5x$, and for the larger triangle, this is $A = \frac{1}{2}5(2x)$. The sum of these is 60, so we write: $60 = (\frac{1}{2})(5x) + (\frac{1}{2})(10x)$. Multiply all terms by 2 for $120 = 5x + 10x$, and simplify for $120 = 15x$, and $x = 8$. The question asks the height of the larger, which is $8 \times 2 = 16$.

11. A. If the area of the square is 16, then each of its sides is $\sqrt{16} = 4$. This means that the side shared by the square and the triangle (the dotted line) has length 4. If the perimeter of the

triangle is 12, then we subtract 4 from the total perimeter to find the length of the remaining 2 sides of the triangle, which must be 8. The other 3 sides of the square have a total length of $3 \times 4 = 12$, so the total perimeter must be $12 + 8 = 20$.

12. F. Since each side of square ACGE has is 4 cm, it has an area of 16 cm. The ACGE square has been split into 4 smaller squares, each with an area of 4. The small triangles in each small square each have an area of 2, since they are half the size of each small square. Triangle CJG is congruent to triangle CHG, so the area of the two triangles together is 8.

13. A. A hexagon has 6 sides. The perimeter of a polygon is the sum of the lengths of its sides. In this case, the lengths of a hexagon are given. The total perimeter can be represented as $54 = 2(x) + 2(3x) + 4x + 6$. Simplify and solve for *x*: $48 = 12x$, and $x = 4$.

14. H. A regular polygon has equilateral sides, meaning all sides have the same length. The hexagon, then, has 6 sides that are each 8 meters long, meaning the total perimeter is $8 \times 6 = 48$ meters. If a square has the same perimeter, but only has 4 sides, then the length of each side is $48 \div 4 = 12$ meters. The area of the square is $12^2 = 144$ square meters.

15. B. Draw this shape. A regular pentagon has 5 sides, so each side must be $15 \div 5 = 3$ mm long. If this is the base of the triangle, and the hypotenuse is 5 mm, then we know that the height of the triangle is 4 mm because this is a special right triangle (a 3-4-5 triangle). This means the area is $0.5(3)(4) = 6$ mm^2.

16. F. We must find the lengths of PQ, QS, ST, and PT. QS is given as 5. We know that PQ = 3 because Q bisects PR, meaning PQ = QR = 3, and that PR has a total length 6. ST = RS because S bisects RT. We know that RS = 4 because it is a special right triangle (a 3-4-5 triangle). Since $b = $ RS = ST = 4, then length RT = 8. Since PR = 6 and RT = 8, and the triangle is a right triangle, we know that PT = 10 (because it is proportional to QRS and also because it is a multiple of the 3-4-5 triangle: a 6-8-10 triangle. Therefore, PQ = 3, QS = 5, ST = 4, and PT = 10. The sum is the perimeter: $3 + 5 + 4 + 10 = 22$.

17. D. The area of a circle can be determined using the formula $A = \pi r^2$, where *r* is the radius of the circle. The radius is given as 10, so the area of the circle is 100π, or approximately 314 sq. ft. Since a gallon of paint can cover 30 sq. ft., $314 \div 30 = 10.46$. We need to round up to the nearest whole gallon; 10 gallons of paint will only cover 300 sq. ft. In order to cover the remaining 14 sq. ft., an 11th gallon would need to be purchased.

18. F. The circumference of a circle is equal to $2\pi r$, or πd. In the figure, KJ is the diameter of the circle. Since JKLM is a square, to find the length of KJ, divide the perimeter 16 by the 4 sides. This tells us that KJ = $\pi(4) = 4\pi$.

19. C. Since we know the area of the circle, we can find the radius, which we know will be the measure of AB. $36\pi = \pi r^2$. Solving for *r*, we can cancel out the π and take the square root of 36, to find that $r = 6$. Now we know that AB = 6. Since AC = 2AB, then AC = $2(6) = 12$. Using the formula for the area of a triangle, $\frac{1}{2}(b)(h)$, we can plug in values for both *b* and *h*: $\frac{1}{2}(6)(12) = 36$.

20. H. Since the area of the circle is 64π, we can solve for the radius of the circle: $64\pi = \pi r^2$. Dividing both sides by π, we arrive at $64 = r^2$. Squaring both sides, we find that $r = 8$. Since the circle is inscribed in the circle, it's center is exactly in the middle of the square. The length of a square is equal to the diameter of the circle, or $2r = 16$. The area of the square is equal to $A = l \times w$, or $16 \times 16 = 256$.

21. B. We can determine the total surface area of a cylinder by using the formula $A = 2\pi rh + 2\pi r^2$, which represents the area of the cylinder including its top and bottom bases. We are given $h = 10$ in., and $d = 4$ in. We can convert *d* diameter into *r* radius by halving the value of *d*, so $r = 2$ in. Substitute the values into the

formula: $A = 2\pi(2)(10) + 2\pi(2)^2$. This simplifies to $A = 40\pi + 8\pi$, or 48π.

22. G. The area of a trapezoid can be determined using the formula $A = \dfrac{a+b}{2}h$, where a and b are the lengths of the top and bottom bases (the parallel sides) and h is the height of the trapezoid (the distance between a and b). Substituting the values from the figure: $A = \dfrac{10 + 20}{2}(10)$, which simplifies to 150.

23. B. Since AB is 12 cm. long, so too is DC. This is because the opposite sides of a parallelogram have the same length. Since E is located at the midpoint of DC, we know DE and CE are both 6. If we can find the height of AE, then we can determine the area of the rectangle. Since $24 = \dfrac{1}{2}(b)(h)$, where $b = $ DE and $h = $ AE, then $\dfrac{1}{2}(6)(h)$. Solving for h, we find that AE = 8. The area of a parallelogram is simply $A = bh$. In this case, $12 \times 8 = 96$.

24. 30. If the length is one more than the width, we can represent this as $l = w + 1$. The perimeter would be $2(w) + 2(w + 1) = 22$, or $4w + 2 = 22$. To find w, subtract 2 from both sides then divide by 4 for $w = 5$. The width is 5, which means the length is $22 = 5 + 5 + 2l$, or $12 = 2l$, for $l = 6$. The area is $l \times w$, or $5 \times 6 = 30$ in^2.

25. 100. The perimeter of the pentagon is 40 inches, since it is regular and has 5 equally long sides (5×8). If a square has the same perimeter as the pentagon, its side length is $40 \div 4 = 10$ inches, and its area is 100 square inches.

26. 4. If the side lengths must all be integers, then the rectangle could only have side lengths of 1 and 24, 2 and 12, 3 and 8, or 4 and 6, which is 4 different combinations. All four of these possibilities render different perimeters, of 50, 28, 22, and 20, respectively.

27. 48. Draw this shape out so that the circle is inside the square (refer to #20 for an example). We know that the circle has a radius of 6, since the area is $36\pi = \pi r^2$. This is half the length of one side of the square, so one side of the square is 12 in long. This means the perimeter is $12 \times 4 = 48$ in.

28. 50. Draw this shape out so that the square is inside the circle, with the corners touching the circle. We know that the circle has a radius of 5, since the area is $25\pi = \pi r^2$. This means the distance from the center of the square to each corner is 5 mm. There are many ways to find the area of the square without knowing the formula for the Pythagorean Theorem. Draw a radius from the center of the circle to the top-right corner of the square, and do the same to the bottom-right corner of the square. Both have length 5, so we know the area of the triangle formed is 0.5(5)(5), or 12.5 mm^2. There are 4 of these triangles in the square, so $12.5 \times 4 = 50$.

29. 4. Two circles that share the same center are called concentric. Draw one circle, and label the radius x. Then, surrounding it, draw a larger radius, and draw a new radius, labeling the radius $2x$. The area of the small circle is πx^2. The area of the larger circle is $\pi(2x)^2$, or $\pi 4x^2$. Choose an easy number to work with (use a small integer that isn't 0 or 1, when using this method), like 2. Substitute this in for x. This means the small circle would have an area of 4π, while the area of the large circle would be 16π. The larger circle has an area that is 4 times as large as the area of the smaller circle.

30. 42. The bases of this parallelogram are 6 units long, and the height from one base to the other is 7 units. The area of a parallelogram is base times height, or $6 \times 7 = 42$.

Volume

1. B. The volume of a rectangular prism like the swimming pool can be determined by the formula length × width × height. We are already given the length × width, which is 350 sq. meters. We need only solve for the height: $4,200 = 350 \times height$. By dividing both sides of the equation by 350, we arrive at a height/depth of 12 meters.

2. F. The volume of a rectangular prism like the swimming pool can be determined by the formula length × width × height. We are given all three dimensions, but must be careful to convert units to feet. The volume, then, is: 20 ft. × 40 ft. × 0.5 ft. = 400 cu. ft.

3. B. First, determine the volume of each package. The volume of a cube measuring 2 feet on all sides is $2^3 = 8$ cubic feet. Next, determine the volume of the storage area: $16 \times 24 \times 4 = 1,536$ (note that the height allows for two layers of packages). 1,536 cubic feet ÷ 8 cubic feet per package = 192 packages.

4. E. The cube has a volume of $3^3 = 27$ cubic inches. The pyramid has a volume of $\dfrac{1}{3}(3)(3)(1) = 3$. In total, $27 + 3 = 30$ in^3.

5. A. The volume of a sphere is given by the formula $A = \dfrac{4}{3}\pi r^3$. If the volume is 36π, first multiply both sides by 3 to simplify, for $108\pi = 4\pi r^3$. Then, divide both sides by 4π for $27 = r^3$. This is the perfect cube of 3, or $3 \times 3 \times 3$.

6. F. If the area is 288π, first multiply both sides by 3 to simplify, for $864 = 4\pi r^3$. Then, divide both sides by 4π for $216 = r^3$. This is the perfect cube of 6, or $6 \times 6 \times 6$. The circumference is $2\pi r$, or 12π.

7. D. The volume of any pyramid can be found by using the formula $\dfrac{1}{3}bh$, where $b = $ area of the triangle's base, and $h = $ the height of the pyramid. Here, we are given that $128 = \dfrac{1}{3}b(6)$. Simplifying, we have $64 = b$. Since the base is a square, we can take the square root of both sides to find that each side is 8 ft. long.

8. G. The volume of any pyramid can be found using the formula $\dfrac{1}{3}bh$, where $b = $ area of the triangle's base, and $h = $ the height of the pyramid. Substituting in known values, we arrive at $36 = \dfrac{1}{3}(12)h$. Simplify and solve: $36 = 4h$, so $h = 9$.

9. D. Using the formula of the volume of a pyramid $\dfrac{1}{3}bh$, we can substitute known values: $144 = \dfrac{1}{3}b(9)$. Isolate b: $48 = b$. The question does not ask for a particular side, only what the possible sides could be. In this case, we know that the area must be 48 in^2. The only combination of dimensions provided that does this is 6 in. by 8 in. ($6 \times 8 = 48$).

10. E. Since we are already given the value of the length × width as being 24 in^2, we solve for the height using the volume: $84 = 24 \times h$. Simplifying, we find that $h = 3.5$ in.

11. B. The volume of a trapezoidal prism can be determined using the formula $\dfrac{a+b}{2} \times h \times l$, where a and b represent the widths of the trapezoid's bases, h represents the height of the prism, and l

represents the length of the prism. We are given all 4 values, and need only to substitute: $\dfrac{4+8}{2} \times 5 \times 10 = 300$.

12. G. The volume of a rectangular prism can be determined by multiplying the length by the width by the height. In the case of the top prism, the volume can be expressed as $y \times y \times y = y^3$. In the case of the bottom prism, we know that the height = y. The length and the width are shown as 2 more than the length and width of the top prism, which we can represent as $y + 2$ and $y + 2$. Thus, the bottom prism has a volume of $y(y + 2)(y + 2)$. We add this to y^3 to arrive at $y^3 + y(y + 2)(y + 2)$.

13. D. The beachball has radius of 3, since $9\pi = \pi r^2$. This means the volume is $\dfrac{4}{3}\pi(3)^3$, or 36π inches^3.

14. 960. The box can fit 12 cubes across, 10 cubes deep, and 8 cubes high, so the total number of cubes is $12 \times 10 \times 8 = 960$.

15. 3. The volume of a cone is $V = \dfrac{1}{3}\pi r^2 h$, or one-third the height of the cone times the area of the cone's base. If the volume is 16π and the radius of the base is 4, then $16\pi = \dfrac{1}{3}(4^2)(\pi)(h)$. This simplifies to $48\pi = 16\pi h$, and $h = 3$.

16. 8. The volume of a cylinder can be found by $V = \pi r^2 h$. If the volume is 48π and the radius is 2, then we have $48\pi = (2^2)(\pi)(h)$. This leaves us with $h = 12$. If the container is $\dfrac{2}{3}$ full, then the depth must be 8 inches.

17. 90. If the pool has a depth of 3 feet, then the volume of water in it is $12 \times 50 \times 3 = 1{,}800$. At a rate of 20 cubic feet per minute, it will take $1{,}800 \div 20 = 90$ minutes.

18. 4. The volume of a pyramid can be found by $V = \dfrac{1}{3} lwh$. If $V = 32$ and $h = 6$, then $32 = \dfrac{6lw}{3}$. Solving for lw, which is the area of the base, we arrive at $96 = 6lw$ and $lw = 16$. Since the base is a square, we know that $l = w = 4$.

19. 6. If the volume of a filled beachball is 36π, then its radius can be found by solving for r in $36\pi = \dfrac{4}{3}\pi r^3$. Multiply both sides by 3 for $108\pi = 4\pi r^3$. Divide both sides by 4π for $27 = r^3$, and $r = 3$. The circumference is $2\pi r$, or 6π. The volume is 6 times bigger.

Triangles

1. B. The longest side of a right triangle is the hypotenuse, or the side that is opposite the 90° angle. In this figure, there are three right triangles: WXY, WYZ, and WXZ. The largest of these triangles is WXZ, which encompasses both of the other right triangles. Therefore, the largest hypotenuse must be opposite the 90° angle XWZ, or length XZ.

2. G. The sum of the interior angles of a triangle always equals 180°. This means that $x + y + z = 180$. Since the question asks for the value of $x + y$, we simply subtract z from both sides to arrive at $x + y = 180 - z$.

3. D. In degrees, the sum of the interior angles of a triangle always equals 180°. Thus, we know that $y° = 180° - 42° - 76°$. So, $y° = 62°$. A straight line has a degree measurement of 180°; 2 angles that add up to 180° are called supplementary angles. So, $w° = 180° - 76°$, or 104°. Similarly, $x° = 180° - 42°$, or 138°. Thus, $62° + 104° + 138° = 304°$.

4. H. Since the sum of interior angles of a triangle is always equal to 180°, then $t + u + v = x + y + z = 180°$. We don't know for sure that any of the other statements are true, since the degree measure individually could vary wildly from one triangle to another.

5. C. Since the sum of interior angles of a triangle is always equal to 180°, and we have the measurement of two of the three angles, we can find the third: $180 - 90 - 40 = 50$. Note that the question asks for the value of y. Note that the 50° angle and angle y are supplementary (they add up to 180°) because the line formed by the base of the triangle extends beyond the triangle itself. The degree measurement of a straight line is 180°. Since the two angles are supplementary, $y = 180 - 50$, or 130°.

6. F. Angle RSQ is supplementary to the exterior angle labeled as 125°. Therefore, angle RSQ = $180 - 125 = 55°$. Knowing this and the fact that angle SQR = 20°, $x = 180 - 55 - 20$, or 105°.

7. B. All angles in an equilateral triangle are congruent, so each angle in triangle ABC is equal to 60°. Triangle BCD is a 30-60-90 right triangle, since we know that BD bisects and is perpendicular to AC. Since BDC = 90°, and BCD = 60°, DBC = 30° (since the sum of interior angles of all triangles must equal 180°).

8. F. We can see that the bigger triangle can in fact be split into two smaller triangles. The triangle on the right has measures 90°, 50°, and $2y°$. Since the sum of all interior angles in a triangle must equal 180°, then $180 = 90 + 50 + 2y$. Solve for y by simplifying to

$40 = 2y$ and $y = 20$. In the triangle on the left, the angle measures are $90° + 3(20)° + x$, which must also equal 180. Simplify and solve for x: $180 = 90 + 60 + x$ becomes $x = 30$.

9. B. If $x = 35$, then the value of angles RQS and QRS = $35 + 70 = 105$. Since we know this, then angle QSR = $180° - 105° = 75°$, since QSR is the vertical angle to angle TSU, which means it too is 75°, then TSU ($y°$) = 75°.

10. F. Since AC is a diagonal that divides the rectangle in half, the area of ACD is $\dfrac{1}{2}$ (15), or 7.5 cm. Applying the formula for area of a triangle, we know that $A = \dfrac{1}{2} bh$. The height in this case is 3 cm, so $7.5 = \dfrac{1}{2} b(3)$, or $7.5 = 1.5b$. If we solve for b, we find that $b = 5$.

11. C. The fact that PQ = QR = PR tells us that the big triangle is an equilateral triangle, meaning its three angles ($\angle QRP$, $\angle PQR$, and $\angle RPQ$) each measure 60°. This is a special property of all equilateral triangles regardless of how long their sides are. The fact that ST = SU and that the measure of $\angle TSU$ = 90° tells us that the small triangle is another special type of triangle, where the remaining angle measures are equal, since the lengths of the other sides are equal. Thus, the other two remaining angles are each 45°. Since $\angle RST$ = 60°, and $\angle QRP$ = 60°, then so too must $\angle RTS$, since the sum of the angles in triangle RST must equal 180°. If we know this, and we know that $\angle STU$ = 45°, then $\angle UTQ$ must equal 180° (the degree measure of the straight line RQ) minus 60°($\angle RTS$) minus $\angle STU$ = 45°. Thus, $\angle UTQ$ = 75°.

12. G. Since QR and TU are parallel, the angles QSR and TSU are vertical and share the same degree measurement. Since both QSR and TSU are triangles, the sum of interior angles in each is 180°. This means that $x + y = 35° + 45° = 80°$.

13. B. AKM is a right triangle comprised of 4 smaller triangles. For one shape to be congruent to another, both shapes must have

exactly the same shape and size, including the lengths of all sides and the degree measurements of all angles. There are 7 triangles congruent with AKM: ACM, CMO, CEO, AKC, KCM, MCE, and MEO.

14. 104. Any exterior angle of a triangle is equal to the sum of the other two angles inside the triangle. So we write $x + 3 + 3x + 5 = 7x - 43$, which simplifies to $4x + 8 = 7x - 43$. Solving for x results in $x = 17$. Exterior angle DBC is therefore $7(17) - 43 = 76$, so the measure of interior angle ABC is $180 - 76 = 104$.

15. 12. The triangles are both 3-4-5 right triangles. The larger triangle has sides three times the size of the smaller triangle, since $5 \times 3 = 15$, so its dimensions are 9-12-15.

16. 4. Angles CDE and CAB are alternate interior angles, so they are congruent. Therefore, $8x + 7 = 39$, meaning $8x = 32$ and $x = 4$.

17. 12. The area of a triangle is $\frac{1}{2}bh$, or $84 = \frac{1}{2}(14)(h)$, which simplifies to $84 = 7(h$. So, the height must be $84 \div 7 = 12$.

Circles

1. B. A circle has a total of $360°$ of arc. In $\frac{5}{6}$ of a circle, then, there are $360° \div 6 = 60° \times 5 = 300°$. $300° - 120° = 180°$.

2. F. The area of a circle is determined by the equation πr^2, where r is the length of the circle's radius. Since the area is given, we need to determine the radius in order to determine the diameter. Set the area equal to the formula: $4\pi = \pi r^2$. Solve for r by dividing both sides by π: $4 = r^2$. Take the square root of both sides: $2 = r$. Since the question asks for the diameter, and the diameter of a circle is twice the radius, $2(2) = 4$.

3. D. The area of a circle is $A = \pi r^2$. The circumference is $C = 2\pi r$. In both equations, r is the radius of the circle. If q is equal to the circumference of the circle, $q = 2\pi r$. If $r = 4$, $q = 2\pi(4)$, so $q = 8\pi$.

4. F. Let x represent the diameter of circle R. If the radius of circle Q is 4 times the diameter of circle R, then in terms of x, the radius of circle Q can be expressed as $4x$. The diameter of circle Q is $2 \times 4x = 8x$. Thus, the ratio is 8:1.

5. C. A tire is a circle that rotates along its circumference. The circumference of a circle is $C = 2\pi r$. In this case, we know that the diameter is 4 feet, so the radius is 2 feet. Thus, $C = 2\pi(2)$, or 4π. This simplifies to approximately $4(3.14) = 12.5$.

6. F. The circumference of each wheel dictates the distance that must be traveled for the wheel to complete one revolution. This formula is $2\pi r$, where r is the radius of the circle. Let x represent the radius of the rear wheel. The circumference of the rear wheel is $2\pi x$. In terms of x, the radius of the front wheel is $3x$. So the circumference of the front wheel is $2\pi(3x)$, or $6\pi x$. The circumference of the front wheel is 3 times greater than that of the rear wheel. This means that in 1 revolution of the front wheel, the rear wheel will spin 3 times.

7. C. If the length of each side is 2, then the radius of the half circle is 1. The area of a circle is represented by πr^2, where r = radius. Since the radius = 1, the area of the full circle would be π. This is only a half circle; divide the area by 2, leaving us with $\frac{\pi}{2}$.

8. G. The circumference of a circle is $C = 2\pi r$. We can use the circumference of circle A to determine its radius. $8\pi = 2\pi r$, so $r = 4$. If the radius of circle B is twice that of circle A, then the radius of circle B is 8. The area of a circle is $A = \pi r^2$. For circle B, this means $A = \pi(8)^2$, or $A = 64\pi$.

9. B. Since we have a circle, and since O is the center of the circle, we know that SR is the diameter of the circle, and that OR, OS, and OQ are all radii of the circle, having equal lengths. And since QS = QR, we know that the angle formed by QOR = $90°$. Since the sum of interior angles of a triangle (for example, triangle QRO) must equal $180°$, the other two angles (of which one is x) must equal 180

$- 90 = 90$. Since OR = OQ because they are both radii, both angles must be equal, and triangle QOR must be an isosceles triangle. Thus, $2x = 90$ means that $x = 45$.

10. H. The diameter of a circle is equal to the 2 times the radius of the circle. Since the radius is represented by $\overline{AO}$, $2\,\overline{AO}$ = the diameter of the circle, which we know to be both $\overline{EC}$ and $\overline{BD}$. Thus, $\overline{EC}$ and $\overline{BD}$ are both equal to 18, not 9 or 16. The chords $\overline{ED}$ and $\overline{BC}$ formed by the two diameters must have equal lengths, so $\overline{ED} \neq 9$ while $\overline{BC} = 7$.

11. D. The radius of the largest circle can be quantified as the radius of circle R + the diameter of circle Q. Since we know the radius of circle R = 3, we need to add to this 2 × the radius of circle Q. This is $3 + 5 + 5 = 13$. This is the radius of the largest circle. The question asks for the diameter, which is simply $13 \times 2 = 26$, since the diameter of a circle is 2 times its radius. This is valid because R is the center of both circle R and the largest circle, and Q is perfectly tangent to circle R and the largest circle (meaning it perfectly overlaps exactly at one point).

12. E. The area of a circle can be determined by the formula πr^2, where r = radius. Substitute the values of each circle's radius. The area of circle X is $\pi\left(\frac{1}{3}\right)^2 = \pi\frac{1}{9} = \frac{\pi}{9}$. The area of circle Y is π. The ratio of the area of circle X to that of circle Y is 1:9, since $\frac{\pi}{9} \div \pi = \frac{1}{9}$.

13. C. The area of a square is the length of the side squared, or in this case, $4^2 = 16$. The area of the circle is given by the formula πr^2. In this case, the radius is half the length of a side of the square, or 2. Thus, the area of the circle is 4π. Subtract the area of the circle from the area of the square: $16 - 4\pi$. Note that 4 can be factored out of this expression, but cannot be cancelled out completely. Thus, the expression $4(4 - \pi)$ would be acceptable, but $4 - \pi$ would not.

14. 25. The area of a circle is $A = \pi r^2$. If the area is 16π, then the radius can be found by solving for r. $16\pi = \pi r^2$. Divide by π on both sides, leaving $16 = r^2$. This gives us $r = 4$. The circumference of a circle is $2\pi r$, or in this case, 8π. $\pi \approx 3.14$, and 8π gives us 25.12, which rounds down to 25.

18. 25. Looking at right triangle ABD, we see that the hypotenuse is 20 and one of the legs is 12. We can use the 3-4-5 right triangle ratio to figure out that side AD is 16. Looking at right triangle BDC, we see that the hypotenuse is 15 and one of the legs is 12. We can use the 3-4-5 right triangle ratio to figure out that side DC is 9. Therefore, AC $= 16 + 9 = 25$.

19. -120. There are $180°$ in every triangle. An equilateral triangle is special in that all angles are also equal. If one angle is x, then we know that $3x = 180°$, so $x = 60°$. 180 less than this is $60 - 180 = -120$.

20. 76. There are $180°$ in every triangle. In an isosceles triangle, we know that two of the angles will be equal, and the other will not be equal. Since we know the smallest is 28, then the other two must each be larger than this, as well as equal to each other. This means the sum of the other two angles is $180 - 28 = 152$. $152 \div 2 = 76$.

15. 3.14. $\frac{1}{4}$ of the circle centered at vertex D will be inside the square.

The other $\frac{3}{4}$ will be outside the square. Therefore, since the circle has radius 2 and area 4π, the section of the circle inside the square will have an area of π, which is 3.14 when rounded to the hundredths place.

16. 120. Since the radius is 6, and the circumference of a circle is given as $C = 2\pi r$, the circumference of this circle is $(2)(6)(\pi) = 12\pi$. If

arc $AB = 4\pi$, then it represents $\frac{1}{3}$ of the circumference. There are 360° in a circle, so $\frac{1}{3}$ of the degrees in a circle is $360 \div 3 = 120°$.

17. 14. If the area of circle O is 81π, then its radius is 9, and the radius of circle P is 7. Therefore, the diameter of circle P is 14.

18. 4. Since the outer circle has a radius of 6, its area is 36π. The area of the shaded region is 20π, so the inner circle must have an area of 16π. Therefore, its radius must be 4.

Angles

1. B. A 90° angle can only be formed by perpendicular lines, in which case the line formed by drawing through G only intersects line l once.

2. G. There are 180° of measure in a straight line like MO. If 45° are taken up by angle LNO, then $180 - 45 = 135°$ remain.

3. D. A straight line, as is represented by $\overline{XW}$, has a degree measurement of 180° in total. If 30° is already the measure of $\angle YQW$, then the remaining degrees in $\angle XQY$ must be equal to $180° - 30° = 150°$. We are told that $\angle XQY$ is bisected (cut in half) by $\overline{QZ}$, forming two smaller, equally sized angles. To find the measure, we divide the total measure of $\angle XQY$ in half: $150° \div 2 = 75°$.

4. H. Since QR is a line, the sum of all angles on the right and left side each equal 180° (since the total degree measure around the line itself equals 360°). On the left side, this means that $5y° = 180°$, which simplifies to $y = 36°$. We can substitute this in on the right side for all instances of y: $180° = x° + 3(36°)$, which simplifies to $180° = x° + 108°$. Solving for x, we find that it equals 72°.

5. C. There are 360° in a circle. Though no circle is shown, we know that the measure of angles around a single point is 360°, formed by an imaginary circle. The degree measures are given individually, but we know that together they form a circle. Thus, $x + 2x + 3x = 6x$ and $360° = 6x$. Solving for x, we arrive at $360° \div 6 = 60°$.

6. G. The measure of angles around a single point (the intersection of the line segments) consists of 360° of arc. This means the only unlabeled angle has a degree measure of $360° - 135° - 65° - 85° = 75°$. The arc y spans this angle as well as the angle given as 65°. Therefore, $65° + 75° = 140°$.

7. B. Make use of vertical and supplementary angles to determine the interior angles of the triangle formed by the intersection of the three lines. The left-most interior angle of the triangle measures 45° because it is the vertical (opposite) angle from the angle given as 45°. The right-most interior angle of the triangle measures 50° because it is supplementary to the angle given as 130°, meaning that the sum of both angles must add up to 180° (because the degree measure of a straight line is 180°). This means that the bottom-most interior angle of the triangle = $180° - 45° - 50°$, which equals 85°, since the sum of all interior angles of a triangle must equal 180°. The bottom-most interior angle of the triangle is supplementary to the angle denoted as $y°$, so $y = 180 - 85 = 95$.

8. F. There are several ways to solve this question. One of the most efficient is to realize that because there are two parallel lines, all angles formed at the intersection of Q and S correspond (are equal to) the respective angles formed at the intersection of R and S. This means that $x° = 65°$, etc. Since the sum of all angles surrounding the intersection of R and S must equal 360°, we need only find the value of the angle not labeled. Since $x° = 65°$, and since the angle not labeled is supplementary to x, the value of the angle not labeled is $180° - 65° = 115°$. Thus, the sum of $x + y + z = 360° - 115°$, which equals 245°.

9. D. Around the intersection of lines r and q, the degree measure equals 360°. At this point, the angle opposite the one given as 125° also equals 125°, since the two angles are vertical angles. The remaining two angles must then have a measure 55° each, since $(2)(55°) + 2(125°) = 360°$. This tells us that the left-most interior angle in the triangle formed by lines q, r, and s is 55°. Since the sum of all interior angles of a triangle must equal 360°, then the right-two interior angles have a sum of $180° - 55° = 125°$. The sum of all angles formed to the left of line s must equal 360°, since there are 4 sets of angles formed at the intersection of s and q and s and r. Since this is the case, and since we know that 2 of these 4 angles already have a combined degree measure of 125°, then the other 2 angles (given as $x°$ and the vertical angle of $y°$) must have a combined degree measure of $360° - 125° = 235°$. This means that $x° + y° = 235°$.

10. H. When two lines intersect, angles that are opposite from each other are called vertical angles, and always have the same degree measurement. In this case, if $x = 40°$, then the vertical angle opposite it is also equal to 40°. The other two angles in the triangle that is formed must then equal $180° - 40° = 140°$. Since the two angles themselves are vertical angles to y and z themselves, then we know that $y + z = 140°$ also.

11. C. Because QT and RS are straight lines, the angle opposite y is a vertical angle, sharing the same angle measurement of y. The sum of interior angles of a triangle is 180°. Since there are two triangles, the total sum of all six interior angles would be 360°. We know that two of these six interior angles must be have a value of $y°$. Thus, the remaining four interior angles would be $360° - 2y°$. Note that you can factor out the 2 from this expression, but you cannot eliminate it entirely. So, $2(180 - y)$ would be a valid answer choice, but $180 - y$ would not be.

12. G. Since the arc is part of a circle centered at Z, WZ = ZV, because both are radii. Thus triangle WZV is an isosceles triangle. $\angle WZV$ has a measure of 45°, since line XZ divides the 90° angle WZY in half. Because this is an isosceles triangle, the remaining angles must be equal, and the angles in a triangle add to 180°, so the two remaining angles add to $180 - 45 = 135$. $135 \div 2 = 67.5$. Thus $\angle ZWV$ and $\angle ZVW$ are each 67.5°.

13. C. Because the trapezoid is isosceles, we know that angles W and X are congruent, and angles Z and Y are congruent. Since the total number of degrees in any quadrilateral is 180, we know that angles W and Z must add up to 180, in which case $2(q + r) = 360$.

14. G. A regular polygon is equilateral (all sides are the same length) and equiangular (all angles have the same degree measure). To find the total measure of interior angles in a regular polygon, use the formula $180(n - 2)$, where n represents the number of sides of the polygon. In this case, substitute 8 (since an octagon has 8 sides) for n to get $180 \times 6 = 1{,}080°$.

15. A. To find the measure of each angle in a regular polygon, use the formula $\dfrac{180(n - 2)}{n}$, where n represents the number of sides of the polygon. In this case, a pentagon has 5 sides, so substitute in for $180 \times 3 \div 5 = 108°$.

The Tutorverse

16. F. In this case, we have a hexagon, which has 6 sides. Substituting 6 in for n and solving, we find that $180° × 4 = 720° ÷ 6 = 120°$. Each angle in the regular hexagon has a degree measure of 120°. The question asks for the value of x, which is a supplementary angle to one of the hexagon's interior angles. Supplementary angles have a sum equaling 180°. Thus, $x = 180° – 120° = 60°$.

17. 4. At the intersection of two perpendicular lines, four right angles are formed, since angles around any points sum to 360 degrees. $360 ÷ 90 = 4$.

18. 120. The total number of degrees in any polygon is equal to $180(n – 2)$, where n represents the number of sides in the polygon. A hexagon has $180(6 – 2) = 720$ degrees, so the average degree measure of each angle is $720 ÷ 6 = 120$ degrees.

19. 72. Angle AEF is an exterior angle of a polygon. In a regular polygon with n sides, all exterior angles measure $360 ÷ n$ degrees. Substituting 5 for n, we get $360 ÷ 5 = 72$.

20. 232. Quadrilaterals have 360°. In an isosceles trapezoid, there are two pairs of congruent angles. If the base angles are both 64°, then they add up to 128°, so the apex angles total $360 – 128 = 232°$.

21. 130. All angles surrounding point E must add to 360°. Therefore, since 220° are already accounted for, angle $BED = 140°$. Since $ABED$ is also a quadrilateral, it also must have 360°. Angle BED is 140° and angle DAB is 90°, so the other two angles must be $360 – (140 + 90) = 130°$.

Measurements

1. C. Since AE = AB + BD + DE, and we know BD = 4 and DE = 7, then we know that AE = 4 + 4 + 7, or 15.

2. G. Count the total number of segments between 5 and 55, as indicated by the tick marks; there are 10 segments formed by the 9 tick marks between 5 and 55. Divide the difference between 55 and 5 (which is 50) by the number of segments. $50 ÷ 10 = 5$. Therefore, each segment represents a separation of 5 units. Since R is 3 tick marks away from 5, we know that $5 + 15 = 20$.

3. B. First, determine the scale of the number line by counting the tick marks between two different numbers. Between –5 and 0 there are 4 tick marks, one each for –1, –2, –3, and –4. So, each tick mark represents 1 unit. Next, determine the value of P, Q, and R. By counting tick marks, we can see that P = –4, Q = –2, and R = 2. Lastly, we need only substitute the values into the expressions given to determine that P – R (or $–4 – 2 = –6$) is the least value. Remember that subtracting a negative results in adding that number. The more negative a number, the less its value.

4. H. Counting the segments between –4 and 6, we can see that the number line is counting by integers. That means A represents –5, and B represents 7, so their distance is 12. If that distance is divided into 4 equal parts, then each section has a length of 3. This means that L is $–5 + 3 = –2$, M is $–2 + 3 = 1$, and N is $1 + 3 = 4$.

5. D. The distance between point A and point B is 12 units (17 – 5).

   The question describes how C is somewhere along $\overline{AB}$, splitting $\overline{AB}$ into two other segments: $\overline{AC}$ and $\overline{CB}$. If $\overline{AC}$ is 3 times longer than $\overline{CB}$, then we know that the distance from C to B must be $\frac{1}{4}$ the entire length from A to B. We can let x = the length of $\overline{CB}$. In terms of x, the length of $\overline{AC}$ is $3x$. So in terms of x, the total length of $\overline{AB}$ is $4x$. This means $4x = 12$, and x must be 3, if we solve for x. The location of C must be 3 less than 17, which is 14.

6. E. The number line shown is divided into 5 segments between each integer. This means that the unit of each tick mark is in fifths, or increments of 0.2. We can prove this by dividing the distance between 0 and 1 (which is 1) by 5 (which is $\frac{1}{5}$). Point A is on the 3rd tick-mark between 0 and 1. This means it is $\frac{3}{5}$ of the way between 0 and 1, or 0.6 (which is also $3 × 0.2$). Similarly, B is on the 2nd tick-mark between 1 and 2. This means it is $\frac{2}{5}$ of the way between 1 and 2, or 0.4 (which is also $2 × 0.2$). So, B is at 1.4 and A is at 0.6.

7. D. Write down the information provided to help solve this question. By doing so, we can tell that, since the length of $\overline{WX}$ is 4, and X is located at point 7, then W must be located at point 3.

We know the entire length of $\overline{WZ}$, is 23, and since now we know that W is located at point 3, we know that Z is located 23 units away, at point 26. Since the length of $\overline{YZ}$ is 6, and we now know that Z is located at point 26, then Y must be 6 less, at 20.

8. F. Write down the information provided to help solve this question. By doing so, we can tell that, since the length of $\overline{RS}$ is 4.75, that the location of point S is 4.75 from R, which is located at 0.25. This means S is at point 5. The entire length $\overline{PS}$ is 9.25 long, so we must subtract 9.25 from 5 to determine the location of P. $5 – 9.25 = –4.25$. Q is 2.5 units farther to the right (less negative, more positive) than P, so we can add 2.5 to –4.25 to arrive at –1.75, the location of Q.

9. C. If C is the midpoint of AB, then AC = BC = 0.5AB. Since we are given AC = 17, then BC = 17.

10. F. Draw the information provided in the question. If Q is the midpoint of $\overline{RS}$, the two distances (RQ and QS) must be equal and must each represent half of the total distance RS. Therefore, 2 times the distance represented by QS must equal the entire length of RS, since QS by itself represents half of the entire length RS.

11. B. The midpoint between two points on a line can be calculated by taking the sum of both points and dividing by 2. In this case, we have $–4 + \frac{3}{4} = –3\frac{1}{4}$. Divide this by two, we arrive at $–1\frac{5}{8}$.

12. H. The best way to tackle this question is to draw the information provided. If X is the midpoint of AB, then AX + XB = AB, and AX = XB. If M is the midpoint of XB, then XM + MB = XB, and XM = MB. Because of this, $XM = MB = \frac{1}{4}AB$. However, the question asks for AM. Since $AX = \frac{1}{2}AB$, then $AX + XM = \frac{3}{4}AB$.

13. C. If 2QR = RS, then we know that QR is exactly half of RS. If T is drawn on the line between R and S, and RT = TS, then T is located at the midpoint of RS. This means that QR = RT = TS. Each of these 3 segments along QS is equally long. If QS = 36, then 36 units ÷ 3 segments = 12 units per segment. QT = QR + RT, so QT = 24.

14. G. If WZ is 16 units apart, then W is located at $13 – 16 = –3$. Since X is the midpoint of WY, then WX = XY. Since WX = $–1 – (–3) = 2$, then XY = 2, and Y is located at 1. The midpoint of YZ = $13 + 1 = 14 ÷ 2 = 7$.

15. B. 1 donut can be glazed in 1 second. To glaze 36,000 donuts would take 36,000 seconds. In hours, this is 36,000 seconds ÷ 60 seconds per minute ÷ 60 minutes per hour = 10 hours.

16. F. We can solve this question algebraically. Let x equal the distance in miles of Yunru's afternoon commute by highway. In terms of x, her morning commute by backroad is $x + 7$ miles long. In total, $x + x + 7 = 57$. Simplify by combining like terms: $2x = 50$

17. B. First, calculate the area of the walls of the room. If the bedroom itself is 10-foot by 12-feet, that means 2 walls have a length of 12, and the other 2 have a length of 10. Each wall is 8 feet tall. So the two walls that have length 10 feet have an area of $8 \times 10 = 80$ sq. ft. each, and the two walls that have length 12 have an area of $8 \times 12 = 96$ sq. ft. each. In total, the square footage of the walls is $160 + 192 = 352$. Since 1 gallon of paint only covers 300 sq. ft., then one would need 2 gallons of paint.

18. G. If the total area of Figure X = 48 sq. in., and there are 16 individual small squares, then each small square equals $48 \div 16 = 3$ sq. in. In Figure Y, there are also 16 small squares, each 3 sq. in. in area. Thus, the area of Figure Y is also 48 sq. in.

19. A. First, convert the measurement of the wall from feet to yards. Since there are 3 feet per yard, we divide each measurement in feet by 3 to arrive at 6 yards and 8 yards. The area in square yards is simply $6 \times 8 = 48$. Note that this is not the same as calculating the square footage then dividing by 3.

20. H. The volume of a box can be measured by multiplying the length by width by height. In this case, $2 \times 3 \times 5 = 30$ cubic meters. For every cubic meter, there 0.4 kg of packing foam. So: $30 \times 0.4 = 12$.

21. B. The total volume of the pool is can be calculated by length times width by height (in this case, depth). Since it is a square, we know that the sides are all 10 m long. Thus, $10 \times 10 \times 3 = 300$ cubic meters. More water per minute is being drained from the pool than is being added to the pool: 8 cubic meters per minute – 3 cubic meters per minute = 5 cubic meters per minute of water being drained. If the pool started at $\frac{2}{3}$ full, then it is 200 cubic meters full. It will take 200 (cubic meters) ÷ 5 (cubic meters per minute) = 40 minutes to fully drain, at 12:40 pm.

22. F. Since there are 60 minutes per hour, we need only multiply: 3.65 hours × 60 minutes per hour = 219 minutes.

23. C. One full cycle consists of 90 minutes where Samson runs for 45 minutes then walks for 45 minutes. The question asks at what time the fourth period of walking will begin. This means 3 full cycles and 1 half cycle will be completed by this time. 3 full cycles × 90 minutes = 270 minutes. Add to this 45 minutes running (for the remainder half cycle) and the total elapsed time is 315 minutes. Since there are 60 minutes per hour, the elapsed time is 300 minutes ÷ 60 minutes = 5 hours, with 15 minutes remaining. Thus, 5 hours and 15 minutes after 9:00 a.m. is 2:15 p.m.

24. F. We know that there are 24 hours in a day. $70 \div 24 = \sim2.9$. So we know that 70 hours after 12:30 p.m. on Monday will be very close to (but 2 hours short of) 3 full days (72 hours) later. Three full days after Monday at 12:30 p.m. would be Thursday at 12:30 p.m. However, only 70 hours, not 72 hours, have elapsed. Instead of a full 3 days, we can count back 2 hours to 10:30 a.m. on Thursday.

25. B. If Byron biked 3 times the distance of Amanda, then he biked a total of $22 \times 3 = 66$ miles. If he did so in 2 times the amount of time as Amanda, then he biked this distance in $3 \times 2 = 6$ hours. In miles per hour, this equals 66 miles ÷ 6 hours = 11 miles per hour.

26. H. The difference in hours between EST and HAST is 1:00 P.M. – 8:00 A.M. = 5 hours. If the first plane arrived in Honolulu at 6:00 P.M. HAST, then the EST equivalent of its arrival in Honolulu is 11:00 P.M. EST. This means that the total flight time was 12:00 P.M. EST – 11:00 P.M. EST = 11 hours. Following this same amount of flight time, the 7:00 A.M. HAST flight from Honolulu would arrive 11 hours later in Newark, at 6:00 P.M. HAST. 6:00 P.M. HAST + 5 hours = 11:00 P.M. EST.

27. –3.5. The best way to solve is to draw a diagram of a number line with W, Y and Z at –12, –5 and 8, respectively. Draw A between X and Y, and draw B between Y and Z. Point A is the midpoint of XY, so it is at –8.5, and point B is the midpoint of YZ, so it is at 1.5. Their midpoint is then –3.5.

28. 8. Point P is at –4, point Q is at 8, and point R is at 24. The midpoint of PQ is then 2, and the midpoint of PR is 10, so the distance between them is 8.

29. 4. J is at –8 and K is at 0. It is 4 tick marks from J to K, so $\frac{1}{4}$ of the way would be at –6. L is at 14, so the midpoint of A and L is 4.

30. 486. 2 yards = 72 inches, and 3 yards = 108 inches. If each tile is 4 inches long, it will take 18 tiles to run the length of the bathroom, and 27 tiles to run the width, requiring a total of $18 \times 27 = 486$ tiles.

Coordinates

1. A. Point A is in the first quadrant, where all x and y values are positive. Point B is in the third quadrant, where all x and y values are negative. The only choice with negative x and y values is represented by $(-x, -y)$.

2. H. Point A is 12 units along the x-axis, and 5 units along the y-axis. This means segment OA actually represents the hypotenuse of a triangle with a height drawn from A up to the x-axis or a leg drawn rom A over to the y-axis. It is a special right triangle with legs 5 and 12. This means its hypotenuse must be 13. The question tells us that OB is $2 \times$ OA, so this is $13 \times 2 = 26$.

3. C. Since the figure is a rectangle, we need only to determine the length of two sides with different lengths. We know that (3, 3) and (3, 1) are 2 units apart on the y-axis, but aligned on the x-axis. Similarly, we know that (3, 1) and (0, 1) are aligned on the y-axis, but are 3 units apart on the x-axis. Therefore, the length and width of the rectangle are 2 and 3. So, the area is 6.

4. H. y values are graphed on the vertical axis. We can tell if more than one point in a graph shares a y-value with another point by visually scanning each graph. Looking left to right, any time we see more than one point at the same vertical distance from the origin (the intersection of the y and x axes), those points have the same y value. This is the case in all graphs but D.

5. D. There are infinite points that are exactly 2 units from the origin. Drawing them all creates a circle about the origin with radius 2.

6. F. Turning (j,k) into $(-k,j)$ means switching the order of the numbers and negating what was originally the y-coordinate.

7. A. The two given vertices create a line segment with a length of 6 units. In any triangle, any two sides must add up to more than the third side. This means that the two other sides must add up to more than 6, so the perimeter must be more than 12.

8. G. A proportional relationship here means that the x and y coordinates should be in the ratio 2:1. Only (14,7) has this relationship.

9. A. The first two vertices are 5 units apart, so every side length should be 5 since it's a square. When a square on the coordinate grid is perpendicular to the axes, each coordinate point should appear twice. There are two 2's and two 3's, meaning the x-coordinate is 7 and the y-coordinate is –2.

10. H. There are four possible squares that can be drawn from the description. The other vertex on the y-axis is either at (0,5) or (0,15). Either way, all vertices are in the top quadrants, so all coordinates must be positive.

11. 24.5. The right triangle has a height of 7 and a length of 7, so the area is $\frac{1}{2} bh$, or $\frac{1}{2} (7)(7) = 24.5$ square units.

12. –3. Since the given endpoint of the diameter is 3 units to the right and 4 units up, the other endpoint must be 3 units to the left and 4 units down, making it (–2, –3).

13. 15. Drawing a rough sketch shows that the triangle has a base of 5 and a height of 6. The area of a triangle = ½(base)(height) = ½(5)(6) = 15.

14. 2. If (4,–2) is reflected over the *x*-axis, the new points are (4,2). If it's then reflected over the *y*-axis, its new coordinates are (–4,2).

15. 16. The trapezoid has a bottom base of 6, a top base of 2, and a height of 4. The area of a trapezoid is (average of the bases) × (height) = 4 × 4 = 16.

Practice Test 2

Part One: English Language Arts

1. A. This sentence is made up of two different, complete thoughts. The first is "Jessica was…park." The second is "She was…sickness." We can combine these sentences together to form one larger sentence using the appropriate conjunction, but we must pay attention to the relationship between the two different ideas. In the first, we are told that Jessica is excited to ride an "extreme rollercoaster." In the second, we are told that she is "deathly afraid" of qualities one normally associates with rollercoasters (heights, motion). Therefore, if she is excited about the roller coast, it must be "in spite of" her fears. In other words, she is excited "even though" she has fears, not "because of" or "since" she has fears. The solution results in an independent clause ("Jessica was…park") followed by a subordinating conjunction and clause ("even though…sickness"). The subordinating clause tells us more information about Jessica's excitement: that she was excited though she had fears.

2. G. Though multiple adjectives describing the same noun should be separated with a comma, there is no need to separate the last adjective from the noun with another comma. In this case, the noun "season" is being described as "cold" and "rainy." "Rainy" does not need to be separated from season by a comma.

3. C. The first two choices leave out important information: that the grapefruits and carrots are Floyd's favorite fruits and vegetables, respectively. When we use the word "respectively," we must be careful that the reference words are aligned in order. In this case, grapefruits are fruits, and carrots are vegetables. Since "grapefruits" was listed before "carrots," then so too must we list "fruit" before "vegetable."

4. G. Sentence 3 describes a process where people find qualities they like about plants or animals and increase the number of those things. The first choice is vague and imprecise, since it describes how people multiply organisms – a strange phrase. In addition, "they" is vague – is it referring to people, or organisms? "It," in the second choice, is also vague. Is the sentence referring to selective breeding, or changing traits in a laboratory? Saying "some people" and "things that they enjoy" is also vague, and helping those things "become part of the plant in the future" is awkward and vague. Instead, the third choice clearly describes what the sentence refers to (the latter being selective breeding), and what it is.

5. A. Sentence 17 brings a different point of view to the passage. Where the preceding paragraph described many benefits, the last paragraph describes reservations and drawbacks. Therefore, we should use a transition word like "nevertheless," which signals a contrast, rather than transitions like "accordingly" and "likewise," which signal a similarity. "Specifically" would be used to expand further upon the ideas in the preceding sentence/paragraph.

6. H. Sentence 4 describes how, over time, organisms like plants develop qualities that people like. Only the last choice describes things that people "love," and how they happen.

7. B. Sentence 5 describes how people can change the traits of organisms quickly thanks to science. Sentence 6 describes how science has also enabled people to combine genes across different domains. The two are related, and can be combined with a "but…as well," which is similar to "but…also." The other choices are nonsensical, using words like "though" and only "but." The first choice changes the meaning of the sentence.

8. H. The noun "genes" is plural, so the verb "to be" should be plural as well. This is "were." "Insect-killing" is properly hyphenated as a compound adjective describing "toxins." The comma after 1995 would separate the sentence in a way that creates fragments on either side of it. The sentence is written in the past tense, so changing "was not" to "is not" is erroneous.

9. D. Sentence 16 lays out several advantages to using GMOs. Only the last choice describes a specific example of "higher nutritional value." The other choices describe drawbacks to the use of GMOs.

10. E. The passage concerns itself with describing what GMOs are, and how they are beneficial, as well as certain negative aspects. Describing more about bacteria and archaea is not important to the main idea. Sentences 11 and 14 are important to describing Bt, the central example of GMOs used in the passage.

Mary Oliver

11. B. The passage shares how Oliver began writing as a child while walking in the woods (paragraph 5), and how her work influenced the masses (paragraph 2). While her poems are known for being emotional, poetry was about empowerment and rising above darkness for Oliver (paragraph 4). And though she was famous – Oprah Winfrey created a special issue of O magazine for her, highlighting a "rare interview that Ms. Oliver gave" – someone that wrote for popular appeal would seek interviews, rather than rarely giving them.

12. G. Prior to this sentence, the passage details her popularity, publications, and honors. After this sentence the passage explores how nature inspired her to write and how combining the two "was [her] salvation" (paragraph 5). This sentence serves as a transition between the two topics. She spent time in the woods in both her old age and in her youth, so there is no contrast.

13. A. Doorways are passages into other rooms. A closed door doesn't share what is behind it; therefore, by Oliver referring to a "thousand opening doors," she illuminates the unknown world by opening them through poetry. Even though poetry was Oliver's chosen artistic medium, prior to the door statement she states that she "did not think of language as the means to self-description" or self-exploration, and the doors open "past" herself.

14. H. The idea in paragraph 4 that Oliver found herself in the woods is echoed by the statement in paragraph 5 about finding her voice in the woods. This is figuratively true, as she found ideas for poetry in the woods, and used it as a way to express her thoughts, confusion, and concerns. The other choices merely describe the reasons why Oliver wished to go into the woods.

15. C. Here the reference to cathedrals elicits connotations of comfort and wonder, given the words "shelter" and "spiritual renewal." Her desperation is described in an earlier sentence.

16. E. Paragraph 6 guides the reader into one of Oliver's poems, explaining how her poetry reflects what she sees in nature. The first quote draws on this idea, and combines it with her personal history to show how poetry and nature were her ways to transform pain into beauty. The other quotations are supporting details, and do not describe the central idea.

17. D. Given the author's positive tone about Oliver (paragraph 5) despite the snubs of "some critics," we can infer that the author believes poets should follow their own interests and not the expectations of others. Even though the author shares Oliver's writing in old age, that was a fact about Oliver and not a main focus of the passage.

Adapted from *The Youngest Girl in the Fifth*

18. F. The simile offers more detail to how Gwen "snatched back her exercise book." The author compares Gwen's motions to "a mother clutching her first-born" to show how deeply invested she is in her work. It may be that Gwen's essay is of very high quality but this quote does not mention the envy of others.

16. –6. The graph shows a line that goes through the origin. Find –2 on the *x*-axis and trace down to the line shown. The *y*-axis value at this point is –6.

17. 1.5. The midpoint of a line segment can be found from the average of its endpoints. Since the *y*-coordinates of the endpoints are 5 and –2, the midpoint must have a *y*-coordinate of 5 + (–2) = 3 ÷ 2 = 1.5.

The Tutorverse

19. A. In paragraph 13, Netta uses examples of how other people cheat, or claim credit for others' work, to seal her argument. Gwen disagrees, and appears to be hurt by Netta's reference to unethical clergymen, but Netta presses her case regardless. Netta has the opposite of a strong sense of fairness. She only cares about getting her way, and will use any justification to get it.

20. G. At this moment, Gwen makes the critical and difficult decision to accept Netta's offer. Up until this point, Netta has been trying to convince Gwen to make a deal (essentially, blackmailing Gwen). After this point, the excerpt describes the consequences of that action: Gwen is miserable. Netta would indeed rather cheat than work hard, but this is supported in other paragraphs, not paragraph 24.

21. C. This quote shows that Gwen is upset at giving away her essay because she wants to be "highly commended." Though paragraph 19 implies that Gwen wants to avoid the consequences of breaking the china, the consequences will be punishment rather than merely being badly perceived.

22. H. In paragraph 15, the excerpt describes Netta's determination to get something – money, or something else – so she blackmails Gwen. Paragraph 16 describes how Netta could be "uncommonly nasty," which factors into Gwen's decision to ultimately give Netta what she wants. The fact that Netta is "neither brilliant nor a hard worker" isn't a reason why Gwen cooperates with Netta – it's a reason why Netta decides to blackmail Gwen for the essay.

23. A. As a result of her agreement with Netta – motivated by Gwen's desire to hide the truth of her actions in Ms. Roscoe's office – Gwen is forced to write a second essay. Had Gwen faced the consequences of her actions, she may have gotten in trouble with Miss Roscoe, but wouldn't have had to give her original essay away.

24. G. The lines in question show that Netta could not have otherwise gotten a chance to receive praise for her work. The fact that she is not known for being the best student is echoed by the students' incredulous reaction to the announcement that Netta wrote the best essay.

25. D. Gwen is filled with frustration because she is witnessing someone else – someone she dislikes – getting the credit she had wanted so badly for working hard on her essay, and she cannot voice the truth. There is no evidence that she is worried about people finding out about her arrangement with Nettie.

The Big One

26. E. The passage discusses the events of the San Francisco earthquake of 1906, and the extent of the damage it caused. This answer option identifies the topic, and describes the quake as "one of the most powerful...ever recorded." Although the passage states facts about the fires that occurred due to the quake (paragraph 4), the fires are a detail rather than the central idea. The passage mentions, but is not primarily about, how San Francisco enjoyed decades of peace after the quake.

27. D. The map highlights the San Andreas Fault's main fracture, and San Francisco's location squarely on top of it, highlighting the main claim of paragraph 1. The map does not illustrate any "man-made factors" that caused the quake or population numbers.

28. H. In paragraph 3, the author states that the quake happened before the development of the Richter scale, and its magnitude was estimated based on later evaluations of the damages and changes it caused. We may infer then that this is not as accurate as having the technology to measure it in present time. The author repeatedly marvels at how short the actual quake was (paragraphs 2 and 8), so the damages were not caused by the sustained length of the quake.

29. B. At the beginning of paragraph 2 the author first mentions "violent shocks" lasting only seconds, then the "rupturing" miles, and finally the "24 feet slip," building the stress and fear felt by the people. Although the paragraph "gives a scientific overview," it is not intended to bore the reader. In addition, the use of a quote at the end of the paragraph drives home the feeling of being there.

30. G. Paragraph 4 describes how the firefighters tried creating "firebreaks by demolishing buildings." They believed that "sacrificing some buildings" would "stop the fires from consuming" more, but the inexperienced firefighters "started more." The statement "caused additional damage […] in efforts to solve the problem" is the best option that describes the firefighters experience. There is no explicit mention of the firefighters being disorganized.

31. A. The author's word choices in the phrase "even knowledge" demonstrates the relentlessness of the fire, and the word "discriminate" implies an intelligence or ability to choose, which personifies the fire. Although the sentence personifies the flames, it does not imply that the flames were capable of intelligent intention.

32. F. This option shows how the House and Senate committees, which are part of the government, sent victims the things they needed. In the previous option, the officials are shown to be identifying, or seeing, the problem, but their action ("passing out clothing") does not match the need of the peoples ("food and shelter were the main concerns").

33. C. Throughout the passage, the events of the 1906 San Francisco earthquake are told in narrative order, and paragraph 9 brings the passage to a close by reaffirming the reader that "San Francisco recovered" and "enjoy[ed] decades of geological peace." Although the paragraph mentions geography, it does not emphasize the destruction, which occurred in previous paragraphs.

Learning Differently

34. F. The passage is primarily concerned with explaining why rote memorization is not as helpful for students as conceptual understanding, despite memorization's role in helping students perform well on standardized tests. The passage offers reasons and explanations supporting the notion that rote memorization does not help students in problem-solving unfamiliar situations, such as those encountered in the workplace, for example. The passage does not say that rote memorization can lead to critical thinking skills, and actually implies the opposite.

35. A. In the second paragraph, the author writes that rote memorization is an ineffective learning tool because it lacks context for the information memorized, and does not develop conceptual understanding. The statement provides an example of how memorizing information (i.e. a formula) does not equal understanding it. It is not a critique of weak math training.

36. F. The word "pitfall" means "an unsuspected or hidden danger." Paragraph three reveals the inadequacies of rote memorization in real learning, contrary to what people expect. Therefore, the use of "pitfalls" to describe rote memorization suggests it has unexpected drawbacks for students. The "dangers" of rote memorization are not obvious, since initially and on tests, it seems to lead to student success.

37. A. The US Department of education study reinforces the idea that high test scores do not correlate to later life success, which is the main claim of paragraph 4. Though the study itself discusses other countries, the paragraph is specifically concerned with education in America, and not how the problem affects children in other countries.

38. G. This statement helps explain how human minds and computers are designed to do different things, and how human minds are ultimately more suited to "process complex information." Though rote memorization is more like how a computer processes information, the passage does not suggest that memorization can make the human brain more like a computer.

39. B. Paragraph 5 introduces the notion of developing critical thinking skills in students, in lieu of encouraging mere rote memorization. Paragraph 6 elaborates on this idea by citing the long-term benefits of critical thinking skills in students' learning, therefore reinforcing its importance. Critical thinking is contrasted with rote memorization, but no mention is made of critical thinking's short-term benefits.

40. H. The notion that idea-sharing (mentioned in paragraph 9 as one type of exercise to develop critical thinking skills) "teaches students how to learn and work in a social setting, which workplaces require" directly supports the claim that critical thinking skills are useful in life beyond school. Though the other answer options state that critical thinking skills are beneficial, they do not show specifically how these skills can be helpful in life after school.

41. C. Paragraph 9 tells us that brainstorming "can reveal seemingly crazy but often creative and novel ways to tackle problems." This highlights the positive, albeit unexpected outcomes of one type of critical thinking exercise. "Crazy" here is used in a positive, not a negative, sense.

"Summer"

42. H. The first several lines describe the relationship between "some" people and nature. To "some," nature is a "closest friend" who they "hold dear communion with." This "dear communion" means that nature benefits man and can be interpreted as the two coexisting peacefully. The speaker does not compare the relationship to a curse, only describing how it benefits people. The fact that nature is beautiful is given, but this by itself does not develop the central idea of the poem. The speaker uses "some" to show that not everyone can take advantage of this relationship.

43. C. The word "voice" tells us that the waters are compared to a person. Notice the preceding and following lines, as well, which describe the hills as one with which people can "hold dear communion" and the winds as bringing "healing in their sound." These are things that only people can do. All of these are positive, not harmful. These do not suggest that people can gain inspiration or advice from them or overcome weaknesses. Instead, this suggests comfort and relief, as mirrored by the word "soothes."

44. F. This metaphor is very powerful. The city, a place where many people live close together, is cast in a negative light, as a "prison house." The speaker doesn't personally hate towns and cities; in these lines, she is describing how people generally perceive summer and cities.

45. A. It is important to read these lines in context. During this part of the poem, the speaker is describing how he agrees with other people about some aspects of summer: nature is beautiful and can do much. But line 18 shows that there is more that nature can provide, which is described later on in lines 34-42. Nature is not described as wild and untamable, but as an ally that helps people.

46. F. Lines 11-12 describe how other people feel, not how the speaker's views differ from those feelings. Lines 18-19 show that the speaker agrees with the idea that nature is beautiful but has deeper thoughts that go beyond nature – that there is beauty to be found amongst people. This is especially true because the lines follow the description of nature's beauty. Lines 20-21 and 25-26 describe an idyllic scene that others would agree with.

47. D. Earlier in the poem, the speaker describes how nature is beautiful and provides inspiration and relief, but that there is more to be found elsewhere. This is what is meant when the speaker says "I love the very human heart of man" (note the preceding line: But more than these, and much, ah, how much more). The answer to this is in lines 35-36, where the speaker describes more of what this means: close contact with others (like living in a city) is "like a lantern shining in the night" – a comforting and reassuring image.

48. G. These lines show a distaste for the season of summer, with negative words like "void," "lags," and "silent." They show that the poet, unlike most people, does not see summer in a completely positive light. Although it mentions how inspiration lags in summer, she is using that as a detail to make her point, and it is not the central idea of the poem.

49. C. To the speaker, summer is a pause, a time for respite – a time when "feeling sleeps." It is not a place or time where "beauty dwells not" – the speaker gives many examples of summer's beauty. And yet, summer does not bring the healing, for the speaker, as it does for other people. The time to gain new

experience is during the winter. As you can see, understanding the context in which the line is written is extremely important.

50. E. The lines toward the end of the poem describe how winter has benefits because it is difficult to be in nature so it is better to spend time with other people. These sentiments are echoed in lines 35-36 and lines 41-42. They are contrasted by lines 11-12, when the speaker describes how some people believe that winter is dreary, and they only endure it for the sake of summer.

Superheated

51. A. The passage is about the life cycle of the sun, starting from when it was first formed 4.5 billion years ago (paragraph 2) to what it will eventually become (paragraphs 5-6). Although it does explain nuclear fusion and the amount of energy given off by the sun, those are supporting details, not the central idea.

52. G. Paragraph 2 states: "Nuclear fusion has sustained the sun ever since, resulting in the release of massive amounts of energy."

53. D. Paragraph 5 discusses how the sun grows in size: "Every 500 million years or so, the sun will double in size until it reaches a size more than 200 times larger than it is today." There is no mention of how much energy other stars output, so we cannot infer that the sun's energy is less than other stars in our galaxy. And while the passage discusses how the Earth's atmosphere absorbs the sun's energy, it does not state whether it absorbs almost all or some of that energy, nor that that energy goes to powering communication efforts specifically.

54. F. The sun will become a red giant once the hydrogen runs out (paragraph 5). After it runs out of helium, it will become a white dwarf star.

55. C. All of the options are true, except that the sun will not begin burning off its supply of hydrogen; it will have already done so, by the time it becomes a red giant.

56. E. The sun is currently a yellow dwarf star (paragraph 1), will become a red giant after burning through its hydrogen (paragraph 5), and will eventually become a white dwarf star (paragraph 6) after its helium supply is exhausted.

57. A. The table shows the mass of each celestial object in our galaxy, and demonstrates how the sun dwarfs all other objects. This supports the claim "The sun alone accounts for more than 99% of all matter in our solar system" (paragraph 1). The table does not show information about the radiation from the sun, nor how its size will change in the future.

Part Two: Math

58. 1.5. We have been given two ratios, one of which can be simplified: if 2 jorps = 4 saffs, then 1 jorp = 2 saffs. Now we know that 1 jorp is equal to both 3 wims and 2 saffs, meaning 3 wims = 2 saffs. We simply divide both sides by 2 to get 1 saff = 1.5 wims.

59. 120. Since 5 students are getting in line, there are 5 options for the first position, 4 remaining options for the second position, 3 options for third position, 2 for fourth position, and only one left for the last position. The answer is $5 \times 4 \times 3 \times 2 \times 1 = 120$.

60. 0. The first statement says x must be greater than −2 and less than 4, so x can be −1, 0, 1, 2, or 3. The second statement says x must be greater than 3 and less than 10, so x can be 4, 5, 6, 7, 8, or 9. There are no numbers that satisfy both statements.

61. 7. Working backwards, if the length of DB is 3, then the length of CB must be 6 and the length of AB must be 12. If B is 12 units to the right of A, then it is −5 + 12 = 7.

62. 4. There are $35 \times 2 = 70$ orange candies, $4 \times 15 = 60$ green candies, and 60 + 70 = 130 purple candies. In total, this is 260 candies. Divided among 65 party bags, this would mean there are $260 \div 65 = 4$ candies per party bag.

63. A. First add up the numbers under the radical. We get the square root of 25. The square root is essentially the opposite operation of raising a number to the second power (also called "squaring" that number). That means we are trying to find a number that we can multiply by itself to get 25. The answer is 5 because $5 \times 5 = 25$.

64. E. The fact that Adina is older than Boaz can be represented by $a > b$. The fact that Adina is younger than Ezra can be represented as a

< e. By combining the two inequalities, we can see that b must be least, e the greatest, and a in the middle. Therefore, b < a < e.

65. B. Notice that all answer choices use the same digits, and only the decimal place changes. We can use logical reasoning to determine that $324 \div 72 = 4.5$. Since the decimal in 0.324 is two places from where it should be, we know we must move the decimal in 4.5 two places to the left, giving us 0.0045.

66. F. One way to solve is to recognize that the value we are looking for, $2m - 10$, is exactly half of the left side of the given equation, $4m - 20$. That means, instead of solving for x, we can simply divide the equation by 2, giving us $2m - 10 = 4.5$.

67. A. The midpoint between A and B is $(3 + (-5)) \div 2 = -1$. The midpoint between A and C is $(7 + (-5)) \div 2 = 1$. The distance between the two midpoints is $1 - (-1) = 2$.

68. H. Each notebook originally costs $\$7.50 \div 3 = \$2.50$ each. If we add $\$0.75$ to this, we get a price of $\$3.25$ each. 5 notebooks would cost a total of $\$3.25 \times 5 = \$16.25$.

69. A. Resolve each exponential term so that the equation becomes $\dfrac{16 + 9}{-8 - 1} = -\dfrac{25}{9}$.

70. H. If x = the number of miles Bob biked, then 3x equals the number of miles Alex biked, in which case they biked a total of 4x miles. Since we know the total is 72, our equation is $4x = 72$, so $x = 18$. But the question is asking for Alex's miles, which is $3(18) = 54$.

71. C. The greatest common factor is 105. Since the greatest common factor cannot be greater than the two numbers, we can eliminate 4,620 immediately. We must test the other answer choices individually. All of them are factors, but of them, 105 is the greatest.

72. E. Since 1.2 euros is equal to 1 dollar, and 102 yen is also equal to 1 dollar, then 1.2 euros = 102 yen. To solve for 1 euro, we need only divide both sides by 1.2. Doing so results in 85 yen.

73. C. An equilateral triangle has sides that are the same length. A regular pentagon is equilateral, meaning all of its five sides are the same length. If one side of the triangle has length 5, and all sides are the same length, then the perimeter of the triangle is 3 sides × 5 = 15. The pentagon has 5 equilateral sides, so each side is 15 ÷ 5 sides = 3. The question asks for the length of 3 sides, so 3(3) = 9.

74. H. To solve, start by combining like terms: $4 - 2x = 14 - 7x$. Then make sure the variable is only on one side of the equation by cancelling out the smaller variable, here by adding 7x to both sides: $4 + 5x = 14$. Isolate the variable by cancelling out the constant and then dividing by the coefficient: $5x = 10$ and $x = 2$.

75. B. 3 fits into 100 approximately 33.333 times, so there are exactly 33 positive multiples of 3 that are less than 100. 3 fits into 50 approximately 16.667 times, so exactly 16 of those 33 multiples are less than 50, so there are 17 multiples of 3 between 50 and 100.

76. G. If they want 60% of their sales to be burgers, that means that 40% of their sales will be hotdogs. The number of hotdogs remains the same at 100, which means that 100 should be 40% of the total number of sales. If x represents the total number of both hamburger and hotdog sales, then we can find x using the equation $100 \div x = 40 \div 100$. Cross-multiply to get $40x = 100 \times 100$. Solving for x we get $x = 250$. This is the total number of sales. Since they sold 100 hotdogs, the number of burgers they need to sell is $250 - 100 = 150$ burgers. They have already sold 100 burgers, so the number of additional burgers they need to sell is $150 - 100 = 50$ additional burgers.

77. D. Let x represent the probability of choosing a black bead out of the box. In terms of x, the probability of choosing a blue bead is 3x. This means the ratio of blue to black beads is 3:1, which we can also represent as fractions. The chance of drawing a blue bead is

$\dfrac{3}{1+3}$; the chance of drawing a black bead is $\dfrac{1}{1+3}$. If there are 12 beads, then $\dfrac{3}{4} \times 12 = 9$.

78. G. If $\dfrac{3}{7}$ of K is 210, then each $\dfrac{1}{7}$ of K is $210 \div 3 = 70$, in which case $\dfrac{5}{7}$ of K is $5(70) = 350$. We can rule out 150 because it is less than 210.

79. B. Students must be familiar with the metric system. 1 gram is equal to 1,000 milligrams. Setting up a proportion, we get $\dfrac{1{,}000 \text{ milligrams}}{1 \text{ gram}} = \dfrac{90 \text{ milligrams}}{x \text{ grams}}$. Cross multiply and solve for x: $90 = 1{,}000x$, so $x = 0.09$.

80. E. If there are s students in total but n students are not going, then they are taken out of the total, leaving $s - n$ students who must pay for the whole trip. The amount each of them must pay is equal to the total amount divided by the number of students going.

81. A. This is a remainder problem. Dividing the total number of bagels by the number of bagels on each tray, we get $163 \div 18$, which results in 9 remainder 1. That means 9 trays will be filled to capacity and there will be 1 bagel left to go on a tray by itself.

82. G. Since MNOP is a rectangle, then PO = MN = 4. The perimeter is 14, so sides NO + MP = 14 - 8. This means NO and MP are each $6 \div 2 = 3$. We have two a special right triangles with sides 3-4-5, meaning the hypotenuse NP is 5.

83. A. The distance between parallel lines is constant, so they will never intersect.

84. G. We can solve this algebraically. $\dfrac{5 + 5 + 8 + 10 + x}{5} = x$. Simplify by combining like terms and canceling denominators: $\dfrac{28 + x}{5} = x$ becomes $28 + x = 5x$. Isolate the variables to one side of the equation and simplify: $28 = 4x$ and $x = 7$.

85. C. The area of a circle is equal to πr^2. AC is a diagonal of the square, and since points A and C both touch the circle, and ABCD is a square, AC is also the diameter of the circle. The radius is equal to half the diameter, so the radius is equal to $36 \div 2 = 18$. Thus $A = \pi(18)^2$, so the area is equal to 324π.

86. F. The only positive integers that leave a remainder of 4 are 8 and 16.

87. A. We know that $2^3 = 8$ from prime factorization. We can substitute 8 in for 2^3, but the original expression is 2^6. Instead of multiplying the exponents, we divide them, arriving at $8^{6 \div 3} = 8^2$.

88. F. If the 7,500 mL bucket is only $\dfrac{2}{5}$, then it currently contains $7{,}500 \times 2 \div 5 = 3{,}000$ mL of water. This means there is $7{,}500 - 3{,}000 = 4{,}500$ mL of water that can be added to fill the bucket. Since there are 1,000 mL in each liter, $4{,}500 \div 1{,}000 = 4.5$ L.

89. C. Since the number must be in all three sets, it must be odd, so we can eliminate 4 and 6. It must be positive, so we can eliminate 0. Thus, 1.

90. E. If the odds of picking the name of a boy out of a hat is 2 out of 5, then the odds of picking the name of a girl out of a hat is 3 out of 5. So, the ratio of girls to boys is 3:2. We can use a proportion to

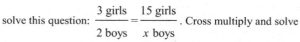

solve this question: $\dfrac{3 \text{ girls}}{2 \text{ boys}} = \dfrac{15 \text{ girls}}{x \text{ boys}}$. Cross multiply and solve

for x: $30 = 3x$, so $x = 10$. But this only tells us the number of boys in the class; the question asks how many more girls there are than boys. $15 - 10 = 5$.

91. B. Substitute 6 for y. This gives us $6 \div 2 = 3$. Then, $2 + 3 = 5$.

92. F. Since the surface area of the red colored sides equals 45 square mms, and there are 5 sides that are painted red, then each side is 45 square mms ÷ 5 sides = 9 square mms. If the area of each side is 9 square mm, then the sides measure 3 mms by 3 mms (the square root of 9). Since the dimensions of the cube measure $3 \times 3 \times 3$, the volume is $3^3 = 27$.

93. A. Let x represent the original number. We can represent the fact that x was decreased by 20% in two different ways: $x - 0.2(x)$, or simply $0.8x$. If from this point, the new number is decreased further by another 20% We repeat the calculations just performed, replacing x with $0.8x$ instead: $0.8x - 0.2(0.8x)$, or simply $(0.8)(0.8)(x)$. Both simplify to $0.64x$, which means that compared with the original number x, the final number is 64% of the original, or 36% less.

94. F. We need simply to divide the coefficients 4.8 and 1.2 as well as the base and exponents. In this case, $4.8 \div 1.2 = 4$. When dividing exponential expressions with the same base, simply subtract the numbers in the exponents. In this case, since the base is 10 for both expressions, subtract 4 from 6. This gives us 10^2. The resulting expression is 4×10^2.

95. B. Setting up a proportion is the most reliable way to solve this question: $\dfrac{7 \text{oz.}}{3.5 \text{ dollars}} = \dfrac{16 \text{oz.}}{x \text{ dollars}}$. Cross multiply and solve for x: $56 = 7x$, so $x = 8$.

96. E. There are 60 minutes in 1 hour. In h hours, this is $60h$ minutes. If there are some remainder m minutes left, then the total number of minutes in h hours and m minutes is $60h + m$.

97. C. To find the correct answer, we first need to solve the inequality algebraically. Subtracting 10 from both sides and then dividing both sides by -5, we get $c < -1$. (*Remember that when you multiply or divide by a negative number, the inequality switches direction!) That means we want an open circle over -1 with the number line shaded to the left.

98. F. We must determine the value of each of the terms in xy^2. We know that $3x = 45$; solving for x, we divide both sides by 3. So, $x = 15$. We know that $5y^2$ also equals 45. We divide both sides by 5 and are left with $y^2 = 9$. Because y^2 is itself a factor of xy^2, we don't need to simplify further to solve for y. Now that we have the values of x and of y^2, we simply substitute and multiply: $(15)(9) = 135$.

99. A. First, determine the value of Q. $|-2| = 2$, and $|-8| = 8$. Therefore, $Q = (-2 - 8) = -10$. Substitute -10 in for Q: $-|(-10)|$. After simplifying, $|10|$ is positive, but the negative on the outside of the absolute value makes it -10.

100. H. Let x represent the extra number that is being added to the set. The total of the new set is $7 \times 12 + x$ because there are 7 numbers with a mean of 12 and we are adding x to them. This total simplifies to become $84 + x$. In order to get the new mean, the total must be divided by 8 because there are 8 numbers including the new one. Therefore, the new mean is $\dfrac{(84 + x)}{8}$. The problem tells us that the new mean is 3 more than the old mean (which was 12) so the new mean is 15. Therefore, we get $\dfrac{(84 + x)}{8} = 15$. To solve this equation, first multiply both sides by 8 and then subtract 84 from both sides. The answer is $x = 36$.

101. C. If a bedroom is 10 feet by 12 feet, then the area of that rectangle is $10 \times 12 = 120$ square feet. Each tile is also a square and is $4 \times 4 = 16$ square inches. However, working with inches and feet is

difficult, so we will convert the tile into square feet. Since there are 12 inches in a foot, the 4-inch tile is $\dfrac{1}{3}$ of a foot on each side.

$\dfrac{1}{3} \times \dfrac{1}{3} = \dfrac{1}{9}$ square foot. To determine how many of these fit into the bedroom, we divide the total square footage of the bedroom by the square footage of a single tile: $120 \div \dfrac{1}{9} = 1{,}080$. Remember that dividing a number by a fraction is the same as multiplying that number by the reciprocal of the fraction (in this case, 9).

102. F. There are 4 different letters in the word "MATH". Since we are asked for different ways to rearrange the letters, the order of the letters is important. We can write out different possible combinations (MATH, MAHT…etc.), but this would take a long time. Instead, we can tell that keeping one letter in the same (in the above, the letter "M") results in 6 different ways to rearrange the remaining letters (in the above, "A," "T," and "H"). We can repeat this for each of the four letters, meaning there are a total of $6 \times 4 = 24$ different combinations.

103. A. Find a power of 2 and a power of 3 that multiply together to make 72. We know $8 \times 9 = 72$. $2^3 = 8$ and the power $3^2 = 9$. This means that $x = 3$ and $y = 2$. Therefore, $x + y = 5$.

104. G. One way to solve is to choose any x-value from the table, plug it into each answer choice, and see if you get the correct corresponding y-value. If we plug 1 in for x in each answer choice, all answer choices work except for $y = x + 5$ and $y = x + 21$. If we then plug 2 in for x, only $y = 3x + 1$ works.

105. B. When two polygons are similar, their corresponding sides are proportional. Here, $\dfrac{AB}{BC} = \dfrac{WX}{XY}$, or $\dfrac{12}{6} = \dfrac{8}{x}$. Using cross multiplication, $12x = 48$, so $x = 4$.

106. E. $\dfrac{3}{5}$ of a packet of iodine tablets, which is what Kevin knows he must use per day, is 3 iodine tablets, since there are 5 iodine tablets in each packet. Kevin has in total 20 iodine packets × 5 iodine tablets per packet = 100 iodine tablets. Since Kevin needs 3 iodine tablets, we know that he has enough iodine for 33 days: $100 \div 3 = 33.33$. The remainder means that Kevin doesn't have enough iodine for the 34th day.

107. B. The angles opposite the 45° and 50° are called vertical angles. Vertical angles have the same degree measurements. So, the triangle formed by the three-intersecting straight lines has to angles that measure 45° and 50°. Since the sum of the interior angles of a triangle equals 180°, the remaining angle (which is the vertical angle of x°) has a measurement of $180 - 45 - 50 = 85$. Therefore, $x = 85°$.

108. H. Since the 4th number is 68, to find the 5th number, first add 2. $68 + 2 = 70$. Then, we double this, for $70(2) = 140$. To find the 6th number, repeat the equation: $(140 + 2)(2) = 284$. To find the 7th number, do the same: $(284 + 2)(2) = 572$.

109. B. The broker earned $9,000, which was 3% of his total sales. If x represents his total sales, we can calculate x using the proportion $\dfrac{9{,}000}{x} = \dfrac{3}{100}$. We cross-multiply this to get $3x = 9{,}000 \times 100$. Solving for x, we get $x = 300{,}000$. This was the broker's total sales over 3 months, so his average sales rate was $300{,}000 \div 3 = 100{,}000$.

110. F. We know that the formula for perimeter is $P = 2l + 2w$. We are told that $P = 70$ and that $l = w + 9$. Plugging those into the equation gives us $70 = 2(w + 9) + 2w$, which we can simplify to $70 = 2w +$

18 + 2w, or 4w = 52, or w = 13. That is the width; we're trying to find the length, which is 13 + 9 = 22.

111. B. Looking at the answer choices, we notice that every choice starts with a^2, so we must distribute the right side of the equation, giving us $y = a^2 - 5a$. To find the value of $y - 1$, we just subtract 1 from both sides, giving us $a^2 - 5a - 1$.

112. F. This problem gives you an equation with several variables, but it also gives you a number to plug in for every variable except one, so just plug in the numbers they've given you: $600 = 25 \times 50 - (12 \times 50 + b)$. Then solve for the remaining variable: $600 = 1{,}250 - 600 - b$. This results in $600 = 650 - b$, or $-50 = -b$ which simplifies to $b = 50$.

113. D. Any problem involving a scale map can be solved using a proportion. We must always make sure we use matching units so we must convert 2.5 feet to 30 inches, giving us $\frac{1}{6} = \frac{30}{x}$, so $x = 180$. However, that number is in yards, but the answer choices are all in feet, so we must convert 180 yards to 540 feet.

114. E. A percent is a part of a whole, with the whole being 100. To find p percent of any value, we must multiply that value by $p \div 100$. The value of two $100,000 houses is $200,000, so the commission earned will be $(p \div 100) \times 200{,}000$, which simplifies to $2{,}000p$.

The Tutorverse

Made in United States
North Haven, CT
06 November 2021